Time Out

Madrid

timeout.com/madrid

Time Out Guides Ltd
Universal House
251 Tottenham Court Road
London W1T 7AB
United Kingdom
Tel: +44 (0)20 7813 3000
Fax: +44 (0)20 7813 6001
Email: guides@timeout.com
www.timeout.com

Published by Time Out Guides Ltd, a wholly owned subsidiary of Time Out Group Ltd.
Time Out and the Time Out logo are trademarks of Time Out Group Ltd.

© Time Out Group Ltd 2010
Previous editions 1995, 1997, 1999, 2000, 2002, 2004, 2007.

10 9 8 7 6 5 4 3 2 1

This edition first published in Great Britain in 2010 by Ebury Publishing.
A Random House Group Company
20 Vauxhall Bridge Road, London SW1V 2SA

Random House Australia Pty Ltd 20 Alfred Street, Milsons Point, Sydney, New South Wales 2061, Australia

Random House New Zealand Ltd 18 Poland Road, Glenfield, Auckland 10, New Zealand

Random House South Africa (Pty) Ltd Isle of Houghton, Corner Boundary Road & Carse O'Gowrie, Houghton 2198, South Africa

Random House UK Limited Reg. No. 954009

Distributed in the US and Latin America by Publishers Group West (1-510-809-3700)
Distributed in Canada by Publishers Group Canada (1-800-747-8147)

For further distribution details, see www.timeout.com.

ISBN: 978-1-84670-120-7

A CIP catalogue record for this book is available from the British Library.

Printed and bound by Firmengruppe APPL, aprinta druck, Wemding, Germany.

The Random House Group Limited supports The Forest Stewardship Council (FSC), the leading international forest certification organisation. All our titles that are printed on Greenpeace approved FSC certified paper carry the FSC logo. Our paper procurement policy can be found at http://www.rbooks.co.uk/environment.

Time Out carbon-offsets its flights with Trees for Cities (www.treesforcities.org).

Contents

Introduction

Spain's two biggest cities – Madrid and Barcelona – go through cyclical phases of each hogging the limelight; while Madrid was the focus during the post-Franco 'transición' in the 1980s, Barcelona stole the show in the '90s and early noughties with its post-Olympics urban design schemes and cosmopolitan outlook. Now, it seems, it's Madrid's turn again. While the country as a whole is struggling to cope with the severe economic crisis, Madrid is still riding on a wave of optimism, partly thanks to the grandiose urban renewal schemes of its ambitious mayor. From the redevelopment of the bank of the Manzanares River to the pedestrianisation of key streets, Madrid's infrastructure has been transformed over the past five years. What's more, the city has witnessed the completion of several high-profile buildings, including Herzog & de Meuron's CaixaForum, extensions to its three world-famous art museums, the revamped Mercado de San Miguel, and the Cuatro Torres development in the financial district, including Norman Foster's Torre Caja Madrid, now the tallest building in Spain. Along with a push by local authorities to promote tourism, these projects have accounted for an increase in visitors and led to a new-found confidence that has inspired the city to push the envelope (as this guide went to press, free Wi-Fi was being implemented in its main squares and even its buses). What's more, widespread immigration during the pre-2008 boom decades has led to a newfound multiculturalism and has transformed the city's eating-out scene.

Yet, despite boasting exciting new architecture, increasingly innovative restaurants and arts centres and the country's best gay scene, this is a city still ruled by traditions and by its distinctive barrios; but herein lies its charm. Whether you're talking about La Latina's Sunday tapas crawl, Malasaña's grungy rock scene or Salamanca's upmarket restaurants, this is a city where social rituals rule supreme. While madrileños are in many ways more forward-thinking than they were a decade ago, they remain loyal to its many atmospheric institutions, with the city's best old bars still packed most nights of the week.

Madrid has experienced a profound shift over the past few years, and its current identity is about attempting to mix the old with the new. With the economic crisis have come testing times, with widespread debt, sky-high unemployment and rising prices. But the local heartbeat is strong, and it's still a great time to visit this historical, culturally rich and supremely fun city.
Anna Norman, Editor

Madrid in Brief

IN CONTEXT

Despite the recession, Madrid is in fine form; mayoral-led urban renewal projects over the past few years have given the city a much-needed facelift and improved its infrastructure, while iconic new architecture and a more outward-looking attitude have freshened up the grandiose vibe it inherited from its Bourbon and Habsburg past. While many traditional features remain, Madrid feels more cosmopolitan and modern than it has in decades.
► *For more, see pp14-49.*

SIGHTS

With the extensions to the Prado, the Thyssen-Bornemisza and the Reina Sofía now complete, Madrid is firmly established as one of the world's best cities for art. But go beyond the frames and you'll find a plethora of excellent small museums, as well as beautiful gardens in the form of the Retiro and the Jardín Botánico. Due to Madrid's compact size, many of its key sights can be reached on foot, via the city's medieval streets or the leafy Paseo del Prado.
► *For more, see pp53-110.*

CONSUME

With increased multiculturalism has come a widening of tastes, reflected most clearly in Madrid's restaurant scene, which now encompasses cuisines from all over the world, as well as the homegrown *nueva cocina*. Lively old tapas joints now rub shoulders with chic bars, while traditional small shops have been joined by a wave of fashion-forward boutiques. The boutique concept also hit the hotels market a few years ago, and hasn't looked back.
► *For more, see pp113-204.*

ARTS & ENTERTAINMENT

Madrid's film and rock music scenes grew out of the 1980s counter-cultural movement, and still fuel its cultural arena – along with new strands of popular music, such as flamenco fusion. A new set of multidisciplinary arts centres, meanwhile, has led to more cutting-edge fare in a city long dominated by tradition. And although Madrid's legendary nightlife is less notorious than it once was, there's still plenty of (extremely) late-night fun to be had.
► *For more, see pp206-266.*

ESCAPES & EXCURSIONS

The stately cities of Toledo and Segovia, and the palaces, monastries and gardens at Aranjuez, La Granja, Riofrío and El Escorial all make excellent escapes from the capital. In summer, the cool mountain air of the *sierras* beckons, with superb hiking and camping and spectacular landscapes; while in winter, head to one of the nearby country towns to hole up in a traditional *mesón*, with red wine, a log fire and some suckling pig.
► *For more, see pp268-292.*

Madrid in 48 Hours

Day 1 Paseo del Prado, the Retiro and Los Austrias

10AM Start the day in the **Puerta del Sol** (*see p66*), Madrid's official centre, by enjoying a coffee and a pastry in **La Mallorquina** (*see p171*) – something of a Madrid institution.

11AM Head south-east down the Carrera de San Jerónimo until you reach the **Paseo del Prado** (*see p82*). Madrid's three world-famous art museums – the Thyssen, the Prado and the Reina Sofía – are all in the vicinity, but we don't suggest you try to tackle them all. The **Museo del Prado** (*see p88*), based on Spain's royal collections, is the absolute don't-miss. Buy a ticket from the machine outside to skip the queues, and head to the Goya rooms. Other highlights include Bosch's *Garden of Earthly Delights* and Velázquez's *Las Meninas*.

2PM Lunch in Madrid is from 2pm, when many restaurants offer a well-priced *menú del día*. Newcomer **Estado Puro** (*see p166*), not far from the Prado, is a good bet if you're looking for local cuisine in a chic space; for cheaper fare, head to the Huertas branch of **Viva La Vida** (*see p171*) for a takeaway box, to be eaten on one of the Paseo del Prado's benches. Then enjoy a post-meal stroll south down the Paseo, taking in the **CaixaForum** (*see p85*) on the right – its vertical garden is now one of the most photographed spots in town.

4PM After a morning of culture, you might like to enjoy some of Madrid's green highlights; the restful **Jardín Botánico** (*see p88*) lies just off the Paseo del Prado, while the **Retiro** park (*see p90*), with its boating lake, buskers and shady avenues, is reached via the recently pedestrianised **Cuesta de Moyano** (*see p85*), lined with upmarket second-hand book stalls.

7PM After a few hours relaxing in the park, head north-west to the historic *barrio* of Los Austrias. In Madrid, afternoon shopping hours are 4pm to around 9pm, and in **Plaza del Conde de Barajas**, near the **Plaza Mayor**, you'll find **Taller Puntera** (*see p196*), Madrid's best shop for artisan leather products. After flexing the credit card, head round the corner to the **Mercado de San Miguel** (*see p162*) for some upmarket tapas – it's a great spot to witness *madrileños* doing what they do best: enjoying food and drink in sociable surroundings.

NAVIGATING THE CITY

One of the most appealing aspects of Madrid is its compact size; the *barrios* where you'll likely spend most of your time are all within walking distance of each other, making the city surprisingly relaxing for a capital. The metro is a reliable and easy way to get around when you do need to resort to public transport. Madrid has several key streets to help you get your bearings (Gran Vía, C/Mayor, Paseo del Prado, Paseo de la Castellana), but its winding medieval alleys can be tricky to navigate. Our street maps (*pp321-329*) make it easier to find your way around, however, while a handful of Spanish phrases might come in useful if you need to ask a (normally friendly) local for help.

SEEING THE SIGHTS

The queues for the Prado museum have been lessened in recent times

Day 2 Madrid's counter-cultural neighbourhoods

10AM Malasaña was the focus of the post-Franco counter-cultural movement known as *La Movida Madrileña*. Although the movement is well and truly over, the neighbourhood retains an atmospheric, grungy feel, with boho cafés and music-led bars. Soak up the vibe with a late breakfast at **El Rincón** (*see p182*) or **Lolina Vintage Café** (*see p181*).

11AM After fuelling up for the day ahead, take a wander around the neighbourhood's laid-back streets. Some of Madrid's best small shops are to be found in this area, including arty **Peseta** and espadrilles-specialist **Antigua Casa Crespo** (for both, *see p194*). The streets around Calle Conde Duque, home to the **Centro Cultural Conde Duque** (*see p81*) – worth a visit if there's an exhibition on – are a good bet for clothes boutiques and record shops.

2PM Although there are plenty of good restaurants in Malasaña, to get a sense of the distinctness of Madrid's different neighbourhoods, cross over Calle de Fuencarral into Chueca for lunch. The famously gay barrio has several good restaurants, but one of the best choices is **Gastromaquía** (*see p147*), which offers a great-value Spanish-fusion *menú del día*.

4PM After a leisurely lunch, you'll have time to explore more of Madrid's *barrios*. The city's compact size means that its central neighbourhoods are all within walking distance of each other. Head south of Gran Vía, through the Puerta del Sol, until you reach Lavapiés, the city's most multicultural *barrio*. It begins at the now spruced-up **Plaza Tirso de Molina** (*see p77*).

6PM A stroll through Lavapiés brings you to Calle de Santa Isabel, home to Madrid's national film theatre in the art nouveau **Cine Doré** (*see p220*). The place has featured in films by Pedro Almodóvar, a key *Movida* figure, and its café is a lively meeting spot for film buffs before a (bargain €2.50) screening – perhaps of a silent movie, or a classic from the national archives.

10PM On the same street as the Cine Doré lies one of Madrid's best tapas bars, **La Musa de Espronceda** (pictured above; *see p164*), a great starting point for a Lavapiés bar crawl.

with more efficient ticketing systems; but it's still best to visit early in the morning or shortly before closing. The Paseo del Arte (*see p54*) is a city council initiative to promote the geographical, historical and thematic links between Madrid's great art triumvirate (the Prado, the Thyssen and the Reina Sofía). After a day of sightseeing, be sure to take respite in the restful royal botanical garden or the Retiro park.

PACKAGE DEALS

The **Paseo del Arte** ticket gives entry to the Prado, Reina Sofía and Thyssen-Bournemisza for €17.60. It can be bought from all three museums; after visiting one you can visit the other two at any time in the same calendar year.

The **Madrid Card** offers free admission for up to 40 of the city's museums. It costs €40 for one day, €62 for two days, or €76 for three. Visit www.madridcard.com.

Madrid in Profile

LOS AUSTRIAS

The Habsburg city, including **Plaza Mayor**, the heart of Golden Age Madrid, lies south-west along Calle Mayor. It's home to newly restored tapas hotspot, the **Mercado de San Miguel** – also great for gourmet gifts.

▶ *For more, see pp55-65.*

LA LATINA

Incorporating the **Cava Baja** and **Plaza de la Paja**, La Latina is a hive of activity on a Sunday, when half the city heads to the area's lively tapas bars for some serious socialising.

▶ *For more, see pp65-66.*

SOL

The Old City's cramped, narrow streets centre on the recently spruced-up **Puerta del Sol**. This is literally the centre of the city, in that all street numbers in Madrid count outwards from Sol.

▶ *For more, see pp66-68.*

GRAN VIA

Madrid's main shopping thoroughfare celebrated its centenerary in 2010. At its western end is the **Plaza de España**, dominated by Franco's bombastic architecture. Some of the city's best cinemas line the nearby streets.

▶ *For more, see pp68-72.*

HUERTAS & SANTA ANA

One of Madrid's most touristy areas, due to its historic and literary past and its plethora of tapas bars and restaurants, Santa Ana's heart is the **Plaza Santa Ana**, just off the pedestrianised **Calle Huertas**.

▶ *For more, see pp72-76.*

LAVAPIES

Madrid's most multicultural *barrio* is home to a sizeable Asian community, reflected in its restaurants and shops. It also contains some of the city's best bars, as well as the Filmoteca at **Cine Doré**, on its border.

▶ *For more, see pp76-78.*

CHUECA

Madrid's gay district, just north of the Gran Vía, and centred around the **Plaza de Chueca**, is rammed during July's Gay Pride. It may have lost some of its edge, but you'll find a host of hip cafés and shops, and some top-notch restaurants.

▶ *For more, see pp78-79.*

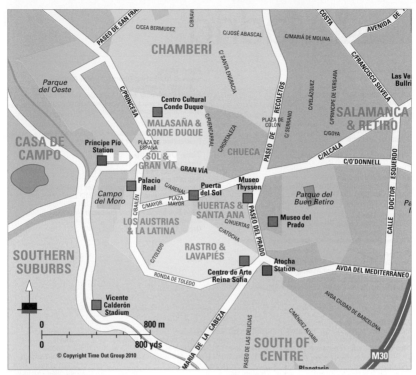

MALASANA & CONDE DUQUE
The original Movida *barrio*, Malasaña's laid-back streets, squares and bars still buzz with a music-led, sociable crowd, while Conde Duque's clothes shops are among the city's most stylish.
▶ *For more, see pp79-81.*

THE RETIRO & AROUND
The **Prado** is here, a short walk along the Paseo del Prado from the **Thyssen**, the **Reina Sofía** and the new **CaixaForum**. The **Retiro** park and **Jardín Botánico** provide some welcome respite.
▶ *For more, see pp82-93.*

SALAMANCA & AROUND
Madrid's most well-to-do neighbourhood is the place to head to for designer garb and swanky restaurants, as well as iconic contemporary architecture and some great small museums.
▶ *For more, see pp93-100.*

BEYOND THE CENTRE
Head beyond the city walls to cool off in the outdoor pool of the verdant **Casa de Campo**, to see the Madrid skyline by cable car or to visit an authentic Egyptian temple, the **Templo de Debod**.
▶ *For more, see pp101-110.*

Time Out Madrid

Editorial
Editor Anna Norman
Copy Editor Edoardo Albert
Listings Editor Matt Norman
Proofreaders Kieron Corless, Holly Pick
Indexer Neelanjona Debnath

Managing Director Peter Fiennes
Editorial Director Ruth Jarvis
Business Manager Dan Allen
Editorial Manager Holly Pick
Assistant Management Accountant Ija Krasnikova

Design
Art Director Scott Moore
Art Editor Pinelope Kourmouzoglou
Senior Designer Kei Ishimaru
Group Commercial Designer Jodi Sher

Picture Desk
Picture Editor Jael Marschner
Acting Deputy Picture Editor Liz Leahy
Picture Desk Assistant/Researcher Ben Rowe

Advertising
New Business & Commercial Director Mark Phillips
International Advertising Manager Kasimir Berger
International Sales Executive Charlie Sokol
Advertising Sales (Madrid) Juan José Bellod
(B2B Communication)

Marketing
**Sales & Marketing Director, North America
& Latin America** Lisa Levinson
Senior Publishing Brand Manager Luthfa Begum
Group Commercial Art Director Anthony Huggins
Marketing Co-ordinator Alana Benton

Production
Group Production Manager Brendan McKeown
Production Controller Katie Mulhern

Time Out Group
Director & Founder Tony Elliott
Chief Executive Officer David King
Group Financial Director Paul Rakkar
Group General Manager/Director Nichola Coulthard
Time Out Communications Ltd MD David Pepper
Time Out International Ltd MD Cathy Runciman
Time Out Magazine Ltd Publisher/MD Mark Elliott
Group Commercial Director Graeme Tottle
Group IT Director Simon Chappell

Contributors

Introduction Anna Norman. **History** Nick Rider. **Architecture** Harvey Holtom, Anna Norman (*Profile: CaixaForum Madrid* Anna Norman). **Madrid Today** David Lennard, Anna Norman. **Seeing the Bulls** Robert Elms. **Movida Movies** Rob Stone. **Flamenco** Rob Stone. **Sights** Sally Davies, Harvey Holtom, Simon Hunter, Robert Latona (*A Saint for All Seasons* Annie Bennett; *El Salón del Prado* Clayton Maxwell, Anna Norman; *Judgement Day* Richard Schweid; *Life After Death* Michael Jacobs; *From the Nile to Parque Oeste* Nick Funnell; *Garden of Enlightenment* Nick Rider). **Hotels** Helen Jones, Danny Wood. **Restaurants** Annie Bennett, Clayton Maxwell, Sally Davies (*Toilet Humour* Simon Hunter). **Tapas** Sally Davies (*Profile: El Mercado de San Miguel* Anna Norman). **Cafés & Bars** Sally Davies (*In the Frame: Tertulias* Michael Jacobs; *The Grape and the Good* Clayton Maxwell). **Shops & Services** Harvey Holtom, Simon Hunter, Anna Norman. **Calendar** Harvey Holtom (*In the Frame: Burial of the Sardine* Clayton Maxwell). **Children** Andrew Wallace. **Film** Rob Stone. **Galleries** Clayton Maxwell. **Gay & Lesbian** Barry Byrne, Pablo Espinoza, Jimmy Shaw (*Pride and Joy* Simon Hunter, Anna Norman). **Music** *Classical & Opera* Delaina Haslam; *Rock, Roots & Jazz* Simon Hunter. **Nightlife** Simon Hunter. **Sport & Fitness** Alex Leith (*Bath Time* Clayton Maxwell, Anna Norman). **Theatre & Dance** Delaina Haslam. **Escapes & Excursions** Sally Davies (*In the Frame: View of Toledo* Nadia Feddo; *Spires and Tyres* Annie Bennett; *Airs and Graces* Nick Funnell). **Directory** Matt Norman, Nathalie Pédestarres. **Additional reviews throughout** Sally Davies, Simon Hunter, Anna Norman, Matt Norman.

Maps Estela Orrego and José Pais, Mapas de Nexolaser (http://mapasdenexolaser.blogspot.com), except: pages 320 and 334 JS Graphics (john@jsgraphics.co.uk); pages 335 and 336 courtesy of Consorcio de Transportes de Madrid.

Photography Jon Santa Cruz, except: pages 3, 5 (centre and bottom left), 8 (top right and centre right), 30, 35 (bottom), 38, 51, 66, 109, 111, 119, 147, 151, 153, 157, 162, 163 (top), 165, 174, 177, 183, 191, 195, 217, 218, 226, 245, 249, 254, 255 Karl Blackwell; pages 4, 6, 7, 8 (top left and bottom left), 9 (top left), 35 (top), 37, 53, 56, 60, 65, 79, 81, 84, 86, 89, 158, 163 (bottom), 171, 189, 192, 197, 198, 206, 211, 219, 220, 221 (bottom), 225, 228, 252, 257, 262, 263, 265 Anna Norman; pages 5 (top right and bottom right), 9 (bottom left), 180, 256, 268 Shutterstock; page 9 (bottom right) Scott Chasserott; page 14 Tupungato; pages 23, 48, 92, 93 Museo del Prado; page 43 Rex Features; page 54 jorgedasi; page 58 Vinicius Tupinamba; page 70 (top), 71 Museo Thyssen-Bornemisza; pages 73, 74 (bottom), 87 rubiphoto; pages 74 (top), 179 Museo Reina Sofia; page 209 la Real Academia de Bellas Artes de San Fernando; page 235 (top) photooiasson; page 267 Ondacaracola; page 269 Walid Nohra; page 272 (top and bottom) Jarno Gonzalez Zarraonandia; page 272 (centre) Richard Semik; page 275 (top) Fred Fokkelman; page 275 (bottom) Serge Lamere; page 279, 287 aguilarphoto; page 280 Graca Victoria; page 283 Matt Tromer; page 291 Silky; page 293 Simone Simone.

The following images were provided by the featured establishments/artists: pages 113, 114, 115, 120, 124, 129, 207, 260.

The Editor would like to thank Annie Bennett, Karl Blackwell, Sally Davies, Bob Francis, Nick Funnell, Nuria Gómez de la Cal, Gonzalo Gil, Matt Hart, Daniel Hermoso at Spain Select, Frank Müller, Matt Norman, John Oakey and Juan Rodriguez.

About the Guide

GETTING AROUND

The back of the book contains street maps of Madrid, as well as overview maps of the city and its surroundings. The maps start on page 320; on them are marked the locations of hotels (❶), restaurants (❶), tapas bars (❶) and cafés and bars (❶). The majority of businesses listed in this guide are located in the areas we've mapped; the grid-square references in the listings refer to these maps.

THE ESSENTIALS

For practical information, including visas, disabled access, emergency numbers, lost property, useful websites and local transport, please see the Directory. It begins on page 294.

THE LISTINGS

Addresses, phone numbers, websites, transport information, opening hours and admission prices are all included in our listings, as are selected other facilities. All were checked and correct at the time that this guide went to press. However, business owners can alter their arrangements at any time, and fluctuating economic conditions can cause prices to change rapidly.

The very best venues in the city, the must-sees and must-dos in every category, have been marked with a red star (★). In the Sights chapters, we've also marked venues with free admission with a FREE symbol.

PHONE NUMBERS

The area code for Madrid is 91. Even if you're in the city, you'll always need to use the code. From outside Spain, dial your country's international access code (00 from the UK, 011 from the US) or a plus symbol, followed by the Spanish country code (34) and the nine-digit number. So, to reach the Prado Museum, dial +34 91 330 28 00.

For more on phones, including details of local mobile-phone access, *see p307*.

FEEDBACK

We welcome feedback on this guide, both on the venues we've included and on any other locations that you'd like to see featured in future editions. Please email us at guides@timeout.com.

Time Out Guides

Founded in 1968, Time Out has grown from humble beginnings into the leading resource for anyone wanting to know what's happening in the world's greatest cities. Alongside our influential weeklies in London, New York and Chicago, we publish more than 20 magazines in cities as varied as Beijing and Beirut; a range of travel books, with the City Guides now joined by the newer Shortlist series; and an information-packed website. The company remains proudly independent, still owned by Tony Elliott four decades after he launched *Time Out London*.

Written by local experts and illustrated with original photography, our books also retain their independence. No business has been featured because it has advertised, and all restaurants and bars are visited and reviewed anonymously.

ABOUT THE EDITOR

Anna Norman has spent several years in Latin America, from Havana to Buenos Aires. In the past few years, she has turned her attention to Spain – and specifically Madrid. She has edited and written for a variety of books for Time Out, including guides to Mallorca & Menorca, Florence and London shops.

A full list of the book's contributors can be found opposite.

Get the local experience

Over 50 of the world's top destinations available.

In Context

Plaza de Toros de Las Ventas. *See p33*.

History

From shanty town to cosmopolitan capital.

TEXT: NICK RIDER

Around 100 years after Madrid had become capital of the Spanish Empire on the whim of Philip II, an attempt was made to construct an ancient past for it, and writers developed the story of its descent from a Roman city called Mantua Carpetana. Though there were Roman towns nearby at Alcalá de Henares (Complutum) and Toledo (Toletum), and Roman villas along the valley of the Manzanares, there is no real evidence that there was ever a local Mantua, or that any of these settlements was the origin of modern Madrid. The story of Mantua Carpetana, however, served to obscure the insignificance of Madrid before Philip II moved his court here in 1561, and, above all, the embarrassing fact that it was founded by Muslims: specifically, in about 860 AD, during the reign of Mohammed I, fifth Emir of Córdoba.

ARABIAN SIGHTS

Following their eruption into the Iberian peninsula in 711, the Arab armies did not occupy the inhospitable lands north of the Sierra de Guadarrama, but established a frontier more or less along the old Roman road linking Mérida, Toledo and Saragossa. The original *qasr* (a word absorbed into Spanish as Alcázar) or fortress of Madrid was one of a string of watchtowers built north of this line in the ninth century, as Christian raids into Al-Andalus became more frequent. The rocky crag on which it stood, where the Palacio Real is today, was ideal for the purpose, since it had a view of the main tracks south from the Guadarrama. It also had excellent water, from underground streams within the rock. Madrid's original Arabic name, Mayrit or Magerit, means 'place of many springs'.

Mayrit became more than just a fortress, with an outer citadel, the eastern wall of which ran along the modern C/Factor, and a wider town or *medina* bounded by the Plaza de la Villa and C/Segovia. A section of wall, the Muralla Arabe on Cuesta de la Vega, and the remains recently excavated next to the Palacio Real are the only remnants of Muslim Madrid visible in the modern city. Both citadel and *medina* consisted of a mass of narrow alleys, like the old quarters of North African cities today.

Mayrit was attacked by Christian armies in 932 and 1047, and in the 970s was used by the great minister of Córdoba, Al-Mansur, as a base for his celebrated 100 campaigns against the north. By the 11th century, it had a population of around 7,000.

CHRISTIAN CONQUEST

In the 11th century the Caliphate of Córdoba disintegrated into a mass of petty princedoms called *taifas*, and Mayrit became part of the Emirate of Toledo. In 1086, Alfonso VI of Castile was able to take advantage of this situation to conquer Toledo, and with it Madrid. The town's main mosque became the church of Santa María de la Almudena, which would survive until the 19th century. For many years, however, Madrid would remain on the front line. In 1109, it was again besieged, by a Moorish army that camped below the Alcázar in the place since known as Campo del Moro (Field of the Moor). A new wall was built, enclosing the area between the Alcázar and Plaza Isabel II, Plaza San Miguel and Plaza Humilladero.

Christian Madrid was a very rural town, and most of the population who worked did so on the land. Madrid did acquire large religious houses, notably the Friary of San Francisco, where the church of San Francisco el Grande still stands, supposedly founded by St Francis of Assisi in 1217. Madrid was still not entirely Christian, however. Many Muslims, known as Mudéjares, had stayed in the conquered areas, retaining their own laws and religion, and were prized by the Castilian monarchs for their skills as builders and masons; their work can still seen today in the towers of San Nicolás de los Servitas and San Pedro el Viejo. In Madrid they were confined to the area known as the Morería. Medieval Madrid also had a smaller Jewish population, concentrated outside the walls in Lavapiés.

Madrid did finally begin to play more of a role in the affairs of Castile in the 14th century. In 1309, the Cortes, or parliament, met here for the first time. Medieval Castile did not have a fixed capital, but instead the Court followed the king around the country. In the 14th and 15th centuries Castile was dogged by a series of social revolts and civil wars, between monarchs, the nobility and rival claimants from the royal family. Against this backdrop, Madrid began to gain popularity as a royal residence, a country retreat more than a centre of power.

Political instability did not prevent substantial economic progress in 15th-century Castile, with Madrid becoming a reasonably prosperous trading centre for the first time. Trade outgrew the old market in Plaza de la Villa, and in the 1460s an area east of the 12th-century wall was built up as a ramshackle new market square, the origin of the Plaza Mayor. A new town wall was built, not for defence but so that taxes could be levied on people living in the new parts of the town. Its eastern entrance was a new gate, the Puerta del Sol.

IN CONTEXT

Madrid retained a degree of royal favour, helped and continued its modest growth, and at the end of the Middle Ages had a population of around 10,000-12,000.

On 11 May 1561, the small-time aristocrats who ran the town of Madrid received a letter from their king, Philip II, warning that he, the entire royal household and all their hundreds of hangers-on would shortly be coming to stay.

CAPITAL IDEA

Philip II (1556-98) was the fundamental figure in Madrid's history. He was a deeply pious, shy, austere man. His father had travelled incessantly about his many dominions, and led his armies into battle. Philip, in contrast, ruled his inheritance from behind a desk, as a kind of king-bureaucrat, sometimes dealing with over 400 documents a day. This extraordinary exercise in paperwork naturally required a permanent base.

Why Philip chose a town without a cathedral, college or printing press as capital remains unclear. The fact that Madrid was near the centre of the Iberian peninsula probably appealed to him, as he was fascinated by geometry and Renaissance ideas of a king as the 'centre' of the state, but his choice made no economic sense at all, since it gave Spain the only major European capital not on a navigable river. Madrid – which for centuries would normally be referred to in Spain as 'La Corte', the Court, never as a city in its own right, which indeed it wasn't – would be a capital of the monarchy's own creation, a pure expression of royal power.

Having established his ideal capital, Philip did little to build or plan it. He had extended the Alcázar when he was still crown prince, then his attention shifted to El Escorial (pictured p19), where he increasingly spent his time. Royal piety was demonstrated by the endowment of new houses for religious orders, such as the Descalzas Reales. Philip II founded 17 convents and monasteries in Madrid, Philip III 14 and Philip IV another 17, and they would cover a third of the city until the 19th century. A wider city wall was put up in 1566, and the Puente de Segovia in the 1580s. Philip's favourite architect, Juan de Herrera, planned the rebuilding of the Plaza Mayor, but the only part built during his reign was the Casa de la Panadería in 1590.

The establishment of the Court and aristocracy in Madrid – the great centres of consumption and patronage – made it a magnet for people from all over Spain and abroad. The population went from under 20,000 in 1561 to 55,000 in 1584 and close to 85,000 by 1600. Building did not keep up with the influx, and a law decreed that in any house of more than one storey, the upper floor could be requisitioned to house members of the Court. In response, people simply put up houses with only one floor, and much of the new Madrid grew as a mass of shabby, low buildings slapped together out of mud.

This improvised capital did not impress foreign visitors. Lambert Wyts, a Flemish aristocrat who arrived in 1571, said that it was 'the foulest and filthiest town in Spain'. Thick mud made it impossible to ride a horse down the main streets in winter until a few cobbles were put down in the 1580s. There were no drains of any kind, and the streets were full of waste thrown out of the houses every night, producing an 'unbearable stench'.

Madrid had taken on a characteristic that would stay with it to this day – that it was a city of outsiders, in which at least 50 per cent of the population was from somewhere else. Another trait for which Madrid would be repeatedly condemned was that it was a city that consumed but did not produce anything. The trades that did develop in Madrid – shoe-making, carpentry, jewellery-making, fan-making, laceworking – were overwhelmingly oriented to servicing the Court and aristocracy.

THE COURT ADJOURNS

The greatest success of Philip II's reign was the defeat of the Turkish fleet off Lepanto in Greece in 1571. In 1580, he became King of Portugal and appeared to be at the height of his strength. However, suspensions of payment on his debts were becoming frequent, and in the 1560s a rebellion broke out in the Netherlands that would develop

IN CONTEXT

'Within a few months Madrid was so deserted "it appeared as if the Moors or the English had sacked and burnt it".'

into a morass into which Spanish armies and wealth would disappear. His dispute with England – leading to the Armada catastrophe – and interventions in France's religious wars were as costly.

As the number of unresolved problems mounted, a gnawing frustration spread through Castilian society, and scapegoats were sought. The former Muslims, nominally converted in 1502, were put under increasing pressure and then expelled from Spain in 1609, and the Inquisition – if not the all-pervading force of Protestant caricature – gained great powers to investigate deviations from Catholic orthodoxy.

Philip II died in 1598 at El Escorial, aged 71. His son Philip III (1598-1621) and grandson Philip IV (1621-65) had neither the intelligence, confidence or normally the motivation to carry on with the awesome burden of work he had set as an example. Philip III began the practice of ruling through a favourite or *valido*, in his case the Duke of Lerma. Spain's impoverished state, aggravated by a devastating plague in 1599, was impossible to ignore, and Lerma responded by making peace with England and the Dutch.

He also committed the ultimate injury to Madrid by moving the Court to Valladolid, in 1601. The stated reason was that this would revive the economy of northern Castile, although Lerma also stood to benefit personally. He also argued that Madrid was so overrun with undesirables that it had become intolerable. The monarchy's purpose-built capital was out of control and it would be best to write it off and start again.

Within a few months Madrid was so deserted 'it appeared as if the Moors or the English had sacked and burnt it'. By 1605, the population had fallen back to just 26,000, little more than before Philip II's arrival in 1561. However, the Valladolid experiment did not work, and it became evident that Madrid had acquired a momentum that was difficult to disregard. In 1606, the Court returned, amid huge rejoicing, and only a year later the population was already back to 70,000.

POMP AND CIRCUMSTANCE

It was after Madrid's definitive establishment as capital, with Philip III's brief declaration *Sólo Madrid es Corte* (Only Madrid is the Court), that more was at last done to give it the look of a grand city. The Plaza Mayor was finally completed in 1619, followed by the Ayuntamiento or city hall and the Buen Retiro palace. The aristocracy, too, began to build palaces around the city once they were assured they would not have to move on again, and Madrid acquired several much more elaborate baroque churches.

The Plaza Mayor was the great arena of Habsburg Madrid. Able to hold a third of the city's population at that time, it was the venue for state ceremonies, bullfights, executions, *autos-da-fé* (the ritual condemnation of heretics), mock battles, circus acts and carnival fiestas, as well as still being a market square.

Habsburg Madrid functioned rather like a giant theatre, a great backdrop against which the monarchy could display itself to its subjects and to the world. On either side were royal estates, which determined the shape of the city left in the middle and its peculiar north-south pattern of growth. Several times a year royal processions took place, with stops for various ceremonies in the Plaza Mayor and High Masses in various churches. For the occasion, buildings were covered in garlands, and temporary arches erected along the route with extravagant decoration extolling the virtues of the dynasty. As the Spanish monarchy slid towards economic collapse the lavishness of these ceremonies only increased, maintaining an illusion of power and opulence.

IN CONTEXT

Away from this ceremonial route, the Habsburgs built few squares and no grand avenues, and old Madrid continued to develop along the tangled street plan it retains today. Even so, the opulence of the Court – and the poverty outside the capital – still attracted more people into the city, and in about 1630 Madrid reached its maximum size under the Habsburgs, with possibly as many as 170,000 inhabitants. In 1656, it was given its fifth and final wall, roughly surrounding the area now considered 'old Madrid', which would set the limits of the city for the next 200 years.

THE PRICE OF WAR

For many years the centre of all the Court pomp was King Philip IV. Throughout the 1620s and 1630s, while the Court maintained its image of grandeur, his *valido*, the Count-Duke of Olivares, struggled to maintain the Spanish empire against threats on every side. In the 1620s, Spain won a series of victories, and for a time it seemed the rot had been stopped. In 1639, though, a Spanish fleet was destroyed by the Dutch, and in 1643 the French crushed the Spanish army at Rocroi in Flanders. Naval defeats made it ever more difficult for Spain to import gold and silver from America. Olivares sought to extend taxation in the non-Castilian dominions of the crown, which led in 1640 to revolts in Portugal and Catalonia. Portugal regained its independence, and the Catalan revolt was only suppressed after a 12-year war.

By mid-century the effects of endless wars on Castile were visible to all, in abandoned villages and social decay. Even Madrid went into decline, so that by 1700 the city's population had fallen back to about 100,000. In the 1660s, the total collapse of the Spanish empire seemed an immediate possibility. Castile, the first world power, had been left poorer than many of the countries it had tried to dominate.

END OF THE HABSBURG LINE

In the Court, meanwhile, life became ever more of a baroque melodrama. Of Philip IV's 12 legitimate children by his two wives, only two girls had survived into adulthood – the youngest the Infanta Margarita, the little princess in Velázquez's *Las Meninas*. In 1661, however, when Philip was already prematurely aged, the queen, Mariana of Austria, had a son.

The new heir, the future King Charles II, was chronically infirm from birth and provided the dynasty with scant consolation. The Habsburgs' marked tendency to ill-health was accentuated by their habit of marrying cousins or nieces. The Habsburg jaw, the growth of which can be followed through family portraits, had in Charles become a real disability. He was unable to eat solid food. Because of this – or, more likely, the endless cures he was subjected to for his many ailments – he suffered uncontrollable diarrhoea, which detracted from the stately dignity of Court ceremonies.

In the meantime, both the economy and the government continued to slide. Concern centred again on the need for an heir, and Charles was married off twice, despite a general belief that he was both impotent and sterile. As it became evident that the throne of the Spanish empire would soon become vacant, the Court was overrun with bizarre intrigues, with different factions and the agents of European powers all waiting on Charles' final demise. In 1695, the French Ambassador reported that the king 'appeared to be decomposing', and could barely walk without assistance. Even so, Charles hung on until the age of 38. In 1700, though, with the pathetic last words, '*Me duele todo*' (It hurts everywhere), he finally died, and the Spanish Habsburg dynasty came to an end.

BOURBON MADRID

Philip V (1700-46), first Bourbon King of Spain, secured his throne in 1714, after the 12-year War of the Spanish Succession. He was the grandson of Louis XIV of France and María Teresa, daughter of Philip IV of Spain. Castile, abandoning its more usual francophobia, gave him complete support. The alternative, Archduke Charles of Austria, was supported by Catalonia and the other Aragonese territories, to whom he had

El Escorial. *See p16.*

promised a restoration of their traditional rights. Twice, in 1706 and 1710, Charles' British, Dutch, Portuguese and Catalan army took Madrid, but was unable to hold it.

Once victorious, Philip reformed his new kingdom along the lines laid down by his illustrious grandfather in France. In 1715, the remaining rights of the former Aragonese territories were abolished, so that it is from this date that Spain can formally be said to exist.

A French king brought with him other innovations. Philip V, raised at Versailles, and his Italian second wife Isabella Farnese were not taken with Madrid or its gloomy Habsburg palaces, and so built their own Franco-Italian villa at La Granja. They were not overly upset when the entire Alcázar burnt down in 1734, and a new Palacio Real was commissioned from Italian architects. Philip V and his administrator of Madrid, the Marqués de Vadillo, also sponsored many buildings by a local architect, Pedro de Ribera.

Reform led to economic recuperation and a recovery in Madrid's population. People still came and went, but it also acquired a more stable resident population, with a merchant community and an artisan and working class. Even so, in many ways Madrid had changed little. Its main function was still to serve the Court, whose ceremonies set the calendar. They were as lavish as ever: until the 1770s the amount spent annually by the Crown in Madrid was greater than the entire budget of the Spanish navy.

Fernando VI (1746-59) was a shy but popular king who gave Spain its longest period of peace for over 200 years. Childless, he was succeeded by half-brother Charles III (1759-88). Previously King of Naples for 20 years, he too was less than impressed by Madrid. However, more than any of his predecessors he set about improving the city, becoming known as Madrid's Rey-Alcalde or 'King-Mayor'.

ENLIGHTENMENT STRIKES

Charles was fascinated by Enlightenment ideas of progress, science and the applied use of reason. No democrat, he sought to bring about rational improvement from the top. Reforms were undertaken in the bureaucracy and armed forces, and to improve trade with Spanish America. He challenged the privileges of the religious orders, and expelled the Jesuits from Spain in 1767 for their refusal to co-operate.

In Madrid, Charles first undertook to do something about the mud in winter, suffocating dust in summer and foul smells at all times – which were noted by every visitor to the city. A 1761 decree banned the dumping of waste in the streets, and Charles' Italian engineer-architect Francesco Sabatini began building sewers and street lighting. A string of major buildings was erected, of which the Casa de Correos in Puerta del Sol and the Puerta de Alcalá are the best-known. A later queen of Spain remarked that it sometimes seemed as if all the monuments of Madrid had been built by Charles III.

'Charles undertook to do something about the mud in winter, suffocating dust in summer and foul smells at all times.'

Charles III's grandest project was the Paseo del Prado (*see p84* **El Salón del Prado**). He sent scientific expeditions to every corner of his empire, and planned to exhibit the fruits of their varied researches in a Museum of Natural Sciences – now the Museo del Prado – and the adjacent Jardín Botánico.

Reform and improved trade did create a feeling of well-being in late 18th-century Madrid. Nevertheless, Spain was still a very feudal society, and the real economy remained backward and frail. And, in an absolute monarchy, a great deal depended on each monarch. Charles IV (1788-1808) had none of his father's energy or intelligence. Also, he chose as his minister the corrupt Manuel Godoy. After the French Revolution, Spain joined other monarchies in attacking the new regime; in 1795, however, Godoy made peace and then an alliance with France, leading to an unpopular war with Britain. Then, in 1808, when Godoy was vacillating over changing sides once again, he was forestalled by anti-French riots that proclaimed Charles IV's son Fernando as king in his place. Napoleon sent troops to Madrid, assuming this decrepit state would be as easy to conquer as any other. It was not to be, at least not initially, and the consequences were horrific (*see p23* **In the Frame**).

Once victory was his, Napoleon made his brother, Joseph Bonaparte, King of Spain. In Madrid he tried in a well-meaning fashion to make improvements, among them some squares for which the city has since been very grateful, notably the Plaza de Oriente and the Plaza Santa Ana. However, this did nothing to overcome the animosity around him. In 1812, the Duke of Wellington and his army arrived to take the city, in a battle that destroyed much of the Retiro palace. The French were finally driven out of Spain in 1813. As well as the fighting itself, the year 1812 brought with it a catastrophic famine, which in Madrid killed over 30,000 people.

The shock of this upheaval initiated a period of instability that continued until 1874 – in fact, it could be said that the instability only really ended with the death of Franco in 1975. Spain withdrew into its own problems, with one conflict after another between conservatives, reformists, revolutionaries and other factions. Each struggled to impose their model on the state and create a political system that could accommodate, or hold back, the pressures for modernisation and some form of democracy.

In 1812, a Cortes had met in Cádiz and given Spain its first constitution. Yet when Fernando VII (1808-33) returned from French captivity in 1814, his only thought was to cancel the constitution and return to the methods of his ancestors. His absolute rule, though, was incapable of responding to the bankruptcy of the country. The regime was also struggling to hold on to its American colonies, by then in complete rebellion. In 1820, a liberal revolt in the army forced Fernando to reinstate the constitution. He was saved three years later, ironically by a French army, sent to restore monarchical rule. Meanwhile, defeat at Ayacucho in Peru (1824) left Spain with only Cuba, Santo Domingo and Puerto Rico of its former American empire.

In 1830, Fernando VII's wife María Cristina gave birth to a daughter, soon to be Queen Isabel II (1833-68). Previously, the most reactionary sectors of the aristocracy, the Church and other ultra-conservative groups had aligned themselves behind the king's brother Don Carlos. When Fernando died in 1833, Carlos demanded the throne, launching what became known as the Carlist Wars. To defend her daughter's rights, María Cristina, as Regent, had no choice but to look for support from liberals, and so was obliged to promise some form of constitutional rule.

IN CONTEXT

OLD ROMANTICS

For the next 40 years Spanish politics was a see-saw, as conservative and liberal factions vied for power, while the Carlists, off the spectrum for most people in Madrid, occasionally threatened at the gates. Madrid was the great centre for aspiring politicians, and the problems of Spain were discussed endlessly in its salons and new cafés, which multiplied around this time. This was the era of Romanticism, and writers such as the journalist Larra and poet José Espronceda were heavily involved in politics. Similarly, many of the politicians of the day were also writers.

Much of the time, though, these reformers were shepherds in search of a flock, for there were no true political parties. The only way a faction could hope to gain power was with the support of a general with troops at his disposal.

This political instability did not mean that life in Madrid was chaotic. Visitors in the early 1830s found a small, sleepy, shabby city, which seemed sunk in the past. Convents and palaces still occupied nearly half its area. It was around this time that Spain acquired its romantic aura. A growing number of foreigners visited, drawn by Spain's timeless, exotic qualities. One was the French writer Prosper Mérimée, who in 1845 wrote his novel *Carmen*, later put to music by Bizet, who himself never visited Spain at all.

EXPANSION AND TURMOIL

The 1830s, however, also saw the single most important change in Madrid during the 19th century. In 1836, the liberal minister Mendizábal took advantage of the church's sympathy for Carlism to introduce his Desamortización or Disentailment law, which dissolved most of Spain's monasteries. In Madrid, the church lost over 1,000 properties. Most were demolished remarkably quickly, and an enormous area thus became available for sale and new building.

Some urban reformers saw this as an opportunity to build broad, airy avenues, following the always-cited example of Paris. Some major projects were undertaken, the most important being the rebuilding of the Puerta del Sol in 1854-62. However, most of the local traders who benefited from Desamortización lacked the capital to contemplate grand projects, and built separate blocks without ever challenging the established, disorderly street plan. The districts of old Madrid took on the appearance they have largely kept until today, with great numbers of tenement blocks. They allowed Madrid to grow considerably in population, without going outside its still-standing wall of 1656.

A few factories had appeared in the city, but for the most part the Industrial Revolution was passing Madrid by. Constitutional governments expanded the administration, and the ambitions of the middle class were focused on obtaining official posts rather than on business ventures. Two more major changes arrived in the 1850s. In 1851, Madrid got its first railway, to Aranjuez, followed by a line running to the Mediterranean. Railways would transform Madrid's relationship with the rest of the country, opening up a realistic possibility of it fulfilling an economic function. Equally important was the completion of the Canal de Isabel II, bringing water from the Guadarrama, in 1858. Madrid's water supply, still part-based on Moorish water courses, had been inadequate for years. The canal removed a crippling obstruction to the city's growth.

Madrid's population was by this time over 300,000. Steps were finally taken for it to break out of its old walls, and in 1860 a plan by Carlos María de Castro was approved for the Ensanche (extension) of Madrid, in an orderly grid pattern to the north and east. However, as with earlier rebuilding, the plan came up against the chronic lack of large-scale local investors. The only major development undertaken quickly was the section of C/Serrano bought up by the flamboyant speculator the Marqués de Salamanca, whose name was given to the whole district.

Meanwhile, the political situation was deteriorating once again, after a long period of conservative rule that began in 1856. Isabel II had become deeply unpopular, surrounded by an aura of sleaze and scandal. In September 1868, yet another military revolt deposed the government and, this time, the queen as well.

IN CONTEXT

There followed six years of turmoil. The provisional government invited an Italian prince, Amadeo of Savoy, to become king of a truly constitutional monarchy. However, in December 1870, General Prim, strongman of the new regime, was assassinated. Carlist revolts broke out in some parts of the country, while on the left new, more radical groups began to appear. At the end of 1868, a meeting in Madrid addressed by Giuseppe Fanelli, an Italian associate of Bakunin, led to the founding of the first anarchist group in Spain. The Cortes itself was riven by factions, and Amadeo decided to give up the struggle and go back to Italy.

On 12 February 1873, Spain became a republic. Rightist resistance became stronger than ever, while many towns were taken over by left-wing juntas, who declared them autonomous 'cantons', horrifying conservative opinion. To keep control, Republican governments relied increasingly heavily on the army. This proved fatal, and on 3 January 1874 the army commander in Madrid, General Pavía, marched into the Cortes, sent all its members home, and installed a military dictatorship.

THE BOURBONS RETURN

At the end of 1874, the army decided to restore the Bourbon dynasty, in the shape of Alfonso XII (1874-85), the son of Isabel II. The architect of the Restoration regime, however, was a civilian politician, Antonio Cánovas del Castillo. He established the system of *turno pacífico*, or peaceful alternation in power (thus avoiding social tensions), between a Conservative Party, led by himself, and a Liberal Party which was made up of former progressives. The control of these 'dynastic parties' over the political system was made secure by election-rigging and occasional repression.

In the late 1870s, the wealthy of Madrid set out on a building boom. They finally overcame their reluctance to leave the old city, and the Salamanca area became the new centre of fashionable life. Most of the district's new apartment blocks had lifts, first seen in Madrid in 1874. In earlier blocks upper floors had been let cheaply, so that rich and poor had often continued to live side by side. With lifts, however, a top floor could be as desirable as a first, and this kind of class mixing faded.

Government and official bodies, too, undertook a huge round of new building. The Banco de España, the Bolsa and the main railway stations are all creations of the 1880s. Madrid meanwhile acquired a larger professional middle class; it also attracted intellectuals from around the country.

At the same time, Madrid was receiving an influx of poor migrants from rural Spain, with over 200,000 new arrivals between 1874 and 1900. Economic growth was reflected in the appearance of yet more small workshops rather than factories. There were also many with next to no work, and the 1880s saw the beginning of a housing crisis, with the growth of shanty towns around the outskirts of the city.

THE EMPIRE STRIKES BACK

Just before the end of the century, however, the preconceptions on which Spanish political life had been based received a shattering blow. The Restoration regime presented itself as having returned the country to stability and some prestige in the world. However, in the 1890s Spain was involved in colonial wars against nationalists in the Philippines and Cuba. In 1898, the government allowed itself to be manoeuvred into a disastrous war with the United States of America. In a few weeks, almost the entire Spanish navy was sunk, and Spain lost virtually all its remaining overseas territories. Known simply as 'The Disaster', this was a devastating blow to Spain's self-confidence. The regime itself was revealed as decrepit and incompetent, based on a feeble economy. Among intellectuals, the situation sparked off an intense round of self-examination and discussion of Spain's relationship with the very concept of modernity. The problems of the regime were not due to the country being backward, however. Rather, they spiralled out of control because after 1900 the country entered an unprecedented period of change.

In the Frame The Third of May

Goya's extraordinary painting of the reality of war.

IN CONTEXT

More than 200 years old, this remains one of the world's most modern paintings. It marked a complete transformation in the portrayal of war. Previously, with very few exceptions, war paintings had presented war as noble contest, glorifying heroic deeds and celebrating kings and commanders – a prime example hangs nearby in the Prado, Velázquez' *Las Lanzas*. In Goya's war images, in contrast – whether the *Tres de Mayo* or the *Desastres de la Guerra* – there is no glory, only misery, brutality and chaos. Death, mutilation and casual savagery are more prominent than victories. There are no generals or famous heroes, only faces in the crowd. There is heroism – again anonymous – but it seems wild, desperate, ultimately futile. It is this searingly honest, unblinking sense of the truth and horror of violence that makes the *Tres de Mayo* so permanently contemporary.

The events portrayed were very real. On 2 May 1808, Madrid awoke to learn that Napoleon had kidnapped the Spanish royal family, and that French troops were taking over the country. The French expected little resistance beyond skirmishes and some manageable grumbling. Instead, uncoordinated Spanish army units and, above all, the people of Madrid fought the invaders street by street, using knives or their bare hands. As the day wore on, the French gradually won control of Madrid, and in the early morning of 3 May – enraged that they had had to fight so hard against a mere street mob, rather than real soldiers – they set out to teach the city a lesson. Captured 'insurgents' were disposed of in mass executions on the hill of Príncipe Pío, which is now at the southern end of the Parque del Oeste.

Goya painted his *Dos de Mayo*, of the struggle in the Puerta del Sol, and *Tres de Mayo* in 1814, just after the French had been driven out of Spain. How much personal observation went into them is an unanswered question. Goya was in Madrid during those days, and one of his gardeners later claimed the artist had watched the executions through a telescope. However, this is impossible to confirm.

Goya's The Third of May 1808 in Madrid *is found at the Prado (see p88).*

CITY WITHOUT LIMITS

Sudden economic expansion was set off by three main factors. One, ironically, was the loss of the colonies, which led to large amounts of capital being brought back to the country. Most important was World War I, which provided unheard-of opportunities for neutral Spain in the supply of goods to the Allied powers. Then, during the worldwide boom of the 1920s, Spain benefited hugely from foreign investment.

Within a few years, Spain had one of the fastest rates of urbanisation in the world. The economic upheaval caused by the world war led to runaway inflation, spurring a huge movement into the cities. Madrid did not grow as rapidly as industrial Barcelona, which had become the largest city in the country. Nevertheless, after taking four centuries to reach half a million, it doubled its population again in just 30 years, to just under a million by 1930. Only 37 per cent of its people had been born in the city.

The most visible manifestation of this growth was a still-larger building boom. Bombastic creations such as the Palacio de Comunicaciones (now called the Palacio de Cibeles) were symptomatic of the expansive mood. Most important was the opening of the Gran Vía in 1910, a project that had first been discussed no less than 25 years previously, which would transform the heart of the old city with a new grand thoroughfare for entertainment, business and banking.

Another fundamental innovation was electricity. The city's trams were electrified in 1898, and the first metro line, between Sol and Cuatro Caminos, opened in 1919. Electricity allowed Madrid, far from any other source of power, finally to experience an industrial take-off in the years after 1910. At the same time, expansion in banking and office work was also reflected in the large number of white-collar workers.

Madrid was also, more than ever, the mecca for intellectuals and professionals from right across the country. This was the background to the enormous vigour of the city's intellectual life at this time, the so-called 'Silver Age' of Spanish literature. From writers of 1898, such as Antonio Machado and Baroja, to the famous poets of the 1927 generation, Rafael Alberti and García Lorca, the city welcomed a succession of literary talent, not to mention painters, historians and scientists. From the 1910s onward, Madrid's cafés were full of talk, forums for discussion multiplied, and any number of newspapers and magazines were published.

In politics, this urban expansion made it impossible for the 'dynastic parties' to control elections in the way they were able to do in small towns and rural areas. In an attempt to move back towards some form of constitutional rule, the government decided to hold local elections on 12 April 1931. They were not expected to be a referendum on the monarchy. However, when the results came in it was seen that republican candidates had won sweeping majorities in all of Spain's cities.

THE SECOND REPUBLIC

On 14 April 1931, as the results of the local elections became clear, the streets of Spain's cities filled with people. In Madrid, a jubilant mass converged on the Puerta del Sol. It was these exultant crowds in the streets that drove the king to abdicate and spurred republican politicians into action, for they had never expected their opportunity to arrive so soon.

The second Spanish Republic arrived amid huge optimism, expressing the frustrated hopes of decades. Among the many schemes of its first government, a Republican-Socialist coalition, was a project for Madrid, the Gran Madrid or 'Greater Madrid' plan, intended to integrate the sprawling new areas around the city's edge. A key part of it was the extension of the Castellana, then blocked by a racecourse above C/Joaquín Costa. The racecourse was demolished, and the Castellana was allowed to snake endlessly northward, forming one of the modern city's most distinctive features. Also completed under the Republic was the last section of the Gran Vía, from Callao to Plaza de España, site of Madrid's best art deco buildings.

'The level of polarisation and of sheer hatred in the country was moving out of control.'

Possibilities of further change and renovation, however, were to be entangled in the accelerating social crisis that overtook the Republic around this time. The new regime aroused expectations that would have been difficult to live up to at the best of times. Instead, its arrival coincided with the onset of the worldwide depression of the 1930s.

THE POLARISATION OF POLITICS

As unemployment and the gap between rich and poor increased, calls for the end of republican compromise in a second, social, revolution increased, especially from the anarchist CNT and the Communist Party. Even the Socialist Party was radicalised. On the right, similarly, the loudest voices – such as the fascist Falange, founded in 1933 by José Antonio Primo de Rivera, son of the former dictator – demanded authoritarian rule as the only means of preserving social order. The vogue for extremism was fed by the mood of the times, in which Nazism, Italian Fascism and Soviet Communism appeared as the most dynamic international models.

In 1933, the coalition between Socialists and liberal republicans broke up. With the left split, elections were won by conservative republicans backed by the CEDA, a parliamentary but authoritarian right-wing party. Reform came to a halt. In October 1934, the CEDA demanded to have ministers in the government, and a general strike was called in response. It was strongest in the mining region of Asturias, where it was savagely suppressed by a rising general called Francisco Franco.

Left-wing parties were subjected to a wave of repression that radicalised their supporters further. In new elections in February 1936, however, the left, united once again in the Frente Popular (Popular Front), were victorious. In Madrid, the Front won 54 per cent of the vote.

A liberal-republican government returned to power, with Manuel Azaña as president. By this time, however, the level of polarisation and of sheer hatred in the country was moving out of control. Right-wing politicians called almost openly for the army to save the country. The military had already laid their plans for a coup.

REVOLUTION AND WAR

On 18 July 1936, the generals made their move, with risings all over Spain, while German and Italian aircraft ferried Franco's colonial army from Spanish Morocco to Andalucia. In Madrid, troops failed to seize the city and barricaded themselves inside the Montaña barracks, the site of which is now in the Parque del Oeste.

The coup was the spark for an explosion of tension. The workers' parties demanded arms. On 20 July, as news came that the army had been defeated in Barcelona and many other cities, the Montaña was stormed and its defenders massacred, despite the efforts of political leaders to prevent it. Among left-wing militants the mood was ecstatic: factories, schools, the transport system and other public services were all taken over, and, although the government remained in place, it had little effective power. Ad-hoc militias and patrols were the only power on the streets, and, amid the paranoia and hatred that were the other side of revolutionary excitement, summary executions of suspected rightists were common.

Meanwhile, the war still had to be fought. Franco's troops were advancing from Seville preceded by stories of reprisals more terrible than anything done by the 'red terror' in Madrid. The militias seemed powerless to stop them. Defeat for the Republic seemed inevitable. German planes bombed the city. On 6 November, as Franco's advance guard arrived, the government left for Valencia, a move widely seen as desertion.

CITY UNDER SIEGE

Without a government, however, a new resolve was seen in the city. In the southern suburbs, troops were resisted street by street. Women, children and the elderly joined in building trenches and barricades. On 9 November the first foreign volunteers, the International Brigades, arrived, doing wonders for morale. After savage fighting, Franco halted the frontal assault on Madrid in November 1936.

Madrid saw little more direct fighting. From the Casa de Campo, where the remains of trenches and bunkers still exist, the army settled in to a siege. Attempts to push them back north and south of Madrid were unsuccessful. The city was regularly bombed, and bombarded by artillery, who took their sights from the Gran Vía, 'Howitzer Avenue'.

General Franco, meanwhile, was advancing on other fronts. During 1937, his forces overran the Basque Country and Asturias, and in March 1938 they reached the Mediterranean near Castellón. In January 1939, they conquered Catalonia. In Madrid, fighting broke out behind Republican lines between the Communists, committed to fighting to the end, and groups who wanted to negotiate a settlement with Franco. Those in favour of negotiation won, but Franco had no intention of compromising. On 28 March 1939, the Nationalist army entered the Spanish capital.

THE LONG DICTATORSHIP

Madrid emerged from the Civil War physically and psychologically battered. Throughout the city, hundreds of buildings stood in ruins. Buildings, however, could be rebuilt fairly quickly; healing the damage done to the city's spirit would take decades.

The Madrid of the 1940s was the sombre antithesis of the expansive city of ten years previously, or its current outgoing, vivacious self. A great many *madrileños* had lost someone close to them, to bombs, bullets, firing squads or prison camps. The black market, rather than art and literature, dominated café conversation, and the figures of earlier years were mostly in exile, or keeping indoors.

The existence of 'two Spains' (right–left, traditional–liberal, rich–poor) was all too apparent. As the victors marched in, they wasted no time in rounding up members (or just suspected sympathisers) of 'enemy' groups, anarchists, Communists, union members and liberals. Some were turned in by neighbours, creating a sordid atmosphere of bitterness and distrust. During the early '40s, while the rest of the world was wrapped up in World War II, thousands were executed in Spain. Others paid the price of defeat by serving as forced labour on fascist landmarks such as the Valle de los Caídos, Franco's victory monument and tomb.

Madrid's loyalty to the Republic almost led to it losing its capital status, as voices were raised calling for a more 'loyal' city to represent the country. Tradition and financial interests bore more weight, however, and the capital stayed put. The Falange, official party of the regime, produced extravagant plans to turn Madrid into a Spanish version of Imperial Rome, but a lack of funding and galloping inflation scotched most of these nouveau-Imperialist notions. The economy was in a desperate state, and Spain went through a period of extreme hardship, the *años del hambre* ('hunger years'); many remember not having eaten properly for ten years after 1936. This poverty also led to the phenomenon that would most shape the face of Madrid in the post-war decades: massive immigration from Spain's rural provinces. Madrid grew faster than any other European capital in the 20th century. A 'big village' of just over half a million at the turn of the century, and 950,000 in 1930, it passed the three million mark by 1970.

Most European countries continued to shun the regime, at least in public, but in 1953, as the Cold War intensified, Franco was saved by the US government's 'our son-of-a-bitch' policy in choosing allies. A co-operation treaty gave the regime renewed credibility and cash in exchange for air and sea bases on Spanish soil, and later President Eisenhower flew in to shake the dictator's hand.

For those not devoted to the regime, life under Franco was a matter of keeping one's head down. Football and other forms of escapism played a huge part in people's lives.

'Life under Franco was a matter of keeping one's head down. Football and other forms of escapism played a huge part in people's lives.'

The national Stabilisation Plan of 1959 gave the fundamental push to Madrid's development, and brought Spain definitively back into the Western fold. The plan revolutionised the country's economy, and especially that of the Madrid region. In the 1960s, tourism began to pump money into Spain, and Madrid trebled in size to become an industrial powerhouse. Quiet tree-lined boulevards were widened to make way for cars, and elegant Castellana palaces were replaced by glass-sheathed monoliths. Madrid took on much more of the look, and feel, of a big city.

LIFE AFTER FRANCO

The 1960s also saw the revival of opposition to the regime in the shape of labour unrest, student protests, and the rise of the Basque organisation ETA. The oil crisis of 1973 coincided with the assassination by ETA of Franco's prime minister, Admiral Carrero Blanco, when a bomb planted beneath a Madrid street launched his car right over a five-storey building. The regime, already challenged by political opposition, now had to deal with rising unemployment, inflation and a moribund Franco. The transition to democracy had begun.

Franco died in November 1975, closing a parenthesis of nearly 40 years in Spanish history. A new age, uncertain but exciting, dawned. In July 1976, King Juan Carlos, chosen by Franco to succeed him, named a former Falange bureaucrat, Adolfo Suárez, as prime minister. Nobody, however, knew quite what was going to happen.

To widespread surprise, Suárez initiated a comprehensive programme of political reform. Clandestine opposition leaders surfaced, parties were legalised and famous exiles began coming home. The first democratic elections since 1936 were held in June 1977, and a constitution was approved in late 1978. Suárez' centrist UCD (Centre-Democratic Union) won the national elections, but local elections in Madrid in 1979 were won by the Socialists, led by Enrique Tierno Galván as Mayor.

The 'other' Spain, however, had not disappeared. In fact, it was starting to feel nervous. Hard-core Francoists were horrified at the thought of Socialists and/or Communists coming to power. Significantly, many of the 'old guard' still held influential positions in the armed forces, and were not inclined to give them up easily.

On 23 February 1981, democrats' worst nightmares appeared to come true when a Civil Guard colonel called Tejero burst into the Cortes with a squad of men, firing his pistol into the air. A little after midnight, King Juan Carlos appeared on TV and assured the country that the army had sworn him its allegiance and that the coup attempt would fail. The next day, people poured on to the streets to demonstrate support for freedom and democracy.

The wolf had shown his teeth, but they were not as sharp as had been feared. Moreover, the coup attempt significantly helped to win Felipe González and the socialist PSOE their landslide victory in the elections of November 1982.

SOCIAL REVOLUTION, CITY RENOVATIONS

The late 1970s and early '80s saw the arrival of democracy and free speech, the loosening of drug laws and the breakdown of sexual conventions. The compulsorily staid Madrid of earlier years gave way to an anything-goes, vivacious city: an explosion of art, counter-culture and nightlife, creativity and frivolity known as the Movida – very roughly translatable as 'Shift' or 'Movement'.

IN CONTEXT

The Socialists used their control of Madrid's Ayuntamiento – led by the fondly remembered Tierno Galván – to renovate the city's weak infrastructure, with long-overdue facelifts in squares and parks. Mayor Tierno also provided unprecedented support for various progressive causes and for the arts, launching a whole string of new festivals.

If Tierno Galván's local administration was happy to be regarded as godfather to the Movida, the national government of Felipe González was still more eager to be seen as leaders of a reborn country. Decades of isolation ended with Spain's entry into the EU in 1986. This had a near-immediate effect on the economy, and in the late '80s the country was the fastest-growing member of the EU. The González governments achieved major improvements in some areas – among them health and the transport system – but also frustrated the expectations of many of their supporters, often giving the impression they believed modernisation would solve all Spain's problems more or less by itself.

The apotheosis of the country's transition was the 'Year of Spain' in 1992, with the Barcelona Olympics, Expo '92 in Seville and, with a somewhat lower profile, Madrid's year as Cultural Capital of Europe. Afterwards, a different mood became apparent. Spain's pre-'92 boom had postponed the effects of the international downturn at the end of the '80s, but it hit Madrid with a vengeance in 1993. Breakneck growth had created its own problems, and land speculation sent property prices spiralling.

Disenchantment with the Socialists and a newly cautious mood that followed the brash overconfidence of the boom years were major factors behind the rise of the re-formed right of the Partido Popular (PP). Even before Spain's great year, in 1991, the PSOE had lost control of the Madrid city administration to the PP.

THE POPULAR VOTE

The 1990s in Spain were markedly different in feel and content from the preceding decade. Led by the deliberately bland José María Aznar, the Partido Popular ably connected with the groundswell of discontent provoked by the later years of Socialist administrations. In the 1993 election Felipe González, long the great survivor of Spanish politics, lost his overall majority, but staggered on for another three years by means of a pact with Catalan nationalists. Next time, however, in 1996, the winners were the PP, even though they too still had to rely on pacts with minority parties to be able to form a sustainable government. The PSOE was sent into opposition for the first time in 14 years.

In Madrid, the PP had already made its mark on local life. Having rallied voters by denouncing the sleaze and corruption that overwhelmed the PSOE, and the Socialists' irresponsible – as many saw it – spending of taxpayers' money, the PP felt it had a clear mandate to cut back and balance the books. In Madrid, this meant cuts in budgets for arts festivals, a tightening up on licences for new bars and clubs and a general attack on the supposed excesses of the nightlife scene.

Despite harsh criticism for its perceived philistine approach to culture, its decidedly un-liberal stance on issues such as immigration or gay rights or its Francoist origins, the PP managed an absolute majority in the 2000 general elections, thanks mainly to its practical, managerial approach to the economy and the disarray of the opposition. Its second term in office was a different story, with the 2002 general strike, closely followed by the sinking of the *Prestige*, Spain's worst-ever ecological disaster. Aznar's flirtation with Bush and Blair led to Spain participating, albeit in a small way, in the Iraq war, against the wishes of 94 per cent of the Spanish people.

The 11 March bombings, and the subsequent media manipulation, were the last straw. The Socialists, under the mild-mannered José Luis Zapatero, had been carefully rebuilding and were now seen as an alternative. On taking power, Zapatero's government immediately brought the Spanish troops back from Iraq and embarked cautiously but firmly on a programme of modernisation of political structures and

EL PAÍS

www.elpais.com · EL PERIÓDICO GLOBAL EN ESPAÑOL

LUNES · EDICIÓN MADRID · **Precio: 1,20 euros**

EUFORIA EN ESPAÑA TRAS CORONAR POR PRIMERA VEZ LA CIMA DEL FÚTBOL

Campeones del mundo

▸ La Roja vence 1-0 en la prórroga a Holanda con un gol de Iniesta
▸ La selección consolida el liderazgo de una generación deslumbrante

Los jugadores de España celebran la victoria tras doblegar a Holanda 1-0 a cuatro minutos del final de la prórroga. Iker Casillas alza la primera Copa del Mundo de La Roja. / ALEJANDRO RUESGA

society. Steps were taken to redefine the nature of relationships between the autonomous regions and the Spanish state; gay marriages have been legalised and a law to provide help for families with income-less dependants has been promulgated. The first steps were taken on the rocky road to peace in the Basque Country. In March 2006, ETA declared a 'permanent ceasefire' but later claimed responsibility for a bomb that exploded at Barajas airport, killing two, in December 2006.

Zapatero won a second term in the 2008 elections. However, with Spain's rate of unemployment increasing from eight per cent to 20 per cent in the past three years of recession, the rising cost of living, and the government's wildly unpopular labour and pensions reforms (part of the 2010 austerity drive), it's no surprise that Zapatero's popularity has slipped badly in recent opinion polls. The World Cup win in summer 2010 lifted flagging spirits, but tough times are ahead.

In Madrid itself, the PP still controls both city and region, under Alberto Ruiz-Gallardón and Esperanza Aguirre respectively. Though belonging to the same party, they represent radically different styles and their mutual aversion is no secret. They have managed to show a united front – albeit somewhat frostily – during the failed campaigns to secure the 2012 and 2016 Olympics, but they will need to bury their differences to face the multiple challenges of Madrid's unbridled growth, the continued regeneration of the centre, the fall-out of the recession, and immigration.

Architecture

The story of Madrid's bricks and mortar.

TEXT: HARVEY HOLTOM & ANNA NORMAN

Madrid's past, turbulent and grand in equal measure, is barely apparent from the city's architecture. The city walls stayed up until the 1860s – longer than in most European cities – meaning that Madrid was forced to build on top of itself, replacing existing constructions at such a rate that by the late 19th century it was a surprisingly modern city.

Its history is, however, reflected in a highly individual, eccentric mixture of architectural styles. To a greater or lesser degree, traces of most of Madrid's past epochs and their influences – Moorish, Flemish, Italian, French and American – are to be found. A truly *madrileño* architectural identity is elusive, but the city can claim one, typically unusual, style as its own – neo-Mudéjar. Madrid also has many totally unique monuments.

The urban planning boom of the past decade, which saw building works blocking up squares and closing off streets for years, has now slowed with the recession, delaying projects such as the high-profile Campus of Justice. But its legacy is some fantastic new architecture (CaixaForum, Matadero Madrid) and a host of revitalised, more pedestrian-friendly public spaces.

IN THE BEGINNING

The first town wall was built by the Moors, and a segment of it (the **Muralla Arabe**) can be found on Cuesta de la Vega, near the Almudena cathedral. For centuries after their 're-conquest', Madrid and most of Castile continued to have large populations of Muslims living under Christian rule, the Mudéjares. The Castilian monarchs were greatly in thrall to their superior building skills, especially in bricklaying and tiling, and throughout the Middle Ages many of the country's important buildings incorporated techniques and styles that had originated in Muslim Andalucia. Hallmarks of the Mudéjar style are Moorish arches and intricate geometric patterns in brickwork, as seen on the 12th-century tower of Madrid's oldest surviving church, **San Nicolás de las Servitas**, built by Arab craftsmen (the body was later rebuilt). Madrid's other Mudéjar tower, on **San Pedro el Viejo**, was built 200 years later. Other medieval buildings in Madrid, such as the 15th-century **Torre de los Lujanes** in Plaza de la Villa, were much plainer in style, reflecting the town's humble status before 1561.

CAPITAL GAINS

Capital status, briefly in 1561 and definitively from 1606, transformed Madrid and its architecture. As royal seat, 'the Court', the tastes of successive rulers were especially important. Philip II's favourite architect, Juan de Herrera, was the first to leave a stamp on the city. He and his royal master had little idea of urban planning, but their major constructions – the **Puente de Segovia** (1584), the first stages of the Plaza Mayor, the widening of Calles Atocha and Segovia – gave Madrid a shape that lasts to this day.

El Escorial, designed by Herrera and Juan Bautista de Toledo, firmly established the 'Herreran' or 'Court' style – austere, rigid and typically employing grey slate for rooftops and the ubiquitous pointed turrets – that became near-obligatory for major buildings in Madrid until the end of the Habsburg era in 1700, despite changes in fashion elsewhere in Europe. Now a symbol of the 'Madrid of the Austrias', it is also known as Castilian baroque, but few of its features are especially 'Castilian': the slate pinnacles came from Flanders, which appealed to the Flemish-born Charles V.

Herrera's chief disciple, Juan Gómez de Mora, modified his master's legacy with a lighter and less monolithic style. He oversaw the completion of the **Plaza Mayor** in 1619 – his original plan is still recognisable in the slate spires, high-pitched roofs and dormer windows – and the 1630 **Casa de la Villa**, the City Hall. Gómez was also structurally innovative, as seen in the massive cellars and housing blocks along Cava San Miguel, which back on to and complete the Plaza Mayor. Due to the abrupt drop in the level of the land, he was obliged to build up to eight storeys high for these blocks to meet the rest of the square, making them Madrid's tallest buildings until the 20th century.

His great rival in Madrid was Gian Battista Crescenzi, an Italian who adopted the 'Court style' – with some Italian flourishes – to please his Spanish masters. Both architects probably worked, at different times, on the **Palacio de Santa Cruz** near the Plaza Mayor, built in 1629-43, nowadays the Foreign Ministry. It shows clear Italian baroque influences, with a façade much more richly shaped than anything Herrera would have tried. Crescenzi also undertook the largest single building scheme of Habsburg Madrid, the **Palacio del Buen Retiro**, parts of which have survived.

Though the Habsburgs commissioned much that was noble and even palatial, 17th-century visitors to Madrid still saw haphazard growth, chaos and dirt rather than a city fit to be capital of the first worldwide empire. Much building was unimpressive owing to the rickety economy, which meant bricks and mortar were favoured over expensive stone.

BOURBON RENEWAL

The expiry of the Spanish Habsburgs with King Charles II in 1700 was followed by war, and the arrival of the Bourbons, under Philip V. The new dynasty endeavoured to embellish and dignify Madrid. The Bourbons were French, and Philip V's second wife, Isabella Farnese, was Italian, and these two influences would long predominate in the dynasty's architectural tastes. Nevertheless, Philip V's administrator in Madrid, the Marqués de Vadillo, commissioned a local architect, Pedro de Ribera, for many projects, among them the 1722 Hospice, now the **Museo de Historia**, the **Cuartel Conde Duque** barracks, now the Centro Cultural Conde Duque, the **Puente de Toledo** and many churches. Ribera's buildings, while following the Herreran tradition, feature exuberant baroque façades centred on elaborately carved entrance porticoes. Many Ribera entrances still survive on buildings that have since been rebuilt, as in the 1734 Palace of the Dukes of Santoña at C/Huertas 3, now occupied by the Cámara de Comercio.

The influence of French and Italian architects was more apparent elsewhere in 18th-century Madrid. After the old grey-spired **Alcázar** burnt down in 1734, Philip V commissioned a new **Palacio Real** from a group of mainly Italian architects led by Filippo Juvarra and Giambattista Sacchetti. Responsible for many projects was Charles III's 'chief engineer', Francesco Sabatini. The great exponents of the sober, 'pure' neo-classicism of the later years of Charles III's reign, however, were Spaniards: Ventura Rodríguez, who had also worked on the Palacio Real, and Juan de Villanueva, architect of the **Museo del Prado** and the **Observatorio**. Like the greatest project of the king's reign, the **Paseo del Prado** – of which these buildings were part – they clearly reflect Enlightenment ideals of architecture and urban planning.

RISE AND SPRAWL

Joseph Bonaparte's brief reign (1808-13) saw the first demolition of monasteries and convents, to be replaced by squares such as Plaza Santa Ana. Generally, though, the first half of the 19th century brought architectural stagnation to Madrid. After the great clearance of monasteries began in the 1830s, many of the buildings that replaced them were simple apartment and tenement blocks, such as the *corralas* (*see p77*). Public buildings of this time, such as the 1840s **Cortes** or the **Teatro Real**, were often conservative and neo-classical in style.

Greater changes came to Madrid after 1860, with the demolition of the walls and Carlos María de Castro's plan for the city's extension or '*ensanche*'. Areas covered by the plan are easy to spot on a map by their grid street pattern. Chief among them is the Barrio de Salamanca, still the most self-consciously grand *barrio* of the *ensanche*. Its wealthiest residents built in an eclectic mix of styles; some of their opulent mansions still stand on Calles Velázquez and Serrano. Other *ensanche* districts – like Chamberí and Argüelles – show rational urban layout, wide thoroughfares and regular-sized blocks.

Public buildings of the first years of the Bourbon Restoration were as eclectic as Salamanca mansions. Madrid's own revivalist style, neo-Mudéjar (*see right* **Moors Code**), was used for official buildings, bullrings, churches, homes and factories. In contrast, one of the most extraordinary constructions of the time, Ricardo Velázquez' **Ministerio de Agricultura** in Atocha, is a remarkable combination of Castilian brickwork and extravagant, French Beaux Arts-style sculpted decoration. This was also the great period of cast-iron architecture in Madrid, with fine structures such as the city markets and the **Estación de Atocha**.

Art nouveau (called '*modernismo*' in Spain), so characteristic of early 20th-century Barcelona, aroused little interest in Madrid, but there are some examples. The **Sociedad General de Autores** (1902), by Jose Grasés Riera, is the best known, but the **Casa Pérez Villamil** at Plaza Matute 6, off C/Huertas, is also impressive.

CUTTING A SWATHE

As the *ensanche* progressed and Madrid's economy boomed from the 1900s to the 1920s, the city's architects looked for inspiration forwards and backwards in time, and both inside and outside Spain. The **Gran Vía**, which celebrated its centenary in 2010, was born of this thinking. An all-modern thoroughfare through Madrid's old centre, the Gran Vía destroyed 14 old streets, becoming grander and more eccentric as it progressed. Writer Francisco Umbral claims it recalls New York or Chicago, but its first

Moors Code

Madrid's neo-Mudéjar architecture was inspired by Moorish styles.

Around 1870, an architectural style emerged in Madrid that the city can claim as its own: neo-Mudéjar. The first example of the style was the new bullring commissioned to replace the plain 18th-century one that stood near the Puerta de Alcalá. In the revivalist atmosphere of the 19th century, architects Ricardo Rodríguez Ayuso and Lorenzo Alvarez Capra decided not to look to Gothic or Egyptian traditions for inspiration, but searched instead for something to revive that was closer to home. They opted for the styles and superb bricklaying techniques that had been employed by the Muslim Mudéjar master builders of medieval Castile.

Neo-Mudéjar uniquely incorporated Moorish horseshoe arches, interlaced brickwork and arabesque tiling, together with a modern use of glass and cast iron. The 1870s bullring no longer stands, but the style became near-obligatory for *plazas de toros* throughout Spain, and Madrid's next ring at **Las Ventas** (*pictured*), completed in 1934, sports many neo-Mudéjar features. The style was extended to other buildings too. Perhaps the best example in Madrid is the **Escuelas Aguirre**, also by Ayuso and

Alvarez Capra, at the intersection of Calles Alcalá and O'Donnell on the north side of the Retiro. Its outstanding feature is a slim minaret-style tower, with a glass and iron lookout-gallery.

Another splendid Arab-inspired tower is the giant spire of the **Santa Cruz** church at the top of C/Atocha (No.6), built in 1899-1902. And the city's new **Matadero Madrid** cultural centre (*see p110*) is a revamped neo-Mudéjar building that was once the city abattoir.

But the style was also used for more everyday buildings, as in the block of flats at C/Barquillo 21 in Chueca, which displays a façade combining diamond-pattern brickwork, neo-Moorish plaster details and iron-work balconies.

IN CONTEXT

building of any standing, the 1905 **Edificio Metrópolis**, shows French inspiration. No.24 is neo-Renaissance, the 1930s **Palacio de la Música** cinema (No.35) has distinctly baroque touches, and the 1929 **Telefónica** building (on the corner of C/Fuencarral) is a New York skyscraper in miniature. The 1930 apartment block at Gran Vía 60 is a classic of *madrileño* cosmopolitanism, by Carlos Fernández Shaw, who in 1927 also built a futuristic petrol station where C/Alberto Aguilera meets Vallehermoso. Also working at this time was the very original Antonio Palacios, main architect of the **Palacio de Cibeles** (1904-18) and the more subtle **Círculo de Bellas Artes**.

During its brief existence the Spanish Republic further encouraged rationalist, rather self-consciously modern architecture, as in the earliest parts of the **Nuevos Ministerios**. Art deco was in vogue, in office blocks like the **Capitol** building on Gran Vía (corner of C/Jacometrezo) or the curious model housing district of **El Viso**.

Civil war and the arrival of the Franco regime brought much destruction, and had an immediate impact in architecture. Falangist architectural thinking was dominated by nostalgia for a glorious past, and so Madrid acquired monster constructions that looked straight back to imperial Spain's Golden Age, combined with ideas from German and Italian Fascist architecture. The results were often grandiose, bombastic and,

'As Spanish society and the economy opened up in the late 1970s, architects felt little inclination to look back with nostalgia.'

probably unwittingly, kitsch. The foremost example is the **Ministerio del Aire**, at the top of C/Princesa. In Plaza de España is the manically colossal **Edificio España**, the work of brothers Joaquín and José María Otamendi, completed in 1953. Conceived along American lines to be a 'small city' in one huge block, with shops, offices, a hotel and apartments, the building acquired all sorts of neo-Herreran decorative touches outside.

By the 1950s, the regime's ideological enthusiasms were fading, although it still sought to impress. Built with no pretence at neo-baroque or anything similar is the tacky 32-floor 1957 **Torre de Madrid** on Plaza de España. These years, though, also saw the beginnings of real modernity in Madrid, most notably with Francisco Cabrero and Rafael Aburto's Casa Sindical at Paseo del Prado 18-20, built in 1948-9 for the Francoist labour unions and now the Health Ministry. Until the 1960s, the floundering Spanish economy still limited the scope for building. When the economy did improve, Madrid opened up to international influences, but much of its newest buildings were dreary apartment blocks, built for a rapidly growing population.

BACK TO THE FUTURE

As Spanish society and the economy opened up with the rebirth of democracy in the late 1970s, one effect of Francoist retro-obsessions was that Spanish architects – and the public – felt little inclination to look back with nostalgia or add neo-classical fronts to new buildings, and welcomed modernity with gusto. The most influential contemporary architects in Madrid have been Alejandro de la Sota and Francisco Sáenz de Oíza, both active since the 1950s, and Sáenz's gifted and original protégé Rafael Moneo.

An important factor in building during the 1980s was the Socialist takeover of the city council in 1979, and the government in 1982. Mayor Tierno Galván's Ayuntamiento was committed to the regeneration of public spaces, and so facilitated the emergence of one of the characteristic features of modern Madrid – daringly imaginative 'grand revamps' of long-decrepit historic buildings. An outstanding example is the **Estación de Atocha**, a run-down, filthy 1880s cast-iron railway terminal that Moneo transformed into a multi-purpose space. The **Reina Sofía** and **Thyssen** museums – also by Moneo – were also rebuilt, and the Centro Cultural Conde Duque created out of Ribera's 1720s barracks.

Outside the public domain, the most vigorous contributions to Madrid since the '80s have been the skyscrapers that line the upper Paseo de la Castellana, the superb white 1988 **Torre Picasso** by Minoru Yamasaki, and the spectacular leaning towers of the **Puerta de Europa** at Plaza Castilla. With Madrid's expansion, much recent building has taken place on the city's edge, such as the **Feria de Madrid** complex, Manuel Delgado and Fernando Vasco's **Estadio de la Comunidad de Madrid**, a dramatic structure in the form of a tilted oval plate, and Richard Rogers' huge Barajas airport terminal, with its undulating Chinese bamboo-insulated roofs, which opened in 2006.

The past few years have also seen some exciting new projects, including Moneo's Prado extension (2007), Herzog & de Meuron's **CaixaForum** (*see right* **Profile**), the remodelling of the old city abattoir for **Matadero Madrid** (p110) and Lord Foster's **Torre Caja Madrid** skyscraper (2009). Foster is also behind the cylindrical structures that will form the High and Provincial Courts at the **Campus of Justice**, near the airport. This complex, also involving Richard Rogers and Zaha Hadid, is already half-complete, but has been delayed due to funding issues.

Profile CaixaForum Madrid

The Paseo del Prado is home to one of the city's new icons.

Sure to become one of the city's landmarks, the CaixaForum is Madrid's new avant-garde cultural centre on the Paseo del Prado, designed by Herzog & de Meuron. The building is the result of a six-year conversion, completed in 2008, of the 1899 Mediodía Electrical Power Station, one of the few examples of industrial architecture in central Madrid.

The building is striking for its rusted metal appearance and its apparent defiance of the laws of gravity, with the front part of the structure appearing to float off the ground. Its adjacent 24-metre-high (79-foot) 'vertical garden', designed in conjunction with French botanist Patrick Blanc, complements the building's intense red, and is now one of Madrid's most photographed spots. Herzog has stated that the aim of the garden is to provide a connection with the botanical gardens opposite, and the leafy landscape of the Paseo del Prado.

The only material from the original power station that the architects were able to use was the building's brick shell, which needed to be fully restored and secured with cast iron. The extraneous parts of the building were removed with surgical precision – including the stone base, the removal of which opened up the new public square in front of the building, while simultaneously providing a sheltered space where summertime visitors can cool off.

The inaugural show at the seven-floor building included 37 contemporary works from the Caixa Foundation's collection, with Cindy Sherman and Georg Baselitz featuring. Since then, the centre has held a host of art exhibitions, film screenings, concerts and educational programmes, and has become one of Madrid's most-visited attractions – as much for its awe-inspiring appearance as the cultural attractions held within.

WHAT'S IN A NAME?

The arts centre's name comes from sponsorship by Catalan bank 'La Caixa', whose Obra Social Fundacíon 'La Caixa' operates community and welfare projects in Spain and abroad.

For more information on the CaixaForum, *see p85.*

IN CONTEXT

Madrid Today

From boom to bust – but there's still plenty to celebrate.

TEXT: DAVID LENNARD & ANNA NORMAN

It's been an eventful past few years in Spain's capital, with much to celebrate, including the completion of several high-profile buildings and urban projects (CaixaForum, the new Prado wing, the Mercado de San Miguel, the pedestrianisation of Calle Fuencarral), a rise in the number of visitors to the city, an increasing tendency to rejoice in Madrid's relatively new-found multiculturalism (especially evident in the city's restaurant and arts scenes), and a World Cup win in 2010 – celebrated to the max in this football-mad city of hedonism. However, these successes have been tempered with a series of big challenges, from the terrorist attacks on the commuter rail network on 11 March 2004, to the severe economic recession that has strangled the country since 2008. The past few years have been marked by the collapse of the country's housing boom, widespread debt and a rising cost of living that's been palpable in the city, even if unemployment, at around 12 per cent, isn't as high here as in the rest of the country (where it currently stands at a shocking 20 per cent). This has led, in turn, to a hardening of attitudes towards immigration.

'The lilting tones of South America and the mangled grammar of other immigrants are everywhere.'

THE BOOM YEARS

If the 1980s was a time to party amid the experimentalism and excesses of the post-Franco Movida, then the 1990s saw many of the Movida generation settle down to a job and a mortgage. After the scandals associated with the Socialists under Felipe González, many voters identified the Partido Popular (PP) with the grown-up business of making money. But what goes around comes around, and the PP, and prime minister José María Aznar, soon became seen as the party of self-interest and arrogance.

Spain's strong economic growth in the first decade of the 21st century, up to the crisis, was driven by Madrid, and the renewal of the historic tension between the centre and the periphery revitalised the city's attitude to itself and to the rest of the country. This revitalised spirit was strengthened further by prime minister José Rodríguez Zapatero. In the first three years of its mandate, Zapatero's socialist government – which dramatically beat Aznar's conservative government in the general election that immediately followed the 2004 terrorist attacks – reversed official attitudes to immigration, legalised gay marriage (to the jubilation of the city's large and vocal gay community), took steps to curb the influence of the Church in education, and redrew the relationship between the centre and the regions. These steps led to Zapatero being reelected for a second term in 2008.

Zapatero has, however, perhaps had less of an influence on present-day Madrid than the city's mayor, Alberto Ruiz Gallardón – a moderate representative of the conservative People's Party (PP). Gallardón has been the figure behind the grandiose urban renewal schemes that have defined Madrid over the past few years, which left large parts of it in what seemed like a permanent state of reconstruction during the first decade of the century. This mayor has been intent on modernising Madrid, and has earned himself the nickname 'Pharaoh', due to his desperation to leave his imprint on the city. Unlike Barcelona and Seville, cities that were revamped for the Olympics and the Expo respectively, Madrid has never had an excuse for a bit of cement-based cosmetic surgery. It was, according to Gallardón, at risk of getting left behind by other European capitals such as London and Paris, but his ambitious urban plans have partly put paid to that.

The schemes have included the redevelopment of the Manzanares River bank, the (€3.5 billion) job of sending part of the M30 motorway underground and into tunnels, the regeneration of historic downtown areas such as Lavapiés (in particular the square at Tirso de Molina), and the pedestrianisation of many of the city's public spaces, such as Huertas and Fuencarral, and the Sol transport developments (which clogged up the square for years, but were finally completed in late 2009). Much of this urban regeneration was propelled by the city's (failed) 2012 and 2016 Olympic bids, which have nonetheless left the city with an improved infrastructure and several already iconic buildings and sports complexes, such as the Caja Mágica (*see p258*) and the city's shiny new skyscrapers. While the construction projects were – and in some cases still are – massively disruptive for ordinary *madrileños*, many of Gallardón's schemes have now been completed, leaving Madrid with a feeling of optimism that has helped temper the recent economic crisis – although cranes and scaffolding are still a common sight in some parts of the centre. Under Gallardón, Madrid also implemented the same-sex marriage legislation approved by the government.

IN CONTEXT

El Mercado de San Miguel.

Both Zapatero and Gallardón remain in power. However, the former's popularity has slipped dramatically; his recent austerity measures to cope with the economic crisis (focused on changes in employment and pensions legislation) brought large numbers of protesters onto Madrid's streets in summer 2010. Gallardón, meanwhile, is still one of Spain's most popular politicians, despite contributing to the severity of Madrid's indebtedness.

THE CHANGING FACES OF MADRID

Walk down any street in Madrid today and listen. Spanish is being spoken, of course, but the accents that you'll hear are not all from Spain; the lilting tones of South America and the mangled grammar of other immigrants are everywhere. You'll hear Romanian, Polish, and every other European language, not to mention Chinese, Arabic, and a medley of African tongues. Suddenly, Madrid seems as multicultural as London, and, although this is a much-celebrated fact for many *madrileños*, for others it has come as an unwelcome shock.

Poll after poll over the past few years has identified immigration as Spaniards' in general, and *madrileños'* in particular, number one concern. This is hardly surprising: the almost daily images of exhausted sub-Saharan men, women and children being eased out of their ramshackle craft and laid in rows, living or dead, on the beaches of the Canary Islands, are a depressing reminder that Spain is on the front line of the refugee exodus from Africa. The fact is, however, that the bulk of immigration is through Barajas airport or over the Pyrenees. From a level of less than two per cent in 1996, the capital's foreign-born population rose to a whopping 15 per cent in 2007, and, although this figure has since stabliised with the economic crisis, it is still the highest in the country. The 'visibility threshold' has long been breached, and attitudes are hardening.

Nationally, Zapatero's government has made determined efforts to square the circle, as is the city administration. Official reports and working papers during the pre-2008 boom years all stressed that the high level of economic growth was a direct result of the incorporation of immigrants into the workforce, leading Zapatero to implement a partial amnesty for illegal immigrants who registered and found employment. However, since the crisis, the focus has shifted to the forced repatriation of illegal immigrants.

'Madrid has never aspired to be Euro-hip in the way that Barcelona has. The important thing has always been to be out and about, afloat in the crowded good humour of the streets.'

However, the legacy of widespread immigration remains, with many bars and restaurants in the city staffed by South Americans, and their kitchens by sub-Saharan Africans and Filipinos. Immigration has also led to an explosion of small businesses, corner shops, specialist food outlets and restaurants over the past decade, which has transformed the city. A decade ago, good Chinese or Indian food was hard to come by, and expensive when you found it. Now, *madrileños* can experiment with the pleasures of non-Spanish cuisine at affordable prices, and the choices are increasing every day. Korean, Lebanese, Uruguayan, Japanese, Thai... they're all available now. And the inner-city heart of immigrant settlement, Lavapíes, is a world community in miniature.

NEW TIMES, NEW MOODS

There's a generation gap at work in people's perception of 'happening Madrid'. To anyone over 30, the scene was better ten years ago than now, but to visitors and the new cohorts of youth, the sparkle of Madrid at night is still irresistible. Maybe this is something that happens to all generations in all cities at all times, but the tensions and changes of the past few years have conspired to make the phenomenon more noticeable here. The fun-zones of the city have become more defined, though the division owes as much to attitude as age, and nowhere is exclusionary. Teenagers and Generation Xers party in Moncloa and Argüelles; older twentysomethings cluster in the bars around Alonso Martínez; the over-30s opt for La Latina. Huertas is for everybody. Unfortunately, the price of partying has soared, with drinks costing up to 50 per cent more than they did five years ago, though they're still fairly cheap compared to some European capitals.

The range of activities available has widened over recent years: not merely restaurant choice, but stimuli for all the senses. High culture and low amusement are still crammed together cheek by jowl, and somehow manage to mingle without too much friction. Madrid is small compared to other European capitals, sitting compactly around its own core (which is perhaps one reason why is was ranked as the tenth most liveable city in the world by *Monocle* magazine in 2010). It has never aspired to be Euro-hip in the way that Barcelona has. This is not a self-regarding city where style and appearance are all, and the important thing has always been to be out and about with friends, afloat in the crowded good humour of the streets. That's not to say it's not looking good, however: the extensions of Madrid's big three art museums are now as good as complete, as are several of the mayor's urban renewal schemes; there is some iconic new architecture to be enjoyed as well as a superb new food market/tapas emporium in the form of El Mercado de San Miguel (*see p200*). What's more, the city's eating, arts and sporting scenes are looking more innovative than ever.

The March 2004 attacks led to a political watershed, turning the country back towards Europe after the Atlanticism of the Aznar government, but it also restarted Madrid's love affair with itself. The city is more expensive, populous and competitive than it was seven years ago, but it's still Madrid. Internationalism is fine. But the local heartbeat is strong and the old lady is kicking up her heels again. To *madrileños*, nothing is more interesting than Madrid. And despite the challenges for the city brought about by the national economic crisis, it's still a great time to visit Spain's capital.

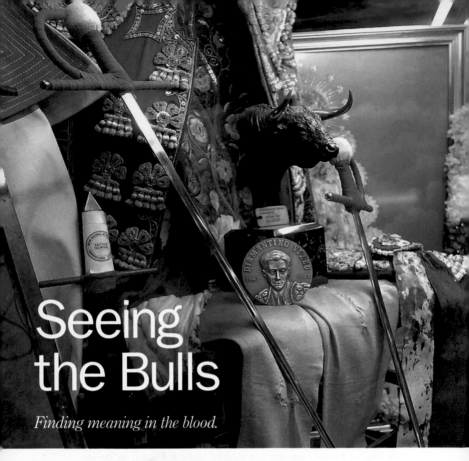

Seeing the Bulls

Finding meaning in the blood.

For many visitors to Spain the bullfight is a barbaric anachronism, a preening blood sport that is dying out in this modern land. Well, they're right about it being bloody: this is not a fun day out for the squeamish. But they're wrong on every other count – at least from Madrid's point of view. First off, it isn't a sport. The essence of sport is an even contest where the end result is unpredictable. The events in the arena are not a competition, and the end result is always the same – the bulls will die. The harsh reality is that you are watching the ritual slaughter of six animals for sheer entertainment. Closest perhaps to opera, and reviewed in the culture section of most newspapers, this is a theatrical performance, a tragedy, involving a truly wild animal and men in *trajes de luces*, 'suits of lights'. Of course it isn't fair; it isn't supposed to be. And, despite the 2010 ban in Catalonia – as well as the terrible goring of José Tomás, Spain's most celebrated bullfighter, some months earlier – in Madrid, it isn't dying out.

Robert Elms is a well-known writer and broadcaster. He has a long connection with Spain and its culture.

'At best the bullfight is a profound lyrical and visceral exploration of the meaning of both death and life.'

In recent years, television has taken the top stars of the ring to new heights and the leading matadors are among the highest-paid performers in the world. On the big days in the big rings, every seat is sold and the atmosphere at this social event is electric.

And it isn't really a bullfight either – that's a mistranslation of *la corrida*, the bull-running. Any man foolish enough to fight a wild bull would die in seconds. The Iberian fighting bull is arguably the most dangerous animal in the world and the idea is to control it and then dance with it before dispatching it; to create a fleeting but profound beauty out of the act of slaughter. To the Spanish this is a celebration of death, which in other countries is hidden away, as countless animals die in ignominy in abattoirs. The bull, which has lived a minimum of four years of absolutely natural existence, on the finest pasture Spain can provide, then gets his chance for a day of destiny and maybe even glory in the sun. 'We are going to see the bulls,' they say.

At heart, the Spanish attitude to the *corrida* comes from a profoundly different view of nature. In Britain, for example, nature is a distant green and fluffy thing that has to be protected. In Spain, a land still tied to agriculture, where the sun is too hot and the soil too poor, nature is a powerful, noble adversary, which has to be respected but dominated. And the fighting bull is its greatest champion. Day after day Spain sends her young men (and the occasional woman) out on to the sand (*arena* simply means sand) to enact this elaborate metaphor of man's continuing struggle with nature, to prove that beauty can still be summoned from the beast.

But that doesn't mean that if you go and see one it will be any good. Even the superstar matadors don't come with a guarantee, and what they are attempting is a difficult business with a genuinely wild and unpredictable animal. The ideal is that the various stages of this highly technical ritual are played out fluently and smoothly, all grace and style. The bull should be brave and noble, and the men controlled and artistic. The emotional high point should be the *faena*, when the matador is in the ring alone with the bull and the true dance of death occurs. This is where man and animal become almost as one as they pass each other time and again, closer and closer, in a heart-stopping blur of crimson and gold. Then the moment of truth arrives and the great beast should be felled with a single blow from the sword. That's how it should be.

But of course it isn't always, and what is supposed to be elegant and honest can end up brutal and clumsy, unworthy of the poetry and the art. Sometimes the bulls are flawed and weak, other times the matadors cowardly and sloppy.

But then, one blazing afternoon, all the fates will fall into place. A bull, fierce, swift and handsome, will come racing out into a packed *plaza*, hear the crowd gasp, and see the matador straighten. He will charge and charge and the men will work with valour and honour to make sure that his death, and therefore his life, is a memorable one. The extraordinary emotion transmitted from the matador, the man in the gleaming gold, charged with the terrible task of dealing death, will infect the crowd. As he cavorts with the bull, *olés* soft and long will start to emerge, a collective exhalation, as a single man takes the primeval power of this beautiful adversary and slows it to a dream with a few sublime swishes of his cape. Then, finally, in frozen silence he will leap over the horns, his sword straight to the heart and his place in the annals assured.

On such, all too rare, days, the dreadful danger and the awesome artistry will touch every soul present, showing why Spain still clings to this ancient and terrible entertainment, as the very soul of its identity, *la fiesta nacional*.

IN CONTEXT

Where and How

The arenas of the corrida.

The 25,000-capacity Plaza de Toros de Las Ventas (C/Alcalá 237, 91, 726 35 70, www.las-ventas.com) holds *corridas* every Sunday from March to October, as well as on various public holidays and festivals. The traditional starting time is 7pm, though some kick off as early as 5pm.

Tickets for Sunday bullfights can be obtained at *taquillas* (ticket windows) near the main entrance of the bullring or online at the official website (see below). Prices vary greatly, from around €4 to as much as €150. As a rule of thumb the nearer the seat is to the arena, the pricier the ticket, and any equivalent ticket is cheaper in *sol* (in the sun) than in *sombra* (in the shade).

If you can't get a ticket at the *taquillas*, there are plenty of authorised agents in Madrid, though they charge 20 per cent commission. Try La Taurina (C/Pasaje Matheu s/n, 91 522 92 16) or Localidades Galicia (Plaza del Carmen 1, 91 531 27 32). There is also an independent online booking service, www.ticketstoros.com, with pages in English. Tickets can then be collected at the TEYCI kiosk, near the main *taquilla*, an hour before the *corrida* begins. You'll need to show your passport, or confirmation email if you booked online.

LAS FERIAS

The best time to watch a top-quality *corrida* is during the Feria de San Isidro. For 20 consecutive evenings from mid May to early June, bullfights are held at 7pm, including *novilladas*, *rejones* (on horseback) and *Goyescas* (in period costume). It is, however, difficult to get tickets for what is the highlight of the season for bullfighting aficionados. Most tickets for the San Isidro are snapped up way in advance by season-ticket holders. Any that are unclaimed are put on sale five days before the corresponding fight; by law 1,000 tickets for each fight must be put up for sale at 10am on the day of the fight, though huge queues form for these. San Isidro is preceded by the Feria de la Comunidad, which has a number of *novilladas* and a major fight on 2 May. Fights are also held daily during the Feria de Otoño, beginning in late September.

OUTSIDE MADRID

Many towns within easy reach of Madrid stage *corridas* on some Sundays during the season and on their annual saint's day. Many also hold bull fairs, with daily bullfights, during their annual fiestas. These small-town fairs often include an *encierro*, in which young bulls are run through the streets first thing in the morning, as in Pamplona's San Fermín. But be warned: bull-running requires a deal of acquired skill, and untrained tourists should be aware that joining in is extremely dangerous. Several have died doing so.

The first bullfights of the year take place in freezing February in **Valdemorillo**, to the north-west of Madrid. **Aranjuez** holds important bullfighting *ferias* on 30 May and in early September. But August is the cruellest month for the bulls: **Chinchón** has *novilladas* in its historic Plaza Mayor, and a smaller event takes place in **Manzanares el Real**. The most spectacular *encierro* close to Madrid is in **San Sebastián de los Reyes**, while the most prestigious fair is the one in **Colmenar Viejo**; both in late August. **Toledo** holds a bullfight on Corpus Christi day.

There is more information on these towns in the **Escapes & Excursions** chapter (*see pp268-292*). For dates and details of transport, *see p308* **Tourist information**.

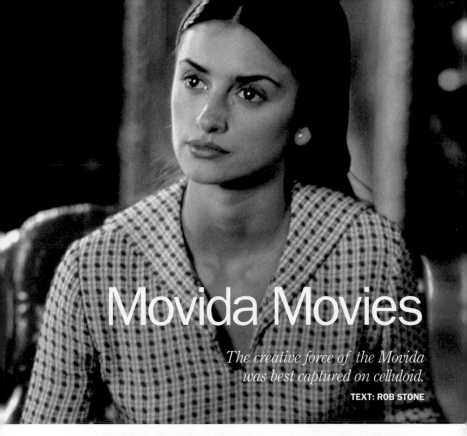

Movida Movies

*The creative force of the Movida
was best captured on celluloid.*

TEXT: ROB STONE

The seasonal skies of Madrid that enthralled Goya and Velázquez have been a similar gift to film-makers. Many foreign epics of the 1960s were made in the studios on the city's outskirts, including Anthony Mann's *El Cid* (1961) and *The Fall of the Roman Empire* (1964), Nicholas Ray's *King of Kings* (1961) and *55 Days at Peking* (1963), and David Lean's *Dr Zhivago* (1965). Recent internationally made films to have employed the city and environs include Milos Forman's *Goya's Ghosts* (2006) and Paul Greengrass's *The Bourne Ultimatum* (2007), the concluding episode of the Euro-tripping, amnesiac spy tale.

But although Madrid makes the top rank alongside such cinematic cities as New York, Paris and Tokyo, it is best understood by Spanish film-makers, who have captured the skies, architecture and contrasts in several classic and modern masterpieces. The creative force of Spanish cinema was especially intense during the Movida, the cultural, sexual and chemical free-for-all that followed Spain's transition to democracy in the 1970s and early '80s – immortalised in Pedro Almodóvar's earliest films.

'The Movida is now long gone, being uniquely of its time and therefore rightly defunct.'

REEL REBELLION

The Movida took its name from a Spanish phrase meaning 'to have a business thing happening', which also doubled as slang for 'a drug transaction'. It was partly an ad hoc translation of British punk that assumed a similarly neo-patriotic stance by assimilating traditional Spanish values into its bizarre new get-up. Unlike British punk, however, the Movida was not so much a working-class movement as a drug-fuelled middle-class pretence of bohemian rebellion against the society of the recent past.

Perhaps the most crucial venue of the Movida's cinematic manifestation was the Alphaville (C/Martín de los Heros 14), which has recently changed its name to Golem. This still-thriving cinema opened in 1977 (when Spain's transition to peaceful democracy and public liberty was assured), and immediately established its revolutionary credentials with a week-long festival of Cuban films. Since then, it has continued to feature politically charged cinema, especially of the contemporary German kind. Wim Wenders' *The American Friend* (1977) still holds the record for the longest continuous run, at an impressive 67 weeks. This pales, however, alongside the ten years of late-night screenings enjoyed by Almodóvar's *Laberinto de pasiones* (*Labyrinth of Passion*, 1982).

ALMODOVAR'S EARLY DAYS

Laberinto de pasiones is a melodramatic, absurdist farce about a nymphomaniac called Sexilia (Cecilia Roth), a gay Islamic terrorist named Sadec (Antonio Banderas) and the son of the exiled Shah of Iran (Imanol Arias). Gobsmacked by the film's outrageousness, most international critics failed to notice the romanticism and compassion that Almodóvar clearly felt for those who had so recently been marginalised from Spanish society.

As well as in film, the Movida was documented in the magazine *La Luna*, in Francisco Umbral's long-running column in the *El País* newspaper, and in TV programmes. There were also alternative music and variety shows presented by Paloma Chamorro and Almodóvar's earliest (and recently reconciled) muse, the actress Carmen Maura.

Maura starred with the punk diva Alaska in *Pepi, Luci, Bom y otras chicas del montón* (*Pepi, Luci, Bom and Other Girls Like Mom*, 1980), which was two years in the making on a £20,000 budget raised by Almodóvar from his friends. In this scatological melodrama of female solidarity, Pepi (Maura) and Bom (Alaska) seek to liberate the masochistic Luci (Eva Siva) from her marriage to a policeman who respects her too much to beat her. Luci becomes a groupie for a band of degenerates, which provokes her jealous husband into beating her senseless, thereby resulting in a happy ending. The perverse yet romantic logic of the film was a faithful reflection of its time and audience, many of whom featured in the scenes set in the legendary Rock-Ola nightclub (a cavernous dive, both garish and grimy, crammed with glam rockers, punk rockers and simply off their rockers) and other venues of the Movida, such as the Alphaville, which hosted the première in October 1980.

THE FALL-OUT

Almodóvar's humour became gradually darker in his later films, when disillusionment with democracy and the repercussions from the drug-fuelled and sex-motivated excesses of the Movida soiled the carefree mood. By *¡Átame!* (*Tie Me Up! Tie Me Down!*, 1989) the director was seeking to reconcile his wayward characters with the more conventional elements of Spain, such as the family unit and fidelity, because the

'Most critics failed to notice the romanticism and compassion that Almodóvar felt for those who had been marginalised from Spanish society.'

human cost of the Movida in terms of drug abuse and AIDS was by then so apparent. Drugs had been the main spur to the fantasy nightlife, but by ¿Qué he hecho yo para merecer esto? (What Have I Done to Deserve This?, 1984) the drug-dealing son of glue-sniffing housewife Gloria (Carmen Maura) is warning her not to graduate to hard drugs and in ¡Átame!, although the psychopathic Ricky (Antonio Banderas) kidnaps ex-junkie porn star Marina (Victoria Abril), he shows great concern for her returning need. Indeed, a prime motor of the plot of Todo sobre mi madre (All About My Mother, 1999) is the effort of the female collective to rescue one of their ilk from her addiction, and there is clearly something desperately retrospective about the wish-fulfilment ending of this film, which culminates in the miraculous birth of a child whose immune system holds a cure for AIDS.

REMAINS OF THE DAYS

Sadly, the Rock-Ola nightclub (C/Padre Xifré 5), which featured in Laberinto de pasiones, is now a supermarket. Several of the most iconic venues of the Movida have also gone, such as the Carolina discotheque (C/Bravo Murillo 202), which became a clothes shop. Nevertheless, the Alphaville (now the Golem) and the clubs El Penta (C/Palma 4), La Vía Láctea (C/Velarde 18) and El Sol (C/Jardines 3) remain, with the latter recently hosting a reunion concert by the leading groups of the period.

La Bobia bar on the edge of the Rastro (C/San Millán 3), where the opening sequence of Laberinto was filmed, is still standing, but now home to a rather dull café. A leisurely walking tour could start from here, after which you could move on up to the Plaza Mayor, where Otto and Ana so narrowly miss each other in Julio Medem's Los amantes del Círculo Polar (Lovers of the Arctic Circle, 1998), and on to the Plaza de España, where Sofía and Jota collide in Medem's La ardilla roja (Red Squirrel, 1993). From here, you can either head up the raucous Gran Vía, so miraculously deserted in Alejandro Amenábar's Abre los ojos (Open Your Eyes, 1997), or head into the sidestreets surrounding the Ópera district, where Matías meets his cousin Violeta in Fernando Trueba's Ópera prima (First Effort, 1980). Either route should get you to Callao in time for an aperitivo beneath the hoarding of the FNAC superstore (C/Preciados 28), which hosted the advertising for Leo's novel in Almodóvar's La flor de mi secreto (The Flower of My Secret, 1995), before a stroll to the Sevilla metro station where Antonio, the rogue ETA terrorist, shoots a cop in Imanol Uribe's Días contados (Running Out of Time, 1994). Enjoy lunch in one of the bars on the Plaza de Colón, close to the María Guerrero Theatre (C/Tamayo y Baus 4) where Becky (Marisa Paredes) performed 'Piensa en mí' in Almodóvar's Tacones lejanos (High Heels, 1991). Then consider an afternoon spent shopping in the chic barrio of Chueca, where Almodóvar filmed La ley del deseo (Law of Desire, 1987) or the bustling Tetuán, where he set much of Volver (2006).

Whatever less truthful guide books might have you believe, the Movida is now long gone, being uniquely of its time and therefore rightly defunct. You can still go from bar to bar in Madrid, check out a gig at El Sol, catch something avant-garde at Alphaville, and pretend along with many avid tourists and nostalgic Spaniards that the Movida is still happening. But resist the pretence – Almodóvar turned 60 in 2009 and, like him, this extraordinary period in Madrid's cultural history is best revisited through his films.

Flamenco

A taste of the south.

TEXT: ROB STONE

The Gypsy *cantaor*, the singer of flamenco *cante jondo*, or 'deep song', is the voice of his race and the keeper of its myths. Although flamenco is commonly perceived and exploited as a joyful and colourful form of song and dance, it is really about suffering and anguish. Its origins lie in the language and traditions of the Andalucían Gypsies, whose beliefs and fears are expressed in a performance style that employs a complex mythology to recount the suffering of their ancient exile, the history of their marginalisation, and the existential anguish that results.

Time was that Madrid's theatres such as the Teatro Real and Teatro Pavón were the equivalent of Carnegie Hall for flamenco artists. Nowadays the big stars play for big money to bigger audiences in concert halls and even stadiums, but you can still see unknowns imitating the legends and trying out new trends in pursuit of *duende*, the somewhat malevolent spirit-guide that is said to possess the greatest performers.

A STORY OF PERSECUTION

Members of a lowly Indian caste once attached themselves to Arabian armies that were moving west into North Africa, serving them as blacksmiths, cooks and entertainers. They moved on through Egypt, from where they took their name ('E-gyptian'), before arriving in southern Spain. The first organised group of Gypsies reached Spain in 1462 pretending to be pilgrims to the Catholic faith, and were consequently afforded protection and provisions by the Spanish nobility. However, by the end of the 15th century, these nomads had outstayed their welcome. Racism was stirred up by clerical propaganda that accused Gypsies of witchcraft and cannibalism, and in 1499 the kingdoms of Castile and Aragon ordered the bands of Gypsies within them to settle within 60 days or be banished.

Clap Your Hands Say Yeah

Audience participation is a requisite part of a flamenco music performance.

Audiences who sit in respectful silence and applaud politely at the end of a performance of flamenco *cante* (song) and *toque* (guitar) might actually be insulting the performers. That's because audience participation – *jaleo* – is an essential part of authentic flamenco, and no truly great performance is ever given or witnessed without it. So this is no time to be shy: give as good as you get and you'll get as good as you give.

Watch and listen how the guitarist bullies the *cantaor*, the singer of flamenco 'deep song', into giving all. The guitarist plucks around the first sounds of the *cantaor* until he hears the right tone being struck by his partner's voice, whereupon his sudden *rasgueo* (strum) alerts the *cantaor* to the fact that this is the direction to be taken. When you hear these single *rasgueos*, you'll know the performance is warming up. Listen closely to the guitarist and the experts around you in the audience. They'll start to goad the singer with phrases such as '*Ezo e*' ('*Eso es*' – 'That's it'), '*Vamos ya*' ('Let's go') and '*Anda ya, chiquillo*' ('Go with it, man'). Any *cantaor* worth his salt will respond by digging deeper.

A rhythmic rapping will begin, soft at first as these complicit torturers tap their palms flat against table-tops. Gradually you'll become aware of their rings and bracelets rapping on the wood and the sound will become sharper. Some will turn their fingers in, forming fists that will punch up the rhythm. When the tattoo is solid and inescapable, the guitarist shows the way to go by tearing off on his own before returning quietly for the *cantaor*, who should by now be humming in time with the rhythm, nodding his head, eyes closed, tapping a foot and summoning up the true voice of deep song as if it were a mix of phlegm and bile, which it is. The audience pushes him to the edge with the calls and rapping, and if he needs an extra shove the clapping (*palmas*) will start, leaving him no place to turn. Now wait. Wait for it.

The sound you'll hear is that of a man falling into the abyss of human existence and landing in a spiritual wasteland that is floating in an indifferent cosmos. If he's any good, that is. Growls, howls and a great range of guttural vocalisations of pain and despair are the true language of the authentic *cante* and the words are not as important as the tone of the performance. How many times will the guitarist scoop up the *cantaor* and make him fall again? How cruel will the audience be in forcing the martyrised *cantaor* to face the pain of their shared existential suffering? It depends on the night and the skill of the performer, for whom alcohol is not just a vice but an anaesthetic. Bruised knuckles, teary eyes and a headache? OK, now you can applaud.

IN CONTEXT

In the Frame The Majas

Goya's portraits of the majas are clothed (or otherwise) with intrigue.

In the 18th century, ordinary people in European cities began to look increasingly similar, wearing more or less the same three-cornered hats, breeches and mop-caps. Not so in Madrid, where this was the era of the *majos* and *majas*. A *majo* wore embroidered shirts, a short jacket with a swathe of buttons, a hair-net, and carried a knife. *Majas* wore short, mid-calf skirts with a mass of petticoats, pearl-white stockings, embroidered bodices, an intricately braided hairstyle and a dramatic lace mantilla. They were drawn from trades such as coach-driving, dressmaking, cigarette rolling or market trading, and most often came from Lavapiés. *Majas* especially were known for their wit, grace and verbal ferocity. In a capital that was still largely a city of servants, but whose servants were renowned for talking back, they deferred to no one.

They were mostly seen in all their finery at fiestas such as the Romería de San Isidro. Goya depicted them often. Also, their cocky elegance led to them being taken up by the upper classes, so that even *grandes dames* like the Duchess of Alba would dress up as *majas*, which is what probably gave rise to the story that Goya's nude and clothed *majas* are portraits of the Duchess herself.

This theory has been discredited by scholars in recent years, but still has many subscribers; the woman depicted does bear a startling resemblance to the Duchess, and the large bow around her waist featured in several of Goya's portraits of her. And, yes, it is possibly true that the Duchess had an affair with the painter, with whom she holed up for several months on one of her country estates after her husband died. It is unlikely, however, that she would allow herself to be painted in such a way, given her standing in society and the certain exposure of the works. Some critics suggest the head was painted on the body later, and this is certainly the visual effect.

What is irrefutable, however, is that Goya was obsessed with Alba, and a more probable explanation for the likeness is simply that he tended to project her image on to an idealised form of female beauty.

Goya's **Clothed Maja** *and* **Nude Maja** *are found at the Prado (see p88).*

'Post-dictatorship, flamenco underwent a revival, thanks to the clusters of migrant Gypsy camps on the outskirts of Madrid.'

Persecution intensified under Charles V, when Gypsies were hunted and enslaved in the galleys. In 1619, all Gypsies were sentenced to death if they refused to settle, inter-marry and live like good Christians. This enforced sedentariness resulted in concentrated settlements in Andalucía, when a national rout of Gypsies in July 1749 caused them to flee towards the south and led to an inevitable deterioration in living conditions in the overburdened areas of Seville, Granada and Cadiz. The brutality of this measure had the desired effect and by 1763 conditions were peaceful enough for Carlos III to declare an amnesty for Gypsies with the objective of transforming them into useful citizens. Fortunately, Andalucía, with its warm climate and fertile earth, was much to their liking and they prospered by smithery, fortune-telling and musicianship. This last skill was especially appreciated by the Catholic church, which employed Gypsies to perform at religious festivals and ceremonies.

Gypsies maintained cordial working relationships with the local populace while preserving their customs, language, song, dance and oral traditions in the privacy of their own homes. On the foundations of Indian traditions of performance, Gypsy musicians, singers and dancers constructed a style that overwhelmed traditional folksong. By the mid 19th century, professionals were performing for public audiences on the stages of *cafés cantantes* (theatre-bars) and *tablaos* (restaurants with a stage). During the Franco years there was an effort to disenfranchise the Gypsies from a song and dance that had become identified with Spanish culture, but when flamenco and folksong proved inseparable, this policy was adapted to claim that flamenco had been indigenous to Spain all along.

THE RESURGENCE AND NUEVO FLAMENCO

Post-dictatorship, authentic flamenco underwent a revival thanks to the growing clusters of migrant Gypsy camps on the outskirts of Madrid and the emergence of such figures as the legendary *cantaor* Camarón de la Isla and the acclaimed guitarist Paco de Lucía. A pop-rock type of flamenco became ubiquitous, but at the other extreme from the wine-bar muzak of the Gypsy Kings and the kitsch spectacles of Joaquín Cortés is *nuevo flamenco*, which started in 1975 with Lole y Manuel's first album *Nuevo Día,* which has since spawned a plethora of innovative and exciting performers. Today's flamenco fan can keep up to date with what's happening by visiting the specialist shop El Flamenco Vive (C/Conde de Lemos 7, www.el flamencovive. com) near the Palacio Real, or by looking at www.flamenco-world.com. The Suma Flamenca festival (*see p208*), now in its fifth year, has given Madrid the country's most high-profile flamenco festival.

CD-wise, for traditional *cante* there is nobody better than Camarón de la Isla (try *Camarón: Antología*, 1996) but since his death in 1992 the more contemporary Enrique Morente (*Lorca*, 1998) has become the reigning *cantaor*. For an equivalent female voice, try the traditional Carmen Linares (*Carmen Linares en antología*, 1996), the decidedly Moorish Estrella Morente (*Mi cante y un poema*, 2001) or the infectious rhythms of Niña Pastori (*Eres Luz*, 1998). For an innovative fusion of flamenco with Cuban rhythms, try Bebo & Cigala (*Lágrimas negras*, 2003), and for the ancient Arabic sounds of flamenco andalusí choose Lole y Manuel (*Nuevo Día: Lo mejor de Lole y Manuel*, 1994), who are now so hip they feature on the soundtrack to Quentin Tarantino's *Kill Bill Vol. 2.0*

IN CONTEXT

www.museothyssen.org

MUSEO THYSSEN-BORNEMISZA
PASEO DEL PRADO, 8
MADRID, SPAIN

Sights

Puerta del Sol. *See p66.*

SEE MORE. BE MORE.

This is NEW YORK CITY

Book Now. Get More.

Tour Madrid

Myriad ways to see the city and its attractions.

A car would be a hindrance in old Madrid and, although public transport is good, walking is often the easiest (and quickest) option. A map is useful but not indispensable: even visitors wandering with no specific destination in mind are easily orientated by the changing flavours of the neighbourhoods. If you prefer to see the city independently, but need extra guidance, then the website **www.descubre madrid.com** (not connected with Descubre Madrid, *below*) has a large number of suggested routes and guided maps that you can print out.

If, on the other hand, you'd like a guided overview of the city, or have a special interest in one particular element of it, then the following organisations are worth checking out.

TOURS

Bus & coach tours/trips

The following run city tours and/or specialised trips focused on bullfights, flamenco and so on, as well as tours of the towns around Madrid.

Juliá Travel
Plaza de España 7 (91 559 96 05, www.julia travel.com). Metro Plaza de España. **Open** 8am-6pm Mon-Fri; 8am-3pm Sat, Sun. **Credit** MC, V. **Map** p323 E10.

Madrid Vision
91 779 18 88, www.madridvision.es. **Tours** Call for times. **Tickets** *1 day* €17.20; €8.60 7-16s & over-65s. *2 days* €21.20; €11.10 7-16s & over-65s. Free under-7s. **No credit cards.**

Trapsatur
C/San Bernardo 5, Malasaña (91 541 63 21, www.trapsatur.com). Metro Santo Domingo. **Open** booking department 9am-1.30pm, 4-7.30pm Mon-Fri; excursions in & around Madrid 8am-8pm daily. **Credit** MC, V. **Map** p323 F10.

Segway & GPS-guided tours

GoCar
C/Santiago 20, Sol & Gran Vía (91 559 45 35, www.gocartours.es/madrid). Metro Opera. **Cars available** *Mar-Oct* 9am-9pm daily. *Nov-Feb* 9am-7pm daily. **Hire price** *1st hr* €35;

2nd hr €30; *3rd hr* €25. *All day* €109. **Credit** AmEx, MC, V. **Map** p327 F12.
Zip around Madrid in a little yellow GoCar – a computer-guide storytelling vehicle that allows you to undertake a personalised sightseeing tour at your own pace. The average tour lasts two to three hours.

Madsegs
Cuesta de San Vicente 10, Los Austrias (659 824 499, www.madsegs.com). Metro Plaza de España. **Segway hire/tour** €65 (plus €15 deposit). **Credit** AmEx, MC, V. **Map** p323 E10.
Madrid's oldest segway tour company offers a two-wheeled way to see the city. The price includes a three-hour tour, a helmet, refreshments and a photo CD.

Walking, bike & alternative tours

Carpetania Madrid
C/Jesús del Valle 11, 4 dcha, Malasaña (91 531 40 18, www.carpetaniamadrid.com). Metro Noviciado. **Open** *July-Aug* 9am-1pm daily. *Sept-June* 9am-9pm daily. **Tours** €9-€14. **Credit** AmEx, DC, MC, V. **Map** p323 G9.
All the guides here are art history specialists. As well as some well-thought-out city routes, there are expert guided tours for art exhibitions.

Descubre Madrid
Centro de Turismo de Madrid, Plaza Mayor 27, Los Austrias (91 588 29 06, www.esmadrid. com/descubremadrid). Metro Sol. **Open** 9.30am-8.30pm Mon-Fri. **Tickets** *On foot or bike* €3.90; concessions €3.12. *By bus* (Oct-Dec and

according to demand) €7.75; €5.65 concessions. **Credit** AmEx, DC, MC, V. **Map** p327 G12. With over 100 different itineraries (by bus and on foot), this service, run by the tourist board, offers tours focusing on architecture, literature and history.

Letango
91 369 47 52, www.letango.com. **Tours** €98.20 (2.5hr private tour); discounts for small groups. Call to arrange time. **Credit** MC, V.
With a knowledgeable team of guides, Letango offers tailored tours taking in Spanish culture and history.

MadWay to Madrid
Paseo de los Melancólicos 28E (650 57 57 56, www.madwaytomadrid.com). Metro Puerta de Toledo. **Tours** Call for details of times and prices. **No credit cards. Map** p326 C14.
Alternative and eco-friendly tours by foot or bike, in English, Dutch, Spanish, French or Italian.

Wellington Society
609 143 203, www.wellsoc.org. **Tours** €60-€85 (plus membership fee of €50); discounts for small groups. Call to arrange time. **No credit cards.**
Private and custom tour packages brought to you by the eccentric Stephen Drake-Jones, and covering themes such as wine, bullfighting, Hapsburg Madrid, Hemingway's Madrid, and the Civil War.

TICKETS

Madrid Card
Information 91 588 29 00, www.madridcard. com. **Prices** (5% discount if you buy online) *1 day* €49. *2 days* €62. *3 days* €76. Buy from tourist offices (*see p308*), train stations and travel agents.
Available for one, two or three days, the Madrid Card offers free admission to up to 40 of the city's museums, and discounts on the Madrid Vision tour bus, shops, restaurants, clubs, theatres and so on.

The Paseo del Arte

Madrid's three world-class art museums are just a stroll apart.

In the **Prado** (pictured; *see p88*), the **Thyssen** (*see p73*) and the **Reina Sofía** (*see p78*), Madrid has three art palaces that are quite simply world class. You'll find them dotted along the Paseo del Prado, in what has increasingly, and slightly facetiously, come to be known as the 'Golden Triangle'. This formidable trio of museums has made Madrid the world's capital of art for many people in the know, and, with extensive revamps of all three museums over the past decade (reckoned to cost some €150 million in total), this label is only set to stick more firmly.

The city council initiative known as the '**Paseo del Arte**' ('art stroll') takes advantage of the proximity of the three art collections, promoting the fact that they are barely ten minutes' walk from one another. The idea echoes Berlin's 'Museum Island', London's 'Museum District' or Washington's 'Museums on the Mall'. The axis that unites the big three – as well as avant-garde newcomer the **CaixaForum** (*see p85*) – is the Paseo del Prado, which is being remodelled by a team of architects under the leadership of Álvaro Siza (*see p84* **El Salón del Prado**).

Of course, it would be far too tiring to approach the Paseo del Arte as a one-day itinerary – a visit to just one of the three museums is likely to take up several hours, and plenty of energy. The idea is more to familiarise visitors with the area – which is becoming more and more pedestrian-friendly – so that the museums can be understood within a historial, geographical and cultural context, and for visits to then be undertaken at one's leisure.

TICKETS
A joint ticket, the **Paseo del Arte**, gives entry to the Prado, the Reina Sofía and the Thyssen-Bornemisza for €17.60. It is available from the ticket desks at all three museums; after visiting one you can visit the other two at any time in the same calendar year. Each museum also has its own 'friends' tickets, giving unlimited entry for a year, which are more expensive and more widely publicised. A better deal is the €48 (concessions €24) annual museum ticket, available from any state-run museum, which gives unlimited entry to all the main museums (except the Thyssen).

The Old City

Habsburg and Bourbon splendour meets the city's lively tapas scene.

The cramped old city, with its narrow medieval streets, contains Madrid's most atmospheric and well-defined *barrios*, as well as its best eating, drinking and nightlife options and many of its landmark buildings. Most visitors spend the bulk of their time here – whether enjoying the Habsburg and Bourbon splendour of Los Austrias and Santa Ana, the laid-back tapas bars of La Latina, the alternative cultural scene of Lavapiés, or the heady nightlife and trendy cafés of Malasaña and Chueca. The heart of the area is the Puerta del Sol, and much of old Madrid converges on this square. Plaza Mayor, the heart of Golden Age Madrid, lies south-west of here, along C/Mayor, while two art museums from Madrid's 'Golden Triangle' – the Reina Sofía and the Thyssen-Bornemisza – lie to the east, bordering the Paseo del Prado.

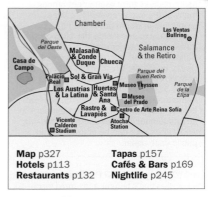

Map p327	**Tapas** p157
Hotels p113	**Cafés & Bars** p169
Restaurants p132	**Nightlife** p245

South of Gran Vía

LOS AUSTRIAS

The oldest part of the city, site of the Muslim town and of most of medieval Madrid, falls between **Plaza de la Cebada**, **Plaza Mayor** and the **Palacio Real**. Even though most of the streets still follow their original medieval lines, this may not be immediately apparent today. Like several other parts of the Old City, this area has been smartened up over the past decade, and is now home to a slew of wine bars and expensive restaurants. Tucked away in side streets are the 12th-century **San Nicolás de los Servitas** (*see p65*) and the city's other Mudéjar tower, the 14th-century **San Pedro el Viejo** (*see p63*). If you continue down C/Segovia beneath the viaduct, you pass a forlorn fragment of the ninth-century **Muralla Árabe** (Arab wall), the only substantial relic of Madrid's Muslim founders. The area around it, known as the **Parque Emir Mohammed I**, has recently been relandscaped, with the addition of information plaques giving interesting historical information.

Back into town, along C/Mayor is the **Plaza de la Villa** (*see p61*), Madrid's oldest square

and home to the city hall, the **Casa de la Villa**. In pre-Habsburg times, the square was also the preferred place of residence for the elite; one such residence, the **Torre de los Lujanes**, can still be seen there. Along with the **Casa de Cisneros**, also on the square, the buildings make up a compendium of the history of the city from provincial town to the imperial capital it was to become.

Despite its ancient beginnings, the area has come to be known as the 'Madrid de los Austrias', after the Habsburgs, although in truth Philip II and his dynasty can scarcely claim responsibility for much of it. The greatest monument they *did* build, however, stands at the area's core: the **Plaza Mayor** (*see p61*) archetypal creation of Castilian baroque (a style also known as 'Herreran', after its key architect). On the north side of the plaza is the city's main **tourist office** (*see p307*), while at the south side, at the corner of C/Toledo, stand the twin baroque towers of **San Isidro** (*see p58*), perhaps Madrid's most important historic church. Continue down here to reach **La Latina** and the **Rastro** flea market.

To the west of the square, off Calle Cava de San Miguel, lies one of the city's most successful new openings, the **Mercado de San Miguel**

SIGHTS

SIDE TRACK
CAPILLA DEL OBISPO

The declared reopening of the Capilla del Obispo (*see p61; pictured below*) in Plaza de la Paja after a 44-year closure has provoked great excitement among many of the city's residents, a large proportion of whom have never had the opportunity to see inside the 16th-century building. The interior of the 'Bishop's Chapel' – one of the city's best-preserved Gothic buildings, which adjoins the church of San Andrés – was closed in a state of ruin in 1966, and has been subject to an intricate restoration since 2005, but from autumn 2010, its finely carved tombs, beautiful inner wooden doors and striking 1550 altarpiece can be enjoyed by the public once again.

(*see p200* and *pp162-163* **Profile**), a refurbished food market that's become a favoured tapas-munching spot for tourists and upper-class *madrileños*. Just down from here is the peaceful **Plaza del Conde de Barajas**, home to the excellent **Taller Puntera** leather goods shop (*see p196*). To the east, leading on from the Calle

Cava de San Miguel, is the **Arco de los Cuchilleros** (Knifemakers' Arch), which runs from the south-west corner of the square via a spectacular bank of steps leading down through C/Cuchilleros to the **Plaza de la Puerta Cerrada**, the walls of which are decorated with some engaging 1970s murals. From here the **C/Cava Baja**, home to many of the most celebrated *mesones*, temples to Madrid's traditional cuisine, runs south, leading to the squares (**Plaza de San Andrés**, **Plaza del Humilladero**, **Plaza de la Paja**) that are prime territory for the traditional Sunday La Latina tapas bar crawl (*see p77* **Inside Track**).

To the south-east of the square, at the **Plaza de la Provincia**, is another major work in the Herreran style: the squatly proportioned **Palacio de Santa Cruz**, which was the work of several architects between 1629 and 1643. Despite its grand appearance, the palace was originally the court prison, with a dungeon so deep that prisoners had to rub their rags with lard and set them alight to stop themselves from going blind. These days the building has a somewhat more dignified role as the Foreign Ministry. In former times, executions often took place in the Plaza de la Cebada, just a tumbril ride away.

For centuries C/Mayor was Madrid's main thoroughfare. The cross-streets between Mayor

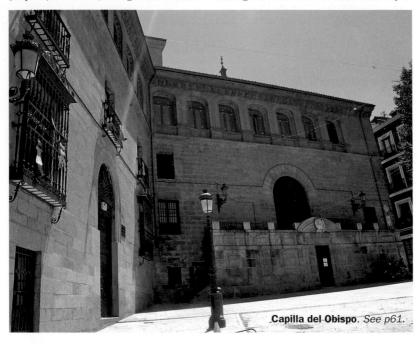

Capilla del Obispo. *See p61*.

Walk Royal Madrid

A stroll through medieval and Habsburg Madrid.

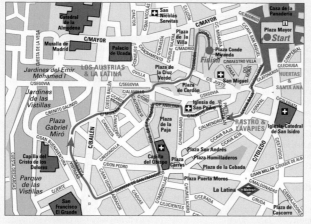

'Straw Square' was the medieval grain and fodder market, and probably marked the most southern point of the Arab wall. Buildings of note that survived 19th-century reconstruction are **San Andrés** church and the **Capillas del Obispo** and **San Isidro**.
Walk up the Costanilla de San Andrés. On the other side of San Andrés is

DURATION: 45MINS

The 16th-century exteriors that once fronted Madrid's interconnecting squares – Paja, Plaza de la Cruz Verde, Plaza de los Carros – were mostly replaced in the 1800s. Nevertheless, these intimate plazas and most of the winding streets of the district of Los Austrias still follow their original Arab and medieval courses, and a walk around these alleys can still be evocative of the Habsburg city, and the medieval town before it.

From Plaza Mayor, walk down the steps under Arco de Cuchilleros in the SW corner.

Walking down C/Cuchilleros, named after the knifemakers who long ago plied their trade here, look out for the 18th-century **El Sobrino de Botín** (*see p137*) on the left, allegedly the oldest restaurant in the world. Continue across the Puerta Cerrada into C/Cava Baja, and you will be walking along the line of the 12th-century wall, now lined with restaurants and tapas bars.

Cut right up C/Almendro, and take the first right down the narrow Pretíl de Santisteban.

At the end is the pretty C/Nuncio, home to several wine bars. Turn left, and on the Costanilla de San Pedro is the dusty 17th-century church of **San Pedro el Viejo**.

Carry on past San Pedro, left down C/Príncipe de Anglona, and veer left to Plaza de la Paja.

what appears to be one rambling square. However, different sections are known by different names. As well as the **Plaza de la Cebada** (Barley Square), once the site for public executions, and the **Plaza de San Andrés**, there is the **Plaza de la Puerta de Moros** (Moors' Gate) – site of the gate to the Muslim quarter (or Morería, under Christian rule).

From there turn right down Carrera de San Francisco.

The dome of **San Francisco el Grande** at the end is seen in some of Goya's skylines.

Right of the church, head along Travesía de las Vistillas to C/Morería, which winds back over C/Bailén to Plaza de la Morería.

The knot of streets between here and **Plaza de la Paja** and **Puerta de Moros** formed the Morería, to which Madrid's community of Mudéjar Muslims were confined for four centuries. The little **Plaza de la Morería** was the site of the mosque and the courts.

From there follow C/Alamillo to C/Segovia. Cross over and head up through C/Conde, then left at C/Cordón. This little alley leads round into the **Plaza de la Villa**, with the city hall. It began life as the Arab souk, and was Madrid's main square until the creation of the Plaza Mayor.

Turn right down C/Codo (Elbow Street) to Plaza Conde de Miranda.

Stop off at the 17th-century **Convento de las Carboneras**, where nuns used to sell own-baked biscuits through a grille.

and Arenal offer an odd mixture of bookbinders, picture-framers and Galician restaurants. The western end of C/Mayor, near the **Palacio Real**, has several old palaces and runs out west into C/Bailén, connected southwards to a splendid 1930s concrete **viaduct** that offers views of the sierra and the Casa de Campo. The viaduct's notoriety as a suicide point has led the city authorities to place giant glass panels all along it, giving it a very strange look and feel – without doing much to deter the jumpers. At the southern end of the viaduct are the hill and park of **Las Vistillas**. The park has more great views and is often used for neighbourhood events, concerts and dances during fiestas and in summer. Beyond the park are the river and the elegant arches of the **Puente de Segovia**, a bridge commissioned by Philip II from Juan de Herrera and completed in 1584 to make it easier for the king to get to El Escorial.

FREE Iglesia-Catedral de San Isidro (La Colegiata)

C/Toledo 37 (91 369 20 37). Metro La Latina or Tirso de Molina. **Open** *Sept-July* 7.30am-1.30pm, 6-9pm Mon-Sat; 8.30am-2.30pm Sun. *Aug* 7.30am-8.30pm Mon-Sat; 8.30am-1.30pm, 7.15-8.30pm Sun. **Map** p327 G13.

Still popularly known as La Colegiata, this massive church, built in 1622-33 once formed part of an important Jesuit college attended by many of the Golden Age playwrights. The high-baroque design by Pedro Sánchez was inspired by the quintessential church of the Jesuits, the Gesù in Rome; the façade was completed by Francisco Bautista in 1664. In 1768, after Charles III expelled the Jesuits from Spain, the church was separated from the college, dedicated to San Isidro and altered by Ventura Rodríguez to house the remains of the saint and his wife, which had been brought here from the Capilla de San Isidro (*see p61*). La Colegiata was the city's provisional cathedral for nearly a century, between 1885 and 1993, when the Catedral de la Almudena (*see p64*) was finally finished and inaugurated.

FREE Museo de los Orígenes (Casa de San Isidro)

Plaza de San Andrés 2 (91 366 74 15, www.munimadrid.es/museosanisidro). Metro La Latina. **Open** *Sept-July* 9.30am-8pm Tue-Fri; 10am-2pm Sat, Sun. *Aug* 9.30am-2.30pm Tue-Fri; 10am-2pm Sat, Sun. **Admission** free. **Map** p327 F13.

Dedicated to the city's patron saint, the well-digger and labourer San Isidro, this museum sits on the spot where he supposedly lived and performed one of his most famous miracles: when his son, Illán, fell into a well, Isidro made the water rise and thus was able to rescue the unfortunate lad. The well – or *a* well, anyway – is preserved inside the house, as is the chapel built in 1663 on the spot where Isidro allegedly died. According to legend, he was originally buried here too. This is, then, a museum that deals in legends as much as in solid artefacts, and the current material on show is a little limited. More interesting are the finds from local archaeological digs, formerly kept in the Museo de Historia and now in the basement here. They include items from lower-Palaeolithic settlements in the area, as well as artefacts from the

Plaza Major. *See p61.*

A Saint for All Seasons

Madrid's church-going public are kept busy all year round.

If you are female and single, you might want to make a discreet pilgrimage to the **Ermita de San Antonio de la Florida** (*see p104*) if you happen to be in Madrid on 13 June (*see also p208*). This is Anthony of Padua's feast day, a saint whose many attributes supposedly include the ability to rustle up boyfriends out of thin air – for Madrid girls at least. The tradition was perhaps started by young seamstresses, as the custom is to turn up at the church with a handful of pins. The girls queue up to drop the pins in the font, then stick their hand into the water. The test is whether the pins stick to their hand. If so, love is just around the corner. It's got to be worth a go.

The **Iglesia de San Antón** on C/Hortaleza, on the other hand is dedicated to Saint Anthony of Egypt, who, like Saint Francis, had quite a way with animals. On 17 January, the people of Madrid commemorate this by bringing not only their pets, but also farm animals to the church to be blessed. This causes something of a livestock bottleneck in the narrow, busy C/Hortaleza, as dogs, cats, rabbits, goats, donkeys and pigs wait to enter the church. Not far away, at the **Iglesia de Santa Pascual** on the Paseo de Recoletos, you might catch sight of a famous face slinking in or out. The church contains a figure of Saint Clare, who in recent times has been appointed the patron saint of television. Actors, actresses and stars of reality TV pop in to ask her to help them get the role that will finally make them a household name.

On 27 July, expect to see a very long queue of people if you are in the vicinity of the **Convento de la Encarnación** (*see p67*). The reliquary of this 17th-century convent contains a phial of blood purportedly belonging to Pantaleón, the doctor saint. On his feast day, the dubious contents of the phial miraculously liquefy, which augurs great things for those who witness the event. Yet more expectant queuing goes on every Friday outside the **Iglesia de Jesús de Medinaceli** (*pictured above*) on Plaza de Jesús. Inside the church is a statue of Jesus of Nazareth that had fallen into the hands of the Moors and was retrieved against all odds by Trinitarian monks in the 17th century. Kissing the foot of the statue is believed to be very auspicious. In fact,

after announcing their engagement in 2003, one of the first things Prince Felipe and his wife-to-be Letizia did was turn up at the church to do just that.

They got married in the **Catedral de la Almudena**, named after a wooden figure now to be found in the crypt. When the Moors arrived in Madrid, they displaced the Visigoths, who before fleeing hid the statue in the wall of their fortress, along with two burning candles. A few centuries later, when the Christians regained power, the hiding place was discovered – and guess what? Those candles were still flickering away. This happy event has led to a public holiday on 9 November, something that has kept Almudena as everybody's favourite saint, with no further miracles required.

SIGHTS

Calle Cava de San Miguel. *See p55*.

Roman villas along the Manzanares, and from the Muslim era. Although the museum was recently renamed, it's still popularly known as the Casa de San Isidro.

Plaza Mayor

Metro Sol. **Map** p327 G12.

The Plaza Mayor began life in the 15th century as a humble market square, then known as the Plaza del Arrabal ('Square outside the Walls'). In the 1560s, after Madrid was made capital of Spain by Philip II, architect Juan de Herrera drew up plans for it to be completely rebuilt, but the only part constructed immediately was the Casa de la Panadería ('the Bakery'). Finished under the direction of Diego Sillero in 1590, it is typical of the Herreran style, with grey slate roofs, spiky pinnacles and two towers which dominate the square. In the early 1990s, in a move unlikely to be contemplated in most countries, this historic edifice was decorated with colourful psychadelic murals. The rest of the plaza was built by Juan Gómez de Mora for Philip III and completed in 1619 although large sections were destroyed by fire in 1790 and had to be rebuilt. Bullfights, carnivals and all the great ceremonies of imperial Madrid were held here. At its centre is a statue from 1616 of Philip III on horseback by Giambologna and Pietro Tacca, which stood originally in the Casa de Campo and was moved here in the 19th century.

The square is still an important hub, with most Madrid-wide celebrations, such as the Veranos de la Villa or San Isidro festivals, centred here and a traditional Christmas fair in December. Best enjoyed on quiet weekday mornings, Plaza Mayor has plenty of pavement cafés from which to contemplate its graceful architecture. On Sunday mornings the plaza bustles with a stamp and coin market. *Photo p58.*

Plaza de la Villa

Metro Ópera or Sol. **Map** p327 F12.

Madrid's oldest square, home to the city's main market place in Muslim and early medieval times,

San Pedro el Viejo. *See p63.*

contains three noteworthy buildings. Dominant is the Casa de la Villa, or City Hall, designed in Castilian-baroque style by Juan Gómez de Mora in 1630, although not completed until 1695. The façade was also altered by Juan de Villanueva in the 1780s. It contrasts nicely with the Casa de Cisneros, which was built as a palace by a relative of the great Cardinal Cisneros in 1537. Restored in 1910, it now also houses municipal offices. Opposite the Casa de la Villa is the simple Torre de los Lujanes, from the 1460s, where one of Madrid's aristocratic families once resided. It is believed that King Francis I of France was kept prisoner in the tower by Charles V after his capture at the Battle of Pavia in 1525.

★ FREE San Andrés, Capilla del Obispo & Capilla de San Isidro

Plaza de San Andrés 1 (91 365 48 71). Metro La Latina. **Open** 8am-1pm, 6-8pm Mon-Thur, Sat; 6-8pm Fri. Open for services only Sun. **Map** p327 E13.

The large church of San Andrés dates from the 16th century, but was badly damaged in the Civil War in 1936 and later rebuilt in a relatively simple style. Attached to it (but with separate entrances) are two of Madrid's most historic early church buildings. The Capilla del Obispo (Bishop's Chapel, 1520-35), with its entrance on Plaza de la Paja, is the best-preserved Gothic building in the

---

INSIDE TRACK RAMON GOMEZ

Few writers have been as central to the life and culture of Madrid as Ramón Gómez de la Serna, one of the most original and influential Spanish authors of the 20th century. Born in Madrid in 1891, he is best remembered for his near untranslatable literary form known as *greguerías* – brief poetic statements in which words, ideas and objects are brought together in almost stream-of-consciousness fashion ('It is only in botanical gardens that trees carry visiting cards').

Walk Literary Madrid

Exploring the city's literature-fuelled Golden Age.

DURATION: 30MINS

The cafés, theatres and churches around Plaza Santa Ana were the centre of literary life during Spain's 16th- and 17th-century Golden Age.

Begin at the junction of C/Atocha with Costanilla de los Desamparados.

C/Atocha 87 was once the printing press where the first edition of *Don Quixote* was published. It is now the **Museo Cervantino**. See the bronze bas-relief of a scene from the book and, above, the head of Cervantes.

Walk up Desamparados and turn right down C/Moratín.

At the **Plazuela de San Juan** is a plaque celebrating poet and playwright Leandro Moratín, born here in 1760.

Turn left up C/Jesús and left again on C/Lope de Vega.

The church ahead of the junction, on the right, is the **Iglesia de Jesús de Medinaceli**, famously a 17th-century centre of rumour and gossip, especially when attended by the great actresses of the time. Up on C/Lope de Vega, on the left, is the **Convento de las Trinitarias**, where Cervantes was buried (his remains have since disappeared). On the anniversary of his death, a mass is held for him and the other great Spanish writers.

Turn right up C/Quevedo.

On the right-hand corner is a plaque marking the house where 17th-century rivals Francisco de Quevedo and Luis de Góngora lived. Quevedo, a satirist, made mincemeat of the hapless and terminally ill poet Góngora in an exchange of verse. He also triumphed posthumously, when the council renamed the street after him, failing to mention Góngora on the plaque. At the end of the street, on C/Cervantes 11, is the **Casa-Museo de Lope de Vega** (*see p73*), where Lope de Vega lived and died. No.2 on this street was built on the site of Cervantes' old house.

Turn left, and right down C/León to C/Prado.

At No.21 is the Ateneo library, with an impressive marble staircase, walls lined with portraits of Spain's greatest figures and delightfully antiquated rooms. Back up C/Prado, you arrive at the Plaza Santa Ana, home to the **Teatro Español** (*see p262*) and bars such as the **Cervecería Alemana** (*see p173*), where writers such as the playwright Ramón del Valle-Inclán and, later, Ernest

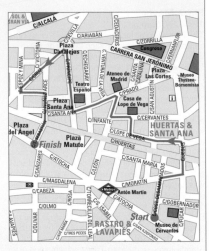

Hemingway were regulars. The theatre itself sits on the site of one of the great open-air *corral* theatres of the Golden Age.

Facing the theatre, turn left up C/Príncipe.

This street was home to many of the literary haunts of the day, but the only one that remains is **Las Cuevas de Sésamo** at No.7 (*see p251*), worth a visit for the quotes painted on the walls and the printed history they will give anyone who's interested.

At Plaza Canalejas turn left down C/Cruz.

C/Victoria on the left has a plaque marking the site of the writers' and politicians' meeting point and subject of Benito Pérez Galdos' eponymous novel, **La Fontana de Oro**. Further up C/Cruz is a mural depicting a reflection of the street, and asking 'Where has the theatre gone? Or is the street the theatre?' The theatre in question is the **Corral de la Cruz**, another open-air theatre that stood on the site.

Turn left down C/Álvarez Gato, through the square and down C/San Sebastián.

What is now a florist in the yard on the corner with C/Huertas used to be the graveyard for the adjacent **Iglesia de San Sebastián**; the ancient olive tree remains a symbol for all the literary luminaries buried there. Opposite is a plaque showing the site of the **Fonda de San Sebastián** – favoured hangout of the 18th-century writers.

SIGHTS

city. It contains finely carved tombs and a 1550 altarpiece by Francisco Giralte. It reopened to the public in late 2010, after being closed for restoration for some 40 years. Further towards Plaza de los Carros is the Capilla de San Isidro, built in 1642-69 by Pedro de la Torre to house the remains of the saint, which were later transferred to the Iglesia-Catedral de San Isidro.

FREE San Pedro el Viejo

Costanilla de San Pedro (91 365 12 84). Metro La Latina. **Open** 6-8pm daily (phone to check). **Admission** free. **Map** p327 F13.
This impressive Mudéjar brick tower dates from the 14th century, although the rest of the church dates from much later, having been rebuilt in the 17th century. *Photo p61.*

Ópera

The area between Plaza Mayor and the **Palacio Real** (*see p64*) is named after the **Teatro Real** opera house at its centre. As well as containing some of the city's most important buildings (the **cathedral** among them), this is one of the most elegant areas of Madrid. A tunnel whisks traffic under the stunning **Plaza de Oriente**, so named because it sits east of the palace, making it one of the most pleasant spots for a coffee. Curiously, Madrid owes this stately square, which seems to complement the Palacio Real ideally, not to the Bourbon monarchs but to Spain's 'non-king', Joseph Bonaparte, who initiated the clearing of the area during his brief reign (1808-13). After his departure it was largely neglected before being laid out in formal style in

1844. During the dictatorship, devotees from all over the country stormed the square for a glimpse of Franco, who addressed his rallies from the palace balcony.

At the square's centre is a fine equestrian statue of King Philip IV that once stood in the courtyard of the Palacio del Buen Retiro. It was made in the 1640s by the Italian sculptor Pietro Tacca, who – on the insistence of the Count-Duke of Olivares – was required to create the first-ever monumental bronze statue featuring a rearing horse, rather than one with four feet on the ground. This remarkable feat was achieved with engineering assistance from Galileo.

On the esplanade between the cathedral and palace, archaeological excavations have recently been undertaken to unearth the remains of the original Muslim fortress and of the foundations of Philip II's Alcázar, covered over by the building of the later Palacio Real. Some of the discoveries, including impressive Moorish arches, have been open to public view. Behind the palace, the delightful **Campo del Moro** gardens run down towards the Manzanares and the Paseo de la Florida.

FREE Campo del Moro

Paseo de la Virgen del Puerto (91 454 88 00). Metro Príncipe Pío. **Open** *Oct-Mar* 10am-6pm Mon-Sat; 9am-6pm Sun. *Apr-Sept* 10am-8pm Mon-Sat; 9am-8pm Sun. **Map** p322 C/D11.
This vast garden was named after a Muslim leader in the Middle Ages, Ali Ben Yusut, who attempted to capture the fortress that is now the Palacio Real. Unfortunately, it is only accessible from the Paseo

SIGHTS

Catedral de la Almudena. *See p64.*

de la Virgen del Puerto side, requiring a fairly long walk down Cuesta de San Vicente or Cuesta de la Vega. As a reward, however, you will see two fine monumental fountains. Nearest the palace is *Los Tritones*, originally made in 1657 for the palace in Aranjuez (*see p288*); the other is *Las Conchas*, designed in the 18th century by Ventura Rodríguez. Both were moved here in the 1890s.

FREE Catedral de la Almudena

C/Bailén 10 (91 542 22 00). Metro Ópera.
Open 9am-8.30pm daily. **Map** p326 D12.
This is not Spain's most impressive cathedral, and it's something of a miracle that it exists at all. For centuries, Church and State could not agree on whether Madrid should have a cathedral; once they did, it took 110 years to complete it. In 1883 work began on a neo-Gothic design by the Marqués de Cubas, but this scheme went off course after only the crypt was completed. Another architect, Fernando Chueca Goitia, took over in 1944, and introduced a neo-classical style. Although the cathedral has failed to win much affection over the years, it was finally finished in 1993 and visited by the Pope. The site once contained the church of Santa Maria de la Almudena, formerly the main mosque of Muslim Madrid (the name comes from the Arabic *al mudin*, 'the mill') until it was knocked down by liberal reformers in 1870. One of its more interesting pieces is the 13th-century polychromatic funerary chest of San Isidro. *Photo p63.*

Palacio Real (Palacio de Oriente)

Plaza de Oriente, C/Bailén (91 454 88 00). Metro Ópera. **Open** *Oct-Mar* 9.30am-5pm Mon-Sat; 9am-2pm Sun. *Apr-Sept* 9am-6pm Mon-Sat; 9am-3pm Sun. **Admission** €10 with guided tour; €8 without; €3.50 concessions. Free to EU citizens Wed. **Credit** AmEx, DC, MC, V. **Map** p327 E11.

Commissioned by Philip V after the earlier Alcázar was lost to a fire in 1734, the Royal Palace is rarely used by the royal family, and many of its 3,000 rooms are open to view. The architects principally responsible for the final design, which reflects the taste of the Spanish Bourbons, were Italian – Giambattista Sacchetti and Francesco Sabatini – with contributions by the Spaniard Ventura Rodríguez. Filippo Juvarra, Philip V's first choice, had planned a palace four times as large, but after his death the project became a little less ambitious. Completed in 1764, the late-baroque palace is built almost entirely of granite and white Colmenar stone, and, surrounded as it is by majestic gardens, contributes to the splendour of the city.

Inside you must keep to a fixed route, but are free to set your own pace rather than follow a tour. The entrance into the palace is awe-inspiring: you pass up a truly vast staircase and then through the main state rooms, the Hall of Halbardiers and Hall of Columns, all with soaring ceilings and frescoes by Corrado Giaquinto and Giambattista Tiepolo. In the grand Throne Room there are some fine 17th-century sculptures commissioned by Velázquez, which were saved from the earlier Alcázar. Other highlights are the extravagantly ornate private apartments of the palace's first resident, Charles III, again decorated by Italians. Particularly striking are the Gasparini Room, the king's dressing room, covered in mosaics and rococo stuccoes by Mattia Gasparini; and the Porcelain Room, its walls covered entirely in porcelain reliefs. A later addition is another giant: the State Dining Room, redesigned for King Alfonso XII in 1880 and still used for official banquets. There are

Palacio Real.

Plaza de la Paja. *See p56.*

also imposing collections of tapestries, table porcelain, gold and silver plates and finally clocks, a particular passion of the little-admired King Charles IV.

One of the real highlights is the Real Armería (Royal Armoury), reached via a separate entrance off the palace courtyard, with a superb collection of ceremonial armour, much of it actually worn by Charles V and other Habsburgs. Look out too for the suits of armour worn by El Cid and his horse – displayed on life-size statues. On the other side of the courtyard, the Royal Pharmacy, is also worth a visit. One of the oldest in Europe, it was wholly dedicated to attending to the many ailments of Spain's crowned heads over several centuries. In years to come, an opportunity to view the excavations of the older Alcázar and Muslim fortress beneath the palace will also form part of the visit. The palace is closed to the public when official receptions or ceremonies are due, so it's a good idea to check before visiting. On the first Wednesday of each month the Royal Guard stages a ceremonial Changing of the Guard in the courtyard, at noon.

There are tours of the Palace throughout the day, but frequency depends on the volume of visitors.

FREE San Nicolás de los Servitas

Plaza San Nicolás (91 559 40 64). Metro Ópera. **Open** 8.30am-1.30pm, 5.30-8pm Mon; 8.30-9am, 6.30-8pm Tue-Sat; 6.30-8.30pm Sun. **Mass** 8pm Mon; 9am & 8pm Tue-Sat; 10.30am, noon & 1pm Sun. **Map** p327 E12.

The oldest surviving church in Madrid stands just a few minutes from Plaza de Oriente. Its 12th-century tower is one of two Mudéjar towers (*see also p63* San Pedro el Viejo), built by Muslim craftsmen living under Christian rule, in the city. Most of the rest of the church was rebuilt later, during the 15th and 16th centuries.

LA LATINA

La Latina – officially the area below Plaza de la Cebada, but many people think of the squares north of here as being part of it – takes its name from the nickname of Beatriz Galindo, teacher of Latin and confidante to Queen Isabella. At the end of the 15th century, she paid for a hospital to be built on the square that bears her name. Its site is now occupied by the **Teatro La Latina**, a stronghold of traditional Spanish entertainment. The district is relatively quiet except during its grand fiestas, around the time of **La Paloma** in August.

Basílica de San Francisco el Grande

Plaza de San Francisco (91 365 38 00). Metro La Latina. **Open** *Sept-June* 11am-12.30pm, 4-6.30pm Tue-Fri; 11am-1.30pm Sat. *July-Sept* 11am-12.30pm, 5-7.30pm Tue-Sun. Last admission half hr before closing. **Admission** (guided tour only) €3; €2 concessions. **Map** p326 D14.

This huge, multi-tiered church between Puerta de Toledo and the Palacio Real is difficult to miss. A monastery on the site, reputedly founded by Saint Francis of Assisi, was knocked down in 1760; between 1761 and 1784 Francisco Cabezas and later Francesco Sabatini built this neo-classical church in its place. Most challenging was the construction of the spectacular dome, with a diameter of 33m (108ft). The dome was restored fairly recently, and work on the rest of the basilica has also now been completed. Inside there is an early Goya, *The Sermon of San Bernardino of Siena* (1781), and several frescoes by other artists.

SOL

The **Puerta del Sol** represents the very heart of Madrid, both because it contains *kilómetro cero* (the mark from which distances from the city are measured) and for its time-honoured role as chief meeting place. Famously, through the centuries people have come to Sol to find out what's going on. Until the 1830s, the block between C/Correo and C/Esparteros was occupied by the monastery of San Felipe el Real, the steps and cloister of which were, in Habsburg Madrid, one of the recognised *mentideros* – literally 'pits of lies', or gossip-mills – where people came to pick up on the latest news, anecdotes or scurrilous rumours. In a city with no newspapers – but where who was in or out of favour was of primary importance – *mentideros* were a major social institution, and rare was the day when at least one of the great figures of Spanish literature, such as Cervantes, Lope or Quevedo, did not pass by here. The

steps of San Felipe were also overlooked by one of the largest brothels of the era, another attraction for men about town. On a more respectable note, the Café Pombo, home to legendary *tertulias* (*see p179* **In the Frame**), stood on the corner of C/Carretas. It is still Madrid's most popular meeting point, particularly the spot by the monument with the symbols of Madrid (a bear and a *madroño* or strawberry tree) at the junction with C/Carmen.

Under the Habsburgs the Puerta del Sol, the main, easternmost gate (*puerta*) of 15th-century Madrid, was surrounded by churches and monasteries. It was rebuilt in its present form in 1854-62. The square's most important building is the **Casa de Correos**, built in 1766 by Jaime Marquet as a post office for Charles III. Today it houses the regional government, the Comunidad de Madrid, but in the Franco era it had much grimmer connotations, as the Interior Ministry and police headquarters. It was altered significantly in 1866, when the large clock tower was added; this is now the building's best-known feature, since it's the clock the whole country sees on New Year's Eve, when revellers crowd into the square to eat their lucky grapes, one for each stroke of midnight. In the 1990s, the tower developed a precarious incline due to rot in its timbers, but it was rebuilt and unveiled once again in 1998. Sol is also where Napoleon's Egyptian cavalry, the Mamelukes, charged down on the *madrileño* crowd on 2 May 1808, as portrayed in one of Goya's most famous paintings.

The building works that saw Sol bristling with JCBs and ringed with iron fencing for

Puerta del Sol.

INSIDE TRACK PICKPOCKETS

Although Madrid isn't a violent city, petty crime such as pickpocketing and bag-snatching is still rife on the metro and buses, as well as in touristy areas such as the Rastro, Retiro park, Puerta del Sol, Plaza Mayor and around the Gran Vía. To avoid being a vicitim, don't leave your belongings on the back of café chairs or on the ground; keep your hand on top of your bag in the metro; be wary if someone pulls out a map to ask or offer directions – thieves often work in pairs, and this could be a way to distract you; and beware of fake policeman – if someone asks to see your ID, ask to see theirs first.

some six years, while the tunnel linking Atocha and Chamartín was being excavated, were finally completed at the start of 2010, leaving the place with a new, and somewhat controversial, Cercanías Renfe Sol rail station stop, shiney new dome entrances to the metro, and a new lease of life.

Tucked in the middle of the area between Sol, Arenal, C/Alcalá and Gran Vía is the **Real Monasterio de las Descalzas Reales**, bursting with artworks and a deliciously unexpected oasis amid the traffic and bustle of Sol. At the west side of the area, just above the Plaza de Oriente, is the peaceful and little visited **Convento de la Encarnación**, also worth a look. Just north of that, occupying the site of another convent, is the old 19th-century **Palacio del Senado** (Senate), now made redundant by its back-to-back counterpart in granite and smoked glass by Santiago Goyarre.

Running almost alongside C/Preciados up to Gran Via is newly pedestrianised but still shabby C/Montera, lined with cheap, dated shops and the main area for street prostitution in the city centre. At the top, parallel with Gran Vía, is C/Caballero de Gracia, with a 19th-century oratory that lays on special Masses for the working girls, many of them Latin American, who operate along the street. While seedy, this area is not generally dangerous, and is heavily policed. Care should be taken when walking around late at night, however, especially if you're on your own.

Convento de la Encarnación
Plaza de la Encarnación 1 (91 547 05 10, information 91 454 88 00). Metro Ópera or Santo Domingo. **Open** 10.30am-12.45pm, 4-5.45pm Tue-Thur, Sat; 10.30am-12.45pm

Fri; 11am-1.45pm Sun. **Admission** €3.60; €2 concessions. Free to EU citizens Wed. **Map** p323 E11.
Before the Alcázar burned down, this understated convent was its treasury, connected by a concealed passageway. In 1611, it was inaugurated as a monastery by Philip III and his wife Margaret of Austria, and rebuilt to a design by Gómez de Mora. However, much of the original building, including the church, was damaged by fire in 1734 and rebuilt in a classical-baroque style in the 1760s by Ventura Rodríguez. It still contains a community of around 20 nuns, but most of the building is open to the public. Although not as lavishly endowed as the Descalzas Reales, it contains a great many pieces of 17th-century religious art, the most impressive of which is Jusepe Ribera's shimmering chiaroscuro portrait of John the Baptist. The Encarnación's most famous and memorable room, however, is the *reliquario* (relics room). In its glass casements are displayed some 1,500 saintly remains, bone fragments and former possessions of saints and martyrs, in extravagantly bejewelled copper, bronze, glass, gold and silver reliquaries. Its prize possession is what purports to be the solidified blood of San Pantaleón, kept inside a glass orb. The blood reportedly liquefies each year from midnight on the eve of his feast day, 27 July (*see p59* **A Saint for All Seasons**). Note that visits are by guided tour only, and tours leave 30 minutes after the first person signs up; so there's little point turning up as it opens.

Real Monasterio de las Descalzas Reales
Plaza de las Descalzas 3 (information 91 454 88 00). Metro Callao or Sol. **Open** 10.30am-12.45pm, 4-5.45pm Tue-Thur, Sat; 10.30am-12.45pm Fri; 11am-1.45pm Sun. **Admission** €5; €2.50 concessions. Free to EU citizens Wed. **Map** p327 G11.
The convent of the Descalzas Reales ('Royal Barefoot Nuns') is the most complete 16th-century building in Madrid and still houses a cloistered community. It was originally built as a palace for Alonso Gutiérrez, treasurer of Charles V, but was converted into a convent in 1556-64 by Antonio Sillero and Juan Bautista de Toledo after Philip II's widowed sister Joanna of Austria decided to become a nun. Founded with royal patronage, the Descalzas became the preferred destination of the many widows, younger daughters and other women of the royal family and high aristocracy of Spain who entered religious orders. Hence it also acquired an extraordinary collection of works of art – paintings, sculptures, tapestries and *objets d'art* – given as bequests by the novices' families. Equally lavish is the baroque decoration of the building itself, belying its sternly austere façade, with a grand painted staircase, frescoed ceilings and 32 chapels, only some of which can be visited.

SIGHTS

Círculo de Bellas Artes.

The largest non-Spanish contingents in its art collection are Italian, with Titian, Bernardino Luini, Angelo Nardi and Sebastiano del Piombo, and Flemish, with Breughel (an *Adoration of the Magi*), Joos Van Cleve and Rubens. The Descalzas is also an exceptional showcase of Spanish baroque religious art, with works by Gaspar Becerra, Zurbarán, Claudio Coello and even a tiny painting attributed to Goya. In addition, as you walk around you can catch glimpses of the nuns' courtyard vegetable garden, which has remained virtually unchanged since the convent was built, and is closed to the public. The monastery was seen by very few until the 1980s, when it was restored and partially opened as a museum. It can be visited only with official tours, which leave every 20 minutes and last around 50 minutes. Frustratingly, the guides rarely speak English, there is no printed information about the convent, and the paintings are not labelled. It is still an enjoyable place to visit, though, for the sheer sumptuousness of its artworks and fittings.

GRAN VIA

The **Plaza de España**, at the western end of the Gran Vía, is dominated by Franco's bombastic architecture. It is flanked by two classic buildings of the type sponsored by the regime when out to impress: the '50s-modern **Torre Madrid** (1957) and the enormous **Edificio España** of 1948-53. The three statues in the middle – of Cervantes, Don Quixote and Sancho Panza – are by Teodoro Anasagasti and Mateo Inurria, from 1928. The square around them is big, noisy and not a particularly relaxing place to sit.

The Gran Vía itself was created in 1910 by slicing through the Old City so that traffic could easily reach Cibeles from C/Princesa. Intended to be a broad modern boulevard, it got grander still when World War I made neutral Madrid a clearing house for international money. With the economy booming, developers and architects set out to embrace modernity as hard as they could to show that if you wanted something impressive, they could provide it. In the following decades, each generation added its own stamp and the result is certainly eclectic.

Heading down the Gran Vía, the area north and east of Sol was originally the city's financial district, hence the number of grand edifices owned by banks and insurance companies. Its other great avenue is **C/Alcalá**, which follows the centuries-old main route into Madrid from the east. In the 18th century, when it was lined by aristocratic palaces, it was described as the grandest street in Europe. It is still pretty impressive today, with a wonderful variety of 19th- to early 20th-century buildings, from the dignified 1882 **Banesto** building (corner of C/Sevilla) to the cautiously modernist **Círculo de Bellas Artes** (*see below*). There are also fine older constructions along the street, such as the austere neo-classical Finance Ministry, built as the **Aduana**, or customs administration, by Francesco Sabatini in 1761-9, and, alongside it, the **Real Academia de Bellas Artes de San Fernando** (*see p72*). At the point where Alcalá and Gran Vía meet, stands Pedro de Ribera's exuberantly baroque church of **San José** (1730-42), with a plaque inside to commemorate the fact that Simón Bolívar was married here in 1802.

Círculo de Bellas Artes

C/Alcalá 42 & C/Marqués de Casa Riera 2 (91 360 54 00, www.circulobellasartes.com). Metro Banco de España. **Open** *Café* 9am-1am Mon-Thur; 9am-3am Fri, Sat. *Exhibitions* 11am-2pm, 5-9pm Tue-Sat; 11am-2pm Sun. **Admission** (excluding exhibitions) €1. Free 2-4pm Mon-Sat. **Map** p328 I11.

The Círculo de Bellas Artes occupies a superb building, designed by Antonio Palacios and completed in 1926. It is a key player in every aspect of the Madrid arts scene: as well as a beautifully airy main floor café, with a gracious pavement terrace, the Círculo offers a plethora of classes, exhibitions, lectures and concerts in its theatre and concert hall, as well as an annual masked ball for carnival.

Walk Working Madrid

A stroll around Lavapiés reveals much about the city's social history.

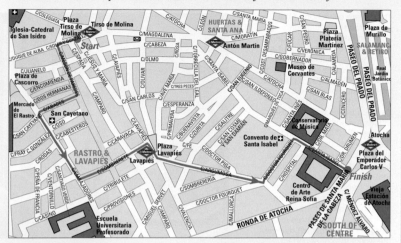

DURATION: 30MINS

Atmospheric Lavapiés shows Madrid's past, present and future. Once the Jewish quarter, long the main working-class area and still home to a large gypsy community, it is now the most racially mixed barrio in the city. It has acquired an often exaggeratedly bad reputation, but it's generally safe by day.

Begin at Plaza Tirso de Molina.

At its eastern end is the **Teatro Nuevo Apolo**, part art deco and part neo-Mudéjar. On the south side of the plaza is the present headquarters of the CNT anarchist workers' union, a reflection of Lavapiés' long-term association with left-wing politics.

Turn down C/Mesón de Paredes.

The street is named after the long-gone inn of Señor Paredes, inventor of the *emparedado* (a type of sandwich). For refreshment today, there is the historic **Taberna de Antonio Sánchez** at No.13 (*see p164*). Mesón de Paredes once boasted all manner of shops, but nowadays these are mostly Chinese-run wholesale shops.

Turn right down C/Abades and left on C/Embajadores.

'Ambassadors' Street' was so named because all Madrid's foreign embassies were moved here during a 17th-century outbreak of the plague. Just by the corner of C/Oso, amid the urban disorder, is the baroque church of **San Cayetano**, built by a variety of architects, including Ribera

and Churriguera, between 1678 and 1761. Despite the many hands involved in its construction, its façade is one of the most finely worked in Madrid. Opposite, a plaque signals the house of the great 18th-century architect Pedro de Ribera.

Turn left at C/Sombrerete.

'Little Hat Street' was named after the hat which Portuguese monk Miguel dos Santos was paraded through the streets in before being hanged in the 16th century. He had been accused of acting as accomplice to chef Gabriel de Espinosa, who claimed to be the missing heir to the Portuguese throne. After the hanging, the hat was left on a muck heap in this street. Where the street becomes the **Plaza Agustín Lara** are the ruins of the 18th-century church/school, **Escuelas Pías de San Fernando**, destroyed in the Civil War. Facing the ruins across from C/Mesón de Paredes is Madrid's most famous *corrala* tenement block (*see p77*).

Continue to Plaza de Lavapiés.

A former stomping ground for the *majos* and *majas* (*see p48* **In the Frame**), and once the centre of the Jewish area, the Plaza has a scruffy appeal. From here runs tree-lined **C/Argumosa**, with its Indian restaurants and pavement cafés.

At the far end, go left into C/Doctor Fourquet.

Home to several galleries, this street leads to C/Santa Isabel and the **Reina Sofía**.

Profile Museo Thyssen-Bornemisza

Hans-Heinrich's private collection is a lesson in Western art history.

The private collection of the late Baron Hans-Heinrich Thyssen-Bornemisza is widely considered the most important in the world. Consisting of some 800 paintings, it came to Madrid on loan, but in 1993 a purchase agreement was signed with the Spanish state. The Baron's decision to sell was doubtlessly influenced both by his wife, Carmen 'Tita' Cervera, and by the offer to house the collection in the Palacio de Villahermosa, an early 19th-century edifice that was superbly converted by architect Rafael Moneo at fantastic cost. Thanks to this revamp, involving terracotta-pink walls, marble floors and skylights, it is possible to view the works with near-perfect illumination. In 2004, the museum unveiled its new wing, containing some 200 works from Carmen Cervera's own collection.

The collection was started by the Baron's father in the 1920s but was dispersed among his heirs when he died. The Baron bought back the paintings from his relatives and then expanded the collection, buying up first Old Masters and then contemporary works during the 1960s. The Baron's home in Switzerland only had space for some 300 works, leading him to look for a larger home for the collection, most of which may now be seen in Madrid, though some paintings are in the MNAC museum in Barcelona.

THE COLLECTION
Works are displayed in chronological order. Beginning on the second floor, you'll find 13th-century paintings, notably by the early Italians, such as Duccio di Buoninsegna. You finish the tour on

the ground floor, where Roy Lichtenstein's *Woman in Bath* is on show. Along the way, you'll have seen examples of all the major schools. The collection partly complements the Prado and Reina Sofía's collections with substantial holdings of 17th-century Dutch painting, Impressionism, German Expressionism, Russian constructivism, geometric abstraction and Pop Art.

The Thyssen's detractors say the collection is a ragbag of every kind of style. However, one of its great attractions is that, while it is extraordinarily broad in scope, it is recognisably a personal collection that reflects a distinct taste, as seen in the room dedicated to early portraits, with works by

CAFE CULTURE
The basement café displays Renato Guttuso's *Caffè Greco* painting. Its El Mirador terrace restaurant, open in July and August, has themed dishes based on temporary shows.

Antonello da Messina and Hans Memling. Equally quirky is the section on early North American painting, including the *Presumed Portrait of George Washington's Cook* by Gilbert Stuart and works by American artists who are rarely seen in Europe, among them Thomas Cole, Frederick Remington and Winslow Homer.

The Thyssen also has its share of real masterpieces. Among the Old Masters, the works of Duccio, van Eyck and Petrus Christus stand out. The museum's most famous painting, however, is the great Florentine master Domenico Ghirlandaio's idealised *Portrait of Giovanna Tornabuoni* (1488) in the Portrait Room. Two rooms further on is Vittore Carpaccio's allegorical *Young Knight in a Landscape* (1510), another gem. Among the masters of the Flemish School represented is the sublime *Annunciation* diptych by van Eyck. The Thyssen is also strong in the German Renaissance, with works by Cranach the Elder and Albrecht Dürer.

From the later 16th century and baroque there are superb paintings, such as Titian's *Saint Jerome in the Wilderness*. There are also representative works by El Greco, Rubens and Tintoretto, and a Bernini marble, *Saint Sebastian*.

The German Expressionists are well represented too, with powerful works by Emil Nolde, Ernst Ludwig Kirchner, Otto Dix, Max Beckmann and Blue Rider group artists Franz Marc and Kandinsky. Also present, on the ground floor, are some more familiar modern masters – Braque, Mondrian, Klee, Max Ernst and Picasso (in the shape of his 1911 *Man with a Clarinet*), among others. The last few rooms focus on the USA, with works by Georgia O'Keeffe and Edward Hopper among others.

THE CARMEN THYSSEN-BORNEMISZA COLLECTION

This extension opened in 2004 and incorporates two adjoining buildings: Nos.19 (the Palacio de Goyeneche) and 21 of the C/Marqués de Cubas. The space exhibits some 220 works of the 300 belonging to the private collection of 'Tita' Cervera, which she has ceded to the Spanish state for an 11-year period. In addition, there is a huge area for temporary shows and the library, restoration workshops and cafeteria have all been enlarged.

Access is from Room 18 on the second floor, which leads straight into rooms with early Italian and Flemish works by the likes of Jan Breughel and van Dyck. Moving on, you will enter a gallery that contains landscapes by Canaletto, Constable, Guardi and van Gogh. In the next room is 18th-century French and Italian painting and beyond that a selection of 19th-century paintings from North America. Downstairs on the first floor you'll find work by North American Impressionists. Two rooms are given over to Gauguin and other post-Impressionists. From then on, you move into German Expressionists, Fauvists and the early 20th-century avant-garde. The collection also contains four Rodin sculptures.

LISTING
For details of opening hours and admission prices, see p73.

SIGHTS

Museo de la Real Academia de Bellas Artes de San Fernando

C/Alcalá 13 (91 524 08 64, Calcografía Nacional 91 524 08 83). Metro Sevilla or Sol. **Open** *Oct-May* 9am-5pm Tue-Sat; 9am-2.30pm Sun. *June, July, Sept* 9am-5pm Tue-Fri; 9am-3pm Sat. *Aug* 10am-3pm Tue-Sun. *Calcografía Nacional* 9am-2.30pm Mon-Fri. *Temporary exhibitions* 10am-2pm, 5-8pm Tue-Fri; 10am-2pm Sat, Sun. **Admission** (excluding exhibitions) €5; €2.50 concessions; free under-18s, over-65s. Free to all Wed. *Calcografía Nacional* free. **No credit cards**. Map p327 H11.

This undervisited museum is in fact one of Madrid's most important and oldest permanent artistic institutions (it was founded in 1794). The eclectic collection is partly made up of works of varying quality donated by aspiring members in order to gain admission to the academy. The museum's greatest possessions, though, are its 13 works by Goya, an important figure in the early years of the Academia. They include two major self-portraits; a portrait of his friend, the playwright Moratín; a portrait of Charles IV's hated minister Godoy; and the *Burial of the Sardine* (see *p209* **In the Frame**), a carnival scene that foreshadows his later, darker works. Another of the academy's most prized possessions is the Italian mannerist Giuseppe Arcimboldo's *Spring*, a playful, surrealistic portrait of a man made up entirely of flowers. It was one of a series on the four seasons painted for Ferdinand I of Austria in 1563: *Summer* and *Winter* are still in Vienna, but the whereabouts of *Autumn* is unknown. There are also important portraits by Velázquez and Rubens, and several paintings by Zurbarán. Among the later works, the best known are some Picasso engravings and a Juan Gris; the most surprising are the colourful fantasies of Múñoz Degrain and the De Chirico-esque work of Julio Romero de Torres. Look out too for Leandro Bassano's superb *La Riva degli Schiavoni*.

The academy also has a valuable collection of plans and drawings, including those of Prado architect Juan de Villanueva, and rare books. In the same building is the Museo de Calcografía Nacional, a similarly priceless collection and archive of engraving and fine printing, which has many of the original plates for the great etching works of Goya.

HUERTAS & SANTA ANA

Spain has more bars and restaurants per capita than anywhere in the world, and you can get the impression that most of Madrid's are crowded into the wedge-shaped swathe of streets between Alcalá and C/Atocha. Oddly enough, this clearly defined area has an identity problem, for the authorities can never agree on a name; however, if anyone suggests a pub crawl down Huertas, or a jar in Santa Ana, it will always bring you – and several thousand others on any weekend – to the right place.

This was once the haunt of Madrid's Golden Age literary set (*see p62* **Walk**), which explains the district's fussy alternative name of Barrio de las Letras ('The District of Letters'). Here were the theatres that provided them with a living, along with whorehouses and low dives for entertainment. It is still the city's most distinctive theatre district. Close by, but not too close, lived the nobles who might have tossed a couple of ducats their way if they buttered them up with a sonnet. Otherwise there were feuds, libellous exchanges and duels to fall back on. A recent tidying up of the area has brought about pedestrianisation of much of Huertas's street, and literary quotes inlaid in bronze underfoot.

Lope de Vega's charming old house, the **Casa-Museo Lope de Vega** (*see p73*), with its tiny garden, is on the street named after his enemy, Miguel Cervantes, the author of *Don Quixote*. Cervantes lived around the corner on C/León, but was buried in the enclosed convent of the **Trinitarias Descalzas** (the 'Barefoot Trinitarians') on C/Lope de Vega, which seems deliberately confusing. Coming upon the massively plain, slab-like brick walls of the Trinitarias amid the Huertas bars is a great surprise, and gives a vivid impression of what old Madrid must have looked like before the great clear-out of religious houses in the 1830s, of which this is a rare survivor.

A reverential nod is in order to the wonderful **Ateneo** library on C/Prado, the literary and philosophical club that became a cultural institution and has been a major centre of discussion and thought at many times in its history, most notably in the years leading up to the Republic of 1931. In the old days, Ateneo members could also find any number of cafés nearby with a suitably literary atmosphere.

The **Carrera de San Jerónimo** borders the north of the district. Once part of the Ceremonial Route of the Habsburg and Bourbon monarchs, today it is one of the centres of official Madrid. On one side is the **Congreso de los Diputados**, Spain's parliament building, while opposite is the **Westin Palace** hotel (*see p119*), where politicians go to mingle and relax. At the bottom of this stretch, where it meets the Paseo del Prado at the last corner of the neighbourhood, is the world-famous **Museo Thyssen-Bornemisza** (*see right* and *pp70-71* **Profile**), containing one of the world's most important private collections of 20th-century (and other) art. Head up the hill in the other direction and you'll reach **Lhardy**, the classic Franco-Spanish restaurant founded in 1839 (*see p143*). North of San Jerónimo, behind the Congreso, is the grand 1856 **Teatro de la Zarzuela**, the city's most characterfully distinguished music theatre.

To the south of the Carrera de San Jerónimo, several streets run back towards Huertas proper.

SIGHTS

Museo Thyssen-Bornemisza.

SIGHTS

On C/Echegaray is the former site of **Los Gabrieles**, until a few years ago a much-loved bar sheathed in perhaps the world's most photographed wall-to-wall tiles, but which has now been converted into luxury flats. However, all is not lost, as another beautifully tiled bar, **Viva Madrid** lies just around the corner on C/Manuel Fernández y González 7 (91 429 36 40), while the nearby **Villa Rosa** on C/Nuñez de Arce also has an impressive tiled exterior.

Last, but in no way least, there is the core of the district, **Plaza Santa Ana**. Like Plaza de Oriente, this popular square was bequeathed to Madrid by poor Joseph Bonaparte, who tore down yet another convent to do so. Somebody should thank him: lined by some of the city's most popular bars and pavement terraces, Santa Ana has long been one of Madrid's favourite places for hanging out for an entire afternoon. On the eastern side of the plaza is the distinguished **Teatro Español**, on a site that has been a theatre continuously since 1583 when the Corral del Príncipe opened its doors to the *mosqueteros*, a heckling mob whose reactions were so violent, they sometimes forced terrified playwrights to change plots mid-play.

Casa-Museo Lope de Vega

C/Cervantes 11 (91 429 92 16). Metro Antón Martín. **Open** *10am-3pm Tue-Sun. Closed Aug.* **Admission** €2; €1 students, over-65s. Free to all Sat. **No credit cards. Map** p328 I12.
Spain's most prolific playwright and poet, Félix Lope de Vega Carpio (1562-1635) spent the last 25 years of his life in this simple, tranquil three-storey house. Oddly enough, the street in which it stands is now named after his arch rival Cervantes (who, confus-

ingly, is buried in a convent on the nearby C/Lope de Vega). The house and charming garden – remarkable survivors from the Golden Age – are the most interesting things to see. The furniture and ornaments are approximations to Lope de Vega's household inventory, rather than the originals. However, even the garden contains the same fruit trees and plants he detailed in his journals. Guided tours are available for groups of no more than ten people. Tours last around 45 minutes and leave roughly every half an hour. Some guides speak English; call in advance to check.

FREE Museo Colecciones Instituto de Crédito Oficial (ICO)

C/Zorrilla 3 (91 420 12 42, www.fundacionico. es). Metro Banco de España. **Open** *11am-8pm Tue-Sat; 10am-2pm Sun.* **Admission** free. **Map** p328 I11.
This small museum is run by the ICO, a state bank. Its collection has three main parts: most important among them is Picasso's *Suite Vollard* series, a milestone in 20th-century prints, dating from 1927 to 1937. There is also a fine selection of modern Spanish sculpture and some international painting from the 1980s.

★ Museo Thyssen-Bornemisza

Palacio de Villahermosa, Paseo del Prado 8, Huertas & Santa Ana (91 369 01 51, 91 420 39 44, www.museothyssen.org). Metro Banco de España. **Open** *Permanent collection* 10am-7pm Tue-Sun. *Temporary exhibitions* Sept-mid July 10am-7pm Tue-Sun. Mid July-Aug 10am-11pm daily. **Admission** €8; €5.50 concessions; free under-12s. *Paseo del Arte ticket* €17.60. *Temporary exhibitions* €8; €5.50 concessions. **Credit** AmEx, DC, MC, V. **Map** p328 J12.
See pp70-71 **Profile.**

Profile Museo Nacional Centro de Arte Reina Sofía

A recent reorganisation aims to keep modern art enthusiasts on their toes.

Occupying an immense, slab-sided building, the Reina Sofía (*see p78*) boasts an impressive façade with glass and steel lift-shafts, designed by British architect Ian Ritchie. And since 2005, the museum has just as impressive a rear, in the form of three buildings arranged around a courtyard and covered by a triangular, zinc-and-aluminium roof, the work of French architect Jean Nouvel. This ambitious extension added almost 30,000 square metres to the already vast space in the patio to the south-west of the main edifice.

The Reina Sofía's great jewel is still unquestionably *Guernica*, Picasso's impassioned denunciation of war and fascism, a painting that commemorates the destruction in 1937 of the Basque town of Guernica by German bombers that flew in support of the Francoist forces in the Spanish Civil War. Certain art historians have seen it more in formal terms, as a reflection on the history of Western painting using elements from the work of the Old Masters. Picasso refused to allow the painting to be exhibited in Spain under the Franco regime, and it was only in 1981 that it was finally brought

to Spain from the Museum of Modern Art in New York. *Guernica* has been in the Reina Sofía since the museum official inauguration in 1992, when it was transferred from the Casón del Buen Retiro amid great controversy. The artist had intended the painting to be housed in the Prado – of which the Casón is at least an annexe – and his family bitterly opposed the change of location. There is no question that the acquisition of *Guernica* hugely boosted the prestige of the Reina Sofía. And with the museum's recent revamp, the painting is now displayed under improved lighting and viewing conditions.

The rest of the Reina Sofía's permanent collection, which came mainly from the old Museo Español de Arte Contemporáneo in Moncloa, has been criticised, with many questioning its claim to be an international centre for contemporary art. At best, it is pointed out, it is a reasonable collection of Spanish modern art, with some thin coverage of non-Spanish artists. It certainly contains works by practically all the major Spanish artists of the 20th century – Picasso, Dalí, Miró, Julio González, Tàpies, Alfonso Ponce de León and Antonio Saura are all present – but even here there are few major works.

OTHER VENTURES

The Reina Sofía also runs the Palacio de Cristal and Palacio de Velázquez exhibition halls (in the Retiro), which present dynamic shows of sculpture and installations. It also houses El Centro para la Difusión de la Música Contemporánea (*see p237*).

In response, an active acquisitions policy adopted in the 1990s has sought to fill some gaps and to add works by major foreign artists.

With the appointment of new director Manuel Borja-Villel at the start of 2008 came a total reorganisation – completed in 2010 – of the collection. It is no longer organised along linear historial or grand thematic lines, but in a way that interweaves common influences, themes and ideas; so works by Luis Buñuel are now displayed alongside works by Picasso, Goya, Solana and even African art.

THE COLLECTION

The permanent collection, comprising more than 1,000 works (paintings, sculptures, photography, installations and audio-visual works), is spread over the first, second and fourth floors of the Sabatini building, while increasingly international temporary shows are weaved throughout. The ground floor also features Espacio Uno, a space for more cutting-edge work.

The second floor is still the most important, housing Collection 1: Historical Avant-Garde. This includes '*Guernica* and the 1930s' in Room 206, with works by Juan Miró, Oskar Schlemmer, Torres García, and, of course, Picasso. Other themes explored on this floor include Modernity, Progress and Decadentism, with works by Picasso and José Gutiérrez Solana; The New Culture in Spain; Dalí, Surrealism and Revolution; Juan Gris; and Cubism, with more works by Picasso, as well as Georges Braque and Sonia Delaunay.

Collection 2: Triumph and Failure of Modernity: the 1950s and 1960s, is on the fourth floor, in Room 405. This section explores themes such as European art after World War II, and the 'End of Painting', with more works by Picasso and Miró.

Collection 3: Paradigm Shift is in Room 104 on the first floor, with works by Yves Klein, Robert Rauschenberg, Eduardo Arroyo and Raymond Hains, mainly from the 1960s and '70s.

BOOKS & SOUVENIRS

The museum has excellent book, music, art and video libraries, and a superior souvenir and bookshop.

El Rastro.

SIGHTS

FREE Palacio del Congreso de los Diputados (Las Cortes)

*Carrera de San Jerónimo (*information *91 390 60 00,* guided tours *91 390 65 25, www.congreso.es). Metro Banco de España or Sevilla.* **Open** *Guided tours* 10.30am-12.30pm Sat. Closed Aug. **Admission** free. **Map** p328 I12.

Spain's parliament, the Cortes, was built in 1843-50 by Narciso Pascual y Colomer on the site of a recently demolished monastery, which has led to no end of problems, as the plot is too cramped to accommodate the legislators' ancillary offices. A classical portico gives it a suitably dignified air, but the building is best distinguished by the handsome 1860 bronze lions that guard its entrance. Tourists can only visit on Saturdays, on the popular free guided tours, which cannot be booked in advance. You'll need to wait outside the iron gates on the Carrera de San Jerónimo to join a tour. Groups of more than 15, however, can book tours for visits between 9am and 2.30pm and 4pm and 6.30pm on weekdays.

LAVAPIES

South of Sol and the Plaza Mayor is the area traditionally considered the home of Madrid's *castizos. Castizos* are something like London's East End cockneys: rough-diamond chirpy types straight out of a Spanish *My Fair Lady.* Many of them materialise round here in best bib and tucker – cloth caps for the men; long, frilly dresses for the ladies – for the city's summer festivals. Since the end of the 1990s, however, Lavapiés has taken on a new characteristic: as a big recipient of non-Spanish immigration – from China, Pakistan,

North and West Africa – it is becoming the city's most multicultural neighbhourhood.

These districts have always been the kind of place where newcomers to the city could find a niche. Historically they were known as the *barrios bajos,* in the double sense of low-lying and full of low life – the closer to the river, the shabbier the surroundings. In imperial Madrid, most of the food brought to the city came in through the **Puerta de Toledo** (*see p78*), and many of the tasks that the upper classes wanted neither to see nor smell, such as slaughtering and tanning, were concentrated here. Consequently, these districts became home to Madrid's first native working class. In the 18th century, the *majos* and *majas* from these streets were admired by the intelligentsia for their caustic wit (for Goya's portraits of them, *see p48* **In the Frame**), sowing the seed for the *castizo* tradition.

On the eastern edge of La Latina is the **Rastro,** Madrid's time-honoured Sunday flea market. It runs all the way down Ribera de Curtidores to the Ronda de Toledo from **Plaza Cascorro,** with its monument honouring a young soldier raised in a nearby orphanage, who volunteered for a suicide mission in Cuba in the 1890s. A true cultural phenomenon, the Rastro is also a district with a strong identity, moulded by centuries of acting as an emporium for goods of all kinds. The market is a social experience more than a shopping destination, but look out for pickpockets. For more on the Rastro, *see p200.*

If, on the other hand, instead of trying to make your way down the Rastro, you head from Plaza Cascorro slightly eastwards down

C/**Embajadores**, you will enter Lavapiés proper. Because of the rapid changes in the area, Lavapiés has sometimes been portrayed, in local conversations and the press, as an urban crisis zone to be avoided. This is one of the areas with a high incidence of petty crime, commonly associated with gangs of North African boys living on the streets, who have especially bad relations with the local Chinese shopkeepers. However, these images have a tendency to get out of proportion: there are places in Lavapiés it's probably best to steer clear of (the small square halfway down Mesón de Paredes, by C/Cabestreros, is the most obvious example), but it would be a shame if this led anyone to avoid the whole neighbourhood, for this web of sloping, winding streets remains one of the most characterful parts of Old Madrid.

Plaza Tirso de Molina, with its statue of the Golden Age dramatist whose name it bears, is the main crossroads between these *barrios bajos* and the city centre proper. It was cleaned up a few years ago and is home to a permanent, fragrant flower market, among other things. From here C/Mesón de Paredes, which is one of the two main arteries of historic Lavapiés (the other is C/Embajadores), winds off down the hill. Along Mesón de Paredes today there are still some of Madrid's most historic *tabernas*, but they stand next to shops selling tropical fruit, Moroccan teahouses, halal butchers, African fabric stores and any number of Chinese-owned wholesale stores selling discount jewellery and T-shirts.

Also on Mesón de Paredes, near the bottom by C/Sombrerete, is **La Corrala**, the city's best surviving example of an 1880s courtyard tenement, predictably garnished with freshly washed sheets and underwear billowing from the balconies. After the demolition of Madrid's monasteries in the mid 19th century, many streets in these districts were rebuilt with these distinctive, open-balconied tenements. *Corralas* always faced an inner patio, multiplying noise

and lack of privacy, factors of urban life that have luckily rarely bothered Spaniards. The *corrala* has become a characteristic of Madrid life; this one, restored in the 1980s, is used in summer as a setting for a season of *zarzuela* comic operas. A later *corrala*, not easily visible from the street, is at C/Embajadores 60. At the bottom of this area is a dynamic exhibition space and cultural centre, **La Casa Encendida** (*see below*).

The **Plaza de Lavapiés** is believed to have been the centre of Madrid's medieval Jewish community, expelled, like all others in her dominions, by the pious Queen Isabella in 1492. Today, the recently renovated square has several good cafés and restaurants, as well as the **Teatro Valle-Inclán** (*see p262*). The narrow, very steep streets between the plaza and C/Atocha are more tranquil than those around Mesón de Paredes, and, with boxes of geraniums on virtually every balcony, often strikingly pretty. Despite all the changes in the area, these closely packed streets of old apartments, shops and workshops still convey the essence of a distinctive urban way of life. At the top of the area by C/Atocha is the Filmoteca Española film theatre, in the **Cine Doré** building (*see p220*).

Running away from the south-east corner of the Plaza de Lavapiés is C/**Argumosa**, known as the 'Costa Argumosa', with shops, restaurants and outdoor-terrace bars that make a popular summer alternative to the more expensive and hectic places further into town. Argumosa leads towards Atocha and the **Museo Nacional Centro de Arte Reina Sofía** (*see p78* and *pp74-75* **Profile**). Its opening in 1992 led to the appearance nearby of attractive one-off shops and galleries, while the Jean Novel extension, completed in 2005, and consisting of three new buildings around a central plaza, is a symbol of modern Madrid. A big reorganisation of the entire museum was recently completed, in 2010. Close by, filling a big stretch of C/Santa Isabel, is the 17th-century **Convento de Santa Isabel**, sponsored, like the Encarnación, by Margaret of Austria, wife of Philip III, and one of the largest religious houses to escape the liberals' axe in the 1830s.

INSIDE TRACK
LA LATINA SUNDAYS

La Latina remains a popular Sunday outing for *madrileños* of all stripes. The tradition is to start at El Rastro flea market, and then to head to the tapas bars around Cava Baja, Plaza de la Paja, Plaza San Andrés and Calle Humilladero for an aperitif of vermouth and some tapas. The hedonistic, sociable affair continues all day long, with some bars resembling scenes normally associated with late-night antics.

★ FREE La Casa Encendida
Ronda de Valencia 2 (90 243 03 22, www.lacasaencendida.com). Metro Embajadores. **Open** 10am-9.45pm daily. **Admission** free. **Map** p328 H15.
This exciting new multidisciplinary centre in a large neo-Mudéjar building was conceived as a space for cultural interchange. Spread over four floors, the 'Burning House' is directed by José Guirao, former director of the Reina Sofía. It offers exhibitions

principally by emerging artists working in all genres, but also features cutting-edge performance art and music (including short seasons of video artists) and activities for kids. The centre also includes a Fairtrade shop, a library and classrooms for courses in, above all, IT and languages.

★ Museo Nacional Centro de Arte Reina Sofía

Edificio Sabatini *C/Santa Isabel 52*. Edificio Nouvel *Plaza del Emperador Carlos V s/n (91 774 10 00, www.museoreinasofia.es)*. Metro Atocha. **Open** 10am-9pm Mon, Wed-Sat; 10am-2.30pm Sun. **Admission** €6; €3 groups of 15 or more; free students, under-18s, over-65s. Free to all 7-9pm Mon, Wed-Fri; 2.30-9pm Sat; all day Sun. *Paseo del Arte ticket* €17.60. **Credit** AmEx, DC, MC, V. **Map** p328 J14/15.
See pp74-75 **Profile**.

Puerta de Toledo

Glorieta de la Puerta de Toledo. Metro Puerta de Toledo. **Map** p327 E15.
Slightly swallowed up in the traffic at the meeting point of the Old City and the roads in from the south-west, this neo-classical gate was one of the monuments commissioned by Napoleon's brother Joseph in his brief span as King of Spain. After his departure, it was rejigged to honour the delegates from the Cortes in Cádiz, and then King Fernando VII.

INSIDE TRACK
SQUAT MOVEMENT

Squatting first arose in Madrid and other Spanish cities during the rural exodus of the 1960s and '70s, and was later revived as the *okupa* movement during La Movida Madrileña in the '80s, when thousands of squats were legalised. In the past decade, the movement has been reignited once again, in a highly politicised form and partly in response to house price inflation. In various squatted buildings around Malasaña and, in particular, Lavapiés, grassroots organisations now offer activities such as yoga and film screenings. One of the most famous of these 'social centres' is Patio Maravillas in Malasaña, which runs a bike repair shop, an internet café, English and art classes, concerts and more from its (new) home in Calle de Pez. It started in a building on Calle del Acuerdo – now famous for its exterior graffitti (*pictured p81*) – but the organisation was famously and controversially evicted by police in January 2010.

North of Gran Vía

CHUECA

The neighbourhood of Chueca, bounded by the Gran Vía, C/Fuencarral and the Paseo de Recoletos, has been through several transformations. In the 18th century, C/Hortaleza was the site of the Recogida, a refuge for 'public sinners', where women could be confined for soliciting on the street or merely on the say-so of a male family member. Release was only possible through marriage or a lifetime tour of duty in a convent. In the 19th century, Chueca became a more respectable, affluent district, but by the 1970s and early '80s it had turned into a shabby, declining area. Since then, though, it has undergone a spectacular revival, due, above all, to it having become the gay centre of Madrid.

The epicentre of the scene is **Plaza de Chueca**; its terraces are packed with buzzing crowds on hot summer nights, and the only limitation on the scene is whether the plaza can actually hold any more people. On the back of the gay scene, many more restaurants, trendy shops, cafés and clubs have opened up, and **Fuencarral**, the borderline between Chueca and Malasaña, is now the heart of Madrid's club-fashion scene. Many gay venues have acquired a fashionable crossover status among the hip non-gay crowd (to the extent that some gays now find some Chueca clubs too 'diluted'). Whatever, Chueca has established itself as a booming free zone for socialising of all kinds, gay and heterosexual.

The north side of the district, above C/Fernando VI, is not really Chueca proper and is often known as **Alonso Martínez**, after the metro station. It's not so much part of 'gay Chueca' either, although it too has many new restaurants and bars. Instead, it's one of the foremost preserves of Madrid's teen scene. Streets such as Fernando VI or C/Campamor and Plaza Santa Bárbara are lined with bars and clubs catering to a young crowd, and on weekend nights the roads are packed too, with noisy (but safe) crowds of kids. Just west of here are the city's history museum, the **Museo de Historia** (previously called the Museo Municipal, and currently closed for lengthy reparations), and the **Museo del Romanticismo** (for both, *see right*).

Towards Recoletos, Chueca also becomes more commercial and more upmarket by day. C/Barquillo is full of hi-fi shops, while C/Almirante and its cross-street C/Conde de Xiquena are important fashion shopping zones. Off Almirante, in C/Tamayo y Baus, is one of Madrid's most important theatres, the **Teatro María Guerrero**.

SIGHTS

Plaza de Chueca.

This area is also part of official Madrid, with the giant **Palacio de Justicia** on C/Bárbara de Braganza. It was formerly the Convento de las Salesas, built in 1750-58 under the patronage of Queen Bárbara, wife of Fernando VI. It has housed law courts since 1870. Its refined classical baroque contrasts nicely with the art nouveau of the **Palacio Longoria**, a few streets away. To the south of Chueca, towards C/Alcalá, there is an isolated relic of Philip II's Madrid, the **Plaza del Rey**, and venerable 1580s **Casa de las Siete Chimeneas**, originally designed by Juan de Herrera, architect of El Escorial.

[FREE] Museo de Historia

C/Fuencarral 78 (91 588 86 72, www.muni madrid.es/museomunicipal). Metro Tribunal.
Open *Sept-July* 9.30am-8pm Tue-Fri; 10am-2pm Sat, Sun. *Aug* 9.30am-2.30pm Tue-Fri; 10am-2pm Sat, Sun. **Admission** free. **Map** p324 H9.
This museum – previously called the Museo Municipal – has been closed for several years for renovation work. Parts of the building may be reopening in 2011; call or see the website for details. The building itself boasts an exuberantly ornate entrance by Pedro de Ribera, one of the finest examples of baroque architecture in Madrid, and worth seeing in itself. For pre-Habsburg Madrid, visit the Museo de los Orígenes (*see p58*).

Museo del Romanticismo

C/San Mateo 13 (91 448 10 45, http:// museoromanticismo.mcu.es). Metro Tribunal.
Open *May-Oct* 9.30am-8.30pm Tue-Sat; 10am-3pm Sun. *Nov-Apr* 9.30am-6.30pm Tue-Sat; 10am-3pm Sun. **Admission** €3; €1.50 concessions. Free to all from 2pm Sat. **Map** p324 H9.
The newly reopened Museo del Romanticismo contains a charming collection of furniture, paintings, ornaments, early pianos and other pieces that evoke the Romantic period of 19th-century Spain. As well as these *objets d'art* there are a paintings from the likes of Francisco Goya and Vicente López Portaña, thousands of prints and lithographs and a substantial number of antique photographs.

Sociedad General de Autores y Editores (Palacio Longoria)

C/Fernando VI, 4 (91 349 95 50). Metro Alonso Martínez. Map p324 I8.
Given the extraordinary output of Catalan *modernista* architects such as Gaudi in Barcelona in the early 20th century, it is remarkable, to non-Spaniards at least, that there is not a single example of their work in Madrid. The only thing at all like it is this building in Chueca, designed by José Grasés Riera in 1902 as a residence for banker Javier González Longoria. The voluptuous façade looks as if it was formed out of wet sand, moulded by an expert in giant cake decoration. It was once thought that Catalan architecture influenced Grasés, but Héctor Guimard and French art nouveau seem to have been a more direct inspiration. It is now owned by the Spanish Writers' and Artists' association.

MALASANA & CONDE DUQUE

By day, the neighbourhood of Malasaña, between C/Fuencarral and San Bernardo, still has a laid-back neighbourhood feel, with grannies watering their geraniums on wrought-iron balconies and idiosyncratic corner shops. By night, though, this has long been an epicentre of Madrid's bar culture. Although less showy than Chueca, this is the city's hipster barrio, albeit with a grungy edge; for Malasaña is still associated with chilled-out cafés, rock bars and cheap, studenty socialising – although the tentacles of Old City gentrification are beginning to take further hold, with a smattering of new boutiques, cafés and bars opening up in the area in the past few years – especially on calle Espíritu Santo.

On 2 May 1808 this area was the centre of resistance to the French. The name of the district comes from a 17-year-old seamstress heroine, Manuela Malasaña, who was shot by the invaders for carrying concealed weapons (her scissors) or ammunition to the Spanish troops – there are various versions of her exploits. The name of the main square, **Plaza Dos de Mayo**, also recalls that day. Where the square is today was then the Monteleón artillery barracks, from where the artillery captains Daoíz and Velarde galvanised the resistance of the people. The last remaining part of the barracks, a gate, stands in the square with a monument to the two men.

The area gained a tough reputation in the 1980s, when needles and broken bottles used to litter the plaza and sidestreets in the mornings, but urban renovation schemes have been very successful, and the neighbourhood feels a lot safer to walk around at night. It is now one of the centres of the San Isidro festivals in May, hosting nightly concerts, fairs and outdoor parties.

The streets between Fuencarral and San Bernardo abound with great cafés, bars and restaurants. There are also indications – such as the broad-arched doorways for carriages – that the 19th-century well-to-do once lived here. One of the most rewarding streets is **C/San Vicente Ferrer**, with jewellery shops and a delightful 1920s tile display advertising long-defunct pharmacy Laboratorios Juanse. Other old ceramic signs on the **C/San Andrés** feature a little boy signalling that his chamber pot is full, and a dramatic, reclining vamp. C/La Palma and C/Divino Pastor, with craft and jewellery shops, are equally worth a stroll. To the north is Glorieta de Bilbao, site of one of Madrid's best traditional cafés, the **Café Comercial** (*see p178*).

The atmosphere gets more lively as you approach the streets near Fuencarral that lead down to the Gran Vía, such as **Corredera Baja de San Pablo**. This is an area of cheap restaurants, wholesale produce dealers in white aprons, shops selling nothing but light bulbs and working-class people who have known each other all their lives. Recent additions are club-style fashion shops, especially towards or on C/Fuencarral. This area contains the triangle (bordered by streets Corredera Baja de San Pablo, Desengaño and Valverde) recently named as **TriBall** by the city council and canny business folk who are looking to create a creative quarter that alludes to New York City's Tribeca. At the corner of the Corredera Baja and C/Ballesta there is an unusual brick church, built by Philip III for his Portuguese subjects in Madrid. Later it was set aside for German Catholic émigrés, and is still known as **San Antonio de los Alemanes**. It is rarely open to visitors. Just a block away along C/Pez, often unnoticed amid the shops, bars and theatres that surround it, is the slab-walled convent of **San Plácido**, another of Madrid's surviving religious houses. Down where C/Fuencarral meets Gran Vía is the **Fundación Telefónica** exhibition space.

The area west of C/San Bernardo is most commonly known as **Conde Duque**, after its finest monument, the **Centro Cultural Conde Duque**, which occupies the giant barracks (*cuartel*) built in 1717-54 by Pedro de Ribera for King Philip V's royal guard. It was wonderfully renovated by the Tierno Galván city council in the 1980s as an arts centre (*see right*). Nearby is the **Museo Municipal de Arte Contemporáneo** (*see right*), and slightly hidden next to it is one of Madrid's least-seen treasures, the **Palacio de Liria**.

Centro Cultural Conde Duque.

Calle del Acuerdo. *See p78.*

SIGHTS

FREE Centro Cultural Conde Duque

C/Conde Duque 11 (91 588 58 34, www.muni madrid.es/condeduque). Metro Noviciado or Ventura Rodríguez. **Open** 10am-2pm, 6-9pm Tue-Sat; 10.30am-2pm Sun. **Admission** free. **Map** p323 F8.

Housed in a former barracks, built in the 18th century for Philip V's guard by Pedro de Ribera, the magnificently restored Conde Duque is a multipurpose cultural centre. Around a dozen shows, both artistic and historical, are held annually in the two exhibition spaces and the two vast patios. Open-air concerts in summer bring in a range of performers. Also housed here are the city's newspaper and video libraries, as well as the Museo Municipal de Arte Contemporáneo *(see below)*, which opened in 2001.

Fundación Telefónica

C/Gran Via 28 (entrance at C/Valverde 2) (91 522 66 45, www.fundacion.telefonica. com/arte_tecnologia). Metro Gran Via. **Open** 11am-9pm Tue-Sun. Closed Aug. **Admission** free. **Map** p323 H11.

Run by Telefónica, the national telephone company, this foundation functions on several levels. The Museo de las Telecomunicaciones is a permanent exhibition illustrating the history of telecommunications. Another large space is used to display selections from its permanent collection of Spanish art, including various works by Eduardo Chillida, Luis Fernández, Miró, Picasso and Tàpies and it also has a permanent show based around post-Civil War Spanish artists of the so-called Madrid and Paris schools, the latter in exile. Temporary exhibitions feature both the arts and technology.

FREE Museo Municipal de Arte Contemporáneo

C/Conde Duque 9 & 11 (91 588 58 61). Metro Noviciado. **Open** Closed until May 2011. *Sept-June* 10am-2pm, 5.30-9pm Tue-Sat; 10.30am-2.30pm Sun. *July, Aug* 10am-2pm, 6-9pm Tue-Sat; 10.30am-2pm Sun. **Admission** free. **Map** p323 F8.

The council's contemporary art collection is currently closed for reparations and expected to reopen in May 2011. It covers painting and graphic work, along with sculpture, photography and drawing. The first floor relates works and artists of different generations and media to show the plurality of Madrid's art scene. Highlights include work by Eduardo Arroyo, Ouka Lele, Eduardo Úrculo, Jorge Oteiza and Eva Lootz.

FREE Palacio de Liria

C/Princesa 20 (91 547 53 02). Metro Ventura Rodríguez. **Open** *Guided tours* 10am, 11am, noon Fri. Booking essential. Closed July-Oct. **Admission** free. **Map** p323 E8.

This sober, neo-classical palace, completed in 1783 and refurbished in the 1910s by Edwin Lutyens, is still the private property of Spain's premier aristocrat, the Duchess of Alba. The extraordinary collection includes work by Rembrandt, Palma Vecchio, Titian and Rubens, and one of the most important Goyas in private hands: his portrait of an earlier Duchess of Alba in red and white. The problem is, the current duchess has no need to open her palace to public view. The Friday guided tours must be booked in advance and in writing. Bookings can be made by email and should be sent to visitas@funacioncasadealba.com. There is currently a waiting list of over a year!

The Retiro & Salamanca

Verdant oases, designer shopping, and that famous royal art collection.

Map pp324-325   **Tapas** p166
   & pp328-329   **Cafés & Bars** p182
Hotels p123   **Nightlife** p254
Restaurants p153

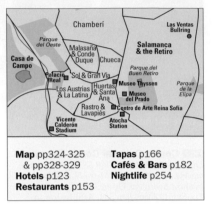

Most visitors encounter the area around the Retiro within the first few days of a trip to the city, seeing as it's home to Madrid's star attraction, the Museo del Prado. The famous art museum – which contains the world's largest and finest collection of Spanish art – is often referred to in relation to the 'Golden Triangle' it forms with the nearby Thyssen-Bornemisza and the Reina Sofía (covered in the Old City chapter). These museums, together with the wide, leafy boulevards of the Paseo del Prado, make up the Paseo del Arte (*see p54*) – the 'art stroll' that has become an even more apt concept with the opening of the postmodern CaixaForum arts centre.

To the east of the museum district is the Retiro park, a verdant oasis of old-fashioned delights, and a perfect post-museum respite – especially in hot weather.

North of here is the barrio of Salamanca, an area known for its designer shopping, expensive restaurants and futuristic architecture (along the Paseo de la Castellana). But it's also home to some of the city's most fascinating small museums.

The Retiro & Around

PASEO DEL PRADO

The most attractive section of Madrid's north–south avenue, and the one that most new arrivals in Madrid first become familiar with, is the oldest: the **Paseo del Prado**, from Atocha up to Plaza de Cibeles. Once an open space between the city wall and the Retiro (*prado* means 'meadow'), it was given its present form in 1775-82, from a design chiefly by José de Hermosilla; it was the most important of Charles III's attempts to give his shabby capital the kind of urbane dignity he had seen in Paris and Italy. The king intended it to be a grand avenue lined by centres of learning and science. Originally called Salón del Prado (*see p84* **El Salón del Prado**), the form of the main section, from Cibeles to Plaza Cánovas del Castillo, was

modelled on Piazza Navona in Rome, with three fountains by Ventura Rodríguez: **Cibeles** at the most northerly point, **Neptune** to the south and a smaller figure of **Apollo** in the middle. The southern stretch of the Paseo, tapering down to Atocha, has another statue, the *Four Seasons*, in front of the Museo del Prado. In the 19th century, the Paseo del Prado was the great promenade of Madrid. Virtually the entire population, rich and poor, took a turn along it each evening, to see and be seen, pick up on the latest city gossip, make assignations and show off new clothes.

Despite the traffic, the tree-lined boulevard still has many attractions on and around it, most notably Madrid's 'big three' great art museums: the **Museo Thyssen-Bornemisza** (*see p73 and pp70-71* **Profile**), near the statue of Neptune, at the border with Santa Ana; Charles III's **Museo del Prado** (*see p88 and pp86-87* **Profile**), with its new wing on Calle Ruiz de

SIGHTS

Retiro. *See p90.*

El Salón del Prado

The tree-lined promenade's 18th-century status is being restored.

Thanks to Charles III's untiring efforts in the 18th century, the Paseo del Prado was to become the social heart of the city. Charles's idea was for this to become a centre of learning, with the main research institutions for arts and sciences, all open to the public, based here. He had it adorned with statues and fountains, and the whole area became known as **El Salón del Prado**. Early photos show women strolling with parasols while men in black bowlers hold ardent discussions. The 19th-century writer Richard Ford effused: 'The Prado, a truly Spanish thing and scene, is unique; and as there is nothing like it in Europe; and oh, wonder! no English on it, fascinates all who passes the Pyrenees.'

Oh, wonder! In time, however, thanks to the invention of the combustion engine, the Paseo del Prado was to become less of a promenade and more of a motorway, with cars speeding through red lights and tour buses blocking the view of the fountains. The mayor's controversial **Plan Especial Prado-Recoletos**, however, has sought to remedy this. The team behind the project, headed by Portuguese architect Álvaro Siza, wants to reclaim the Paseo for pedestrians, widening the pavements, planting new trees and reducing traffic lanes. The plan – initiated in 2005, but which didn't get underway until 2008 – is now partially complete. But in 2010, the project stalled due to political rows. When it is finished – hopefully in 2012, but this date is now unconfirmed – a broad expanse of walkable promenade will link the Plaza de Colón and the big three museums (the 'Golden Triangle') to Atocha train station, with minimal interference from passing traffic.

So far, the stretch from Colón along Paseo Recoletos to Cibeles is the only

part that has been remodelled, however, along with isolated spots around the Retiro, such as the now-pedestrianised bookstall-lined Cuesta de Moyano. The towering statue of Columbus in the Plaza de Colón has also been transferred back to its original spot in the centre of the adjacent roundabout. (The story goes that the pointing finger of the Columbus statue was intended to point towards the Dominican Republic, his first settlement, but an error in calculations meant that he was, until his move in 2008, pointing towards Greenland.) But the Paseo del Prado itself is still waiting for its facelift.

In fact, the remodelling of the Paseo has been the most contentious and disruptive element of the project. The plan to cut the number of traffic lanes from 12 to six has sparked intense opposition from right-wing politicians over fears of reduced north-south traffic mobility, and a new proposal arose in 2010 for one or two tunnels to be built between Atocha and Cibeles.

Whether or not the controversial tunnel proposal is approved, the eventual completion of the Prado-Recoletos plan will mean that strollers will, at some point in the future, be able to amble leisurely between Madrid's best art museums and extraordinary new architecture (the CaixaForum), and that the fountain-filled Prado 'salon' will be returned to its 19th-century self as Madrid's best place to see and be seen.

Alarcón; and, at the very bottom, in the south-east corner of Lavapiés, the **Museo Nacional Centro de Arte Reína Sofía** (*see p78 and pp74-75* **Profile**). Together with the cutting-edge **CaixaForum** (*see p85 and p35* **Profile**), which opened in 2008, these spaces form the Paseo del Arte (*see p54* **The Paseo del Arte**).

To the left of the Paseo, looking up, streets lead off into Huertas and the Old City, while to the right is the tranquil district of the Retiro. The knot of elegant streets in between the Paseo and the Retiro make up Madrid's most concentrated museum district, with, as well as the Museo del Prado, the **Museo Naval** (*see p88*), the **Bolsa de Comercio de Madrid** (*see below*) and the **Museo Nacional de Artes Decorativas** (*see p88*).

Heading south from here, other highlights include the **Real Jardín Botánico** (*see p88*), on the Paseo del Prado itself; the rows of second-hand bookstalls on the newly pedestrianised **Cuesta de Moyano**, which runs alongside the southern side of the botanical garden; the magnificently grandiose 1880s **Ministry of Agriculture**, right on Glorieta de Atocha, and designed by Ricardo Velázquez, the same architect who created the delicate exhibition halls inside the Retiro itself; and the landmark 19th-century **Atocha** station (*see right*).

A few blocks east from here along the (traffic-ridden) Paseo Reina Cristina, a turn right down C/Julián Gayarre leads to the **Real Fábrica de Tapices** (*see p88*). On Julián Gayarre there is also the much rebuilt **Basílica de Atocha** and the odd, often deserted, **Panteón de Hombres Ilustres** (*see p95*) containing the elaborate tombs of Spanish politicians of the 19th century.

FREE Bolsa de Comercio de Madrid

Plaza de la Lealtad 1 (91 589 22 64, www. bolsamadrid.es). Metro Banco de España. **Open** (By guided tour only) *Sept-June* Individuals noon Thur. Groups 10am Mon-Fri. **Admission** free. **Map** p328 J11.
In the same plaza as the Hotel Ritz, Madrid's stock exchange is a landmark as well as a business centre. Enrique María Repullés won the competition to design it in 1884, with a neo-classical style chosen to reflect that of the nearby Prado. The building has two distinct areas: one is the trading area; the other, open to the public, houses an exhibition on the market's history. Guided tours last 60 minutes; phone to arrange a visit.

★ FREE CaixaForum Madrid

Paseo del Prado 36 (91 330 73 00, http://obrasocial.lacaixa.es). Metro Atocha. **Open** 10am-8pm daily. **Admission** free. **Map** p328 J13/J14.
Housed in the former Mediodía Electric Power Station, remodelled by Herzog & de Meuron archi-

tects to striking effect, this cutting-edge cultural centre runs a lively programme of events and exhibitions. Contemporary and traditional temporary art exhibitions are run alongside engaging and stimulating music and poetry events, as well as lectures, debates and workshops. Federico Fellini, Fotopres photojournalism, and the Fairtrade movement have all been the focus of recent shows. By virtue of its location, CaixaForum can be considered a new addition to the 'Paseo del Arte', sitting as it does inside the 'Golden Triangle' formed by the Prado, Reina Sofia and Thyssen on the Paseo del Prado. It replaces the Fundación La Caixa, previously located on Calle Serrano. *See also p35* **Profile**.

★ FREE Estación de Atocha

Glorieta del Emperador Carlos V. Metro Atocha. **Map** p328 K15.
Madrid's classic wrought-iron and glass main rail station was built in 1888-92, to a design by Alberto del Palacio. It remained much the same, gathering a coating of soot, until the 1980s, when Rafael Moneo – he of the Museo Thyssen and Prado extension – gave it a complete renovation in preparation for Spain's golden year of 1992. Entirely new sections were added for the AVE high-speed train to Andalucia and Barcelona, and the *cercanías* local rail network, and an indoor tropical garden installed, in an imaginative blend of old and new.

Museo Nacional de Antropología

C/Alfonso XII 68 (91 539 59 95, http://.mn antropologia.mcu.es). Metro Atocha. **Open** 9.30am-8pm Tue-Sat; 10am-3pm Sun. **Admission** €3; €1.50 students; free under-18s, over-65s. Free to all 2-8pm Sat & all Sun. **No credit cards. Map** p328 K15.
This three-storey building between the Retiro and Atocha station houses several levels, each devoted to a specific region or country. The first level has an extensive collection from the Philippines (a former Spanish colony), dominated by a 6m (20ft) dugout canoe. Among the bizarre highlights are a 19th-century Philippine helmet made from a spiky blowfish, shrunken human heads from Peru and the skeleton of Don Agustín Luengo y Capilla, an Extremaduran

SIGHTS

Profile Museo Nacional del Prado

Madrid's top tourist attraction contains the world's finest collection of Spanish art.

Housed in a gigantic neo-classical building begun by Juan de Villanueva for King Charles III in 1785, the Prado is Madrid's best-known attraction. Charles originally wanted to establish a museum of natural sciences, but by the time it opened, in 1819, this plan had changed: the Prado was a public art museum – one of the world's first – displaying the royal art collection.

The main phases of the Prado's highly ambitious expansion programme of the past decade have now been brought to fruition, making the collection more comprehensive than ever before. In 2007, after long delays, the new extension opened, on the site of the San Jerónimo cloisters behind the main building. The highly controversial cube-shaped edifice designed by Rafael Moneo houses the museum's temporary galleries, as well as a huge foyer containing the café/restaurant, information points, book and gift shop and, on the first floor, the restoration workshops.

Director Miguel Zugaza's action plan for the 2009-2012 period – known as its 'second expansion' – has involved a massive internal reorganisation, with the aim of increasing the number of works displayed by 50 per cent (to around 1,500 works by 2012). In autumn 2009, the first step was reached, with the opening of 12 new rooms (arranged chronologically) on the ground floor, containing a total of 176 pieces from the museum's 19th-century collection (many moved from El Casón del Buen Retiro), and inaugurated with the '19th Century at the Prado' exhibition.

In spring 2010, a further seven new rooms opened containing newly restored works. Dedicated to Medieval and Renaissance Spanish art, they complete the ground floor collections of the Villanueva building, and significantly expand the museum's displays of 12th- to 16th-century Spanish painting. Six more new rooms are due to open by 2012.

THE COLLECTION

The Prado embraces art from the 12th to the 20th century, and contains the world's largest collection of Spanish works. Its core is still the royal holdings, however, so it reflects royal tastes and political alliances from the 15th to the 17th centuries: court painters Diego de Velázquez and Francisco de Goya are well represented. Political ties with France, Italy and the southern, Catholic Netherlands also assure the presence of works by Titian, Rubens and Hieronymous Bosch.

But Spanish monarchs had begun collecting long before this time. By the 1500s, Queen Isabella already had a substantial collection of works by Flemish artists. During the reigns of Emperor Charles V (1516-56) and Philip II (1556-98), Italian and Flemish works continued to dominate. Titian was a favourite of both kings, and the eclectic Philip II also purchased several works by Bosch, among them the triptych *Garden of Earthly Delights*

SUGGESTED ROUTES
The museum has devised three routes that focus on 15, 30 or 50 masterpieces to be seen in one, two or three hours respectively. Visit the website for details before you go, or enquire at one of the museum's information points.

(*see p92* **Judgement Day**), which he had hanging on his bedroom wall in El Escorial.

Philip IV (1621-65), a major patron of Rubens, is seen as the greatest of the Habsburg art collectors. He was contemptuous of Spanish painters until he saw the work of the young Velázquez, who would serve him as court painter for nearly 40 years (1623-60). Velázquez also supervised the acquisition of other works, adding some 2,000 paintings by Renaissance and 17th-century masters.

Spain's first Bourbon King, Philip V (1700-46), brought with him one of the museum's most extraordinary possessions, displayed in the basement: the Tesoro del Delfín ('Treasures of the Grand Dauphin') – mostly 16th- and 17th-century Italian *objets d'art*.

The last monarch to add significantly to the royal collection was Charles IV (1788-1808), the employer of Goya, possibly the least respectful court painter who ever lived, as evidenced by his portraits of Charles IV's family.

HIGHLIGHTS AND BASIC FLOOR PLANS

It is impossible to do the Prado justice in a single visit, and we don't suggest you try. Pick up a floor plan when you arrive to help you track down the don't-misses. Rooms are being renumbered 1 to 100, and more reorganisation of works is still taking place as part of the 2009-2012 'second expansion'.

The ground floor contains Flemish and Italian works from the 14th to the 16th centuries, including Breughel the Elder's *Triumph of Death* and Bosch's *Garden of Earthly Delights* (Room 56A, which will become Room 3), as well as Spanish art from

the 12th to the 19th centuries, including some of Goya's major works, and in particular his masterpiece *The Third of May* (Room 64, which will become Room 89; *see also p25* **In the Frame**). The ground floor central gallery also displays many works from the museum's sculpture collection.

The highlight of the first floor is the Velázquez rooms, in the Central Gallery. Here you'll find the Prado's most famous work, *Las Meninas* (Room 12, which will become Room 50), often described as the greatest painting in the world, because of its complex interplay of perspectives and realities. Elsewhere on this floor are Italian paintings from the 16th century and Spanish art from the 16th to the 19th centuries, including several works by El Greco, a room dedicated to Joaquín Sorolla (Room 60A, which will become Room 99) and Goyas from the period 1780 to 1800.

The second floor is devoted to Spanish art from the 18th century, with works by Paret, Meléndez and Goya, and will soon also have new rooms for European art from the 17th, with more paintings by Rubens, among others.

SIGHTS

TICKETS & OPENING HOURS
For details of opening hours and admission prices, *see p88.* Tickets are now also available from self-service machines outside the museum.

JEN RETIRO

n Retiro in the Retiro
t of the Museo del
he Prado's Villavueva
extension, the Casón's 19th-century
paintings were transferred to the main
building, and, after a 12-year and €40-
million restoration, it is now used as
a centre for art research, housing
the Prado's library. Its ceiling has a
magnificent fresco by Luca Giordano.

who was 2.25m (7ft 4in) tall. Even more enticing is a shrivelled tobacco leaf-skinned mummy, said to have once been in Charles III's royal library. Both are in the annexe to the first level.

Museo Nacional de Artes Decorativas
C/Montalbán 12 (91 532 64 99, http://mnartes decorativas.mcu.es). Metro Banco de España.
Open 9.30am-3pm Tue-Sat; 10am-3pm Sun. 3rd and 4th floors closed July, Aug. **Admission** €3; €1.50 students; free under-18s, over-65s. Free to all Sun. **No credit cards. Map** p328 K11.
The Decorative Arts Museum houses more than 15,000 *objets d'art*, furniture and tapestries from all over Spain, plus many from China. One of the most prized rooms is the fifth-floor tiled kitchen, painstakingly transferred from an 18th-century Valencian palace, whose 1,604 painted tiles depict a domestic scene, with a huddle of servants making hot chocolate. Also of great interest is the second floor, where the Spanish baroque pieces are concentrated, among them ceramics from Talavera and Teruel, textiles, gold and silver work and jewellery cases from the Tesoro del Delfin (Treasure of the Grand Dauphin), the rest of which is in the Prado. Elsewhere are 19th-century dolls' houses, antique fans, an ornate 16th-century four-poster bedstead and a Sèvres jug given to Queen Isabel II by Napoleon III.

★ Museo Nacional del Prado
C/Ruiz de Alarcón 23, off Paseo del Prado, Retiro (91 330 28 00, 91 330 29 00, 90 210 70 77, www.museodelprado.es). Metro Atocha or Banco de España. **Open** 9am-8pm Tue-Sun. **Admission** €8; €4 concessions; free under-18s, EU students under 25. Free to all 6-8pm Tue-Sat; 5-8pm Sun. *Paseo del Arte ticket €17.60.*
Credit AmEx, DC, MC, V. **Map** p328 J12/13.
See pp86-87 **Profile.**

FREE Museo Naval
Paseo del Prado 5 (91 532 87 89, www.armada.med.es). Metro Banco de España.
Open 10am-2pm Tue-Sun. Closed Aug.
Admission free. **Map** p328 J11.

Madrid's naval museum contains examples of the booty accumulated by Columbus and other mariners during Spain's period of maritime expansion, and an array of navigational instruments, muskets, guns and naval war paintings. Glass displays enclose primitive weapons, some of which, like the swords lined with sharks' teeth from the Gilbert Islands, promise greater damage than their Western counterparts. The most impressive room is dominated by a huge mural-map that traces the routes taken by Spain's intrepid explorers; in front of it are two equally impressive 17th-century giant globes. This same room also holds the museum's most valuable possession: the first known map of the Americas by a European – a parchment paper drawing by royal cartographer Juan de la Cosa, believed to have been made for Ferdinand and Isabella in 1500. Worth a look also is the room occupied by items salvaged in 1991-3 from the *Nao San Diego*, which sank in the China Seas in 1600. You'll need to show your passport or other form of ID to gain entry.

FREE Puerta de Alcalá
Plaza de la Independencia. Metro Retiro.
Map p324 K11.
A short distance along C/Alcalá from Cibeles, in the middle of another traffic junction, stands one of the most impressive monuments built for King Charles III, a massive neo-classical gate designed by his favourite Italian architect, Francesco Sabatini, to provide a grand entrance to the city. It was built between 1769 and 1778, using granite and stone from Colmenar. Possible to miss in daytime traffic, it is unavoidably impressive at night.

Real Fábrica de Tapices
C/Fuenterrabía 2 (91 434 05 50, www.real fabricadetapices.com). Metro Menéndez Pelayo.
Open *Guided tours only* 10am-2pm Mon-Fri (last tour approx 1.30pm). Closed Aug. **Admission** €4; €3 under-12s. **No credit cards. Map** p329 M15.
Goya created some of his freshest images as designs for Madrid's royal tapestry factory, founded in 1721. Originally it was in Chueca, but has been here since 1889. The hand-working skills and techniques used haven't changed, and are evident from the intricate, painstaking work carried out in its two sections – the carpet room and the tapestry room. Goya designs are a mainstay of the work that's done here today (the factory also maintains carpets for royal palaces and the Ritz, as well as undertaking work for private clients). Guided tours are normally in Spanish, but if you call in advance an English-speaking guide can always be arranged. *Photos pp90-91.*

★ Real Jardín Botánico
Plaza de Murillo 2 (91 420 30 17, www.rjb.csic.es). Metro Atocha. **Open** *Nov-Feb* 10am-6pm daily. *Mar, Oct* 10am-7pm daily. *Apr, Sept* 10am-8pm daily. *May-Aug* 10am-9pm daily. **Admission** €2.50; €1.25 student. Free under-10s.
No credit cards. Map p328 K13/14.

Real Jardín Botánico.

SIGHTS

Real Fábrica de Tapices. *See p88.*

Madrid's luscious botanical gardens were created for Charles III by Juan de Villanueva and the botanist Gómez Ortega in 1781. They are right alongside the Paseo del Prado, just south of the Prado museum, but inside this deep-green glade, with over 30,000 plants from around the world, it's easy to feel that city life has been put on hold. A sign at the entrance asks that you treat the gardens as if they were a museum, but don't feel bad about getting comfortable with a book for a while; it is one of the best spots in Madrid to do so. The building in the middle of the gardens is used as a gallery space. *Photo p89.*

FREE San Jerónimo el Real

C/Moreto 4 (91 420 30 78). Metro Banco de España. **Open** *Oct-June* 10am-1.30pm, 5-8.30pm daily. *July-Sept* 10am-1pm, 6-8.30pm daily. **Map** p328 K12.

**INSIDE TRACK
CUESTA DE MOYANO**

The Cuesta de Moyano (*see p85*) – the hilly pathway linking the Paseo del Prado with the Retiro park – has now been pedestrianised as part of the Plan Especial Prado-Recoletos (*see p84*). Lined with traditional book stalls, it makes for a lovely, browsing-infused stroll.

Founded in 1464 and rebuilt for Queen Isabella in 1503, this church near the Retiro was particularly favoured by the Spanish monarchs, and used for state ceremonies. Most of the original building was destroyed during the Napoleonic Wars, and the present church is largely a reconstruction that was undertaken between 1848 and 1883. The cloisters at the side of the church have been taken over for use as galleries by the Prado.

THE RETIRO

When Philip II ruled Madrid, this whole area was just open country, apart from the church of **San Jerónimo** (*see left*) and a few other royal properties. In the 1630s, it was made into gardens – unprecedented in size for the era, at nearly 122 hectares (300 acres) – that became part of the **Palacio del Buen Retiro**, built by the Conde Duque de Olivares for Philip IV to impress the world. Gardeners were brought in from across Europe to create the park and its lake, and to ensure that it would feature shade and flowers throughout a Madrid summer. Charles III first opened sections of the park to the public in 1767, but it was only after the fall of Isabel II in 1868 that the gardens became entirely free to the public. After it became a park, the Retiro acquired most of its many statues, particularly the giant 1902 monument to King Alfonso XII presiding over the lake.

Since it was made open to all, the Retiro has found a very special place in the hearts and habits of the people of Madrid. On a Sunday morning stroll, especially before lunch, you will see multigenerational families watching puppet shows, dog-owners and their hounds, children playing on climbing frames, vendors hawking everything from *barquillos* (traditional wafers) to etchings, palm and tarot readers, buskers from around the world, couples on the lake in hired boats, kids playing football, elderly men in leisurely games of *petanca* (boules), cyclists, runners, and a good many bench-sitters who want nothing more than to read the paper. During the week it's much emptier, and it's easier to take a look at some of the 15,000 trees, the rose garden and the park's fine exhibition spaces: the **Palacio de Cristal** (*see p93*), the **Palacio de Velázquez** (*see p122*) and the **Casa de Vacas** (*see right*). Built in the 19th century, they were extensively renovated during the 1980s.

At the southern end of the park is the **Observatorio Astronómico** (*see right*), a fine neo-classical building. However, the greatest curiosity of the park is Madrid's monument to Lucifer, in the moment of his fall from heaven. Known as the **Angel Caído** (Fallen Angel), this bizarrely unique statue on the avenue south of the Palacio de Cristal is thought to be the only monument to the devil in the world.

After the death of Philip IV in 1665, little use was made of the Retiro, although the palace gained a new lease of life when the Alcázar burned down in 1734, as it became the primary royal residence in Madrid until the Palacio Real was completed in 1764. However, in 1808 Napoleon's troops made it a barracks, and when the British army arrived in 1812 to fight over Madrid, much of it was destroyed.

On the north side of the park, forming a bridge between it and Salamanca, is the grand **Puerta de Alcalá** (*see p88*), still imposing despite being surrounded by the hectic traffic of the Plaza de la Independencia. The districts around and south of the Retiro are in some ways similar to Salamanca, but less emphatically affluent and more mixed.

FREE Centro Cultural Casa de Vacas
Parque del Retiro (91 409 58 19). Metro Retiro.
Open 11am-2pm, 5-9pm Mon-Fri; 11am-9pm Sat.
Times may vary. **Admission** free. **Map** p329 L11.
This exhibition space in the Retiro, close to the boating lake, is run by the local council and offers shows on a variety of subjects, ranging from children's books to wildlife photography.

FREE Observatorio Astronómico Nacional
C/Alfonso XII 3 (91 527 01 07, www.oan.es).
Metro Atocha. **Open** *Guided tours* 10am-1pm
Fri. **Admission** free. **Map** p329 L15.

Judgement Day

Two of the Prado's not-to-be-missed masterpieces are depictions of the Last Judgement.

In Room 56A of the Prado are two of the greatest paintings ever done of the Last Judgement: Pieter Breughel the Elder's *The Triumph of Death* (*above*) painted in 1562, and *The Garden of Earthly Delights* (*below*), the triptych by Hieronymous Bosch (El Bosco to the Spanish), thought to have been completed around 1501. The latter is one of the greatest canvases of all time. And the *Triumph of Death* is no lightweight effort either; even if Breughel had not also been Flemish and an unabashed admirer of Bosch's painting, it would still be a good choice to display near *Earthly Delights*. It is smaller, a single canvas, but imagined in hallucinatory detail that is every bit a counterweight to the Bosch. In it, hundreds of skeletons herd the living into a huge coffin. The humans are terrified, helpless, shoved, pushed and prodded along by skeletons. There is a huge bony horse and astride it is a skeletal general in death's army, huge scythe in one hand, reaping as he tramples through the waves of terrified human beings. A dog feeds on a dead woman's body. The horizon is high on the painting, the whole shocking scene in the foreground fades into dark spectral colours punctuated by pockets of leaping flames.

On the facing wall is Bosch's triptych, two metres high, the centre panel twice the width of the wings, which fold in over it. Painted on the back of the wings, so as to form another scene when they are covering

the centre panel, is the third day of creation as described in Genesis. The main triptych depicts our peopled world in its implacable fullness and flesh, its joys and sufferings, all in amazingly modern detail.

The left panel shows the Garden of Eden in its innocence, but even here all is not peace and light, as beasts swallow other beasts, hinting at the savage brute world on which ours is built. In the centre panel is the antediluvian world of the senses – the world as we know it, a variety of human pleasure as modern as television or Hollywood's latest scandal. Sensual romps we have no trouble recognising as our own. The pleasures of the flesh in trysts, threesomes, group gropes, everyone indulging. Beside it, in the last panel, hell itself, Judgement Day, when the former revellers are tied and tortured by ghouls and animals: miserable, dominated, impaled, ensnared and enslaved, their cities burning in the implacable darkness of the last days.

The Garden of Earthly Delights is full of the most modern of physical forms, from a round earth to airships. The power of its images is undimmed across the centuries, and its images still resonate to this day.

One of Charles III's scientific institutions, the Observatorio was completed after his death in 1790. Beautifully proportioned, it is Madrid's finest neo-classical building, designed by Juan de Villanueva. It still contains a working telescope, which can only be seen by prior request. One room is also open to the public, but only on Fridays and as part of a guided tour; tours should be requested by fax (91 527 19 35).

FREE Palacio de Cristal
Parque del Retiro (91 574 66 14). Metro Retiro. **Open** *Oct-Apr* 10am-6pm Mon, Wed-Sat; 10am-4pm Sun. *May-Sept* 11am-8pm Mon, Wed-Sat; 11am-6pm Sun. **Admission** free. **Map** p329 M13. This 1880s glass and wrought-iron construction, an outpost of the Reina Sofia, is a lovely, luminous space for viewing art. Shows here often involve large-scale installations, sculpture or pieces conceived specifically for the space.

FREE Palacio de Velázquez
Parque del Retiro (91 573 62 45). Metro Retiro. **Open** *Oct-Apr* 10am-6pm Mon, Wed-Sat; 10am-4pm Sun. *May-Sept* 11am-8pm Mon, Wed-Sat; 11am-6pm Sun. **Admission** free. **Map** p329 M12. Built by Ricardo Velázquez for a mining exhibition in 1883, this pretty brick and tile building amid the trees of the Retiro is topped by large iron and glass vaults. Another Reina Sofia annexe, its galleries are wonderfully airy, and host very good temporary shows, including a recent one by Julian Schnabel. Contemporary dance has also featured recently.

Salamanca & Around
PLAZA DE CIBELES

Midway between the Puerta del Sol and the Retiro, this four-way intersection and its statue signify Madrid to Spaniards as much as the Eiffel Tower or the Empire State Building identify their particular cities. It is surrounded by some of the capital's most prominent buildings: the **Palacio de Cibeles** (*see p94*) – formerly the Palacio de Comunicaciones (the main post office), but which is now government offices – the **Banco de España** (*see p94*, the **Palacio Buenavista** (now the Army headquarters) and the Palacio de Linares, which houses the **Casa de América** (*see p94*). The Ventura Rodríguez statue in the middle is of Cybele, the Roman goddess of fertility and symbol of natural abundance, on a chariot drawn by lions. The goddess and the fountain around her have traditionally been the gathering point for victorious Real Madrid fans (Atlético supporters soak themselves in the fountain of Neptune, by the Thyssen museum) and the place where wins by the Spanish national football team have been celebrated – most recently for the World Cup winning team in 2010.

SIGHTS

SIGHTS

Plaza de Cibeles. *See p93.*

PASEO DE RECOLETOS

While other cities have rivers cutting through them as navigational points of reference, Madrid has two great avenues: the Gran Vía and its continuation, C/Alcalá, running east–west, and the **Paseo de la Castellana** – which becomes the **Paseo de Recoletos** and the **Paseo del Prado** as it runs north–south. The leg that runs north of Cibeles, Paseo de Recoletos, was mostly added in the 1830s and '40s. The Palacio de Linares, now the **Casa de América** (*see below*), is perhaps the best preserved of the palaces built by wealthy families after the Restoration. The curiously grand marble palace a little further north on the right, which is now the **Banco Hipotecario**, was once the residence of the Marqués de Salamanca, 19th-century Madrid's huckster-in-chief. It famously had the first flushing toilets in Madrid, an amenity the marquis later offered to residents in his new housing developments.

At the north end of Recoletos, on the right, stands the huge building housing the **Biblioteca Nacional** and, behind it, the **Museo Arqueológico Nacional** (*see p100*). The most ambitious project of the reign of Isabel II, the building was commissioned in 1865, but only completed in 1892. It overlooks the **Plaza de Colón**, which has recently been remodelled, and whose Columbus statue now sits in the central roundabout. The square houses the **Fernán Gómez** theatre and arts centre (formerly the Centro Cultural de la Villa; *see below*).

FREE Casa de América
Palacio de Linares, Paseo de Recoletos 2 (91 595 48 00, www.casamerica.es). Metro Banco de España. **Open** 11am-8pm Mon-Sat; 11am-3pm Sun. *Guided tours* 11am, noon, 1pm Sun. Closed Aug, except for cinema. **Admission** free. *Guided tour* €7; €4 concessions; free under-12s. **Map** p324 J11.
Housed in the 1872 Palacio de Linares, the Casa de América showcases Latin American art, both by established figures and emerging talents. It also has the important role of promoting cultural contacts between Spain and the Continent. As well as this, there are film seasons (*see p218*), music, theatre and talks given by leading writers, film directors, playwrights and political figures. There are also print and video libraries, a good bookshop and a terrace – the Terraza Jardín Brugal – with arts events in summer. Tours of the Palacio de Linares must be taken with a guide.

FREE Museo del Biblioteca Nacional
Biblioteca Nacional, Paseo de Recoletos 20 (91 580 77 59, www.bne.es). Metro Colón. **Open** 10am-9pm Tue-Sat; 10am-2pm Sun. **Admission** free. **Map** p324 K9/10.

Banco de España
Plaza de Cibeles. Metro Banco de España. **Map** p324 J11.
This grandiose pile on the corner of Calle Alcalá was designed in 1882 by Eduardo Adaro and Severiano Saínz de la Lastra to house the Bank of Spain. The eclectic style was most influenced by French Second Empire designs, with a few Viennese touches. The decorative arched window and elaborate clock above the main entrance are best appreciated from a distance.

Palacio de Cibeles
Plaza de Cibeles (91 588 10 00). Metro Banco de España. **Map** p324 J11.
This extraordinary construction, which dwarfs the Plaza de Cibeles, and which is regularly compared to a sandcastle or wedding cake, was arguably the world's most spectacular post office until 2007, when it became the city council headquarters. Formerly known as the Palacio de Comunicaciones, it was designed in 1904 by Antonio Palacios and Joaquín Otamendi. Completed in 1918, it is the best example of the extravagant style favoured by Madrid's elite at its most expansive. The design was influenced by Viennese art nouveau, but it also features many traditional Spanish touches, with a grand entrance (complete with oversized revolving door), a Hollywood film-set staircase, soaring ceilings, stunning columns and grand marble floors. Sadly, however, the interior is now closed to the general public.

Life After Death

Spain's pantheons for its famous figures have been something of a dead weight.

The Spanish philosopher Miguel de Unamuno famously wrote that the dead in Spain were never allowed to rest. The truth of this observation will become apparent to anyone who wonders what has happened to the tombs of famous Spaniards who have died in Madrid. Remarkably, the remains of none of the city's outstanding Golden Age figures, including Cervantes, Lope de Vega and Calderón de la Barca, have survived, though there was a brief moment of excitement in 1999 following the discovery of bones wrongly believed to be those of Velázquez and his wife.

Even those Spaniards wealthy enough in the past to have paid for *sepultura perpetua* (others still have their bodies automatically removed from their tombs after ten years) have not been guaranteed a tranquil posthumous life. The expansion or destruction of churches have led to constant transferences of corpses, during the course of which a high proportion of these have been mislaid or misidentified.

In view of this unfortunate situation, a decision was finally taken in 1869 to create what Spain so obviously lacked – a national pantheon for its heroes. The domed late 18th-century **Basílica de San Francisco** was set aside for this purpose, and on 19 June, the remains of Calderón and other famous Spaniards were taken to the church in a triumphant procession involving cannon-fire and horse squadrons. But barely had the corpses had time to recover from their journey than the parishes from where they had come began to reclaim them. In the case of Calderón, the body would be moved several more times before disappearing altogether.

The fiasco of San Francisco did not put an end to the idea of a Spanish pantheon. In the 1890s, next to the then ruined 16th-century Basilica and Monastery of Atocha, the **Panteón de Hombres Ilustres** (*photo above*) was built. However, this too proved a failure, and most of the illustrious corpses for whom it was intended were taken away, leaving just the remains of largely forgotten politicians. Today, it's one of Madrid's least visited sites, but nonetheless worth a look for its inappropriately Italianate architecture, and its splendidly elaborate tombs by Benlliure and other fashionable Spanish sculptors of the period.

While the Panteón de Hombres Ilustres is centrally located, visitors with a love of cemeteries will find themselves travelling to some of the city's poorest outlying districts. The largest of the city's cemeteries is that of the **Almudena**, out to the east (metro García Noblejas), the terrifying scale of which, not to mention the dusty, grim surroundings, gives it a compelling morbid appeal. Across the road is the comparatively intimate **Civic Cemetery**. Tidied up in the early 1990s following the burial here of the Communist leader Dolores Ibarruri ('La Pasionaria'), this contains the tombs of hundreds of opponents to Franco and the Catholic Church. At the end of the Civil War numerous Republican prisoners were shot here and thrown into a mass grave.

But the most absorbing of Madrid's cemeteries is the **Sacramental de San Justo**, attached to the cemetery of the Hermitage of San Isidro (bus 17) out west. In a state of poignant neglect, this overgrown, cypress-shaded wasteland is the resting place of some of the more distinguished writers of 19th- and 20th-century Spain, from the romantic Madrid poet Mariano José de Larra to prolific writer and man-about-town Ramón Gómez de la Serna. Luis Buñuel was greatly drawn to this cemetery; his memory of coming across the hair of a woman protruding from a cracked grave here was used by him in his film *The Phantom of Liberty*.

SIGHTS

Museo al Aire Libre de la Castellana.

SIGHTS

With over three million volumes, Spain's national library has been called the 'Prado of paper'. Among the wealth of printed matter is every work published in Spain since 1716, Greek papyri, Arab, Hebrew and Greek manuscripts, Nebrija's first Spanish grammar, bibles, and drawings by Goya, Velázquez, Rembrandt and many others. Given the precious and fragile nature of the texts, access was limited to scholars, but in 1996 the administration opened this museum to allow the public a glimpse of the library's riches. The displays are conceived as interactive, steering visitors through bibliographical history via multimedia applications including laser shows, videos and holographs.

FREE Teatro Fernán Gómez, Centro de Arte
Plaza de Colón 4 (91 436 25 40, http://teatro fernangomez.esmadrid.com). Metro Colón. **Open** *Exhibitions* 10am-9pm Tue-Sat; 10am-7pm Sun. **Admission** *Exhibitions* free. *Shows* €14-€22. **Map** p324 K9.

Previously called the Centro Cultural de la Villa, the city council's only purpose-built cultural centre has been renamed after the late Spanish actor and director Fernán Gómez, who died in 2007. On offer is a mixed bag of theatre, puppets, opera and *zarzuelas* in the summer, as well as art exhibitions, usually featuring important Hispanic artists.

PASEO DE CASTELLANA

Sights along the Castellana are listed here from bottom to top, south to north. The metro system partly avoids the avenue, but the 27 bus runs up and down the whole stretch, covering the Paseo del Prado, Recoletos and the Castellana.

In 1860, when he designed Madrid's 'extension', Carlos María de Castro took the significant decision, since the Paseo del Prado and Recoletos were already there, to continue along the same route with the main avenue of the new district. Thus the Castellana was born. Until the Republic of 1931 demolished Madrid's old racetrack, the avenue reached only as far as C/Joaquín Costa. Today it snakes away freely northwards, through thickets of office blocks. It also contains, near the junction with C/Juan Bravo (location of the recently renamed **Museo al Aire Libre de la Castellana**, *see right*), Madrid's 'beach' of upmarket terrace bars, at the height of fashion in the mid 1990s and still thronged with *pijos* (something like Sloanes). To the east is the Salamanca district, the heart of affluent Madrid, and the city's most upscale shopping area.

In the 1970s and '80s banks and insurance companies vied with each other to commission in-vogue architects to create corporate showcases along the upper Castellana; see the **Bankinter** building at No.29 and **Bankunión** at No.46. Beyond the latter, the **Museo de Ciencias Naturales** (*see p98*) is set back from the road on a grassy hill; further still, on the left, is the Kafkaesque grey bulk of the enormous **Nuevos Ministerios** government complex. Begun in 1932, it contains many government ministries, and is one of the largest projects bequeathed by the Spanish Republic to Madrid. It was designed by a team led by Secundino Zuazo, chief architect of the Gran Madrid (*see p23*) plan, in a monolithic '30s rationalist style; then, after the victory of General Franco, the same architect added to the still-unfinished building some curving, traditionalist details more to the taste of the new regime. Inside it has a park-like garden, open to the public.

Beyond that, a huge branch of the Corte Inglés signals your arrival at the **AZCA** complex. The Asociación Zona Comercial A, known to some as 'Little Manhattan', is a glitzy skyscraper development first projected during the Franco regime's industrial heyday in the '60s, but it gained extra vigour in democratic Spain's 1980s boom to become a symbol of Madrid yuppiedom. At its centre is the **Plaza Picasso**, a small park, and amid the office blocks are a chic shopping mall, restaurants and other facilities to make it a self-contained 'workers' city'. At its north end is the **Torre Picasso**, designed by Japanese architect Minoru Yamasaki (also responsible for New York's World Trade Center) in 1988 and, at 157-metres (515-feet), Madrid's tallest building. Beyond it is the circular **Torre Europa**.

A little further up again, opposite each other, are the **Real Madrid** stadium, Estadio Bernabéu (*see p256*), and the **Palacio de Congresos** conference centre. By this time, the view up the Paseo de la Castellana is dominated by the two leaning towers officially known as the **Puerta de Europa** at Plaza Castilla. These remarkable smoked-glass blocks, leaning in at 15 degrees off the perpendicular, are perhaps the greatest monument to Spain's 1980s boom. They were begun with finance from the Kuwait Investment Office (so that the towers are often called the **Torres KIO**; *photo p99*) and left unfinished for years after a financial scandal in 1992. With their rather phallic fountain in the middle, they have now joined the landmarks of modern Madrid.

★ FREE Museo al Aire Libre de la Castellana
Paseo de la Castellana 41. *Metro Rubén Darío.* **Map** p325 L6.

An unconventional museum, this '70s space at the junction of the Castellana with C/Juan Bravo was the brainchild of engineers José Antonio Fernández Ordoñez and Julio Martínez Calzón. Designing a bridge across the avenue, they thought the space underneath would be a good art venue, and sculptor Eusebio Sempere convinced fellow artists to

SIGHTS

donate their work. All the major names in late 20th-century Spanish sculpture are represented – including Pablo Serrano, Miró, Chillida – and much of their work is spectacular, especially the dynamic stainless-steel *Mon per a infants* ('A world for children') by Andreu Alfaro and the spectacular cascade by Sempere that forms a centrepiece. *Photo p96.*

Museo de Ciencias Naturales

C/José Gutiérrez Abascal 2 (91 411 13 28, www.mncn.csic.es). Metro Gregorio Marañón. **Open** *Sept-June* 10am-6pm Tue-Fri; 10am-8pm Sat; 10am-2.30pm Sun. *July, Aug* 10am-6pm Tue-Fri; 10am-3pm Sat; 10am-2.30pm Sun. **Admission** €5; €3 concessions. Free over-65s and under-3s. **No credit cards**.

The Natural Science Museum occupies two spaces in a huge building overlooking a sloping garden on the Castellana. Much of the north wing is given over to temporary exhibitions, which tend to be hands-on, interactive and fun for kids. Permanently in this wing is 'Mediterranean Nature and Civilisation', a large exhibition of Mediterranean flora and fauna, illustrating the region's biodiversity. The smaller space to the south contains a simpler, more old-fashioned presentation of fossils, dinosaurs and geological exhibits. A replica of a diplodocus dominates the two-floor space, surrounded by real skeletons of a glyptodont (giant armadillo) and other extinct animals. The most distinguished skeleton here, though, is that of the *Megatherium americanum*, a bear-like creature from the pleistocene period unearthed in Luján, Argentina, in 1788.

SALAMANCA

In the mid 19th century, as it became evident that Spanish cities needed to expand beyond their old walls, attempts were made to ensure that this happened in an orderly way. Madrid and Barcelona had plans approved for *ensanches* ('extensions'). Carlos María de Castro's 1860 plan for Madrid envisaged the expansion of the city north and east in a regular grid pattern, with restrictions on building height and public open spaces at regular intervals within each block to ensure a healthy, harmonious landscape. The problem, however, was that for a good while few members of Madrid's middle classes seemed to have the money or motivation to invest in such a scheme, and they preferred to stay within the cramped, noisy Old City. That Madrid's *ensanche* got off the ground at all was due to a banker, politician and speculator notorious for his dubious business practices, the Marqués de Salamanca.

The marquis had previously built his own vast residence, now the **Banco Hipotecario**, on Paseo de Recoletos in 1846-50. He spent one of the several fortunes he made and lost in his lifetime building a first line of rectangular blocks along C/Serrano, from C/Goya up to Ramón de la Cruz. However, his ambitions overstretched his resources, the apartments proved expensive for local buyers, and he went terminally bankrupt in 1867. Nevertheless, it is to the rogue Marqués, not the old Castilian university town, that Madrid's smartest *barrio* owes its name.

It was only after the Restoration of 1874 that Madrid's wealthier citizens really began to appreciate the benefits of wider streets and residences with more class than the musty old neighbourhoods could supply. Once the idea caught on, the exodus proceeded apace, and the core of Salamanca was built up by 1900. The wealthiest families of all built individual palaces along the lower stretch of the Paseo de la Castellana, in a wild variety of styles – French imperial, Italian Renaissance, neo-Mudéjar. The block on C/Juan Bravo between Calles Lagasca and Velázquez contains a magnificent example: the neo-baroque palace of the **Marqueses de Amboage**, now the Italian Embassy. From the C/Velázquez side it's possible to see the extraordinarily lush gardens. Other mansions are scattered around the district, tucked in between apartment blocks. Those who could not quite afford their own mansion moved into giant apartments in the streets behind. The area has been the centre of conservative, affluent Madrid ever since.

Salamanca is a busy area, with streets that often boom with traffic, and so the best time to explore it is Saturday morning, when the shops are open but traffic has slackened. Streets such as Calles Jorge Juan, Ortega y Gasset, Goya and Juan Bravo yield top designers, art galleries and dealers in wine, silver or superior leather goods. Salamanca also has its own social scene, based around C/Juan Bravo, with shiny, smart bars and discos. Towards the east end of C/Goya there is a slightly more affordable shopping area; on the very eastern flank of Salamanca is Madrid's bullring, **Las Ventas**; and south of here is the numismatic **Museo Casa de la Moneda** (for both, *see p100*).

Art buffs are advised to head for the marble tower with sculpture garden at C/Castelló 77, base for the **Fundación Juan March**'s

SIGHTS

Torres KIO. *See p97.*

first-rate collection of modern art, which also hosts great contemporary art shows and free classical concerts (*see below*). For private art galleries, C/Claudio Coello, parallel to C/Serrano, is the city's most elegant centre. At the north end of Serrano is the eclectic **Museo Lázaro Galdiano** (*see below*).

The blocks of Serrano, Claudio Coello and Lagasca below C/Ortega y Gasset are the oldest part of Salamanca, the first section built up by the Marqués in the 1860s. Streets here are narrower, traffic less intense and shops closer together, making the area more amenable for strolling, browsing and snacking. There are charming buildings with intriguing details – such as the glass-galleried block on the corner of Claudio Coello and C/Ayala. The block between Claudio Coello and Lagasca on C/Ayala also contains the **Mercado de la Paz**, Salamanca's excellent market.

FREE Fundación Juan March

C/Castelló 77 (91 435 42 40, www.march.es). Metro Núñez de Balboa. **Open** *Mid Sept-June* 11am-8pm Mon-Sat; 10am-2pm Sun. *July, Aug* 11am-8pm Mon-Fri. **Admission** free. **Map** p325 N6.
This cultural foundation, set up by the wealthy financier Juan March in 1955, is one of the most important in Europe. Each year, a couple of major exhibitions are held here, and a decent selection of the foundation's 1,300 works of contemporary Spanish art is also on permanent display. The regular free concerts are also worth checking out.

Museo Arqueológico Nacional

C/Serrano 13 (91 577 79 12, http://man.mcu.es). Metro Serrano. **Open** 9.30am-8pm Tue-Sat; 9.30am-3pm Sun. **Admission** Currently free to all while the museum is being renovated; call for details once these are completed. **No credit cards**. **Map** p324 K10.
One of Madrid's oldest museums, dating back to 1867, the Museo Arqueológico Nacional shares the same building as the Biblioteca Nacional and Museo del Libro. It is currently undergoing long-term renovations (with no confirmed date for completion), but access is still permitted, although some areas may be closed to the public. It traces the evolution of human cultures, from prehistoric times up to the 15th century, and the collection of artefacts includes finds from the Iberian, Celtic, Greek, Egyptian, Punic, Roman, Paleochristian, Visigothic and Muslim cultures. Remarkably, the great majority of pieces came from excavations carried out within Spain, illustrating the extraordinary continuity and diversity of human settlement in the Iberian peninsula. Begin in the basement, which holds palaeontological material such as skulls, tombs and a mammoth's tusks, still attached to its skull. Some of the most interesting relics are from the area around Madrid itself, such as the many 4,000-year-old neolithic bell-shaped pottery bowls. The first

floor holds the museum's most famous possession, the *Dama de Elche*, the stone bust of an Iberian priestess, believed to date from 500BC. In the garden, steps lead underground to a reproduction of the renowned Altamira prehistoric cave paintings in Cantabria.

FREE Museo Casa de la Moneda

C/Dr Esquerdo 36 (91 566 65 44, www.fnmt.es). Metro O'Donnell. **Open** *Sept-July* 10am-5.30pm Tue-Fri; 10am-2pm Sat, Sun. *Aug* 10am-2pm Mon-Fri. **Admission** free.
This museum, dedicated to coins and currency, boasts a huge collection, dating from the 18th century, that is among the most important in the world. The history of coins is represented in chronological order, and complemented by various displays of seals, bank notes, engravings, rare books and medals, plus around 10,000 sketches and drawings from Spain, Italy and Flanders, ranging from the 16th to 18th century.

Museo Lázaro Galdiano

C/Serrano 122 (91 561 60 84, www.flg.es). Metro Gregorio Marañón. **Open** 10am-4.30pm Mon, Wed-Sun. Third floor closes at 2pm Mon, Wed-Fri. **Admission** €4; €2 concessions; free under-12s. Free to all Sun. **No credit cards**. **Map** p321 L6.
This unjustifiably little-known museum holds the extraordinarily eclectic collection of 15,000 paintings and *objets d'art*, covering 24 centuries, that was accumulated over 70 years by the financier and bibliophile José Lázaro Galdiano (1862-1947). Its holdings include paintings by Goya and Bosch, an important collection of work from the Dutch and English schools, and some wonderful Renaissance ornamental metalwork. The four-storey mansion and its gardens are a sight in themselves.

FREE Plaza de Toros de Las Ventas

C/Alcalá 237 (91 356 22 00, museum 91 725 18 57, www.las-ventas.com). Metro Ventas. **Open** (Museum) *Nov-Feb* 9.30am-2.30pm Mon-Fri. *Mar-Oct* 9.30am-2.30pm Tue-Fri; 10am-1pm Sun. **Admission** (Museum) free.
More than 22,000 spectators can catch a bullfight in this, Spain's largest arena, completed in 1929. Like most early 20th-century bullrings, it is in neo-Mudéjar style, with often playful use of ceramic tiling. Around it there is ample open space to accommodate the crowds and food vendors, so it's easy to get a good look at the exterior. It's not necessary to go to a *corrida* to see the ring from within. When the bulls are back on the ranch, concerts are often held here, and alongside the ring there is the small Museo Taurino. The museum holds portraits of famous matadors, as well as *trajes de luces* (suits of lights), including the pink-and-gold outfit worn by the legendary Manolete on the afternoon of his death in the ring in 1947. Among the 18th-century paintings is a portrait of *torero* Joaquín Rodríguez Costillares, once thought to be by Goya but now labelled as anonymous.

Beyond the Centre

Cross the city walls to find museums, parks and an Egyptian temple.

City walls and building restrictions over the centuries have kept even Madrid's more far-flung attractions within reasonably easy reach of the city centre. Many visitors never stray out of the Old City and the triangle defined by the big three art museums. That's all very well – and if this is your first visit it's certainly a reasonable decision – but go further afield and you can take in the Madrid skyline by cable car, visit an authentic Egyptian temple or inspect General Franco's old home. The more distant areas also provide welcome green escapes from the urban density of Madrid's centre, with the woods and hills around El Pardo serving as a refuge to wildlife and humans seeking respite from the summer heat.

But this is Madrid, so there's some magnificent art to see as well, ranging from the frescoes adorning Goya's tomb to the finest collection of pre-Columbian American art to be found in Europe. And away from the attractions there are the quiet pleasures of suburbs like Vallecas secure in their own identity.

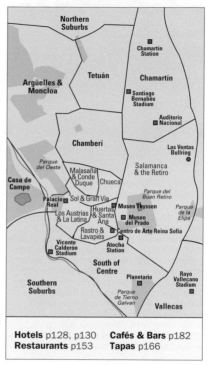

| Hotels p128, p130 | Cafés & Bars p182 |
| Restaurants p153 | Tapas p166 |

Hotels p128, p130 Cafés & Bars p182 Restaurants p153 Tapas p166

NORTH & WEST

Casa de Campo

Once a royal hunting estate, the verdant, sprawling parkland of the **Casa de Campo**, to the west of the city, was only opened to the public under the Republic in 1931. Five years later, it became a key site for Franco's forces in the Civil War battle for Madrid, its high ground being used to shell the city centre and the university. Remains of trenches still exist.

Today, the Casa is home to the **Parque de Atracciones** funfair (*see p212*) and the **Zoo** (*see p214*), as well as **swimming pools** (*see p259*) and **tennis courts** (*see p261*), and a large boating lake. The cafés that ring the lake are good for an outdoor lunch, and cyclists should note that most of the park's roads are closed to cars on Sunday mornings.

Once you stray away from the criss-crossing roads much of the park is surprisingly wild, and it's possible to have a real country walk through its woods and gullies. A favourite way to visit is via the **Teleférico** cable car (*see p102*) from the **Parque del Oeste** (*see p102*), which runs over the trees almost to the middle of the Casa, where there are viewpoints, an (undistinguished) bar-restaurant and picnic spots.

Couples seeking seclusion favour the Casa de Campo, both by day and night, and the area by the Teleférico has been a gay cruising spot, although police have been cracking down on this. In contrast, one new feature of the modern

SIGHTS

Ermita de San Antonio de la Florida.
See p104.

SIGHTS

Casa is that Madrid's city authorities seem near set on turning the roads from Lago metro to the Zoo into a semi-official prostitution zone, with the aim of moving prostitution from the city centre. Consequently, by night, and often by day, there are female and transvestite prostitutes along these roads, displaying their assets pretty outrageously to cruising drivers, and leaving some pretty unpleasant debris behind them. One very Spanish aspect of this is that many of the other users of the park, by day at least, don't let this bother them, but carry on lunching, cycling or whatever, regardless.

Teleférico de Madrid

Paseo del Pintor Rosales (91 541 74 50, www.teleferico.com). Metro Argüelles. **Open** *June-Aug* noon-1.45pm, 3-9pm Mon-Fri; noon-9.30pm Sat, Sun. Opening times for rest of year change on a weekly and monthly basis (see website). **Tickets** (return) €5.20; €4.60 concessions. Free under-3s. **Map** p322 B8.
An extraordinary 2.5km (1.5-mile) trip over the Casa de Campo and Parque del Oeste in a cable car. The views of the Palacio Real, Río Manzanares, city skyline and park are breathtaking. There are even interesting close-ups of the park's seedier goings-on. In the winter, the cable cars rarely operate on week days.

Argüelles & Moncloa

West of Conde Duque lie the districts known as Argüelles and Moncloa. **Argüelles**, properly speaking, is the grid of streets between Plaza

de España, C/Princesa, Plaza de Moncloa and Paseo del Pintor Rosales. The Paseo is known for its *terrazas* – open-air bars that are ideal for taking the air on summer evenings. The Paseo sits above the **Parque del Oeste**, which, designed by Cecilio Rodríguez in the 1900s, is one of Madrid's most attractive spaces. The park was completely relaid after forming part of the front line in the Civil War. **La Rosaleda**, the rose garden, is beautiful in spring. The Montaña del Príncipe Pío, at its southern end, is one of the city's highest points, with great views of the Palacio Real and the incongruous **Templo de Debod** (*see p105* **From the Nile to Parque Oeste**), an Egyptian temple that was presented to Spain in 1968. This was the site of the Montaña barracks, the Nationalists' main stronghold at the start of the Civil War, before it was demolished and the hill incorporated into the park. Below the Teleférico stop a path leads to the **Ermita de San Antonio de la Florida**, with its Goya frescoes (*see p104*), and beyond that, the river. The fountain below the Teleférico used to preside over the roundabout at Príncipe Pío station, but was moved to the park in 1994. In its place by the station there is now the **Puerta de San Vicente** – an entirely new, quite convincing reconstruction of the 18th-century gate that once stood on this side of the city. On Sundays Madrid's Andean community takes over the Parque del Oeste, organising volleyball tournaments and picnics; after dark, the area around the fountain, like the Casa de Campo, becomes a prostitution zone.

In the southern corner of the district, just off Plaza de España, is the **Museo Cerralbo** (*see p104*). In the opposite, northern corner, unmissable at the end of C/Princesa, stands one of the biggest, most significant creations of the Franco regime, the **Ministerio del Aire** or Air Ministry, built in the 1950s, in kitsch-Castilian baroque style and popularly known as the 'Monasterio del Aire', thanks to its resemblance to El Escorial.

Alongside the Ministry is the Plaza de Moncloa, Moncloa metro station and the departure points for many bus services to towns north and west of Madrid. There is also Franco's fake-Roman triumphal arch, built to commemorate victory in the Civil War. To the north of the plaza, in the **Moncloa** district lies the sprawling campus of the Universidad Complutense, the **Ciudad Universitaria**. Consequently, the streets just to the south and east have plenty of studenty bars. Within the university, specific attractions are the **Museo de América** (*see p104*) and the **Faro de Madrid** observation tower, and, beyond that, the new **Museo del Traje** (*see p105*).

From the Nile to Parque Oeste

How an Egyptian temple ended up in a Madrid park.

For two millennia the ancient Egyptian Templo de Debod stood on the banks of the River Nile in Lower Nubia, southern Egypt. Then in 1968, the Egyptian government dismantled the structure brick by brick, shipped it across the Med and reassembled it on the Montaña del Príncipe Pío, at the southern tip of Parque Oeste – as thanks for Spain's help in saving Abu Simbel's temples from immersion in Lake Nasser (the artificial lake created by the building of the Aswan High Dam).

There, unassumingly, the temple remains. Visitors are free to step inside its cool, sometimes disorientingly dark interior and explore the ancient stone corridors and chambers; adventurous types will enjoy getting down on their hands and knees to crawl through some of the smaller passageways. Audiovisual presentations and relics help conjure up a sense of the past. Upstairs, a diorama shows the temple's original location: near the first cataract of the Nile and close to a key religious centre dedicated to Isis (goddess of magic and wife and sister of Osiris), on the island of Philae.

First built as a temple to Isis and Amun, the principal god of the Egyptian and Meroitic (Kushite) religions, construction took place between 200BC and 180BC at the instigation of Adikhalamani, king of the Meroitic people. The Meroites occupied what is now southern Egypt and northern Sudan from 800BC to AD350. Reliefs on the temple's wall record Adikhalamani worshipping and making offerings to Amun, Isis and other gods. Later, pharaohs of the Ptolemaic dynasty (305-30BC) and Roman rulers, including Augustus, Tiberius, and perhaps Hadrian, added futher chapels, an entrance hall, stairs, a terrace, a processional way and a landing quay.

In ancient times it was believed that the gods physically lived in the temple, so only the pharaoh and his priests could enter. Every day in the main chapel at sunrise, the priest would begin the important dawn ritual of cleaning, decorating and making offerings to the statues of Amun and Isis. He would offer meat, beer and other foodstuffs, then finally, to Amun, a statue of Maat, personification of the concepts of Egyptian order and justice. The priest would then exit, carefully cleaning away all traces of his activity, including his own footprints. Such ceremonies – others were performed at midday and dusk, and at specific times of the year – continued in the Templo de Debod into the sixth century AD, when it was abandoned after Byzantine emperor Justinian ordered the closure of the centre on Philae (an event generally taken to mark the end of ancient Egypt).

Today, a thousand miles from home, Templo de Debod remains one of the few ancient Egyptian architectural works that can be seen in its entirety outside Egypt.

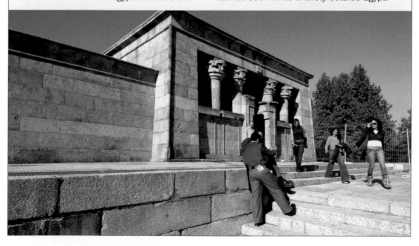

SIGHTS

Ermita de San Antonio de la Florida

Glorieta de San Antonio de la Florida 5 (91 542 07 22). Metro Príncipe Pío. **Open** 9.30am-8pm Tue-Fri; 10am-2pm Sat, Sun. **Admission** free. **Map** p322 B9.

This plain neo-classical chapel was completed by Felipe Fontana for Charles IV in 1798. Quite out of the way, north of Príncipe Pio station on the Paseo de la Florida, it is famous as the burial place of Goya, and for the unique, and recently restored, frescoes of the miracles of St Anthony, incorporating scenes of Madrid life, which he painted here in 1798. In contrast to the rather staid exterior, the colour and use of light in Goya's images are stunning. Featuring a rare mix of elements, including his unique, simultaneously ethereal and sensual 'angels', they are among his best and most complex works. On the other side of the road into the park is a near-identical second chapel, built in the 1920s to allow the original building to be left as a museum. There are free guided tours of the Ermita, in Spanish and English, at 11am and noon on Saturdays. *Photo p102.*

Faro de Madrid

Avda de los Reyes Católicos. Metro Moncloa. **Open** Currently closed for restoration work. Expected to reopen in spring 2011. **Admission** €1; 50¢ concessions.

This radio and communications tower, at 92m (302ft), provides one of the best views of the whole of the city and the sierras in the distance. Diagrams along the floor point out highlights of the city, though with

age they're becoming increasingly difficult to decipher. The best bit, though, is the stomach-lurching ride up in the glass lift.

Museo de América

Avda de los Reyes Católicos 6 (91 543 94 37, http://museodeamerica.mcu.es). Metro Moncloa. **Open** 9.30am-3pm Tue, Wed, Fri, Sat; 9.30am-3pm Sun. **Admission** €3.01; €1.50 concessions. Free to all Sun. **No credit cards.**

This museum comprises the finest collection of pre-Columbian American art and artefacts in Europe, a combination of articles brought back at the time of the Conquest and during the centuries of Spanish rule over Central and South America, plus later acquisitions generally donated by Latin American governments. The collection includes near-matchless treasures: there is the *Madrid Codex*, one of only four surviving Mayan illustrated glyph manuscripts in the world; the *Tudela Codex* and illustrated manuscripts from central Mexico, which depict the Spanish Conquest; superb carvings from the Mayan city of Palenque, sent back to Charles III by the first-ever modern survey expedition to a pre-Hispanic American ruin in 1787; and the Gold of the Quimbayas, a series of exquisite gold figures from the Quimbaya culture of Colombia, which were presented to Spain by the Colombian government. All the main pre-Columbian cultures are represented – further highlights include Aztec obsidian masks from Mexico, Inca stone sculptures and funeral offerings from Peru, and finely modelled, comical and sometimes highly sexual figurines from the Chibcha culture of Colombia. There are also exhibits from the Spanish colonial period, such as the *Entry of the Viceroy Morcillo into Potosí* (1716) by the early Bolivian painter Melchor Pérez Holguín, a series of paintings showing in obsessive detail the range of racial mixes possible in colonial Mexico, and a collection of gold and other objects from the galleons *Atocha* and *Margarita*, sunk off Florida in the 18th century and only recovered in 1988.

The collection is arranged not by countries and cultures, but thematically, so that rooms are dedicated to topics such as 'the family', 'communication' and so on, with artefacts from every period and country alongside each other. Without some knowledge of the many pre-Columbian cultures this can be confusing and uninformative. Frustrating, then, but it's still a superb, intriguing collection, and temporary shows are usually interesting.

Museo Cerralbo

C/Ventura Rodríguez 17, Argüelles (91 547 36 46, http://.museocerralbo.mcu.es). Metro Plaza de España. **Open** 9.30am-3pm Tue-Sat; 10am-3pm Sun. **Admission** €3; €1.50 concessions. Free under-18s & over-65s. Free to all Sun. **No credit cards. Map** p323 E10.

Laid out in a sumptuous late 19th-century mansion in Argüelles is the incredible private collection of

Parque Oeste. *See p102.*

artworks and artefacts assembled by Enrique de Aguilera y Gamboa, the 17th Marqués de Cerralbo. A man of letters, politician and traveller who collected pieces everywhere he went, he bequeathed his collection to the state with the stipulation that it should be displayed exactly how he had arranged it himself. Thus the contents are laid out in a crowded manner, with paintings in three levels up the walls, and few items labelled. Among the many paintings, though, there are El Greco's *The Ecstasy of St Francis of Assisi* – the real highlight – and works by Zurbarán, Alonso Cano and other Spanish masters. The upstairs area contains an astonishing collection of European and Japanese armour, weapons, watches, pipes, leather-bound books, clocks and other curiosities. The mansion itself is of interest; it gives a good idea of how the aristocracy lived in the Restoration period – look out for the lavish ballroom.

Museo del Traje (Museum of Clothing)

Avda Juan de Herrera 2 (91 550 47 00, http://museodeltraje.mcu.es). Metro Moncloa. **Open** *Sept-June* 9.30am-7pm Tue-Sat; 10am-3pm Sun. *July, Aug* 9.30am-7pm Tue, Wed, Fri, Sat; 9.30am-10.30pm Thur; 10am-3pm Sun. **Admission** €3; €1.50 concessions. Free to all 2.30-7pm Sat & all Sun. **No credit cards.**

This museum is a must for those interested in any aspect of clothing. The collections comprise around 21,000 garments covering six centuries of Spanish fashion, though there are some much older items, among them fragments of Coptic cloth and Hispano-Muslim pieces. The permanent exhibition shows up to 600 items at any one time, rotating them frequently both to protect them and to allow returning visitors to appreciate the breadth and diversity of the collection. It is arranged chronologically, in 14 spaces, among which are two outstanding monographic rooms, one covering regional costume, the other containing pieces by Mariano Fortuny y Madrazo, son of the painter, whose creations were worn by the likes of Isadora Duncan. Other rooms cover costume from the Enlightenment and the *castizo* (Madrid's working classes); early 19th-century French influences; Romanticism; belle époque, the avant-garde, post-Civil War fashion and the modern era. A room is dedicated to the great couturier Balenciaga and another to Spanish haute couture. Visitors can learn about how clothes are made in 'didactic areas' and a further exhibition space shows temporary displays, the first showcasing a century of *Vogue* photography. Facilities include reading and rest rooms, a bookshop, a café and a restaurant

Templo de Debod

Montaña del Príncipe Pío (91 366 74 15). Metro Plaza de España or Ventura Rodríguez. **Open** *Apr-Sept* 10am-2pm, 6-8pm Tue-Fri; 10am-2pm Sat, Sun. *Oct-Mar* 9.45am-1.45pm, 4.15-6.15pm Tue-Fri; 10am-2pm Sat, Sun. **Admission** free. **Map** p322 D9.

Museo Sorolla.

This Egyptian structure, which sits on the outskirts of the Parque del Oeste, dates back 2,200 years and is dedicated to the gods Amun and Isis. It was sent, block by block, by the Egyptian government in 1968 in thanks for Spain's help in preserving monuments threatened by the Aswan Dam. *See also p103* **From the Nile to Parque Oeste.**

Chamberí

Directly north of Malasaña is the *barrio* of Chamberí, one of the first working-class districts outside the walls to be built up in the second half of the 19th century. Consequently, and generably justifiably, it has become one of the few areas outside the old city considered to have genuine *castizo* character. A pleasant place to while away an evening in this area is the circular **Plaza de Olavide**, ringed with pavement cafés. Just to the east of here is the charming **Museo Sorolla**. On the north side of Chamberí is Madrid's main water supply, the Canal de Isabel II. On C/Santa Engracia, a neo-Mudéjar water tower has been converted into a unique photography gallery, the **Sala del Canal de Isabel II** (*see p107*).

Museo Sorolla

Paseo del General Martínez Campos 37 (91 310 15 84, http://museosorolla.mcu.es). Metro Gregorio Marañón or Iglesia. **Open** 9.30am-8pm Tue, Sat; 10am-3pm Sun.

SIGHTS

Garden of Enlightenment

Where poets and painters hobnobbed with the nobility.

SIGHTS

Just to the north of the A-2 motorway, now surrounded by Madrid's eastern sprawl, there is a jewel of a romantic fantasy garden, a remarkably preserved monument to 18th-century taste, the **Parque El Capricho de la Alameda de Osuna**. Within its 14 hectares is an artificial river leading between lakes, woods, rose gardens, mock temples and a whole range of cool, surprising corners. The gardens were begun in the 1780s for the Duke and Duchess of Osuna, the most cultivated couple among the Spanish aristocracy of their day, enthusiastic promoters of the ideas and enquiring spirit of the Enlightenment and great patrons of the artists, writers and musicians of their day. The Capricho was their country estate and, under the direction of the Duchess, became a special combination of salon and pleasure garden. In the 1790s an invitation to spend a day there was the hottest ticket in Madrid, for both the aristocracy and the intelligentsia.

The Capricho has been called 'the essence of a feminine garden', and its design closely reflected the Duchess's

personal taste. Her main architect was Jean-Baptiste Mulot, a French gardener who had previously worked for Marie Antoinette, although much of the Capricho is in the English style, with simulated natural landscapes between smaller formal gardens. An Italian theatre designer, Angelo Maria Borghini, was brought in to construct many of the Capricho's fanciful buildings. Wandering visitors were to be surprised and delighted by a succession of different ambiences: from secluded alcoves to broad vistas; from the tranquillity of boat rides on the lakes out to tiny artificial islands to sampling the simple life at the Casa de la Vieja, a mock peasants' cottage. Also waiting to be discovered were replica Greek and Egyptian temples, a ballroom, an open-air theatre and the Abejero and even an ornate beehive in the shape of a classical temple. Within the Capricho, the Osunas' aristocratic friends, men and women, could mingle with artists and intellectuals and talk freely, whether of gossip or great ideas, in an atmosphere that was very different from the paralysing etiquette of the royal court. New poems were read, and operas and music performed: Haydn was a favourite composer. This liberal informality encouraged by the Duchess – already deeply suspect for her 'French' ideas – also soon led to unstoppable rumours that far more illicit activities were going on among the Capricho's intimate arbours than just chat.

The Duke and Duchess of Osuna were also among the first important patrons of Goya, and their support played a major part in winning him acceptance among high society. Among the several paintings that Goya produced for the Osunas' house at El Capricho were two oddities, the Aquelarre ('Witches' Sabbath') and Escena de Brujas ('Witchcraft Scene') – both now in the Museo Lázaro Galdiano – precursors of his later macabre, sensual paintings, which could indicate a more decadent taste in the Duke and Duchess alongside their more celebrated Enlightenment rationalism. The Capricho is also famous as the place where Goya, then aged 40, met the 23-year-old Duchess of Alba, in 1786, and so where his obsession with her began. Scandalous and impulsive, known for breaking whichever social conventions suited her, dressing as a Madrid maja or street girl and having a string of male escorts from aristocrats to bullfighters, the Duchess of Alba was nevertheless a good friend of the high-minded Duchess of Osuna, and a frequent visitor to El Capricho.

The gardens were badly knocked about by Napoleon's troops – who also shot the head gardener, the French émigré Pierre Prévost – but were later reclaimed by the Duchess of Osuna, who lived on there until her death, aged 82, in 1834. El Capricho then suffered decades of decay and occasional destruction – during the Civil War – before it became the property of the city of Madrid, in the 1970s.

Parque El Capricho de la Alameda de Osuna

Paseo de la Alameda de Osuna (information 91 588 01 14). Metro El Capricho. **Open** *Oct-Mar* 9am-6.30pm Sat, Sun. *Apr-Sept* 9am-9pm Sat, Sun.

Admission €3; €1.50 concessions. Free to all Sun. **No credit cards. Map** p321 J6.

Often considered a neo-Impressionist, Valencia-born Joaquín Sorolla was really an exponent of 'luminism', the celebration of light. He was renowned for his iridescent, sun-drenched paintings, including portraits and family scenes at the beach and in gardens. Sorolla's leisured themes and greetings-cardesque (and indeed they are often used as such), aesthetic are easy to dismiss, but most find his luminous world at least a little seductive. This delightful little museum, housed in the mansion built for the artist in 1910 to spend his latter years, has been recently restored and boasts 250 works. The works are exhibited on the main floor, in his former studio areas. The salon, dining room and breakfast room are furnished in their original state with the artist's eclectic decorative influence in evidence. The garden, Moorish-inspired but with an Italianate pergola, is a delightful, peaceful oasis of calm, seemingly miles away from the roaring traffic outside.

Sala del Canal de Isabel II

C/Santa Engracia 125 (91 545 10 00, www.cyii.es). Metro Ríos Rosas. **Open** 11am-2pm, 5-8.30pm Tue-Sat; 11am-2pm Sun. **Admission** free.

This water tower, built in elaborate neo-Mudéjar style in 1907-11 is considered a gem of Madrid's industrial architecture. It is now home to a stylish exhibition space that specialises in photography, ranging in quality from good to world-class. Two kilometres north of here, just off the Plaza de Castilla, is the Fundación Canal (www.fundacioncanal.com), another arts and education centre run by the Canal de Isabel II.

Tetuán & Chamartín

North of Chamberí is **Tetuán**, a modern, working area centred on C/Bravo Murillo, and, to the east, **Chamartín**, which contains the major business area of modern Madrid. The main point of interest for visitors is the local market, the **Mercado de Maravillas**, at C/Bravo Murillo 122, just north of Cuatro Caminos – it's the largest market in the city. On Sunday mornings, too, a 'Rastro' gets going on C/Marqués de Viana. Also well worth a visit is the **Museo Tiflológico** just north of here. A museum designed especially for blind and partially sighted visitors, it by no means excludes other visitors; in fact, it's hands-on approach is particularly suitable for those with children in their group.

Across the Castellana, north-east of Nuevos Ministerios, is **El Viso**, an anomaly in high-rise Madrid. It was developed in the 1920s as a model community on garden-city lines, on the fringes of the city at that time, and some of its individual houses are museum-worthy examples of art deco. Unsurprisingly, the district has

El Pardo.

retained its desirable (and expensive) status. At the southern tip of this area is the incongruously political cultural centre, the **Residencia de Estudiantes**. Further east again is **La Prosperidad**, also once a model housing development, although most of its early buildings have been replaced by modern blocks. Within it is the **Auditorio Nacional de Música** (*see p234*).

Museo Tiflológico

C/La Coruña 18 (91 589 42 19, http://museo. once.es). Metro Estrecho. **Open** 10am-2pm, 5-8pm Tue-Fri; 10am-2pm Sat. Closed Aug. **Admission** free.
Owned and run by ONCE, the organisation for blind and partially sighted people, this special museum presents exhibitions of work by visually-impaired artists (the name comes from the Greek *tiflos*, sightless). Work here is intended to be touched, and is generally sculptural, three-dimensional, rich in texture and highly tactile. As well as temporary shows the museum has a large permanent collection of instruments devised to help the blind over the years, and a series of scale models of monuments from Spain and around the world.

La Residencia de Estudiantes

C/Pinar 21-23 (91 563 64 11, www.residencia. csic.es). Metro Gregorio Marañón. **Open** (during exhibitions, phone to check) 10am-8pm Mon-Sat; 10am-3pm Sun. **Admission** free.
From its foundation in 1910 until the war in 1936, the Residencia de Estudiantes was the most vibrant cultural centre in Madrid, and a powerful innovative force in the whole country. Though it was a students'

residence – García Lorca, Buñuel and Dalí all stayed there in the early days – 'La Resi' also organised visits to Madrid by leading artists and scientists of the day and was active in the propagation of avantgarde ideas from outside Spain. The Civil War and subsequent regime severely stifled intellectual freedom and the Residencia languished until the late 1980s, when it was resurrected as a private foundation sponsored by Spain's official scientific research council. It hosts talks by international figures, conferences and exhibitions, recitals, films and concerts.

The northern suburbs

The northern and western *extrarradio* offers a radical contrast to the south. The thing to do for those with the necessary cash in Madrid has been to adopt the Anglo-Saxon way of life and move out of city flats into house-and-garden districts like **Puerta de Hierro**, north of the Casa de Campo. Named after the 1753 iron gate to the royal hunting reserve of El Pardo, its posh homes are no match for **La Moraleja**, off the Burgos road, an enclave for executives and diplomats.

The growing districts to the east are not nearly so lush. The area along the A-2 motorway towards the airport is intended to be Madrid's major commercial development zone, with the Feria de Madrid trade fair complex and the **Parque Juan Carlos I**, which lies between the airport and the Feria de Madrid centre. Oddly enough, the area already contains, swallowed up in the urban spread, one of Spain's most appealing and neglected 18th-century gardens, the **Capricho de la Alameda de Osuna** (*see p106* **Garden of Enlightenment**).

Parque Juan Carlos I

Avda de Logroño & Avda de los Andes.
Metro Campo de las Naciones.
This huge park, Madrid's newest green (and brown) space, lies between the airport and the Feria de Madrid trade fair centre. With time it should become one of the city's more attractive spaces, but it has taken a while for the trees to grow to provide shade. That said, the park's current draws include a series of different gardens within a circle of olive trees, an artificial river and other water features.

El Pardo

Around ten miles (15 kilometres) to the northwest of the city lies a vast expanse of verdant and well-looked after parkland. This area contains the main residence of the Spanish royal family, the **Palacio de la Zarzuela**, but the reason most people will venture up here is for the peculiar sensation of nosing around in the house where General Franco lived and worked for the 35 years up to his death in 1975, the **Real Palacio de El Pardo**, situated in the peaceful 18th-century town of El Pardo. Today the place serves mainly to host foreign dignitaries and heads of state, most notably in recent years during the 2004 wedding of the heir to the throne, Prince Felipe.

The hills and woodlands are also worth a visit, however, being remarkably unspoilt thanks to those long protected years of dictatorial and regal status, and they contain an amazingly rich array of wildlife. It therefore comes as no surprise that game features on many restaurant menus in the town.

Real Palacio de El Pardo

C/Manuel Alonso (91 376 15 00,
www.patrimonionacional.es). Bus 601 from
Moncloa. **Open** *Apr-Sept* 10.30am-5.45pm Mon-Sat; 9.30am-1.30pm Sun. *Oct-Mar* 10.30am-4.45pm Mon-Sat; 10am-1.30pm Sat. **Admission** €4; €2.70 concessions. Wed free to EU citizens. **No credit cards.**
In 1405, Henry III constructed a hunting lodge here, but the first monarch to take a really serious interest in El Pardo's excellent deer and game hunting estate was Charles I of Spain (Charles V of the Holy Roman Empire), who built a sizeable palace here. His successor, Philip II, added many important works of art but most of these were lost in a fire in 1604, and after various architectural changes the building was finally reconstructed on Charles III's orders by 18th-century architect Francesco Sabatini; superb murals by Bayeu and Maella were added at this time. The current furnishings, paintings and tapestries were added during the 19th and 20th centuries.

In addition to its main role today as a diplomatic rendezvous, the palace is partially open to the public and there are tours of its ornate and gaudy interior with its ornamental frescoes, gilt mouldings and some fine tapestries, many of which were woven in the Real Fábrica de Tapices to Goya designs. There's an ornate theatre, built for Charles IV's Italian wife María Luisa of Parma, where censorious film fan Franco used to view films with his cronies before deciding on their suitability for the great unwashed, but in truth the only rooms of real fascination are the Generalísimo's bedroom, dressing room and '70s bathroom – decorated to his own specifications.

Outside you can wander in the palace's attractive gardens or explore or picnic in at least part of the

Matadero Madrid. *See p110.*

SIGHTS

magnificent surrounding parkland known as Monte de Pardo – even though much of this is still closed to the public. Other nearby highlights include the Convento de los Capuchinos del Pardo (Ctra del Cristo, 91 376 08 00, open 8am-1pm, 4.30-8pm daily), famed for Gregorio Fernández's wooden baroque sculpture of Christ; the Quinta del Pardo, a small 18th-century summer house, and the single-storey Casita del Príncipe, built in 1785 by Juan de Villanueva and noted for its lavish lounges, though both have been closed to the public for some years.

SOUTH
South of the centre

The *barrios* of southern **Embajadores** – namely **Delicias**, **Arganzuela** and **Legazpi** – occupy a triangular chunk of land just south of the old city, bordered by the Manzanares river, the M-30 motorway and the rail lines from Atocha. Low rents attract a fair number of resident foreigners. Conventional attractions are few – the **Museo del Ferrocarril** (*see below*) and the **Parque Tierno Galván**, with the **IMAX Madrid** (*see p212*) and **Planetario de Madrid** (*see p213*) – but the area contains the **Estación Sur** bus station, and two symbols of Madrid, the **Atlético Madrid** stadium and, alongside it, the Mahou brewery. It's also now home to new cultural centre **Matadero Madrid** (*see below*), in the city's old abattoir (hence the name). Beyond that is the river and the **Puente de Toledo**, which was built by Pedro de Ribera for Philip V in 1718-32.

Just south of the river is the **Parque de San Isidro**, containing a charming 18th-century hermitage dedicated to the city's patron saint. The hermitage is the traditional focus of the Romería (Procession) de San Isidro. The park still fills with life and crowds during the **San Isidro** fiestas every May (*see p207*). At other times it's very tranquil; the view from the hill of San Isidro is familiar as one painted many times by Goya, and is still recognisable, despite the tower blocks.

★ Matadero Madrid
Paseo de la Chopera 14 (91 517 73 09, www.mataderomadrid.com). Metro Legazpi. **Open** 6-10pm Tue-Fri; 11am-10pm Sat, Sun. **Admission** varies. **No credit cards.**
A century-old neo-Mudéjar building that was once the city's municipal slaughterhouse is now showing its sensitive side in Matadero Madrid, the city's new innovative and multidisciplinary arts centre. The vast, ambitious space consists of ten different buildings, and the Madrid City Council hopes it will be a key socio-cultural symbol for the city. Just bear in mind that the place is something of a work in progress until it's finalised sometime in 2011. *Photo p109.*

Museo del Ferrocarril
Paseo de las Delicias 61 (91 506 83 33, www.museodelferrocarril.org). Metro Delicias. **Open** 10am-3pm Tue-Sun. Closed Aug. **Admission** €5; €3.50 concessions. Free to all Sat. **No credit cards.**
Housed in the elegant but disused Delicias station, with ironwork by Gustave Eiffel, Madrid's railway museum has an evocative collection of models, old locomotives, railway equipment and memorabilia. There is also a room dedicated to clocks, including the one that marked time when Spain's first ever train chugged from Barcelona to Mataró. You can climb on the trains, have a drink in an old restaurant car or watch film footage of Spanish railways. This great museum for kids offers occasional theatre performances, a bring-and-buy market for model train enthusiasts, and more. It is located about 100 yards off the main road, behind the national railway offices.

Vallecas

Vallecas, beyond the M-30 south-east of the city, was already an industrial suburb in the 1930s and remains an area of Madrid with a firm sense of its own identity.

The area has its own football team, **Rayo Vallecano**, which is forever struggling to keep up with its money-laden neighbours. Car stickers proclaim 'Independence for Vallecas' (spelt 'Vallekas' by hipper natives, who have their own punky sense of cool). It also has a pleasant tree-lined main drag, more than enough to mark it out from the other areas around it. There are problem districts not far away, such as **Entrevías**, home to some of Madrid's largest Gypsy communities.

OUTER LIMITS
Southern suburbs

Carabanchel, **Leganés**, **Getafe**, **Móstoles** and **Alcorcón** form the southern industrial belt of Madrid, virtually all of it built up since the 1960s. Areas still within the city, such as **Orcasitas**, blend into the towns of the *extrarradio*, the outskirts, and concrete flyovers and tower blocks make up the urban landscape.

These areas are now better connected thanks to the extension of the metro system, and central city dwellers occasionally come down here for entertainment: **Alcorcón** holds a flamenco festival, and **Fuenlabrada** has a clutch of teen-macro-discos. The popularity of hard rock in these suburbs is also attested to by Calle AC/DC in Leganés, inaugurated by the rock legends themselves in 2000. On the street is a converted bullring that has become one of the most important music venues in Madrid, **La Cubierta de Leganés** (*see p239*).

Consume

Gaudeamus Café. *See p174*.

Hotels

From family-run hostales to designer hotels.

For a compact city, Madrid has an unusually large number of hotels. In fact, so many new properties have opened in the past few years that there are concerns that there are too many, in the centre at least. For visitors, of course, this can only be a good thing. Intense competition means higher standards of accommodation and service, even in the lower-priced places. In particular, the difference between budget and mid-range hotels is becoming increasingly marginal, with the newer *hostales* now offering en suite bathrooms in most rooms. And, across all price brackets, staff are friendlier and keener to help than ever before. Fans of boutique hotels, meanwhile, will be pleased to hear that the concept has finally made it to Madrid.

STARS, PRICES & DISCOUNTS

Star ratings are somewhat arbitrary in Spain, and the difference between four- and five-star hotels can be hard to spot. Mid-range hotels have not been the city's strong point, but this is beginning to change thanks to chains such as **Room Mate** and **High Tech Hotels**.

In this chapter we have arranged hotels and *hostales* by area and price category, according to the cost of a standard double room. Hotels charging over €250 are categorised as 'luxury'; those costing between €170 and €250 are classed as 'expensive'; 'mid-range' is between €70 and €170; 'budget' is less than €70. Breakfast is not included unless stated. All prices shown are for online advance bookings. Where a scale is shown, this represents the cheapest available double room between low and high season. Prices tend to be highest in January (somewhat surprisingly), when some hotels require a minimum of two to three nights. Also note that the cheapest online rate is often for a non-refundable booking.

LOS AUSTRIAS & LA LATINA
Mid-range

chic&basic Mayerling
C/Conde de Romanones 6 (91 420 15 80, www.chicandbasic.com). Metro Tirso de Molina.
Rates (incl breakfast) €69-€130. **Map** p327 G12 ❶

CONSUME

This former textiles warehouse, on the border of Lavapiés, houses the second Madrid hotel from the chic&basic mini chain. The chic&basic Mayerling opened in 2009, and offers 22 simple but stylish lodgings (with an abundance of white, plus glass-walled bathrooms with power showers) in M, L and XL. Complimentary continental breakfast, tea- and coffee-making facilities and a great sun terrace with loungers add to the appeal. *Photo p115.*
Disabled-adapted room. No-smoking rooms.
Internet (free wireless). TV.
Other locations *C/Atocha 113, Huertas & Santa Ana (91 369 28 95). Chic&basic Colors, C/Huertas 14, Huertas & Santa Ana (91 429 69 35).*

★ Hostal Gala
C/Costanilla de los Ángeles 15 (91 541 96 92, www.hostalgala.com). Metro Santo Domingo.
Rates €50-€100 double. **Credit** MC, V.
Map p327 F11 ❷
This well-located new boutique *hostal* on a quiet but central street is run by a very friendly couple. The 22 rooms are comfortable and tasteful, with wooden floors, air-conditioning, retro-modern wallpaper and spacious bathrooms with power showers. Some rooms have balconies, while the superior double has a lounge area. An excellent option. *Photo p114.*
Internet (free wireless). TV.

❶ Red numbers given here correspond to the location of each hotel on the street maps. *See pp321-329.*

Hostal Gala. *See p113.*

CONSUME

Hotel Palacio San Martín

Plaza de San Martín 5 (91 701 50 00,
www.intur.com). Metro Ópera or Sol. **Rates**
€80-€100 double. **Credit** AmEx, DC, MC, V.
Map p327 G11 ❸

The Hotel Palacio San Martín is, in fact, housed in a
19th-century former palace, but it was only established as a hotel in 2001. It is located on a tranquil
but central square and has maintained much of the
glory of its previous palatial career, with period
façade, high stucco ceilings, wood panelling and an
attractive central courtyard. A quite lovely rooftop-
terrace restaurant looks out over the surrounding
area, while a huge presidential suite, also on the
rooftop, comes complete with jacuzzi – and more of
those striking views.
Business centre. Gym. Internet (wireless broadband).
Restaurant. Room service. TV (pay movies).

INSIDE TRACK HOSTALES

Note that a *hostal*, also known as
a *pensión*, is closer in meaning to
'guesthouse' than 'hostel'. Not all
hostales have someone on the door 24
hours a day, so check how to get back in
at night. These places tend to be family-
run affairs, and while some owners speak
English, any effort on your part to attempt
a few words of Spanish will be well
received. It's also worth noting that many
hostales and *pensiones* are located up
several flights of stairs in old buildings
without a lift. If this is likely to be a
problem, check before you book.

Petit Palace Arenal

C/Arenal 16 (91 564 43 55, www.hthoteles.
com). Metro Sol. **Rates** €73-€131 double.
Credit AmEx, DC, MC, V. **Map** p327 F11 ❹

Fans of chintz should steer well clear, but the good-
value High Tech chain of hotels is perfect for techno
fiends on a budget. The Arenal's compact but sleekly
designed rooms have flat-screen TVs and free ADSL
connection, and more expensive rooms come
equipped with a PC (also with free net access) and an
exercise bike. Some of the superior rooms have showers fitted with solariums, saunas and radios.
Business centre. Disabled-adapted rooms (1).
Internet (high-speed). No-smoking floors (5). TV.
Other locations Posada del Peine, C/Postas 17,
Sol (91 523 81 51); Tres Cruces, C/Tres Cruces 6,
Sol & Gran Via (91 522 33 27); Puerta del Sol,
C/Arenal 4, Sol (91 521 05 42), and throughout
the city.

Budget

Hostal Oriente

C/Arenal 23 (91 548 03 14,
www.hostaloriente.es). Metro Ópera. **Rates** €65-
€68 double. **Credit** DC, MC, V. **Map** p327 F11 ❺

Right on the doorstep of the opera house, and just a
short walk from Sol, the comfortable Oriente is in an
excellent location. The 19 rooms all have compact
bathrooms, TVs and air-conditioning, and the
friendly staff are a further draw.
TV.

Hostal Riesco

Third floor, C/Correo 2 (91 522 26 92,
www.hostalriesco.es). Metro Sol. **Rates** €60
double. **No credit cards. Map** p327 G11 ❻

The Riesco is a *hostal* that feels more like a hotel, what with its dark wood lobby, stucco ceilings and chintzy curtains. All rooms come with en suite bathrooms, and several have balconies bedecked with flowers. The location is hard to beat – it's rare to find such good-value accommodation so close to Sol and the Plaza Mayor.

SOL & GRAN VIA
Expensive

Hotel Emperador
Gran Via 53 (91 547 28 00, www.emperadorhotel.com). Metro Santo Domingo. **Rates** €93-€150 double; €353-€560 suite. **Credit** AmEx, DC, MC, V. **Map** p323 F10 ❼
While the traffic speeds by on the Gran Via outside, the Emperador has to deal with a flow of student groups and tourists that is almost as unrelenting. It's little surprise that it's so booked up, since the hotel is well situated for visiting the city's major sights and has a wonderful rooftop swimming pool (which is also open to non-residents for a fee). Rooms are conservatively decorated; the renovated bathrooms are a huge improvement on the old brown 1970s-style suites. *Photo p120.*
Bar. Business centre. Concierge. Disabled-adapted rooms (9). Gym. No-smoking floors (3). Internet (wireless). Parking (€22.47 per day). Room service. Pool (outdoor). TV (satellite).

Tryp Ambassador
Cuesta de Santo Domingo 5-7 (91 541 67 00, www.trypambassador.solmelia.com). Metro Santo Domingo. **Rates** €89-€210 double. **Credit** AmEx, DC, MC, V. **Map** p323 F11 ❽

Located in a former palace, the Ambassador manages to retain a vaguely baronial air despite being part of a chain. Suits of armour stand guard in the corridors, while plush upholstery adorns the public spaces and the large, light-filled atrium. Breakfast is expensive (€17) but abundant and good.
Bar. Business centre. Internet (free wireless). No smoking rooms. Restaurant. Room service. TV (satellite).

Mid-range

Hotel Arosa
C/Salud 21 (91 532 16 00, www.bestwesternarosa. com). Metro Gran Via. **Rates** €64-€148 double. **Credit** AmEx, DC, MC, V. **Map** p323 H11 ❾
This friendly, well-equipped and good-value 134-room hotel is situated right in the heart of the action. The spacious, air-conditioned rooms all come with clean, modern, wooden furnishings and bright marble bathrooms, and some of the more expensive doubles have a private seating area looking out on to the busy Gran Via. The public areas include a kitschy fake leopard-skin reception, and a restaurant and bar that Almodóvar would be proud of.
Bar. Concierge. Internet (free wireless). Parking (€27 per day). Restaurant. Room service. TV (satellite, pay movies).

Hotel Carlos V
C/Maestro Victoria 5 (91 531 41 00, www.bestwesternhotelcarlosv.com). Metro Sol. **Rates** €73-€159 double. **Credit** AmEx, DC, MC, V. **Map** p323 G11 ❿
The corporate feel is avoided in this Best Western hotel with homely touches, from the motley but charming crew running reception and the *trompe*

CONSUME

chic&basic Mayerling. *See p113.*

l'oeil lift door, to the tapestries in the corridors and the botanical prints in the colourful and elegant breakfast room. The rooms on the top floor are the nicest, and some have their own large, Astroturfed terraces (though you pay a bit extra for this).
Bar. Internet (free wireless). Room service. TV (satellite).

★ Hotel de las Letras
Gran Vía 11 (91 523 79 80, www.hotel delasletras.com). Metro Gran Vía. **Rates** €80-€167 double. **Credit** AmEx, DC, MC, V. **Map** p324 H11 ⑪
The new Hotel de las Letras laughs in the face of the current hotel vogue for teak and slate, and plumps instead for bold paintwork in red, orange and purples, with literary quotations strewn across its walls. It does this with remarkable aplomb, thanks to stylish furniture and well-designed rooms. Bathrooms are huge, and even standard rooms come with balconies. Downstairs is a comfortable spa and gym, along with a small library with free internet access. The ground floor bar hums with bright young things day and night. A gem.
Bar (2). Disabled-adapted room. No-smoking floor. Internet (wireless). Restaurant. Room Service. Spa. TV (satellite).

★ Hotel Mercure Santo Domingo
C/San Bernardo 1 (91 547 98 00, www.hotelsantodomingo.es). Metro Santo Domingo. **Rates** €86-€167 double. **Credit** AmEx, DC, MC, V. **Map** p323 F11 ⑫
Courteous staff welcome guests to this well-located, slick hotel, which is part of the Mercure chain. The hotel features a small(ish) but appealing rooftop pool and 80 individually decorated rooms – which will jump to 200 rooms once the hotel is merged with the Best Western Santo Domingo in the near future (the two buildings will be linked via passageways on the ground and first floors). The huge white lobby hints at the design-focus found within, yet the modern feel is tempered with displays of classical 19th-century paintings belonging to the hotel's owner. Huge walk-in showers are a real indulgence. *Photo p119.*
Bar. Disabled-adapted room. No smoking rooms. Internet (free wireless). Parking (€27 per day). Pool (outdoor). Restaurant. Room service. TV (satellite).

Budget

Hostal Andorra
7th floor, Gran Vía 33 (91 532 31 16, www.hostalandorra.com). Metro Gran Vía. **Rates** €62 double. **Credit** AmEx, DC, MC, V. **Map** p323 G11 ⑬
Brightly painted rooms, floral bedspreads and comfortable leather recliners confirm the homely atmosphere of this centrally located *hostal*. While the roar of the Gran Vía's traffic is unforgiving, the interior

CONSUME

Hotel de las Letras.

is calm, with cleanliness and facilities that belie the rates. Every room has satellite TV, and the bathrooms, while compact, are clean and modern.
Bar. Internet (wireless). TV room.

Hostal Triana
1st floor, C/Salud 13 (91 532 68 12, www.hostal triana.com). Metro Gran Vía. **Rates** €57 double. **Credit** MC, V. **Map** p323 H11 ⓮
A popular and efficiently run business, this traditional, good-value 40-room *hostal* has been open for more than four decades, and attracts guests of all ages. Rooms are sparklingly clean with modern en suite bathrooms. It's worth booking early.
Disabled-adapted room. Internet (wireless). TV.

What's Where.

Madrid's centre is small but varied.

Though Madrid is pretty small for a capital city, its accommodation is spread over a wide area, so it's a good to have an idea of what you want before you book.

Sol and **Gran Vía** are the best areas for mid-range accommodation right in the thick of things, and, though pretty touristy, are home to a clutch of decent bars and restaurants. Heading north of here, **Malasaña** has a choice of good budget *pensiones*, particularly along C/Palma. Bordering Malasaña to the east, **Chueca** is home to some great one-off properties. Both areas, especially Malasaña, boast a real neighbourhood vibe.

South of Chueca, lively **Huertas** and **Santa Ana** are both great areas for cheap *pensiones* and, increasingly, boutique hotels. On the edge of here, the Paseo del Prado provides a variety of budget accommodation right on the doorstep of the Big Three art museums. Upmarket areas include **Retiro** and **Los Austrias**. Though located across town from each other (Retiro is between the Prado and the Retiro park in the east, Los Austrias is adjacent to the Royal Palace to the west), both are home to Madrid's old money, and both are peaceful – though bars and restaurants can be expensive.

Just north of the Parque del Retiro, around the chic shopping street C/Serrano, is **Salamanca**. If you feel at home among the smart, wealthy set, you'll blend in well here. Business travellers should head for **Chamberí**, to the north of the centre, and, further north, to **Chamartín**, both of which are convenient for transport to the airport.

HUERTAS & SANTA ANA
Expensive

Hotel Urban
Carrera de San Jerónimo 34 (91 787 77 70, www.derbyhotels.com). Metro Sevilla or Sol. **Rates** €175-€225 double. **Credit** AmEx, DC, MC, V. **Map** p328 I11 ⓯
The Derby chain (which the Hotel Villa Real is also part of; *see below*) is owned by Catalan archaeologist Jordi Clos, and ancient figurines and artworks are found throughout the rooms, common areas and in the Egyptian museum in the basement. This cultural treasure trove is a perfect counterpoint to the painfully hip surroundings – a glass and steel atrium, rooms sexily designed with teak and leather and what must be the coolest doormen in the city. Other pluses include extremely friendly staff and a much needed plunge pool on the roof.
Bar. Business centre. Gym. Internet (high-speed, pre-pay wireless). Parking. Pool (outdoor). Restaurant. Room service. Smoking rooms. TV (satellite).

Hotel Villa Real
Plaza de las Cortes 10 (91 420 37 67, www.derbyhotels.com). Metro Banco de España. **Rates** €140-€210 double. **Credit** AmEx, DC, MC, V. **Map** p328 I12 ⓰
The Villa Real – as the name suggests – reflects owner Jordi Clos's interest in Roman archaeology. The guest rooms are elegant, with marble bathrooms boasting large picture windows, and many have panels of Roman mosaics. Most double rooms have split-level sitting areas, some duplex suites come with their own jacuzzi and the luxury suites have private terraces. The Hotel Urban (*see above*) is also part of the same chain.
Bar. Business centre. Internet (high speed, wireless). No-smoking floor. Parking (€26.75 per day). Restaurant. Room service. TV (satellite).

★ ME Madrid
Plaza Santa Ana 14 (91 701 60 00, www.memadrid.com). Metro Sevilla or Sol. **Rates** €150-€243 double. **Credit** AmEx, DC, MC, V. **Map** p328 H12 ⓱
Although plans to turn this into Europe's first Hard Rock hotel didn't quite come off, the Melia chain appropriated the lovely old Hotel Reina Victoria to showcase its 'ME' brand. Despite being on the small side, rooms are supremely comfortable, with luxury bed linen, Aveda toiletries and lots to keep gadget-fiends happy, not only with plasma screens, CD and DVD players, but even iPod adapters. The rooftop bar has amazing views of the city.
Bar. Business centre. Disabled-adapted rooms (4). Gym. No-smoking floors (5). Internet (high speed, wireless). Parking (€30 per day). Restaurant. Room service. TV (pay movies, satellite).

Hotel Mercure Santo Domingo. *See p117.*

CONSUME

★ Westin Palace

*Plaza de las Cortes 7 (91 360 80 00,
www.westinpalacemadrid.com). Metro Banco de
España.* **Rates** €189-€259. **Credit** AmEx, DC,
MC, V. **Map** p328 I12 ⑱

One of the most famous hotels in Madrid, the
Palace successfully combines old-world elegance
with cutting-edge facilities. The lounge areas and
stunning atrium have an air of sumptuousness, and
the latter features opera performances once a
month. The hotel's reasonably priced, comfortable
bars and restaurants are popular with visiting
celebs and politicians from the parliament buildings across the road, and, luckily for non-residents,
they're open to all. The hotel is brought into the
21st century with a fully equipped fitness centre,
sauna and solarium.

*Bar. Business centre. Disabled-adapted room.
Gym. Internet (high speed, wireless). No-smoking
floor. Parking (€34.15 per day). Restaurant (2).
Room service. TV (satellite, pay movies).*

Mid-range

Hotel Lope de Vega

*C/Lope de Vega 40 (91 360 00 11,
www.hotellopedevega.com). Metro Antón Martín.*
Rates €82-€127 double. **Credit** AmEx, DC, MC,
V. **Map** p328 J12/13 ⑲

A stone's throw from the Prado, this anonymous-
looking hotel's rooms are done up in standard-issue
mid-range decor, but are a good size, comfortable
and many have large balconies. Posted outside each
one is information about playwright Lope de Vega,
and the corridors are lined with pictures of his productions. Other nice touches on the landings include
books about the great man himself and other literary giants, along with bowls of fruit.

*Bar. Cafeteria. No-smoking floors (5). Internet
(high-speed, wireless). Meeting rooms. Parking
(€24.84 per day). Room service. TV (satellite).*

Hostal Persal

*Plaza del Ángel 12 (91 369 46 43, www.
hostalpersal.com). Metro Sol or Antón Martín.*
Rates €65-€84 double. **Credit** AmEx, MC, V.
Map p328 H12 ⑳

The Persal's rooms don't quite live up to the first
impressions given by the glass front and swish
lobby, but thankfully they're modern, spotlessly
clean and more than functional (it's well worth paying the extra for a nicer one on the upper floors). If
you're travelling as a family or a group, the hard-
working staff are especially welcoming and helpful.
*Bar. Internet (wireless). Meeting rooms. TV
(satellite).*

Hotel El Prado

*C/Prado 11 (91 369 02 34, www.pradohotel.com).
Metro Antón Martín.* **Rates** €76-€122 double.
Credit AmEx, DC, MC, V. **Map** p328 H/I12 ㉑

The sister hotel to the Lope de Vega (*see p119*), the
Prado too has an anonymous look from the outside,
but the rooms are prettily furnished, this time with
a wine theme. Curtains and upholstery are adorned
with vine patterns and the downstairs lounge is
filled with books, videos and magazines about viti-
culture. There are bowls of fruit to munch on in the
public areas and free internet access in the lounge.
*No-smoking rooms (40). Internet (free wireless).
TV (satellite).*

Hotel Santander

*C/Echegaray 1 (91 429 95 51, www.hotelsantander
madrid.com). Metro Sevilla or Sol.* **Rates** €47-
€86 double. **Credit** MC, V. **Map** p328 H11 ㉒

Hotel Emperador. *See p115.*

The Santander's glamorous, gilded entrance makes for a foyer with character, and if you can get over the rather offputting list of house rules (no visitors after midnight, no noise after 11pm, for example) you'll enjoy your stay. The rooms are elegant, kitted out with decent furniture and wooden floors. Some are more like suites, with small seating areas where you can have breakfast.
TV.

Budget

Hotel Asturias

C/Sevilla 2 (91 429 66 76, www.hotel-asturias.com). Metro Sevilla. **Rates** €48-€70 double. **Credit** AmEx, MC, V. **Map** p328 H11 ㉓
Within spitting distance of Sol, this bustling 19th-century hotel is nothing to write home about from the outside. Inside, though, the 170 rooms are bright and spacious, decorated in simple whites and creams, with carpets and furnishings that blend well with the wooden floors and fittings. Some have views over the gorgeous Teatro Reina Victoria, but ask for an interior room if noise bothers you.
Bar. Concierge. Restaurant. TV (satellite).

Hotel Mora

Paseo del Prado 32 (91 420 15 69, www.hotelmora.com). Metro Atocha. **Rates** €58-€83 double. **Credit** AmEx, DC, MC, V. **Map** p328 J13 ㉔
If you like marble, you'll love the Mora's foyer, with its caramel-coloured columns and chandeliers. The rooms are functional but comfortable, and some have views over the tree-lined Paseo del Prado. Not surprisingly, given the location and price, it can be hard to get a room, so try to book early.
Bar. Internet (wireless). TV.

Hostal Alaska

4th floor, C/Espoz y Mina 7 (91 521 18 45, www.hostalalaska.com). Metro Sol. **Rates** €52-€55 double. **Credit** MC, V. **Map** p327 H12 ㉕
Exceptionally large rooms for this price range, decorated with splashes of bright blue, give this comfortable, colourful *hostal* a bit of a beachside feel. The atmosphere is homely, and guests have use of a fridge and washing machine. The five doubles and one single all come with bathrooms, and many have balconies. It's on the fourth floor but there's a lift.
Internet (wireless). TV.

Hostal Armesto

1st floor, C/San Agustín 6 (91 429 90 31, www.hostalarmesto.com). Metro Antón Martín. **Rates** €59 double. **Credit** MC, V. **Map** p328 I12 ㉖
This great-value six-room *hostal* in the centre of Huertas is run by a friendly husband and wife team. Rooms are spotless and all of them have their own small bathroom with shower; some boast views over the garden of the San Agustín palace next door. The Armesto is a good choice for art lovers on a budget, being well situated for the art museum triumvirate.
TV.

Hostal Astoria

2nd floor, Carrera de San Jerónimo 30-32 (91 429 11 88, www.hostal-astoria.com). Metro Sevilla or Sol. **Rates** €53-€70 double. **Credit** AmEx, DC, MC, V. **Map** p328 H11 ㉗
Managed by (mostly) friendly staff, the Astoria is a good choice if you want to be centrally located, with access to basic facilities at a very good price. All 26 rooms are relatively spacious and have en suite bathrooms, but try to get the biggest available, and preferably one facing away from the street.
Business centre. Internet (free wireless). TV.

CONSUME

Hostal Casanova

1st floor, C/Lope de Vega 8 (91 429 56 91).
Metro Antón Martín. **Rates** €45 double.
Credit MC, V. **Map** p328 I12 ❷⑧
Run by a friendly family and in a quiet street just off newly pedestrianised C/Huertas, this *hostal* is especially good value for those travelling in threes. Rooms are basic but bright, some with bathrooms, and all with air-conditioning.
TV.

Hostal Delvi

Plaza Santa Ana 15 (91 522 59 98, www.
hostaldelvi.com). Metro Sevilla or Sol. **Rates**
€45 double. **Credit** MC, V. **Map** p328 H12 ❷⑨
Located on lively Plaza Santa Ana and in a delightfully eccentric building, the Casa de Guadalajara, the Delvi is ideal for backpackers. An entrance hall decorated with ceramics of winged cherubs leads you past the Guadalajara Club, then up to the third floor (there's no lift) where an elderly couple run this good-value *hostal*. Rooms are basic, but some have showers and a toilet, and others boast views of the square.

Hostal Horizonte

2nd floor, C/Atocha 28 (91 369 09 96, www.
hostalhorizonte.com). Metro Antón Martín. **Rates**
€44-€72 double. **Credit** MC, V. **Map** p327 H13 ❸⓪
One of the oldest *pensiones* in Madrid, the Horizonte has stayed in the same friendly family throughout its 65-year history. The manager is the young and helpful Julio César, a font of knowledge about the history and cultural life of the city. Rooms are colourfully decorated, clean and comfy, and the welcoming atmosphere is unbeatable.
Internet (free wireless).

Hostal Martín

1st floor, C/Atocha 43 (91 429 95 79,
www.hostalmartin.com). Metro Antón Martín.
Rates €39-€66 double. **Credit** AmEx, DC, MC,
V. **Map** p327 H13 ❸①

THE BEST HIGH-END HOTELS

ME Madrid
The slick ME Madrid in Plaza Santa Ana hotel was designed to raise eyebrows.
See p118.

Hotel Santo Mauro
Palatial luxury, in a hidden-away spot.
See p127.

Westin Palace
One of Madrid's most famous hotels, and a haven for the rich and powerful.
See p119.

This very friendly, first-floor *hostal* has a pleasantly rough-and-tumble family feel about it. The 20 high-ceilinged, air-conditioned rooms all come with an en suite bathroom and decent shower. The helpful couple who run it speak various languages between them and can book you into other hotels if you're moving on to other parts of the country. The hearty breakfast includes plenty of fresh fruit and very good coffee.
Internet (free wireless). Parking. TV (satellite).

Hostal San Antonio

2nd floor, C/León 13 (91 429 51 37, www.hostal
sanantonio.net). Metro Antón Martín. **Rates** €53 double. **No credit cards. Map** p328 I12 ❸②
A clean, quiet and cool modern *hostal,* tranquil by day, buzzing on weekend nights. Rooms are comfortable and generously sized for the price, and all come with air-conditioning, and en suite toilet and shower room. Most look out on to a busy street, so it can get quite noisy at night.
Internet (free wireless). TV.

★ Hostal Sud-Americana

Paseo del Prado 12 (91 429 25 64, http://hostalsud
americana.com). Metro Banco de España. **Rates**
€29-€57 double. **Credit** MC, V. **Map** p328 J12 ❸③
This place has a real feel of Old Madrid, with mini Goya reproductions lining the creaky, wooden-floored hallway. Whitewashed walls, high ceilings and dark wooden furniture give the rooms a centuries-old atmosphere and some have lovely views over the tree tops of the Paseo del Prado. One bathroom is shared between eight rooms, but all have their own washbasin. You'll find it very difficult to find this sort of old-world elegance elsewhere at such a cheap price, particularly if you're after a single.

LAVAPIES
Budget

Hostal Apolo

C/Juanelo 24 (91 360 08 00, www.hostalapolo
madrid.com). Metro Tirso de Molina. **Rates** €45-
€55 double. **Credit** MC, V. **Map** p327 G13 ❸④
This is the best of the few hotel options in the lively and multicultural Lavapiés area. The new owner is eager to please and proud of his establishment. Rooms are rather functional but clean and good value, and all have en suite bathrooms.
Bar. Internet (€6 per day high speed, wireless). TV.

CHUECA
Mid-range

Petit Palace Ducal

C/Hortaleza 3 (91 521 10 43, www.hthoteles.com).
Metro Gran Vía. **Rates** €63-€118 double. **Credit**
AmEx, DC, MC, V. **Map** p324 H11 ❸⑤

CONSUME

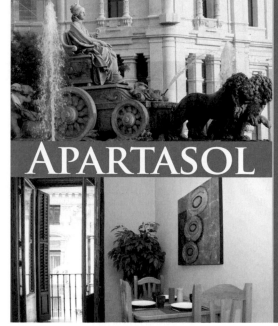

The Petit Palace Ducal blends seamlessly into its cool Chueca surroundings. Staff are young and friendly, and the striking red and black design eye-catching. So-called High Tech rooms come with flat-screen PCs, exercise bikes and sauna or hydromassage showers. The Ducal is also practical in its provision of family rooms. Given all this, the prices are reasonable, and it's even worth spending extra for a sixth-floor room with small terrace. The High Tech chain manages other hotels in the city; see the website for details. *Bar. Business centre. No-smoking floors (5). Internet (free high speed, wireless). Restaurant. TV (satellite).*

★ Room Mate Oscar

Plaza Vázquez de Mella 12 (91 701 11 73, www.room-matehotels.com). Metro Chueca or Gran Vía. **Rates** (incl breakfast) €78-€143 double. **Map** p324 H11 ⊕

The latest in a chain of stylish, mid-range hotels, especially popular among a design-appreciative public (for which, often, read 'gay'). Room Mate Oscar oozes affordable chic, from the ergonomic white plastic chairs to the smart chequered grey and white bathrooms. The staff (black-shirted, naturally) are as welcoming and easy on the eye as the spacious rooms, and the location in one of Chueca's main squares in unbeatable. The huge roof terrace – complete with bar and pool – is also a big plus, and a prime hangout for the city's gay scene. *Photo p124. Bar (2). Business centre. Disabled-adapted room. No smoking rooms. Internet (free wireless, free shared terminal). Restaurant. Telephone. TV.* **Other locations** Room Mate Alicia, C/Prado 2, Santa Ana (91 389 60 95); Room Mate Laura, Travesía de Trujillos 3, Sol & Gran Vía (91 701 16 70); Room Mate Mario, C/Campomanes 4 (91 548 85 48).

Budget

Hostal Benamar

2nd floor, C/San Mateo 20 (91 308 00 92, www.hostalbenamar.es). Metro Alonso Martínez or Tribunal. **Rates** €49.90 double. **Credit** MC, V. **Map** p324 I9 ⊕

Well situated between Chueca and Alonso Martínez, this *hostal* can be divided into two different parts. The friendly owners promote the recently renovated section, which has marble floors, modern en suite bathrooms and computers in every room. The other section is older but clean, with shared bathrooms and cheaper rates. *Internet (highspeed). TV.*

Hostal Santa Bárbara

3rd floor, Plaza de Santa Bárbara 4 (91 446 93 08, www.hostalsantabarbaramadrid.com). Metro Alonso Martínez. **Rates** €42-€60 double. **Credit** MC, V. **Map** p324 I8 ⊕

This well-connected *hostal* provides friendly service in a secure building. The rooms are basic but they are also clean and every one has walk-in shower facilities. The friendly Italian owner and the staff all speak good English. *TV.*

MALASAÑA & CONDE DUQUE
Budget

Hostal Sil & Serranos

C/Fuencarral 95 (91 448 89 72, www.sil serranos.com). Metro Bilbao. **Rates** €55-€59 double. **Credit** MC, V. **Map** p323 H8 ⊕

Clean and smartly decorated, these *hostales* are well located for night-time revelling – indeed, rooms looking out on to C/Fuencarral will bear witness to the *madrileño* enthusiasm for partying well into the early hours. Although interior rooms are a little darker, the noise is minimal and the price slightly lower. All rooms have air-conditioning, small bathrooms and digital TV, and the properties are run by a fun couple and their English-speaking children. *Internet (high-speed). TV (satellite).*

Hotel Abalu

C/Pez 19 (91 531 47 44, www.hotelabalu.com). Metro Noviciado. **Rates** €69-€139 double. **Credit** AmEx, DC, MC, V. **Map** p323 G9 ⊕

The Abalu is near the Gran Vía and metro, but its extravagant interior design pull in as many visitors as its location. The rooms range from restrained to gloriously over the top; the staff are generally friendly although sometimes hard to pin down. *Internet (wireless). TV.*

Hotel Alexandra

C/San Bernardo 29-31 (91 542 04 00, www.halexandra.com). Metro Noviciado. **Rates** €45-€74 double. **Credit** AmEx, DC, MC, V. **Map** p323 F10 ⊕

A few minutes' walk from the Gran Vía and the metro, the Alexandra is well located for sightseeing. All rooms are clean and pretty quiet, but you can request an interior room to avoid the traffic noise from C/San Bernardo. Although the hotel is slightly anonymous in its style, the staff are friendly and the area and prices just that little bit less touristy than if you cross the Gran Vía towards Sol. *No-smoking rooms (21). TV.*

THE RETIRO & SALAMANCA
Luxury

AC Palacio del Retiro

Alfonso XII 14 (91 523 74 60, www.ac-hotels.com). Metro Banco de España or Retiro. **Rates** €238-€302 double. **Credit** AmEx, DC, MC, V. **Map** p328 K11 ⊕

CONSUME

Room Mate Oscar. *See p123.*

CONSUME

With their palette of greys and browns, the rooms can seem a little dour and masculine after the frothy extravagances of the belle époque building in which they are housed. The hotel is beautifully located near the park and Prado, however, and the staff eager to please. Amenities are good – rooms feature plasma-screen TVs and CD players – as is breakfast (as one would expect for €29).

Bar (2). Business centre. Concierge. Disabled-adapted rooms (2). No-smoking floors (3). Internet (free wireless). Restaurant. Spa. Room Service. TV (satellite).

Hotel Ritz

Plaza de la Lealtad 5 (91 701 67 67, www.ritzmadrid.com). Metro Banco de España. **Rates** €248-€346 double. **Credit** AmEx, DC, MC, V. **Map** p328 J12 ❸

Madrid's Ritz was built in 1910, thanks to a personal intervention by King Alfonso XIII, who had been embarrassed at the time of his wedding to Princess Victoria four years earlier because his guests could not find a hotel that was up to scratch. When the hotel first opened, the handful of bathrooms, one telephone per floor and lift were considered the height of luxury, and it soon attracted politicians, royalty and writers. Today, the 167 rooms maintain some of the original belle époque style, though the swirly carpets and occasionally shabby fittings are incongruous in such a setting. And, for the price, it has fairly minimal fitness facilities (and no pool). The Ritz has shaken off its slightly stuffy image and now welcomes celebs it once shunned; however, guests must abide by a strict dress code in the restaurant.

Bar (2). Business centre. Concierge. Disabled-adapted room. Gym. Internet (free high-speed, wireless). No-smoking floors (2). Restaurant. Room service. TV (satellite).

Villa Magna

Paseo de la Castellana 22 (91 587 12 34, www.villamagna.es). Metro Rubén Darío. **Rates** €248-€416 double. **Credit** AmEx, DC, MC, V. **Map** p324 K7/8 ❹

Although it's a modern, rather nondescript building from the outside, the lavishly entitled Villa Magna, a Park Hyatt Hotel, more than lives up to its reputation – and tariffs – on the inside. The huge lobby, full of jewellery displays, international businessmen and polite staff, leads to two excellent restaurants and a champagne bar, whose lunch menu is surprisingly reasonably priced. The 150 rooms and suites, looking out over the busy Paseo de la Castellana or the exclusive C/Serrano, have good facilities and, like the rest of the hotel, are spacious and elegantly decorated. There's also a top-notch gym.

Bar (2). Business centre. Concierge. Disabled-adapted rooms (10). Gym. Internet (free high-speed, wireless). No-smoking floors (7). Parking. Restaurant (2). Room service. Spa. TV (DVD, satellite).

Expensive

★ Hotel Selenza Madrid

C/Claudio Coello 67 (91 781 01 73, www.selenzahotelmadrid.com). Metro Serrano. **Rates** €155-€250. **Credit** AmEx, DC, MC, V. **Map** p325 L8 ❺

The new Hotel Selenza Madrid achieves the perfect blend of modern and classic. It's housed in a graceful 19th-century Salamanca building, it has slick black-and-white chequered tiles and upholstered chairs in the public areas, impressive staircases that are perfect for making a grand entrance, and mod cons throughout. The 44 spacious rooms and suites are comfortable and well-designed, with huge comfy

beds, wooden floors, muted tones and patterns, slick bathrooms, and Molton Brown toiletries. The Michelin-starred restaurant is another plus.
Bar. Business centre. Concierge. Disabled-adapted rooms. No-smoking floors. Internet (free high-speed, wireless). Parking. Restaurant. Room service. TV (DVD, satellite).

Hotel Wellington

C/Velázquez 8 (91 575 44 00, www.hotel-wellington.com). Metro Retiro. **Rates** €140-€232 double. **Credit** AmEx, DC, MC, V. **Map** p325 M10 ㊻
More than half a century after it opened, the Wellington remains an extremely graceful place in which to stay, with chandeliers, marble and murals, and groups of guests in formal eveningwear milling around the lobby. The hotel is just a stone's throw from the city's most expensive shopping area, Salamanca, and has a summer pool with terrace – an ideal location for relaxing after all that retail therapy. Rooms vary in size and are decorated in a conservative but classic style.
Bar (3). Business centre. Internet (free high-speed, wireless). No-smoking floors (4). Parking (€20 per day). Restaurant (2). Room service. Pool (outdoor). Spa. TV (satellite).

Mid-range

Hostal-Residencia Don Diego

C/Velázquez 45 (91 435 07 60, www.hostaldondiego.com). Metro Velázquez. **Rates** €50-€93 double. **Credit** AmEx, DC, MC, V. **Map** p325 M8 ㊼
The Hostal-Residencia Don Diego lies above a row of upmarket private apartments on one of Madrid's most exclusive streets. Rooms are plain but clean and good value, and, because of the location, the *hostal* is popular with the business crowd and those attending trade shows at the IFEMA.
Internet (free wireless). No-smoking rooms (37). TV (satellite).

Hotel Alcalá

C/Alcalá 66 (91 435 10 60, www.nh-hoteles.com). Metro Príncipe de Vergara. **Rates** €59-€133 double. **Credit** AmEx, DC, MC, V. **Map** p325 M/N10 ㊽
Even though the chain status of this hotel gives it uniformity and a certain anonymity, the Hotel Alcalá provides visitors with modern accommodation, supplemented by good facilities and thoroughly professional staff. Not surprisingly, its location (right near the Retiro) and style (rooms with contemporary decor and good sound-proofing) make it a popular choice.
Bar (4). Concierge. Internet (free wireless). No-smoking floors (5). Parking (€22 per day). Restaurant. Room service. TV (pay movies, satellite).

Hotel Meliá Galgos

C/Claudio Coello 139 (91 562 66 00, www.meliagalgos.com). Metro Rubén Dario. **Rates** €70-€162 double. **Credit** AmEx, DC, MC, V. **Map** p325 L6 ㊾
This large, glitzy and bustling hotel is part of the Sol Meliá group. It's located in the heart of the business district, so it comes as no surprise that there are 11 conference rooms – but it is also popular with the well-heeled leisure set. The 'Servicio Real' floor offers a separate reception, a free bar, yet more mod cons in the rooms and secretaries for hire, and even the standard rooms are large and comfortable – if somewhat dated in decor. The gym comes complete with sauna and whirlpools, while the breakfast spread is spectacular.
Bar. Business centre. Concierge. Gym. No-smoking rooms (120). Internet access (high-speed, wireless). Restaurant (2). Room service. TV (pay movies, satellite).

Radisson Blu, Madrid Prado

C/Moratín 52, Plaza de Platería Martínez (91 524 26 26, www.radissonblu.com/prado hotel-madrid). Metro Antón Martín. **Rates** €98-€190 double. **Credit** AmEx, DC, MC, V. **Map** p328 J13 ㊿
In prime tourist territory, on the corner of the Paseo del Prado and just steps from the Prado Museum and the CaixaForum, the new Radisson Blu is a useful new addition to the city's hotel offerings, with a slick interior, modern artwork and comfortable rooms (54 bedrooms and six suites), equipped with all mod cons, black-slate bathrooms and great views. The Cask restaurant offers Spanish fare made with good-quality ingredients.
Bar. Business centre. Concierge. Disabled-adapted rooms. Gym. Internet (free high-speed, wireless). No-smoking floors. Restaurant. Room service. Spa. Swimming pool (indoor). TV (pay movies, satellite).

INSIDE TRACK TAKE A PLUNGE

Considering how hot Madrid gets in the summer months, it's disappointing that there are relatively few hotels in the city with outdoor swimming pools. However, due to reasons of space in this cramped city, the hotel pools that do exist are high up on the roofs, and often have fantastic views. If you're visiting between May and September, and a pool and lounge terrace are a priority, then check in to the **Hotel Emperador** (*see p115*; the pool is also open to non-guests for a fee), **Hotel Mercure Santo Domingo** (*see p117*), **Hotel Wellington** (*see above*) or **Room Mate Oscar** (*see p123*).

CONSUME

World Class

Perfect places to stay, eat and explore.

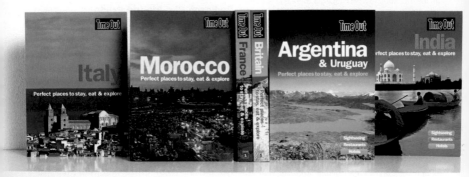

**TIME OUT GUIDES
WRITTEN BY
LOCAL EXPERTS**
visit timeout.com/shop

Budget

Hostal Arco Iris

Sixth floor, C/O'Donnell 27 (91 575 50 15, www.hostalarcoiris.com). Metro O'Donnell. **Rates** €45-€75 double. **Credit** AmEx, DC, MC, V. **Map** p325 O10 ❺

Although it's a little more expensive than most *hostales*, the Rainbow's colour schemes make a refreshing change when compared with the dark corridors of the other budget accommodation in the city centre. Rooms are modern and bright, with clean bathrooms, and the friendly staff are happy to add extra beds to make triples or twins. Stays of two nights or more receive a discount. Well worth a look. *Internet access (free wireless). No-smoking rooms (all). TV.*

ARGUELLES

Expensive

Hotel Husa Princesa

C/Princesa 40 (91 542 21 00, www.hotel husaprincesa.com). Metro Ventura Rodríguez. **Rates** €86-€300. **Credit** AmEx, DC, MC, V. **Map** p322 D8 ❷

Beyond the Plaza de España and the hustle and bustle of Gran Vía lies the Husa Princesa, decorated with large reproductions of Goya and Velázquez classics in each room. Two floors are known as 'club class', providing extra amenities such as a pillow menu, butler service and mid-morning snacks. The hotel's gym and large sports complex are impressive, incorporating an indoor pool, saunas, steam baths and 150 exercise machines, plus a beauty treatment area. The hotel is a favourite of airline staff, who can often be seen sunning themselves on the outdoor terrace. *Bar. Business centre. Concierge. Disabled-adapted rooms. Gym. Internet. No-smoking floors (6). Parking. Restaurant. Room service. Swimming pool (indoor). TV (pay movies, satellite).*

Mid-range

Hotel Tirol

C/Marqués de Urquijo 4 (91 548 19 00, www.t3tirol.com). Metro Argüelles. **Rates** €55-€75 double. **Credit** AmEx, MC, V. **Map** p322 D7 ❸

The most child-friendly hotel in the city features family rooms with separate spaces for kids, a children's play area and discounts for family stays. Situated within easy reach of the Parque del Oeste, the Tirol is also well located for those wishing to discover the greener side of Madrid. The hotel is now part of the T3 chain. *Business centre. No-smoking rooms. Internet (€4 per hour, high-speed, wireless). Gym. Parking (€22 per day). TV (satellite).*

CHAMBERI

Luxury

Hotel Hesperia Madrid

Paseo de la Castellana 57 (91 210 88 00, www.hesperia-madrid.com). Metro Gregorio Marañón. **Rates** €109-€319. **Credit** AmEx, DC, MC, V. **Map** p321 K5 ❺

Part of a Catalan chain, Hesperia Madrid is what you'd call 'contemporary luxury'. The dimly lit entrance gives way to white and cream surroundings, while plants lend a necessary splash of colour. In contrast, guest rooms feature dark wood and strong tones. Interior rooms have larger bathrooms, though guests wanting a jacuzzi and terrace will have to move up to the Executive and Presidential levels. The Catalan restaurant, Santceloni, has been awarded two Michelin stars. *Bar (3). Business centre. Concierge. Garden. Internet access (free high-speed, wireless). No-smoking floors (5). Parking (€28.89 per day). Restaurant (2). Room service. TV (pay movies, satellite).*

Hotel Orfila

C/Orfila 6 (91 702 77 70, www.hotelorfila.com). Metro Alonso Martínez or Colón. **Rates** €202-€437 double. **Credit** AmEx, DC, MC, V. **Map** p324 J8 ❺

This small mansion in a tranquil residential area has been transformed into an elegant five-star hotel. Built in the 1880s as a private home for an artistic family, the Orfila also contained a theatre and a literary salon during the 1920s. Thankfully, the hotel has held on to its 19th-century decor, not to mention its façade, carriage entrance and dramatic main stairway. Bedrooms are wonderfully quiet. The elegant restaurant looks on to the lovely garden patio, and guests take tea in the lobby in the afternoon. *Bar. Concierge. No smoking rooms. Internet access (wireless). Parking (€25 per day). Restaurant. Room service. TV (pay movies, satellite).*

★ Hotel Santo Mauro

C/Zurbano 36 (91 319 69 00, www.hotel acsantomauro.com). Metro Rubén Darío. **Rates** €237-€324 double. **Credit** AmEx, DC, MC, V. **Map** p324 J7 ❺

Famous in recent times as the Beckhams' first residence in Madrid, this exquisite hotel is discreetly hidden away in the embassy-lined streets that separate the Castellana from busy C/Santa Engracia. The elegant and peaceful entrance prepares guests for the experience to come. The 51 rooms, housed in two parts of what was the residence of the Duke of Santo Mauro, are luxuriously decorated, and boast king-size beds and floor-to-ceiling picture windows hung with opulent silk drapes. The old palace library has been converted into a high-class

CONSUME

THE BEST BARGAIN BEDS

chic&basic

The fun chain of simple but stylish hotels now has three locations in Madrid. *See p113.*

Hostal Gala

A new boutique *hostal*, with friendly owners. *See p113.*

Hotel Mora

If you want to be near the Golden Triangle, but can't afford the Ritz. *See p120.*

restaurant and former ballrooms are now conference rooms opening on to an immaculately kept garden. *Bar. Business centre. Concierge. Disabled-adapted room. Gym. Internet (wireless). No-smoking rooms (35). Parking (€20.90 per day). Restaurant. Room service. Parking (€28.89 per day). Pool (indoor). Smoking rooms. TV (satellite).*

Expensive

Gran Hotel Conde Duque

Plaza Conde del Valle Suchil 5 (91 447 70 00, www.hotelcondeduque.es). Metro San Bernardo. **Rates** €97-€201 double. **Credit** AmEx, DC, MC, V. **Map** p323 F7 ⑤⑦

A quiet, out-of-the-way hotel with front rooms facing a pretty, leafy plaza. Rooms are tastefully kitted out with yellow and green upholstery, while the belle-époque salon downstairs serves afternoon tea. Beds are king-size and one room, 315, has a waterbed. Previous guests have included Celia Cruz and Marcel Marceau, and Pedro Almodóvar has been spotted in the bar. Guests can use the gym on the other side of the square. *Bar. Business centre. Concierge. Gym. Internet access (high-speed, web TV). No-smoking floors (5). Parking (€20 per day). Restaurant. Room service. TV (pay movies, satellite).*

Hotel Zurbano

C/Zurbano 79-81 (91 441 45 00, www.nh-hoteles. com). Metro Gregorio Marañón. **Rates** €49-€232. **Credit** AmEx, DC, MC, V. **Map** p321 J5 ⑤⑧

Part of the NH chain, the Zurbano is split between two buildings. Rooms are immaculate (if a little bland) and incredibly well soundproofed, given the location right next to the chaotic C/José Abascal and its never-ending traffic jams. The size of the rooms varies according to the building (the one furthest up on the street tends to have the biggest bedrooms). For travellers needing to be near the northern business district or within easy reach of Barajas airport, the location couldn't be better.

Bar. Business centre. Concierge. Disabled-adapted room. Internet access (wireless). No-smoking floor. Parking (€16.05 per day). Restaurant. Room service. TV (pay movies, satellite).

InterContinental Madrid

Paseo de la Castellana 49 (91 700 73 00, www.madrid.intercontinental.com). Metro Gregorio Marañón. **Rates** €120-€184 double. **Credit** AmEx, DC, MC, V. **Map** p321 K6 ⑤⑨

The InterContinental is a long-standing Madrid favourite. The elegant decor in the lobby extends to the rooms, most of which overlook the Paseo de la Castellana. The hotel appeals to a wide-ranging clientele, being well located for the business districts but also offering special packages for fans visiting the Bernabéu football stadium. In terms of eating and drinking options, the modern Bar 49 is perfect for a cocktail or two before dinner, the El Jardín restaurant serves French cuisine outdoors during the summer months, and the café serves light meals overlooking the lovely garden. *Bar. Business centre. Concierge. Disabled-adapted rooms (4). Gym. Internet (high-speed, wireless). No-smoking floors (5). Parking (€30 per day). Restaurants (2). Room service. Smoking rooms. TV (pay movies, satellite).*

OTHER AREAS

Expensive

Hotel Puerta América

Avda America 41, East of centre (91 744 54 00, www.hoteles-silken.com) Metro Cartagena. **Rates** €100-€201 double. **Credit** AmEx, DC, MC, V.

The Puerta América will not be to all tastes, least of all, probably, those business travellers attracted by its proximity to the airport, but it is a wonderland for design buffs. Each of its 12 floors and public spaces is designed by an all-star cast of architects, including Norman Foster, Richard Gluckman, Marc Jewson and Ron Arad. Guests can select the floor of their choice on arrival, but most popular tend to be Zaha Hadid's rooms (which appear to be sculpted from snowdrifts) or Arata Isozaki's studies in Japanese minimalism. The building itself (along with the pool and gym) was designed by Jean Nouvel. *Bar (2). Disabled-adapted rooms (8). Gym. No-smoking floors (2). Internet (wireless). Pool (indoor). Restaurant (3). Spa. Room service. TV (satellite).*

Mid-range

Hotel Don Pío

Avda Pío XII 25, Chamartín (91 353 07 80, www.hoteldonpio.com). Metro Pío XII. **Rates** €110-€160 double. **Credit** AmEx, MC, V.

Quite a way from the centre but right opposite Pío XII metro and Chamartín railway station, and just

CONSUME

A Home from Home

Apartment rentals and aparthotels are gaining popularity in Madrid.

Spain Select.

located properties. Most properties sleep between two and six people. If you want to stay in the heart of the action, in luxurious surroundings, then opt for the Plaza Mayor apartment (€1,190-€1,260 per week, based on two people sharing) housed in an 18th-century building, and with a balcony overlooking the square. An equally attractive apartment in the characterful Plaza de la Paja, in the heart of the city's tapas scene, costs between €875 and €945 for two people. There are hundreds more options all over town, with a good number in the traditional barrio of Salamanca.

Another agency with plenty of apartments on its books is **Friendly Rentals** (www.friendlyrentals.com, 34 93 268 80 51). Less focused on luxury and personal service than Spain Select, it's nevertheless a good option for those looking for a nicely decorated home from home in a central Madrid location.

APARTHOTELS

Aparthotels are generally made up of self-catering suites or small apartments, usually with kitchen facilities (sometimes basic), as well as standard hotel services, such as a reception, maid service, concierge and room service. They're normally available on weekly, monthly or longer-term rates, so are handy if you're staying in town for a while.

Halfway between a conventional hotel and apartment, the **Aparto-Hotel Rosales** (C/Marqués de Urquijo 23, Argüelles, 91 542 03 51, www.apartohotel-rosales.com) provides accommodation ranging from spacious and comfortably furnished bedsitters to suites. All boast kitchens and marble-clad bathrooms, and larger rooms also have a lounge. Other facilities include a coffee shop and a decent restaurant. Double studios cost between €85 and €175 per night, while double apartments are between €124 and €235.

A more centrally located option is the **Apartamentos Príncipe 11** (C/ Príncipe 11, Santa Ana, 91 429 44 70, www.atprincipe11.com), on a pleasant street not far from Plaza Santa Ana. The 36 apartment rooms have a kitchen area (with hob, microwave, fridge and basic utensils), while rates for double rooms vary from €48 to €87 per night. There are also larger family rooms.

APARTMENT RENTALS

An increasing number of properties in Madrid – most equipped with fully-fitted kitchens, balconies or terraces, and all mod cons – are now available for tourists to rent on a daily, weekly or monthly basis as an alternative to hotels. If you're in town for a week or more, this can work out as a more economical way to lodge in the city than staying in hotels; even with the luxurious apartments, the fees can work out the same as many mid-range hotels if you stay for one week or more. They're also a godsend for those who like to actually get a sense of what it's like to live in the city they're visiting – or who simply want a sense of independence or privacy. What's more, you'll save money on food if you cook for yourself on some nights.

Apartment-rental agencies save you the hassle of contractual negotiations or guarantees that you'd encounter if you were to rent an apartment independently, and include a cleaning service, 24-hour assistance and free Wi-Fi. For short-term rentals all over town, the best agency to try is **Spain Select** (www.spain-select.com, 91 523 74 51), which offers a host of hand-picked, high-quality and centrally

CONSUME

15 minutes from the airport, this hotel offers good facilities for the price. The lobby is decorated with dark wooden panelling and antique furniture, while the 41 spacious rooms, arranged round a glass-roofed atrium, are clean, bright and spacious. The marble bathrooms have hydromassage baths. *Bar. Business centre. Disabled-adapted room. Gym. No-smoking floors (2). Internet (free wireless). Parking (€14.98 per day). Restaurant. Room service. TV (satellite).*

Hotel Eurobuilding
C/Padre Damián 23, Chamartín (91 353 73 00, www.nh-hoteles.com). Metro Cuzco. **Rates** €69-€134 double. **Credit** AmEx, DC, MC, V.
The very name conjures up images of blandness, but this hotel is set in an appealing residential area. Yes, it's a twin-tower giant, with 459 rooms, but for sports fans and business travellers the location is hard to beat, right near the Palacio de Congresos and Real Madrid's Estadio Bernabéu. The hotel offers a range of services including a spa and beauty salon. Apartment-size suites are available for long stays. *Bar (2). Business services. Concierge. Disabled-adapted rooms. Gym. Internet (wireless). No-smoking floors (2). Restaurant (2). Room service. Spa. TV (satellite).*

YOUTH HOSTELS

Much of Madrid's youth hostel accommodation is situated outside the city centre, within easy reach of the mountains – great if you're into walking or skiing.

Albergue Juvenil Municipal
C/Mejía Lequerica 21 (91 593 96 88, www.ajmadrid.es). Metro Bilbao or Alonso Martínez. **Rates** (incl breakfast) €19.07 per person under-25s; €20.60 over-25s. **Credit** AmEx, DC, MC, V. **Map** p324 H8 ⑥⓪
Open since 2007, this is the only council-run hostel in the city centre. Conditions are well above average and communal areas include a multimedia room with free internet access, a room full of exercise bikes, a games and TV room, and a diner.

Albergue Juvenil San Fermín
Avda de los Fueros 36, South of centre (91 792 08 97, www.san-fermin.org). Metro San Fermín/bus 23 from Plaza Mayor. **Rates** (incl breakfast) €15.15 per person; €13 under-26s. €35.35 double. *Locker* €3. *Towel* €3. **Credit** AmEx, DC, MC, V.
This great-value hostel is aimed specifically at young people and is part of a local regeneration project for the San Fermín area, which lies to the south of the city. The modern building houses clean and bright dorms as well as computer facilities, a TV room, gardens and a hall for cultural events. It is non-smoking throughout.

Barbieri International Hostel
2nd floor, C/Barbieri 15, Chueca (91 531 02 58, www.barbierihostel.com). Metro Chueca or Gran Vía. **Rates** (incl breakfast) €17-€19.50 per person. *Daytime use incl storage & facilities* €5. *Locker* €1. **Credit** MC, V. **Map** p324 I10 ⑥⓵
Right in the middle of Chueca, this hotel is popular with budget travellers of all nationalities. The double rooms and dorms for three or seven people are basic but clean, and there are kitchen facilities, a TV room with DVD player and a book exchange service. Staff are very friendly, the atmosphere relaxed and there's no curfew.

CAMPSITES

There's a fair sprinkling of campsites around Madrid and towards the Guadarrama and Gredos mountains. Most are open year-round. A full list is available from tourist offices.

Camping El Escorial
Ctra de Guadarrama a El Escorial, km 3.5 (91 890 24 12, www.campingelescorial.com). Bus 664 from Moncloa. **Rates** €6.65 per person, per car, per tent. *Electricity* €3.75. *Plots* (incl tent, car and electricity) €19-95-€25.95. **No credit cards.**
This luxury campsite, in the foothills of the Sierra de Guadarrama around 45 minutes from Madrid, is set in 40 hectares (99 acres) of grounds. There are wooden chalets (€70-€143) that accommodate five people and have heating for winter stays, as well as pitches for caravans, tents and motorhomes. Facilities are ample: four swimming pools, various sports courts (football, basketball, tennis and more), two discos, a restaurant, café-bar, launderette and supermarket, plus organised activities for children.

Camping Osuna
Avda de Logroño s/n, Northern suburbs (91 741 05 10). Metro Canillejas. **Rates** €6.90 per person, tent, car or caravan; €6 bike. *Electricity* €5.70. **No credit cards.**
This is the closest campsite to central Madrid, and the only one within reasonable distance of a metro station. Services include a supermarket, laundry facilities, a restaurant and a bar with a summer terrace that features live entertainment in the evenings.

INSIDE TRACK
CALL THE COUNCIL

A list of council-owned youth hostels in and around the city can be found on the website **www.esmadrid.com** (go to 'Services' then 'Hotels', then select 'Youth Hostels' in the 'Accommodation Guide' box). The site also has a long list of hotels.

Restaurants

Gastro bars and international influences are reinventing Madrid's gourmet scene, but suckling pig is still on the menu.

Not so long ago, it used to be that even dishes from Asturias were thought exotic here in the capital. However, the times they are a changin' and, thanks in part to immigration, these days *madrileños* have become Spain's unlikely flag-bearers for culinary globalisation. Mexican, of course, has always been around, and Asian, particularly, has become *de rigueur*. But add to this list the overwhelming popularity of Italian, French, Cuban, Middle Eastern, Thai and Japanese restaurants in town and wonder at the future of the paella.

Among the pluses of these newcomers, three advantages stick out: style, spice and vegetables. Where the dining scene used to be all red-checked tablecloths or old-style elegance, now those who fancy the chic and minimal have a place to go and look glam. If your taste buds are inclined to more nuances of spice, you can now rest easy in Madrid. And it's also good news for vegetarians, in that the options are no longer limited to tortilla, or green beans with the ham picked out.

CAPITAL MAINSTAYS

That said, this city remains a bastion of unreconstructed Spanish cuisine and what has often been described as 'brown food'. The famous *cocido madrileño* – a stew of various bits of meat, offal and vegetables served up in three courses – is still eaten religiously, particularly at weekends. The down-home *casas de comida* (eating houses) are packed daily with regulars who are perfectly happy with a plain *ensalada mixta* followed by a greasy pork chop and the ubiquitous *flan* for dessert. Even the young and cool are faithful to the less expensive classic *mesones* (old-style taverns), while the most upscale traditional places still require you to join a waiting list.

Gastro bars now alternate with temples to the most traditional *madrileño* cuisine in the area around Los Austrias and La Latina – particularly along C/Cava Baja, leading south from the Plaza Mayor. Chueca is packed with stylish restaurants offering international as well as Spanish cuisine (many of which offer great value at lunchtime).

Round these parts, one restaurant closes as another opens, but many have stood the test of time. The most upmarket restaurants, on the other hand, can be found in the Salamanca area, and particularly in the expensive business hotels around the Paseo de la Castellana.

TIMING

Rule number one for visitors to Madrid: don't go out too early. *Madrileños* rarely eat lunch before 2pm, although go after 4pm and you may find people sweeping up around you. Probably due to a combination of substantial lunches and the heat, dinner is usually eaten late as well – around 10pm, and even later in summer. It's advisable to book a table in most places for Friday and Saturday night, and at other times if you're in a big group. Many restaurants close on Sunday evening and all of Monday. August is livelier than it used to be, but most restaurants still close for at least two weeks. Where possible, we've indicated this, but it's best to ring and check.

❶ Blue numbers given here correspond to the location of each restaurant on the street maps. *See pp321-329.*

By law, restaurants are obliged to declare on the menu if VAT (IVA) is included and if there's a cover charge. In practice, however, they almost never do, and there almost always is (strictly speaking cover charges are illegal, but are often disguised as a charge for bread).

LOS AUSTRIAS & LA LATINA

La Botillería de Maxi

C/Cava Alta 4 (91 365 12 49, www.labotilleriade maxi.com). Metro La Latina. **Open** 12.30-4pm, 8.30pm-12.30am Tue-Sat; 12.30-6pm Sun. Closed last 2wks Aug. **Main courses** €7-€10. **Set lunch** €9 Tue-Fri. **No credit cards.** **Map** p327 F13 ❶ Castilian

Fashionably scruffy young waiting staff and blaring flamenco in a no-frills classic setting make for an unpretentious blend of old and new. While the *callos a la madrileña* (tripe in a spicy sauce) are acknowledged as the best in town, there's no shame in going for the *pisto manchego* (aubergine, courgette, pepper and tomato stew) with fried eggs, the partridge pâté or the *mojama* (air-dried tuna).

La Camarilla

C/Cava Baja 21 (91 354 02 07, www. lacamarillarestaurante.com). Metro La Latina. **Open** 1.30-5.30pm, 9pm-midnight Mon, Tue, Thur; 1.30-5.30pm, 9pm-1am Fri; 1pm-1am Sat; 11.30am-midnight Sun. **Main courses** €16-€20.50. **Set lunch** €11.50 Mon, Tue, Thur. **Credit** MC, V. **Map** p327 F13 ❷ Castilian

Of the many traditional restaurants on this stretch of road, La Camarilla offers the most innovative versions of Spanish home cooking: gazpacho with mango,

---

INSIDE TRACK MENU DEL DIA

While the *menú del día* is aimed at workers looking for a cheap three-course lunch, the concept also works well for hungry tourists after a morning's sightseeing. It can be a great way to eat cheaply and well, and all but the swankiest restaurants are obliged to offer one. It usually consists of a starter, main course, dessert, bread and wine. Dishes cost much less than they would do à la carte (although portions tend to be smaller) and the *menú del día* also provides a chance to sample upmarket places on a budget. Standard Spanish restaurants tend to offer typical *comida casera* (home cooking), however, so don't expect fireworks.

The *menú del día* should not be confused with the *menú degustación*, a meal featuring tasters of various dishes.

---

revuelto (scrambled egg) with mushrooms and parmesan, and tasty cod dishes. The setting is reminiscent of a genteel 1930s hotel and the staff are incredibly friendly. Creative tapas and a hearty *menú del día* are served in a relaxed front room and luxurious gourmet meals in an adjoining formal dining room.

Casa Ciriaco

C/Mayor 84 (91 548 06 20). Metro Ópera or Sol. **Open** 1-4.30pm, 8pm-12.30am Mon, Tue, Thur-Sun. Closed Aug. **Main courses** €12-€24. **Set lunch** €20 Mon, Tue, Thur, Fri. **Credit** DC, MC, V. **Map** p327 E12 ❸ Castilian

Pick your way down the side of the open kitchen to a deep dining room hung with pictures of visiting royals and celebrities, along with rather grimmer photos of the 1906 bombing of the wedding procession for Alfonso XIII and his English wife Victoria Eugenie – which happened right outside the door. Undamaged and still going strong, Casa Ciriaco was a meeting place for the intelligentsia in pre-Civil War days, and although it no longer attracts many thinkers, the Castilian fare is a taste of days gone by. *Gallina en pepitoria* (chicken in an almond and white wine sauce) is the speciality. The waiters are very friendly.

★ Casa Lucio

C/Cava Baja 35 (91 365 32 52, www.casalucio.es). Metro La Latina. **Open** 1.15-4pm, 9pm-11.30pm Mon-Fri, Sun; 9pm-midnight Sat. Closed Aug. **Main courses** €18-€25. **Credit** AmEx, DC, MC, V. **Map** p327 F13 ❹ Castilian

A restaurant unsurpassed by any other in Madrid for its famous patrons: King Juan Carlos, Bill Clinton and Penélope Cruz among them. This is the place of historical rendezvous, where Aznar and Bush's wives did lunch back when alliances were in the making. It also knows how to cook up one cracking *solomillo* (beef). The key to Lucio's glory is the use of a coal-fired oven and the best olive oil. Another star dish is a starter of lightly fried eggs laid on top of a bed of crisp, thinly cut chips – the King always orders it. Be sure to ask for a table on the first floor. *Photo p137.*

★ Casa Marta

C/Santa Clara 10 (91 548 28 25, www. restaurantecasamarta.com). Metro Ópera. **Open** 1.30-4pm Mon; 1.30-4pm, 9pm-midnight Tue-Sat. Closed Aug. **Main courses** €9-€15. **Set lunch** €10.50 Mon-Fri. **Credit** AmEx, DC, MC, V. **Map** p327 F11 ❺ Castilian

Every Saturday, according to the novel, Don Quixote ate *duelos y quebrantes* (scrambled eggs, ham, bacon, chorizo and brains) and you can still try them at Casa Marta – although they usually leave out the brains these days. A quaint old place, it's been a favourite since the beginning of the 20th century, when operagoers and singers would stop in for a tipple after performances. The satisfying *platos de cuchara* ('spoon food') – warming bowls of *cocido*, beans and lentils – are another star turn that always pulls in the crowds.

CONSUME

Toilet Humour

Which door's which?

It's a nerve-racking choice. S or C? A-ha, you say, S must be *señor*! The men's room! Well, no. S is in fact '*señora*', and C, '*caballero*', meaning gentleman. But what if you see C and D? Who is the D? That would be '*dama*', meaning 'lady'. It's not always so simple. Many bars and restaurants in Madrid seem to have spent hours dreaming up original ways to designate their lavatory doors.

Stromboli (C/Hortaleza 96), for example, has abridged the words *chicos* (boys) and *chicas* (girls), labelling the doors simply 'OS' and 'AS'. That one has even the natives scratching their heads (or should that be scratching their 'ads'?). In cases such as these, it's important to know that words ending in O are male, and words ending in A are female. In **Alqamara** on C/Espíritu Santo it's useful to know that the bar is run by lesbians, hence '*Vosotros*' (meaning 'you', masculine plural), and '*Nosotras*' (meaning 'us', feminine plural).

Then there are those that opt for pictures or symbols. Much simpler, you'd think – well, no. Take **Jellyfish Café** on C/Pelayo. There, a fish tail means men's and a jellyfish means women's. Or then there's **Olsen** (*see p143*), where the Nordic theme extends to the lavs, with a wooden stag representing the gents' (*pictured*) and an antlerless deer for the ladies'. **La Soberbia** on C/Espoz y Mina keeps it nice and Spanish with a small version of roadside Osborne sherry bulls for the men. Easy. The ladies' version is exactly the same

as the men's, just painted with a Friesian pattern and with a pink udder attached.

Then there's the really obvious. At **Matador** on C/Cruz you will see a graphic pencil drawing of a staggeringly ugly pair of male and female genitals. But however confusing these pictorial or textual signs may be, they're still infinitely preferable to the labelling chosen by **La Ida** (*see p180*), where the absence of anything written on either door makes for an entertaining toilet roulette.

CONSUME

Emma y Júlia

C/Cava Baja 19 (91 366 10 23). Metro La Latina. **Open** 8pm-midnight Tue; 2-4pm, 8pm-midnight Wed-Thur; 2-4pm, 8pm-1am Fri, Sat; 2-5pm, 9-11.30pm Sun. Closed July. **Main courses** €9.50-€14. **Credit** AmEx, DC, MC, V. **Map** p327 F13 ❻ **Italian**

Smack in the middle of a street flanked with traditional restaurants and gourmet tapas bars is this incongruous and popular Italian eaterie – a sound option when a big salad and pizza are in order. The staff are friendly, the environment laid-back, and the food solid. The breaded artichokes are divine and the house red is good and cheap. It's often wise to reserve in advance.

▶ *Marechiaro (see p134) is another excellent restaurant for pizza, as is Pizzeria Cervantes (see p145).*

El Estragón

Costanilla de San Andrés 10, Plaza de la Paja (91 365 89 82, www.elestragonvegetariano.com). Metro La Latina. **Open** 1.30-4.15pm, 8-11.45pm Mon-Thur, Sun; 1.30-4.15pm, 8pm-12.45am Fri, Sat. **Main courses** €12-€18. **Set lunch** €14 Mon-Fri. **Credit** AmEx, DC, MC, V. **Map** p327 E13 ❼ **Vegetarian**

El Estragón's underlying concept appears to be 'vegetarian food for meat-eaters', and thus there is no shortage of soya 'meatballs', 'hamburgers' and so on. Where this place really excels, however, is in its straightforward vegetarian dishes, such as a fabulous towering heap of *risotto verde* containing every green vegetable you can think of, topped with stringy Emmental. It's a delightful spot, with terracotta tiles, blue-and-white gingham and views over Plaza de la Paja, on which tables are set in summer.

Menu Glossary

A guide to some of the key words you'll find on a menu.

Basics

Primer plato (**entrante**) first course; **segundo plato** second or main course; **postre** dessert; **plato combinado** quick, one-course meal, with several ingredients served on the same plate; **aceite y vinagre** oil and vinegar; **agua** water (**con gas/sin gas** fizzy/ still); **pan** bread; **vino** wine (**tinto** red, **blanco** white, **rosado** rosé); **cerveza** beer; **la cuenta** the bill; **servicio incluído** service included; **propina** tip.

Cooking styles & techniques

Adobado marinated; **al ajillo** with olive oil and garlic; **al chilindrón** (usually chicken or lamb) cooked in a spicy tomato, pepper, ham, onion and garlic sauce; **a la marinera** (fish or shellfish) cooked with garlic, onions and white wine; **a la parilla** charcoal-grilled; **al pil-pil** (Basque) flash-fried in sizzling oil and garlic; **a la plancha** grilled directly on a hot metal plate; **al vapor** steamed; **asado** (**al horno de leña**) roast (in a wood oven); **crudo** raw; **en salsa** in a sauce or gravy; **escabechado, en escabeche** marinated in vinegar with bay leaves and garlic; **estofado** braised; **frito** fried; **guisado** stewed; **hervido** boiled; (**en**) **pepitoria** casserole dish, usually of chicken or game, with egg, wine and almonds; **relleno** stuffed.

Sopas y potajes (soups & stews)

Caldo (**gallego**) broth of pork and greens; **fabada** rich Asturian stew of beans, chorizo and *morcilla* (black blood sausage); **gazpacho** cold soup, usually of tomatoes, red pepper and cucumber; **purrusalda** (Basque) soup of salt cod, leeks and potatoes; **sopa de ajo** garlic soup; **sopa castellana** garlic soup with

poached egg and chickpeas; **sopa de fideos** noodle soup.

Huevos (eggs)

Huevos fritos fried eggs (sometimes served with chorizo); **revuelto** scrambled eggs; **tortilla asturiana** omelette with tomato, tuna and onion; **tortilla francesa** plain omelette; **tortilla de patatas** Spanish potato omelette.

Pescado y mariscos (fish & shellfish)

Almejas clams; **atún, bonito** tuna; **bacalao** salt cod; **besugo** sea bream; **bogavante** lobster; **caballa** mackerel; **calamares** squid; **camarones** small shrimps; **cangrejo, buey de mar** crab; **cangrejo de río** freshwater crayfish; **dorada** gilthead bream; **gambas** prawns; **kokotxas** (Basque) hake cheeks; **langosta** spiny lobster; **langostinos** langoustines; **lubina** sea bass; **mejillones** mussels; **mero** grouper; **merluza** hake; **ostras** oysters; **pescadilla** whiting; **pescaditos** whitebait; **pulpo** octopus; **rape** monkfish; **rodaballo** turbot; **salmonete** red mullet; **sardinas** sardines; **sepia** cuttlefish; **trucha** trout; **ventresca de bonito** tuna fillet; **vieiras** scallops.

Carne, aves, caza y embutidos (meat, poultry, game & charcuterie)

Bistec steak; **buey, vacuno** (cuts **solomillo, entrecot**) beef; **butifarra** Catalan sausage; **callos** tripe; **capón** capon; **cerdo** pork, pig; **chorizo** spicy sausage, served cooked or cold; **choto** kid; **chuletas, chuletones, chuletillas** chops; **cochinillo** roast suckling pig; **cocido** traditional stew of Madrid;

Julián de Tolosa

C/Cava Baja 18 (91 365 82 10, www.casajuliandetolosa.com). Metro La Latina. **Open** 1.30-4pm, 9pm-midnight Mon-Sat; 1.30-4pm Sun. **Main courses** €20-€30. **Credit** AmEx, DC, MC, V. **Map** p327 F13 ⑧
Basque
Probably the most modern restaurant in the *barrio*, this upscale Basque establishment is all smooth wood, glass and brick, housed in a 19th-century building. With a very limited, simple menu, the main attraction here is the grilled steak (*chuletón de buey*), a contender for the city's best. Try the smoky idiazábal sheep's cheese, a speciality from the little

Basque town of the same name. The maître d' will steer you through an excellent selection of more than a hundred wines.

★ Marechiaro

C/Conde de Lemos 3 (91 547 00 42). Metro Ópera. **Open** 9pm-midnight Mon; noon-4.30pm, 9pm-1am Tue-Sat. Closed 2wks Aug. **Main courses** €10-€15. **Set lunch** €12. **Credit** AmEx, DC, MC, V. **Map** p327 F11 ⑨
Italian
It's a standard definition of pizza worth, but it still holds up: you know a pizzeria is good when it attracts this many Italians. Two Neapolitans are

codillo knuckle (normally ham); **codornices** quails; **conejo** rabbit; **cordero** lamb; **costillas** ribs; **estofado de ternera** beef stew; **faisán** pheasant; **gallina** chicken; **hígado** liver; **jabalí** wild boar; **jamón ibérico** cured ham from Iberian pigs; **jamón serrano** cured ham; **jamón york** cooked ham; **lacón** gammon ham; **lechazo, cordero lechal** milk-fed baby lamb; **liebre** hare; **lomo (de cerdo)** loin of pork; **morcilla** black blood sausage; **pato** duck; **pavo** turkey; **perdiz** partridge; **pollo** chicken; **riñones** kidneys; **salchichas** frying sausages; **sesos** brains; **ternera** veal (in Spain it is slaughtered much later than most veal, so is more accurately young beef).

Arroz y legumbres (rice & pulses)
Alubias, judías white beans; **arroz a banda** rice cooked in shellfish stock; **arroz negro** black rice cooked in squid ink; **fideuà** seafood dish similar to a paella, but made with noodles instead of rice; **fríjoles** red kidney beans; **garbanzos** chickpeas; **judiones** large haricot beans; **lentejas** lentils; **pochas (caparrones)** new-season kidney beans.

Verduras (vegetables)
Acelgas Swiss chard; **alcachofas** artichokes; **berenjena** aubergine/eggplant; **calabacines** courgettes/zucchini; **cebolla** onion; **champiñones** mushrooms; **col** cabbage; **ensalada mixta** basic salad of lettuce, tomato and onion; **ensalada verde** green salad, without tomato; **espárragos** asparagus; **espinacas** spinach; **grelos** turnip leaves; **guisantes** peas; **habas** broad beans; **judías verdes** green beans; **lechuga** lettuce; **menestra** braised mixed vegetables; **patatas fritas** chips; **pepino** cucumber; **pimientos** sweet peppers; **pimientos de piquillo** slightly hot red peppers; **pisto** mixture of cooked vegetables, similar to ratatouille; **setas** oyster mushrooms; **tomate** tomato; **zanahoria** carrot.

Fruta (fruit)
Arándanos cranberries, blueberries, redcurrants or blackcurrants; **cerezas** cherries; **ciruelas** plums; **fresas** strawberries; **higos** figs; **macedonia** fruit salad; **manzana** apple; **melocotón** peach; **melón** melon; **moras** blackberries; **naranja** orange; **pera** pear; **piña** pineapple; **plátano** banana; **sandía** watermelon; **uvas** grapes.

Postres (desserts)
Arroz con leche rice pudding; **bizcocho** sponge cake; **brazo de gitano** swiss roll; **cuajada** junket (served with honey); **flan** crème caramel; **helado** ice-cream; **leche frita** custard fried in breadcrumbs; **membrillo** quince jelly (often served with cheese); **tarta** cake; **tarta de Santiago** sponge-like almond cake; **torrijas** sweet bread fritters.

Quesos (cheeses)
Burgos, villalón, requesón white, cottage-like cheeses, often eaten as dessert; **cabrales** strong blue Asturian goat's cheese; **idiazábal** Basque sheep's milk cheese; **mahón** cow's milk cheese from Menorca; **manchego (tierno, añejo, semi, seco)** hard sheep's-milk cheese (young, mature, semi-soft, dry); **tetilla** soft cow's milk cheese; **torta del casar** tangy sheep's milk cheese from Extremadura.

CONSUME

behind this modest little restaurant that provides some of the best pizzas in the city. Cooked in wood-fired ovens, they have thin, flavourful crusts and fresh ingredients. Pastas are good too, but they definitely play second fiddle. Decor is pungent-orange walls sporting a mix of Venetian masks and old photos of Maradona.

▶ *Emma y Júlia (see p133) is also good for pizza.*

La Musa Latina
Costanilla San Andrés 12 (91 354 02 55, www.lamusalatina.com). Metro La Latina. **Open** noon-midnight Mon-Thur; noon-2pm Fri; 1pm-2am Sat; 1pm-1am Sun. **Main courses** €6.50-€16. **Set lunch** €8-€11 Mon-Fri. **Credit** MC, DC, V. **Map** p327 E13 ❿ Global
A laid-back vibe, tasty tapas and stir-fries, and a great location on the Plaza de la Paja all contribute towards making La Musa Latina into a tempting package. Try the fried green tomatoes and the prawn tempura with avocado. There are plenty of indulgent desserts – go for the chocolate brownie or the *dulce de leche* pannacotta. Waiters are supercool but friendly, and the diners well-heeled and hip (note the Junk Club downstairs). There is a sister restaurant in Malasaña, but this one is roomier.
Other location La Musa, C/Manuela Malasaña 18 (91 448 75 58).

YOU KNOW WHO YOU ARE.

MADRID • PASEO DE LA CASTELLANA 2
+34-91-436-43-40 • HARDROCK.COM

Hard Rock
CAFE

Casa Lucio. *See p132.*

CONSUME

★ El Sobrino de Botín

*C/Cuchilleros 17 (91 366 42 17, 91 366 30 26,
www.botin.es). Metro Sol.* **Open** 1-4pm, 8pm-
midnight daily. **Main courses** €10-€30. **Set
meal** €39.40. **Credit** AmEx, DC, MC, V.
Map p327 F12 ⑪ **Castilian**
The world's oldest restaurant is still coming up with
the goods after nearly 300 years. For all its popularity as a tourist destination, its nooks and crannies add
up to an atmospheric – if cramped – dining spot over
several floors. Ask for a table in the vaulted cellar for
the full effect. Order the suckling pig or the lamb,
which are roasted in a huge wood-fired oven. And,
yes, seeing as you asked, Hemingway did come here.

La Taberna del Alabardero

*C/Felipe V 6 (91 547 25 77, www.alabardero.eu).
Metro Ópera.* **Open** 1-4pm, 9pm-midnight daily.
Main courses €15-€50. **Set lunch** €32.10
daily. **Credit** AmEx, DC, MC, V. **Map** p327 F11
⑫ **Basque**
Father Lezama first started up his traditional tavern in 1974, when he put underprivileged boys to
work as waiters in this converted 16th-century townhouse. With a quiet *terraza* on the street that runs
along the north side of the Teatro Real, it is still one
of the most popular post-theatre dining spots, serving traditional tapas at the bar and Basque cuisine
in the restaurant in the back. Lezama is now a very
prosperous restaurateur – he has opened six more
restaurants in Spain and one in Washington, DC.
Some of those original boys are now shareholders.

Taberna Salamanca

*C/Cava Baja 31 (91 366 31 10). Metro La
Latina.* **Open** 1-4pm, 8.30pm-midnight Tue-Thur;
1-4pm, 8.30pm-1am Fri, Sat; 1-4.30pm Sun. Closed

mid July-mid Aug. **Main courses** €7-€15. **Set
lunch** €9.50 Tue-Sun. **No credit cards**. **Map**
p327 F13 ⑬ **Castilian**
On a street crammed with high-priced eateries, this
is where the cool, young, and more frugal set comes
to eat. There are three lunch *menús* to choose from,
offering the usual Spanish pickings – the *croquetas*,
courgette tortilla and endives with roquefort cheese
are all pretty dependable. The staff are friendly and
young, with a tendency to whack up the stereo.

Vadebaco

*C/Campomanes 6 (680 132 538,
www.vadebaco.com). Metro Ópera.* **Open**
noon-4.30pm, 6pm-midnight Mon-Sat; noon-
4.30pm Sun. **Main courses** €9-€18. **Set
lunch** €12. **Credit** AmEx, MC, V. **Map** p327
F11 ⑭ **Modern Spanish**
With more than 350 wines – and at least 40 by the
glass – you'll probably spend longer choosing what
to drink than what to eat at Vadebaco. The wall as
you enter is a huge blackboard listing just some of
the food and wine on offer, giving you an idea of what
to expect in the supercool space. Share a few things
to get the best experiece: maybe slices of cured beef
from León, a really excellent tortilla, lamb meatballs
or oyster mushroom ravioli. Stick around after dinner for a cocktail too. The set lunch is great value.

El Viajero

*Plaza de la Cebada 11 (91 366 90 64).
Metro La Latina.* **Open** 2-4.30pm, 9pm-12.30am
Tue-Thur; 2-4.30pm, 9pm-1am Fri, Sat; 2-4.30pm
Sun. Closed 3wks Jan & last 2wks Aug. **Main
courses** €7-€18. **Set lunch** €12 Tue-Fri.
Credit AmEx, DC, MC, V. **Map** p327 F13 ⑮
Mediterranean

MERCADO DE LA REINA

C/Gran Via 12 (91 521 31 98)
Metro Gran Via.

Open 9am-midnight.
Fri & Sat: 9am-2am. Sun: 10am-midnight.
www.mercadodelareina.es

Packed with trendy *Madrileños*, Mercado de la Reina is the brainchild of three friends who successfully created one of the new "all day kitchens" – open from breakfast to late night drinking. The food is a mix of traditional and new cuisines and is based around the market concept: all fresh ingredients, constantly changing menus, and *puesto* with different foods – the butcher's stall, the fishmonger's stall etc.

Mercado a Reina is also a place to go to for delicious tapas, with a nice red from the impressive wine list. The cosmopolitan crowd sits around the bar and eats imaginative pinchos, chatting loudly with traditional *Madrileño* boisterousness.

As the hours pass, the Gin Club – the third element of the Mercado de la Reina – comes into its own. Gin Tonic is a particular favourite in the Spanish capital, and in this cosy space you can find the best one in town, choosing from over 30 varieties of gin to go with your tonic, ice and citrus oil.

_a Latina scenesters in sideburns and retro couture still flock to this three-storey bar/restaurant famous for its rooftop *terraza*. The food, a mixed array of Mediterranean dishes and barbecued meats, is delicious, if a little expensive. The carpaccios are melt-in-the-mouth and the pastas, particularly the *taglioni marinera*, drip with flavour. Discriminating carnivores love El Viajero for the high-quality, hormone-free Argentine meat, while sweet-tooths rejoice over the scrumptious tiramisu. *Photo p140.*

Viuda de Vacas

C/Águila 2 (91 366 58 47). Metro La Latina. **Open** 1.30-5pm, 9pm-1am Mon-Wed, Fri, Sat; 1.30-4.30pm Sun. Closed July. **Main courses** €9-€16. **Credit** MC, V. **Map** p327 F13 ⑯ **Castilian**

Viuda de Vacas has moved from its location on Cava Alta, where Pedro Almodóvar has filmed on several occasions, but the unpretentious authenticity has survived just about intact at its new home nearby. Classic Castilian home cooking has been in the Canova family for three generations; it was established by the feisty grandmother (the widow of Señor Vacas). Favourite dishes include the stuffed courgettes and the baked hake or sea bream.

Xentes

C/Humilladero 13 (91 366 42 66). Metro La Latina. **Open** 2-5pm, 9pm-midnight Tue-Sat; 12.30-5pm Sun. Closed Aug. **Main courses** €6-€25. **Credit** AmEx, DC, MC, V. **Map** p327 F14 ⑰ **Galician**

With the TV blaring and some half-hearted nautical decor, this is a rather strange setting for some of the best seafood in Madrid. But the Galician patrons at the bar happily gulp down oysters and beer, and the diners in the back are just as delighted with their *pulpo a gallega* (octopus with paprika) and *arroz con bogavantes* (lobster paella). Well worth seeking out.

SOL & GRAN VÍA

19 Sushi Bar

Salud 19 (91 524 05 71, www.19sushibar.com). Metro Gran Vía. **Open** 1.30-4pm, 8-11.30pm Mon-Thur; 1.30-4pm, 8.30pm-midnight Fri; 8.30pm-midnight Sat. Closed 2 wks Aug. **Main courses** €6.90-€18.60. **Set lunch** €14.85-€24.75. **Credit** DC, MC, V. **Map** p323 H11 ⑱ **Japanese**

Going strong since 2005, 19 Sushi Bar is a favourite among aficionados of Japanese cuisine. The Kobe beef sashimi, tuna fillet with wasabi and the king prawn tempura roll are just three of the star dishes. Just off the Gran Vía, the decor is typically cool and minimalist, but at least there's nothing on display to distract you from the food.

▶ *Nodo (see p153) also has its supporters in the contest for best sushi in Madrid.*

La Bola Taberna

C/Bola 5 (91 547 69 30, www.labola.es). Metro Ópera or Santo Domingo. **Open** 1-4pm, 8.30-11pm Mon-Sat; 1-4pm Sun. Closed Aug. **Main courses** €12-€23. **Set meal** €24.80. **Credit** MC, V. **Map** p323 F11 ⑲ **Castilian**

Holding court on a quiet backstreet, this dignified, classic Madrid restaurant is considered by many to be the home of *cocido*, the huge and hearty stew beloved of *madrileños* and a test for the biggest of appetites. La Bola is still run by the same family that founded it in the 19th century, and the *cocido* (which is only served at lunchtime) is still cooked traditionally in earthenware pots on a wood fire. Unfortunately, this impressive pedigree has led to a certain complacency in some of the waiting staff.

Caripén

Plaza de la Marina Española 4 (91 541 11 77). Metro Santo Domingo. **Open** 9pm-2am Mon-Sat. Closed Aug. **Main courses** €12-€35. **Credit** DC, MC, V. **Map** p323 E11 ⑳ **French**

At first glance, this French bistro seems a wee bit run down, but nonetheless it's all class – in a campy, Broadway kind of way. Behind the dangling blue Christmas-tree lights are tables occupied by singing, dancing, canoodling patrons having a very good time, oblivious to the excellent skate in black butter or crêpe with salmon and caviar. The merry atmosphere owes a lot to the staff, particularly Juanjo, who floats through the restaurant spreading his charm.

Delfos

Cuesta de Santo Domingo 14 (91 548 37 64). Metro Santo Domingo. **Open** 1.30-4.30pm, 8.30pm-midnight Tue-Sat; 1.30-4.30pm Sun. **Main courses** €9-€18. **Set lunch** €10.95 Tue-Fri. **Credit** AmEx, DC, MC, V. **Map** p323 F11 ㉑ **Greek**

Delfos is here to prove that Greek food is not all kebabs and salads. In taverna-style surroundings, with just-on-the-right-side-of-tacky Greek details, friendly waiters serve up an unexpected variety of dishes. A good start is the *pikilia megali*, a platter of garlicky Greek olives, rich fried feta cheese, refreshing tsatsiki, lemony taramasalata, stuffed vine leaves and more. The moussaka and lamb with nut and honey are also scrumptious.

Don Paco

C/Caballero de Gracia 36 (91 531 44 80). Metro Gran Vía. **Open** 1.30-4pm, 8-11pm Mon-Fri; 1.30-4pm Sat. Closed Aug. **Main courses** €9-€12. **Set lunch** €13 Mon-Sat. **Set dinner** €35 Tue-Fri. **Credit** MC, V. **Map** p324 I11 ㉒ **Andalucían**

Don Paco, now in his 80s, is a former bullfighter from Jérez, and the Andalucían matador in him is charmingly apparent in his 45-year-old restaurant. With photos of famous visitors (the King and his parents were regulars) and Andalucían memorabilia

CONSUME

covering the walls, it oozes southern style. *Tinto de verano* ('summer wine' cut with lemonade) on tap, ample sherry options… who needs Seville? Don't miss the *tortillitas de camarones* (shrimp fritters).

Gula Gula

Gran Vía 1 (91 522 87 64, www.gulagula.net). Metro Banco de España or Sevilla. **Open** 1-4.30pm, 8.30-midnight daily. **Lunch buffet** €9-€12. **Dinner buffet** €25-€30. **Credit** AmEx, DC, MC, V. **Map** p324 I11 ㉓ **International**

Prepare yourself for muscled waiters in scant clothing, singing drag queens and bawdy humour – this is Gula Gula (Greedy Greedy). It's all about the show, darling, less about the food, but even that isn't half-bad. Most people skip the hot dishes (though they have shown some moments of inspiration lately) and stick to the all-you-can-eat salad buffet, which is fair to middling. But what's truly inspiring here are the tiny leather shorts worn by the waiters.

Taj

C/Marqués de Cubas 6 (91 531 50 59, www.restaurantetaj.com). Metro Banco de España. **Open** 1-4pm, 8.30-11.30pm Mon-Thur; 1-4pm, 8.30pm-midnight Fri-Sun. **Main courses** €7.95-€16.50. **Set lunch** €10.95 Mon-Fri. **Credit** AmEx, DC, MC, V. **Map** p328 I11 ㉔ **Indian**

Everything about Taj promises serious curry – from the jingly-jangly muzak to the fanned linen napkins and plastic flowers. The menu includes all the usuals, but the *degustación* of samosa, pakora, tandoori chicken, lamb curry, pilau and naan is a good bet. Try to get the curries *picante* (hot), though the waiters may decide that that can't be what you really mean and give you *medio* anyway. Desserts are a bit limited and the decor slightly naff, which is curiously reassuring.

La Terraza del Casino

C/Alcalá 15 (91 532 12 75, www.casinodemadrid.es). Metro Sevilla. **Open** 1.30-4pm, 9-11.45pm Mon-Fri; 9-11.45pm Sat. Closed Aug. **Main courses** €28-€40. **Credit** AmEx, V. **Map** p328 H11 ㉕ **Nueva cocina**

The sumptuous environs of this gentlemen's club provide the setting for a restaurant inspired and partly overseen by gourmet god Ferran Adrià. Paco Roncero, a former disciple, is at the helm in the kitchen, and has put his own stamp on the cooking, winning two Michelin stars along the way. The tasting menu changes seasonally, but might include such delights as lobster sashimi, crunchy black algae or false popcorn. *See also right* **New Kids on the Block**.

HUERTAS & SANTA ANA

Arrocería Champagnería Gala

C/Moratín 22 (91 429 25 62, www.arroceriagala.hostoi.com). Metro Antón Martín. **Open** 1-4pm, 8.30-10.30pm Tue-Thur; 1.30-3.30pm, 8.30-11pm Fri-Sun. **Main courses** €15-€25. **No credit cards**. **Map** p328 I13 ㉖ **Paella**

This garden atrium, dripping in ivy and gaudy chandeliers, is a festive place to stick your fork in one of 28 varieties of paella. But it's the *porrón* – a long-spouted jug from which you pour a stream of wine down your throat – that makes this really fun: everyone must try their turn at this subtle art. The Champagnería Gala has ever so slightly

El Viajero. *See p137.*

CONSUME

New Kids on the Block

Nueva cocina continues to make waves in the capital.

When Jake and Brett are about to part ways in Madrid, at the end of Hemingway's *The Sun Also Rises*, what do they do? Go eat suckling pig and drink three bottles of Rioja at the world's oldest restaurant, **El Sobrino de Botín** (*see p137*), more commonly known as Botín. Back in the late 19th century, when King Alfonso XII's sister needed a break from the palace, she would wander over to **La Bola Taberna** (*see p139*) to get a bowl full of her favourite dish – a gutsy *cocido madrileño*. Every Saturday Don Quixote would tuck into a plate of *duelos y quebrantes* – a mess of scrambled eggs, ham, chorizo, brains and tripe – at **Casa Marta** (*see p132*).

Cocido, suckling pig and offal. This is Madrid's culinary history and, happily, her culinary present. The pig and Rioja at Botín are still great, despite the crowds of tourists and the demise of Lady Brett and Jake. The *cocido* is still eaten regularly at La Bola, though the Infanta has long gone. And Antonio Roiloa, the owner of Casa Marta, is still proud to serve Quixote's Saturday dish, though he often takes the brains out to appease more delicate tastebuds. These heavy dishes are as much Madrid as the Prado and Plaza Mayor.

So what does Madrid's ardent traditionalism mean for *nueva cocina*, the new wave of experimental cooking blowing this way from the Basque Country and the Catalan coast? Spearheaded by Catalan culinary legend Ferran Adrià, *nueva cocina* is renowned for its fantastical repertoire of edible foams, air and hot jellies, improbable pairings of flavour, and twists of texture and temperature. Can this surrealist revolution of food as we know it make any sense in a city in which the

hearty stew continues to reign supreme? Paco Roncero, a *madrileño* and one of Spain's finest chefs, thinks so. Roncero, the man behind the Michelin-starred **La Terraza del Casino** (*see p140*), is one of the ambassadors of *nueva cocina* in the capital. Adrià actually oversees the restaurant, with himself and Roncero working in tandem to concoct whimsical creations like a 'lollipop' parmesan wafer, and barnacles in aspic with tea.

Things were slow to take off and Madrid was reluctant to embrace these Catalan culinary imports. But Roncero is seeing an attitude shift: *madrileños* are showing curiosity, he says, and they come to the restaurant already knowing about the famous foams and strange textures and wanting to journey through the *menú de degustación* – an array of the team's best inventions.

One of Roncero's specialities lies in reinventing the traditional dishes. Take his *croquetas de jamón* (ham croquettes) – quivering globes of exquisitely tasty liquified ham, coated in fine breadcrumbs, that explode in the mouth. *Madrileños* love them. They're not so much croquettes as the essence of them, in much the same way that Miró isn't exactly painting a bird, but its essence. The *cocido*, however, remains untouched: he explains, speaking with quiet reverence, that it is one dish he is not quite ready to take on. 'That one is still too difficult,' he says, 'but maybe in the future.'

'We must always have respect for our traditional cooking,' insists Roncero. 'Leaving it behind is like leaving behind a part of who we are. But that doesn't mean we can't have fun with new things.'

become a victim of its own success, however, and the quality of the food has diminished in recent years as the number of tourists has grown.

Artemisa

C/Ventura de la Vega 4 (91 429 50 92, www.restauranteartesmisa.com). Metro Sevilla. **Open** 1.30-4pm, 9pm-midnight daily. **Main courses** €8.75-€15.65. **Set lunch** €10.50 Mon-Fri. **Credit** AmEx, DC, MC, V. **Map** p328 H/I12 **㉗ Vegetarian**

With the nondescript decor so typical of Madrid's vegetarian restaurants, Artemisa might seem no

different from the rest. But the salads are bigger and more creative, and the soy burgers have more flavour. The satisfying *menú de degustación* lets you try it all: veggie paella, *croquetas*, aubergine salad and more. They also have a few non-veggie options, such as the (organic) chicken Armagnac.

Other location: C/Tres Cruces 4, Sol & Gran Vía (91 521 87 21).

★ El Cenador del Prado

C/Prado 4 (91 429 15 61, www.elcenador delprado.com). Metro Antón Martín. **Open** 1.30-4pm, 9pm-midnight Mon-Fri; 9pm-midnight Sat;

CONSUME

1.30-4pm Sun. Closed 1wk Aug. **Main courses** €14.50-€19.50. **Set meal** €15-€51 Mon-Thur; lunch Fri, Sat. **Credit** AmEx, DC, MC, V. **Map** p328 H12 ❷ **Castilian/Nueva cocina**
Don't let the design extravagance – fuschia walls, explosive murals of fruit and gilt mirrors – distract you from the Herranz brothers' culinary talents: tasty Spanish cuisine with imaginative twists. Several decadent *menús de degustación*, one for vegetarians, offer good value. The *patatas a la importancia* (potatoes fried in garlic, parsley and clam sauce) are superlative, and the wine list is good and well priced. Dishes are artistically prepared and some are veritable sculptures.

★ Come Prima
C/Echegaray 27 (91 420 30 42). Metro Antón Martín. **Open** 9pm-midnight Mon; 1.30-4pm, 9pm-midnight Tue-Sat. Closed 3wks Aug. **Main courses** €15-€30. **Set lunch** €12-€15 Tue-Fri. **Credit** AmEx, DC, MC, V. **Map** p328 H12 ❷ **Italian**
The toothsome risottos and own-made pastas here are a godsend for Italian gastronomes. Don't miss the risotto with mushrooms, parmesan and white-truffle oil, or the perfectly executed pasta with lobster. Since it opened a few years ago, Come Prima has brought in a classy crew of Spaniards, who pack the place out every night, even on a Monday. With white curtains and tablecloths, green wood-panelled walls and Italian opera posters, you could almost be in the Tuscan countryside.

Lhardy
Carrera de San Jerónimo 8 (91 521 33 85, www.lhardy.com). Metro Sol. **Open** 1-3.30pm, 8.30-11pm Mon-Sat; 1-3.30pm Sun. Closed Aug. **Main courses** €28-€40.50. **Credit** AmEx, DC, MC, V. **Map** p327 H11 ❸ **Castilian/French**
This landmark restaurant, which opened in 1839, is credited with having introduced French haute cuisine into the culinary wilderness of Madrid. Founder Emile Lhardy is said to have been enticed to the city by none other than *Carmen* author Prosper Mérimée, who told him there was no decent restaurant in the Spanish capital. These days, it's rated as much for its history and belle-époque decor as for the food. The menu is as Frenchified as ever, although there's also a very refined *cocido*, good game and *callos* (tripe), in addition to an excellent, if pricey, wine list.
▶ *Lhardy has a permanent takeaway branch at upmarket food market El Mercado de San Miguel (see p200 and pp162-163 Profile).*

Midnight Rose
Hotel ME Madrid, Plaza Santa Ana 14 (91 701 60 20, www.memadrid.com/MidnightRose.html). Metro Sol or Sevilla. **Open** 1-4pm, 9pm-12.30am daily. **Main courses** €12-€25. **Set lunch** €15. **Credit** AmEx, DC, MC, V. **Map** p328 H12 ❹ **Fusion**

With shimmering scarlet lamps and shimmying gorgeous staff, Midnight Rose is fashionista heaven. The restaurant is located on the ground floor of the ultrahip ME hotel and if there isn't a famous face dining at the next table, you should ask for your money back. And the food? Surprisingly good, in a sort of Mediterranean-Asian fusion way. It's good value at lunchtime too.

★ Olsen
C/Prado 15 (91 429 36 59, www.olsenmadrid.com). Metro Antón Martín or Sevilla. **Open** 1-5pm, 8pm-2am Mon-Thur, Sun; 1-5pm, 8pm-2.30am Fri, Sat. **Main courses** €14-€17. **Set lunch** €10 or €15 Mon-Fri. **Credit** AmEx, MC, DC, V. **Map** p328 I12 ❸ **Scandinavian**
Olsen is a hugely successful, if rather strange sounding, Argentinian-run but Scandinavian-flavoured restaurant and vodka bar. The decor is all moulded beech and curiously hip snow scenes. Somehow it all serves to throw into sharper relief a selection of the freshest food ideas around. Especially good are the hot corn blinis served with dishes of caviar, sour cream, smoked salmon and shredded wild trout, while the selection of Nordic canapés paired with shots of various vodkas comes a close second. Bread is also excellent. *Photo p145.*

Le Petit Bistrot
Plaza Matute 5 (91 429 62 65, www.lepetitbistrot.net). Metro Antón Martín. **Open** 1.15-4pm, 9.15-11.30pm Tue-Sat. Closed 2wks Aug. **Main courses** €13.70-€21.50. **Set lunch** €13.50 Mon-Fri. **Credit** AmEx, MC, V. **Map** p328 H12/13 ❸ **French**
A cosy corner of traditional France tucked away in the capital of Spain, with bare-bricked walls, yellow paintwork and a roll-call of dishes that verges on the parodic: deep-fried brie; garlicky snails, coquilles St Jacques, Châteaubriand and so on. The Gallic desserts do not disappoint either, and this may be the only place where you can get decent tarte tatin or profiteroles in the city. On Sundays the vibe is a lazy one, with many people settling down to a protracted brunch involving pastries, eggs and a copy of *Le Monde*.
Other locations C/Ponzano 60, Chamberí (91 399 04 51); C/Príncipe de Vergara 210, Salamanca (91 411 29 21).

INSIDE TRACK
SMOKE SIGNAL

Madrid's anti-smoking laws require bars and restaurants over 100sq m to have separate non-smoking areas; larger venues have (mostly) complied, but many smaller affairs are still as smoky as ever.

CONSUME

Pizzeria Cervantes

C/León 8 (91 420 12 98). Metro Antón Martín.
Open 9am-1pm Mon, Wed-Sun; 6pm-1am Tue.
Closed 2wks July. **Main courses** €8.50-€18. **Set
lunch** €10 Mon-Fri. **Credit** AmEx, DC, MC, V.
Map p328 I12 **③** **Italian**
Despite the name, this place exceeds the definition
of pizzeria, with a long list of salads, crêpes, risottos
and standard fare such as roast beef and *solomillo*.
The neighbourhood regulars are fans of the cheap
breakfast deal and love to linger over *café con leche*
and the papers.

La Vaca Verónica

*C/Moratín 38 (91 429 78 27, www.lavaca
veronica.es). Metro Antón Martín.* **Open** 1-
4.30pm, 8.30pm-12.30am Mon-Sat; 1-4.30pm Sun.
Main courses €10-€35. **Set lunch** €15 Mon-
Fri. **Credit** AmEx, DC, MC, V. **Map** p328 J13 **③**
Pan-European
With canary-yellow walls, puffed-up banquettes,
bright paintings and a certain Gallic charm, Veronica
the Cow is a whimsical reprieve from the bustling
streets of Huertas. Attracting business types and hip-
sters alike, it's a fine choice for a quality *menú del día*.
Pesto pasta, the abundant 'cow's platter' of chorizo,
morcilla (black blood sausage) and other meats, and
various salads are just some of the options.

LAVAPIES

Baisakhi

C/Lavapiés 42 (91 521 80 31). Metro Lavapiés.
Open 12.30pm-4pm, 8pm-midnight daily. **Main
courses** €4.50-€6. **Set lunch** €7-€9.25. **Credit**
MC, V. **Map** p328 H14 **③** **Indian**
For good-value Indian food, Baisakhi is probably the
best bet along what has become Madrid's answer to
Brick Lane. The waiters all speak English, and the
dishes on the menu include all the old faves. If you
like a bit of poke in your curry, then be sure to ask
for a spicier version of your chosen dish, as
Spaniards don't generally like their food hot. The
terrace is preferable to the slightly shabby interior.

★ Casa Lastra

*C/Olivar 3 (91 369 08 37, www.casalastra.
com). Metro Antón Martín.* **Open** 1-4pm, 8pm-
midnight Mon, Tue, Thur-Sat; 1.30-4pm Sun.
Closed July. **Main courses** €9-€20. **Set lunch**
€12.50 Mon-Fri. **Credit** AmEx, DC, MC, V.
Map p327 H13 **③** **Asturian**
Asturian food is now gaining international acclaim,
but the regulars at Casa Lastra have known how
good it is for a long time. Always packed with happy
locals munching *cabrales* (a strong Asturian blue
cheese) and *pote asturiano* (a stew with cabbage,
haricot beans, black pudding, chorizo and potato) at
the bar, or dining on *perdiz* (partridge) and *merluza
a la sidra* (hake in cider) at the back, this is the place
for good cooking and a glass of still cider.

Olsen. *See p143.*

CONSUME

★ El Económico Soidemersol

*C/Argumosa 9 (91 528 16 55, http://restaurant
eeleconomico.es). Metro Atocha or Lavapiés.*
Open 9am-2am Tue-Sun. **Main courses** €8-
€17. **Set lunch** €8.95-€9.95 Mon-Fri; €10.50-
€11.50 Sat; €12-€13 Sun. **Credit** AmEx, DC,
MC, V. **Map** p328 H14 ❸ **Castilian**
Also confusingly known as Los Remedios (turn it
backwards to see why), the Soidemersol is something of an institution. In recent years, the premises
have had a bit of a facelift, but it retains a friendly
neighbourhood feel, along with the wooden furniture and original tiling. Try the seafood risotto, calf's
liver and onions, or beef ragoût with vegetables.
There are tables outside in summer.

★ Freiduría de Gallinejas

*C/Embajadores 84 (91 517 59 33,
www.mformacion.com/gallinejas). Metro
Embajadores.* **Open** 11am-11pm Mon-Sat.
Closed 3wks Aug. **Main courses** €4.50-€8.
No credit cards. Map p327 H16 ❸ **Castilian**
Still going strong after a century, this is the best
place in the city for deep-fried lamb intestines and
other tasty titbits. Not for weak stomachs, this offal
institution offers superbly prepared testicles, glands
and stomach linings, all accompanied by strong red
wine. Worth checking out just for the lively scene
and for a taste of Old Madrid's innard circle.

Moharaj

*C/Ave María 26 (91 467 86 02, http://
moharajcomidaindiamadrid.com). Metro
Lavapíes.* **Open** noon-5pm, 8pm-midnight
daily. **Main courses** €6.50-€12. **Credit**
AmEx, DC, MC, V. **Map** p328 H14 ❹ **Indian**
It may not look fancy, but among curry lovers
Moharaj is widely believed to serve the best Indian
food in Madrid. The secret is that most dishes are
made from scratch when ordered, avoiding that
greasy gloop so prevalent in some establishments.
If there are four of you, order the Moharaj platter to
start, which has samosas, bhajis and more, then
maybe prawns rezala, lamb jalfrezi, beef madras and
matar paneer. But everything is really tasty, so you
can't go wrong.

CHUECA

El 26 de Libertad

C/Libertad 26 (91 522 25 22). Metro Chueca.
Open 1-4pm Mon, Sun; 1-4pm, 8pm-11pm Tue-
Thur; 1-4pm, 9pm-midnight Fri, Sat. **Main
courses** €9.40-€18. **Set lunch** €10.90-€16 Mon-
Sat. **Credit** AmEx, DC, MC, V. **Map** p324 I10 ❹
Castilian/International
With its deep colours and lavishly set tables, El 26
de Libertad is over-the-top elegance bordering on the
camp. But it's not too fine to be fun, and is a favourite
in the *barrio* – the bar is often brimming with *caña*
drinkers. The food is Spanish, but dishes such as

morcilla (black pudding), cannelloni and anchovies
filled with spinach and pine nuts have a creative
edge. At lunchtime only a simple *menú* is available,
so book for dinner to put them through their paces.

El Armario

*C/San Bartolomé 7 (91 532 83 77, www.
elarmariorestaurante.com). Metro Chueca or
Gran Vía.* **Open** 1.30-4pm, 9pm-midnight daily.
Closed 3wks July. **Main courses** €11.85-€18.75.
Set menu €21.40. **Credit** AmEx, DC, MC, V.
Map p324 I10 ❷ **Mediterranean**
Aptly named 'The Closet', this restaurant in the
heart of Chueca makes up for its diminutive size
with generous portions. This is Mediterranean food
with a twist; soups and salads are above the norm.
The *menú del día* is a find, and might include cream
of spinach soup to start, followed by some oriental
chicken and a pud. It's always packed, so get there
before the crowds, especially for lunch. Charming
service is a real plus when eating at close quarters.

El Bierzo

C/Barbieri 16 (91 531 91 10). Metro Chueca.
Open 1-4pm, 8-11.30pm Mon-Sat. **Main
courses** €9-€18. **Set lunch** €11 Mon-Fri.
Set dinner €15. Closed Aug. **Credit** MC, V.
Map p324 I10 ❸ **Castilian**
El Bierzo is one of the best of Madrid's long-established *casas de comida* – honest, dependable neighbourhood joints where you can get a good *menú del
día* at a reasonable price. It buzzes, particularly during lunch, with a loyal crowd feasting on simple
dishes: roast chicken, seven types of tortilla and
excellent *setas al ajillo* (wild mushrooms fried in garlic). It's worth coming here just for a chat with the
friendly owner, Miguel.

El Bogavante del Almirante

*C/Almirante 11 (91 532 18 50, www.bogabar.
com). Metro Banco de España.* **Open**
1.30-5.30pm, 9pm-12.30am Mon-Sat;
1-4pm Sun. Closed 2wks Aug. **Main courses**
€12-€23. **Credit** AmEx, DC, MC, V. **Map** p324
J10 ❹ **Seafood**
Almirante wins the award for most fanciful set
design. Nestled in a cave-like basement, a ponderous
lobster claw hangs from the ceiling, while black out-
lines of sea creatures swirl across shrimp-pink walls.
The staff, clad in black, add to the scene, which feels
more Manhattan than Madrid. Seafood is the forte.
The fish specials are always excellent, but the *arroz
con bogavante* (lobster paella) takes the prize.

Café Oliver

*C/Almirante 12 (91 521 73 79, http://
cafeoliver.com). Metro Colón.* **Open** 1.30-4.30pm,
9pm-midnight Mon-Thur; 1.30-4.30pm, 9pm-1am
Fri, Sat; 11.30am-4pm Sun. **Main courses**
€16.50-€21.50. **Set lunch** €14. **Credit** AmEx,
DC, MC, V. **Map** p324 J10 ❹ **Pan-European**

urban mex restaurant

Tepic. *See p149.*

Still an 'in' spot for the international crowd, Café Oliver runs the gamut of French, Spanish, Italian and Moroccan without falling into the dreaded (con)fusion trap. Highlights include the *bomba de chocolate*, definitely a candidate for top all-time pudding. The plush red velvet banquettes and large windows looking out on the street make Café Oliver an ideal place for Chueca people-watching. Ideal on a Sunday for American brunch. The downstairs cocktail bar is cool and loungy.

★ Casa Manolo
C/Orellana 17 (91 308 73 78, www.comidascasamanolo.es). Metro Alonso Martínez. **Open** 1.30-4.30pm Mon-Thur; 1.30-4.30pm, 9pm-midnight Fri; 2-4.30pm, 9pm-midnight Sat. Closed Aug. **Main courses** €14-€23. **Set lunch** €15. **Credit** MC, V. **Map** p324 J9 **46** **Castilian**
One of the best sources of *cocina casera*, or home cooking, in Madrid, Casa Manolo has an endearing, homely atmosphere. But even though it's all about tradition, this place prepares creative mouthwatering salads that put the usual *ensalada mixta* to shame – the aubergine with tomato and goat's cheese, for example, must be one of the best in the city. And then there's lentil soup, *cocido* and other hearty stews, all supremely well prepared.

★ Extremadura
C/Libertad 13 (91 531 82 22, 91 521 03 17, www.restauranteextremadura.com). Metro Chueca. **Open** 1.30-4.30pm Mon; 1.30-4.30pm, 9pm-midnight Tue-Sun. Closed 3wks Aug. **Main courses** €10.50-€35. **Credit** DC, MC, V. **Map** p324 I11 **47** **Extremaduran**

With festive live piano accompaniment, this is the spot to try out specialities from one of Spain's least-known regions, Extremadura. The place is both classy and country – beautifully set tables with enormous glasses (for the excellent wines) combine with painting and pottery from the region. The food is marked by Extremadura's former days of austerity, with game that could be hunted on the dry plains. The trademark dish, *migas*, is a mix of breadcrumbs, chorizo and peppers that shepherds concocted to make use of old bread. Try the *torta del casar*, a soft, pungent regional cheese.

★ Gastromaquia
C/Pelayo 8 (91 522 64 13). Metro Chueca. **Open** 1-4pm, 9-11.30pm Tue-Sat; 1-4pm Sun. **Main courses** €15-€25. **Set lunch** €10.80. **Credit** AmEx, DC, MC, V. **Map** p324 I10 **48** **Spanish fusion**
Filling the space left by the old Don Pelayo taverna, Gastromaquia has been getting rave reviews since opening a few years ago. The restaurant, located in the heart of Chueca, is run by Catalans Hugo Escolies and Ramón Figuls, and the compact interior is minimalist in style, with a red, white and black colour scheme and bare-brick walls artistically lined with old soda syphons. The Spanish-fusion food is expertly executed and beautifully presented: guacamole and plantain chips, and grilled octopus with potato foam are examples of some of its most celebrated dishes. The set lunch menu is great value, and this is also a popular spot for tapas. The downside, at least for some, is that smoking is allowed.

CONSUME

Zara.

12.30-4pm, 9pm-midnight Tue-Sat; 12.30-4pm Sun. Closed Aug. **Main courses** €6.50-€22. **Set lunch** €8.60. **Credit** MC, V. **Map** p324 I10 🐵 **Andalucían**

Refreshingly unpretentious, Los Jiménez was serving no-frills food long before Chueca became the gay capital of Spain. Ghastly fluorescent lights overhead, the smell of frying and a menu board that spans the wall behind the bar – basically, it's a good old-fashioned greasy spoon. Popular with old-time locals and new kids, who come here for all the Andalucían staples: oxtail stew, tripe, *cocido* and generous, if basic, salads.

La Mordida
C/Belén 13 (91 308 20 89, www.lamordida.com). Metro Chueca. **Open** 1.30-5pm, 8.30pm-1am daily. **Main courses** €10-€10.95. **Credit** AmEx, DC, MC, V. **Map** p324 I9 🐵 **Mexican**

Joaquín Sabina, the gravelly voiced Madrid musician and legend, does restaurants, too, but who'd have expected it to be Mexican food? And such good authentic Mexican food too, straight from the heart of Tenochtitlan. Usually full to bursting with high-spirited tequila drinkers, this is the place to embrace *mole*, the Mexican chocolate sauce that often scares the uninitiated away.

Other locations throughout the city.

★ La Piazzetta
Plaza Chueca 8 (91 523 83 22). Metro Chueca. **Open** 1.30-4pm, 8pm-12.30am Tue-Sat; 1.30-4pm Sun. **Main courses** €8-€12. **Set lunch** €14 Mon-Thur. **Credit** DC, MC, V. **Map** p324 I10 🐵 **Italian**

Plaza Chueca has plenty of bars, but only one great restaurant, and this is it. The place is attractively decked out in warm beige tones, with plenty of natural light streaming in from the square. The menu boasts tasty but simple Italian cuisine, with starters such as grilled vegetables or buffalo mozzarella with tomato and aubergine salad, and great pasta main courses such as ravioli with pecorino and pear, or tortellini with pumpkin and mushrooms. The tiramisu is a must. It's especially perfect for summer evenings, when you can dine on the terrace.

Other location Boccondivino, C/Castelló 81, Salamanca (91 575 79 47).

El Puchero
C/Larra 13 (91 445 05 77, www.elpuchero.com). Metro Bilbao or Tribunal. **Open** 2-4pm, 9pm-midnight Mon-Sat. Closed Aug. **Main courses** €11-€22. **Credit** AmEx, DC, MC, V. **Map** p324 H8 🐵 **Castilian**

Excitingly for El Puchero, red gingham is making a comeback after 30 years in the cold. Here it had never gone away – in tablecloths, cushions, lampshades and curtains. Almost unchanged too is the range of tasty country classics – from *civet de liebre*

Indochina
C/Barquillo 10 (91 524 03 17). Metro Banco de España. **Open** noon-4pm, 8pm-midnight daily. **Main courses** €9.75-€25. **Set lunch** €20. **Credit** AmEx, DC, MC, V. **Map** p324 J11 🐵 **Asian**

Yes, it's Asian fusion with modern design, but Indochina is more relaxed and less style-conscious than most. It's best for a lunchtime *menú del día*: enjoy piquant sweet and sour soup followed by some decent pad thai and then – the most interesting part – green-tea ice-cream with caramelised walnuts on top (trust us, it's good). If you're going à la carte, the Peking duck is a safe bet. Ask for a table in the front, near the tall windows looking out on C/Barquillo; the back rooms are a bit dreary.

Los Jiménez
C/Barbieri 14 (91 521 11 86, http://losjimenez. restaurantesok.com). Metro Chueca. **Open**

INSIDE TRACK ORDER, ORDER

When the food arrives, if one person hasn't ordered a starter, it is considered polite in some places in Madrid (and in Spain in general) to bring their main course to the table with the other diners' starters.

(hare stew) to *criadillas* (don't ask) – and some excellent seafood. It's a good idea to reserve at lunchtime. **Other location** C/Padre Damián 37, Chamberí (91 345 62 98).

Ribeira Do Miño
C/Santa Brígida 1 (91 521 98 54, www.maris queriaribeiradomino.com). Metro Tribunal. **Open** 1-4pm, 8-11.30pm Tue-Sun. Closed 2wks Jan & all Aug. **Main courses** €10-€17. **Set lunch** €11. **No credit cards. Map** p324 H9 **54 Galician/Seafood**
Galician in origin, this one's for seafood lovers. Heaped platters of prawns, crab, goose-necked barnacles, lobster and other sea creatures make it the ideal place to roll up your sleeves and get cracking shells. Other typical *gallego* dishes that add a little heat to the fun are pancakes doused in *orujo* (a fiery spirit very similar to grappa) and set aflame, and the *queimada* – a bowl of *orujo* set on fire and then cooled with black coffee. No reservations are allowed, so grab a ticket and wait.

Salvador
C/Barbieri 12 (91 521 45 24). Metro Chueca. **Open** 1.30-4pm, 9-midnight Mon-Sat. Closed Aug. **Main courses** €12-€28. **Set lunch** €20 Mon-Fri. **Credit** AmEx, DC, MC, V. **Map** p324 I10 **55 Castilian**
Every inch of this old classic is crammed with bullfighting memorabilia. You'll find good traditional fare – lentil soup, *revueltos* (concoctions with scrambled egg, often with seafood or asparagus), hake, *solomillo* (sirloin steak) with french fries – but the real treat is the atmosphere.

Tepic
Pelayo 4 (91 522 08 50, www.tepic.es). Metro Chueca. **Open** 1.15-4.30pm, 9pm-midnight Mon-Thur, Sun; 1.15-4.30pm, 9pm-12.30am Fri, Sat. **Main courses** €11-€13.90. **Credit** AmEx, DC, MC, V. **Map** p324 I10 **56 Mexican**
The name comes from the capital of Nayarit state in Mexico and a huge photo of a typical Mexican takes up one wall of this chic restaurant. There is no doubt about what you're going to eat here: quesadillas, guacamole, tacos, enchiladas, enmoladas… all of a much higher standard than at most Mexican joints in Madrid. It's no wonder Tepic is so popular. And the margaritas are so good, there's no way you're going to have just one. *Photo p147.*

Tienda de Vinos (El Comunista)
C/Augusto Figueroa 35 (91 521 70 12). Metro Chueca. **Open** noon-4pm, 8pm-midnight Mon-Sat. Closed Aug-mid Sept. **Main courses** €5.50-€9. **No credit cards. Map** p324 I10 **57 Castilian**
This restaurant's popular name comes from its role as a lefty meeting point years ago, under Franco (but Tienda de Vinos is all you'll see above the door). It's one of the city's real classics and a visit is essential,

but no one makes any grand claims about its unchanging and unchallenging menu. To start, there are soups: gazpacho, lentil or own-made broth, followed by liver and onions, lamb cutlets, kidneys in sherry and plenty of fish. Service is known for being deadpan, but if you're lucky, you'll get one of the two charming great-grandsons of the original owner.

Zara
C/Infantas 5 (91 532 20 74, http:// restaurantezara.com). Metro Chueca or Gran Vía. **Open** 1-5pm, 8.30-11.30pm Mon-Fri. Closed Aug. **Main courses** €7-€14. **Set menus** €20-€25. **Credit** AmEx, DC, MC, V. **Map** p324 H10/11 **58 Cuban**
It's easy to walk right past these wooden doors and miss the little Havana with red-chequered tablecloths that lies within. Inés, the owner, left her home city over 30 years ago, but brought the best Cuban recipes with her – try the 'Typically Tropical' dishes like *ropa vieja* (literally, 'old clothes', but actually shredded beef), black beans and rice with pork, and minced beef with fried bananas. Daiquiris are the drink of the house. Good Cuban food, low prices: you may have to wait in line as they don't take reservations.

MALASAÑA & CONDE DUQUE

Adrish
C/San Bernardino 1 (91 541 15 41, www. restauranteadrish.com). Metro Noviciado or Plaza de España. **Open** 1-4pm, 8.30pm-midnight Mon-Thur, Sun; 1-4pm, 8.30pm-1am Fri, Sat. **Main courses** €7.60-€28.20. **Set lunch** €9.50. **Credit** AmEx, DC, MC, V. **Map** p323 F9 **59 Indian**
The looks of the place may be a tad dreary, but you'll forget all about the mauve tablecloths when you taste the tandoori chicken with almonds. Adrish was one of the first restaurants to appear on the global restaurant street that is C/San Bernardino, and although it rarely seems full, it has survived with dignity. The large tandoori oven and charcoal grill produce some tasty dishes and a variety of naan breads, even if the spiciness has dropped to a level acceptable to local palates.

Bufalino
C/Puebla 9 (91 521 80 31, www.bufalino.es). Metro Gran Vía or Tribunal. **Open** 1pm-1am Tue-Sat. Closed 1wk Aug. **Main courses** €8.50-€12. **Set lunch** €10.50 Mon-Sat. **Credit** MC, DC, V. **Map** p323 H10 **60 Argentinian/Italian**
Run by an Italian and Argentine couple, Bufalino takes the cuisines of their countries and fuses them, offering a fine selection of fresh pastas made on site, along with panini and polenta. The restaurant gets packed at around 11pm as regulars pop by for a few drinks, and the noise levels in the small space go through the roof. The service always comes with a big smile, and a refurbishment has added sparkle.

CONSUME

HOME
BURGER BAR

BEST ORGANIC BURGERS*
*IN TOWN SINCE 2006

C/ Espíritu Santo, 12
28004 Madrid
tel: 91.522.97.28

C/ Silva, 25
28004 Madrid
tel: 91.115.12.79

C/ San Marcos, 26
28004 Madrid
tel: 91.521.85.31

*CERTIFIED ORGANIC B

www.homeburgerbar.com

Gumbo

C/Pez 15 (91 532 63 61). Metro Noviciado. **Open** 2-4pm, 9pm-midnight Tue-Sat; 2-4pm Sun. Closed 2wks Aug. **Main courses** €10-€16.50. **Set lunch** €9.50. **Credit** DC, MC, V. **Map** p323 G10 (61) **North American**

Bona fide N'Awlins chef Matthew Scott has some good Creole spices simmering in his gumbo pot. In a simple locale tastefully decorated (with a poster of *Gone With the Wind*), you can sample scrumptious New Orleans classics: fried green tomatoes, seafood gumbo, black steak. For festive group dinners, ask Matthew to bring out a parade of tapas-like dishes to share. And only a fool would make any attempt to resist the desserts.

Other location Gumbo Ya-Ya, Calle de la Palma 63, Malasaña (91 532 54 41).

Home

C/Espíritu Santo 12 (91 522 97 28, www.homeburgerbar.com). Metro Tribunal. **Open** 1.30-4pm, 9pm-midnight Tue-Sat; 1-4pm, 8.30pm-midnight Sun. **Main courses** €6-€10. **Credit** AmEx, MC, V. **Map** p323 H9 (62) **Burger bar**

If you associate burger bars with junk food, then this restaurant's aim is to make you think again. Home is the brainchild of a French Canadian restaurateur, who has created a carefully thought-out menu using 100% organic produce. The attention to detail is fantastic, from the diner-style decor complete with cheesy table lamps to the menus, which come printed on American supermarket paper bags. There are quite a few vegetarian dishes, and even vegans can enjoy a marinated tofu club sandwich.

Other locations C/San Marcos 26, Chueca (91 521 85 31); C/Silva 25, Sol & Gran Vía (91 115 12 79).

► *For more burger action, head to Peggy Sue (C/Santa Cruz de Marcenado 13, 91 521 85 60, www.peggysue.es), a classic US diner and handy lunch spot if you've been to the Conde Duque cultural centre.*

★ La Isla del Tesoro

C/Manuela Malasaña 3 (91 593 14 40, www.isladeltesoro.net). Metro Bilbao or San Bernardo. **Open** 1.30-4pm, 9pm-midnight daily. **Main courses** €9.50-€11. **Set lunch** €11. **Credit** AmEx, DC, MC, V. **Map** p323 H8 (63) **Vegetarian**

One of Madrid's few vegetarian eateries not stuck in a circa-1978 gastronomic time warp, La Isla del Tesoro (Treasure Island) is often declared hands-down the best veggie restaurant in Madrid. Matching the international collectibles decor, dishes come from across the globe: try the locally renowned couscous *seitan* or the *buen rollito* (fresh pasta stuffed with spinach, apple, leek, cheese and nuts). The *menú del día* features dishes from a different nation – which can range as far afield as Pakistan and Mexico – each day.

Siam

C/San Bernardino 6 (91 559 83 15). Metro Noviciado or Plaza de España. **Open** noon-4.30pm, 8pm-midnight daily. **Main courses** €12-€20. **Set lunch** €14. **Credit** AmEx, DC, MC, V. **Map** p323 F9 (64) **Thai**

Texan David Haynes has poured his heart and the experience of years spent in Thailand into this restaurant, and the investment has paid off with a loyal and enthusiastic clientele. Authenticity is his thing (please don't ask for bread) and he imports vegetables and spices that he can't get hold of in the

Taberna Agrado. See p152.

city. Try the spicy Thai green curry, or just ask him to recommend a dish. There is also a fabulous range of cocktails and special teas.

▶ *The same company runs Bangkok (C/Arenal 15, Sol & Gran Vía, 91 559 16 96).*

★ Subiendo al Sur

C/Ponciano 5 (91 548 11 47, www .subiendoalsur.org). Metro Noviciado or Plaza de España. **Open** *Food served* 2-5pm Mon; 2-5pm, 9pm-midnight Tue-Sat. **No credit cards. Map** p323 F9 ❻❺ **International**
Easily missed, this co-operative-run fair trade café-restaurant and shop is a gem. All profits go to good causes, and the charming co-owners take turns in the kitchen, each lending ideas from their home country to the daily-changing menu. A wide selection of *empanadas* and pastries sit alongside Zambian *babotie*, Peruvian ceviche, Brazilian *moqueca*, and kebabs. Highly recommended.

★ Taberna Agrado

C/Ballesta 1 (91 521 63 46). Metro Gran Vía or Callao. **Open** 10am-2.30am Mon-Sat. **Main courses** €8-€14. **Set lunch** €12-€13.50. **Credit** MC, V. **Map** p323 H10 ❻❻ **Nueva cocina**
Named after a character in Pedro Almodóvar's film *The Flower of My Secret*, Agrado opened in early 2010 and immediately caused a bit of a stir. Although located on an unpromising street just off the Gran Vía, this area, recently rebranded 'TriBall', is undergoing a bit of a renaissance. The chef, Byron Canning, is British, with experience in some of London and Madrid's top restaurants. Behind the bar, Héctor Monroy from Mexico shakes up some mean cocktails. The speciality is the melt-in-the-mouth beef and Iberian pork hamburger. There's also octopus carpaccio and, of course, fish and chips. *Photo p151.*

★ La Tasquita de Enfrente

C/Ballesta 6 (91 532 54 49, www.latasquita deenfrente.com). Metro Gran Vía or Callao. **Open** 1.30-3.30pm, 8.30-11pm Tue-Sat. Closed Aug. **Main courses** €19-€32. **Credit** AmEx, DC, MC, V. **Map** p323 H10 ❻❼ **Nueva cocina**
One of Madrid's best restaurants, La Tasquita de Enfrente is run by Juanjo López Bedmar, a former executive who chucked it all in to devote himself to cooking. There are only half a dozen tables, so you need to book well ahead. The menu changes according to what is best at any given time, but don't miss the *pochas* (white beans) with clams, if they're available. Also fabulous are the squid gnocchi, and the slow-cooked acorn-fed Iberian pork cheeks. But the best idea is to go for the special menu of the day.

Toma

C/Conde Duque 14 (91 547 49 96). Metro Noviciado or Plaza de España. **Open** 9pm-12.30am Tue-Fri; 1-4.30pm, 9pm-12.30am Sat,

INSIDE TRACK QUICK FIXES

It's a phenomenon often noted by visitors that Madrid lacks the sandwich bars found on every corner of most European capitals. The Spanish have always been appalled by the idea of lunch as refuelling, let alone – horror of horrors – eating at one's desk. No, lunch here is a leisurely affair. However, if time is short, or if you're eating alone and don't fancy a drawn-out affair, then head to Chueca's C/San Marcos, for café/takeaway hotspot **Diurno** (No.37), or noodle bar **The Wok** (No.31-33). Another street to note is Malasaña's C/Espíritu Santo, which now has a good Italian café-takeaway in the form of **La Vita é Bella** (No.13), a half-decent crêpe joint, **Crêperie La Rue** (No.18), and the popular **Home** (*see p151*) for gourmet beef in a bun. For more sophisticated fast food, there's Ferran Adrià's **Fast Good** (*see p155*).

Sun. **Main courses** €11-€20. Closed 1wk end Dec, 1wk Jan. **Credit** MC, V. **Map** p323 F9 ❻❽ **International**
A tiny restaurant with cherry-red walls and an informal feel, Toma has quickly become a real favourite of the neighbourhood. Its homely, laid-back atmosphere can make the prices seem rather high, especially if you end up having to sit at the bar, but the food is commensurately good. From duck magret with pak choi to tuna tartare with lemon and soy, or rack of lamb with honey and mustard, the preparation is equally assured, and the results often divine. If it's available on the night you visit, be sure to finish your meal with the creamy cappuccino cheesecake.

THE RETIRO & SALAMANCA

La Brasserie de Lista

C/Serrano 110 (91 411 08 67, www. labrasseriedelista.com). Metro Núñez de Balboa. **Open** noon-4pm Mon, Sun; noon-4pm, 9pm-midnight Tue-Sat. **Main courses** €10.50-€29. **Set lunch** €12.90, €18.50. **Set dinner** €37-€45. **Credit** AmEx, DC, MC, V. **Map** p325 L6 ❻❾ **French**
La Brasserie de Lista is a throwback from the obsession with French cuisine that gripped Spain after the end of the dictatorship. In fact, the restaurant could be mistaken for one of the hundreds of similar establishments in Paris, all wood panelling and parlour palms. On the menu: Caesar salad, onion soup with Emmental, sirloin steak with pepper sauce and hamburgers. The set menu is excellent, or there is a bar at the front where you can just enjoy some tapas.

Casa Portal

C/Doctor Castelo 26 (91 574 20 26, www.casa-portal.com). Metro Goya. **Open** 1.30-4.30pm, 8.30-11pm Mon-Sat. Closed Aug. **Main courses** €12.40-€43.20. **Credit** AmEx, MC, V. **Map** p325 O11 **70** **Asturian**

Casa Portal specialises in all things traditional from Asturias, hence the mountain of cheeses in the window and the cider being poured from a great height. Apart from cider, this spot has been serving *fabada* (an Asturian bean stew with chorizo), tortilla, fish and shellfish for more than 50 years. Choose between the sawdust-strewn bar at the front and the dining room behind.

Nodo

C/Velázquez 150 (91 564 40 44, www.restaurantenodo.es). Metro República Argentina. **Open** 1-4pm, 9pm-midnight daily. **Main courses** €11-€20. **Credit** AmEx, MC, V. **Map** p321 M3 **71** **Japanese/Mediterranean**

With minimalist decor and food to match, Nodo keeps the famous and the fashionable coming back for more. Style aside, some say it's the best sushi in town. Chef Albert Chicote's beef carpaccio with foie gras and coriander coulis typifies the menu, a successful blend of Japanese and Mediterranean. The sashimi and the tuna tataki with garlic get high marks; the service scores lower, but that might be a part of the minimalist serving ethic.

OTHER DISTRICTS

A'Casiña

Avda del Ángel, Casa de Campo (91 526 34 25, www.acasina.com). Metro Lago. **Open** 1.30-4pm, 8.30pm-midnight Mon-Sat; 1.30-4.30pm Sun. **Main courses** €12-€22. **Credit** AmEx, DC, MC, V. **Galician**

A Casiña is one of several restaurants specialising in regional cuisine – in this case Galician – in the Casa de Campo. The restaurant is a reconstruction of a *pazo*, a Galician manor house, and really comes into its own in summer, with tables outside in the garden. Expensive but top-quality fish, shellfish and beef are the highlights, along with favourites from the region, such as *caldo gallego*, a broth made with pork, potatoes and cabbage. There is also a tapas bar, for a cheaper seafood experience.

Asador Donostiarra

C/Infanta Mercedes 79, Tetuán (91 579 08 71, www.asadordonostiarra.com). Metro Tetuán. **Open** 1-4pm, 9pm-midnight Mon-Sat; 1-4pm Sun. **Main courses** €20.50-€39.50. **Credit** AmEx, DC, MC, V. **Steakhouse**

If you love meat and you love Real Madrid, you may want to splurge on a night out at the once-preferred *asador* (steakhouse) of David Beckham and the rest of the team, located near the Bernabéu stadium. The celeb crowd is as legendary as the *solomillo*, and they often give away signed photos and other goodies from the team. Dissenting voices say that all the press has had an adverse effect, and the run-of-the-mill salad, steak and potato offerings are not commensurate with the hefty prices; others still claim it's the best *asador* in Madrid, years after El Becks has disappeared over the pond.

Bar Tomate

C/Fernando El Santo 26, Chamberí (91 702 38 70, http://www.grupotragaluz.com/rest-tomate.php).

Bar Tomate.

CONSUME

Santceloni.

Metro Colón. **Open** 8.30am-midnight Mon-Wed, Sun; 8.30am-2.30am Thur-Sat. Closed Sundays Aug. **Main courses** €8-€10. **Credit** MC, V. **Map** p324 K8 ⑫
Mediterranean
Open all day, this establishment is great for breakfast, a snack, lunch or dinner. Part of the wildly successful Tragaluz group, which has several restaurants in Barcelona, Bar Tomate specialises in light and tasty Mediterranean cuisine, such as gorgonzola croquettes, anchovies and red piquillo peppers on toast, asparagus tempura and individual tortillas. There are good deals available at breakfast time, with a selection of little rolls and pastries, and later on you can have cocktails.

★ Casa Mingo
Paseo de la Florida 34, Casa de Campo (91 547 79 18, www.casamingo.es). Metro Príncipe Pío. **Open** 11am-midnight daily. **Main courses** €4-€10. **No credit cards. Map** p322 B9 ⑬
Asturian
A vast and noisy Asturian cider house, open since 1888. This is a great opportunity to rub elbows with madrileños really enjoying themselves at one of the long wooden tables. The restaurant does only three things: roast chicken, salad and cider. Turn up before the city gets hungry (around 1.30pm) if you want a terrace seat, or take out a chicken and a bottle of cider and head for the River Manzanares for a picnic. At other times, expect to queue.

★ El Comité
Plaza de San Amaro 8, Chamartín (91 571 87 11). Metro Santiago Bernabéu. **Open**

1.30-4.30pm, 9pm-1am Mon-Fri; 9pm-1am Sat. Closed 1wk Aug. **Main courses** €18-€37. **Credit** AmEx, DC, MC, V. **French**
Yes, it's out of the way and has the feel of an elite club, but this somehow enhances the appeal. A romantic French restaurant offering exceptionally good food at a price, El Comité also offers the chance to see Madrid's discreetly elegant top people at play. Great starters include Harry's Bar carpaccio and a tempura of langoustines; a main-course highlight is the steak tartare, and the snails bourguignonne are legendary. A classic.

★ Fast Good
C/Padre Damián 23, Chamartín (91 343 06 55, www.fast-good.com). Metro Cuzco. **Open** 12.30-11.30pm daily. **Main courses** €2.95-€7.95. **Set lunch** €9.50-€9.95. **Credit** AmEx, DC, MC, V. **Nueva cocina/Fast food**
A fast food joint devised by culinary wizard Ferran Adrià has to be worth trying. In a colour-crazy, super-designed deli you can pick out innovative salads like the foie with green beans or panini with brie and spinach. The crowning glory, however, is the Fast

---

INSIDE TRACK TOP TIPS

The Spanish tend to tip very little, often simply rounding up to the nearest euro, but there are no hard and fast rules and tourists – who are known for being generous tippers in comparison – should let their conscience decide.

is used for cooking, and there is even olive oil ice-cream (surprisingly good, since you ask). Specialities include the lobster and herb salad, the *solomillo* with foie, and a fine tarte tatin.

★ Santceloni
Hotel Hesperia Madrid, Paseo de la Castellana 57 (91 210 88 40, www.restaurantesantceloni.com). Metro Gregorio Marañón. **Open** 2-4pm, 9-11pm Mon-Fri; 9-11pm Sat. Closed Aug. **Main courses** €37-€65. **Credit** AmEx, DC, MC, V. **Map** p321 K5 ⑦ **Nueva cocina**
Named after the village where the famed Barcelona restaurateur Santi Santamaria was born, and run by his protégé Oscar Velasco, the Santceloni was given its first Michelin star after less than a year. Santamaria's success is due to the use of only the best local ingredients. The menu changes frequently to make the most of the best seasonal ingredients, but might include crab in sherry with creamed onion and celery, or one of Santamaria's trademark dishes: ravioli of sliced raw prawn with a filling of ceps. The tasting menu will set you back a pretty penny, but it's a chance to relish the talents of one of Spain's celebrity chefs.

★ Sergi Arola Gastro
C/Zurbano 31, Chamberí (91 310 2169, www.sergiarola.es). Metro Rubén Darío. **Open** 2-3.30pm, 9-11.30pm Mon-Fri; 9-11.30pm Sat. Closed 3 wks Aug, 10 days Dec. **Set menu** €95-€160. **Credit** AmEx, DC, MC, V. **Map** p324 J7 ⑦ **Nueva cocina**
This is the flagship restaurant of Sergi Arola, one of Spain's top chefs, and has two Michelin stars. There is no menu as such, just a fixed range of courses that changes according to seasonal availability of ingredients. The Art Deco dining room makes a change from the bland beigeness of his previous premises at the Hotel Miguel Angel. Sergi's wife, Sara, runs the front of house with sommelier Daniel Poveda and barman Diego Cabrera, who mixes fierce cocktails in the downstairs lounge. Together, they make quite a team.

Sudestada
C/Ponzano 85, Chamberí (91 533 41 54). Metro Ríos Rosas or Cuatro Caminos. **Open** 1-4pm, 9.30pm-midnight Mon-Sat. **Main courses** €8-€20. **Set menu** €30. **Credit** MC, V. **Asian**
Run by young Argentines with a passion for Asian food, Sudestada is the new Madrid branch of a Buenos Aires favourite. In its short life it has already received a hugely respected Spanish restaurant award, and is packed out every night. Given the authentic spiciness of its curries – from all over South-east Asia – this gives the lie to the idea that Spanish diners prefer their food bland. Less *picante* options include Vietnamese rolls and dim sum from Singapore. Reservations are all but essential, especially at weekends.

Good hamburger – a superlative specimen, and now there's an organic version too. Everything is made fresh and light – even the fries are cooked in olive oil. It's been a big success, despite the clunky name. **Other location** C/Orense 11, Tetuán (91 555 82 49).

La Favorita
C/Covarrubias 25, Chamberí (91 448 38 10, www.restaurante-lafavorita.com). Metro Alonso Martínez or Bilbao. **Open** 1.30-4pm, 9pm-midnight Mon-Fri; 9pm-midnight Sat. **Main courses** €20-€24. **Set lunch** €15. **Set dinner** €25. **Credit** AmEx, DC, MC, V. **Map** p324 I7 ⑦ **Castilian/Navarran**
Opera fanatic Javier Otero converted this charming 1920s mansion into a restaurant and filled it with singing waiters – conservatoire students or artists just starting out on their careers. It's a surprisingly fun way to dine. And the food, made using fresh ingredients from Navarra, also hits a high note. Reservations are essential.

El Olivo
C/General Gallegos 1, Chamartín (91 359 15 35/359 03 52). Metro Cuzco. **Open** 1.30-4pm Mon; 1.30-4pm, 9pm-midnight Tue-Sat. Closed last 2wks Aug. **Main courses** €18-€35. **Credit** AmEx, DC, MC, V. **Mediterranean**
Frequented by an over-50 crowd and decorated in a sombre olive-green, this old-school Mediterranean restaurant still ranks high with more discriminating gastronomes. Olive oil is the keystone: the kindly, very formal waiters wheel a cart of bottles over to the table for you to sample with bread; only the best

CONSUME

JUANALALOCA

PINTXOS - BAR

PLAZA PUERTA DE MOROS, 4 - 28005 MADRID - 91 366 55 00 / 91 364 05 25

Tapas

Madrid's best spots in which to tapear.

In their more fanciful moments, Spaniards will describe them as 'the world on a plate'. They will tell you that the eating of tapas is proof of the country's gregarious nature, its need to share and the importance it places on spending time in good company. Thanks to the *tapa*, it is possible to spend the whole night in a bar without requiring help to get home. This is the point so often missed by those outside the country, those who reproduce them for dinner parties or nibble them in expensive restaurants in London. For the Spanish, it's not about what you eat, it's about how you eat.

TAPAS TRADITIONS

Tapas vary from region to region, and examples of most are available in Madrid. Galician bars highlight octopus, prawns and seafood, traditionally with white Ribeiro wine, served in little ceramic bowls. In Extremaduran bars you will always find *migas* (crumbs), fried and mixed with chorizo. Asturian bars specialise in cider (*sidra*), theatrically poured from above the head to separate out sediment, accompanied by blood sausage, *morcilla*, or blue *cabrales* cheese. Andalucian bars offer cold dry *fino* sherry with *mojama* (dry-cured tuna) or sardines. Madrid's own specialities are *patatas bravas*, offal (particularly *callos*, tripe), and snails in a hot sauce.

INSIDE TRACK
THE TAPAS STORY

An accidental invention, tapas originated in Andalucía and were originally pieces of ham or chorizo that were placed on top of the plate, or slice of bread, used to cover a glass of wine and keep out the dust and flies. The word *tapa*, in fact, means 'lid'. The idea became widely established during the 19th century, with the principal objective of making the customer thirsty in order to sell more drinks. The tapas boom really occurred, however, in the 1940s after the Civil War, when many of Madrid's existing bars first appeared.

❶ Yellow numbers given here correspond to the location of each tapas bar on the street maps. *See pp321-329.*

Tapas have become more sophisticated and and thus expensive in recent times, and an evening's *tapeo* can cost more than a full meal in a restaurant.

LOS AUSTRIAS & LA LATINA

El Almendro 13

C/Almendro 13 (91 365 42 52). Metro La Latina. **Open** 1-4pm, 7.30pm-12.30am Mon-Thur; 1-4pm, 7.30pm-1am Fri; 1-5pm, 8pm-1am Sat; 1-5pm, 8pm-12.30am Sun. **No credit cards.** **Map** p327 F13 ❶
A sleepy, traditional bar during the week, it hots up at weekends, and drinkers often drift on to the pavements. A peculiar speciality is the *rosca*, a sort of oversized, filled bagel. These are invariably accompanied by a glass of the house *manzanilla*.

Bodegas Ricla

C/Cuchilleros 6 (91 365 20 69). Metro Ópera. **Open** 1-4pm, 7pm-midnight Mon, Wed-Sun. **Credit** AmEx, MC, V. **Map** p327 F12 ❷
A tiny, bright and friendly mother-and-son operation, Bodegas Ricla does a great line in garlicky *boquerones* and an incongruous one in soft rock. Cheap but good wine and sherry are available by the litre, poured from tall clay urns, or there is vermouth on tap. Also worth trying are the *cecina* (thin slices of cured venison) and *cabrales* cheese in cider.

CONSUME

La Cabra en el Tejado

C/Santa Ana 29 (91 142 46 43). Metro La Latina. **Open** 6-11pm daily. **No credit cards.** **Map** p327 F14 ❸

A clear fave among creative types, 'The Goat on the Rooftop' is a little hidden away, but worth seeking out for its selection of good, cheap and unusual tapas – including quiches, humous, crêpes, *tostas*, salads, and sweet options, such as the delicious chocolate brownie. The space is nicely decorated, with a huge mural painted on one wall, and a retro feel.

La Casa de las Torrijas

C/Paz 4 (91 532 14 73). Metro Sol. **Open** 10am-4pm, 6-10pm Mon-Thur; 9.30am-4pm, 6-11pm Fri, Sat. Closed Aug. **No credit cards.** **Map** p327 G12 ❹

Formerly known as the As de los Vinos, this is a charmingly old unkempt bar, tiled and mirrored,

---

INSIDE TRACK SUNDAY'S BEST

In Madrid, Sunday feels like Friday. Preparing for Monday isn't given much thought; *madrileños* like to squeeze the most out of their weekends, hence the Sunday post-Rastro drinking tradition in La Latina. On sunny days, the barrio's squares brim with hedonism. On rainy days, the best bars in the area burst with smoking, drinking, talking *madrileños*. The essence of the tradition is vermouth, and the whole ritual, tapas and all, sometimes known as '*haciendo el vermut*' – 'doing vermouth'.

---

with table-tops constructed from old enamel adverts. Since 1907, it has served little more than *torrijas* – bread soaked in wine and spices, coated in sugar and deep-fried – and house wine. There is a handful of other, simple, tapas, however, and a basic set lunch.

★ Juanalaloca

Plaza Puerta de Moros 4 (91 364 05 25). Metro La Latina. **Open** 1.30-5.50pm, 8.30pm-12.30am Mon-Thur; 1.30-5.30pm, 8.30pm-1am Fri-Sun. **No credit cards.** **Map** p327 E13 ❺

Where the hip go to *tapear*, this Uruguayan-run tapas bar attracts a stylish mix of Argentinians, Uruguayans, locals and tourists. It's kind of pricey, but offers undeniably creative cooking – such as wild mushroom and truffle croquettes, tuna carpaccio with almond oil and rice, and vegetables in a 'Hindu tempura'. Its delicious tortilla is also renowned.

Taberna Matritum

C/Cava Alta 17 (91 365 82 37, www.matritum. es). Metro La Latina. **Open** 8.30pm-12.30am Mon-Wed; 1-4.30pm, 8.30pm-12.30am Thur-Sun. **Credit** DC, MC, V. **Map** p327 F13 ❻

Its name is Latin for Madrid, but Matritum has a great selection of tapas and wine from other regions of Spain, most notably Catalonia. Try *gambas all cremat* (prawns with burnt garlic) or fabulous canapés such as *cabrales* cheese with apple compôte. The wine list, too, is dominated by Catalan labels, with many notably good bottles from the Penedes.

Taberna Según Emma

C/Conde de Miranda 4 (91 559 08 97). Metro Ópera. **Open** 1-5pm, 8pm-12.30am daily. **Credit** AmEx, DC, MC, V. **Map** p327 F12 ❼

Tapas Glossary

Madrid's tapas bars are about more than just patatas bravas

There are three basic sizes of *tapa* portion: a *pincho* (more or less a mouthful), a *tapa* (a saucerful or so) and a *ración* (a small plateful). Some bars offer *media raciones* (a half-*ración*). If there's something you like the look of that isn't identifiable on the menu or the list behind the bar, just point to it. Bread (*pan*) normally comes automatically, but if not, just ask. Most often, you let a tapas bill mount up and pay when you've finished, not when you order; it's usually about 25 per cent more expensive if you sit at a table rather than eat at the bar.

For more food terms, *see pp134-135*.

Basics
Bocadillo sandwich in a roll or part of a French loaf; **cazuelita** small hot casserole; **montados** canapé-style mixed tapas, often a slice of bread with a topping; **pincho/pinchito** small titbit on a toothpick, or mouthful-sized *tapa*; **pulga/pulguita** small filled roll; **ración** a portion (small plateful); **tabla** platter (of cheese, cold meats); **tosta** slice of toast with topping; **una de gambas, chorizo…** one portion of prawns, chorizo…; **por unidad** per item.

Carne, aves y embutidos (meat, poultry & charcuterie)
Albóndigas meat balls; **alitas de pollo** chicken wings; **callos** tripe; **cecina** dry-cured beef; **chistorra** Navarrese sausage with paprika; **chorizo** spicy sausage, eaten cooked or cold; **criadillas** bulls' testicles; **flamenquines** ham and pork rolls in breadcrumbs; **longaniza, fuet** mild but chewy, often herby, salami-type sausages; **mollejas** sweetbreads; **morcilla** a black, blood sausage; **oreja (de cerdo)** pig's ear; **pincho moruno** grilled meat brochette; **riñones al Jerez** kidneys cooked in sherry; **salchichón** a large, fatty, soft, salami-type sausage; **San Jacobo** fried ham and cheese escalope; **sobrassada** soft Mallorcan paprika sausage; **torrezno** grilled pork crackling; **zarajo** grilled sheep's intestine on a stick.

Pescado y mariscos (fish & shellfish)
Ahumados smoked fish; **almejas** clams; **anchoas** salted conserved anchovies; **anguilas** eels; **angulas** elvers; **berberechos** cockles; marinated fried fish; **b** vinagre/fritos** pickled **calamares a la roman** in batter; **calamares en su tinta** squid cooked in their ink; **carabineiros** large red ocean prawns; **centollo** spider crab; **chanquetes** tiny fish, served deep fried; **chipirones en su tinta** small Atlantic squid in their ink; **chopito** small cuttlefish; **cigalas** crayfish; **croqueta de bacalao** salt cod croquette; **fritura de pescado** flash-fried fish; **gambas al ajillo** prawns fried with garlic; **gambas en gabardina** prawns deep-fried in batter; **huevas** fish roe; **mojama** dried and salted tuna fish; **navajas** razor clams; **nécora** swimming crab; **percebes** goose-neck barnacles; **pulpo a feira/a la gallega** octopus with paprika and olive oil; **quisquillas** shrimps; **salpicón** cold chopped salad, often with some shellfish; **sepia** large squid; **soldaditos de pavía** strips of salt cod, fried in light batter; **tigres** mussels cooked with a spicy tomato and béchamel sauce; **zamburiñas** small scallops.

Vegetales (vegetable tapas)
Aceitunas, olivas (adobados, rellenos) olives (pickled, stuffed); **almendras saladas** salted almonds; **pan con tomate** bread rubbed with fresh tomato and olive oil; **patatas bravas** deep-fried potatoes with hot pepper sauce; **perdiz de huerta** lettuce hearts; **pimientos de Padrón** fried, and occasionally hot small green peppers; **queso en aceite** cheese marinated in olive oil; **setas** wild mushrooms.

Other tapas
Caracoles snails; **croquetas** potato croquettes (which may be made with chicken, ham, tuna, and so on); **empanada** flat pies, usually made with a tuna filling; **empanadilla** small fried pasties, usually with a tomato and tuna filling; **ensaladilla rusa** potato salad with onions, red peppers, usually tuna and other ingredients in mayonnaise, now a completely Spanish dish that's still called a Russian salad; **huevos rellenos** stuffed cold hard-boiled eggs; **migas (con huevo frito)** fried breadcrumbs (with fried egg); **pisto manchego** ratatouille with meat (usually ham) and egg; **revuelto** scrambled eggs.

...a small, lively space with lime-green wooden tables – run by thirtysomethings ...ysomethings. It used to be an Asturian bar and ...ses from the region and favourites such as clams ...th haricot beans remain, alongside newer tapas.

Taberna del Zapatero
C/Almendro 22 (91 365 37 57). Metro La Latina. **Open** 8pm-midnight Tue-Sun. **No credit cards. Map** p327 F13 ❽
Occupying the shop of an old shoemaker (*zapatero*), this is now a boisterous and smoky tapas bar. Old cobblers' tools are dotted about the place, and the excellent canapés are known as *suelas*, 'soles'. Fill your boots with asparagus with brie or cod brandade.

★ El Tempranillo
C/Cava Baja 38 (91 364 15 32). Metro La Latina. **Open** 1-4pm, 8pm-midnight Tue-Sun. Closed Aug. **Credit** V. **Map** p327 F13 ❾
Never less than rowdy, decorated in bullring ochre and bare brick, with flamenco on the sound system, El Tempranillo offers an impressive range of labels from nearly every wine-producing region in Spain. The tapas are addictive too: try the wild mushrooms in scrambled egg or the sweetbreads.

La Torre del Oro
Plaza Mayor 26 (91 366 50 16). Metro Sol. **Open** noon-1am daily. **Credit** AmEx, DC, MC, V. **Map** p327 F12 ❿
It's smack on the Plaza Mayor, so don't expect any bargains, especially if you sit out in the square, but this Andalucian bar is the real deal, with bullfighting memorabilia and incomprehensible waiters. If you can understand and make yourself understood, ask for prawns or whitebait (*pescaítos*), and accompany them with a cold, dry *fino*.

★ Txirimiri
C/Humilladero 6 (91 364 11 96, www.txirimiri.es). Metro La Latina. **Open** noon-4.30pm, 8.30pm-midnight Mon-Sat; 11am-midnight Sun. Closed Aug. **Credit** MC, V. **Map** p327 F13 ⓫
The popular Txirimiri specialises in Basque *pintxos*, and despite its aspirational-sounding tag line of 'haute cuisine in miniature', it's a laid-back, friendly place, and always rammed on a Sunday. The thirtysomething crowd is drawn by the excellent, well-priced tapas (don't miss the croquettes and ravioli) and sociable atmosphere. There's a restaurant area at the far end. **Other location** C/General Díez Porlier 91, Salamanca (91 401 43 45).

SOL & GRAN VIA

Las Bravas
Pasaje Matheu 5, off C/Victoria (91 521 51 41). Metro Sol. **Open** 12.30-4.30pm, 7.30pm-midnight Mon-Thur, Sun; 12.30-5pm, 7.30pm-12.30am Fri, Sat. **No credit cards. Map** p327 H12 ⓬

La Torre del Oro.

Decorated in the luminous orange that characterises its mass-produced sauce, Las Bravas still merits a mention for having, allegedly, invented the *patata brava*. These days, you'll do better elsewhere, unless you're attracted to supermarket lighting. **Other locations** throughout the Sol area.

Casa Labra
C/Tetuán 12 (91 531 00 81). Metro Sol. **Open** *Taberna* 9.30am-3.30pm, 5.30-11pm daily. *Restaurant* 1.15-3.30pm, 8.15-10pm daily. **Credit** AmEx, DC, MC, V. **Map** p327 G11 ⓭
Famously the birthplace of the Spanish Socialist Party back in 1879, this legendary bar, with its brown 1950s paintwork and luggage racks, is worth a visit for its history alone. The speciality of the house is the cod *croquetas* served up by dour whitejacketed waiters.

El Escarpín
C/Hileras 17 (91 559 99 57). Metro Ópera or Sol. **Open** 9am-4.30pm, 8pm-midnight daily. **Credit** AmEx, DC, MC, V. **Map** p327 F11 ⓮
So vast that you'll always find a seat, this Asturian cider bar has the look – bare bricks and long wooden tables – to go with the regional tapas. Natural cider (*sidra*) should be followed by *lacón* (gammon), *fabada asturiana* (bean and pork stew) or chorizo.

HUERTAS & SANTA ANA

Alhambra
C/Victoria 9 (91 521 07 08, http://taberna alhambra.es). Metro Sol. **Open** 11am-1.30am Mon-Wed, Sun; 11am-2am Thur; 11am-2.30am Fri, Sat. Closed Aug. **Credit** MC, V. **Map** p327 H12 ⓯

INSIDE TRACK FINGER FOOD

Don't be afraid to dispose of the debris (olive stones, prawn shells and screwed-up napkins) by dropping them on the floor, except in the more upmarket places where you should copy what the locals are doing; and remember that a lot of tapas are designed to be eaten with the fingers.

Named after Granada's magical palace and done up in suitably Andaluz-Moorish style, this is a pretty and peaceful spot during the day, serving basic tapas along with oxtail stew and gazpacho, and a simple set lunch. It's a different place at night, though; awash with Spanish pop, techno and hormones.

Casa Alberto

C/Huertas 18 (91 429 93 56, www.casaalberto.es). Metro Antón Martín. **Open** *Sept-June* noon-1.30am daily. *July* noon-1.30am Mon-Sat. Closed Aug. **Credit** AmEx, DC, MC, V. **Map** p328 H12 ⑯
One of the city's most evocative *tabernas*, hung with oil paintings and presided over by a septuagenarian. It still has its old zinc bar complete with running water trough to keep the wine cool and a draught beer head with five founts. Try lambs' trotters, garlicky prawns, chorizo in cider or oxtail stew as tapas, or as more substantial dishes in the restaurant at the back.

★ Los Gatos

C/Jesús 2 (91 429 30 67). Metro Antón Martín or Sevilla. **Open** 11am-2am daily. **Credit** MC, V. **Map** p328 I13 ⑰
With their reputation for staying out all night, *madrileños* are popularly known as '*los gatos*' (the cats) and there's nowhere better than here to begin a night prowling the tiles. The bar is hung with all manner of paraphernalia from gramophones to choirboy mannequins – here you can get a selection of tasty canapés, and a good frothy beer.

La Platería

C/Moratín 49 (91 429 17 22). Metro Antón Martín. **Open** 7.30am-1am Mon-Fri; 9.30am-2am Sat, Sun. **Credit** MC, V. **Map** p328 J13 ⑱
Everything from the smoked salmon and red peppers to *caldo gallego*, grilled asparagus or baked potatoes with eggs and garlic, is available in half portions, so this is a perfect place for a quick snack 'twixt two of the big three museums. The bar is rather cramped, but there are tables outside.

Taberna de Conspiradores

C/Moratín 33 (91 369 4741, www. conspiradores.com). Metro Antón Martín. **Open** 1pm-1am Mon-Thur, Sun; 1pm-2am Fri, Sat. **Credit** AmEx, MC, V. **Map** p328 I13 ⑲

The food, wine and liqueurs on offer here are all from Extremadura, unusually. The speciality is *migas* – fried breadcrumbs baked with sausage, garlic and pancetta – and a dense venison stew. The small space is lined with black and white photographs from the Magnum greats, and occasionally hosts world music or flamenco gigs.

★ Taberna La Dolores

Plaza de Jesús 4 (91 429 22 43). Metro Antón Martín. **Open** 11am-1am Mon-Thur; 11am-2am Fri-Sun. **No credit cards. Map** p328 I12 ⑳
Another Madrid classic, with wonderful tiling outside and rows of dusty beer steins inside, La Dolores has been serving ice-cold frothy beer since the 1920s. There's a short list of tapas, which are good if a bit expensive. Specialities are smoked fish, anchovies and *mojama* (wind-dried tuna).

Vinoteca Barbechera

C/Príncipe 27 (91 555 07 54, www.vinoteca-barbechera.com). Metro Antón Martín or Sevilla. **Open** noon-1am Mon-Thur, Sun; noon-2am Fri, Sat. **Credit** AmEx, MC, V. **Map** p328 H12 ㉑
It looks a lot grander than it is, which is not to say that the tapas aren't good, just that the bill is a pleasant surprise in these rather lofty surroundings. *Pinchos* include smoked salmon with cream cheese, *cabrales* with quince jelly and goose liver with apple. **Other locations** C/Gravina 6, Chueca (91 523 9816); C/Hermosilla 103, Salamanca (91 575 5664).

RASTRO & LAVAPIES

Café Melo's

C/Ave María 44 (91 527 50 54). Metro Lavapiés. **Open** 8pm-1.30am Tue-Sat. Closed Aug. **No credit cards. Map** p328 H14 ㉒
It's got all the aesthetic charm of a kebab shop, but this bright little bar is something of a classic. It's famous for its *zapatillas* – huge, open sandwiches (the word, like ciabatta, means 'slipper') with a variety of toppings. A big favourite for late-night munchies with the bohemian element of the *barrio*.

Casa Amadeo Los Caracoles

Plaza de Cascorro 18 (91 365 94 39). Metro La Latina. **Open** 10.30am-3.30pm, 7-10.30pm Tue-Sat; 10.30am-4pm Sun. **No credit cards. Map** p327 F14 ㉓
Again, this is no looker, but it's a popular post-Rastro stop. Its specialities include the eponymous snails in spicy sauce, knuckle of ham, and *zarajo*, the lamb's intestines wrapped round sticks without which your Madrid trip would not be complete.

La Casa de las Tostas

C/Argumosa 29 (91 527 08 42). Metro Lavapiés. **Open** noon-4pm, 7.30pm-1am Tue-Thur, Sun; 7.30pm-2am Fri, Sat. **No credit cards. Map** p328 I15 ㉔

CONSUME

Profile El Mercado de San Miguel

The city's revamped central food market is an upmarket hotspot for tapas.

One of Madrid's biggest success stories of recent times, El Mercado de San Miguel (www.mercadodesanmiguel.es) is the daily food market/tapas emporium in Plaza de San Miguel – immediately south-west of the Plaza Mayor – which reopened its polished-up glass doors in May 2009 after a decade-long restoration. The 1915 wrought-iron and glass structure, with boutique-like food stands inside, has created a new culinary buzz in the city; the place is often heaving at lunchtimes and in the evening, and it continues in this vein until well after midnight (when you can nab bargain tapas). Some say it's lost some of its original soul and that it's overpriced, yet the slick operation – one of the few covered markets in the city – is always rammed with smart-looking *madrileños* and tourists enjoying *bacalao pinchos* (saltcod on bruschetta), oysters, tortillas, olives, wine, sherry, vermouth and, just as important, conversation.

Have a wander around the market to check out the different options before you make your choices, and then take your tapas selection to one of the perches or tables in the centre. It's difficult to make a bad choice here with so many delicious options, but there are some essential don't-miss highlights.

An excellent starting point is also one of San Miguel's best-loved spots: **El Yantar de Ayer** (www.elyantardeayer.es), a four-shop affair specialising in aperitifs – namely vermouth and sherry – and nibbles by which to accompany them. With 15 different types of *vermút*, it's an excellent place to initiate yourself in the quintessential *madrileño* tradition. Sherry – known in Spain simply as *vino de Jerez* – is also taken seriously here. Whichever tipple you go for, be sure to accompany it with some *encurtidos* (pickles) to help lessen the alcoholic punch.

Once you've whet your appetite here, you'll want to move on to more solid fodder. Saltcod specialist **La Casa de Bacalao**, just along from El Yantar, offers some of the market's most popular tapas: *pinchos* (small rounds of toast) topped with puréed *bacalao* in a range of different guises, such as with caviar. At €1 per pincho, it's tempting to order several, but be sure to save room for the market's other temptations.

Two more stands not to be missed are upmarket Lhardy, on the opposite side to La Casa de Bacalao, and, a little way along, the oyster stand. A classic Spanish tortilla from **Lhardy** will set you back €7, but rest assured it's the real (delicious)

OPENING HOURS
For the market listing, *see p200.*

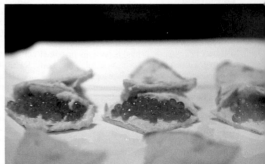

deal. The traditional food store also sells a tempting range of *empanadas*, quiches and meals.

Ostra Sorlut (www.ostrasorlut.com), meanwhile, is a great spot in which to undertake the oyster rite of passage, or, if you're already an aficionado, to enjoy the slippery molluscs (€1.20-€2.50) in suitably salubrious surroundings, knocked back with a cold glass of white wine.

La Alacena de Victor Montes *croquetas* stand is a stall on wheels that's always to be found somewhere in the market – it sells Basque croquettes (filled with saltcod, mushroom, leek et al, at €1 each), either ready to eat, or uncooked to take home.

Spanish tapas tend to be fairly heavy, with copious quantities of oil. For a lighter snack, there's **Sushimarket**, next to Lhardy; sushi is becoming more popular in the city as locals have steadily expanded their culinary horizons. Just around the corner from here, there's the equally healthy **Jugosa** juice stall, selling *licuados* (smoothies), *batidos* (milkshakes), lassi and gazpacho.

If you want to go in a distinctly unhealthy vein, however, head to the opposite corner. Here you'll find a little block of tempting bakeries, including the **Horno San Onofre**, offering artisanal ice-cream, with original flavours, such as cava and lemon, as well as meringues, sugared almonds and more. Next door, the **Horno La Santiaguesa** is the place for chocolate from Valrhona, and classic *madrileño* churros.

Whichever option you go for, the market is an excellent place to people-watch and marvel at *madrileños* doing what they do best: enjoying food in a civilised fashion, and being social – as if it were a duty, a passion and a performance, all rolled into one.

Welcome to the House of Toast. Toast with scrambled eggs, prawns and wild mushrooms; toast with salmon in white vermouth; toast with gammon and melted cheese; toast with anchovies and roquefort; toast with cod pâté. And most importantly, toast with wine, many available by the glass.

Casa de Granada

C/Doctor Cortezo 17 (91 369 35 96/reservations 91 420 08 25). Metro Tirso de Molina. **Open** noon-midnight Mon-Sat; 11am-8pm Sun. **Credit** AmEx, DC, MC, V. **Map** p327 G/H13 ㉕
A very ordinary bar serving very ordinary food, which has an extraordinary view. To get in, ring the buzzer on street level, and then ride the lift all the way up to the sixth floor – in summer you'll have to fight tooth and nail for a seat on the terrace.

Los Hermanos

C/Rodas 28 (91 468 33 13). Metro Tirso de Molina. **Open** 7am-11pm Mon-Fri; 7am-5pm Sun. Closed Aug. **Credit** MC, V. **Map** p327 G14 ㉖
Just off the main drag of the Rastro is this bar with a strong neighbourhood feel, generous complimentary tapas, a huge range of *raciones* or a great range of *bocadillos*, including a hangover-busting bacon and egg. On Sundays, there's a well-priced *menú del día* for the market crowd, available in a quieter side room.

★ La Musa de Espronceda

C/Santa Isabel 17 (91 539 12 84). Metro Antón Martín. **Open** 1.30-4pm, 8pm-midnight daily. **Credit** DC, MC, V. **Map** p328 I14 ㉗
Just along from the Filmoteca (*see p220*), La Musa is known for its *pinchos* – don't miss the butternut squash, goat's cheese and caramelised onion version, or the brie wrapped in bacon. The tortilla is also excellent, while the mojitos are well made and priced. Blackboards, literary posters and globe lights around a central bar lend the place an arty vibe.

La Taberna de Antonio Sánchez

C/Mesón de Paredes 13 (91 539 78 26). Metro Tirso de Molina. **Open** noon-4pm, 8pm-midnight Tue-Sat; noon-4pm Sun. **Credit** MC, V. **Map** p327 G13 ㉘
Little changes at this historic bar, from the zinc bar to the bull's head on the wall. Its various owners have all been involved in bullfighting, and *tertulias* of critics, *toreros* and aficionados are still held here. It's local and friendly, with superior tapas (the best is the scrumptious salad you get free with a drink).

Taberna El Sur

C/Torrecilla del Leal 12 (91 527 83 40). Metro Antón Martín. **Open** 8pm-midnight Tue-Thur; 1-5pm, 8pm-1am Fri-Sun. **Credit** MC, V. **Map** p328 H13 ㉙
Named after Victor Erice's seminal film, decorated with cinematic posters and popular with long-haired soulful types returning from the nearby Filmoteca.

Juan, the friendly owner, offers an interesting selection of *raciones*: try *ropa vieja* (shredded beef, Cuban style) with fried potatoes or 'Arabian' lentils.

CHUECA

La Bardemcilla

C/Augusto Figueroa 47 (91 521 42 56, www.labardemcilla.com). Metro Chueca. **Open** noon-5pm, 8pm-2am Mon-Fri; 8pm-2am Sat. **Credit** AmEx, MC, V. **Map** p324 I10 ㉚
A fun, mellow place, owned by the royal family of Spanish cinema, the Bardems. There are filmic references everywhere, from the doll's house set from *Before Night Falls* to the names of the tapas. *Jamón, Jamón* is *croquetas* (geddit?); *Victor o Victória* is *gazpacho* or consommé, depending on the season. **Other location** Corazon Loco, C/Almendro 22, Los Austrias (91 366 57 83, www.corazonloco.com).

El Bocaíto

C/Libertad 4-6 (91 532 12 19, www.bocaito.com). Metro Chueca. **Open** 1-4.30pm, 8-30pm-midnight Mon-Fri; 8.30pm-midnight Sat. Closed Aug. **Credit** DC, MC, V. **Map** p324 I11 ㉛
Film-set traditional, from the bullfight posters and Andalucían ceramics to the old-school tapas and unsmiling, white-jacketed waiters. If you're famous, though, they'll grin for the camera, just as they did with Pedro, Hugh and, goddammit, Mark Knopfler.

El Tigre

C/Infantas 30 (91 532 00 72). Metro Banco de España or Chueca. **Open** 10.30am-2am Mon-Thur, Sun; 12.30pm-2.30am Fri, Sat. **Credit** V. **Map** p324 I11 ㉜
If you can actually make it through the door, order a beer or cider and marvel at the hefty tapas that come with it – patatas bravas, *jamón serrano*, tortilla… it's all free, and each plate varies with each round. The bar itself is noisy, smoky and always rammed.

MALASANA & CONDE DUQUE

Albur

C/Manuela Malasaña 15 (91 594 27 33, www.restaurantealbur.com). Metro Bilbao. **Open** 12.30-1am Mon-Thur; 12.30pm-2am Fri, Sat; 1.30pm-1am Sun. **Credit** MC, V. **Map** p323 H8 ㉝
The speciality is *revueltos* (scrambled egg) with prawns, wild mushrooms and so on, but there's also good ham, chorizo, black pudding, and a variety of wines to accompany them. Generally a quiet place, with soothing buttercup-yellow walls, it gets quite lively later on with a young Malasaña crowd.

Casa do Compañeiro

C/San Vicente Ferrer 44 (91 521 57 02). Metro Noviciado. **Open** 1.30pm-2am Tue-Sun. **No credit cards.** **Map** p323 G9 ㉞

Estado Puro. *See p166.*

A tiny jewel among tapas bars, with wonderful tiling. The tapas are mainly from Galicia, with lots of octopus, gammon, pig's ear and, of course, *caldo gallego*, a broth made with cabbage and pork. A glass of crisp, dry *fino* makes the perfect accompaniment.

Conache

Plaza de San Ildefonso, C/Santa Barbara 11 (91 522 95 00). Metro Tribunal. **Open** 10am-1am Mon-Thur; 10am-2am Sat; 11-6pm Sun. **Credit** AmEx, MC, V. **Map** p323 H9 ⑤
The Conache look is casually hip, even though the bright lighting and fruit machines keep scenesters at bay. The food, however, is absolutely where it's at. Try stir-fried vegetables with prawns, little rolls of venison and apple, or spinach and brie with figs, and be sure to finish with the cheese mousse with fruits of the forest.

El Maño

C/Palma 64 (91 521 50 57). Metro Noviciado. **Open** 7.30pm-12.30am Mon-Thur; 12.30-4.30pm, 7.30pm-1.30am Fri, Sat. **No credit cards**. **Map** p323 F8 ⑥
A relaxed place, with french windows opening on to the street in summer, marble-topped tables, faded yellow paintwork and art deco touches. A good selection of wine is chalked up on the walls, some of it poured from ancient barrels, and there are tortillas served with *pisto*, ragu or squid, brochettes of chicken and lamb and a small selection of canapés.

La Taberna de la Copla

C/Jesús del Valle 1 (91 522 44 22). Metro Tribunal. **Open** *Sept-June* 1-4pm, 8pm-midnight Tue-Thur; 1-4pm, 8pm-1am Fri, Sat; 1-4pm Sun.
July, Aug 1-4pm, 8pm-midnight Tue-Thur; 1-4pm, 8pm-1am Fri, Sat. **No credit cards**. **Map** p323 G9/10 ⑦
Copla is a form of Spanish ballad, as sung by those depicted here in the dozens of crumbling photos. Tapas are named for famous *coplas* – Juanita Reina is ham with tomato; Principe Gitano is tuna with peppers, and a range of tortillas includes La Zarzamora (plain); Ojos Verdes (with ham), and Cinco Farolas (with tuna).

Taberna El 9

C/San Andrés 9 (91 319 29 46). Metro Tribunal. **Open** *Sept-June* 7.30pm-1am Tue-Thur, Sun; 7.30pm-2.30am Fri, Sat. *July, Aug* 8.30pm-2am Tue-Thur, Sun, 8pm-2.30am Fri, Sat. **No credit cards**. **Map** p323 G9 ⑧
Fun, funky and very much of its neighbourhood, with a young crowd. Taberna El 9 has a straightforward list of canapés, including good scrambled egg with chorizo, and serves house wine by the very cheap *chato* – a small glass.

La Tabernilla del Gato Amadeus

C/Cristo 2 (91 541 41 12). Metro Noviciado. **Open** 1pm-midnight Mon-Wed, Sun; 1pm-1am Thur-Sat. **No credit cards**. **Map** p323 F8 ⑨
Named after a late, great, Persian cat, this is a tiny, welcoming bar, whose *croquetas* are legendary. The other favourite is the *patatas con mojo picón* (baked new potatoes with a spicy sauce). Although there's not much seating inside the premises (the sister bar nearby is bigger), in summer there are tables outside.
Other location C/Limón 32, Malasaña & Conde Duque (91 542 54 23).

THE RETIRO & SALAMANCA

Cervecería Santa Bárbara

C/Goya 70 (91 575 00 52, www.cerveceria
santabarbara.com). Metro Goya. Open 8am-
midnight daily. Credit MC, V. Map p325 O9 ⑳
The prawns are the thing here, consumed in rosy
platefuls by the uptown shoppers crowded round
the horseshoe-shaped bar. Always full, with a loyal
clientele, it is one of the city's meeting places, with
a good selection of beers, and tables outside.
Other locations Plaza de Santa Bárbara 8 (91
319 04 49); C/José Castán Tobeñas 1 (91 570 09
71); C/Padilla 4 (91 577 95 76).

Estado Puro

Plaza Cánovas del Castillo 4 (91 330 24 00,
www.tapasenestadopuro.com). Metro Banco
de España or Sevilla. Open 11am-1pm Mon-
Sat; 11am-5pm Sun. Credit AmEx, DC, MC,
V. Map p328 J12 ㊶
Chef Paco Roncero mans the kitchen at this NH Hotel
initiative , which turns out classic tapas with a modern twist, as well as gazpacho, salads, sandwiches,
meat and fish courses. The cool interior is the real
attraction, however, evoking an upmarket diner, with
a colourful 1950s-style mural and high tables with bar
stalls, and with white mantilla combs arranged artfully
over one wall. And with a terrace at the top of the Paseo
del Prado, it's no surprise that this is a popular tourist
lunch spot – despite the high prices. Photo p165.

Estay

C/Hermosilla 46 (91 578 04 70, www.estay
restaurante.com). Metro Velázquez. Open
8am-2am Mon-Sat. Credit AmEx, DC, MC, V.
Map p325 M9 ㊷
Estay's bright, air-conditioned interior, usually filled
with baying young mothers heavily laden with
shopping bags, does not immediately suggest gastronomic promise. Stick with the place, however, and
you'll enjoy scrumptious and sophisticated tapas
and cheap wines by the glass.

Hevia

C/Serrano 118 (91 561 46 87, www.hevia
madrid.com). Metro Gregorio Marañón.
Open Sept-July 9am-1am Mon-Sat. Aug 8pm-
1am Mon-Sat. Credit AmEx, DC, MC, V.
Map p321 L6 ㊸
A quiet, well-heeled crowd frequents this smart bar.
Tapas are correspondingly sophisticated – foie gras,
caviar, crab and duck liver pâté – and correspondingly pricey. During the summer the tables outside
can prove irresistible.

José Luis

C/Serrano 89 (91 563 09 58, www.joseluis.es).
Metro Núñez de Balboa. Open 9am-1am Mon-
Sat; noon-1am Sun. Credit AmEx, DC, MC, V.
Map p321 L6 ㊹

Probably one of Madrid's most famous tapas bars
and name-checked in a song by the Catalan folk
singer Serrat, the food here is little changed since the
1950s and of a high standard. If your appetite is up
to it, try the brascada (sirloin with ham and onions).
Other locations throughout the city.

NORTH & WEST

Argüelles

Alhuzena

C/Martín de los Heros 72 (91 294 08 37,
http://alhuzena.com). Metro Argüelles. Open
Sept-June 8pm-2am Mon-Thur, 8pm-3am Fri, Sat.
July 8pm-3am Mon-Sat. Closed Aug. Credit DC,
MC, V. Map p322 C7 ㊺
A quirky basement bar, kicking to the strains of flamenco and with wooden painted furniture and a
Gaudiesque mosaic bar. Wine is served in little chatos,
and the tapas are outstanding: artichokes filled with
jamón ibérico, mozzarella with tomato and pesto, and
crêpes with spinach and ricotta among them.

Chamberí

Bodegas la la Ardosa

C/Santa Engracia 70 (91 446 58 94). Metro
Iglesia. Open 9.30am-3pm, 6-11.30pm daily.
Closed mid July to end Aug. No credit cards.
A tiny local bar with a lovely old tiled exterior (confusingly marked No.58) and walls lined with bottles
of wine. There are especially good patatas bravas and
fried pigs' ears, as well as sardines, an array of wonderful shellfish and good beer. Not to be confused
with the Malasaña bar of the same name (see p177).

Taberna de los Madriles

C/José Abascal 26 (91 593 06 26, www.los
madriles.com). Metro Alonso Cano. Open
11am-midnight Mon-Sat. No credit cards.
The speciality of this diminutive bar is the pincho
Los Madriles, with red pepper and anchovies. Also
worth trying are the tuna and prawn pinchos, the
fried potatoes and the callos. Decorated with hundreds of black and white photos of its regulars as
kids, this old-style bar can get a bit cramped, but has
tables outside in summer.

INSIDE TRACK
PLAZA DE OLAVIDE

Chamberí's Plaza de Olavide (see p105)
is something of a neighbourhood hub,
and a great place to enjoy tapas alfresco.
On summer evenings, the place buzzes
with relaxed conversation. Try Arco
Iris (No.2), renowned for its excellent
tortilla de patata.

Cafés & Bars

Madrileños love a drink among friends. Here's where to join them.

The outrageous claims abound: Madrid has over 100,000 bars (about one per 100 residents); the Calle Alcalá has more bars than Belgium; the city has more bars per square metre than anywhere else in Europe. The amazing thing is that they're probably all true. *Madrileños*, even by normal Spanish standards, are a very sociable bunch who place a lot of importance on eating and drinking in company. Consequently the first coffee of the day tends to be drunk in a bar on the way to work, and the second (sometimes accompanied by a glass of wine) will happen at around 10.30am or so when groups of office workers head out for breakfast.

OTRAS D.O.
MASCONTAL "PENEDES"
PAGOS DEL GALIR" VALDEORRA
CASTIZO "MADRID"
VIÑA ALBALI "VALDEPEÑAS"
ESTOLA "LA MANCHA"
CASTELAR "RIBIRA DEL GUADI"
A. SANTAMARÍA "CIGALES"

COFFEE AND TEA

A *café con leche* is a largish, milky coffee, which can also be served in a glass (*vaso*); ask for a *taza grande* if you want it even bigger. An espresso is a *café solo*; the same with a dash of milk is *un cortado*, while *un americano* is diluted with twice the normal amount of water. With a shot of alcohol, a *solo* becomes a *carajillo*. A true *carajillo* is made with coffee, sugar, some coffee beans and brandy, which s then set alight on top so that the mixture gets mulled a little; a *carajillo* can also be just a *solo* with a shot of *coñac*, and you can equally ask for a *carajillo de whisky, de ron* (rum), *de Bailey's* (pronounced 'bye-lees'), *de anís* or anything else you fancy. Decaffeinated coffee is *descafeinado*, and you will normally be asked if you want it from a sachet (*de sobre*), or the machine (*de máquina*). In summer, a great alternative is *café con hielo* – iced coffee.

Tea in bars is usually awful, and, unless you specifically request otherwise will often come as a glass of hot milk with a teabag on the side. Very popular, however, are herbal teas (*infusiones*), such as *menta* (mint) or *manzanilla* (camomile) and nowadays, if the cloud of globalisation has a silver lining, it is that there are a few more cafés around that have some awareness of what decent tea might be.

BEER

Draught beer (*de barril*) is served in *cañas*, a small measure that varies but is less than half a pint, *tubos* in a tall thin glass, or as *dobles* (a little bigger). Some places even serve *pintas* (pints), often in a *jarra*, a large heavy glass with a handle. Bottled beer usually comes in *tercios*, a third of a litre, or in *botellines*, a quarter of a litre. Spain produces some good-quality beers. In Madrid, the favourite is the local Mahou, with two basic varieties – green label Mahou Clásica and the stronger red label Cinco Estrellas. San Miguel is less common, while Andalucian favourite Cruzcampo is growing in popularity. A darker Mahou beer (*negra*) is also available. Shandy is *clara*, and is made with bitter lemon. Imported beers are now common, too, but nearly always cost more.

WINES, SPIRITS AND OTHER DRINKS

All bars have a sturdy cheap red wine (*tinto*) on offer, and usually there's a white (*blanco*) and a rosé as well (*rosado*). Madrid's traditional summer drink is *tinto de verano* (red in a tall glass over ice, with a slice of lemon and topped up with lemonade). Most bars listed here will have at least one decent Rioja and probably a cava, but truly good wines are normally only found in the new-style *tabernas* that take pride in their lists.

Sherry is *jerez*. The type virtually always drunk in Spain is dry *fino*, served very cold. A good fuller-bodied variety is *palo cortado*. Sweet sherries have traditionally been only for export.

---

❶ Green numbers given here correspond to the location of each café and bar on the street maps. *See pp321-329.*

CONSUME

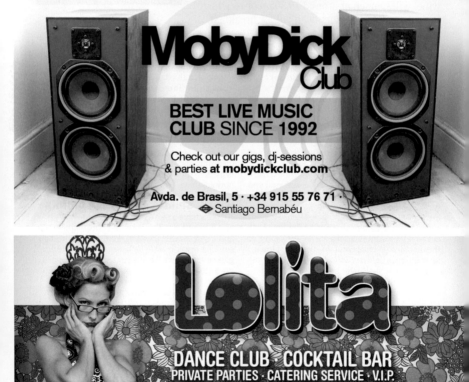

INSIDE TRACK
LOCAL ETIQUETTE

In bars in Spain it is customary to pay at the end, although different rules apply in touristy places or on outdoor terraces. To get a waiter's attention, try a firm, but questioning, '*oiga*' (literally, 'hear me', a perfectly polite way of attracting someone's attention). Once you've got him/her, ask '¿*Me pones un...?*' ('Could you bring me a...?'). Tipping is discretionary. Change is usually returned in a small dish, and people generally leave just a few coins, regardless of the amount spent. In most bars, you can throw olive stones on the floor, along with toothpicks, paper napkins and so on, but watch what the locals are doing.

Red vermouth (*vermut*) with soda is another Madrid tradition, usually as an aperitif, and has recently come back into fashion a little. For a powerful after-dinner drink, try Galician *orujo*, a fiery spirit similar to grappa, that normally comes plain (*blanco*) or *con hierbas*, in a luminous green colour. Other *digestivos* include *patxarán*, a fruity aniseed-flavoured liqueur from Navarra, and the more Castilian *anís*, the best of which hails from Chinchón and is available dry (*seco*) or sweet (*dulce*).

NON-ALCOHOLIC DRINKS

Low- and alcohol-free beers (Laiker, Buckler, Kaliber) have an important niche in the market; other favourites for non-alcohol drinkers are the Campari-like but booze-free Bitter Kas, and plain tonic (*una tónica*) with ice and lemon. Fresh orange juice, *zumo de naranja*, is often available. Trinaranjus is the best-known bottled juice brand; favourite flavours are orange (*naranja*), pineapple (*piña*) and peach (*melocotón*). *Mosto* is grape juice, served in small glasses, sometimes with ice and a slice. A great and unappreciated Spanish speciality, though, are its traditional summer refreshers: most unusual is *horchata*, a milky drink made with tiger nuts. It has to be drunk fresh, from a specialised shop, as it curdles once made. The same places also offer *granizados* – crushed ice with fresh lemon, orange or coffee. Mineral water (*agua mineral*) can be ordered anywhere, either sparkling (*con gas*) or still (*sin gas*).

Many entries in the **Nightlife** and **Tapas** chapters are also good all-rounders, acting as cafés or bars for at least part of the day.

LOS AUSTRIAS & LA LATINA

El Anciano Rey de los Vinos
C/Bailén 19 (91 559 53 32, www.elanciano reydelosvinos.es). Metro Ópera. **Open** 10am-midnight Mon-Sun. Closed mid Feb-mid Mar. **Credit** MC, V at table. No credit cards at bar. **Map** p327 E12 **❶**

Delic. *See p171.*

Café de Oriente.

CONSUME

Kept much as it has been for the last century – very simple, but spacious and light inside with a wide counter and mirrored walls – the King of Wines serves good canapés, and is a great place for a drink after visiting the cathedral. Prices are quite high, especially if you sit outdoors.

Café del Nuncio
C/Nuncio 12 & C/Segovia 9 (91 366 08 53). Metro La Latina. **Open** noon-1.30am Mon-Thur; noon-2.30am Fri, Sat; noon-1am Sun. **No credit cards. Map** p327 F13 **2**
Split into two halves at either end of the narrow Escalinata del Nuncio, the Café del Nuncio has lovely cool, dark interiors with gently rotating ceiling fans and soft classical music. The real charm of

---

THE BEST
MADRID INSTITUTIONS

Bar El Palentino
This Malasaña local is loved by all ages.
See p178.

Café Gijón
Madrid's definitive literary café; it's been fuelling bookish discussions since 1888.
See p182.

Chocolatería San Ginés
Half of Madrid heads here for hot chocolate and *churros* at the end of a heavy night. *See right.*

---

the place, however, lies in the terrace outside on the stepped slope dividing the two spaces; this is one of the most picturesque streets in the old city.

Café de Oriente
Plaza de Oriente 2 (91 541 39 74). Metro Ópera. **Open** 8.30am-1.30am Mon-Thur, Sun; 9am-2am Fri, Sat. **Credit** AmEx, DC, MC, V. **Map** p327 E11 **3**
The belle époque interior is entirely fake yet entirely convincing, making this one of the most peaceful and elegant spots to flick through the newspapers or recover from the exertions of the Palacio Real opposite. Despite its location, with tables outside on the stunning Plaza de Oriente, the café seems to be more popular with locals than with tourists, who are perhaps put off by its air of grandeur.

Café del Real
Plaza de Isabel II (91 547 21 24). Metro Ópera. **Open** 9am-1am Mon-Thur, Sun; 10am-3am Fri, Sat. **No credit cards. Map** p327 F11 **4**
This likeable, cramped café with a lovely façade is a good place to come for coffee and cake (chocolate or carrot), though prices are a tad on the high side. Head upstairs to a low-beamed room with red leather chairs and old opera posters, overlooking the plaza. The café was a particular haunt of intellectuals, artists and actors in the '80s, but it's popular with a wider crowd these days.

★ Chocolatería San Ginés
Pasadizo de San Ginés 5 (91 365 65 46). Metro Ópera or Sol. **Open** 9.30am-7am daily. **No credit cards. Map** p327 G11 **5**

Serving chocolate and *churros* (deep-fried batter sticks) to the city night and day since 1894, this veritable institution has had to introduce a ticketing system – pay before you order – to deal with the 5am queues of exhausted clubbers and chipper old ladies. The lighting is a bit much if you fall into the former category, but there are at least tables outside.

★ Delic

Costanilla de San Andrés 14, Plaza de la Paja (91 364 54 50). Metro La Latina. **Open** 10am-11.45pm Mon-Thur; 10am-12.30am Fri, Sat. Closed last 2wks Aug. **No credit cards**. **Map** p327 E13 ⑥

A perennial favourite with seemingly everybody; from those looking for a peaceful morning coffee on the leafy Plaza de la Paja to those meeting up for a few bolstering cocktails before a big night out. A globe-trotting menu includes tabouleh, Japanese dumplings and filled ciabatta, and the Chilean chocolate cake is utterly irresistible. *Photo p169.*
▶ *Right next door is vegetarian café Viva La Vida (see below).*

La Fontanilla

Plaza Puerta Cerrada 13 (91 366 27 49). Metro La Latina. **Open** 11am-2am daily. **Credit** DC, MC, V. **Map** p327 F12 ⑦

La Fontanilla claims to be not the biggest or the best or the oldest, but the smallest Irish pub in Madrid. There's no disputing this singular claim, but it does manage to cram in a couple of wooden tables alongside wide hatches opening on to the street. The myriad beers racked up the walls are sadly not for sale, but there is Murphy's and Guinness, at least, along with some incongruous canapés to nibble at.

Taberna Gerardo

C/Calatrava 21 (91 221 96 60). Metro Puerta de Toledo. **Open** noon-4pm, 8pm-12.30am Mon-Sat; 12.30-6pm Sun. **No credit cards**. **Map** p327 E14 ⑧

A lively and unpretentious wine bar, Taberna Gerardo is an essential part of the neighbourhood, offering excellent sausage, ham and seafood tapas, as well as a particularly good selection of cheeses.

★ El Ventorillo

C/Bailén 14 (91 366 35 78). Metro Ópera. **Open** 10am-1am daily. **No credit cards**. **Map** p327 E13 ⑨

Just down from the Palacio Real, this terraza offers the finest sunsets in Madrid, with a magnificent location looking out over the Casa del Campo and all the way to the Guadarrama. Not cheap, however.

★ Viva La Vida

Costanilla de San Andrés 16 (91 366 33 49). Metro La Latina. **Open** noon-midnight Mon-Wed; 11am-2am Thur-Sun. Closed last 2wks Aug. **Credit** AmEx, DC, MC, V. **Map** p327 E13 ⑩

This recently opened vegetarian café has been a great success. Take a plate (or take-away box) and make your selection from the buffet, which includes delicious, creative salads, sautéed vegetables, wholegrains, dips and hot meals, such as veggie lasagna. The staff then weigh the plate to get the price. A typical main course plate costs €10. There's also a good range of juices and sweet things.
▶ *There's a take-away only branch on C/Huertas (No.57, 91 369 72 54), not far from the Paseo del Prado – which makes for a nice spot to take your lunch.*

SOL & GRAN VIA

Café del Círculo de Bellas Artes

C/Alcalá 42 (91 521 69 42). Metro Banco de España. **Open** 9am-1am Mon-Thur; 9am-3am Fri, Sat; noon-1am Sun. **Admission** €1; free 2-4pm. **Credit** DC, MC, V. **Map** p328 I11 ⑪

A quintessential point of reference in the city's café society, the Bellas Artes is utterly elegant. Under new ownership, it is now free to enter at lunchtime for the *menú del día*. Otherwise take a seat amid the columns and female nudes and frown over *El País* with coffee and a croissant to fit right in.

★ La Mallorquina

Puerta del Sol 8 (91 521 12 01). Metro Sol. **Open** 9am-9.15pm daily. Closed mid July-Aug. **No credit cards**. **Map** p327 G11 ⑫

While the atmospheric bakery downstairs supplies box after ribbon-tied box of flaky *ensaïmada* pastries, croissants and *napolitanas* to what seems like

CONSUME

diurno

cafe take away video&dvd

Chueca c/San Marcos 37 (91 522 00 09)
Metro Chueca

Mon-Thur: 10am – midnight
Fri: 10 am – 1am
Sat: 11 am – 1 am
Sun & holidays: 11am – midnight

www.diurno.com

The chaps at Diurno like to call the place a gourmet video-club. Indeed it is one of those places where cultural *Madrileños* go to rent the latest (or the oldest) high-brow movie, and discuss them till late.

With a rich selection of coffees, sandwiches, salads, sushi and desserts, it is easy to see why the city's smart alternative set likes to hang out in this "cultural drugstore." With a modern decor and an unhurried atmosphere, Diurno makes an excellent break from hectic Chueca.

half of Madrid, the upstairs *salón* crackles with the animated chat of *madrileña* blue-rinses and savvier tourists. Windows overlooking the Puerta del Sol make this an unbeatable central spot for breakfast. The coffee is cheap and very good.

★ Museo Chicote

Gran Vía 12 (91 532 67 37, www.museo-chicote. com). Metro Gran Vía. **Open** 8am-3am Mon-Sat. **Credit** AmEx, DC, MC, V. **Map** p324 I11 ⑬
Its art deco interior is starting to look a bit shabby around the edges, but Chicote is still the doyen of Madrid cocktail bars. This was famously where Hemingway and other international press hacks would spend their days sheltering from the artillery shells flying down the Gran Vía during the Civil War. Grace Kelly and Ava Gardner, along with just about every Spanish writer, actor or artist of the last 60 years have passed through too. These days, the place is run by Trip Family, one of the biggest promoters on the Madrid nightlife scene. On a Thursday night you can catch Spain's answer to Gilles Peterson, DJ Sandro Bianchi, playing electrosoul, funk, hip hop and anything with a groove.

HUERTAS & SANTA ANA

Casa Pueblo

C/León 3 (91 420 20 38). Metro Antón Martín. **Open** 5pm-2.30am daily. **Credit** AmEx, MC, V. **Map** p328 I12 ⑭
A handsome, old-fashioned jazz bar hung with antique clocks and black and white photos, Casa Pueblo is popular with a slightly older crowd that knows its whisky. Occasional live music includes jazz and tango (on a Wednesday).

Cenador del Prado

C/Prado 4 (91 429 15 61, www.elcenador delprado.com). Metro Antón Martín. **Open** 8am-midnight Mon-Wed; 8am-2.30am Thur-Sat; noon-midnight Sun. Closed 2wks mid Aug. **Credit** AmEx, DC, MC, V. **Map** p328 H12 ⑮
Under new ownership but with the same air of hauteur, Cenador del Prado (formerly Prado 4) emulates, with no little success, one of the grand cafés of the Habsburg empire. And after a recent refurb, it's looking noticeably fresher.

Cervecería Alemana

Plaza Santa Ana 6 (91 429 70 33). Metro Sol. **Open** 11am-midnight Mon-Thur, Sun; 11am-2am Fri, Sat. **Credit** DC, MC, V. **Map** p328 H12 ⑯
Famous for being Ernest Hemingway's daily haunt (his table, should you be wondering, is the one in the near right-hand corner). The decor is *fin-de-siècle* German bierkeller, with dusty old paintings and dark wood. The tapas can be uninspired and the waiters are unfailingly gruff, but for many this will be an essential stop.

THE BEST APERITIF SPOTS

La Palmera
With vermouth on tap, this is a lovely pre-meal spot if you're dining in Malasaña. *See p181.*

La Venencia
This shabby but atmospheric old-school joint only serves sherry. *See p174.*

El Yantar de Ayer
This vermouth and sherry bar is located in the Mercado de San Miguel. *See p200.*

Cervecería Santa Ana

Plaza Santa Ana 10 (91 429 43 56, www.cervecariasantaana.es). Metro Antón Martín or Sol. **Open** 11am-1.30am Mon-Thur, Sun; 11am-2.30am Fri, Sat. **No credit cards.** **Map** p328 H12 ⑰
Another on this strip of beerhouses (the most exotic brew on offer here is Guinness), this one was never frequented by Hemingway and is consequently cheaper. Two entrances lead into two different spaces; one with seating and one without, and there are tables outside. Good for a light lunch, with decent salads and a range of *pulgas* (small rolls).

Dos Gardenias

C/Santa María 13 (mobile 627 003 571). Metro Antón Martín. **Open** *Oct-May* 8pm-2am Tue-Sun. *June-Sept* 10pm-2am Tue-Sun. **No credit cards.** **Map** p328 I13 ⑱
There's no sign on the door – just look out for this mellow little space painted in warm yellow, orange and blue and the emanating chilled-out vibes, soft flamenco and Brazilian jazz. Kick back on a velvet sofa with the house speciality: a mojito made with brown sugar and Angostura bitters.

Naturbier

Plaza Santa Ana 9 (91 429 39 18, www.naturbier.com). Metro Antón Martín or Sol. **Open** 11am-12.30am Mon-Thur, Sun; 11am-1.30am Fri, Sat. **Credit** MC, V. **Map** p328 H12 ⑲
The least exciting-looking of all the beer cellars lining this side of the Plaza Santa Ana, Naturbier's big draw is its own-made organic beer – in fact, it's the only place in Madrid to brew its own. The tapas are also worth checking out, despite the pricing, which is somewhat creative.

Sol y Sombra

C/Echegaray, 18 (91 542 81 93, www.solysombra.name). Metro Sevilla or Sol. **Open** 10pm-3.30am Tue-Sat. **Credit** V. **Map** p328 H12 ⑳

CONSUME

Gaudeamus Café.

CONSUME

A curious fusion of neon lighting and taurine decor (the name refers to the seats at a bullfight), which just about comes off. It's certainly very popular with the mix of thirtysomething minor celebs and their well-heeled friends. Live acts feature every night from Wednesday to Saturday, with a mix of Spanish cheese, flamenco-chill and lounge on offer. A sniffy door policy discourages scruffy trainers.

★ La Venencia

C/Echegaray 7 (91 429 73 13). Metro Sevilla or Sol. **Open** 1-3.30pm, 7.30pm-1.30am daily. **No credit cards**. Map p328 H12 ㉑
Totally unreconstructed, La Venencia is gloriously shabby, with old, peeling sherry posters, barrels behind the bar and walls burnished gold by decades of tobacco smoke. It serves only sherry (locals will order a crisp, dry *fino* or *manzanilla*, leaving the sweet stuff to the occasional tourist that stumbles in here), along with manchego cheese, *cecina* (air-dried beef) and chorizo by way of tapas. Orders are still chalked up on the bar, and an enamel sign asks customers not to spit on the floor.

RASTRO & LAVAPIES

★ Gaudeamus Café

C/Tribulete 14 (91 528 25 94, www.gaudeamus cafe.com). Metro Lavapiés. **Open** 6pm-midnight Mon-Sat. **No credit cards**. Map p327 H15 ㉒
On the corner of Tribulete and Mesón de Paredes, in the heart of the Rastro, Gaudeamus has attracted cultured types in their droves since it first opened in 2007. They come for the large roof terrace, with spectacular views of the *barrio*'s rooftops, and the 'in-the-know' vibe (the place isn't visible from the

outside – you have to walk through the university building to reach the lift that takes you up to the café). The partitioned-off restaurant area has two seatings – at 8.30pm and 10.15pm.

La Heladería

C/Argumosa 7 (91 528 80 09). Metro Lavapiés. **Open** 10am-midnight Mon-Thur, Sun; 10am-1am Fri, Sat. Closed Nov-Mar. **No credit cards**. Map p328 H14 ㉓
Peruvian owner Yoli is unfailingly charming, and happy to let you try her excellent ice-creams before you buy – blackberry (*mora*) and lemon come recommended. Try the *blanco y negro*, a delicious café-frappé with ice-cream, or one of her milkshakes.

Nuevo Café Barbieri

C/Ave María 45 (91 527 36 58). Metro Lavapiés. **Open** 4pm-2am Tue-Thur, Sun; 4pm-2.30am Fri, Sat. **No credit cards**. Map p328 H14 ㉔
An airy and peaceful space with high ceilings and a dusty elegance, its marble-topped tables slightly chipped and its red-velvet banquettes a little worn. A favourite haunt of journos and wannabe travel writers, Barbieri has plenty of newspapers and magazines, but its ordinary coffee comes at a premium and the service lacks much verve.

★ Oliveros

C/San Millán 4 (91 354 62 52). Metro La Latina. **Open** 1-4pm, 8pm-midnight Tue-Sat; noon-6pm Sun. Closed mid Aug-mid Sept. **Credit** MC, V. Map p327 F13 ㉕
Oliveros is the genuine article, and although it was closed for years, it has been miraculously preserved in its original mid 19th-century bare-bricked state,

complete with tiles and zinc bar. However, it might be worth ringing before going there especially, as opening hours can be somewhat erratic.

Taberna de Tirso de Molina
Plaza de Tirso de Molina 9 (91 429 17 56).
Metro Tirso de Molina. **Open** 8am-2am daily.
Credit MC, V. **Map** p327 G13 ㉖
It has a good stab at looking traditional with tiles, nautically uniformed waiters and exposed brickwork, but this *taberna* is, in fact, quite new. There are plenty of tables where you can eat a decent breakfast on the way to the Rastro, or a very generous set lunch for €8.25. Tapas are available all day, along with heftier dishes such as the towering *parillada de marisco* (seafood platter).

Vinícola Mentridana
C/San Eugenio 9 (91 527 87 60). Metro Antón Martín. **Open** 1pm-1am Mon-Thur, Sun; 1pm-2am Fri, Sat. **No credit cards. Map** p328 I14 ㉗
Frequented by the bohemian hip element of the Lavapiés, this cool wine bar, with tall windows opening on to the street, is gently evocative of the old *bodega* it used to be. An impressive list of well-priced wines by the glass is complemented by tasty canapés, along with mulled wine and *caldo* (broth) in winter, or gazpacho and *granizado* in the summer months.

CHUECA

Ángel Sierra
C/Gravina 11 (91 531 01 26). Metro Chueca.
Open 12.30pm-2.30am Mon-Sat; 12.30pm-2am Sun. **No credit cards. Map** p324 I10 ㉘
This battered old bar with its tiled walls, zinc bar top, overflowing sink and glasses stacked on wooden slats has become the Chueca meeting-place *par excellence*, thanks to its position overlooking the main square. A newer room to the back of the bar, however, has a faux pub look enhanced with amplified MOR radio and a rule that only doubles and pints are served after midnight.

Bar Cock
C/Reina 16 (91 532 28 26, www.barcock.com).
Metro Gran Vía. **Open** *Sept-June* 7pm-3am

INSIDE TRACK HIGH SPIRITS

Be warned: spirit measures in Madrid are much more generous than they are in the UK. When ordering a *gin tonic* (or vodka equivalent), it's customary for the barman to keep pouring the gin into the glass until the customer tells him or her to stop, meaning that you'll often end up with half gin, half tonic.

Mon-Thur, Sun; 7pm-3.30am Fri, Sat. *July,* 9pm-3am Mon-Thur, Sun; 9pm-3.30am Fri,
Credit AmEx, DC, MC, V. **Map** p324 I11 ㉙
A former brothel, Bar Cock is pricey and very s⬛ furnished in what Spaniards think to be the sty⬛ an 'English pub' (red-velvet curtains, embos⬛ leather armchairs and a fake half-timbered effect⬛ still continues to attract those who like to think themselves as being in the know. As a result it ca⬛ get extremely crowded.

★ Le Cabrera
C/Bárbara de Braganza 2 (91 319 94 57,
www.lecabrera.com). Metro Colón. **Open** *Cocktail bar* 4pm-2am Mon-Thur; 4pm-2.30am Fri, Sat. *Gastro bar* 1.30-4pm; 8.30pm-midnight Tue-Thur; 1.30-4pm, 8.30pm-2am Fri, Sat. **Credit** AmEx, DC, MC, V. **Map** p324 J10 ㉚
This excellent new two-storey cocktail bar opened in 2010, with the aim of revolutionising Madrid's cocktail scene through the heady talents of barman and namesake Diego Cabrera. The ground floor bar serves wine and quality tapas, while the basement area has a smaller, intimate feel and is the place to sample the bar's long list of both classic and innovative cocktails. *Photo p177.*

Del Diego
C/Reina 12 (91 523 31 06). Metro Gran Vía.
Open *Sept-July* 7pm-3am Mon-Thur; 7pm-3.30am Fri, Sat. Closed Aug. **Credit** AmEx, MC, V.
Map p324 H11 ㉛
Not to all tastes, with an unchanging, late 1980s, steel-and-blonde-wood *Wall Street* vibe, Del Diego is nevertheless deservedly renowned for its consummately smooth barmen and superb cocktails. Pull up a stool and try a zingy mint *julep del Diego* to kickstart a night's wheeling and dealing.

Finnegan's
Plaza de las Salesas 9 (91 310 05 21). Metro Alonso Martínez. **Open** 11am-1.45am Mon-Fri; 1pm-2am Sat, Sun. **Credit** DC, MC, V.
Map p324 J9/10 ㉜
One for rugby fans, Finnegan's has its own team, the Madrid Lions, and a talent for sniffing out every conceivable match to show on its large screens. In lean sporting times, the void is filled with pub quizzes and DJs (mostly rock) at weekends. Pints of Beamish, Newky Brown and John Smith's complement burgers and other pub grub.

Isolée
C/Infantas, 19 (91 524 12 98, www.isolee.com).
Metro Banco de España. **Open** 10am-10pm Mon-Wed; 10am-9pm Thur-Sat; 3.30pm-10.30pm Sun.
Credit AmEx, DC, MC, V. **Map** p324 I11 ㉝
The tendrils of cool emanating from Chueca are creeping ever further afield. As evidence, we cite Isolée, a multi-faceted café, CD, clothes and kitchenware shop. The café is a little on the pricey side, but

Le Cabrera. See p175.

it does serve decent sushi and bagels. Mostly, though, Isolée is a place for the hip to sip espressos and make use of the Wi-Fi.

Olivera
C/Santo Tomé 8 (no phone). Metro Chueca. **Open** 6pm-2am Mon-Thur, Sun; 6pm-2.30am Fri, Sat. **No credit cards. Map** p324 J10 ❸
A relaxed lounge bar, presided over by a portrait of the owner's mother, Yugoslav film star Olivera Markovic. The musical mood is nu jazz and funk, and the mismatched armchairs and sofas make it an easy place to end up staying all night. Increasingly, though, it's become a stop-off on the pre-club round.

★ Stop Madrid
C/Hortaleza 11 (91 521 88 87, www.stopmadrid. es). Metro Chueca or Gran Vía. **Open** noon-2am daily. **Credit** MC, V. **Map** p324 H11 ❸
When it opened in 1929, this was the first ham and charcuterie shop in Madrid. It's undergone a few changes since then, but many of the original fittings have been retained, and great pride is taken in sourcing the best ingredients for tapas. Of the 50-strong wine list, all are available by the glass.

Zanzíbar
C/Regueros 9 (91 319 90 64, http:// 212.34.146.165/~zanzibar). Metro Alonso Martínez. **Open** *Sept-July* 8pm-3am Mon-Thur, Sun; 8pm-3.30am Fri, Sat. *Aug* 8pm-2am Thur; 8pm-3.30am Fri, Sat. **No credit cards. Map** p324 I9 ❸
Good causes and ethnic chic combine to create a cute and colourful hangout for right-on revellers. On a small stage at the back there are frequent appearances by bossa nova bands, singer-songwriters and storytellers; at other times soft flamenco and reggae tickle the speakers. A few bar snacks are available, along with fair-trade coffee.

MALASAÑA & CONDE DUQUE

★ La Ardosa
C/Colón 13 (91 521 49 79, www.laardosa.com). Metro Tribunal. **Open** 8.30am-2am Mon-Fri; 11.50am-2.30am Sat, Sun. **No credit cards. Map** p323 H9/10 ❸
Having an affair? Then simply duck under the counter to find the most intimate bar-room you could wish for. Out front, meanwhile, this is a lovely old tiled *taberna* lined with dusty bottles, old black and white lithographs and beer posters. A range of canapés has just been added, and the speciality of the house is its draught beer – Bombardier, Budvar and, especially, Guinness.

★ Bar El 2D
C/Velarde 24 (91 448 64 72). Metro Tribunal. **Open** *Sept-June* 1pm-2am Mon-Wed, Sun; 1pm-3am Thur-Sat. *July, Aug* 6pm-2am Mon-Wed, Sat; 1pm-3am Thur, Fri. **No credit cards. Map** p323 H8 ❸
The emblematic Malasaña hang-out, packed at weekends and drowsily mellow in the afternoons, with a tiled bar and engraved mirrors, nicotine-stained walls and lazily circling ceiling fans. To drink there's vermouth, lager and Beamish on tap, plus plenty of bottled beers and a small range of wines, served (if you dare) in *porrones*, long-spouted drinking jars.

CONSUME

★ Bar El Palentino

C/Pez 12 (91 532 30 58,
www.myspace.com/barpalentino). Metro Callao
or Noviciado. **Open** 8.30am-2am Mon-Sat.
No credit cards. Map p323 G10 ⓷⓽
Something of a Madrid institution, this old-school
neighbourhood bar is popular with seemingly everyone – the place is always packed with every. A
Wooden panelling, fluorescent strip ceiling lamps, a
much-loved owner and notoriously cheap (but good)
drinks attract punters of all ages, creating a buzzing,
sociable and quintessentially *madrileño* vibe.
Sandwiches help to soak up the *cañas.*
▶ *Calle del Pez is home to several other much-*
loved bars, including El Pez Gordo (No.6, 91 522
32 08), known for its creative tapas; Argentinian-
run Antorcha (No.4, 91 532 44 29), popular for
weekend brunch; the two-storey Cafeina (No.18,
91 522 03 31), which has DJs at night, and El
Hombre Moderno (No.2, 91 521 44 32),
something of a home-from-home.

★ Café Comercial

Glorieta de Bilbao 7 (91 521 56 55). Metro
Bilbao. **Open** 7.30am-midnight daily. **No credit**
cards. Map p323 H8 ④⓪
Café Comercial still rates as one of the classic Madrid
bars, with its original battered brown leather seats,
revolving doors and marbled walls. A cursory nod
to the modern age comes in the shape of the internet
terminals upstairs, where American gap-year students write home about the old men playing chess
alongside them.

Café Isadora

C/Divino Pastor 14 (91 445 71 54). Metro Bilbao.
Open 4pm-2am Mon-Thur, Sun; 4pm-2.30am Fri,
Sat. **No credit cards. Map** p323 G8 ④①
An elegant shrine to the dancer, Isadora Duncan,
with a chequered floor, marble-topped tables and an
eerie collection of prints of 'that scarf', alongside frequently changing exhibitions. Along with a range
of *patxaráns,* many of them own-made, is a list of
'aguas' (cocktails made with cava). *Agua de Valencia*
is the original and best, featuring orange juice, gin,
Cointreau and vodka. (Duncan was killed when the
the scarf she was wearing got caught in the rear
wheel of her car, strangling her.)

Café Manuela

C/San Vicente Ferrer 29 (91 531 70 37). Metro
Tribunal. **Open** *Oct-May* 6pm-2am Mon-Thur;
4pm-2am Fri, Sat. *June-Sept* 6pm-2.30am daily.
Credit MC, V. **Map** p323 H9 ④②
Stacked to the rafters with board games, Café
Manuela has been a hive of activity since the Movida
days. Its handsome art nouveau decor and conveniently nicotine-coloured walls are still the backdrop
to occasional live music and other performances, but
otherwise it's a great place to reacquaint yourself
with Cluedo and Mastermind.

Café El Moderno

Plaza de las Comendadoras 1 (91 531 62 77, 91
522 48 35). Metro Noviciado. **Open** *Sept-July* 3pm-
1.30am Mon-Thur, Sun; 3pm-2.30am Fri, Sat. *Aug*
5.30pm-1.30am Mon-Thur, Sun; 5.30pm-2.30am Fri,
Sat. **No credit cards. Map** p323 F8 ④③
El Moderno's art deco look is entirely fake, but none
the worse for it, and, along with its large terrace,
attracts a mixture of local characters and curious
tourists. The specialities are teas, milkshakes and hot
chocolates, with an impressive 30 varieties of each.
Fans of *Sex and Lucia* will recognise the building as
Lorenzo's apartment block.
▶ *Café Comendadoras, under the same*
ownership and with similar fare, is located right
next door (91 532 11 32).

Café de Ruiz

C/Ruiz 11 (91 446 12 32). Metro Bilbao. **Open**
2.30pm-2am Mon-Thur, Sun; 2.30pm-2.30am Fri,
Sat. **Credit** MC, V. **Map** p323 G8 ④④
A quiet favourite with the smarter denizens of the
neighbourhood, Café de Ruiz is an elegant place, with
comfortable sofas and dramatic flower arrangements. A big draw is its own-made ice-cream and
other tempting sweet treats, such as hot chocolate
with *churros,* milkshakes, lemon tart and cheesecake.

Café Rustika

C/Limón 11 (91 542 15 67, www.rustikacafe.es).
Metro Noviciado. **Open** 6.30pm-midnight Tue-
Thur, Sun; 6.30pm-2.30am Fri, Sat. **Credit**
AmEx, DC, MC, V. **Map** p323 F9 ④⑤
Whimsical interiors, funky lo-fi music and lots of
hanging lanterns make this one of the most relaxing
cafés in a neighbourhood full of them. New ownership brings a randomly international menu with
dishes from couscous to chop suey to chocolate cake
and a wide selection of teas.

Casa Camacho

C/San Andrés 4 (91 531 35 98). Metro Tribunal.
Open noon-2am Mon-Thur, Sun; noon-2.30am
Fri, Sat. Closed mid Aug-mid Sept. **No credit**
cards. Map p323 G/H9 ④⑥
A rough diamond, the diminutive Casa Camacho has
changed little since it opened in 1928, except for the
addition of a fruit machine and a TV – both in constant use. Pre-war dust coats the bottles and plastic

---

INSIDE TRACK EARLY TIPPLES

Although Madrid's bar scene is a
notoriously late-starting affair, there have
been moves in recent years to popularise
after-work drinking – with some success.
Many bars now adopt 'after-work' happy
hours and promotions, so you won't
necessarily need to adjust your timetable.

In the Frame Tertulias

The rise of Madrid's café society was beautifully captured by Solana.

The intellectual life of Spain once revolved around the ephemeral institution known as the *tertulia*. Originating in the humanist salons of 16th-century Seville, the *tertulia* is a gathering of people united by a common interest, which can range from mathematics to gastronomy, but has traditionally been literature. And Spain being a country where people tend to go out rather than meet in each other's houses, these gatherings have invariably been held in bars and cafés.

The rise of the *tertulia* in Madrid, as depicted in many paintings of the time, coincided with the city's emergence in the early 19th century as the centre of a café life rivalling that of Paris and Vienna. Café life has always flourished at times of great political repression, the café being a place whose proverbial smoky gloom has provided a suitably furtive retreat for dissidents. During the grey, autocratic rule of Spain's Ferdinand VII, the *tertulia* became an expression of political and cultural freedom.

Tertulias took place in many of the cafés that by the 1830s had almost entirely encircled the Puerta del Sol. But the most influential of these gatherings was the one associated with a tiny, rat-infested basement café next to the neo-classical Teatro Español (the present bland reconstruction bears little resemblance to the original establishment). The place was officially called the Café del Príncipe, but everyone came to know it as the 'Parnasillo' or 'Little Parnassus', on account of its attracting all the fashionable writers of the day. Among these were the much revered satirical essayist Mariano José de Larra and the writer Ramón de Mesonero Romanos, who famously wrote that in 'this miserable little room' they succeeded in shaking the very foundations of Spanish life and culture.

With the evolution towards the end of the 19th century of Madrid's idiosyncratically late eating and drinking hours, *tertulias* proliferated as never before, reaching their apogee in the 1920s under the guidance of a writer sometimes referred to as 'the second of the Ramones', Ramón Gómez de la Serna. Every Saturday night, from around 10pm until dawn, a *tertulia*, presided over by Gómez de la Serna, was held in what was soon dubbed 'The Sacred Crypt of the Pombo', a now vanished café off the Puerta del Sol. The solemnity of these celebrated meetings was captured in a sombre painting by José Gutiérrez Solana (*pictured*). La Serna is pictured standing, in the centre. These gatherings were also slightly ridiculed by the film-maker Luis Buñuel, who later described how 'we used to arrive, greet each other, and order a drink – usually coffee, and a lot of water – until a meandering conversation began about the latest literary publications or political upheavals.'

Most liberal and avant-garde associates of the Pombo went into exile after the Civil War, thus radically diminishing the cultural life of the capital. Subsequently many of the cafés in the centre of Madrid were succeeded by the HQs of large banks, and many more suffered the humiliation of being transformed into Formica-lined, American-style cafeterias.

La Tertulia del Café Pombo, *by José Gutiérrez Solana, is found at the Reina Sofía (see p78).*

CONSUME

The Grape and the Good

Fine wines at fine prices, and a pleasing lack of pomp.

Madrid is an oenophile's playground, with none of the solemnity and hefty price-tags attached to wine-drinking elsewhere. Everyone drinks it here, from builders to nuns. It so pervades daily life, in fact, that the Spanish Ministry of Agriculture categorises wine as food rather than an alcoholic beverage.

Wine-lovers around the globe have now caught on to the fact that Spanish labels are the best value for your euro. *Wine Spectator* and American wine tsar Robert Parker claim Spain is one of the hottest regions in Europe. The sad fact remains, however, that a lot of bars serve plonk. To taste the good stuff, get thee to a wine bar. Madrid has a number of cosy little *enotecas* where you can settle in at the bar and try different wines by the glass. **La Cruzada** (C/Amnistía 8, 91 548 01 31), for example, offers a delectable selection of reasonably priced *vinos*. King Alfonso XII reportedly used to frequent this bar when he needed to escape the nearby royal palace for a clandestine tipple. Check out the lovely carvings of bare-breasted women on the bar, dating back to 1827. Other reliable spots for quality wines include **La Taberna de Cien Vinos** (C/Nuncio 17), **González** (*see p197*), **Entrevinos** (C/Ferraz 36, 91 548 31 14) and **Vinoteca Barbechera** (*see p161*).

An entertaining way to dive into Spanish wine is to attend one of Madrid's many wine-tasting classes, known as *cursos de cata*, which get you happily swirling,

sniffing and sipping good wine. **La Carte des Vins** (C/Hermosilla 85, 91 577 19 71, www.lacartedesvins.com) is the Madrid branch of a French franchise that offers weekly wine-tasting courses in English and Spanish. These include the 'Wine: Basic Notions' course, a 90-minute introduction, costing €15, as well as personalised tastings.

AtSpain (91 547 50 91, www.atspain. com), an online shop for Spanish gifts and gourmet products, also arranges fun English wine and tapas classes with sommeliers from Madrid's best wine stores. You might also pay a visit to the Torres Bodega's **Centro Cultural del Vino** (C/Martires Concepcionistas 19, 91 401 77 62, www.torres.es) for its professional wine classes covering everything from soil types to food pairing, over the course of two nights. The city's best wine shops, **Reserva y Cata**, **Lavinia** and **Bodegas Santa Cecilia** (for all, *see p200*), also offer regular *cursos de cata* in Spanish.

---

flowers on display and the floor is a sea of toothpicks and cigarette ends, but for a slice of real neighbourhood life it can't be beat.

★ La Ida
C/Colón 11 (91 522 91 07). Metro Tribunal. **Open** 1pm-2am daily. Closed Aug. **No credit cards. Map** p323 H9/10 **47**
La Movida meets *Friends* in this cramped but jolly little café, where everybody knows everybody else. This is where the painfully cool neo-punks from the nearby Mercado Fuencarral come to let their guard down, tucking into courgette tart and canapés at the scrubbed pine tables amid perky green walls. .

★ El Jardín Secreto
C/Conde Duque 2 (91 541 80 23). Metro Plaza de España or Ventura Rodríguez. **Open** 6.30pm-

1.30am Mon-Thur; 6.30pm-2.30am Fri, Sat; 5.30pm-12.30am Sun. **Credit** DC, MC, V. **Map** p323 E9 **48**
Although it also functions as a restaurant, El Jardín Secreto – decked out with mismatched furniture and arty knick-knacks – is most popular as a *merienda* (afternoon tea) spot. The crowds tend to show up at 6.30pm, right when the place opens. Its cakes and desserts – in particular the chocolate orgasm – are much talked about, and there's a large selection of chocolate drinks, teas and coffees on the menu. Open late, it's also popular as a cocktail spot.

Laydown
Plaza Mostenses 9 (91 548 79 37, www.laydown.es). Metro Plaza de España. **Open** 9.30pm-2.30am Tue-Sat; noon-6pm Sun. **Credit** AmEx, DC, MC, V. **Map** p323 F10 **49**

This flashy, minimalist bar, restaurant and club – which also has branches in Barcelona and Valencia – is known for its chic lounge chairs with comfy mattresses (the clue is in the name). Dinner is a set meal and there is live music or theatre performances most nights. Once dinner is over, it's DJ time, as everyone clambers out of bed to bust a few grooves. The Sunday brunch is very popular.

Lola Loba
C/Palma 38 (91 522 96 16). Metro Noviciado. **Open** noon-2am Mon-Sat. **No credit cards.** **Map** p323 G8/9 ⑩

Lola Loba is named after a *copla* singer who ran away from her abusive American millionaire husband and opened this bar. In 1872 he found her and murdered her, and 'tis said her ghost still prowls within the red-brick walls. What is not known is whether she approves of the jazz, funk and house, or the fab *tostas*, slathered in mozzarella, tomato and basil; caramelised onion with brie, or smoked salmon with camembert.

★ Lolina Vintage Café
Espíritu Santo 9 (91 523 58 59, www.lolinacafe.com). Metro Tribunal. **Open** 9am-2am Mon-Thur, Sun; 9am-2.30am Fri, Sat. **Credit** AmEx, DC, MC, V. **Map** p323 H9 ㉜

Now a couple of years' old, Lolina was among the new wave of openings on Calle de Espíritu Santo. The cute, retro space – with its 1970s wallpaper and vintage floor lamps – is a popular hangout for arty types and young expats, drawn by its pan-European vibe, brunch-style menu and large selection of teas, coffees and juices. The good-value breakfasts start from €2.50; and if you visit in the evening, be sure to order a mojito or caipirinha – the house specialities.

★ La Palmera
C/Palma 67 (mobile 630 884 470). Metro Noviciado. **Open** 8pm-2am Mon-Thur; 8pm-2.30am Fri, Sat. **No credit cards.** **Map** p323 F8 ㉛

The tiles in this tiny, crowded bar date back to its opening at the beginning of the last century, and have featured in various magazines. For years it lay in terminal decline, until it was bought in the late 1990s by a long-term regular. It almost exclusively serves vermouth and beer to a loyal crowd made up of both locals and expats.
▶ *Just up the street is La Caracola (C/Palma 70, 91 521 11 56), another excellent bar in the same vein, with a dark, intimate interior, top-notch cocktails and friendly bar staff.*

El Parnasillo
C/San Andrés 33 (91 447 00 79). Metro Bilbao. **Open** 2.30pm-3am Mon-Thur, Sun; 2.30pm-3.30am Fri, Sat. **No credit cards.** **Map** p323 H8 ㉝

Long frequented by writers, artists, journalists and intellectuals, the art nouveau El Parnasillo was very much at the centre of Madrid's cultural renewal in the '70s and '80s, to the extent that it was bombed by a far-right group. It's unlikely to excite the same emotion these days, but is still an evocative place for a cocktail, sarnie or *pa tumaca* (bread rubbed with tomato) topped with cheese, ham or smoked salmon.

★ Pepe Botella
C/San Andrés 12 (91 522 43 09). Metro Tribunal. **Open** *Sept-July* 10am-2am Mon-Thur, Sun; 11am-3am Fri, Sat; 11am-2am Sun. *Aug* 3pm-2am Mon-Thur, Sun; 3pm-3am Fri, Sat. **No credit cards.** **Map** p323 H8 ㉞

CONSUME

La Ida.

A cineaste's delight, the colourful Pepe Botella is frequented by the likes of director Alejandro Amenábar and actor Eduardo Noriega. For all that, it's wonderfully unpretentious, and attracts an intelligent bunch of mainly thirty- and fortysomethings, who engage in lively debate while smoking for Spain. The place has free Wi-Fi.

★ El Rincón
C/Espíritu Santo 26 (91 522 19 86). Metro Tribunal. **Open** 10am-2am daily. **Credit** DC, MC, V. **Map** p323 H9 ❺❺
Popular with both locals and expats, laid-back El Rincón has a classic new-wave Malasaña feel, with chequered floors, powder blue walls, black and white photos on the walls, mismatched wooden tables and a boho vibe (a sign outside reads *'No fumen porros en la terraza'* – 'Don't smoke joints on the terrace.'). For a bite to eat, try the house gazpacho (€3.50) or the quality sandwiches and cakes. There's also good coffee and a large range of loose teas, and this must be one of the few places in Madrid that serves Chegworth Valley apple and pear juices.

THE RETIRO & SALAMANCA

El Botánico
C/Ruiz de Alarcón 27 (91 420 23 42). Metro Banco de España. **Open** 8.30am-midnight daily. **Credit** AmEx, DC, MC, V. **Map** p328 K13 ❺❻
Confusingly, this quiet bar-restaurant actually sits on C/Espalter, just around the corner, and overlooking the botanical gardens. Tucked away from the tourist drag, it's very quiet considering its proximity to the Prado, and has a peaceful, shaded terrace. It's a good spot for breakfast, and there are tapas later in the day.

★ Café Gijón
Paseo de Recoletos 21 (91 521 54 25, www.cafegijon.com). Metro Banco de España or Colón. **Open** 7am-1.30am Mon-Fri, Sun; 7am-2.30am Sat. **Credit** AmEx, DC, MC, V. **Map** p324 J10 ❺❼
Still charming after all these years, this is Madrid's definitive literary café, open since 1888. It still holds poetry *tertulias* on Monday nights, and publishes a

magazine filled with doodles and thoughts from visiting writers. A pianist tinkles the ivories to a packed terrace in summer, while in winter it's heaving inside.

Castellana 8
Paseo de la Castellana 8 (91 578 34 87, www.castellana8.es). Metro Colón. **Open** 11.30am-2.30am daily. **Credit** AmEx, MC, V. **Map** p324 K8 ❺❽
Previously known as Jazzanova, Castellana 8 remains a supremely smooth bar-restaurant-club, its black walls softened by clever uplighting, orange velvet cushions and a mellow soundtrack of jazz and blues. Brunch on Sundays is dished up with cocktails and live music, though not, sadly, on the terrace outside, which is limited to drinking only. The upmarket location and older clientele mean predictably higher prices.

James Joyce
C/Alcalá 59 (91 575 49 01, www.jamesjoyce madrid. com). Metro Banco de España. **Open** 10am-2am Mon-Thur, Sun; 10am-2.30am Fri, Sat. **Credit** AmEx, DC, MC, V. **Map** p324 K11 ❺❾
Previously known as Kitty O'Shea's, this is the Madrid outpost of what is now a global chain of Oirish theme pubs. With both Guinness and Murphy's on tap, pub grub, chatty staff and plenty of rugby and Premier League matches showing on two big screens and three TVs, it's all much as you'd expect. Of more interest, perhaps, is that the pub sits on the site of the historic Café Lion, a haunt of post-Civil War literati.

El Pavellón del Espejo
Paseo de Recoletos 31 (91 319 11 22, www.restauranteelespejo.com). Metro Colón. **Open** 9am-1am Mon-Thur; 9am-2am Fri-Sun. **Credit** AmEx, DC, MC, V. **Map** p324 K9/10 ❻❶
Not nearly as historic as the neighbouring Gijón, although it may look it: when it opened in 1978, 'the Mirror' ('*el Espejo*') set out to be the art nouveau bar Madrid never had, with positively Parisian 1900s decor. Its terrace bar out on the Paseo de Recoletas occupies a splendid glass pavilion reminiscent of a giant Tiffany lamp. Fashionable and comfortable, it has excellent tapas at reasonable prices.

ARGUELLES

Bruin
Paseo del Pintor Rosales 48 (91 541 59 21). Metro Argüelles. **Open** 11am-11pm Tue-Thur, Sun; 11am-2am Fri, Sat. **No credit cards.** **Map** p322 C8 ❻❶
A wonderfully old-fashioned ice-cream parlour, with a terrace overlooking the Parque del Oeste. In contrast to its 1950s feel, some of its 40 own-made flavours are decidedly modern: try olive oil, tomato, idiazábal cheese, tomato or sherry. Diabetics get a look-in, too, with the sugar-free varieties.

INSIDE TRACK
ALFONSO OF CAFE GIJON

Alfonso, who sold cigarettes, matches and lottery tickets just inside the entrance of Café Gijón (*see above*) for over 30 years, sadly died in 2006; a portrait and plaque – above the cigarette machine that replaced him – commemorate his life and long contribution to the café.

CONSUME

Shops & Services

A new wave of hip boutiques aims to defy the recession.

The high streets of Madrid have undeniably taken on the identikit look of most European capitals, albeit with Spanish chains – Zara, Mango, System Action – proliferating; but get off those main thoroughfares and what strikes you is the curious mix of the traditional and the new. Here the chains and international franchises rub shoulders with museum-piece, family-run businesses and ancient shops dedicated to just one product – espadrilles, maybe, or Spanish ceramics.

Visitors from cities with cutting-edge fashion scenes, such as London, New York and Berlin, are sometimes disappointed by Madrid's clothes shops; however, the scattering of hip new openings around Malasaña, Conde Duque and Alonso Martínez is starting to heighten consumer expectations.

WHERE TO SHOP

Madrid is not a large city, and its main shopping areas break down into several distinctive zones, all conveniently within walking distance – or a short metro ride – of each other. Between Sol and Gran Vía are **C/Preciados** and **C/Carmen**, always bustling with shoppers, and boasting a mix of chains and smaller stores selling cheap and mid-price clothes, shoes and accessories. Several branches of El Corte Inglés are to be found in this area. **Gran Vía** itself is given over to the flagship stores of many a household name – H&M, Zara and the Nike Store, to name but three. After battling through the crowds of dawdling shoppers, the tranquil area of **Los Austrias** comes as a welcome respite, with its musical instrument stores, bohemian gift shops and treasure troves of decorative items. If you're all about labels, then **Salamanca** is the place to be, in particular C/Serrano, where on the same block you will find Loewe, Yves St Laurent and La Perla, as well as smaller designer boutiques throughout the area. **Chueca** houses a host of

hip independents, such Bunkha (*see p192*), vintage store Lotta (*see p192*) and bookshop Panta Rhei (*see p188*), as well as the youth-orientated brands of **C/Fuencarral** (home to MAC, Diesel, Puma, Fornarina, as well as Spanish brands Hoss Intropia and Hakei). Here you'll also find the shopping mall **El Mercado de Fuencarral**, a popular hangout for the city's fashion-conscious teens and twentysomethings, hosting streetwear shops with names like Fuck, Alter-nativa and Cannibal, as well as tattoo parlours and trendy hairdressers. For shoes, head down C/Augusto Figueroa, and then continue north up C/Barquillo for the more refined fashion boutiques, most of which are squeezed into the area between C/Argensola and Plaza Santa Barbara. West of here, the trendy triangle recently named **triBall**, just west of where C/Fuencarral meets Gran Vía, and the area around **C/Conde Duque** are now home to some of the city's most interesting boutiques. The city's flea market, the **Rastro**, is an obligatory visit, but more for the atmosphere than the goods – you will almost certainly walk away empty-handed.

INSIDE TRACK QUEUING

Spaniards do queue (although it may not look like it) – just ask '¿Quién es el último/la última?' ('Who's last in the queue?') before joining.

OPENING HOURS

Opening times are changing, as is the traditional August break. While smaller stores will still close for two or three hours at lunch and stay shut on Saturday afternoons, some mid-size and nearly all large outlets will remain

vices

y. If you have yet to get used to ⸘ck lunch and can face the heat in ⸘er, head to the bigger stores in the ⸘n and you will miss the crowds.

⸘e from large retailers brought about ⸘ation of the laws on Sunday opening ⸘l amid much grumbling from small ⸘nesses, who find it very hard to compete ⸘ such timetables. As a result, large retailers ⸘ – and do – open every first Sunday of the ⸘onth. A further bonus on these Sundays is ⸘he closure of Gran Vía to private transport. As revenue from tourists becomes more vital to the shopkeepers of Madrid, August is no longer a month where the city closes down.

ONE-STOP SHOPS

El Corte Inglés
C/Preciados 1-3 & 9, Sol & Gran Vía (all branches 91 379 80 00/Tel-entradas ticket phoneline 90 240 02 22, www.elcorteingles.es). Metro Sol. **Open** 10am-10pm Mon-Sat; 11am-9pm 1st Sun of mth except Aug. **Credit** AmEx, DC, MC, V. **Map** p323 G11.

Spain's biggest retail concern has blown all the rest of the competition out of the water. El Corte Inglés is the solution when all else fails for some, but the first choice for many. You can get practically everything you need, be it clothes, household goods, books or multimedia products, and the store also offers a range of services from cutting keys to booking tickets. Most outlets also have well-stocked, if expensive, supermarkets. Information points staffed by multilingual employees are a plus as is the post-sale, money-back guarantee. The branches on C/Preciados specialise in film, music, electronics, books, fashion and sports. This branch on the Plaza de Callao has homewares, toys and electronics.
Other locations throughout the city.

FNAC
C/Preciados 28, Sol & Gran Vía (91 595 61 00/ 91 595 62 00, www.fnac.es). Metro Callao. **Open** 10am-9.30pm Mon-Sat;

11.30am-9.30pm Sun, public hols. **Credit** AmEx, MC, V. **Map** p323 G11.

The French giant offers a huge range of CDs, DVDs, videos and books, plus computer hardware and software, all at competitive prices and under one roof. Among the CDs there are good world music and flamenco sections, and the helpful staff can look up titles on the database. There is a reasonable English-language book section, with recent paperbacks as well as classics. On the second floor is a room to sit and read while listening to music. Downstairs there's a ticket booking service, a café and paper shop with a good range of foreign press and magazines, and the FNAC Forum, which hosts readings and film and record launches.

After hours

Three names dominate after-hours shopping in Madrid. The most ubiquitous, and open 24 hours a day, is **Sprint** (7/11 re-branded), which sells prepared food, hot and cold drinks, plus press and magazines. **OpenCor** and **Vip's** have shorter hours (8am-2am and 9am-3am respectively), but have a greater selection of goods, including supermarket products, fresh food, CDs, DVDs, books and gifts. In Vip's, Spanish and English-language press is sold, and you can get films processed. After-hours shops are not allowed to sell alcohol after 10pm (9pm on Sundays). All have branches throughout town, but below are the most central.

OpenCor
C/Fuencarral 118, Chamberí (91 591 38 96). Metro Bilbao. **Open** 8am-2am daily. **Credit** AmEx, DC, MC, V. **Map** p323 H7.

Sprint
C/Arenal 28, Los Austrias (no phone). Metro Ópera. **Open** 24hrs daily. **No credit cards.** **Map** p327 F11.

Vip's
Gran Vía 43 (91 559 66 21). Metro Callao or Santo Domingo. **Open** 9am-3am daily. **Credit** AmEx, DC, MC, V. **Map** p323 G11.

SHOPPING CENTRES

ABC Serrano
C/Serrano 61 & Paseo de la Castellana 34, Salamanca (91 577 50 31, www.abcserrano.com). Metro Rubén Darío. **Open** 10am-9pm Mon-Sat; noon-8pm 1st Sun of mth. **Map** p325 L6/7.

Occupying the building that once housed the ABC newspaper, this upmarket and well located shopping mall has eight floors. Four of them are dedicated to fashion, designer and high street, sportswear, jewellery, crafts and hi-fi. There are three restaurants on

CONSUME

On Easy Street

Madrid's shopping streets have traditionally specialise[...]

Up until Madrid's promotion to capital status in 1561, and the construction of the Plaza Mayor, guilds of tradespeople and artisans tended to cluster together in certain streets or quarters. A brief glance at a map of the higgledy-piggledy street layout in the environs of the Plaza Mayor shows this clearly: many streets are named after the guilds, *gremios*, that were concentrated in the immediate vicinity.

A little north of the Plaza Mayor, just across the Calle Mayor, is the Plaza de Herredores, 'Blacksmiths' Square', and running from there to Calle Arenal is the Calle de las Hileras, or 'Spinners' Street'. Parallel to this is Calle Bordadores, 'Embroiderers' Street', whose artisans presumably bought their supplies of *hilo*, thread, one street over. Also serving the textile trade were the *coloreros*, purveyors of dyes, who were established in the tiny street of the same name just a few yards away. To the west of Plaza Mayor is the Calle Sal, thus named because salt was sold from the royal deposits there. A few yards away is the minuscule Calle Botoneras, where buttons were sold, and close by is the Calle de los Esparteros, where mats were manufactured from esparto grass, still used nowadays to make espadrilles. To the south of the square is the Calle Latoneros, where the brassmongers traded. This street feeds into the Calle de los Cuchilleros, 'Knifemakers' Street', where Plaza Mayor butchers bought their cleavers. A little further south, what is nowadays the main drag of the Rastro, the Ribera de Curtidores, 'Tanners' Alley', was close to the city's slaughterhouse. The name 'Rastro' very possibly has its origin in the blood-stained trail, or *rastro*, left by the slaughtered animals.

As the centuries went by and Madrid expanded, these trades slowly disappeared or moved out and other commercial establishments sprang up. During the 19th and 20th centuries other shopping thoroughfares became associated with vendors of certain types of product, even though the street names now had nothing to do with the wares on sale. Right up until the advent of the PC, if you wanted to buy a typewriter you headed for Hortaleza and Hernán Cortés streets (a couple of shops selling Remington portables are still on the

latter). If you needed anything orthopaedic you went to the Carretas street, where there are still a couple of establishments selling these items. Books – both new and second-hand – you found in the Calle de los Libreros and the Cuesta de Moyano, as you still do today. The Calles de la Paz and Postas have long had a tradition of shops dealing in religious artefacts and the Plaza de Pontejos still has several haberdashers and remnants shops.

More recently, specialised streets have started to deal in modern goods. Walk along the Calle Barquillo in Chueca, and you'll notice an abundance of shops selling hi-fi equipment, hence the nickname Calle del Sonido ('Sound Street'). From here runs the Calle Almirante, which since the '80s has been colonised by a number of designer fashion shops, earning it the moniker 'Calle de la Moda', a title for which C/Claudio Coello in the Salamanca neighbourhood would now contend. More fashion, of the street- and clubwear variety, is concentrated along the C/Fuencarral, riding the Mercado de Fuencarral wave of the last few years. They may not be tinsmiths or button sellers any more, but many of Madrid's retailers still seem happier having their direct competitors just across the street.

CONSUME

the upper floors, a café on the ground floor and a lively summer *terraza* on the fourth, plus a gym at the top.

Centro Comercial La Vaguada
Avda Monforte de Lemos 36, Barrio del Pilar (information 91 730 10 00, www.enlavaguada. com). Metro Barrio del Pilar. **Open** 10am-10pm Mon-Sat, 1st Sun of month. *Leisure area only* 10am-12.30am Mon-Fri; 10am-2.30am Sat, Sun.
Madrid's first giant mall, and still the largest in the city, La Vaguada has around 350 outlets. There's a branch of El Corte Inglés (*see p184*), and the upper floor is given over to leisure, with cinemas and a bowling alley. A bit of a trek, but the metro line is fast.

Centro Comercial Príncipe Pío
Paseo de la Florida s/n, Moncloa (91 758 00 40, www.ccprincipepio.com). Metro Príncipe Pío. **Open** 10am-10pm Mon-Sat; 11am-10pm Sun. *Leisure area only* 10am-1am Mon-Thur; 10am-2am Fri, Sat; 11am-1am Sun. **Map** p322 C11.
A welcome addition to one of the city's main transport hubs. Built into the shell of the old train station, the mall manages to pack in a deceptively large amount of shops and eateries – from the Body Shop and H&M to a Vip's restaurant and the obligatory Starbucks.

El Jardín de Serrano
C/Goya 6-8, Salamanca (91 577 00 12, www.jardindeserrano.es). Metro Serrano. **Open** 9.30am-9.30pm Mon-Sat. **Map** p325 L9.
This mall may be small but it's a gem, with designer boutiques, expensive shoe shops and a classy café.

Las Tiendas de Serrano
C/Serrano 88, Salamanca (no phone). Metro Rubén Darío. **Open** 10.30am-2.30pm, 5-8.30pm Mon-Sat (shops may vary). **Map** p325 L7.
Another small shopping mall, dominated by shops selling upmarket designer fashion, party clothes and accessories, mainly for women.

ANTIQUES
If you want antiques, head to the **Rastro** (*see p200*). On the main drag, C/Ribera de Curtidores, are several arcades where you'll find everything from old junk to authentic antiques. The adjoining streets, such as C/Mira el Río Alta and C/Carnero, are more downmarket and can yield real bargains. Elsewhere, there are a handful of antique shops in the C/Prado and, over in Salamanca, on and around C/Claudio Coello, are lots of upmarket, specialist dealers.

Galerías Piquer
C/Ribera de Curtidores 29, Rastro (no phone, www.dai.es/piquer). Metro Puerta de Toledo. **Open** 10.30am-2pm, 5-8pm Mon-Fri; 10.30am-2pm Sat, Sun. **Credit** varies. **Map** p327 G15.

The antique shops in this Rastro arcade stock pieces for punters who don't want to have to brush the dust off their purchases. Opening times may vary.

Tiempos Modernos
C/Arrieta 17, Los Austrias & La Latina (91 542 85 94, www.tiempos-modernos.com). Metro Ópera. **Open** 11am-2pm, 5-8.30pm Mon-Fri; 11am-2pm Sat. Closed 1st 3 wks of Aug.
Credit AmEx, DC, MC, V. **Map** p323 E11.
Tiempos Modernos deals in modern Spanish painting and hosts temporary shows and exhibitions of photography and artwork. The main line of business, though, is the great range of 1940s, '50s and '60s furniture. *Photo p188.*

El Transformista
C/Mirá el Río Baja 18, Rastro & Lavapiés (91 539 88 33). Metro Puerta de Toledo. **Open** 11am-2pm Tue-Sun. **No credit cards**. **Map** p327 F15.
Original '50s and '60s furniture and collectibles are up for grabs at this shop. Almodóvar is rumoured to source items for his movies here.

BOOKS
FNAC (*see p184*) has an excellent general selection. A traditional centre of the book trade is **Calle de los Libreros** ('Booksellers' Street') off Gran Vía, with many specialist bookshops.

★ La Casa del Libro
Gran Vía 29 (91 521 66 57, www.casadellibro.com). Metro Gran Vía. **Open** 9.30am-9.30pm Mon-Sat; 11am-9pm Sun. **Credit** AmEx, DC, MC, V. **Map** p323 H11.
Madrid's most comprehensive bookshop by far, La Casa del Libro covers just about every subject imaginable in Spanish, but also has good sections of literature, reference and teaching material in English and other languages.

Librería de Mujeres
C/San Cristóbal 17, Los Austrias (91 521 70 43). Metro Sol. **Open** *Oct-June* 10am-2pm,

INSIDE TRACK
MUSEUM SHOPS

Madrid's 'Paseo del Arte' museums all have excellent book- and souvenir shops. The Reina Sofía's is particularly good for books, while the Prado, in addition to its main shop inside the museum, also has a mobile shop outside the gallery before you enter. The new CaixaForum cultural centre is great for quirky gifts and useful gadgets.

CONSUME

Tiempos Modernos. *See p187.*

5-8pm Mon-Fri; 10am-2pm Sat. *July-Sept* 10am-2pm, 5-8pm Mon-Fri. **Credit** MC, V. **Map** p327 G12.

Madrid's best women's bookshop goes by the motto '*Los libros no muerden, tampoco el feminismo*' – 'Books don't bite, neither does feminism'.

★ Ocho y Medio

C/Martín de los Heros 11, Argüelles (91 559 06 28, www.ochoymedio.com). Metro Plaza de España. **Open** 10am-2pm, 5-8.30pm Mon-Sat. **Credit** AmEx, DC, MC, V. **Map** p323 E9.

This superb cinema bookshop is an absolute treat for film buffs, with plenty of works in English and other languages, plus DVDs and film paraphernalia. *See also p221* **Profile**.

★ Panta Rhei

C/Hernán Cortés 7, Chueca (91 319 89 02, www.panta-rhei.es). Metro Chueca. **Open** 10.30am-8.30pm Mon-Fri; 11am-8pm Sat. **Credit** MC, V. **Map** p324 H10.

This friendly Chueca bookshop sells an excellent range of illustrated and photography books, many in English and many with a humorous bent. Its stylish cotton totes make nice, cheap souvenirs too.

La Vida es Sueño

C/Mayor 59, Sol & Gran Vía (91 364 16 82). Metro Sol. **Open** 11am-8.30pm Mon, Wed-Fri; 11am-2pm, 5-8pm Sat, Sun. **Credit** MC, V. **Map** p327 F12.

The Museo Municipal's bookshop offers a wealth of written materials, mainly in Spanish, covering all aspects of the city's history and culture, some of them beautiful coffee-table editions.

Children

Mar de Letras

C/Santiago 18, Los Austrias (91 541 71 09, www.lamardeletras.com). Metro Ópera. **Open** 10.30am-2pm, 5-8.30pm Mon-Fri; 10.30am-2.30pm Sat. Closed 1wk Aug. **Credit** DC, MC, V. **Map** p327 F11/12.

Mar de Letras is a well-stocked bookshop specialising in kids' editions. Look out too for the English titles, regular English storytelling evenings and educational toys.

English-language specialists

Panta Rhei and **Ocho y Medio** (for both, *see above*) both stock lots of English-language books; the former specialises in art and design, the latter in film.

Booksellers

C/Fernández de la Hoz 40, Chamberí (91 442 79 59, www.booksellers.es). Metro Iglesia. **Open** 9.30am-2pm, 5-8pm Mon-Fri;

CONSUME

Moyano book fair.

CONSUME

10am-2pm Sat. Closed on Sat in Aug.
Credit AmEx, DC, MC, V. **Map** p324 J6.
Madrid's best English-language bookshop sells a
wide selection of literature, videos and DVDs, as well
as materials for TEFLers. The branch below also
has a children's book section.
Other location Plaza de Olavide 10, Chamberí
(91 702 79 44).

J&J Books & Coffee

*C/Espíritu Santo 47, Malasaña (91 521 85 76,
www.jandjbooksandcoffee.com). Metro Noviciado.*
Open 11am-midnight Mon-Thur, Sat; 11am-2am
Fri; 4-10pm Sun. **Credit** AmEx, DC, MC, V.
Map p323 G9.
J&J is at once a relaxing little café (at ground-floor
level) and a well-stocked second-hand bookshop (in
the basement). Activities held here include open-mic
sessions, language exchanges (Wednesdays and
Thursdays from 8pm) and quizzes (Fridays from
11pm). Staff can source books that aren't in stock.
The daily 'happy hour' is from 4pm to 7pm.

Pasajes

*C/Génova 3, Chueca (91 310 12 45, www.pasajes
libros.com). Metro Alonso Martínez.* **Open** 10am-
8pm Mon-Fri; 10am-2pm Sat. **Credit** MC, V.
Map p324 J8.
This linguists' treasure trove sells a great range of
fiction and non-fiction, language-learning materials,
maps, audio books and videos. Most things are in
English, French, German and Spanish.

Petra's International Bookshop

*C/Campomanes 13, Sol & Gran Vía
(91 541 72 91). Metro Ópera or Santo*

Domingo. **Open** 11am-9pm Mon-Sat.
Credit MC, V. **Map** p327 F11.
A great range of second-hand books in English and
other languages is on offer in this laid-back little
shop. Here you can offload excess books or trade
them for others. Sadly, Petra the cat, who gave the
shop its name, has now passed on.

Second-hand & rare

Most bookshops dealing in rare and
antique books are around the pedestrianised
C/Huertas. A great place for cheap second-
hand books is the **Cuesta de Moyano**, on
C/Claudio Moyano, by the Jardín Botánico
(map p328 J11). It has a line of kiosks (*pictured
above*) selling second-hand books, from rare
editions to remainders. Some are open all
week, but Sunday mornings are busiest.
See also p90.

Librería San Ginés

*Pasadizo de San Ginés 2, Sol (91 366 46 86).
Metro Ópera or Sol.* **Open** 11am-8pm Mon-Sat.
Credit MC, V. **Map** p327 G11.
This Old Curiosity Shop-type place, in an atmos-
pheric passageway, sells everything from scruffy
English paperbacks to antique editions.

Travel & maps

Librería Desnivel

*Plaza Matute 6, Santa Ana (91 429 97 40,
www.libreriadesnivel.com). Metro Antón
Martín.* **Open** 10am-2pm, 4.30-8pm Mon-Sat.
Credit AmEx, MC, V. **Map** p328 H13.

This excellent travel and adventure bookshop sells a wide range of maps and books covering Spain and other countries. Desnivel's own publications include walking and climbing guides, and the shop also has information on organised walks, hikes and so on.

La Tienda Verde

C/Maudes 23 & 38, Chamberí (91 534 32 57, www.tiendaverde.es). Metro Cuatro Caminos. **Open** 9am-2.30pm, 4.30-8.30pm Mon-Fri, 9.30am-2pm, 5-8pm Sat. **Credit** AmEx, DC, MC, V.
Madrid's original and best shop for travel books and maps, the 'Green Shop' now occupies two premises on the same street. At No.23 you will find tourist and nature guides, while No.38 sells maps and specialised mountaineering books.

CHILDREN

Clothes

Max Kinder

C/Carretas 8, Los Austrias (91 521 69 47, www.maxkinder.es). Metro Sol. **Open** 10am-9pm Mon-Sat. **Credit** MC, V. **Map** p327 H11.
This shop is the junior version of Max Moda, across the street, and does a reasonable range of basic clothes for children from three months to 16 years.

Toys

Don Juego

C/Alcalá 113, Salamanca (91 435 37 24, www.donjuego.es). Metro Príncipe de Vergara. **Open** Sept-July 10am-2pm, 5-8.30pm Mon-Sat. *Aug* 10am-2pm Mon-Sat. **Credit** MC, V. **Map** p329 M10.
This shop specialises in board games for both kids and adults – as well as mah-jong, solitaire, Chinese chequers and chess, it specialises in Go.

Sanatorio de Muñecos

C/Preciados 19, Sol (91 521 04 47). Metro Sol. **Open** 10am-2pm, 5-8pm Mon-Fri. **Credit** AmEx, DC, MC, V. **Map** p323 G11.
The 'dolls' hospital' does indeed mend dolls, but also functions as the oldest toy shop in Madrid, full of parents gazing nostalgically at the old-school model cars, teddy bears and so on.

CLEANING & LAUNDRY

Self-service *lavanderías* (launderettes) are rather thin on the ground in Madrid: in most there will be an attendant.

Lavandería Automática

C/Don Felipe 4, Malasaña (91 523 32 45). Metro Tribunal. **Open** 10am-9pm daily. **No credit cards. Map** p323 H9.

Lavandería Donoso Cortés

C/Donoso Cortés 17, Chamberí (91 446 96 90). Metro Quevedo or Canal. **Open** *Sept-July* 9am-2pm, 3.30-8pm Mon-Sat. *Aug* 9am-2.30pm Mon-Sat. **No credit cards.**

CRAFTS & GIFTS

★ Antigua Casa Talavera

C/Isabel la Católica 2, Sol & Gran Vía (91 547 34 17). Metro Santo Domingo. **Open** 10am-1.30pm, 5-8pm Mon-Fri; 10am-1.30pm Sat. **Credit** AmEx, MC, V. **Map** p323 F11.
This long-standing family business specialises in traditional blue and white Spanish ceramics. Every available space is crammed with hand-painted designs all sourced from small Spanish producers. The charming owner speaks good English.

Madrid al Cubo

C/Cruz 35, Sol & Gran Vía (627 45 20 53, www.madridalcubo.com). Metro Tirso de Molina. **Open** 10.30am-2pm, 5-10pm Mon-Sat; 11am-3pm, 6-11pm; 11am-3pm Sun. **Credit** AmEx, MC, V. **Map** p327 H12.
New tourist shop Madrid al Cubo sells cool alternative souvenirs, including graphics-based prints, T-shirts and mugs, coffee-table books, tote bags and original postcards.

Piedra de Luna

C/Príncipe 14, Santa Ana (91 521 63 73). Metro Sevilla. **Open** 10am-2.30pm, 5-10pm Mon-Sat; 4-8pm Sun. **Credit** DC, MC, V. **Map** p328 H12.
A treasure trove of good-quality craftwork from around the world. Tuareg kilims, Moroccan ceramics and Indian silver jewellery and painted wooden furniture all feature.

Popland

C/Manuela Malasaña 24, Malasaña (91 591 21 20, www.popland.es). Metro Bilbao. **Open** 11am-8.30pm Mon-Sat. **Credit** DC, MC, V. **Map** p323 G8.
For times when only a Jesus action figure will do, Popland saves the day. The shop is packed with all things pop-culture and plastic, but also film posters, shower curtains and T-shirts. There's also a good range of greetings cards – quite a rarity in Madrid.

DESIGN & HOUSEHOLD

BD Madrid

C/Villanueva 5, Salamanca (91 435 06 27, www.bd madrid.com). Metro Serrano. **Open** 9.30am-1.30pm, 4.30-8pm Mon-Fri; 10am-1.30pm Sat. Closed Aug. **Credit** AmEx, DC, MC, V. **Map** p325 L10.
BD carries a stunning selection of contemporary furniture designs from Spanish and international names, many with a retro feel. The company is now

CONSUME

producing its own pieces, including a kitchen range. Hefty price tags, but worth a visit if only to peruse.

Expresión Negra
C/Piamonte 15, Chueca (91 319 95 27, www.expresionnegra.org). Metro Chueca. **Open** 11am-2.30pm, 5-8.30pm Mon-Sat. **Credit** AmEx, DC, MC, V. **Map** p324 J10.
Expresión Negra is a great place to indulge in a spot of retail therapy and help the environment at the same time. As well as breathing new life into recycled objects – briefcases, lamps and other objects made out of used Coke cans, sardine tins and so on – the shop also puts a different spin on African handicrafts, with brightly coloured throws, textiles and some unusual metalwork.

PlazAAarte
Costanilla de los Capuchinos 5, Chueca (91 522 85 93, www.plazaarte.com). Metro Chueca. **Open** *Sept-July* 11.30am-2pm, 5.30-9pm Mon-Sat. *Aug* 6.30-9.30pm Mon-Sat. **Credit** AmEx, DC, MC, V. **Map** p324 H10.
This is a trendy, Swedish-owned shop/gallery that specialises in contemporary items for the home by up-and-coming national and international designers.

Víctimas de Celuloide
C/Ave Maria 18, Lavapiés (91 547 61 35, www. victimasdeceluloide.com). Metro Lavapiés. **Open** 11am-2.30pm, 5.30-9.30pm Mon-Sat. **Credit** AmEx, DC, MC, V. **Map** p327 F12.
'Because we are all victims of celluloid,' says the proprietor of this shop selling interior design pieces

with a twist, mainly from Nordic suppliers. A pop art influence is noticeable in the selection.

Vinçon
C/Castelló 18, Salamanca (91 578 05 20, www.vincon.com). Metro Velázquez. **Open** 10am-8.30pm Mon-Sat. **Credit** AmEx, MC, V. **Map** p325 M10.
The Madrid outpost of the classic Barcelona design store occupies a former 1920s silver factory. It has everything for the cred-seeking homeowner – furniture, home and garden accessories and attractive gift ideas, often at surprisingly low prices.

FASHION
Boutiques & designer

Agatha Ruiz de la Prada
C/Serrano 27, Salamanca (91 319 05 01, www.agatharuizdelaprada.com). Metro Serrano. **Open** *Sept-June* 10am-8.30pm Mon-Sat. *Aug* 10am-2pm, 5-8pm Mon-Sat. **Credit** AmEx, MC, V. **Map** p325 L8.
Loud and colourful designs distinguish this designer's work, many emblazoned with her trademark hearts and flowers. The childrenswear range is hugely popular, as is the homeware.

Amaya Arzuaga
C/Lagasca 50, Salamanca (91 426 28 15, www. amayaarzuaga.com). Metro Serrano. **Open** *Sept-June* 10.30am-8.30pm Mon-Sat. *Aug* 10.30am-2pm, 5-8.30pm Mon-Fri;

CONSUME

Madrid al Cubo.

10am-2pm Sat. **Credit** AmEx, DC, MC, V.
Map p325 L9.
One of the few Spanish designers who has an inter-national presence. The clothes are not for everyday wear, but there are some great outfits to be discovered, with a hard-edged punky look. The knitwear is of excellent quality.

★ Bunkha
C/Santa Bárbara 6, Malasaña (91 522 09 50, www.bunkha.com). Metro Tribunal or Gran Vía. **Open** 11am-9pm Mon-Sat. **Credit** MC, V. **Map** p323 H9.
This newish addition to Calle Santa Bárbara, on the borders of Chueca and Malasaña, opened in 2009. The stylish boutique stocks a host of upmarket yet hip labels, such as Danish brand Won Hundred, Spanish brand Marlota and Italian label Camo. Menswear is in the front space, while womenswear is in the mezzanine area.

★ HAND
C/Hortaleza 26, Chueca (91 521 51 52, www.hand-haveaniceday.com). Metro Chueca. **Open** 11am-2.30pm Mon-Sat. **Credit** AmEx, DC, MC, V. **Map** p324 H10.
HAND stands for Have a Nice Day, and is run by two discerning Frenchmen. An interesting boutique, it mixes French labels with bits and pieces brought back from their travels.

★ Lotta
C/Hernán Cortés 9, Chueca (91 523 25 05, www.lottavintage.com). Metro Chueca or Tribunal. **Open** *Sept-July* 11am-2.30pm,

5-8.30pm Mon-Sat. *Aug* 6-10pm Mon-Sat. **Credit** MC, V. **Map** p324 H10.
The Swedish proprietor of Lotta set up her first vin-tage clothing store in the Rastro in 1992. The shop carries vintage clothing from the '50s to the '80s and also stocks colourful dresses designed by the owner herself, using materials from Scandinavia.

Sybilla
Callejón de Jorge Juan 12, Salamanca (63 274 97 76, www.sybilla.es). Metro Retiro or Serrano. **Open** 10.30am-8.30pm Mon-Sat. Closed 2wks Aug. **Credit** AmEx, DC, MC, V. **Map** p325 L10.
As well as her usual eye-catching outfits for actresses attending the Goyas (the Spanish equiva-lent of the Oscars), Sybilla also stocks a new range, Jocomomola, aimed at a younger crowd.

Chains & high street

For famous Spanish leather specialist **Loewe**, *see p196.* International high street chains are to be found on Gran Vía (with H&M at no.32) and C/Fuencarral. The global Spanish chains **Mango** (C/Fuencarral 70) and **Zara** (C/Fuencarral 126-128 and Gran Vía 34) are slightly cheaper here than in shops outside Spain. There's a branch of **Topshop** at Puerta del Sol 6.

Adolfo Domínguez
C/Ortega y Gasset 4, Salamanca (91 576 00 84, www.adolfodominguez.es). Metro Núñez de Balboa. **Open** 10.30am-9pm Mon-Sat. **Credit** AmEx, DC, MC, V. **Map** p325 L7.

Peseta. *See p194.*

CONSUME

INSIDE TRACK
BOUTIQUE BROWSING

The best spots for browsing independent boutiques are **Conde Duque**, around Plaza Guardias de Corps; the Alonso Maríinez part of **Chueca**, between C/Argensola, C/Genova, Plaza Santa Bárbara and C/Fernando VI; and the trendy triangle now known as **triBall** (meaning 'triangle of Ballesta', after one of the area's best streets), formed by C/Corredera Baja de San Pablo, C/Valverde and C/Desngaño.

Simple, classic clothing from the well-known Galician designer. The suits are well cut and long-lasting, while the accessories and shoes are also some of the brand's strong points.
Other locations throughout the city.

Custo

C/Fuencarral 29, Chueca (91 360 46 36, www. custo-barcelona.com). Metro Gran Vía or Chueca. **Open** 10am-9pm Mon-Sat. **Credit** AmEx, DC, MC, V. **Map** p324 H10.
This Catalan designer is famous for his funky patterned T-shirts, but has expanded the range to include creative and flattering dresses, skirts and coats. Custo sells in boutiques around the world, but is also rapidly expanding its own network of shops, with a new branch on C/Mayor.
Other locations throughout the city.

Hakei

C/Fuencarral 35, Chueca (91 522 09 34, www.hakei.com). Metro Chueca. **Open** 11am-9pm Mon-Sat; noon-8pm Sun. **Credit** AmEx, MC, V. **Map** p324 H10.
This nationwide womenswear chain – similar in style to the UK brand Jigsaw – has yet to venture beyond the Spanish borders. Clothes, shoes and accessories are stylish, feminine and well-priced, with the large range of well-priced leather bags especially covetable.
Other locations C/Arenal 8 (91 521 47 26); C/Ayala 34 (91 575 45 75); C/Goya 41 (91 575 05 11).

Purificación García

C/Serrano 28, Salamanca (91 435 80 13, www.purificaciongarcia.es). Metro Serrano. **Open** 10am-8.30pm Mon-Sat. **Credit** AmEx, DC, MC, V. **Map** p325 L9.
Purificación García is where Madrid's older but elegant woman heads when she wants something smart for the office. Well cut and using natural materials, the clothes are very well priced for the quality of the fabrics.
Other locations throughout the city.

Street, casual & clubwear

The shopping mall **El Mercado de Fuencarral** (*see p183*) is home to a large number of the city's indie streetwear brands.

Desigual

C/Fuencarral 36-38, Chueca (91 521 49 07, www.desigual.com). Metro Tribunal or Gran Vía. **Open** 10am-9pm Mon-Sat. **Credit** AmEx, MC, V. **Map** p323 H10.
Desigual has become a real hit with the club-kids, and it's easy to see why: gorgeous shop assistants, pumping house music and affordable, quality club and streetwear for men and women.

Flip

C/Mayor 19, Los Austrias (91 366 44 72, www. flipmadrid.com). Metro Sol. **Open** 10.30am-9pm Mon-Sat. **Credit** AmEx, MC, V. **Map** p327 G11/12.
Well-chosen stock from the likes of g-sus, Miss Sixty, Kangol and Black Flys, all presided over by über-hip and highly pierced, highly tattooed staff.

Gas

C/Fuencarral 16, Malasaña (91 701 05 01, www. gasjeans.com). Metro Gran Vía. **Open** 10am-9pm Mon-Wed; 10am-10pm Thur-Sat; noon-9pm Sun. **Credit** MC, V. **Map** p324 H10.
'Keep it simple' is the Gas motto and it certainly does, with collections of crisp cotton and linen separates, but mainly denim.

Lanikai

C/Alberto Aguilera 1, Malasaña (91 591 34 13, www.lanikai.es). Metro San Bernardo. **Open** *Sept-July* 10.30am-2pm, 5-9pm Mon-Sat. *Aug* 10.30am-2.30pm. **Credit** AmEx, MC, V. **Map** p323 G7.
This three-storey emporium has all the essentials for the keen snowboarder, surfer and skateboarder, or anyone looking for streetwear by the likes of Etnies, Carhartt, Diesel and Stylelab.

★ Nonstop Sneakers

C/Pez 14, Malasañu (91 523 26 46). Metro Callao or Noviciado. **Open** 11am-2.30pm, 5-8.45pm Mon-Sat. **Credit** AmEx, DC, MC, V. **Map** p323 G10.
Madrid's best trainers shop sells a good range of New Balance and Nike, with plenty of rare editions and exclusive models.
▶ *Calle del Pez has seen various hip new openings of late, including Japanese Closet, opposite Nonstop Sneakers, at No.11 (91 522 97 72), selling stylish labels such as Sessún; and La Antigua Shop (No.2), selling new and vintage womenswear. Check out the street's myriad cafés and bars afterwards (such as El Palentino; see p178), for a post-shopping pick-me-up.*

CONSUME

Pepita is Dead

C/Doctor Fourquet 10, Lavapiés (91 528 87 88, www.pepitaisdead.es). Metro Atocha. **Open** 11am-2pm, 5-8.30pm Mon-Sat. Closed 3wks Aug. **Credit** AmEx, DC, MC, V. **Map** p328 I14.
Pepita is Dead specialises in vintage clothing. These items – mens-, womens- and childrenswear, plus accessories – are all unworn originals, carefully chosen from the '60s to the '80s.

Snapo

C/Espíritu Santo 5, Malasaña (91 532 12 23, www.snaposhop.com). Metro Noviciado or Tribunal. **Open** 11am-2pm, 5-9pm Mon-Sat. **Credit** AmEx, DC, MC, V. **Map** p323 H9.
Snapo stocks streetwear with attitude. Designs are funny and cheeky. The collection is mainly T-shirts, plus some bags, caps and womenswear.

★ Sportivo

C/Conde Duque 20, Malasaña (91 542 56 61, www.gruposportivo.com). Metro San Bernardo. **Open** 10am-9pm Mon-Sat. **Credit** AmEx, MC, V. **Map** p323 F8.
With a great range of menswear labels, including Cantskate, Burro, Levi's Red and Vintage, New York Industries, YMC and Duffer of St George, Sportivo is an unmissable stop. The staff are extremely helpful.
▶ *The area of Conde Duque around Plaza Guardias de Corps is now home to a host of stylish independents, including unisex clothing shops Polar (C/Conde Duque 5 (91 559 46 49) and Clean (C/Acuerdo 36, 91 593 94 52), record shop Radio City (see p202) and artisan bag shop Peseta (see right).*

Lingerie & underwear

¡Oh, qué luna!

C/Ayala 32, Salamanca (91 431 37 25, www.ohqueluna.com). Metro Serrano. **Open** 10am-2pm, 5-8.30pm Mon-Fri; 11am-2pm, 5-8.30pm Sat. **Credit** AmEx, DC, MC, V. **Map** p325 L8.
Glam, sexy lingerie, negligées and dressing gowns. It also does a line in bedlinen and swimwear.

FASHION ACCESSORIES
Jewellery & accessories

Concha García

C/Goya 38, Salamanca (91 435 49 36, www.concha-garcia.com). Metro Goya. **Open** 10.30am-8.30pm Mon-Fri; 10.30am-2.30pm, 5-8.30pm Sat. **Credit** AmEx, DC, MC, V. **Map** p325 N9.
Concha García's two shops-cum-galleries are important showcases for contemporary and ethnic jewellery design, both national and international.

Joaquín Berao

C/Claudio Coello 35, Salamanca (91 577 28 28, www.joaquinberao.com). Metro Serrano. **Open** *Sept-July* 10am-2pm, 5-8.30pm Mon-Fri; 10.30am-2.30pm, 5-8.30pm Sat. *Aug* 10am-2pm, 5-8.30pm Mon-Fri; 10am-2pm Sat. **Credit** AmEx, DC, MC, V. **Map** p325 L9.
Chunky, twisted and contorted, but also fluidly elegant, Joaquín Berao's solid silver bracelets, necklaces, earrings and chokers are increasingly the choice of those in the know.

★ Peseta

C/Noviciado 9, Conde Duque (91 521 14 04, www.peseta.org). Metro Noviciado or Plaza de España. **Open** 10am-8.30pm Mon-Fri; 10am-3pm Sat. **Credit** AmEx, DC, MC, V. **Map** p323 F9.
This cute shop-atelier in a creative quarter of Conde Duque sells artisan bags, purses, laptop and passport cases, bicycle caps, handkerchiefs, keyrings and badges from the Peseta range, all made using vintage-style fabrics. It also sells Harinezumi 2 Japanese digital cameras. The shop itself is lovingly kitted out with retro furniture, and its owners, Laura and Jaime, are often at work in the attached atelier (you might need to ring the bell at such times). Collaborations with Marc Jacobs in 2008 and '09 raised the brand's profile. *Photo p192.*
▶ *Upstairs is vintage bicycle workshop AA Ciclos (www.aaciclos.com), specialising in fixed-gear models. It's open on Fridays evenings (6-9pm) and Saturday mornings (11am-2pm).*

Scooter Hombre

C/Jorge Juan 12, Salamanca (91 576 47 49, www.scooterhombre.com). Metro Serrano. **Open** 10.30am-8.30pm Mon-Fri; 10.30am-2.30pm, 5-8.30pm Sat. **Credit** DC, MC, V. **Map** p325 L10.
Accessories are the focus of this French store, with funky, chunky jewellery, Anya Hindmarch bags and gorgeous flip flops by Dorotea. The clothes – a mix of funky and ethnic – are worth a look too.

Shoes, bags & leather products

Spain is a major producer of footwear, with the Valencia and Alicante areas dominated by shoe factories. As a result, Madrid is a haven for the confirmed shoe addict. The street to head for is **Augusto Figueroa**, in the heart of Chueca. Here you'll find a street packed with factory '*muestrarios*' (selling samples) such as Vime or Caligae.
Artisan shop **Peseta** (*see above*) sells a beautiful range of fabric bags.

★ Antigua Casa Crespo

C/Divino Pastor 29, Malasaña & Conde Duque (91 521 56 54, www.alpargateriacrespo.com).

Who's Who

The lowdown on Madrid's fashion clans.

Heavies

Pronounced with a guttural, Scottish 'ch' at the beginning, these are the rockers that time forgot. Look for leather and studs, heavy metal T-shirts and boots.
Where to find them: In a *plaza* engaging in a *botellón* (piss-up), and in the suburbs. The famous 'heavies of Gran Vía' twins always stand outside the former Madrid Rock shop – now a branch of Bershka.
Essential accessories: Bottle of Mahou beer, cigarettes and unruly facial hair.
Seen at: the **Rastro** for Metallica T-shirts, **Sprint** (*see p184*) for beer and baccy.

Muscu-locos

The Muscle-Boys. A play on words – a mix of 'muscular' and 'crazy about muscles'. Tight tops and vests for this lot; biceps as big as your head warrant showing off. These boys are mad about their image and cultivate it in the gym and Chueca's boutiques.
Where to find them: Chueca is the place to marvel at their chiselled features and sculpted torsos. Here they shop, bar-hop and admire each other from afar... and sometimes not so afar.
Essential accessories: Very short shorts, Speedos for the pool, and a roving eye.
Seen at: **Amantis** for toys, **Berkana** for books and **SR** for leather goods (for all, *see p231*).

Fiesteros

The party people. Pierced and tattooed to the hilt, this polysexual crew are the hippest of the hip kids.
Where to find them: Their natural habitat is Malasaña and the Fuencarral market, where they shop, chat and get more piercings.
Essential accessories: VIP passes for the next big party, fashionable mullet haircuts from Juan ¡por Diós!, and sunglasses.
Seen at: The Malasaña boutiques on Calle del Pez and Corredora Baja de San Pablo.

Pijos & pijas

The posh kids. Big, floppy '80s-style barnets – and that's just the boys. Lacoste polo shirts, a jumper tied around the shoulders, white jeans and espradilles top off the look.
Where to find them: Branches of El Corte Inglés in the designer sections, Calle Serrano and any bar or club that was cool with the fiesteros two months previously.

Essential accessories: Daddy's credit card, a Mini Cooper and a comb to keep that floppy hair in check.
Seen at: **ABC Serrano** (*see p184*) shopping centre, **Adolfo Domínguez** (*see p192*) for sporty sweaters and **Sana Sana** (*see p202*) for a post-shopping massage.

Señores y señoras

The mature couple. For *él*, distinguished grey hair will be slicked back and the obligatory moustache neatly trimmed. For *ella*, an immaculately coiffed 'do is a must, with the make-up erring on the heavy side. A camel-hair jacket for him, a fur coat for the lady. Cigars and cigarettes respectively.
Where to find them: Salamanca, where they'll double park for an hour while *la señora* gets a new bag.
Essential accessories: A small yappy dog, a Mercedes and plenty of bling.
Seen at: **Purificación García** (*see p193*) for something smart, **Mantequerías Bravo** (*see p197*) for some posh nosh and **Loewe** (*see p196*) for indulgent leather accessories.

CONSUME

letro Bilbao. **Open** *Sept-Apr* 10am-1.30pm,
-8pm Mon-Fri. *May-Aug* 10am-1.30pm,
5-8.30pm Mon-Fri; 10am-1.30pm Sat.
Closed last 2wks Aug. **No credit cards.**
Map p323 G8.
This perfectly preserved old-fashioned, family-run
store, founded in 1863, is dedicated to espadrilles of
all sizes and colours.

Camper
*C/Serrano 24, Salamanca (91 578 25 60,
www. camper.com). Metro Serrano.* **Open**
9.30am-9pm Mon-Sat. **Credit** AmEx, DC,
MC, V. **Map** p325 L10.
Branches of the Mallorcan family firm continue to
spring up all over the city. At this one, two large
plinths display the entire men's and women's collection – brightly coloured, fun shoes and sandals.
Other locations throughout the city.

Farrutx
*C/Serrano 7, Salamanca (91 577 09 24,
www.farrutx.com). Metro Serrano.* **Open**
Sept-June 10am-2pm, 5-8pm Mon-Fri; 10.30am-
2pm, 5-8.30pm Sat. *July, Aug* 10.30am-2pm, 5.30-
8.30pm Mon-Sat. **Credit** AmEx, DC, MC, V.
Map p324 K10.
Innovative and sharply elegant leather designs
from this popular Mallorcan company, with bags
and shoes too.
Other locations throughout the city.

Loewe
*C/Serrano 26 & 34, Salamanca (91 577 60 56,
www.loewe.com). Metro Serrano.* **Open** 10am-
8.30pm Mon-Sat. **Credit** AmEx, DC, MC, V.
Map p325 L8/9.
The world-famous, elite Spanish leather goods company, selling bags, shoes, cases and a small range
of clothes. Prices are very high.
Other locations throughout the city.

Piamonte
*C/Piamonte 16, Chueca (91 523 07 66,
www.piamonteshop.com). Metro Chueca.*
Open 11am-8.30pm Mon-Sat. **Credit** AmEx,
DC, MC, V. **Map** p324 J10.
Desirable bags in all shapes, sizes and fabrics,
from denim to super-soft leather.
Other locations C/Lagasca 28, Salamanca
(91 575 55 20); C/Marqués de Monasterio 5,
Chueca (91 308 40 62); C/Villanueva 16,
Salamanca (91 435 37 47).

INSIDE TRACK DOWN AT HEEL

All markets and most streets have a shoe
repairer – look out for *rápido* or *reparación
de calzados* signs.

★ Taller Puntera
*Plaza Conde de Barajas 4, Los Austrias (91
364 29 26, www.puntera.com). Metro Ópera,
La Latina or Tirso de Molina.* **Open** 10am-2pm,
5-8pm Mon-Sat; 10am-2pm Sun. **Credit** DC,
MC, V. **Map** p327 F12.
This lovely leather accessories shop/workshop
opened on Plaza Conde de Barajas – near the
Mercado de San Miguel – in 2009, but its sister shop
in Malasaña was established over a decade ago.
Simple but stylish bags, satchels, rucksacks, wallets,
notebooks and more, all in top-quality leather, are for
sale in a range of tasteful colours. Each 'piece' has a
story behind it, and you can personalise it by getting
your name engraved for free. What's more, the staff
are genuinely friendly and the prices excellent for
this level of workmanship. A gem. *Photo p198.*
Other location C/Cristo 3, Malasaña
(91 541 33 60).

★ Vialis
*C/Colón 3, Malasaña (91 575 99 33,
www.vialis.es). Metro Tribunal.* **Open** 10am-2pm,
5-8pm Mon-Sat. **Credit** AmEx, DC, MC, V. **Map**
p324 H10.
Madrid's only branch of the stylish Spanish
footwear brand is located just off the Fuencarral, on
the edges of Malasaña. Expect chunky but hip shoes
and boots in solid shapes, and a small selection of
high-quality leather bags.

FOOD & DRINK
Chocolates, cakes & sweets

★ Cacao Sampaka
*C/Orellana 4, Huertas (91 319 58 40, www.
cacaosampaka.com). Metro Alonso Martínez.*
Open *Shop* 10am-9.30pm daily. *Café* 10am-9pm
Mon-Fri; 10am-2pm, 3.30-9pm Sat, Sun. Closed
2wks Aug. **Credit** AmEx, MC, V. **Map** p324 J9.
Hand-made choccies arrayed in dazzling displays
and for sale singly or in themed boxes, such as
'Spices of the Americas' or 'Flowers and herbs'.
There are also chocolate jams, chocolate sauces and
chocolate ice-creams and a café on hand to sample
its delights over a cup of coffee. *Photo p200.*

★ La Duquesita
*C/Fernando VI 2, Chueca (91 308 02 31). Metro
Alonso Martínez.* **Open** 9.30am-2.30pm, 5-9pm
Tue-Sun. Closed Aug. **Credit** MC, V. **Map** p324 I9.
This traditional *pastelería*, dating from 1914, has fea-
tured in lots of period-piece movies. Gorgeous choco-
lates and cakes are up for grabs, along with *turrón*
in the run-up to Christmas.

Happy Day
*C/Espíritu Santo 11, Malasaña (91 522 91 33).
Metro Tribunal.* **Open** 10am-2pm, 5-8pm Mon-
Sat. **Credit** MC, V. **Map** p323 H9.

CONSUME

Antigua Casa Crespo. *See p194.*

Happy Day is aiming to bring the cupcake phenomenon to Madrid. The 1950s-style *pastelería* is kitted out in pastel shades, and has a café table if you want to indulge your sweet tooth in-store.
Other location C/Cuchilleros 14, Los Austrias (same phone as above).

★ La Mallorquina
*Puerta del Sol 8, Sol & Gran Vía (91 521 12 01).
Metro Sol.* **Open** 9am-9pm daily. Closed mid July, Aug. **No credit cards. Map** p327 G11.
Always bustling with people, La Mallorquina occupies a prime location right on the Puerta del Sol. Downstairs, the pastry shop sells great cakes and savouries, all baked on the premises. The upstairs café has a pre-war feel and a team of old-school waiters in attendance.
▶ *For the review of the café, see p173.*

El Riojano
*C/Mayor 10, Los Austrias (91 366 44 82,
www.confiteriaelriojano.com). Metro Sol.*
Open Sept-July 10am-2pm, 5-9pm daily.
Closed Aug. **Credit** MC, V. **Map** p327 G11.
El Riojano has been in business since 1885, selling irresistible cakes, pastries, meringues and seasonal goodies. All are made in the traditional way, with meringues a particular speciality. Enjoy one with a coffee in the café out back.

Delicacies

Magerit, stand No.20/21 in La Cebada market (*see p199*), is an excellent place to buy cheese. For olives of all varieties, **F Illanas**, stalls 33-44, in the Mercado de Chamberí, C/Alonso

Cano 10 (91 446 95 89), is a good bet. Several branches of **El Corte Inglés** (*see p184*) and most **OpenCor** outlets (*see p184*) have luxury food sections called El Club del Gourmet. But for the most atmospheric experience, head along to sample the goods from the gourmet-food specialists at **El Mercado de San Miguel** (*see p200* and *pp162-163* **Profile**).

La Boulette
*Stands 63-68, Mercado de La Paz, C/Ayala 28,
Salamanca (91 431 77 25, www.laboulette.com).
Metro Serrano.* **Open** 9am-2.30pm, 5-8pm
Mon-Fri; 9am-2.30pm Sat. **Credit** MC, V.
Map p325 L8.
La Boulette probably has the largest selection of cheeses in Madrid and possibly the country, with over 400 varieties, both Spanish and imported, on sale. The range of goods in the charcuterie section is similarly impressive.

González
*C/León 12, Huertas & Santa Ana (91 429 56
18). Metro Antón Martín.* **Open** Sept-June 9am-
midnight Tue-Thur; 9am-1am Fri, Sat. *July-Aug*
5pm-1am Tue-Sat. **Credit** AmEx, DC, MC, V.
Map p328 I12.
Once a local grocer's, González is now a smart delicatessan with a fine range of cheeses, charcuterie, preserves, fruit and nuts, olive oils and plenty more besides. The back room is now a pleasant, well-stocked wine bar.

Mantequerías Bravo
*C/Ayala 24, Salamanca (91 576 02 93). Metro
Serrano.* **Open** 9.30am-2.30pm, 5.30-8.30pm

CONSUME

Taller Puntera. *See p196.*

Mon-Fri; 9.30am-2.30pm Sat. Closed Aug.
Credit AmEx, DC, MC, V. **Map** p325 L8.
A marvellous selection of foodstuffs is on sale in this
Salamanca shop, including meats and cheeses,
wines and spirits and coffees and teas. Homesick
Brits will be pleased with imports such as English
mustard and cream crackers.
Other locations Paseo General Martínez
Campos 23, Chamberí (91 448 09 18).

Museo del Jamón

*Carrera de San Jerónimo 6, Huertas & Santa
Ana (91 521 03 46, www.museodeljamon.es).*
Metro Sol. **Open** 9am-midnight daily.
Credit MC, V. **Map** p327 H11.
Dotted around town, the various branches of the
'Ham Museum' are a sight to behold, with dozens of
hams dangling from the ceiling. Sample their wares
at the bar or in their restaurants.
Other locations throughout the city.

Patrimonio Comunal Olivarero

*C/Mejía Lequerica 1, Chueca (91 308 05 05,
www.pco.es). Metro Alonso Martínez.* **Open**
10am-2pm, 5-8pm Mon-Fri; 10am-2pm Sat.
Closed Aug. **Credit** MC, V. **Map** p324 I9.
Olive oil from every region of Spain that produces
the stuff is on sale at Patrimonio Comunal Olivarero.
Quantities go from two-litre bottles to five-litre cans,
and some make lovely gifts.

Health & herbs

NaturaSí

*C/Doctor Fleming 1, Chamartín (91 458 32 54,
www.naturasi.eu). Metro Santiago Bernabéu.*
Open 10am-8.30pm Mon-Sat. **Credit** AmEx,
DC, MC, V.
This 'natural' supermarket sells a huge range of ecological and natural foodstuffs, among them fresh
fruit and veg, cheese and herbal products.

Salud Mediterranea

*Paseo Santa María de la Cabeza 3, Atocha
(91 527 89 29, www.saludmediterranea.com).
Metro Atocha.* **Open** 10am-8pm Mon-Fri; 10am-
2pm Sat. **No credit cards. Map** p328 J15.
The huge selection of organic and macrobiotic
products at this shop includes hard-to-find
Japanese items and pollen from the bees in the
Sierra de Madrid.
Other locations C/Ortega y Gasset 77,
Salamanca (91 309 53 90).

Markets

Madrid's markets are a noisy, colourful way
to get close to the locals – and to stock up on
cheap food. They offer a vast range of fruit
and veg, meat, wet fish, cheese, charcuterie
and offal. All the following markets are open
from around 9am-2pm and 5-8pm (15 May-15
Sept until 8.30pm) during the week, and 9am-
2pm on Saturdays.

Anton Martín

C/Santa Isabel 5, Lavapiés (91 369 06 20).
Metro Antón Martín. **Map** p328 I13.

La Cebada

*Plaza de la Cebada s/n, La Latina (91 365
91 76). Metro La Latina.* **Map** p327 F13.

Chamartín

*C/Bolivia 9, Chamartín (91 457 53
50/http://mercadodechamartin.com).*
Metro Colombia.
In an upmarket neighbourhood with many affluent
foreign residents, and produce to match.

Chamberí

C/Alonso Cano, 10, Chamberí (no phone).
Metro Iglesia.
Big, with lots of variety. The fruit and veg stalls in
the middle are among the best in town.

Mercado de Maravillas

C/Bravo Murillo 122, Tetuán (no phone).
Metro Alvarado.
Madrid's biggest market, and the best for fish.

★ Mercado de la Paz

*C/Ayala 28, Salamanca (91 435 07 43,
http://mercadodelapaz.blogspot.com).*
Metro Serrano. **Map** p325 L8.
An high-end market, with a dazzling range of products. Don't miss gourmet cheese stall La Boulette.

THE BEST ARTISAN SHOPS

Antigua Casa Talavera
Traditional blue and white Spanish
ceramics. *See p190.*

Antigua Casa Crespo
Espadrilles, or *alpargatas,* cover the
walls of this old-school shop. *See p194.*

Cacao Sampaka
Handmade chocolates in beautiful
packaging. *See p196.*

Guitarrería F Manzanero
This master guitar-maker's shop is sure
to get you strumming. *See p202.*

Taller Puntera
Lovely artisan leather bags and purses
are sold in this spacious shop-atelier.
See p196.

Mercado de San Miguel

*Plaza de San Miguel, Los Austrias (91 548 12
). Metro Sol.* **Map** p327 F12.
This posh market, with a restored 19th-century
wrought-iron façade, has been a huge success story
since reopening in 2009. There's a good selection of
quality produce, but the market is designed more as
a spot for tapas munching than as a place to stock
up on essentials. For details of the market's outlets,
see pp162-163 **Profile**.

Los Mostenses

*Plaza de Los Mostenses, Malasaña (no phone).
Metro Plaza de España.* **Map** p323 F10.
A huge market in Malasaña with an international
atmosphere: Chinese and Mexican products are
much in evidence.

El Rastro

*C/Ribera de Curtidores, between Plaza de
Cascorro & Ronda de Toledo (no phone,
www.elrastro.org). Metro La Latina.*
Open dawn-approx 2pm Sun. **Map** p327 G14.
The city's most famous flea market dates back
nearly five centuries. Stalls start setting up from
8am, with the hardcore bargain-hunters arriving
soon afterwards, though trading officially begins at
9am. In truth, there are few real deals to be had these
days, but in among the tat are Moroccan stalls selling lovely leather bags (though be sure to haggle
hard), and antiques stalls and shops that are worth
a trawl (*see also p187*). In any case, it's still a quintessential stop on the tourist map – especially as a
pre-La Latina tapas bars jaunt (*see p77* **Inside
Track**). Do keep an eye on your bag though.

Cacao Sampaka. *See p196.*

Supermarkets

Hypermarkets are mostly to be found on the main roads around the edge of the city, and are mainly accessible only by car. If you're mobile and need to stock up, look for ads for Alcampo, Continente or Pryca. Many branches of **El Corte Inglés** (*see p184*) also have (pricey) supermarkets. For information on Sunday opening, *see p184*. In town, look out for branches of **Caprabo** (www.caprabo.es), **Carrefour Express** (www.carrefour.es), **Sabeco** (www.simply.es) and **Lidl** (www.lidl.es).

Wine & drink

Bodegas Santa Cecilia

C/Blasco de Garay 72-74, Chamberí (91 445 52 83, www.santacecilia.es). Metro Islas Filipinas. **Open** 10am-9pm Mon-Sat. **Credit** AmEx, DC, MC, V. **Map** p323 E6.

This *bodega*, occupying two almost-adjacent locales, stocks a vast array of wines, beers and spirits – over 4,000 in total. They're mainly Spanish, while beers and spirits come from all over. The gourmet shop, No.72, hosts frequent tasting sessions.
Other locations C/Bravo Murillo 50, Cuatro Caminos (91 442 35 32).

★ Lavinia

C/José Ortega y Gasset 16, Salamanca (91 426 06 04, www.lavinia.es). Metro Nuñez de Balboa. **Open** 10am-9pm Mon-Sat. **Credit** AmEx, DC, MC, V. **Map** p325 M7.

No oenophile should miss visiting Lavinia, which claims to be Europe's largest wine shop. In stark contrast to many of Madrid's dusty old *bodegas*, it's bright, airy and spacious, and staff are knowledgeable and helpful.

Mariano Madrueño

C/Postigo de San Martín 3, Sol & Gran Vía (91 521 19 55, www.marianomadrueno.es). Metro Callao. **Open** 10am-2pm, 5.30-8.30pm Mon-Fri; 11am-2.30pm, 5.30-8.30pm Sat. Closed 2wks Aug. **Credit** MC, V. **Map** p327 G11.

This classic old *bodega*, dating back to 1895, has a charming interior, with wrought-iron columns and carved wooden shelves. As for the books on sale, the selection is enormous, with wines and spirits, plus the *bodega*'s own (lethal) coffee and orange liqueurs.

Reserva y Cata

C/Conde de Xiquena 13, Chueca (91 319 04 01, www.reservaycata.com). Metro Chueca. **Open** 11am-2.30pm, 5-9pm Mon-Fri; 11am-2.30pm Sat. **Credit** AmEx, DC, MC, V. **Map** p324 J10.

This shop is crammed full of wines from Spain and abroad, all displayed with helpful information and often at prices lower than in the supermarkets. Tasting sessions and courses are also offered.

HAIR & BEAUTY
Cosmetics & perfumes

Branches of upmarket international cosmetics and skincare brands, such as **MAC**, **Kiehls** and **Korres**, can be found on C/Fuencarral. There are branches of the Parisian cosmetics and perfume shop **Sephora** in Conde Duque (C/Alberto Aguilera 62, 91 550 20 50) and on the Puerta del Sol (No.3, 91 523 71 71).

Hairdressers

Jofer

C/Galileo 56, Chamberí (91 447 51 60, www.jofer.com). Metro Quevedo. **Open** 8am-10pm Mon-Sat. **Credit** AmEx, DC, MC, V. **Map** p323 F6.

A good bet if you just want a quick trim or a blow-dry. Prices vary but are generally reasonable, and at most branches you don't need an appointment. Waxing, tanning and other beauty services are also on offer, and you can also arrange for a home visit.
Other locations throughout the city.

Juan, ¡por Diós!

C/Pérez Galdós 3, Chueca (91 523 36 49). Metro Chueca or Gran Vía. **Open** 10am-9pm Mon-Sat. **Credit** AmEx, DC, MC, V. **Map** p324 H10.

Currently the place to get your hair cut in Madrid's trendiest quarter, this innovative place also stocks international style magazines, CDs and even has a Wi-Fi connection.

Spas & massages

See also p258 **Bath time**.

Chi Spa

C/Conde de Aranda 6, Salamanca (91 578 13 40, www.thechispa.com). Metro Retiro. **Open**

INSIDE TRACK 'BLANKET-TOPS'

A common sight in Madrid is people running with sheets in their hands, especially around the areas of Sol, Atocha and Bravo Murillo. They're not taking part in the capital's version of the running of the bulls, but rather they are '*los top manta*' ('the blanket-tops'), who sell their pirated CDs and DVDs laid out on squares of material. Once a policeman is spotted, strings tied to the corners of the material are hastily pulled and off they sprint.

CONSUME

10am-9pm Mon-Fri; 10am-6pm Sat.
Credit AmEx, DC, MC, V. **Map** p325 L10.
A sleek, sophisticated space that has separate areas for men and women offering specialised body and relaxation treatments, massages with essential oils and spices, hydrotherapy and aromatherapy.

Masajes a 1,000
C/Carranza 6, Malasaña (91 447 47 77, www.masajesa1000.es). Metro Bilbao.
Open 8am-midnight daily. **Credit** AmEx, MC, V. **Map** p323 G7/8.
That's Masajes for €6 to you and me. While it tries to come up with a new and catchy euro-based name, Masajes a 1,000 (pesetas) continues to rub, knead, pluck and tweeze its way through its loyal clientele. Tanning, waxing and pedicures are also offered. Buy books of vouchers if you intend to make multiple visits.
Other locations throughout the city.

Sana Sana
C/General Martínez Campos 40, Chamberí (91 310 54 24, www.sanasaludsana.es). Metro Rubén Darío. **Open** 11am-9pm Mon-Fri; 11am-3pm Sat. **Credit** AmEx, DC, MC, V. **Map** p324 J6.
An instant massage chain that offers a ten-minute workover for the harassed exec using specially designed chairs. It also offers shiatsu, sports and anti-stress massage, and beauty treatments. No booking is necessary for the short massage.

Tattoos & body piercing

Factory Tattoo
C/Montera 24, Sol & Gran Vía (91 521 44 69). Metro Gran Vía or Sol. **Open** 10am-10pm Mon-Sat; 5-10pm Sun. **Credit** AmEx, DC, MC, V. **Map** p327 H11.
Factory is the most popular of the city's tattoo parlours, its seedy location no doubt adding to its allure. If your pain threshold is low, it's worth a visit just to see – and wince at – photos of piercings past.

MUSIC

For wannabe DJs, **C/La Palma** and the surrounding streets are the places to be, with all genres of dance and rock music covered in a plethora of record shops. Head to **FNAC** (*see p184*) for the best selection of DVDs and music CDs; El Corte Inglés has an ineffective classification system and sprawling layout.

El Flamenco Vive
C/Conde de Lemos 7, Los Austrias (91 547 39 17, www.elflamencovive.es). Metro Ópera.
Open 10am-2pm, 5-9pm Mon-Sat. **Credit** AmEx, DC, MC, V. **Map** p327 F11.

Even if you harbour only a passing interest in flamenco, the brilliant range of CDs, guitars, books and other paraphernalia at this shop will lure you in.

★ Radio City
Plaza Guardias de Corps 1, Conde Duque (91 547 77 67, www.radiocitydiscos.com). Metro Noviciado or Plaza de España or Ventura Rodríguez. **Open** 11am-2pm, 5-9pm Mon-Sat.
Credit MC V. **Map** p323 F8.
One of the city's best record shops, with a host of independent labels covering everything from indie folk to rare soul and R&B via Latin beats, on both vinyl and CD. A selection of vintage LPs is also stocked.
▶ *Nearby, on the other side of C/San Bernardo, is CD Drome (C/Pozas 6, 91 521 83 88, www. cddrome.com), selling a good range of rock, pop and electronica CDs, as well as DVDs.*

Up Beat Discos
C/Espíritu Santo 6, Malasaña (91 522 76 60, www.upbeat.es). Metro Noviciado or Tribunal. **Open** 11am-2pm, 5-8.30pm Mon-Sat.
Credit MC V. **Map** p323 G9.
Soul, jazz and reggae dominate the shelves here, with a hand-picked collection of CDs and vinyl, along with a sideline in donkey jackets, parkas, Dr Martens, and so on. The shop has a fab '60s feel, with a space dedicated to scooter parts. Staff can track down rarities.

Musical instruments

Guitarrería F Manzanero
C/Santa Ana 12, La Latina (91 366 00 47, www.guitarrasmanzanero.com). Metro La Latina. **Open** *Sept-June* 10am-1.30pm, 5-8pm Mon-Fri. *July* 10am-1.30pm Mon-Fri. Closed Aug. **Credit** AmEx, DC, MC, V. **Map** p327 F14.
For a real taste of Spanish guitar-making, drop by at this master guitar-maker's shop, which also has a great display of old and rare string instruments. Call first to avoid disappointment.

OPTICIANS

+ Visión
Puerta del Sol 14, Sol (91 701 49 80, www. masvision.es). Metro Sol. **Open** 10am-9pm Mon-Sat. **Credit** AmEx, DC, MC, V. **Map** p327 H11.
This high-street optician is part of the same group as the UK's Vision Express. There's a wide range of frames and contacts. Prescription glasses or sunglasses take an hour to make up.
Other locations throughout the city.

PHARMACIES

For general information on pharmacies, *see p301.*

CONSUME

Farmacia Central
*Paseo de Santa María de la Cabeza 64,
Embajadores (91 473 06 72). Metro Palos de la
Frontera.* **Open** 24hrs daily. **No credit cards.**

Farmacia Lastra
*C/Conde de Peñalver 27, Salamanca (91 402
43 01). Metro Goya.* **Open** 8am-11pm daily.
Credit AmEx, DC, MC, V. **Map** p325 O9.

PHOTOGRAPHIC

FNAC *(see p184)* has a good photography
department, with helpful staff.

Fotocasión
*C/Ribera de Curtidores 22, Rastro (91 467 64
91, www.fotocasion.es). Metro Puerta de Toledo.*
Open 10am-2pm, 4.30-8.30pm Mon-Fri; 10am-
2pm Sat, Sun. **Credit** MC, V. **Map** p327 F/G15.
A treasure trove for photographers and camera collectors. Owner José Luis Mur is a walking encyclo-
pedia on cameras; he also has great offers on spare
parts and new and second-hand cameras.

SPECIALITY SHOPS

Almirante 23
*C/Almirante 23, Chueca (91 308 12 02,
www.almirante23.net). Metro Chueca.*
Open 11am-1.30pm, 5-7.30pm Mon-Fri; 11am-
1.30pm Sat. **Credit** MC, V. **Map** p324 J10.
This curiosity shop is packed full with all manner
of old stuff, including toys, tacky postcards, prints,
cameras, watches, bull-fighting programmes and
more. Brilliant for browsing – and buying gifts.

Belloso
*C/Mayor 23, Los Austrias (91 366 42 58,
www.belloso.es). Metro Sol.* **Open** 9.45am-2pm,
4.45-8pm Mon-Fri; 9.45am-2pm Sat. **Credit**
AmEx, DC, MC, V. **Map** p327 G11.
This neighbourhood has an abundance of shops selling Catholic paraphernalia, but Belloso is one of the
best. The gear on offer covers a huge range, including rosaries, crucifixes and statues of the Virgin.

La Casa de los Chales
*C/Duque de Sesto 54, Salamanca (91 574 25
73, http://lacasadeloschales.com). Metro Goya
or O'Donnell.* **Open** 8am-1.30pm, 5-9pm Mon-
Sat. **Credit** AmEx, MC, V. **Map** p325 O10.
The 'House of Shawls' has a huge range of *mantones
de Manila*, beautifully made fringed and embroidered shawls. Capes, handbags and feather boas
complete the stock.

Casa de Diego
*Puerta del Sol 12, Sol (91 522 66 43, www.casa
dediego.com). Metro Sol.* **Open** 9.30am-8pm
Mon-Sat. **Credit** AmEx, DC, MC. **Map** p327 H11.

This much-loved shop specialises in hand-painted
fans, umbrellas and classy walking sticks.

Guantes Luque
*C/Espoz y Mina 3, Santa Ana (91 522 32 87).
Metro Sol.* **Open** 10am-1.30pm, 5-8pm Mon-Sat.
Credit MC, V. **Map** p327 H12.
This old-fashioned glove shop in Santa Ana has
been open for more than 125 years. Luque sells
gloves in all sizes, colours and materials, covering
all types of wool, silk and leather. If you can't find
them here you won't find them anywhere. Prices
range from €20 to €300.

Objetos de Arte Toledano
*Paseo del Prado 10, Huertas (91 429 50 00,
www.armasmedievales.com). Metro Banco
de España.* **Open** 10am-7.45pm Mon-Sat.
Credit AmEx, DC, MC, V. **Map** p328 J12.
Located across from the Prado, this souvenir shop
par excellence sells traditional *españoladas* such as
fans, flamenco and bullfighting dolls. A great place
to find that gift for your kitsch-loving friends.

SPORT

For trainers, *see also p193* **Nonstop
Sneakers.**

Área Real Madrid
C/Carmen 3, Sol (91 521 79 50). Metro Sol.
Open 10am-9pm Mon-Sat; 10am-7pm Sun.
Credit AmEx, MC, V. **Map** p327 G/H11.
A true emporium for the Real Madrid-inclined. On
sale are, naturally, replica shirts and all manner of
other stuff bearing the club's logo, from ashtrays to
mouse mats, bath towels to undies.

Supporters Shop
*C/Goya 50, Salamanca (91 575 88 68). Metro
Goya.* **Open** 10.15am-2pm, 5-8.30pm Mon-Sat.
Closed Aug. **Credit** AmEx, DC, MC, V. **Map**
p325 N9.
Selling shirts and other memorabilia from over 500
clubs worldwide, Supporters Shop can usually kit
out fans of even the most obscure teams.

Tornal Moya Deportes
*Ronda de Valencia 8, Lavapiés (91 527 54 40,
www.tornalmoya.com). Metro Embajadores.*
Open 10am-2pm, 5-9pm Mon-Sat. **Credit** MC, V.
Map p328 H15.
This big, well-laid-out shop stocks the lot: top-name
sportswear, trainers, walking boots, swimwear, ten-
nis rackets, replica football shirts and bags.

STAMPS & COINS

Stamp & coin market
Plaza Mayor, Los Austrias. Metro Sol.
Open *approx* 9am-2pm Sun. **Map** p327 G12.

CONSUME

CONSUME

On Sunday mornings, an avid mass of stamp and coin collectors swarm over the Plaza Mayor, buying, selling and eyeing up each others' wares. This also acts as a Sunday-morning attraction for anyone out for a stroll in town, whether or not they are really bothered about tarnished old pesetas, stamps of all nations and 19th-century share certificates. Other traders sell old magazines, second-hand books, postcards, badges and ex-Soviet bloc military regalia. You can even get phonecards nowadays, along with just about anything else that someone, somewhere, considers collectable.

TICKET AGENTS

There are all manner of ways of avoiding queues to buy tickets (*entradas*) for shows and gigs these days, among them telesales, online purchase and cashpoints. Some of the biggest players in this game are savings banks (*cajas de ahorro*) such as the Caixa de Catalunya and La Caixa, who do advanced sales by phone, as does the all-embracing Corte Inglés.

Each of these services is associated with different venues, so check in a listings magazine such as the *Guía del Ocio* to see which of them handles the telesales for the show you want to attend. The *Guía del Ocio* itself offers online sales for cinemas and other venues via its website, www.guiadelocio.com. **FNAC** (*see p184*) is a useful place to pick up concert tickets.

El Corte Inglés

90 240 02 22, www.elcorteingles.es. **Open** 10am-10pm daily. **Credit** AmEx, DC, MC, V.
El Corte Inglés sells tickets for a huge range of shows and events, either by phone, online or at any of its stores.

Entradas.com

90 248 84 88, www.entradas.com. **Open** 24hrs daily. **Credit** AmEx (some venues), DC, MC, V.
This 24-hour ticketing service functions both by telephone and online. When dialling, depending on the type of event you wish to buy a ticket for, you get put through to a different number, and it's generally easier to book via the net. Tickets can be collected at the event box office.

Servicaixa/La Caixa

www.serviticket.com. **Credit** AmEx, DC, MC, V.
Servicaixa has a limited share of the theatre ticket sales market to purchase online. Group bookings (ten people or more) can also be made by telephone; call 902 88 80 90.

Tel-entradas/Caixa de Catalunya

902 10 12 12, www.telentrada.com.
Open 24hrs daily. **Credit** MC, V.

Through the Caixa de Catalunya you can book tickets for theatres, venues and concerts, pay by credit card and pick them up either at a branch of the bank or from the venue's box office itself (depending on the show and the venue). Some staff members speak minimal English, but don't bank on it. Online purchasing, with pages in English, is another option.

TOBACCO & SMOKING

The easily spotted maroon-and-yellow *Estancos* (tobacco shops) can be found all over town.

La Cava de Magallanes

C/Magallanes 16, Chamberí (91 446 28 17).
Metro Quevedo. **Open** *Sept-June* 8.30am-8.30pm Mon-Sat. *July, Aug* 8.30am-2.15pm, 5-8.30pm Mon-Fri; 8.30am-2pm Sat. **Credit** MC, V.
Map p323 G6.
A temple to tobacco, La Cava de Magallanes stocks over 350 different types of cigars, all maintained at optimum temperature in a special humidified room. The knowledgeable owner speaks a little English. There is a good range of accessories too. Note that some credit cards incur a small extra charge.

La Mansión del Fumador

C/Carmen 22, Sol & Gran Vía (91 532 08 17).
Metro Sol. **Open** 10.30am-2pm, 5.30-8.30pm Fri; 10am-2pm Sat. **Credit** AmEx, MC, V.
Map p327 G11.
Not a place to buy tobacco or cigarettes, La Mansión del Fumador does, however, stock a big range of accessories such as cigar-cutters, lighters, humidors, pipes and ashtrays.

TRAVEL SERVICES

Forocio

3rd floor, C/Mayor 4 (office 6) (91 522 56 77, 90 236 36 33, www.forocio.com). Metro Sol.
Open *Sept-July* 10.30am-7.30pm Mon-Fri. *Aug* 11.30am-5.30pm Mon-Fri. Closed 1 wk in Aug.
Credit DC, MC, V. **Map** p328 H11.
This multi-purpose agency offers services for young foreigners, such as hosting 'International Parties' and providing Interrail and student cards, setting up language exchanges, and organising budget flights, day trips and weekend tours. The 'Tarjeta Forocio' gives a 10% discount on trips. English and other languages are spoken.

Viajes Zeppelin

Plaza de Santo Domingo 2, Sol & Gran Vía (91 758 10 40, www.v-zeppelin.es). Metro Santo Domingo. **Open** 9am-8pm Mon-Fri; 10am-1pm Sat. **Credit** AmEx, DC, MC, V. **Map** p327 F11.
This well-established agency with friendly service specialises in cheap European charter flights and long-haul youth fares. You can also book online.

Arts & Entertainment

Marula. *See p246.*

Calendar

This most sociable of cities has an unsurpringly full calendar.

Practically all year round, apart from perhaps during the late winter lull (when everybody is worn out and broke from Christmas, New Year and Reyes) and the end of the summer, anyone coming to Madrid is likely to encounter an arts festival, a music fest, a fiesta or a themed film season. There is something here to suit all tastes, but, to make sure you catch one you like, it's worth doing a little forward planning.

PHOTO**ESPAÑA**2010

XIII Festival Internacional de Fotografía y Artes Visuales
9 junio - 25 julio
www.phe.es

Events and festivals that receive official sponsorship come under the aegis of either the Ayuntamiento (city council) or the Comunidad de Madrid (regional government), and the influence of politics, inevitably, is felt in culture. Municipal events have looked less tawdry and more upbeat with the Mayor Alberto Ruiz-Gallardón at the helm, and Comunidad cultural policy has maintained a consistently high standard in recent years.

Other events, such as the photographic extravaganza PHotoEspaña, are independent and still more are semi-independent, functioning with a mix of public and private money.

SPRING

See also p236 **Airs and Graces**, for the Música Antigua Aranjuez festival.

Día de la Mujer/Semana de la Mujer
Various venues. Route normally starts at Plaza Jacinto Benavente, Huertas & Santa Ana. Metro Sol or Tirso de Molina. **Information** Dirección General de la Mujer (91 420 85 92) & Centro de la Mujer (91 700 19 10). **Date** 8 Mar & surrounding week.
International Women's Day is celebrated in Madrid with a march, usually from Plaza Jacinto Benavente to the bottom of C/Atocha. Some of the many other related events taking place over the week include short film seasons and concerts.

Festival de Arte Sacro
Various venues. **Information** Tourist offices & 012, www.madrid.org. **Date** Last 3wks Mar.

For more on music festivals, *see p234, p237 and p242*; for art events, *see p224*; for performing arts festivals, *see p266*. For a full list of public holidays, *see p308*.

This three-week festival of music, dance, theatre, poetry, movies and conferences focuses on the role of religion in art over the centuries. The most recent festival looked at religious traditions throughout the world, from Buddhism to Catholicism and Islam.

Teatralia
Various venues. **Information** Tourist offices & 012, www.madrid.org. **Date** Last 3wks Mar.
A regional jamboree of performing arts, including theatre, puppet shows, circus and cinema as well as workshops and other activities aimed at children and young people. In Madrid itself the main venues are the Teatros Pradillo and Triángulo, the Sala Cuarta Pared (for all, *see p266*), the Círculo de Bellas Artes (*see p68*) and the Carpa de Los Malabaristas (Jugglers' Tent) in the Casa de Campo.

Semana Santa (Holy Week)
All over Madrid. **Information** Tourist offices & 010, www.esmadrid.com. **Date** wk leading up to Good Friday and Easter weekend (Mar/Apr). Easter is usually a good time to be in Madrid, as many *madrileños* get out of town for the long weekend, and the weather is usually good. In Madrid and nearby towns, there are many parish processions in which hooded *penitentes* schlep figures of Christ and the Virgin around. Regarded as the most impressive

is that of Jesús Nazareno el Pobre from San Pedro El Viejo and around La Latina. All over town there are organ and choral performances in churches.

Klubbers' Day

Madrid Arena (see p240). **Information** www.klubbers.com. **Dates** 14-16 April 2011.
This dance festival sets out to be a Madrid equivalent to Andalucía's Creamfields. Despite its name, it's actually a two-day event in Madrid Arena, which, when not being used for sporting events, converts nicely into a giant club. Local and international talent steps up to the decks or does live sets, with names such as Sven Väth, Ellen Allien, DJ Hell, Slam and Cycle on the bill.

Fiesta del Trabajo (May Day)

City centre & Casa de Campo. Metro Batán or Lago. **Date** 1 May.
The largest May Day march, attracting upwards of 60,000 people, is called jointly by the communist-led CCOO and the socialist UGT unions, which converge on Sol. Smaller in scale but quite animated is the anarcho-syndicalist CGT's march from Atocha to Plaza Jacinto Benavente. The anarchist purists CNT/AIT, meanwhile, march up C/Bravo Murillo from Cuatro Caminos. Many of the participants then head to the Casa de Campo where the UGT organises a lively party with stalls run by the *casas regionales*, clubs representing Spain's regions.

Dos de Mayo

District of Malasaña. Metro Bilbao, Noviciado or Tribunal. **Map** p323 G8. *Parque de las Vistillas.* *Metro Ópera.* **Map** p326 D13. **Information** Tourist offices & 012. **Date** 2 May.
Commemorating the fateful day in 1808 when the people of Madrid rose up against Napoleon's occu-

pying troops and paid for their audacity by being massacred, 2 May is now the region's official holiday and kick-starts a nearly continuous series of fiestas that go on throughout the rest of the spring and summer. Things get going in the Malasaña neighbourhood – named after the uprising's teenage heroine, Manuela Malasaña – in the Plaza Dos de Mayo, where the Monteleón barracks, a main bastion of resistance, then stood. Live gigs are held in the Plaza and in the Las Vistillas park and there are events at a number of other spots around town.

★ San Isidro

Plaza Mayor, Los Austrias, & all over Madrid. **Information** Plaza Mayor tourist office & 010, www.madrid.es. **Date** 1wk around 15 May.
For six days either side of 15 May, this is the time to see *madrileños* doing what they do best: taking to the

San Isidro.

ARTS & ENTERTAINMENT

streets and having a rollicking good knees-up. The fiestas celebrate San Isidro, Madrid's patron saint, a humble 12th-century labourer and well-digger to whom all manner of miracles are attributed and whose wife, María de la Cabeza, was also canonised, making them the only sainted couple in history. The action centres on the Plaza Mayor, where the fiestas are officially declared open and nightly gigs are held (with the odd classical performance thrown in). There is more music in Las Vistillas park; music, theatre, painting workshops and more are put on for kids in the Retiro; classic *zarzuela* arias get an airing in the Conde Duque Cultural Centre; the Auditorium in the Museo de la Ciudad programmes classical music; in the Planetarium there are performances of early, medieval and baroque music, and lovers of Spanish Golden Age theatre are catered for in the Plaza de San Andrés. An associated event is the Feria de la Cacharrería, a ceramics market, held in the Plaza de las Comendadoras, close to Conde Duque. Recent additions to the programming are Documenta, a short season of international documentary films; + Arte, a mixed bag of installations, performances, hip hop, electronic music and sanctioned graffiti, and Universimad, a rock festival at the Complutense.

Throughout the week there are also numerous religious ceremonies in various churches. The 15th itself sees a procession of vintage cars in the Castellana. Possibly most fun of all is the traditional *romería* (pilgrimage) at and around the Ermita de San Isidro, in the park of the same name; families in traditional *castizo* garb, looking like something out of a Goya painting, drink from wine skins and stuff themselves with traditional *madrileño* delicacies such as chorizo, morcilla and other offal dishes.

Feria del Libro Antiguo y de Ocasión
Paseo de Recoletos, Salamanca. Metro Banco de España or Colón. **Information** 91 420 34 21. **Dates** 2wks Apr-May.
This old and second-hand book fair, spanning a week either side of the San Isidro weekend, has been held annually for more than 30 years. Here you may stumble across rare treasures, out-of-print editions or recent remainders. Don't expect much in English.

Festimad Sur
Estadio Butarque, Leganés. Bus 483/484 or Metro Sur San Nicasio. **Information** 91 522 37 87, www.festimad.es. **Dates** late Apr/early May.
Despite problems with funding and various other ups and downs in recent years, including changes of venue, Festimad, Madrid's biggest rock festival, is certainly still alive and kicking, featuring a line-up of national bands as well as some, often fairly obscure, international names.

★ Documenta Madrid
Various venues. **Information** 91 517 98 17, www.documentamadrid.com. **Dates** 1wk early May.

This popular international documentary film festival, organised by the Ayuntamiento de Madrid, is now in its seventh year. It consists of one week of screenings, workshops and related activities, in high-profile venues such as Matadero Madrid (also the festival's main office; *see p110*), Cine Doré (the Filmoteca; *see p220*) and Casa de América (*see p94*).

SUMMER

La Feria del Libro (Book Fair)
Parque del Retiro. Metro Atocha or Ibiza. **Information** 91 533 51 84. **Date** 2wks end May-June. **Map** p329 L-N, 11-14.
First celebrated in 1933, the Book Fair is now a major international event. Hundreds of publishers are present and well-known writers show up to sign copies of their works.

★ PHotoEspaña
Various venues. **Information** 91 360 13 20, www.phedigital.com. **Dates** June, July.
Every spring/summer since 1998, PHotoEspaña has swept through Madrid's major museums and galleries, redefining the city as an international photography epicentre. Each year has a different theme; the 2010 theme was Time. In recent years, the retinue of photographic stars, many of whom give workshops and lectures throughout the festival, has included Nan Goldin, Joel Peter Witkin, Philip Lorca di Corcia, and Paul Graham. PHotoEspaña also transforms C/Huertas into an active outdoor exhibition space and puts on slide projections in Plaza Santa Ana and Centro Cultural Conde Duque. *Photo p211.*

★ Suma Flamenca
Various venues. **Information** www.madrid. org/sumaflamenca. **Date** June.
Now five years old, the month-long Suma Flamenca is Madrid's high-profile flamenco festival, a feast of music, dance and intense emotion. The 15 different concert venues include Teatros del Canal (Sala Roja; *see p265*) and the Centro Cultural Pilar Miró in Plaza Antonio María Segovia, as well as a host of municipal buildings and theatres.

San Antonio de la Florida
Ermita de San Antonio de la Florida (see p104). **Information** 91 547 07 22. **Date** 13 June. **Map** p322 A9.
One of the first of the summer's biggest street parties, the San Antonio celebrations can trace their history back a very long way. June 13 is the feast day of San Antonio, the patron saint of seamstresses. Single girls used to place 13 pins in the baptismal font of the hermitage. If one stuck to her finger she would marry within a year. The main party, including events for kids, takes place across the Paseo de la Florida, in the Parque de la Bombilla. *See also p59* **A Saint for All Seasons.**

In the Frame Burial of the Sardine

Goya's depiction of Madrid's bizarre Ash Wednesday ritual.

It doesn't get any weirder than this. On Ash Wednesday, the last day of Carnival, Madrid mourns the death of a sardine. In Pythonesque absurdity, his scaly little corpse, dressed in Sunday best, is somberly paraded through the streets of old Madrid by La Alegre Cofradía de la Sardina (the Happy Brotherhood of the Sardine). They carry his diminutive coffin from bar to bar, enjoying a tongue-in-cheek display of funereal ceremony along with their cañas. The route changes annually, but always winds up at the Fuente de los Pajaritos in the Casa de Campo.

The origins of this wacky pageant are sadly unclear. Some say that it derives from the days when abundant sardines were sold on the last day in which eating meat was permitted before Lent began, and that the ripe little fellow came to symbolise the many sacrifices that lay ahead until Easter.

The fish may also have phallic implications, and its burial could be a harbinger of sexual abstinence during Lent. Other sources link it to the reign of Carlos III (1759-1788), when a shipload of rotten sardines arrived at his court and he ordered that they be buried immediately.

Despite the ritual's uncertain roots, Goya's masterful and macabre painting suggests that the custom was in full swing by the early 1800s (although the concrete date of the painting is unknown). Goya depicts a frenzied bacchanal of cavorting, masks and partner-swapping, overseen by a gruesome death mask. Despite the title of the painting, no sardines are in sight.

The sardine, its burial and other carnival merriment were suppressed during the dictatorship. La Alegre Cofradía, a small group of high-spirited friends, thought they'd chance it anyway. One Ash Wednesday in the early 1950s, they marched the fish to the Casa de Campo, singing and dancing en route. The police were summoned by a priest, who felt this spectacle to be sacrilegious. The police found the entourage to contain so many venerable old lawyers, doctors and journalists, however, that they simply joined the throng.

Nowadays, the Cofradía has more than 90 members and a sister organisation, La Peña del Boquerón (the Anchovy Club), for the widows of the dead sardine. The march usually begins at 6pm, from sardine HQ at C/Rodrigo de Guevara 4 in La Latina (you will know the building by the fish on the door). But be prepared for a mournful moment, as all of the ornately painted miniature coffins from previous years are on display at the Cofradía site, and you will be expected to pay proper respects to the dearly departed fish.

Goya's **Burial of the Sardine** *is found at the Real Academia de Bellas Artes de San Fernando, see p72.*

ARTS & ENTERTAINMENT

★ **Orgullo Gay (Gay Pride)**
Around Chueca (see p78). **Information** www.cogam.org, www.orgullolgtb.org. **Date** 1wk late June/early July.
One week of partying in Chueca, Madrid's gay neighbourhood, and a huge parade on the Saturday that runs from Puerta de Alcalá to Plaza de España. *See also p230* **Pride and Joy**.

★ **Veranos de la Villa**
Various venues. **Information** 91 758 92 70, www.esmadrid.com. **Dates** July/Aug.
As part of the 'Summers in the City' festival, a good selection of top names have appeared at the patio of the Centro Cultural Conde Duque, which acts as the festival's main stage. Among them are Brazilians Milton Nascimento, Caetano Veloso and Carlinhos

Brown, the fabulous Cape Verdean singer Cesaria Évora, many top flamenco artists, Youssou N'Dour and Femi Kuti, Cubans like Ibrahim Ferrer and some gnarled old rockers. Interspersed among them, however, there has also been a fair amount of dross. Elsewhere, *zarzuelas* are programmed in both the Centro Cultural de la Villa and in the Sabatini Gardens beside the Royal Palace, the 'Titirilandia' puppet season for kids takes place in the Retiro, while Golden Age or more contemporary theatre productions may be seen outdoors beside the Muralla Árabe and in the Centro Cultural Galileo, and fringe venues all over town offer plenty more 'alternative' shows. Also outdoors is a two-screen cinema in the Parque de la Bombilla, down on the Paseo de la Florida.

Verbenas de San Cayetano, San Lorenzo & La Paloma

La Latina & Lavapiés. Metro La Latina. **Information** Tourist offices & www. madrid.es. **Date** 6-15 Aug. **Map** p327 F/G/H14.

Madrid popular culture at its best – the streets and squares of the Lavapiés, Rastro and La Latina neighbourhoods are dolled up with flowers and bunting and the locals don their *castizo* gear for some serious street partying. San Cayetano is first, on 7 August, followed by San Lorenzo on the 10th and La Paloma on the 15th. Daytime sees parades and events for kids; by night there are organ grinders, traditional *chotis* dancing, the aroma of grilled chorizo and *churros*, sangría by the bucketful and a lot of good clean fun.

AUTUMN

Metrorock

Campus de la Universidad Complutense de Madrid, Avda de Séneca 2, Moncloa. **Information** www.metrorock.net. **Dates** mid Sept.

As the name may suggest, this festival started its life as a series of free concerts taking place in Madrid's underground stations. In recent years though, it has grown into a full-sized even. The line-up includes a good mix of international and Spanish acts – Beck,

Franz Ferdinand, Paul Weller, The Charlatans and OK Go have all paid a visit, while the Red Hot Chilli Peppers were among the 2010 line-up.

Fiestas del Partido Comunista

Recinto Ferial de la Casa de Campo. Metro Lago. **Information** Partido Comunista de España (91 300 49 69, www.lafiestadelpce.es). **Date** mid Sept.

Now in the political minority, the Spanish Communist Party still has enough clout, however, to stage a three-day fiesta. There are performances by flamenco and rock bands, theatre shows, stalls run by political groups, debates on many political and social issues and lots of regional cuisine in the *casas regionales*.

★ La Noche en Blanco

Various venues. **Information** www.es madrid.com/lanocheenblanco. **Date** Sept.

To have *'una noche en blanco'* means to spend a sleepless night, and this is insomniac heaven. In Madrid, as in Paris, Rome, Brussels and Riga, for one night only you can wander from exhibition centre to museum, from fashion show to concert all night long and all for free. See the website for a list of participating venues.

★ Festival de Otoño

Various venues. **Information** Comunidad de Madrid (91 720 81 94/3), tourist offices & 012, www.madrid.org. **Date** 4-5wks Oct-Nov.

The impressive and always enjoyable 'Autumn Festival' offers somewhere in the region of 60-odd theatre, dance and music spectacles and remains one of the city's major performing arts events. The range throughout the festival is quite wide. Acts as diverse as the Brodsky Quartet, Ballets Trockadero de Monaco, musical groups from Rajasthan, La Comédie Française, Eddie Palmieri and the Spanish Orquesta Nacional de Jazz have all popped up in recent years, with *Tartuffe* and *Romeo and Juliet* big theatrical draws in previous years. Events take place both in the capital and surrounding towns, making a trip out quite tempting. Around ten venues in Madrid itself have shows, among them the Teatros Albéniz and Zarzuela, the Círculo de Bellas Artes and fringe spaces such as Teatro Pradillo and Sala Cuarta Pared.

WINTER

Estampa

Palacio de Cristal, Avda de Portugal s/n, Casa de Campo. Metro Lago. **Information** 91 544 77 27, www.estampa.org. **Dates** late Nov-Dec.

A firm fixture on the arts calendar, Estampa is a well-attended show that brings together galleries and collectors from around the world to exhibit prints and contemporary art editions.

Feria de Artesanía

Plaza de España. Metro Plaza de España, Sol & Gran Vía. **Information**

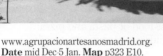

PHotoEspaña. *See p208.*

www.agrupacionartesanosmadrid.org.
Date mid Dec-5 Jan. **Map** p323 E10.
This large and crowded crafts fair is an ideal place to look for original presents and coincides with Christmas, New Year and Reyes.

Navidad (Christmas)
All over Madrid. **Date** 25 Dec.
Less hyped than in northern climes, Christmas begins, very reasonably, in December, and is traditionally less important than Epiphany (Reyes; *see below*). Consequently, you are not reminded of the number of shopping days left until Christmas at every turn and the absence of piped carols is almost eerie. Father Christmas, tinsel, flashing lights and baubles are far more evident than a few decades ago, however; all these trappings, plus lots of other cheap festive junk, are sold in the Christmas market in Plaza Mayor throughout December. The big family blow-out is usually on Noche Buena (Christmas Eve) with shrimps, red cabbage and either roast lamb, sea bream or both. Some families exchange presents on the otherwise fairly quiet Christmas Day, but the big ones are usually saved for 6 January.

Noche Vieja (New Year's Eve)
Puerta del Sol, Sol & Gran Vía. Metro Sol.
Date 31 Dec. **Map** p327 H11.
New Year's Eve is celebrated with gusto, usually *en familia*, and involves another blow-out meal, litres of cava and the curious tradition of eating 12 grapes as the clock chimes midnight. Ever resourceful, many supermarkets now sell seedless grapes pre-packed in dozens for the occasion. The Puerta del Sol is where thousands throng – not recommended with kids or for misanthropes. Clubs and bars organise parties, often starting at 12.30am or later.

Reyes (Three Kings)
All over Madrid. **Date** 6 Jan.
On the evening of 5 January, Noche de Reyes, thousands of children and their parents line up along C/Alcalá to watch the annual *cabalgata* (parade), which is also televised. Dozens of elaborate floats pass by and the riders hurl sweets to the children. Later, most families have a big dinner, and the following day presents await those who have been good. Those who haven't get a piece of coal.

Festival de Flamenco Caja Madrid
Casa Encendida (see p77). **Information**
Cultyart 91 553 25 26, www.cultyart.com.
Dates 2wks Jan/Feb.
Brings in the top names in flamenco for sessions of *cante jondo*, foot-stomping and guitar playing.

Carnaval
Various venues. **Date** wk of Shrove Tuesday.
Carnival is a very good excuse for dressing up and partying, either in the street or in Madrid's many bars and clubs. It opens in the Plaza Mayor, followed by a parade around old Madrid. On Ash Wednesday, the last day, there is a ribald ceremony during which a fish is carted around to the strains of a marching band, before being interred (*see p209* **In the Frame**).

INSIDE TRACK TRADE FAIRS

The Juan Carlos I exhibition centre (www.ifema.es) hosts Madrid's trade fairs, such as **ARCO** (*see p224*), and **International Fashion Week** in February and September.

Children

Madrid's compact size and amiable locals make it a top spot for los niños.

This is a city where children are welcome almost everywhere. *Madrileños* are, in general, a friendly bunch and if you have kids in tow their amiability is sure to go up a notch. The care of children is considered everybody's business. Waitresses will scoop your baby up to show to the kitchen staff and old ladies will happily advise you that your child is wearing too few/too many clothes for the season.

Taking children to restaurants or pavement cafés is considered the norm, but be prepared to adapt to Spanish meal times; lunch is normally eaten around 2pm, and dinner is from 10pm. If your kids really can't wait, then the numerous fast-food or pasta and pizza places are your best hope, and high chairs and children's menus can usually be found in these joints.

MANAGING THE DAY

In summer, afternoon temperatures can hover around a very uncomfortable 40°C and so outdoor activities are best in the morning. After a late lunch, a siesta is the best option before venturing out into the relatively cool evening air. The city comes alive again in the hour or two before dusk when families come out to stroll, eat ice-cream and watch the world go by.

Be warned that few metro stations have lifts, and buses will only admit pushchairs if they are folded. Baby-changing facilities are limited to shopping centres, the department store El Corte Inglés (*see p184*), and the airport.

Note that prices for Madrid's theme parks and similar attractions are often ten per cent cheaper if you buy tickets online before your visit.

ATTRACTIONS

Kids also enjoy the **Teleférico** cable-car (*see p102*) that runs from the Parque del Oeste deep into the Casa de Campo, and the dizzying **Faro de Madrid** (*see p104*).

Faunia

Avda de las Comunidades 28, Eastern suburbs (91 301 62 10, www.faunia.es). Metro Valdebernardo. **Open** Opening times are subject to weekly variations, so it's worth checking the website or calling before a visit. *Most of Jan, Feb* 10am-6pm Sat, Sun; *Mar* 10am-6pm Mon-Fri; 10am-7pm Sat, Sun; *most of Apr* 10am-6pm Mon-Fri; 10am-8pm Sat, Sun; *May* 10am-7pm Mon-Fri; 10am-9pm Sat, Sun; *June-Aug* 10am-8pm Mon-Fri; 10am-9pm Sat, Sun; *Sept* 10am-7pm Mon-Fri; 10am-8pm Sat, Sun; *Oct* 10am-6pm Mon-Fri; 10am-7pm Sat, Sun; *Nov-Dec* 10am-6pm daily. **Admission** €25.50 over-8s; €19.50 3-7s & over-65s; free under-3s. **Credit** AmEx, MC, V.

Part zoo, part theme park, Faunia recreates the world's different ecosystems in a series of domes. Best of the bunch is the Amazon jungle house, which echoes with the screech of exotic birds; an intense tropical storm is simulated every half hour. And in summer, Penguin World, an impressive reconstruction of a polar zone, where you can see the little fellas zipping about, is wildly popular. Faunia is not a cheap day out and queues can be long.

IMAX Madrid

C/Meneses s/n, Parque Tierno Galván, Legazpi, South of centre (91 467 48 00, www.imaxmadrid.com). Metro Méndez Álvaro. **Admission** €7.10-€12.20. **Credit** AmEx, MC, V.

The hourly wildlife and scientific shows are only in Spanish, but the 3D and Omnimax presentations are awesome enough to be enjoyed by all children.

Palacio de Hielo

C/Silvano 77, Eastern suburbs (ice rink 91 716 01 59, www.palaciodehielo.com). Metro Canillas. **Open** *Ice rink* Sept-May 8.45pm-10.15pm Wed, Thur; 5.30pm-midnight Fri; 12.30-3pm, 5.30-midnight Sat;

12.30-3pm, 5.30-10.30pm Sun. Closed June-mid Sept. *Bowling alley* 3-11pm Mon-Thur; 11am-2am Fri, Sat; 11am-11pm Sun. **Admission** *Ice rink* €5-€11. *Bowling alley* €2.90-€5.20. **No credit cards**.

The Ice Palace is a huge leisure complex dominated by a 1,800-sq-m ice rink. With a curling and skating school, a 24-lane bowling alley and a 15-screen cinema, it's a good option for a rainy day with teenagers. The site, out towards Barajas Airport, also has a shopping centre (10am-10pm Mon-Sat), numerous cafés and restaurants and a nursery for kids aged three to 11.

Parque de Atracciones

Casa de Campo (90 234 50 09, 91 526 80 30, www.parquedeatracciones.es). Metro Batán. **Open** varies (see website), but generally 11am-7pm daily. **Admission** €10.60 over-3s; €4 over-65s. **Credit** MC, V.

A funfair with something for everyone. The wildest ride is El Abismo, The Abyss, which is a 49-metre high roller that follows a 450m route of scary drops at 100kph. There is now a children's version too, so nobody has to miss the terror. Other new features include indoor paintball and a 4D cinema. There are long queues for some rides.

Planetario de Madrid

Avenida del Planetario 16, Parque Tierno Galván, Legazpi, South of centre (91 467 38 98, 91 467 34 61, www.planetmad.es). Metro Arganzuela-Planetario. **Shows** vary; phone to check. Closed 1st 2wks Jan. **Admission** €3.55; €1.55 2-14s, over-65s. **No credit cards**.

Close to the IMAX (*see above*), the Planetarium has seasonal exhibitions on the solar system as well as 45-minute shows. Like the IMAX, the narration here is only in Spanish and may test your kids' interest in the heavens if they are non-Spanish speakers.

The Tooth Mouse

Spain's rodent counterpart to the tooth fairy is a madrileño.

Ask any Spanish child to name the most famous mouse in the world and few of them will come up with Mickey. By far the most celebrated rodent in Spain and much of South America is **Ratoncito Pérez**, the mythical mouse who sneaks into children's rooms at night to slip money under the pillow when a tooth falls out. What few people know is that El Ratón (the mouse) Pérez is actually a *madrileño*.

Stroll half a minute from the Puerta del Sol and you can see a plaque marking the house where Pepito Pérez lived in a biscuit tin in the basement of a pastry shop. The ground floor of C/Arenal 8 is now a small arcade of shops. Inside, you'll find a mouse-sized statue (well, hamster-sized, perhaps). There are also illustrated panels telling the story of Pepito and his creator, a Jesuit priest, Father Coloma.

Juan Coloma, who found God after nearly killing himself while cleaning his revolver as a young man, first published the story of *Ratoncito Pérez* in 1902. He dedicated the book to the young King Alfonso XIII, to whom he had told the story while the monarch was a sickly child.

According to the story, the mouse would frequently escape from the basement by means of the sewers. From this labyrinth he could find his way into the bedroom of any child from the boy-king to the poorest *niño* in the land, exchanging a lost tooth for money or a

small gift. The story sparked the tradition that continues to this day.

In 2003, the mayor of Madrid unveiled the plaque to Ratoncito Pérez, announcing rather grandly that, just as the Americans have Mickey, Pepito 'deserves recognition as a symbol of the hopes and dreams of all children, and because he is *our* mouse'.

ARTS & ENTERTAINMENT

CosmoCaixa.

Zoo Aquarium Madrid

Casa de Campo (91 512 37 70, www.zoo madrid.com). Metro Batán. **Open** 11am-dusk daily. **Admission** €18.80 over-8s; €15.25 3-7s & over-65s; free under-3s. **Credit** V.

This attractively landscaped zoo is located slap bang in the heart of the Casa de Campo. The animals look as happy as can be expected of beasts held in captivity, although the big cats could really do with a bit more leg-room. At the Tierra de Gorilas ('Land of Gorillas') a sheet of reassuringly thick glass separates you from the massive, glowering silverbacks that prowl about. Children will enjoy walking through the shark tank and dolphinarium. There is also a petting zoo and a train ride.

BABYSITTING & CHILDCARE

English-speaking babysitters can be found through local English-language publications; for a list of magazines and newspapers in English published in Madrid, *see p302*. Alternatively, parents can leave children aged from four to 12 for short periods at any of the following *ludotecas* (play centres) around town.

Centro de Recreo Infantil Dinopeppino

C/Mártires de Alcalá 4, Malasaña & Conde Duque (91 559 22 04, 91 559 61 21, www. dinopeppino.com). Metro Ventura Rodríguez.

Open 4.30-8.30pm Mon-Fri; 11.30am-2pm, 4.30-8.30pm Sat, Sun. **Admission** (per hr) €6.20; €50 10hr multi-entry. **No credit cards**. **Map** p323 E8. A well-equipped and spacious play centre.

Chiqui Tin Centro Infantil

C/Sebastian Elcano 16, Lavapiés (91 528 55 36, www.escuelachiquitin.com). Metro Embajadores. **Open** 9am-5pm Mon-Fri. Closed Aug-mid Sept. **Admission** (per hr) €7. **Credit** MC, V. One of the most centrally located branches of this chain of play centres.

Gorongoro

Avda de Felipe II 34, Salamanca (91 431 06 45, www.gorongoro.es.tl). Metro Goya. **Open** *Sept-June* 4.30-9pm Tue-Fri; 11.30am-2.30pm, 4.30-9pm Sat, Sun. *July* 6-9.30pm Mon-Fri; 11.30am-2.30pm, 6-9pm Sat. Closed Aug. **Admission** (per hr) €6.60 over-4s; €6 under-4s. **Credit** AmEx, DC, MC, V. **Map** p325 O9/10. This well-equipped play centre is close to the Retiro and the Goya shopping area.

ENTERTAINMENT

Events aimed at children are dotted around the year, starting in January, with a parade on the fifth of January – the eve of **Reyes**, when Spanish children traditionally get their Christmas presents. The parade features floats from which the Three Kings throw sweets to children along the route. During **Carnaval** (*see p211*), kids' activities are organised, and there are also children's events during **San Isidro** (*see p207*) and **Veranos de la Villa** (*see p209*). In April, festivities for **El Día del Niño** (Day of the Child) are held in C/Bravo Murillo in Tetuán. The street is taken over by bouncy castles, puppet shows, foam-spraying firemen and candy floss stalls.

Look out, too, for children's theatre. **Teatro San Pol** in the Casa de Campo (C/San Pol de Mar 1, 91 541 90 89, www.teatrosanpol.com, closed July & Aug) puts on occasional shows in English. The **Madrid Players**, an English-language theatre group (91 326 24 39, www.madridplayers.org), puts on a pantomime at Christmas and hosts occasional theatre workshops for kids (check website for details).

In the Retiro park the permanent **Teatro Municipal de Titeres** (91 792 41 12, mobile 670 72 33 60, www.titirilandia.org), near the boating lake, has puppet shows most weekends, albeit in Spanish. **La Casa Encendida** (*see p77*) runs children's workshops on diverse subjects. Storytelling sessions are on Fridays and at weekends there are puppet shows in the patio.

MUSEUMS

The **Museo del Ferrocarril** (*see p110*) houses steam, diesel and electric locomotives. Children's activities include theatre at weekends, a mini-train on Saturdays and a monthly market for model train enthusiasts.

CosmoCaixa

C/Pintor Velázquez s/n, Alcobendas (91 484 52 00, www.fundacio.lacaixa.es). Bus 157 from Plaza Castilla. **Open** 10am-8pm Tue-Sun. **Admission** €3; €2 under-16s and concessions. **Credit** MC, V.

Kids and adults uncover the mysteries of science via hands-on interactive exhibits. The *clik de los niños* (three- to eight-year-olds), where processes can be tried out, is popular, as is the *toca, toca* (touch, touch) area for small children, where there are animals to stroke.

Museo de Cera (Wax Museum)

Paseo de Recoletos 41, Salamanca (91 319 26 49, www.museoceramadrid.com). Metro Colón. **Open** 10am-2.30pm, 4.30-8.30pm Mon-Fri; 10am-8.30pm Sat, Sun. **Admission** €16; €9 over-10s; €12 4-10s & over-60s. **No credit cards.** **Map** p324 K9.

Madame Tussaud's it isn't (there's no queueing for starters), yet this wax museum still has a certain tacky charm. Along with the usual rogues, celebrities and statesmen – among them the Beatles, Clark Gable and George W Bush – there's a Tren de Terror (ghost train).

PARKS & PLAYGROUNDS

Small neighbourhood parks are not Madrid's strong point; play areas have improved in recent years but are still a little tame. One of the better play areas is in the **Plaza de Oriente**, next to the Palacio Real. The **Paseo del Prado** central boulevard has safe wooden climbing frames and slides and **Dos de Mayo** in Malasaña has play areas for toddlers and *terrazas* for adults, as does the nearby **Plaza de las Comendadoras**. **C/Fuencarral** was done up a few years ago, with widened pavements, and now boasts six small play areas.

The **Retiro** (*see p90; photos p83*) has a boating lake, cafés around the edge, buskers, artists, puppet shows, sports facilities and a good play area by the Puerta de Alcalá entrance. To the east is the Parque del Oeste, which has great views, decent play areas, ice-cream parlours and the Teleférico. The huge **Casa de**

Retiro.

Campo (*see p101*) has the Zoo, the Parque de Atracciones funfair, an even bigger boating lake and the best outdoor pools in Madrid (*see p259*), with a shaded and shallow kids' pool.

OUT OF TOWN

Most rides in the waterparks around town are suited to older kids, but there are usually areas for small children. For general pools, *see p259*.

Aquópolis de San Fernando de Henares

Crta de Barcelona (A-2), km 15.5, San Fernando de Henares (91 673 10 13, www.aquopolis.es). Bus (Continental) to Alcalá de Henares or Torrejón from Avda de América/by car A-2. **Open** *Last 2 wks June* 12.30-7pm Mon-Fri; noon-7pm Sat, Sun. *July, Aug* 12.30-8pm Mon-Fri; noon-8pm Sat, Sun. Closed Sept-mid June. **Admission** €19.50 adults taller than 1.4m; €14.50 over-65s and children shorter than 90cm. **Credit** MC, V.
Madrid's first waterpark, with giant water slides, pools for smaller and larger kids, wave pools and wilder attractions for reckless youths.

Aquópolis de Villanueva de la Cañada

Avda de la Dehesa, Villanueva de la Cañada (91 815 69 11, 90 234 50 06, www.aquopolis.es). Bus 627 from Moncloa/by car Ctra de La Coruña (A-6), exit 41, then M503. **Open** *Last 2 wks June & first wk Sept* noon-7pm daily; *July-Aug* noon-7pm Mon-Fri; noon-8pm Sat, Sun. Closed mid Sept-mid June. **Admission** €22.95 adults taller than 1.4m; €17.50 over-65s & children between 0.9m and 1.4m. **Credit** AmEx, MC, V.
One of the largest waterparks in Europe, run by the same company as the Aquópolis-San Fernando and with similar attractions.

De Pino a Pino

Área Recreativa del Chorro, Navafría (mobile 659 45 45 68, www.depinoapino.com). By car A-6/AP-61 to Segovia (100km), then N110 to Navafría (20km). **Open** *Feb* (prior bookings only) 11am-7pm daily. *Mar* 11am-7pm daily. *Apr, May, Oct* 11am-7.30pm daily. *June, Sept* 11am-8pm daily. *July, Aug* 11am-3pm, 4.30-8pm Mon-Fri; 11am-8pm Sat, Sun. *Nov* 11am-6.30pm daily. *Dec* 11am-6pm daily. Closed Jan. Last entry 2hrs prior to closure. **Admission** €23; €21 14-18s; €17 9-13s; €13 7-8s. **No credit cards**.
A way from Madrid, but well worth the trip, 'From Pine to Pine' is a forest-based adventure park where logs, hanging bridges and tree platforms are incorporated into routes that criss-cross the pine forests. Courses are designed with varying levels of difficulty according to kids' ages and each takes an hour.

Madrid Xanadú

Autovía A-5, km 23.5, Arroyomolines (90 226 30 26, www.madridxanadu.com). Bus 528, 534

from *Príncipe Pío, or 498, 498A, 524, 529, 531, 531A from Móstoles.* **Open** 10am-10pm Mon-Thur; 10am-2am Fri-Sun. **Admission** (excluding equipment hire) *1hr* €19, €16 under-13s. *4hrs* €27, €24 under-13s. **Credit** AmEx, DC, MC, V.
Billed as 'Europe's largest destination for snow, shopping and leisure', Madrid Xanadú is home to Madrid SnowZone (91 648 23 65, www.madridsnowzone.com), which boasts 24,000sq m of indoor ski slopes. All the necessary equipment can be hired. There are also go-karts, a 15-screen cinema, 200 shops and around 30 restaurants.

Parque Warner Madrid

San Martín de la Vega (91 821 12 34, 90 202 41 00, www.parquewarner.com). By car A-4 to km 22, then M-506 to San Martín de la Vega/ by train C-3 from Atocha to Parque de Ocio. **Open** varies (see website). **Admission** €38.50 adults & children over 120cm; €29.50 children under 120cm & over-60s. Free for children shorter than 90cm. **Credit** AmEx, DC, MC, V.
The park has five themed areas with rides to match: Hollywood Boulevard, Cartoon Village, Old West Territory, DC Super Heroes and Warner Brothers Studios. Popular rides can have long, hot queues, and it's an expensive day out, especially as visitors are not allowed to bring in their own food. Tickets are valid for two days but you must validate your entrance bracelet for a second day before you leave the park on your first day.

Safari de Madrid

Aldea del Fresno, Ctra de Extremadura (A-5), km 32 (91 862 23 14, www.safarimadrid.com). By car A-5 to Navalcarnero, then M-507 to Aldea del Fresno. **Open** *Nov-Mar* 10.30am-5.30pm daily; *Apr-June* 10.30am-6.30pm daily. *July, Aug* 10.30am-8pm daily; *Sept-Oct* 10.30am-7pm daily. **Admission** €13; €9 3-10s. **Credit** AmEx, DC, MC, V.
A drive-through safari park where giraffes, elephants, big cats and monkeys roam free. In summer there's a swimming pool, a lake with pedalos for rent, a go-kart track, mini-motorbikes and a giant slide.

Tren de la Fresa (Strawberry Train)

Paseo de las Delicias 61 (902 22 88 22, www.renfe.com). Metro Delicias. **Open** departs from Museo del Ferrocarril. *May, June, Sept, Oct* 10am Sat, Sun (return from Aranjuez 6.25pm). Closed mid Oct-late Apr, mid July-mid Sept. **Tickets** €26; €18 4-12s; under-4s free (as long as they don't occupy a separate seat). **Credit** MC, V. **Map** p329 L15/16.
A relaxing and enjoyable steam train ride to Aranjuez. The 1920s 'strawberry' train departs from the Museo del Ferrocarril (*see p110*) and the ticket price includes visits to the palaces and gardens. Aranjuez's famous strawberries are served by hostesses in period costume.

Film

Multiplexes, arthouse fare – and an excellent shop.

Madrileños and movies go together like
chocolate and *churros*. Indeed, this happy
foursome is all that's needed for a perfect night
out. Tickets are reasonably cheap, even for the
plushest screens, and the range of film fare is
easily a match for Paris or London.

Spanish film goes from strength to strength, but
it's been a mixed few years for Madrid's cinephiles,
with several of the city's old movie-houses closing
down. However, the opening of Sala Berlanga in
June 2010, in the refurbished California cinema in
the district of Argüelles, has been something of a
silver lining, promising to offer Spanish, Iberoamerican and European films in
their original (undubbed) versions. The cinema joins the still-adequate list of
arthouse cinemas in the city – including the excellent Cine Doré Filmoteca (the
national film theatre) in Lavapiés and the Enana Marrón in Chueca, showing
old films in VO (*versión original*) – as well as a host of multiplexes.

SPANISH CINEMA

Spain has no film censorship and its movie
aficionados have long indulged their considered
taste for avant-garde cinema, which, in turn,
has inspired the works of homegrown masters
such as Pedro Almodóvar and Julio Médem.
Once the enfant terrible of Spanish cinema, the
deservedly garlanded Almodóvar now makes
mature and richly textured films that are
both emotionally and stylistically audacious.
The metaphysical Médem, whose thrilling
documentary on the Basque conflict, *Basque
Ball*, made him a controversial figure in
Spain, produced one of his most interesting
works in 2007, in the shape of the eagerly
awaited *Caótica Ana*.

Other names to watch for are the social realists
Iciar Bollaín and Fernando León de Aranoa;
Catalan director Isabel Coixet; the satirist Álex
de la Iglesia, and the precocious maestro that is
Alejandro Amenábar – director of Nicole Kidman
in *The Others*. Added to this roster are veterans
such as Carlos Saura, who is still going strong.

Due to complex funding and distribution
policies, an enormous number of films are made
in Spain when compared with how many
eventually make it into mainstream cinemas.
However, a plethora of film festivals of every
persuasion provide a springboard for new

filmmakers and the production of short films is
booming, with arthouse cinemas programming
some of the best before their main features.

For more on Spanish film, *see pp43-45*
Movida Movies.

VENUES

There is no shortage of multiplexes showing
Hollywood fodder dubbed into Spanish
throughout the city, but for a more refined
experience, try the commercially viable
arthouse cinemas showing Spanish auteurs,
documentaries, foreign films in VO (*versión
original* – ie, undubbed and with subtitles),
and an exhilarating variety of quirky, classic
and controversial features. For film seasons
and older films, both Spanish and VO, choose
the grand Filmoteca or the Enana Marrón.

Tickets & times

Daily newspapers, the weekly *Guia del Ocio*
and the http://madrid.lanetro.com website
have film reviews and full listings. Screenings
(*pases*) usually start at around 4pm. The 8pm
screening is the most popular, though the late
screenings (*sesiones de madrugada*) at midnight
and 1am can be surprisingly packed if they're
showing cult films or current favourites.

Sala Berlanga.

Read the newspapers for VO listings, and once there check whether your seating is allocated (*numerada*) before paying. Be warned of the rarity of adequately tiered seating – Spaniards are getting taller but the screens are yet to be put any higher. Monday and Wednesday are often *días del espectador* ('spectator days'), offering special discounts, though every cinema has its own policy on price reductions. Internet reservations are available through www.entradas.com and many cinemas will take advance bookings for busy times and popular films.

VO CINEMAS

Casa de América
Plaza de la Cibeles 2, Salamanca (91 595 48 00, www.casamerica.es). Metro Banco de España. **Tickets** €5; concessions €3. **No credit cards. Map** p324 J11.
This cultural centre has its own cinema screening classic and contemporary Spanish and Latin American cinema as themed seasons and special events. *See also p94.*

Cine Estudio de Bellas Artes
C/Alcalá 42, Huertas & Santa Ana (91 360 54 00, www.circulobellasartes.com). Metro Banco de España. **Tickets** €5; €3.40 members and concessions. **No credit cards. Map** p328 I11.
Originally a theatre, this repertory cinema is part of the grand Círculo de Bellas Artes building. The sound system is excellent, and the programme of themed film seasons goes down well with the trendy audience.

La Enana Marrón
Travesía de San Mateo 8, Chueca (91 308 14 97, www.laenanamarron.org). Metro Tribunal. **Tickets** €4; €2.60 members. **No credit cards. Map** p324 I9.
A side street in Chueca is the hip and lively location of the strangely named Brown Dwarf microcinema, specialising in experimental films, retrospectives, shorts and repertory classics. A meeting place for movie folk, fans and students with debates and discussions, it also boasts a witty website.

Golem
C/Martín de los Heros 14, Argüelles (information 91 559 38 36, box office 90 222 16 22, www.golem.es). Metro Plaza de España. **Tickets** €5.60 Mon; €7 Tue-Fri; €7.20 Sat, Sun. **No credit cards. Map** p323 E9.
This legendary four-screener, until recently known as the Alphaville, was the first of Madrid's art-house cinemas and played a crucial role in the Movida during the 1980s. The screens and sound systems are showing their age and tiering is inadequate, but the basement café is still a fashionable meeting place with a bohemian atmosphere.

INSIDE TRACK
SCREENING TIMES

Screenings tend to start promptly with few trailers or ads, though a brisk turnover means that credits are curtailed and latecomers are a constant hazard.

Ideal Yelmo Cineplex

*C/Doctor Cortezo 6, Lavapiés (information
91 369 25 18, box office 902 22 09 22,
www.yelmocineplex.es). Metro Tirso de Molina.*
Tickets €8; €6-€7 concessions. **Credit** MC, V.
Map p327 H13.
This hugely popular nine-screen multiplex is an efficient if somewhat characterless venue for international mainstream films in *versión original.*

Pequeño Cine Estudio

*C/Magallanes 1, Chamberí (91 447 29
20, www.pcineestudio.es). Metro Quevedo.*
Tickets €7; €5 Mon and concessions.
No credit cards. Map p323 G6.
It's always worth keeping an eye on this peculiar little VO cinema because its rapid turnover means that rarely viewed classics from Hollywood and world cinema often make it on to the programme.

Renoir Plaza de España

*C/Martín de los Heros 12, Argüelles
(information 91 541 41 00, box office 90 222
91 22, www.cinesrenoir.com). Metro Plaza de
España.* **Tickets** €7.50 Tue-Fri; €8 Sat, Sun;
€5.60 Mon & concessions; €5.10 members.
Credit MC, V. **Map** p323 E9.
The flagship cinema of the enterprising Renoir chain. Screens are on the small side and the queuing

system in the cramped foyer is haphazard, but good sound systems and a keen crowd of film fans ensure enjoyable viewing. The Cuatro Caminos branch is also worth a mention for its larger screens, decent bar and intelligent balance of Spanish and world cinema, while the Princesa also has an eclectic mix of Spanish, European and independent American cinema.
Other locations Renoir Cuatro Caminos, Raimundo Fernández Villaverde 10, Chamberí; Cines Princesa C/Princesa 3, Moncloa; Renoir Retiro C/Narváez 42. For all Renoir cinemas ring 91 541 41 00 for information and 90 222 91 22 for the box office.

★ Sala Berlanga

*C/Andrés Mellado 53, Argüelles (91 349 97
73, www.arteria.com). Metro Argüelles, Islas*

Filmoteca at Cine Doré. *See p220.*

Filipinas or Intercambiador de Moncloa.
Tickets €4-€8. **Credit** AmEx, MC, V.
Map p323 E6.
The old California cinema, refurbished to a tune of €2 million by SGAE, reopened as Sala Berlanga in June 2010 – much to the delight of local cinephiles. Named after Spanish film director Luis García Berlanga, the 250-seat VO-only cinema is one of the city's most technologically advanced. It runs special seasons and festivals, with a strong focus on documentary, shorts and underground films. *Photo p218.*

Verdi

C/Bravo Murillo 28, Chamberí (information 91 447 39 30, www.cines-verdi.com/madrid). Metro Canal or Quevedo. **Tickets** €7.50 Tue-Sun; €5 Mon and first screening Tue-Fri; €5 concessions. **No credit cards.**
This relative newcomer to the ranks of VO cinemas has five screens showing a lively mix of arthouse, Spanish, independent and mainstream foreign films.

THE FILMOTECA

★ Cine Doré (Filmoteca Española)

C/Santa Isabel 3, Lavapiés (box office 91 369 11 25, information 91 369 21 18, bookshop 91 369 46 73). Metro Antón Martín. **Open** *Bar-cafés* 5pm-12.30am Tue-Sun. *Bookshop* 5.30-10pm Tue-Sun. **Tickets** €2.50; €2 concessions. 10 films €20, €15 concessions. **No credit cards. Map** p328 I13.
Known affectionately as *la filmo* and featured in films by Almodóvar, this chic art nouveau national film theatre was founded more than 50 years ago. The neon-lit foyer/café is a lively meeting place and the tiny bookshop is always full of browsers. A free, expansive, fold-out monthly programme features

Alejandro Amenábar.

details of its eclectic seasons of films from the Spanish National Archive and world cinema. The grand auditorium is an especially marvellous place to see silent movies, sometimes accompanied by live music. The outdoor rooftop cinema and bar are open – and unsurprisingly very popular – during the summer months. Note that the box office opens at 5.15pm and stays open until 15 minutes after the start of the last performance of the night. Advance tickets can only be bought for the following day's performance and then only up until a third of capacity has been booked. Note also that you can only buy three tickets per person for each performance.

OPEN-AIR MOVIES

Fescinal (Cine de Verano)

Parque de la Bombilla, Avda de Valladolid, La Florida (91 541 37 21, www.fescinal.es). Metro Príncipe Pío. **Tickets** €5; €4 concessions; free under-5s. **No credit cards. Map** p322 B6.
An open-air night-time venue in Parque de la Bombilla for catching double bills of mainstream films during the Veranos de la Villa festival, which takes place between July to September. As well as the massive screen (with wayward sound), Fescinal also offers a smaller one for kids, plus the opportunity to munch on *bocadillos* washed down with *cerveza* for that truly communal experience of movie-watching.

**INSIDE TRACK
ALEJANDRO AMENÁBAR**

Alejandro Amenábar (born 1972; *photo above*) is one of the city's most precocious directors. He studied cinema at Madrid's Universidad Complutense, and, despite not completing the course, has gone on to direct such celebrated films as Academy Award-winning *Mar Adrento* (*The Sea Inside*), *Abre Los Ojos* (*Open Your Eyes*) and, most recently, *Agora* (2009), starring Rachel Weisz. In addition to writing and directing his own films, Amenábar has composed several film scores, such as for José Luis Cuerda's *La Lengua de las Mariposas*. Widely regarded as one of the film world's most sincere and modest hot shots, he came out to the media in 2004, and is often spotted in bars around town.

ARTS & ENTERTAINMENT

Profile Ocho y Medio

Madrid's excellent film bookshop is a don't-miss for movie buffs.

Cinéfilos will find a mecca of moviedom at Madrid's Ocho y Medio bookshop (*see p188*). Rolling since 1996, in larger premises near Plaza de España since 2006 and renovated with the addition of a smart café in 2009, the store's empire is now well established.

Stock includes over 20,000 books with titles in Spanish, English, Italian, French and even Japanese, and anything not on the shelves can be ordered. The DVD section is also excellent and visitors will find film posters, T-shirts, calendars and all sorts of filmic gadgets. Not surprisingly, the shop has become something of a living museum for lovers of Spanish cinema – even the bags, re-designed every few months by an actor or director, have become collectors' items.

Framed posters of recent films are scrawled with thanks and blessings from cast and crew and the walls sport signed dedications from various famous film folk. Frequent guest signings and launch parties have made the store the hub of the Spanish film industry.

Given its reputation, it's not surprising that Ocho y Medio's enthusiastic owners, Jesús Robles and María Silveyro, have been awarded several prestigious prizes and are often recipients of thanks during film awards ceremonies. Both of them speak English and are founts of information.

Just across the street are some of the city's best multi-screen arthouse and VO cinemas – the Golem, the Renoir Plaza de España and the Renoir Princesa – while a range of tapas bars, tabernas and restaurants serves the film-going crowds.

LOCATION SCOUTING
With scores of arthouse cinemas nearby, the location is perfect for when the shop closes and you're turfed onto the streets... at 8.30pm (in line with the Felliniesque name).

ARTS & ENTERTAINMENT

Galleries

Madrid's commercial art scene has broadened its horizons.

Madrid's galleries generally exist in clusters, with many lining the same streets. The grandest galleries tend to be around Alonso Martínez and Colón metros, with plenty of interesting places in the environs of C/San Pedro and C/Doctor Fourquet in the Antón Martín and Lavapiés areas. However, in a complementary blend of institutional muscle from the big guys and spunk from the smaller galleries, the streets surrounding the Reina Sofía have been gradually transforming into the city's art nexus over the past decade. Enhancing the artsy vibe, each June PHotoEspaña (*see p208*) adorns nearby C/Huertas with photography in the streets and hosts popular summer slide shows in Plaza Santa Ana.

HUERTAS & SANTA ANA

Ángel Romero
C/San Pedro 5 (91 429 32 08, www.galeriaangel romero.com). Metro Atocha. **Open** 11am-2pm, 5.30-8.30pm Mon-Sat. Closed July-mid Sept. **No credit cards. Map** p328 J14.
A beautiful gallery with a cavernous basement, which has previously shown some of Spain's most intriguing young artists. In recent years its scope has become more international, with artists from Cuba, France and Germany. Keep an eye out for young German painter Barbara Stammel.

★ Galería La Fábrica
C/Alameda 9 (91 360 13 20/5, www.lafabrica galeria.com). Metro Atocha. **Open** 11am-2pm, 4.30-8.30pm Tue-Sat. Closed Aug. **No credit cards. Map** p328 J13.
La Fábrica is a hub of the Madrid art world, heavily involved in exhibitions such as PHotoEspaña. It exhibits major-league as well as up-and-coming artists and is known for its insights into photography. It also publishes art books and, in collaboration with website www.notodo.com, organises art competitions.

LAVAPIES

Cruce
C/Dr Fourquet 5 (91 528 77 83). Metro Atocha. **Open** 5-9pm Tue-Sat. Closed Aug. **Map** p328 I14.
More than just a gallery, Cruce is a community hub for young Spanish artists, poets and intellectuals. In addition to fun and outlandish exhibitions, it hosts

book presentations, concerts and poetry readings. Pick up the monthly schedule to see what's on.

Espacio Mínimo
C/Dr Fourquet 17 (91 467 61 56, www.espacio minimo.net). Metro Atocha. **Open** 10am-2pm, 3.30-7.30pm Tue-Fri; 10am-6pm Sat. Closed Aug. **Map** p328 I14.
This contemporary gallery shows a good selection of national and international works, from graphics-based artist Gamaliel Rodríguez to English photographer Martin Parr.

Helga de Alvear
C/Dr Fourquet 12 (91 468 05 06, www.helgade alvear.net). Metro Atocha. **Open** Sept-June 11am-2pm, 4.30-8.30pm Tue-Sat. *July* 11am-2pm, 4.30-8.30pm Tue-Fri; 11am-2pm Sat. Closed Aug. **Map** p328 I14.
Run by a feisty, fashionable German owner, this gallery has been a leader in internationalising the city's art climate. The artists she selects come from all over, and have included British filmmaker Isaac Julien and Canadian artist Christine Davis.

CHUECA

Arnés y Röpke
C/Conde Xiquena 14 (91 702 14 92, www. galeria arnesyropke.com). Metro Chueca. **Open** 10am-2pm, 4-7pm Tue-Fri. **No credit cards. Map** p324 J10.
The owners of this gallery are a Spanish/German duo who aim to promote abstract and figurative art

(photography is a forte). They have been successful in bringing European contemporary art to Spain and Spain's avant-garde to the rest of the world. If you can, try to catch a show by Arnold Odermatt.

Edurne

C/Libertad 22 (91 521 52 52, www.galeria edurne.com). Metro Chueca. **Open** 11am-2pm, 6-9pm Mon-Fri; by appointment Sat. Closed Aug. **No credit cards. Map** p324 I10.

In 1964, despite the controlling eyes of the dictatorship, Margarita de Lucas and Antonio de Navascues opened Edurne, the first gallery of its kind. This engaging pair is credited with promoting many of Spain's top artists when they were just starting out. Luis Gordillo, Antonio Saura and Gerardo Rueda are among the earlier protégés; recent exhibitions include Enrique Veganzones and Andrés Monteagudo.

Elba Benítez

C/San Lorenzo 11 (91 308 04 68, www.elba benitez.com). Metro Tribunal. **Open** 10am-6pm Tue-Sat. Closed Aug. **No credit cards. Map** p324 I9.

Located in the courtyard of a faded old villa, this is a pleasant gallery to wander through. Elba Benítez promotes Spanish art abroad, although her repertoire also includes international artists. The art is very modern, with an emphasis on photography, video and installation pieces.

Elvira González

C/General Castaños 3 (91 319 59 00, www. galeriaelviragonzalez.com). Metro Colón. **Open** 10.30am-2pm, 4.30-8.30pm Mon-Fri; 11am-2pm Sat. Closed Aug. **No credit cards. Map** p324 J9.

One of Madrid's most distinguished galleries, this is an appealing enclave of Spanish and international contemporary art. LeWitt, Lichtenstein, Warhol, Judd, Rothko and Picasso have all featured in the past.

Galería La Caja Negra

C/Fernando VI 17, 2° izq (91 310 43 60, www.lacajanegra.com). Metro Alonso Martínez. **Open** 11am-2pm, 4.30-8.30pm Mon-Fri; 11am-2pm Sat. Closed Aug. **Credit** AmEx, DC, MC, V. **Map** p324 I9.

Something of a leader on the local art scene, representing international mega artists in addition to famous Spanish contemporary artists. It specialises in original graphic works, photography and illustrated books. Chillida, Tàpies, Barceló, Antonio Saura, Richard Serra and even Picasso are all to be found here, while the internationals include Braque, LeWitt, Rauschenberg, Robert Motherwell and Keith Haring.

★ Galería Juana de Aizpuru

C/Barquillo 44, 1° (91 310 55 61, www.juana deaizpuru.com). Metro Chueca. **Open** 4.30-8.30pm Mon; 10.30am-2pm, 4.30-8.30pm Tue-Sat. **No credit cards. Map** p324 I10.

Madrid's *grande dame* of vanguard photography has been setting the standard since 1983. Juana is known worldwide and represents such local photography luminaries as Alberto García Alex and Cristina García Rodero. Foreign artists who grace the walls include Joel Peter Witkin, William Wegman and Sol Lewitt. Installation work and sculpture also feature.

Heinrich Ehrhardt

C/San Lorenzo 11 (91 310 44 15, www. heinrich ehrhardt.com). Metro Chueca. **Open** 4-8pm Mon; 10am-6pm Tue-Fri; 10am-2pm Sat. **Credit** AmEx. **Map** p324 I9.

This contemporary gallery originally endeavoured to introduce Madrid to German artists such as Joseph Beuys and Baselitz. In the past few years, however, it has expanded its scope to include young Spanish artists such as Ángel Borrego.

Moriarty

C/Libertad 22 (91 531 43 65, www.galeria moriarty.com). Metro Chueca. **Open** 11am-2pm, 5-8.30pm Tue-Sat. Closed mid July-mid Sept. **Credit** V. **Map** p324 I10.

Established in 1981, Lola Moriarty's gallery was a prime hangout and showcase for artists on the Movida scene, and today still supports the Spanish avant-garde and contemporary art scene. Some of her current top artists are photographers: the renowned duo Walter Martin and Paloma Muñoz, the surrealist talent Chema Madoz, and Atsuko Arai.

Sen

C/Barquillo 43 (91 319 16 71, www.galeriasen. com). Metro Chueca. **Open** 4.30-8.30pm Mon;

Elba Benítez.

ARTS & ENTERTAINMENT

11am-2pm, 4.30-8.30pm Tue-Fri; 11am-2pm Sat. Closed Aug. **No credit cards. Map** p324 I10.
Sen is another Movida-related gallery, and helped fringe artists like Costus and Ceesepe earn the respect of critics. It exhibits established and emerging names in various media – painting, sculpture and photography. Its list of artists includes photographer Carlos García-Alix and cult Movida cartoonist Nazario.

SALAMANCA

Guillermo de Osma
C/Claudio Coello 4, 1° izq (91 435 59 36, www. guillermodeosma.com). Metro Retiro. **Open** 10am-2pm, 4.30-8.30pm Mon-Fri; noon-2pm Sat. **No credit cards. Map** p325 L10.
A classic on the Madrid art scene, Guillermo de Osma specialises in artists from the avant-garde movements of 1910-40 and holds five to six shows a year, always accompanied by a superb catalogue. In the past it has worked with the crème de la crème of the art world: think Picasso, Braque and Torres García.

Oliva Arauna
C/Barquillo 29 (91 435 18 08, www.oliva arauna.com). Metro Banco de España. **Open** *Sept-June* 11am-2pm, 4.30-8.30pm Mon-Sat. *July* 11am-2pm, 4.30-8.30pm Mon-Fri; 11am-2pm Sat. Closed Aug. **No credit cards. Map** p324 I10.
Another empress of contemporary art, Oliva Arauna has a taste for large, bold, challenging photographs and slick minimalist sculpture. A small but impressive gallery, this is a good place to get a glimpse of Spain's most inventive photographers. Concha Prada, in particular, is one to watch.

CHAMBERI

Estiarte
C/Almagro 44 (91 308 15 69/70, www.estiarte. com). Metro Rubén Darío. **Open** 10am-2pm, 4.30-8.30pm Mon-Fri; 10am-2pm, 5-9pm Sat. Closed Aug. **Credit** DC, MC, V. **Map** p324 K6.

This gallery has specialised in original graphics for 30 years and represents many big names, past and present – Miquel Barceló, Max Ernst, José María Sicilia, Eva Lootz, Calder, Chillida and Picasso.

Galería Javier López
C/José Marañón 4 (91 593 21 84, www. galeriajavierlopez.com). Metro Alonso Martínez. **Open** 11am-2pm, 4.30-8.30pm Tue-Fri; 11am-2pm Sat. Closed Aug. **No credit cards. Map** p324 I8.
Javier López is a well-known figure on the Madrid art circuit. The gallery originally opened in London, but moved to Madrid in 1996 (relocating to its current space in 2007), and shows artists as prestigious – and diverse – as Donald Judd, Andreas Gurskey, Edward Ruscha and Hiroshu Sugimoto.

Galería Soledad Lorenzo
C/Orfila 5 (91 308 28 87, www.soledadlorenzo. com). Metro Alonso Martínez. **Open** 4.30-8.30pm Mon; 11am-2pm, 4.30-8.30pm Tue-Sat. Closed Aug. **No credit cards. Map** p324 J8.
A forerunner among Madrid's galleries, this large, beautiful space shows highly contemporary installation work, video, painting and photography. Artists are primarily Spanish, and include the likes of Miguel Barceló, Tàpies and Julian Schnabel.

Marlborough
C/Orfila 5 (91 319 14 14, www.galeria marlborough.com). Metro Alonso Martínez. **Open** *Sept-June* 11am-2pm, 4.30-8.30pm Mon-Sat. *July* 11am-2pm, 4.30-8.30pm Mon-Fri; 11am-2pm Sat. Closed Aug. **Credit** MC, V. **Map** p324 J8.
This luminary of the Madrid art world represents major Spanish artists (Antonio Saura, Blanca Muñoz, Luis Gordillo), and has branches in London, New York, Monte Carlo and Santiago. The expansive space, designed by US architect Richard Gluckman, is a work of art in itself.

ART FAIRS

ARCO
Feria de Madrid (91 722 50 00, 90 222 15 15, www.arco.ifema.es). Metro Campo de las Naciones. **Dates** 1wk mid Feb. **Open** noon-9pm Mon-Sat. **Admission** €30. Tickets online at www.entradas.com. **Credit** varies.
While the Arte Contemporáneo (ARCO) fair has been around since 1982, it has only recently gained major international kudos. Now scores of Spanish and foreign art heavyweights pack into the city each February, seeking out the latest art trends. In 2010 the spotlight was on Los Angeles, and Russia is due to follow in 2011, with hundreds of galleries from various different countries setting up stalls at the Parque Ferial Juan Carlos I, transforming the pavilion into a colourful sea of contemporary art.

Gay & Lesbian

Out and about in one of Europe's most exciting gay hubs.

The transformation of Chueca from a haven for winos and junkies into a vibrant gay quarter has let Madrid establish itself as one of the world's most gay-friendly cities. What's more, Prime Minister José Luis Rodríguez Zapatero came good on his first pre-election promise to legalise same-sex marriage, making Spain the third country to do so after Belgium and Holland. Further positive legislative changes have included the Law of Gender Identity, which gives transsexuals the right to have their change of sex reflected on their ID cards and passports.

ARTS & ENTERTAINMENT

THE SCENE

The throbbing heart of the scene (*el ambiente*) is the Plaza de Chueca. Tightly packed around what is an otherwise nondescript square in the centre of town, it's home to a dazzling array of bars and services aimed almost exclusively at one of Madrid's most vociferous and dynamic communities. With bars, cafés, hotels, saunas, travel agencies and bookshops, the formerly run-down neighbourhood has emerged as one of the city's most lively and trendy areas. But Chueca has become, perhaps, a victim of its own success, its hip hangouts attracting a non-gay crowd in recent years. Now, many want their ghetto back, at least for cruising, and plenty of shag-and-go gay male-only bars have popped up all over the place. Special events aimed at specific subcultures are a growth industry too: there are camping weekends for bears in the nearby mountains, an action-packed 'Sleazy Madrid' long weekend every spring, plus lesbian raves with dykey darkrooms, body-shaving bashes and sloppy mud parties.

CAFES & RESTAURANTS

As well as the places listed below (all of which are in Chueca), other restaurants that are noticeably popular among the gay community include **El Armario** (*see p146*), **Gula Gula** (*see p140*) and **El 26 de Libertad** (*see p146*). **Ángel Sierra** (*see p175*), while not a gay bar per se, is smack on the Plaza de Chueca and therefore an ideal place to start the evening.

Café Acuarela
C/Gravina 10 (91 522 21 43). Metro Chueca. **Open** 2pm-2am daily. **Credit** MC, V. **Map** p324 I10.
By day a quiet, mixed haven to duck into and catch your breath: curl up with a book and sample one of the teas. After sundown, sip a cocktail, sink into a deep sofa and admire the decor – a mix of kitsch, retro glamour and exuberant baroque.

★ Café Figueroa
C/Augusto Figueroa 17 (mobile 67 754 17 16). Metro Chueca. **Open** *Oct-May* noon-1am Mon-Thur; noon-2.30am Fri, Sat; 4pm-1am Sun. *June-Sept* 4.30-11.30pm daily. **No credit cards.** **Map** p324 H10.
Madrid's original gay café is a sedate place where the lace curtains, 19th-century chandeliers and winding wooden staircase lend themselves nicely to a cosy destination for those who want gay in an old Spain way. There's a pool table upstairs.

Café La Troje
C/Pelayo 26 (91 531 05 35). Metro Chueca. **Open** 5pm-2am Mon-Thur, Sun; 5pm-2.30am Fri, Sat. **No credit cards. Map** p324 I10.
A romantic and popular stop, with friendly service and big screens playing chill-out videos. It gets chock-a-block at weekends with an amiable and mixed crowd, who are generally on their way somewhere else.

Colby Urban
C/Fuencarral 52 (91 521 25 54, www.restaurante.colby.com). Metro Chueca. **Open** 9.30am-1.30am Mon-Thur;

9.30am-2.30am Fri, Sat; 11.30am-1am Sun.
Credit AmEx, DC, MC, V. **Map** p324 H10.
It's red, it's urban, it's aspirational. Colby Urban is
the flagship of a string of cool eateries and chilled-
out cafés with a concept. We're not sure what the
concept is, but the location is handy, the custom is
pretty and the diner-style food hits the spot.

D'Mystic

*C/Gravina 5 (91 308 24 60, www.dmystic.net/
dmystic3d.html). Metro Chueca.* **Open** 9.30am-
2.30am daily. **Credit** DC, MC, V. **Map** p324 I10.
This den of cool is located at a strategic crosssroads,
with bigger-than-average cocktails that make up for
the aloof staff. Watch the real world stroll by outside or gaze at the natural world on the New Agey
videos on the screens inside. Relax, listen to the
whale songs and the waterfalls. Then get out and
head for Eagle (*see p228*).

★ Diurno

*C/San Marcos 37 (91 522 00 09, www.
diurno.com). Metro Chueca.* **Open** 10am-
midnight Mon-Thur; 10am-1am Fri; 11am-1am
Sat; 11am-midnight Sun. **Credit** AmEx, DC,
MC, V. **Map** p324 I10.
A minimalist and sexy film-rental café spinning all-
day chill-out sounds (and occasional techno). As well
as a fabulous selection of movies, there are delicious
sandwiches, salads, pasta dishes and cakes. A peaceful place to start the day, upbeat and lively at night.

Mama Inés

*C/Hortaleza 22 (91 523 23 33). Metro Gran
Via.* **Open** 10am-2am Mon-Thur, Sun; 10am-
3am Fri, Sat. **No credit cards. Map** p324 H10.
Another place to successfully combine a decent
breakfast with plenty of eye candy. Chill-out and nu
flamenco waft through this modern but surprisingly
intimate café during the day, while at night house
takes over and the T-shirts get progressively tighter.

XXX Café

*C/Clavel, corner C/Reina (91 522 37 77).
Metro Gran Via.* **Open** 3.30pm-2am Mon-Thur,
Sun; 3.30pm-2.30am Fri, Sat. **No credit cards.**
Map p324 I11.

INSIDE TRACK
KIKE SARASOLA

Hotel magnate (he's the owner of the
Room Mates chain), three-times Olympic
horseriding champion and darling of the
Spanish gossip rags, Kike Sarasola's
2006 wedding – attended by politicians
and members of the Spanish royal family
– was the first high-profile gay marriage
to be featured in *¡Hola!*.

Room Mate Oscar. *See p230.*

Quiet until the pre-dinner crowd arrives to shake it
up, this is a small and popular meeting point where
the staff are gorgeous and the regulars friendly. Park
yourself by the window for the best view – with any
luck, you'll be snapped up in no time.

CLUBS & DISCOBARES

A *discobar* treads the line between club and
regular drinking den. Admission is generally
free (exceptions are noted below), and there is
normally a diminutive dancefloor to justify
the pricier-than-average drinks.
    As well as the venues below, **Ohm** (*see p248*)
and **Weekend** (*see p248*) also have a big gay
following, as does Space of Sound on Sundays
at **Macumba** (*see p255*). Unless otherwise
stated, all of the following are in Chueca.

Black & White

*C/Libertad 34 (91 531 11 41, www.discoblack-
white.net). Metro Chueca.* **Open** 10pm-5.30am
Mon-Thur, Sun; 10pm-6am Fri, Sat. **No credit
cards. Map** p324 I10.
The grubby upstairs bar is a hit with cocky *latino*
rent boys and their older prospective patrons, and
plays host to some of the best cabaret shows in town.
Downstairs things really liven up in the heaving *discobar* that is popular with revellers of all ages and
orientations. A classic.

★ Liquid
C/Barbieri 7 (91 523 28 08, www.liquid.es).
Metro Chueca. **Open** 9pm-3am Mon-Thur;
9pm-3.30am Fri, Sat. **Credit** AmEx, DC, MC, V.
Map p324 I11.
A cool, happening place in which to see and be
seen, with a contemporary, minimalist interior, lit
up with megascreens showing the latest dance
music videos. It might be a bit tame for some, but
it's a friendly crowd.

Rick's
C/Clavel 8 (91 531 91 86). Metro Gran Vía.
Open 11.30pm-5.30am daily. **Admission**
(incl 1 drink) €8. **No credit cards.**
Map p324 I11.
Expensive drinks and an expensive, older crowd are
the hallmarks of this friendly late-night alternative
to the discos. With hi-NRG beats and camp Spanish
hits, it's standing-room only at weekends.

★ Sala Cool
C/Isabel la Católica 6, Sol (91 542 34 39).
Metro Santo Domingo. **Open** midnight-6am
Fri, Sat; 9pm-2am Sun. **Admission** (incl 1 drink)
€10-€15. **Credit** MC, V. **Map** p323 F11.
The *número uno* place to be on Friday and Saturday
nights. Snarling caged gogos, preening Muscle Marys,
serious shirtless studs with sweaty torsos, spaced-out
twentysomethings and gorgeous waiters are all part
of the coolture at this slick, designerish two-floored
club. Join them on the throbbing dancefloor or bop to
the handbag music upstairs. *Photo p228.*

Teatro Kapital
C/Atocha 125, Huertas & Santa Ana
(91 420 29 06, www.grupo-kapital.com).

Metro Atocha. **Open** 11.30pm-6am Thur-Sun.
Admission €12-€16. **Credit** AmEx, DC,
MC, V. **Map** p328 J14.
Another palace to brighten up dull Sundays. Keep
your bearings as you make your way through the
main dancefloor and bars of Madrid's seven-storey
megaclub, and head for the gay corner of this empire
of decadence and dance. There's a cinema on the fifth
floor and a rooftop terrace. *See also p251.*

EXCLUSIVELY MALE/HARDCORE

Bangalá
C/Escuadra 1, Lavapiés (no phone, www.
bangalamadrid.com). Metro Lavapiés.
Open 9pm-2.30am Mon-Fri, Sun; 9pm-3am
Sat. **Admission** (incl 1 drink) €10-€15.
No credit cards. Map p328 H14.
It's sleek. It's black. It's red. Bangalá is the latest
addition to the Lavapiés scene and promises to
outdo its rivals with fetisho-licious nights such as
Night of Tongues or Dawn of the Vampires. Behind
the bar are cabins and two pristine darkrooms.

Copper
C/San Vicente Ferrer 34, Malasaña (no phone,
www.copperbar.net). Metro Tribunal. **Open**
2pm-3am Mon-Thur, Sun; 2pm-3.30am Fri-Sat.
Admission (incl 1 drink) €9.40. **No credit
cards. Map** p323 G9.
The friendly guys at this sloppy and sweaty club
got tired of trying to enforce the dress code so now
it's a self-styled 'nudist bar', except on Saturdays
when it's Underwear Night. The place can get pretty
hardcore, but there's a chatty crowd out front, and
a popular large backroom.

ARTS & ENTERTAINMENT

Café Acuarela. *See p225.*

ARTS & ENTERTAINMENT

Sala Cool. *See p227.*

Cruising

C/Pérez Galdós 5, Chueca (91 521 51 43).
Metro Chueca. **Open** 8pm-3.30am Mon-Fri;
8pm-4.30am Sat, Sun. **No credit cards.**
Map p324 H10.

A fun, sleazy cruising club that puts the 'laid' into
'laid-back'. Upstairs there's a quieter pub-like area,
and a diminutive porn cinema; downstairs there's a
dancefloor and a spacious public loo-like darkroom.
The place could do with a lick of paint, but its faded
glory is part of its enduring charm.

Eagle

C/Pelayo 30, Chueca (no phone, www.eagle
spain.com). Metro Chueca. **Open** 2pm-2am
Mon-Fri; 2pm-2.30am Fri; 5pm-2.30am Sat; 5pm-
2am Sun. **Admission** free. **No credit cards.**
Map p324 I10.

This is the nerve centre of the fetish scene in Madrid.
For a visit to the Eagle, boots, leather chaps and
handcuffs are all that the well-dressed devotee need
worry about packing. The small and cramped downstairs gives way to an even tighter squeeze in the
upstairs play area, which is where the real boys are
to be found. Among the entertainments, you might
chance upon Leather Night, Uniform Night or – if
you really hit the jackpot – Golden Night.

Hell

C/Buenavista 14, Lavapiés (no phone,
www.hell sexclub.com). Metro Antón Martín.
Open 10.30pm-3am Tue-Thur; 11.30pm-3.30am
Fri, Sat; 10pm-3am Sun. **Admission**
€8-€10. **No credit cards.** **Map** p328 I14.

A tiny and rough fetish club whose denizens get
down to some hard cruising. Each month there is a
changing programme of themed nights, though
every Sunday is Noche Sport, when the dress code
is sneakers, jockstraps, underwear or, if any of that
seems a little over-dressed, naked. On Tuesdays the
dress code is naked, thus removing the agony of
choice. Some nights are devoted to private parties
or special events. Log on to the titillating website for
the latest details.

Hot

C/Infantas 9, Chueca (91 522 84 48, www.bar
hot.com). Metro Chueca. **Open** 6pm-3am Mon-
Thur, Sun; 6pm-3.30am Fri, Sat. **Admission**
free. **No credit cards.** **Map** p324 H11.

Hot, hairy, homo heaven at this fun bear den for hir-
sute late thirty- and fortysomethings. Things get
even hotter downstairs in the darkroom. Two drinks
for the price of one, every day until midnight.

Leather Club

C/Pelayo 42, Chueca (91 308 14 62). Metro
Chueca. **Open** 8pm-3am daily. **Admission**
free. **No credit cards.** **Map** p324 I10.

The name of this big, two-floor hangout is a bit mis-
leading as little leather is in evidence, but the crowd
is raunchy, and can be found in the large darkroom
or lurking in anticipation in the cabins. Check out
the individual movie screens over the urinals.

Odarko

C/Loreto Chicote 7, Malasaña (no phone,
www.odarko.com). Metro Callao. **Open** 10pm-
4am Mon-Fri; 10pm-very late Sat; 6-11pm Sun.
Admission (incl 1 drink) 10pm-1am €8;
midnight-close €10. **Credit** DC, MC, V.
Map p323 G10.

The seedy backstreets off Gran Via make the perfect approach to this lively sex club, where chains
chink, bars rattle and boots scuff the soiled floor.
Dress code is strictly enforced on weekends and
some of the nights are pretty full-on. Check the website in advance, lest you turn up in a crisp Fred Perry
top to find it's the Wild & Wet Piss session.
Improbably, the owners run a little B&B upstairs.

The Paw

C/Calatrava 29, La Latina (91 366 60 93,
www. thepawmadrid.com). Metro Puerta de
Toledo. **Open** 8pm-6am Mon-Sat; 5pm-4am
Sun. **Admission** (incl 1 or 2 drinks) €10-€12.
No credit cards. Map p327 E14.

Formerly known as Into The Tank, this louche little joint is off the beaten track but well worth the
effort for dress code and fetish fans. If you forgot to
pack your cop uniform, don't worry, you can go
naked every night. Check out the hot underwear parties: log on to the website for all the lurid details.

Strong Center

C/Trujillos 7, Sol & Gran Via (91 541 54 15,
www.strong-center.com). Metro Ópera. **Open**
midnight-6am daily. **Admission** (incl 1 or 2
drinks) €12 midnight-2am; €11 2am-close Mon-
Thur, Sun; €13 Fri; €15 Sat. **No credit cards.**
Map p327 G11.

The dancefloor at the Strong Center is a forlorn,
empty place. Don't dismay, however, as no one

INSIDE TRACK PUBLICATIONS

Some of the best of the free publications
lying around in bars are *Shangay Express*
newspaper – or its pocket-sized
companion *Shanguide* – with listings
on the gay and lesbian scene throughout
Spain; *Odisea*, which deals more with
social and political issues and publishes
a handy map, and *Revista Mensual*, sold
at news kiosks (its personal ads are
riveting). Fetish fans (men only) should
look out for *Phetix*, a free quarterly guide
to sex clubs and parties.

There are also some good websites,
all with guides to the scene, plus nifty
extra features such as personals and
access to chat. Try www.chueca.com,
www.guiagay.com, www.gaymadrid4u.com,
www.gaymadrid.com and www.cogam.org.

---

comes here for the music, and you're just about to
discover Spain's biggest and most labyrinthine
darkroom, where you can lose yourself among hundreds of hot, horny men.

Saunas

Balneario Paraíso

C/Norte 15, Conde Duque (91 522 58 99,
www.mundoplacer.com). Metro Noviciado.
Open 1pm-midnight Mon-Thur; 24hrs Fri-
Sun. **Admission** €15. **No credit cards.**
Map p323 F9.

Located in what used to be a popular flamenco club,
this extensive, spotlessly clean sauna has maintained its original evocative mosaics. The young,
hunky clients often seem more interested in their
own well-toned pecs than in you, but there is a small
pool, porn cinema, bar, darkroom and cabins as consolation. Massage and sunbeds are also available.

Men

C/Pelayo 25, Chueca (91 531 25 83, www.sauna
men.es). Metro Chueca. **Open** 3.30pm-midnight
Sun-Wed; 3.30pm-7am Thur, Fri; 4pm-9am Sat.
Admission €10; €5 18-25s; €5 for 2 people Tue;
€8 Wed, Thur. **No credit cards. Map** p324 I10.

A small, dowdy sauna with a perplexing door policy (though cute young guys are usually safe).
Located right at the heart of the gay scene, Men is
always rammed with a cross-section of gay Madrid.
There's a bar, darkroom and a few cabins in which
to spend a steamy hour or two.

Sauna Príncipe

Travesia de las Beatas 3, Malasaña (91 559
02 59, www.mundoplacer.com. Metro Plaza
de España. **Open** noon-midnight daily.
Admission €13. **No credit cards.**
Map p323 F10.

This sauna is better equipped than its rivals and
caters for a varied crowd, though it's particularly
popular with bears, not to mention tourists.

GAY & LESBIAN SHOPS

A Different Life

C/Pelayo 30, Chueca (91 532 96 52, www.
differentlife.es). Metro Chueca. **Open** 10.30am-
9.30pm daily. **Credit** AmEx, DC, MC, V.
Map p324 I10.

A well-stocked bookshop, with some titles in
English, plus magazines and a range of cheesy gay
gifts. Downstairs you'll find an eye-popping range
of porn videos, which can be bought or rented.

Amantis

C/Pelayo 46, Chueca (91 702 05 10,
www.amantis.net). Metro Chueca. **Open** 10am-
10pm Mon-Sat; 4.30-9pm Sun. **Credit** AmEx,
DC, MC, V. **Map** p324 I10.

ARTS & ENTERTAINMENT

Pride and Joy

Madrid's Gay Pride is one of the world's biggest, wildest and most symbolic.

On seizing power in 2004, Spain's Socialist government wasted no time in addressing gay rights, legalising gay marriage and allowing transsexuals to choose whichever gender they wished on their identity cards. Milestone achievements that were celebrated with leather, rubber, bears, tanned toned flesh and non-stop hedonism in the 2004 Gay Pride (Orgullo Gay) parade. In recognition of his efforts for equality, Zapatero was awarded the Civic Courage Prize from Berlin-based gay-rights association Christopher Street Day.

Orgullo Gay (*see p209*), organised by COGAM and FELGBT, has continued to grow since then, despite continued threats to the event by some Chueca residents, who want the week-long June party to be moved to the outskirts of the city. From 2006, the parade itself was extended, running from the Puerta de Alcalá to Plaza España. It attracts some 1.5 million people. For an entire week, the city is invaded by visitors from all over the world, partying hard at night, and sporting an array of ludicrously coloured banana hammocks at the swimming pools by day, with the rooftop terrace of the Room Mate Oscar hotel (*see p123*) a popular hotspot. In 2010, Kylie Minogue gave a free concert in Plaza España on the Saturday evening.

As well as the parties and the parades, the week boasts some 300 cultural, artistic and sporting events – kicking off with the Carrera en Tacones (a running race where contestants run in stilettos) – as well as off-site parties at the end of the week.

Despite such leaps, bounds and high-heeled trotting towards an equal Spain, there is much still to be done, according to Madrid's numerous gay-rights associations. As a reaction to the passing of the same-sex marriage legislation, 166,000 protesters (1.5 million if you believe the organisers), convened by the 'Family Forum' in June 2006, took to the streets to voice their deep disapproval of same-sex marriage. The protesters, who were made up mostly of right-wing families and their children, members of the clergy and politicians from the opposition Popular Party (PP), carried slogans that claimed that the traditional family unit was at stake, and demanded the resignation of Zapatero. The PP hasn't stopped there, going so far as to bring the legislation before the constitutional courts to contest its legitimacy. Throw in the occasional news story of continuing homophobia, such as the refusal of a popular Madrid restaurant to host a reception for a gay wedding, and it's clear that while, in the words of the major gay associations, Madrid is 'one of the most tolerant cities in the world', there is still plenty to march for.

The most discreet of the city's sex shops in terms of location, Amantis has a sunny feel and seems rather like a small-town shop. Albeit a small-town shop filled with condoms, lube, improbable dildos, porn mags, videos and DVDs.

Berkana

C/Hortaleza 64, Chueca (91 532 55 99, www. libreriaberkana.com). Metro Chueca. **Open** 10.30am-9pm Mon-Fri; 11.30am-9pm Sat; noon-2pm, 5-9pm Sun. **Credit** AmEx, DC, MC, V. **Map** p324 H10.

There are books and videos in English here, and members of staff are friendly and helpful. Browsing is encouraged and you can linger over some of the erotica at the in-store café.

City Sex Store

C/Hortaleza 18, Chueca (91 181 27 23). Metro Chueca. **Open** 11am-10pm Mon-Fri; 11am-11pm Sat; 12.30-9.30pm Sun. **Credit** AmEx, DC, MC, V. **Map** p324 H10.

Bright, shiny and well organised, City Sex Store is a veritable supermarket of porn, with merchandise spread out over two floors.

SR

C/Pelayo 7, Chueca (91 523 19 64, www.sr-shop.es). Metro Chueca. **Open** 5.30-9pm Mon; 11am-2pm, 5-9pm Tue-Sat. **Credit** AmEx, DC, MC, V. **Map** p324 I10.

Everything for the discerning leather and fetish fan. Leatherwear, uniforms, rubber and SM gear, plus indispensable accessories – masks, slings, chains and handcuffs to help you turn that unused boxroom into your very own dungeon. And no, we don't know what the live crocodiles are for, either.

Lesbian Madrid

All those places for the boys, and barely enough bars to make a decent pub crawl for lesbians – what's a girl to do? Keep her eyes peeled, that's what. Madrid's lesbian scene is growing, but it still has a long way to go before catching up with the gay male *ambiente*. There are lots of one-nighters throughout the year, one organised by the Supernenas and another by Diversité – ask around, or look for flyers in the venues on and near Plaza de Chueca. The square is where you should start off, in any case: every bar here seems to be owned by lesbians, even though the clientele is mixed.

CAFES, BARS & CLUBS

As well as the following, another venue popular with lesbians is **Café Acuarela** (*see p225*).

Escape

C/Gravina 13, Chueca (91 532 52 06, www.escapechueca.com). Metro Chueca. **Open** midnight-5.30am Mon-Thur, Sun; midnight-6am Fri, Sat. **Admission** (incl 1 drink) €8-€10. **Credit** MC, V. **Map** p324 I10.

This cavernous dancehall draped in bullfighter red is one of the most popular destinations for women and is filled to the brim with the sexiest *chicas* in the city at the weekends. In fact, its popularity has spiralled to the extent that it's now one of the more boisterous clubs around Plaza de Chueca.

Medea

C/Cabeza 33, Lavapiés (91 369 33 02). Metro Antón Martín or Tirso de Molina. **Open** 11pm-7am Tue-Sun. **Admission** €10 (incl 1 drink) or €12 (incl 2 drinks). **Credit** AmEx, DC, MC, V. **Map** p327 H13.

Decorated in muted rainbow colours, this welcoming women's disco is one of the clear favourites on the lesbian scene. Men are admitted only in the company of Sapphic sisters.

★ El Mojito

C/Olmo 6, Lavapiés (no phone). Metro Tirso de Molina or Antón Martín. **Open** 9pm-2.30am daily. **Admission** free. **No credit cards. Map** p328 H13.

This cute Lavapiés locale has a retro vibe (Barbie dolls in compromising positions are part of the decor) and excellent cocktails. It attracts a friendly, mixed crowd of both gays and metrosexuals.

Muse

C/Pelayo 31 (mobile 600 265 236). Metro Chueca. **Open** 10pm-3.30am Mon-Sat. **Admission** varies. **No credit cards. Map** p324 I10.

Britney and Madonna engaging in that famous kiss take pride of place on the wall at Muse, which is a mostly lesbian disco-bar on bustling Calle Pelayo. The white walls here are adorned with mirrors shaped like naked ladies and bathed in pink lighting, helping to create a warm setting in which to get your groove on to the vocal house classics that roar out of the bar's sound system. Be sure to get there for around 1am, when the venue really starts to pack out.

Truco

C/Gravina 10, Chueca (91 532 89 21, www.trucochueca.com). Metro Chueca. **Open** 5pm-3am Mon-Thur; noon-3am Fri, Sat. **Credit** V. **Map** p324 I10.

Truco is often very crowded and usually with an extremely young and loud crowd. No matter: this high-octane corner joint remains *the* place for gals who are looking for gals in the earlier part of the evening. It is also a stone's throw from the very popular girl bar Escape (*see above*).

Music

Classical, rock, flamenco and all that jazz.

Madrid's cultural clout has steadily increased over recent years, with the city finally shaking off a reputation for producing stuffy composers, ensembles with limited scope, a limited contemporary classical scene and a reactionary public. Credit must go, too, to a city that depends predominantly on public funds to bring in top-class international musicians and ensembles to its worthy concert venues.

And despite the introduction of stricter licensing laws in the past few years, Madrid still has a multitude of venues to hear live rock music (whether home-bred or international), with Malasaña – the original Movida barrio – still home to plenty of intimate and atmospheric spots. Lavapiés, meanwhile, as the multicultural melting-pot of the city, is the place to head to to hear both traditional and fusion flamenco and rumba, as well as tango, electronica and world music.

Classical & Opera

Traditionally, the scene orbits around three main venues: the modern and austere (and arguably the best-quality classical venue in Europe) **Auditorio Nacional** (*see p234*) the grand **Teatro Real** (*see p236*), hosting opera, and the **Teatro de la Zarzuela** (*see p237*), for a decent selection of classical concerts (as well as for *zarzuela*, Madrid's traditional operetta art form).

INSIDE TRACK
AUDITORIO AUDIENCES

One-off attendees to concerts at the **Auditorio Nacional de Música** (*see p234*) will find themselves joining an ageing audience, the majority of them being serious season-ticket holders, who tend to be particularly expressive. Many make their feelings known when pleased with the odd exultant cheer of '*bravo*', but more save themselves for when they want to voice their disapproval – boorings have been known in reaction to particularly offensive contemporary compositions, especially when the composer is present.

A word of advice for attending classical concerts in Madrid – get there early. The stereotypical Spanish tardiness is not a trait shared by classical music lovers.

ZARZUELA

Zarzuela is an ineffable part of *madrileño* culture, though tricky for the outsider to get a grip on. It was Spain's early answer to the Italian opera – shorter and funnier and incorporating elements of theatre, slapstick and dance. Golden Age playwrights Félix Lope de Vega and Pedro Calderón de la Barca were early pioneers of the genre, which was later developed by the likes of Ramón de la Cruz and the composer Federico de Chueca and, moving into the 20th century, Amadeo Vives and Jacinto Guerrero. *Zarzuela* is full of local jokes (usually rhyming and rattled off at speed) and traditional songs with which the public will sing along, so be prepared. Catch it in its home ground of the Teatro de la Zarzuela, in the Centro Cultural de la Villa in July or August, or at a summer open-air performance.

INFORMATION & TICKETS

Check venue websites detailing current and future seasons, as well as any last-minute changes or cancellations. You can pick up leaflets from most of the venues – often quicker than trying to get through by phone – or check the *Guía del Ocio* or daily newspapers. Tickets can usually be bought via phone or internet from the venue itself (check venue listings) or from Tel-entrada or Caixa de Catalunya (902 10 12 12, www.telentradas.com). Tickets for state-run venues such as the Auditorio Nacional and the Teatro de la Zarzuela are sold at one another's box offices as well as ServiCaixa (902 33 22 11, www.serviticket.com).

ORCHESTRAS & ENSEMBLES

Orquesta y Coro de la Comunidad de Madrid

www.orcam.org

Madrid's state-funded regional orchestra is one of the city's most highly regarded. It provides accompaniment for the shows at the Teatro de la Zarzuela, but also performs at the Auditorio Nacional. The orchestra's artistic director, José Ramón Encinar, provides an occasionally erratic programme of mainly Spanish composers.

Orquesta & Coro Nacionales de España (OCNE)

http://ocne.mcu.es

A certain element of instability has hounded Spain's national orchestra and choir over the years, with numerous strikes carried out by the state-employed members when asked to practise at home outside their set paid hours. They take to the stage every weekend at the Auditorio Nacional, occasionally performing world premières of contemporary pieces. Josep Pons is the current artistic director of the

orchestra and the choir, and is attempting to renovate programme content. He has even shown an interest in adding jazz, tango and ethnic music to the orchestra's traditionally classical and Romantic repertoire.

Orquesta y Coro de RTVE

www.rtve.es/rtve/orquesta-coro

The orchestra and choir of Spain's national state-run television and radio stations (Radio Televisión España) was originally founded for broadcasting. Its home is in the Teatro Monumental and concerts are usually Thursdays and Fridays at 8pm. Season tickets, running from October till late March, are reasonably priced and the programme is consistently good. Carlos Kalmar is to take over from Adrian Leaper as artistic director in September 2011.

Orquesta Sinfónica de Madrid

www.osm.es

The *orquesta titular* of the Teatro Real and oldest existing symphonic ensemble in Spain has a reputation within classical music circles for proposing odd, irregular seasonal programmes. Recent years have looked more stable, however, with a proposed series of chamber concerts, *zarzuelas* and symphonic concerts. At the Teatro Real the major operas are also usually complemented by related concerts put on by the orchestra and performed in a new concert space in one of the upstairs rooms.

As well as all the top Spanish conductors, the OSM has also worked with international greats such as Peter Haag, Pinchas Steinberg and Kurt Sanderling. Its artistic director is the esteemed Jesús López Cobos, but his work at the Teatro Real is so demanding that his commitment to orchestral work can sometimes play second fiddle.

Teatro de la Zarzuela. *See p237*.

INSIDE TRACK
FESTIVE SOUNDS

With such good weather, music festivals are understandably popular. San Isidro is a good place to catch free concerts in Las Vistillas park. July sees the Veranos de la Villa festival, and Madrid's indie festival, Festimad Sur, is still going strong in its new home in Leganés. The Carnaval and Dos de Mayo holidays see live acts performing for free, as do the Fiestas del Partido Comunista in September and the May Day celebrations. For all these and more, *see pp206-211* **Calendar**.

Proyecto Guerrero

This is one of the more interesting ensembles covering the much ignored contemporary spectrum. Having said that, professional opinions as to its real competence are mixed. Under the artistic direction of Javier Güell, Proyecto Guerrero is the main component of the Auditorio Nacional's Música de Hoy programme (www.musicadhoy.com).

VENUES

The **Círculo de Bellas Artes**' classical and contemporary music programme has broadened immensely over the last decade (*see p68*). The **Teatro Español** (*see p264*) occasionally holds *zarzuelas* and performances by chamber and symphonic orchestras. A handful of cafés and restaurants around town offer an opera-accompanied dining experience. Try the **Café Viena** (C/Luisa Fernanda 23, 91 559 38 28) for its Monday night sessions, called Lunes Líricos (consisting of dinner followed by a short *zarzuela* or opera performance, all for €30 plus wine). Also, check out the professional singing waiters at **La Favorita** (*see p155*) and **La Castafiore** (C/Marqués de Monasterio 5, 91 319 42 21, www.lacastafiore.net). Another place to keep an eye on is the **Centro Asturiano** (C/Farmacia 2, 4°, 91 532 82 81, www.info negocio.com/casturmadrid), which runs a cycle called Lunes Musicales with concerts performed by small ensembles on Mondays. **Café La Fídula** (C/Huertas 57, 91 429 29 47) is a cosy café with concerts on Fridays and Saturdays.

Auditorio Nacional de Música

C/Príncipe de Vergara 146, Prosperidad (information 91 337 01 40, tickets 91 337 03 07, www.auditorionacional. mcu.es). Metro Cruz del Rayo or Prosperidad. **Open** *Box office* 4-6pm Mon; 10am-5pm Tue-Fri; 11am-1pm Sat.

Closed Aug. **Main season** Oct-June. **Tickets** €10-€47. **Credit** MC, V.
This impressive concert hall has capacity in its main auditorium for over 2,000, and a smaller chamber hall, La Sala de Cámara. As well as the OCNE, the Auditorio hosts the Comunidad de Madrid's orchestra, ORCAM, and is the provisional home of the Joven Orquesta Nacional de España (worth checking out for their youth and enthusiasm – in contrast to the OCNE). In addition, there are ensembles such as that of the Universidad Politécnica de Madrid who invite orchestras to accompany the university's choir, performing selected Friday and Saturday evenings at 10.30pm. But the best concerts are those by invited international orchestras – which are, happily enough, something the Spanish state likes to invest its music budget in. The best seasons are the Grandes Intérpretes, the Liceo de Cámara (Fundación Caja Madrid), Ibermúsica, Ciclo de Cámara y Polifonía and the contemporary Música de Hoy programme (*see left* **Proyecto Guerrero**). Look out too for organ recitals.

Tickets for the Auditorio usually go on sale about a fortnight before the performance, and can be hard to get hold of. Tickets are generally cheaper for Sunday morning concerts.

Real Academia de las Bellas Artes de San Fernando

C/Alcalá 13, Sol & Gran Vía (91 524 08 64, http://rabasf.insde.es) Metro Sevilla or Sol. **Concerts** *Sept-June* noon Sat. **Admission** free. **Map** p327 H11.
This beautiful building right in the heart of Madrid is a must for a concert experience. It hosts three or four cycles of free concerts a year, usually organised through the Radio Nacional de España for broadcast with musicians from the Escuela Superior de Música Reina Sofía. One well-reputed cycle is the short baroque season, which usually takes place in March.

Teatro Monumental

C/Atocha 65, Lavapiés (91 429 12 81, www.rtve.es). Metro Antón Martín. **Open** *Box office* 11am-2pm, 5-7pm daily. *Concerts* Oct-May 8pm Thur, Fri. **Main season** Oct-March. **Tickets** €9-€22. **Credit** AmEx, DC, MC, V. **Map** p328 H13.
Located in slightly seedy Antón Martín, the Monumental has more character than most, but is functional rather than beautiful. Its main purpose is to record broadcast concerts by the RTVE Orchestra and Choir – consequently it may not have the glitz of the Teatro Real, but it does have excellent acoustics and high-quality performances. The principal diet here is generally concerts, with a side order of opera and *zarzuela*. The Monumental opens to the public free of charge for rehearsals on Thursday mornings and chamber music concerts around midday on Saturdays.

Teatro Real. *See p236.*

Teatro Real

Plaza de Isabel II, Los Austrias (information 91 516 06 60, box office 902 24 48 48, www.teatro-real.com). Metro Opera. **Open** *Box office* 10am-8pm Mon-Sat, from 2hrs before show Sun. *Visits* 10.30am-1pm Mon, Wed-Fri; 11am-1.30pm Sat, Sun. **Main season** Sept-July. **Tickets** *Ballet* €10-€107. *Opera* €6-€156. *Visits* €5; concessions €3. **Credit** AmEx, DC, MC, V. **Map** p327 F11.

Shaped like a compressed oval, the interior of the city's opera house is breathtakingly ornate compared with its sombre façade, and one of the most technologically advanced in Europe. Productions are impressive, with complicated revolving sets and attention to detail in costume and props, and enjoy funding from some of Spain's biggest companies, as well as the Comunidad de Madrid. Projection screens at either side of the stage show the full-stage action, though this does not quite compensate for the lack of vision at the far ends of the top galleries (the *tribunas* and part of the *anfiteatro*). There is also a screen above the stage showing Spanish surtitles for non-Spanish operas. The acoustics are so good that the quality of the sound is practically the same everywhere in the hall.

The annual Festival de Verano runs alongside the theatre's regular programme in June and July but offers a more orchestra- and dance-orientated programme as well as children's shows (tickets for these events are much cheaper and easier to obtain). Guided tours run every day except Tuesday, and take visitors through the main dressing room and auditoria. Tours last 50 minutes and a minimum of ten people is required for a tour to take place (call 91 516 06 96 for all tour enquiries/booking).

Airs and Graces

Concert programmers in and around Madrid are slowly waking up to the charms of the region, taking music out of the theatres and lighting up monasteries, palaces and gardens. What could be more inviting than a soirée of Rachmaninoff, Fauré, Mozart and Schumann in one of the cool churches of the Sierra when the temperature is in the 40s in Madrid?

The **Clásicos en Verano** (www.madrid.org/clasicosenverano) concerts may not bring the greatest musicians, but their range is broad. Come July and August, it seems every nook and cranny, every old church and town hall around Madrid is filled with the sweet sounds of piano concertos, percussion groups, choirs, wind ensembles, string quartets, accompanied poetry and medieval music by local groups. The apparently random programming has led to Bach and Handel arias being performed at the San Andrés church in Rascafría, while in nearby Alameda del Valle, young men climbed stepladders to read names and numbers from the phone book as if they were poetry.

Not only are these concerts widespread and plentiful (there are nearly 100 of them in 53 different towns), they're also free. Pass by a tourist information office (*see p208*) or the Consejería de Cultura y Deportes on C/Alcalá 31 to pick up a full programme. Some of the more striking venues include the Castillo de los Mendoza in Manzanares el Real (*see p282*); and the Iglesia de San Bernabé and Iglesia de los Arroyos in El Escorial (*see p273*).

There are a couple of other options in historical settings that are more highly respected in classical music circles. Care for a turn about the charming gardens of the Aranjuez Palace (*see p288*) serenaded by *zarambeques*, *folías*, *marionas*, *fandangos* and *pasacalles*? The festival of **Música Antigua Aranjuez** (www.musicaantiguaaranjuez.net) keeps the music live in the place that inspired Joaquín Rodrigo's haunting *Concierto de Aranjuez*, but with sounds from much earlier in the palace's history. At weekends during the months of May and June the palace hosts concerts of medieval, renaissance and baroque music played on original instruments from the period. Many of the composers featured do not enjoy wide exposure today, although they were well known in their day. Concerts are held inside the palace (in the chapel and the Sala de Teatro), as well as in the palace grounds. The much-loved guided 'musical walks' have pauses for concerts along the way. Tickets are around €20 for concerts and €18 for musical walks and can be bought from Tel-entradas (902 10 12 12, www.telentradas.com).

The Fundación Caja Madrid (www.fundacioncajamadrid.es) is behind several impressive classical music cycles throughout the year in places of interest. The **Fiestas Reales** festival puts on very good concerts in El Escorial (*see p273*), Madrid's Real Monasterio de las Descalzas Reales (*see p67*) and San Jerónimo El Real (*see p90*). This foundation is the most active and positively focused in Madrid and these concerts are of an excellent standard.

Performances usually begin at 8pm, or 6pm on Sundays, with ballet and family opera matinées at noon. Tickets go on sale approximately ten days before the première, and standby tickets are available on the day. With the cheapest tickets, for rows F and G, vision is seriously reduced; check the website for a detailed plan.

Teatro de la Zarzuela

C/Jovellanos 4, Huertas & Santa Ana (box office 91 524 54 10, http://teatrodelazarzuela.mcu.es). Metro Banco de España. Open Box office noon-6pm (8pm before shows) daily. Main season Sept-July. Tickets €5-€42. Credit AmEx, DC, V. Map p328 I11.

The Teatro de la Zarzuela, which served as an opera house for many years previous to the Teatro Real's renovation, is now principally devoted to its *raison d'être* – staging *zarzuela*, the home-grown Spanish operetta. Despite *zarzuela*'s uncool image and lack of credibility among serious music lovers, it retains considerable popularity, drawing in audiences for daily 8pm performances from October to July. Accompanying the Teatro's packed *zarzuela* programme are performances of dance (often by the Ballet Nacional), music, plays, conferences and special family-orientated shows. The well-reputed annual Ciclo del Lied pays tribute to the lesser-known 19th-century German song form.

Institutions

Institutions such as the **British Council** (www.britishcouncil.org/es), the Institut Français (www.ifmadrid.com), the **Istituto Italiano di Cultura** (www.iicmadrid.com) and the **Goethe Institut** (www.goethe.de/ins/es/mad/esindex. htm) are also worth checking for classical music concerts and related activities. *See also p266* **Centro Cultural de la Villa**.

Centro para la Difusión de la Música Contemporánea

5th floor, Centro de Arte Reina Sofia, C/Santa Isabel 52, Lavapiés (91 744 10 72/http://cdmc.mcu.es). Metro Atocha. Main season Oct-May. Map p328 J14/15.

Founded by Luis de Pablo, this pioneering institution boldly goes where few others in Madrid dare to go – into the dangerous world of the contemporary. The Centro gives 30 or so commissions annually to students who debut at the Auditorio Nacional, the Círculo de Bellas Artes or at the Reina Sofía museum. The centre also organises an interesting music festival, La Música Toma el Museo, with free concerts around the museum as well as out on the pleasant patio.

Fundación Canal

C/Mateo Inurria 2, Chamartín (91 545 15 06, www.fundacioncanal.com). Metro Plaza de Castilla. Main season Oct-July.

Set up by Madrid's water company, the Canal Isabel II, in recent years this foundation has become active in all areas of the arts, programming various types of occasionally excellent exhibitions and concerts year-round. Music programming has included seasons of chamber music performed by musicians from the Orquesta de la Comunidad de Madrid and several one-off recitals by virtuosos such as the Russian pianist Alexander Moutouzkine. Non-classical music gets a look-in too; the regular 'conFUSIÓN' series has featured genres as diverse as bossa nova, gospel and jazz.

Fundación Carlos Amberes

C/Claudio Coello 99 (91 435 22 01, www.fcamberes. org). Metro Serrano. Main season Sept-July. Map p325 L7.

The Carlos Amberes foundation dates back to 1594, when it was founded by a 16th-century Flemish benefactor. Today, as well as exhibitions and conferences, it hosts an average of 15 to 20 concerts per year in three cycles (one at the beginning of the year, another in May and one at the end of the year), both in its rather dingy basement and sometimes upstairs in a converted church, which is pretty but has bad acoustics. The programme tends to nod towards the music of the Low Countries.

Fundación Juan March

C/Castelló 77, Salamanca (91 435 42 40, www. march.es). Metro Núñez de Balboa. Main season Oct-June. Map p325 N7.

Set up in 1955, this charitable foundation and hive of musical, artistic and scientific activity was one of few such organisations in Spain for a good many years. These days the Fundación Juan March remains a key player in Madrid's classical world, putting on around 150-200 free concerts per year. These usually consist of soloists or chamber ensembles and take place on Mondays at midday and 7pm, Wednesday evenings from 7pm (the most popular slot, with better-known professional musicians and broadcast on Radio Nacional) as well as some Saturdays and Sundays at midday featuring performances ranging from jazz and classical to world music. The concert hall seats 300; when it fills up a second hall with a big screen is opened, and then the bar. The programme in general is pretty much free from restrictions as it does not depend on ticket sales; there is a leaning towards Spanish composers, but with a lot of flexibility. Take in some good art exhibitions while you're there.

CLASSICAL FESTIVALS

Fiesta season in Madrid kicks off in May with the week of merriment leading up to **San Isidro** on the 15th. The council provides annual free concerts including *zarzuela* in the Centro Cultural Conde Duque (*see p80*) as well as in parks to the west of the city and the Plaza

ARTS & ENTERTAINMENT

Café la Palma.

Mayor. Classical concerts, given by ensembles such as the Banda Sinfónica Municipal, are sometimes held in the Teatro Español (*see p264*). See the council's website www.madrid.es or ask at tourist offices for a San Isidro programme.

The international **Día de la Música** on June 21 involves 12 hours of non-stop dance, musical theatre, cinema, photography and, of course, music in an increasing number of museums and other venues across the city, organised by the Circulo de Bellas Artes, and all for free. June also sees classical concerts in **Alcalá de Henares** on some Sundays, performed by local orchestras in the Plaza

Cervantes bandstand. For the summer festivals **Clásicos en Verano** and **Festival de Música Antigua**, *see p236* **Airs and Graces**.

Rock, Roots & Jazz

It's been a difficult past decade for live music in Madrid. As part of the local authority's crusade against what it apparently deems to be low culture, bar and venue owners continue to fight a sometimes insurmountable battle in order to put on live music. In another bizarre twist to the tale, as part of the anti-alcohol drive, the council has also banned under-18s from concerts, something which some lament as the beginning of the end of rock in Spain.

Surprisingly, in the face of such fervent opposition, Madrid's live music scene continues to thrive, with bigger and bigger names coming to the city in the past few years – receiving a warm reception from all but the council.

VENUES

In the centre of Madrid there is not one concert venue that holds more than 2,500 spectators. Intimacy is the order of the day then, with many big names coming to play in surprisingly small auditoria. As well as those listed here, the bullring at Las Ventas (see p42 **Where and How**) sometimes hosts gigs, and being outdoors is perfect for the concerts put on there in July. The Parque de Atracciones (see p212) in the Casa de Campo is another summer venue where you can catch some local rock groups.

Venues listed do not charge admission unless otherwise stated. If there is no charge on the door, there will most likely be a supplement on your first drink, which usually goes straight into the pocket of the band. Few venues will accept credit cards on the door, although we have noted those that do in our listings. To make licensing issues easier, many of these venues stay open as nightclubs after the concerts end, while some clubs in the **Nightlife** chapter (see pp245-255) often host live music.

ROCK/WORLD MUSIC

La Buena Dicha
C/Santa Hortensia 14, Chamartín (91 413 60 14, www.labuenadicha.com). Metro Alfonso XIII or Prosperidad. **Open** 10pm-6am Thur-Sat. Closed Aug. **Admission** (incl 1 drink) €7 for concerts.
A medium-sized venue with a large stage and lots of smoke and light tricksiness, La Buena Dicha programmes little-known local pop and rock outfits, usually of a pretty good standard. Be warned, it can be hard to find, so allow plenty of time.

Búho Real
C/Regueros 5, Chueca (91 308 48 51, www.buhoreal. com). Metro Alonso Martínez or Chueca. **Open** 7pm-3am daily. Closed Aug. **Credit** MC, V. **Map** p324 I9.
The lights go down very low in the Búho Real, and the spots come up on a tiny stage. The size limitations here dictate the acts – expect local jazz or acoustic groups, most of them just two- or three-piece bands. The name means the 'Royal Owl', which goes some way towards explaining the large collection of minature owls on display.

Café la Palma
C/Palma 62 (91 522 50 31, www.cafela palma.com). Metro Noviciado. **Open** 4pm-3am Mon-Thur, Sun; 4pm-4am Fri, Sat. *Concerts & club nights* from 10pm & midnight Thur-Sat. **Admission** *Concerts* (minimum consumption) €7. **No credit cards. Map** p323 F8.
This is a longstanding favourite among the Malasaña crowd. Choose from an area with tables, a chill-out zone where everyone lazes on cushions on the floor or the main room, where from Thursday to Saturday you can catch concerts from local up-and-comers such as Raíces y Puntas.
▶ *Calle de la Palma is home to a host of good bars, including local fave La Palmera and the friendly late-night cocktail den La Caracola (for both, see p181).*

La Coquette
C/Hileras 14, Los Austrias (91 530 80 95). Metro Ópera or Sol. **Open** *Sept-Apr* 8pm-3am Mon-Thur, Sun; 8pm-3.30am Fri, Sat; *May-July* 9pm-3am Mon-Thur, Sun; 9pm-3.30am Fri, Sat. Closed Aug. **Admission** varies. **Map** p327 F11.
This basement bar, going for some 20 years now, was Madrid's first dedicated exclusively to blues. Run by a Swiss-Spanish guy called Albert, who has a large collection of old records that won't disappoint, there are live acts featuring local bluesers from Tuesday to Thursday. Can get very smoky.

La Cubierta de Leganés
C/Maestro 4, Leganés (91 689 87 15, box office 91 694 78 46, www.la-cubierta.com). Metro Leganés Central. **Open** varies. **Admission** varies.
La Cubierta is a bullring with retractable roof south of the centre in Leganés. Bullrings often double as concert venues, but sadly the shape of a bullring is not conducive to good acoustics, leaving a crisp kick-drum distorted into a nebulous throb. That said, it's a magnet for rock and heavy metal groups, plus dance acts too: Chemical Brothers, Deep Purple and Tool have all paid a visit.

**INSIDE TRACK
ANTONIO VEGA**

The *madrileño* Antonio Vega, who died of lung cancer in 2009, aged 51, was one of the key figures of the Movida Madrileña movement in the 1980s. His song 'La Chica de Ayer' ('Yesterday's Girl') – recorded by Nacha Pop, the band he formed with his cousin Nacho García Vega – was the anthem of a generation, and now exists in a multitude of versions recorded by different Spanish and Latin American artists.

Garibaldi Café

C/San Felipe Neri 4, Los Austrias (91 559 27 33, www.salagaribaldi.com). Metro Ópera.
Open 9.30pm-6am daily. **Admission** varies.
Map p327 F12.

A roomy venue with a good sound system and a varied programme. Its staple fare is new bands doing the rounds on the local scene, but in addition there are DJ sessions from Thursday to Sunday. Midweek you'll find stand-ups, storytelling, theatre and dance.

Gruta 77

C/Cuchillo 6, Southern suburbs (91 471 23 70, www.gruta77.com). Metro Oporto. **Open** 8pm-6am daily. **Admission** varies.

A mix of local unsigned groups and touring bands from the States, Australia and Japan pass through this 300-seater *sala*, on the corner of Cuchillo and Nicolás Morales. Punk, rock, ska and *mestizaje* tastes are catered for, with regular rock competitions, the prize being the chance to professionally record an album. An excellent sound system makes it worth the trip out to the 'burbs.

Honky Tonk

C/Covarrubias 24, Chamberí (91 445 61 91, www.clubhonky.com). Metro Bilbao. **Open** *Sept-June* 9.30pm-5am daily. *July, Aug* 10.30pm-5am. Concerts start 12.30am. **Admission** free.
Map p324 I7.

Honky Tonk programmes local country, blues and rock acts nightly, and its own Gary Moore/Rolling Stones-influenced band performs regularly. Ignore the intimidating-looking doormen and get here early, as the large pillars that hold up the building tend to restrict the views of those not at the front.

Madrid Arena

Casa del Campo, Avda de Portugal s/n (91 722 04 00, www.madridarena.org). Metro Alto de Extremadura or Lago. **Open** varies. **Admission** varies.

INSIDE TRACK GIG GUIDES

The listings mags *Guía del Ocio, Salir Salir* and the Friday supplements of many Spanish newspapers have details of forthcoming gigs. Otherwise, concert information comes on posters, flyers and in free magazines found in bars and music and fashion shops. Magazines to look for include *MondoSonoro, Punto H, Rockdelux, GO* and the irregular *Undersounds*. Concert information is also available on the web if you speak Spanish at: www.lanetro.com, www.madridmusic.com and www.mondosonoro.com.

A behemoth of a venue, refurbished just a few years ago, and well laid out, with good facilities and great acoustics. There are plenty of macro-raves here too — it's not all just about the guitars.

Moby Dick

Avda del Brasil 5 (91 555 76 71, www.mobydickclub.com). Metro Cuzco or Santiago Bernabéu. **Open** 10pm-3am Mon-Thur, 10pm-5am Fri, Sat. **Admission** €5-€15. **Credit** (bar only) MC, V.

With two different levels for music, Moby Dick caters for plenty of tastes. Mainly a venue for local groups and touring Spanish bands, it can still pull a few surprises. The Long Blondes, the Libertines and the Feeling have all paid a visit, as have the sublime Fat Freddy's Drop. Warm up next door with a pint of Guinness in its sister bar the Irish Rover first.

Orange Café

C/Serrano Jover 5, Conde Duque (91 542 28 17, www.soyorangecafe.com). Metro Argüelles. **Open** 9pm-5am Tue-Sat. Concerts start between 8.30pm & 11pm. **Admission** *Concerts* €6-€25. **Map** p323 E7.

What was once the Chesterfield, a small concert venue with an impressive track record in live music, has been remodelled and reopened under the corporate sponsorship of mobile phone company Orange. The programme remains more or less the same, however, with mostly local but sometimes international acts appearing most Thursdays, Fridays and Saturdays.

Palacio Municipal de Congresos

Avda de la Capital de España Madrid 7 (91 722 04 00, www.madrideyc.es/palacio). Metro Campos de las Naciones. **Open** varies. **Admission** varies.

This Ricard-Bofill designed auditorium looks to have been purpose-built for a symphony orchestra, but that doesn't mean pop and rock acts can't make use of it. Antony and the Johnsons played here, as did the Woody Allen New Orleans Band. Crosby and Nash defied the security guards to pull the audience on stage. Various awards ceremonies are held here, from the Goyas (the Spanish Oscars) to the annual Canadian Aboriginal Music Awards.

Palacio Vistalegre

C/Utebo 1, Southern suburbs (91 422 07 81, www.palaciovistalegre.com). Metro Oporto or Vista Alegre. **Open** varies. **Admission** varies.

This stadium is what the Spanish call *multi-usos*, so it serves as a basketball stadium and a conference hall as well as a concert venue. Some of the slightly dubious names to have rocked a crowd here in recent times include Judas Priest, Bryan Adams and Spanish rockers Extremoduro.

Ritmo & Compás

C/Conde de Vilches 22, Salamanca (91 355 28 00, www.ritmoycompas.com). Metro Cartagena

El Junco. *See p243.*

or Diego de León. **Open** *Bar* 4pm-end of concert programme. **Admission** varies.

A music fanatic's paradise, Ritmo & Compás boasts 160 rehearsal rooms over two sites, recording studios, its own record label and courses and seminars. As a live venue it has a programme as diverse as the facilities, including pop-rock, reggae, northern soul, metal, blues, funk, techno and breakbeat. The stage and auditorium are well designed, allowing a good view from any angle.

La Riviera
Paseo Bajo de la Virgen del Puerto s/n, Los Austrias (91 365 24 15, www.salriviera.com). Metro Puerto del Ángel. **Open** *Gigs* varies. *Club* midnight-5am Fri, Sat. **Admission** varies. **Map** p326 B/C12.

This club on the banks of the Manzanares is a major player on the Madrid music scene and is ranked by many as the city's best medium-sized venue. It's certainly popular, and comes equipped with an excellent sound system. All manner of acts have passed through in recent times, among them Missy Elliot, Yo La Tengo, Bloc Party and Jet.

La Sala
Avda Nuestra Señora de Fátima 42, Carabanchel (91 525 54 44, www.lasala.biz). Metro Carabanchel. **Open** 8pm-5am daily. **Admission** varies.

The neon and neo-classical columns in the entrance, the torch-lighting inside – it's all a bit strip joint, but don't let that, or the suburban location, put you off.

La Sala's mixed bag of gigs mainly features Spanish pop, but there have also been performances from the likes of Deacon Blue and Ron Wood. There is a concert space with room for 700 on the first floor, while downstairs there are pinball machines, a pool table and a loud but louche atmosphere.

Sala Caracol
C/Bernardino Obregón 18, Embajadores (91 527 35 94, www.salacaracol.com). Metro Embajadores. **Open** 9pm-3am concert nights. **Admission** varies. **Map** p327 H16.

The much-cherished Caracol is a cosy venue, but nevertheless big enough to have hosted Queens of the Stone Age, Papa Roach, Placebo and The Editors since it opened over 20 years ago. Once known for flamenco and world music, it is now more likely to feature rock, and has its own competition for up-and-coming bands.

Sala Heineken
C/Princesa 1, Argüelles (91 547 57 11, www.sala rena.com). Metro Plaza de España. **Open** midnight-6am Fri, Sat (concert days opens 10pm). **Admission** varies. **Map** p323 E9.

The venue formerly known as Arena (but not to be confused with Madrid Arena, for which see above), Sala Heineken plays host to several club nights, but is also a fairly hot live music venue. The layout is not especially conducive to everyone getting a good view of the action, but it's an intimate venue, with recent visitors including the likes of !!!, Peaches and the Kaiser Chiefs.

Siroco

*C/San Dimas 3, Malasaña (91 593 30 70,
www.siroco.es). Metro Noviciado or San
Bernardo.* **Open** 9.30pm-5am Thur; 9.30pm-6am
Fri, Sat. Closed 3 wks Aug. **Admission** (incl 1
drink) €5-€8. **No credit cards. Map** p323 F8.
Regulars at this long-established joint know just what
they want, and management are more than happy to
provide it, programming a steady schedule of well-
established local rock, indie, pop and funk outfits and
providing a stage for young hopefuls. In addition,
there are late-night DJ sessions covering a broad range
of styles. The club has its very own record label and
tends to be frequented by A&R types from others.

El Sol

*C/Jardines 3, Sol & Gran Via (91 532 64 90,
www. elsolmad.com). Metro Gran Vía.* **Open**
midnight- 5.30am Tue-Sat, doors open for
concerts at 11pm. **Admission** (incl 1 drink)
€9. **Credit** (bar only) MC, V. **Map** p327 H11.
A steady flow of top live acts passes through El Sol,
another remnant of the Movida. The decor is not up
to much, but the vibe and the programme make up
for that – a mixture of rock, rhythm and blues, punk,
soul, and hip hop from national outfits, complemented by visits from international acts such as the
Bellrays, Snow Patrol and Gigolo Aunts.

JAZZ

The **Festival de Otoño** (*see p210*) includes
a jazz section and many top international names
(especially from the field of Latin jazz) appear
here. Other venues with occasional live jazz acts
include **Marula** (*see p246*), and the otherwise
sleepy **Café El Despertar** (C/Torrecilla del
Leal 18, 91 530 80 95, www.cafeeldespertar.com)
in Lavapiés. Fair-trade café **Zanzíbar** (*see
p177*) in Chueca has a varied programme of
jazz, blues, singer-songwriters and bossa nova.

Café Berlin

*C/Jacometrezo 4 (91 521 57 52, www.cafe
berlin.es). Metro Callao or Santo Domingo.*
Open noon-4am Tue-Sun. **Admission** varies.
No credit cards. Map p323 G11.
In 2003 the Berlin was another venue to fall foul of
enforced closure by the council but has since
bounced back impressively, with its own jazz school.
While it is mainly a jazz venue showcasing local
groups, bigger names such as Eddie Henderson also
come to call. These days you can also get a bite to
eat – burgers, pasta and desserts with names like
Tarta Miles Davis. The premises also hosts the club
Oba-Oba, offering up DJ sessions of Brazilian beats,
and the best caipirinhas in the city.

Café Central

*Plaza del Ángel 10, Huertas & Santa Ana
(91 369 41 43, www.cafecentralmadrid.com).*

Metro Antón Martín or Sol. **Open** 1.30pm-
2.30am Mon-Thur, Sun; 1.30pm-3.30am Fri,
Sat. *Concerts* 10pm-midnight. **Admission**
gigs €7-€12. **Credit** AmEx, DC, MC, V.
Map p327 H12.
For many years now, this beautiful place with high
ceilings and elegant decor has been *the* place to
get your jazz fix in Madrid. The artists that come
here put it among the best of its kind in Europe.
George Adams, Don Pullen, Ben Sidran and
Bob Sands have all taken the stage, as well as
Spanish stalwarts such as Chano Domínguez,
Jorge Pardo and the oldest and greatest of them
all, Pedro Iturralde.

Café Populart

*C/Huertas 22, Huertas (91 429 84 07,
www.populart. es). Metro Antón Martín.*
Open 6pm-2.30am Mon-Thur, Sun; 6pm-3.30am
Fri, Sat. *Concerts* 10.15pm-11.30pm. **Admission**
free. **Map** p328 I12.
Escape from the beer-crawl route that is Huertas
slipping into this superb jazz club. There's no cover
charge, but the drinks are a bit pricey. A strong
backer of Spanish jazz and host to many an international artist, Populart features jazz and blues every
night with two shows, one at 11.30pm and the other
at 12.30am.

Clamores

*C/Alburquerque 14, Chamberí (91 445 79
38, www.salaclamores.com). Metro Bilbao.*
Open 7pm-2am Mon-Thur, Sun; 7pm-4am Fri,
Sat. **Admission** *Concerts* €6-€15; students
€5-€8. **Map** p323 H7.
This emblematic jazz club opened in 1979, and for
eight years served as the set for the TV programme
Jazz Entre Amigos. Stocking what is apparently the
widest range of cavas and champagnes in Madrid,
it has a very varied programme these days, with
tango, pop, rock, bossa, samba and folk all on the
bill as well as the jazz that made its name. The live
acts sprawl into late-night jam sessions on Friday
and Saturday nights. There are no live performances
on Monday or Sunday nights.

INSIDE TRACK
FLAMENCO FESTIVALS

A great way of experiencing flamenco
dance is as part of the city festivals in
honour of **San Isidro** (*see p207*) and the
summer's **Veranos de la Villa** (*see p209*),
while the **Festival Flamenco Cajamadrid**
is held in February and March in the Teatro
Albéniz (C/Príncipe 25, Huertas & Santa
Ana, 91 360 14 80). The biggest flamenco
festival, though, is the month-long **Suma
Flamenca** (*see p208*).

El Johnny

Colegio Mayor Universitario San Juan Evangelista, C/Gregorio del Amo 4, Moncloa (91 534 24 00, http://cmusanjuan.com). Metro Metropolitano. **Open** *Oct-May* 10pm Fri-Sun. Closed June-Sept. **Admission** varies (sometimes free).

This auditorium, located in a student residence, is actually much more prestigious than you might think. Contrary to its appearance, it's one of the city's most discerning jazz clubs – hundreds of great names have passed through the doors here in the 30-plus years of its existence. Look out for the annual spring jazz festival and the Flamenco por Tarantos festival in April.

★ El Junco

Plaza Santa Bárbara 10 (91 319 20 81, www. el junco.com). Metro Alonso Martínez. **Open** 11pm-6am daily. **Credit** AmEx, DC, MC, V. **Map** p324 I8.

This is the late-night jazz spot in the city, boasting jam sessions on Sundays and Tuesdays, and gigs on most other weeknights. When there are not live musicians for your listening pleasure, a carefully selected roster of DJs, such as Frenchman Fedi Petit, will be spinning vinyl with just the right amount of off-beats.

Segundo Jazz

C/Comandante Zorita 8, Cuatro Caminos, Tetúan (91 554 94 37, www.segundojazz.es). Metro Cuatro Caminos or Nuevos Ministerios. **Open** 7pm-4am daily. **Admission** (minimum consumption) €5.

Founded many years ago by the owner of the legendary Whisky Jazz Club, this is Madrid's longest standing jazz joint. Nowadays, as well as jazz, the programme takes in Brazilian groups, singer-songwriters and '60s cover bands banging out Beatles and Stones songs. A great atmosphere and friendly staff make it an essential stop, but don't get there too early: concerts start at midnight.

LATIN

La Bodeguita de Beny

C/Tres Cruces, 8, Sol & Gran Vía (91 521 34 82). Metro Gran Vía. **Open** 7pm-3am daily. **Admission** free. **Map** p323 H11.

This rather narrow bar, adorned with pictures of Beny Moré, specialises in Cuban cocktails and sounds, and attracts a lively crowd. From Wednesday through to Sunday there are performances on the tiny stage. Expect to find acoustic duos and trios (there's no space for full bands) playing *son*, *guaracha* and Latin jazz.

Galileo Galilei

C/Galileo 100, Chamberí (91 534 75 57, www.sala galileogalilei.com). Metro Islas Filipinas

or Quevedo. **Open** 6pm-3am Mon-Sat. **Admission** €6-€16 Mon-Fri; €23 Sat.

Galileo Galilei presents possibly the widest range of artists to be seen under one roof in all of Madrid. Whatever kind of music you like, you'll likely find it here, since all the bases seem to be covered. There's Latin jazz, flamenco, salsa, singer-songwriters and myriad types of fusion. There are also occasional comedy nights. It's a former cinema, and as such is very spacious, though the mock-Hellenic decor can be a bit over the top. It's non-smoking throughout.

Oba-Oba

C/Jacometrezo 4, Sol & Gran Vía (no phone). Metro Callao. **Open** 11pm-5am Mon-Thur, Sun; 11pm-6am Fri, Sat. **Admission** €8. **Map** p323 G11.

An old favourite, the larger than life Oba-Oba has been serving up ice-cold caipirinhas and fabulous samba for over 25 years to its good-time clientele. There are live acts jamming here several nights a week, and, given the theme, it's perhaps less than surprising that almost all of them are Brazilian, as are many of its patrons.

Flamenco

The most authentic flamenco inhabits a closed world and is proud of it; but if you know where to go and are lucky on the night you might be granted a peek. Madrid's original *cafés cantantes* are long gone but visitors can still catch a feel by crawling the bars around the district of Huertas and the Plaza Santa Ana, where a lucky dip of extravagantly nicknamed performers can sometimes yield a future star. These shows are mostly spontaneous so don't expect them to be advertised. The best way to see flamenco is to bar-hop in streets that live and breathe it, such as C/Echegaray. Rule of thumb: the more the punters look like the performers, the more chance there is that you're in the right place.

Where people are most likely to see flamenco, though, is at a *tablao,* of which there are several in Madrid; below is a selection of those with more genuine performances. As well as the show, you can dine or just drink; both are appallingly expensive, but if you stay till closing you may get your money's worth. The fun really starts around midnight, when most tourists go off to bed and the major artists appear; until then you may just get the kitsch jollity of the *cuadro de la casa* (the house musicians and dancers). Flamenco purists are notoriously snobbish about what's on offer in Madrid, but even they are thrilled by the performances at **Casa Patas**, where guitarists are skilled, dancers ooze power and grace, and singers are as they should be – bloody terrifying.

For more information on flamenco music, see the **Flamenco** chapter (*pp46-49*).

ARTS & ENTERTAINMENT

VENUES

Café de Chinitas

*C/Torija 7, Sol & Gran Vía (91 559 51 35/
91 547 15 02, www.chinitas.com). Metro
Santo Domingo.* **Open** 8pm-1.30am Mon-Sat.
Performances 8.30pm & 10.30pm. **Admission**
(incl dinner) €65 and up; (incl drinks) €31.
Credit AmEx, DC, MC, V. **Map** p327 F11.
An indulgent evening's entertainment for those who
like to play at being 19th-century aristocrats – and
don't mind paying 21st-century prices. At least this
self-styled 'Cathedral of Flamenco' makes an effort,
with sumptuous decor that contributes to the experience. The food and floorshow are expensive, yes,
but at least it means the owners can afford to pay
top euro for flamenco stars, who may not break a
sweat but will still send you reeling into the night.

★ Candela

*C/Olmo 2, Lavapiés (91 467 33 82). Metro
Antón Martín.* **Open** 11pm-5.30am Mon-Thur,
Sun; 11pm-6am Fri, Sat. **No credit cards.**
Map p328 H13.
An ideal place to soak up atmosphere, though performances are impromptu and only take place downstairs and after hours. Still, this in-the-know watering
hole for professional musicians and amateurs is welcoming to knowledgeable and respectful aficionados.

Las Carboneras

*Plaza del Conde de Miranda 1, Los Austrias
(91 542 86 77, www.tablaolascarboneras.com).
Metro Sol.* **Open** 8.30pm-midnight Mon-Sat.
Performances 10.30pm Mon-Thur; 9.30pm,
11pm Fri, Sat. **Admission** (incl 1 drink) €22.
Credit AmEx, MC, V. **Map** p327 F12.
Packed with tourists, this bar-restaurant still offers
good value for money, with an energetic, passionate
show performed by a troupe of enthusiastic dancers.
The set menus comprise typical fare, and diners
are exempt from the admission charge. Highly
polished flamenco for that inauthentic but
unashamedly fun night out.

Cardamomo

*C/Echegaray 15, Santa Ana (91 369 07 57,
www.cardamomo.es). Metro Sevilla.* **Open** 9pm-
4am Mon-Sat. Closed Aug. **Admission** Shows
(incl 1 drink) €32, (incl dinner) €68. **No credit
cards. Map** p327 H12.
A firm fixture on the scene, this frenetic flamenco
bar plays a mixture of flamenco and rumba tunes,
often to thundering effect.

★ Casa Patas

*C/Cañizares 10, Lavapiés (91 369 04 96,
www.casapatas.com). Metro Antón Martín.*
Open 1-4.30pm, 8pm-midnight Mon-Thur;
1-4.30pm, 7.30pm-1am Fri, Sat. **Performances**
10.30pm Mon-Thur; 9pm, midnight Fri, Sat.

Closed 3 wks Aug. **Admission** (incl 1 drink)
€31. **Credit** AmEx, DC, MC, V. **Map** p327 H14.
This is a plush and somewhat pricey place to
savour traditional or nuevo flamenco. Recent topliln-
ers have included Chaquetón, Remedios Amaya and
Niña Pastori. A highly prized venue with a reputation to maintain, Casa Patas is deservedly proud of
its standing and treats its loyal, knowledgeable and
sometimes intimidating audience with respect. The
same owners have a bar, Pata Chico, alongside, for
pre-flamenco drinks.

Corral de la Morería

*C/Morería 17, Los Austrias (91 365 84 46,
www.corraldelamoreria.com). Metro La Latina.*
Open 8pm-2am daily. **Performances** from
10.30pm. **Admission** (incl drinks) €36-€41.
Credit AmEx, DC, MC, V. **Map** p327 E13.
More serious and exacting than Las Carboneras,
this longstanding *tablao* sports seemingly authentic Arab decor and an atmosphere to match. A
relaxed mix of tourists, fans (Hemingway, Che
Guevara and Picasso have all paid a visit) and professionals enjoy a solid, expensive and sometimes
exhilarating show.

Corral de la Pacheca

*C/Juan Ramón Jiménez 26, North of centre
(91 353 01 00, www.corraldelapacheca.com).
Metro Cuzco.* **Open** 9pm-midnight daily.
Performance 10.30pm. **Admission** €30-
€32 (incl 1 drink); €70-€95 (incl dinner).
Credit AmEx, MC, V.
This grand centre of popular and traditional flamenco
boasts a history of star performers and even starrier
punters. Built on the site of a 17th-century theatre, it
began life as a *tablao* but grew into an imposing venue
with a large auditorium and stage.

La Soleá

*C/Cava Baja 34, Los Austrias (91 366 05 34).
Metro La Latina.* **Open** 10pm-6am Tue-Sat.
Credit MC, V. **Map** p327 F13.
This small but amiable bar in the centre of Madrid
boasts a constant babble of flamenco aficionados and
a roster of performers that alternate with spontaneous
(and variable) songs from the clientele. Great fun on
a good night, but it can also be surprisingly dull.
Watch out, too, for the occasional rough element.

Torres Bermejas

*C/Mesonero Romanos 11 (91 532 33 22,
www.torresbermejas.com). Metro Callao.*
Open 8.30pm-2am daily. **Performance** 9.30pm.
Admission (incl drink) €35. **Credit** AmEx, DC,
MC, V. **Map** p327 H11.
Modelled somewhat kitschly on the Alhambra, this
bar plays hosts to authentic Gypsy flamenco and a
faithful in-crowd, managing to absorb the tour par-
ties without spoiling the mood. The paella and the
Rioja veal are, like the flamenco, rich and satisfying.

Nightlife

Time to adjust your body clock.

Sleep is almost a dirty word to this most fun-loving of people: Macbeth didn't murder sleep, Madrid did. The Spanish love to party, and they have always partied harder and later than any other nationality you'd care to mention.

In recent years, however, it seems as if things have changed somewhat. The hedonistic days of La Movida – the libertine backlash against the repression of the Franco era – are gone. Instead, the scene is facing its own backlash, as the local government, and in turn the police, crack down on the giant night-time playground that is Madrid.

This is mainly due to the unwanted by-products of excess: the noise and mess left by the party people, and the political pressure brought on by consistent complaints from the city's residents.

WHAT HAPPENS WHEN

Nightlife here has distinct stages. In the early evening, from 6pm until midnight, teenagers take to the streets. Most of them congregate in parks and squares and engage in what is known as the *botellón* (*see p246* **Inside Track**).

At around 11pm a more mature crowd starts to spill out of the restaurants and hits the bars.

INSIDE TRACK
SURVIVAL TIPS

Having changed your body clock around to suit your schedule in Madrid, there are just a few more things you need to bear in mind before you go out seeking *la marcha*, or a good time. Firstly, don't get too dolled up; with some exceptions, Madrid is not a town where people dress to impress. Creativity is more important than couture. Secondly, be careful with the drinks; measures poured here are such that you may, for once, actually ask the bartender to put a little less in. And lastly, be aware that there is a specific window of time for every venue in Madrid, so if you turn up to a club or bar and it's empty, it doesn't necessarily mean it isn't popular – you might just have arrived at the wrong hour.

Generally, bars break down into several distinct categories. *Bares de copas* sell spirit-based drinks with or without a DJ in the corner. Then come the *discobares,* which may require a cover charge and bang out international and Spanish pop, perfect for their alcohol-fuelled clientele. Then there are the funkier pre-club bars, often with a house DJ warming you up for a night on the town. Thanks to recent legislation, bars must close at around 3am: precisely the moment when the clubs or *discotecas* fill. (*Discoteca* carries no cheesy connotations in Spanish; in fact be careful what you ask for when talking to locals – *club* in Spanish usually means brothel.)

Time was when the party kept on going through the morning and into the afternoon, as numerous dodgy after-hours would fling open their doors at a truly ungodly hour to welcome in revellers for whom sleep was not an option. But the police crackdown has put paid to that, and now there are only a few places to go should you want to dance from dawn.

LOS AUSTRIAS & LA LATINA

Danzoo @ Maxime
Maxime, Ronda de Toledo 1 (902 49 99 94). Metro Puerta de Toledo. **Open** midnight-6am Sat. **Admission** (incl 1 drink) €13; free before 2am. **No credit cards. Map** p327 F15.
Progressive and tech-house with an edge. This is not one for the handbag housers out there, rather this is a hard session; like Spinal Tap's amplifiers, the

Marula.

volume here goes up to 11. The crowd is grungy and tends to be predominantly male. On a Friday, Danzoo is at Macumba (*see p255*).

Kathmandú

C/Señores de Luzón 3 (no phone, http://kathmanduclub.com). Metro Ópera or Sol. **Open** midnight-6am Thur-Sat. **Admission** (incl 1 drink) €10 Fri, Sat; free Thur. **No credit cards**. **Map** p327 F12.
This basement club is cosy, friendly and nicely chilled. The DJs spin a delicious mix of funk, soul, jazz and hip hop, luring the friendly clientele on to

the dancefloor by about 3am. Non-dancers take to ample seating in the cave-like venue and nod along.

Marula

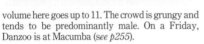

C/Caños Viejos 3 (91 366 15 96, www.marula cafe.com). Metro La Latina. **Open** 11pm-6am daily. **Admission** varies. **No credit cards**. **Map** p327 E13.
This small venue serves as bar, club and live music venue. Tuesday nights are concert nights, and there are late-night jams midweek, but the place really hots up at weekends, attracting DJ sessions from local talent such as Señorlobo, Chema Ama and Javi Kalero. The summertime terrace is a big pull, filling up by midnight and staying that way.

FREE El Nuevo Barbú

C/Santiago 3 (91 542 56 98, www.elbarbu club.com). Metro Ópera or Sol. **Open** 10.30pm-3.30am Mon-Thur; 10.30pm-4am Fri, Sat. **Admission** free. **Credit** DC, MC, V. **Map** p327 F12.
A sumptuous red velvet curtain separates the chilled front bar from two spacious candlelit chambers at the back where a swirling wash of intensely coloured psychedelic projections bathe the walls and ceilings. The DJ keeps the easygoing, urbane crowd happy with a slick mixture of funk, salsa and African beats. This is more the kind of a place to give you a warm glow than to really light your fire.

Shôko Restaurant & Lounge Club

C/Toledo 86 (91 366 87 41, www.shoko madrid.com). Metro Puerta de Toledo. **Open** midnight-6am Thur-Sat. **Admission** varies. **Credit** DC, V. **Map** p327 F14.

INSIDE TRACK
EL BOTELLÓN

Despite an attempted crackdown by local authorities and the police, the *botellón* – basically a pre-club piss-up of teenagers and young people in public spaces – is still a phenomenon in Madrid. Thousands of litres of red wine are mixed with Coke, to make a sticky mix known as *calimocho*, the drink that launched a million teen-hangovers. Officially, the *botellón* is now illegal in the city; the focal point of a stand-off between the police and wannabe revellers is Malasaña's Plaza Dos de Mayo, one of the most popular sites for *botellón*. However, 15 squad cars can't be there every night, nor can they cover the hundreds of other squares in Madrid, ensuring that it still goes on every weekend.

This popular 1,600-metre space houses an Oriental restaurant (at the top) and slick lounge-club with high ceilings and minimalist decor made up of bamboo, water pools, Japanese panels and contemporary furniture. DJs spin 1990s disco, deep house and electronica. There's sometimes a dress code of shirts (for men) and no trainers. Events are often held here.

SOL & GRAN VIA

For the much-loved cocktail/DJ bar **Museo Chicote**, *see p171.*

Adraba

C/Alcalá 20 (902 49 99 94). Metro Sevilla.
Open 12.30am-6am Wed-Sun. **Admission** varies. **Credit** AmEx, MC, V. **Map** p328 I11.
Adraba opened in spring 2010, on the site of the former Alcalá 20 club – the place where 81 people tragically died in a fire in 1983. Huge sums of money have been spent to ensure that the club is now one of the safest – and most aesthetically impressive – in Europe. Inside the modern space, DJs spin commercial house and a sophisticated clientele knocks back expensive cocktails.

Bash

Plaza Callao 4 (91 541 35 00, www.trip family.com). Metro Callao. **Open** midnight-6am Wed. **Admission** (incl 1 drink) €10-€12. **No credit cards. Map** p323 G11.
Wednesday is firmly established as hip hop night in Madrid, and judging by the turnout these clubs get, Thursdays must see a massive drop in Madrid's productivity thanks to what must surely be some cracking hangovers. Bash doesn't really get going until after 1am, but once it does there's no room to move. The residents specialise in the latest R&B and hip hop and the guest DJs have featured Funk Master Flex among others.

Joy Eslava

C/Arenal 11 (91 366 54 39/reservations 91 366 37 33, www.joy-eslava.com). Metro Ópera or Sol. **Open** Club nights midnight-5.30am Mon, Tue, Sat. **Admission** €12 Mon-Thur, Sun; €15 Fri, Sat (incl 1 drink). **Credit** AmEx, DC, MC, V. **Map** p327 G11.
Unusual in that it retains some original trappings of its former incarnation as a 19th-century theatre, in every other respect this is an ordinary high-street club. The vast crammed dancefloor runs the gamut from teenage tribes through housewives, enjoying staple disco house. Also a concert venue and cinema.

Ocho y Medio

C/Mesonero Romanos 13 (91 541 35 00, www.tripfamily.com). Metro Callao or Gran Vía. **Open** 1-6am Fri. **Admission** €10-€12 (incl 1 drink). **No credit cards. Map** p323 H11.

Independents' Day

What's the perfect remedy for a city plagued by a tired and flabby dance-music scene and the closure of several of its best medium-sized concert venues? An indie revival, that's what. And it's not just floppy haircuts and baggy-ness that have exploded all over Madrid; goth has made a major comeback too, with black PVC trenchcoats and safety pins replacing cool clubwear.

If you're pining for the UK, try stepping into the teleportation device that is **Supersonic** (C/Campoamor 3, www.myspace.com/supersonicmadrid), an always-rammed indie bar in Alonso Martínez, where Cool Britannia still rules. The bar moved from its previous address on C/Meléndez Valdes in September 2010, but its DJs still bang out the same cocktail of indie, Beatles tracks and punk. This is the after-show venue par excellence when any of the big international bands plays Madrid, often attracting the band members themselves.

For choice of name alone, a visit to **Dark Hole** (C/Mesonero Romanos 13, Sol & Gran Vía, 91 758 04 50, www. tripfamily.com) must be on your gothic agenda when in Madrid. Slap that eyeliner on, make sure your piercings are in place, and leave the handbag behind in favour of one of those coffin backpacks – this is the really dark deal. But if you've satanic leanings, there's **666** (C/Aduana 21, Sol & Gran Vía, no phone, www.gothic666.net), where free entry and slightly cheaper drinks than the big clubs will have you playing devil's advocate.

Kitsch reigns supreme at legendry indie-pop bar **Tupperware** (*see p258*), where there are more plastic figures, neon lights and gaudy posters on display than in a 12-year-old's bedroom. One of the staple bars on the Malasaña route, this place is always packed and always banging out top rock and indie tracks. *Star Wars* memorabilia is merely the icing on the cake.

Tucked away in a backstreet parallel to Gran Vía, **Home Bar** (C/Fomento 30, no phone, Los Austrias) is a shrine to Basildon's finest export. Depeche Mode are worshipped in this indie haven, which pulls in the Britophile punters thanks to the singular musical selection and the distinctly Depeche decor.

Although somewhat anachronistic, Ocho y Medio is the perfect stop on your hedonistic tour of the town if you're looking for an alcohol-fuelled mass of party energy. DJ Smart makes it all sound very '80s and '90s, thrashing out an eclectic mix of indie, electro-clash, electro-pop, new wave and New York rock. It takes a master to meld Blur and Depeche Mode.

Ohm
Bash, Plaza Callao 4 (91 541 35 00, www. tripfamily. com). Metro Callao. **Open** midnight-6am Fri, Sat. **Admission** (incl 1 drink) €10. **No credit cards. Map** p323 G11.
While some nights come and go with alarming frequency, Trip Family's Ohm is one that's here for the duration. Strictly speaking it's a gay night, but it's too much fun (and too central) for the straight crowd to stay away. The result is a friendly party atmosphere with soulful, vocal-driven house tracks mixed to perfection by residents Kike Boy and Tetsu.

Palacio de Gaviria
C/Arenal 9 (91 526 60 69, www.palaciogaviria. com). Metro Ópera or Sol. **Open** 11pm-3am Mon-Wed; 11pm-6am Thur-Sat; 11.30pm-3.30am Sun. **Admission** (incl 1 drink) €10 Mon-Thur, Sun; €15 Fri, Sat. **Credit** AmEx, DC, MC, V. **Map** p327 G11.
Prepare to go large in a stately 19th-century palace. Ascend the splendid sweeping staircase, and enter a multitude of rooms with three dancefloors playing pumping dance tunes, Spanish pop and 1980s favourites. Portraits hang on the walls and frescoes adorn the ceilings… imagine the Ministry of Sound in Kensington Palace and you're halfway there. Thursdays see the International Party attracting foreign students, expats and a smattering of tourists. There are tango and salsa classes too (Mon-Fri, 8pm).

★ Sala de Nombre Público
Plaza de los Mostenses 11 (no phone, www. intromusica.com). Metro Plaza de España. **Open** 12.30am-6am Fri, Sat. **Admission** (incl 1 drink) €13. **No credit cards. Map** p323 F9.
A nice and grimy basement club, of which the main room is Low Club – capitalising on the recent mainstream interest in the experimental side of electronica. The DJs – resident and otherwise – spin a varied mix, taking in everything from electro to indie, and making the venue one of the most forward-thinking in the city when it comes to dance music. The large venue doesn't fill up until 3am, though, so don't rush. The building also houses the Pop Room club.

Sala Wind
Plaza del Carmen s/n (no phone, www.sala wind.com). Metro Gran Vía or Sol. **Open** midnight-6am, Thur-Sat. **Admission** (incl 1 drink) €10-€14. **Map** p327 H11.
After the closure of several of the city's finer nighteries, Madrid needed a new club. The answer, my

friend, was blowing in the Wind: this old venue got a serious makeover and flung open its doors four nights a week. Wednesdays see drum and bass or hip hop, Thursdays are turned over to tech and electro house, Fridays are gay night Spank, while Saturdays are Elástico, mixing up rock, electro, indie and everything in between.

★ El Sol
C/Jardines 3 (91 532 64 90, www.elsolmad.com). Metro Gran Vía or Sol. **Open** 11pm-5.30am Tue-Sat. **Admission** (incl 1 drink) €9. **Credit** (bar only) MC, V. **Map** p327 H11.
To call this music joint and club 'no-frills' is an understatement – as its faded yellow walls and middle-aged bar staff attest. However, as anyone knows, it's the music and crowd that make a night, and that's where El Sol is a winner. The DJ serves up an eclectic selection of unmixed rock, soul, funk and R&B. Before long you're lured on to the floor and there you will stay, getting down alongside a varied crowd of twenty- and thirtysomethings. The venue is the city's classic climax to a big night out.

FREE Terraza Atenas
C/Segovia & C/Cuesta de la Vega (91 765 12 06, mobile 650 50 67 93). Metro Ópera or Puerta del Ángel. **Open** noon-3am daily. Closed Nov-Mar. **Admission** free. **No credit cards. Map** p326 D12.
A super-cool *terraza* set in its own small park. The plentiful tables in the front bar are filled by midnight and the overflow swells on to the surrounding gentle slope of grass. With no complaining neighbours to worry about, the crowd can enjoy the easy sounds of Latin house mixed by the DJ long after other *terrazas* have called it a night.

Weekend
Bash, Plaza Callao 4 (91 541 3500, www. tripfamily.com). Metro Callao. **Open** midnight-5am Sun. **Admission** (incl 1 drink) €10-€12. **No credit cards. Map** p323 G11.
Weekend is one of the longest standing and most successful Sunday club nights, with a funky feel. Resident DJ Roberto Rodríguez downshifts a gear from the harder revolutions of his other appearances and cruises with Latin and nu jazz, taking the mixed gay and straight crowd through to Monday morning.

HUERTAS & SANTA ANA

FREE La Alhambra/El Buscón
C/Victoria 5 & 9 (91 521 07 08/91 522 54 12). Metro Sol. **Open** 11pm-1am Mon-Wed, Sun; 11pm-2.30am Thur-Sat. **Admission** free. **No credit cards. Map** p327 H12.
Typically Spanish tapas bars by day, these two adjacent eateries assume a whole new identity come the weekend as DJs play a mix of everything from new flamenco and '80s pop to handbag house.

Shôko Restaurant & Lounge Club. *See p246.*

Joy Eslava. *See p247.*

Heavily Andaluz, the south of Spain leaps out from every ornately tiled alcove and arch. This place pulls in all sorts, from the international crowd to pony-tailed flamenco aficionados.

La Boca del Lobo

C/Echegaray 11 (91 429 70 13, www.labocadel lobo.com). Metro Sevilla. **Open** midnight-3.30am Tue, Thur-Sun. **Admission** (incl 1 drink) €5-€10, otherwise free. **Credit** V. **Map** p327 H12.
Unselfconsciously hip and unremittingly friendly, La Boca del Lobo combines live bands with a heady mix of house, breakbeats and R&B. Emerge from the sweaty downstairs dancefloor to the cramped bar area by the entrance or retire upstairs to find a seat (almost impossible after midnight at weekends) and watch the DJ spin a beguiling cocktail of music.

FREE El Burladero

C/Echegaray 19 (no phone, www.elburladero copas.com). Metro Sevilla or Sol. **Open** 8pm-4am daily. **Admission** free.
No credit cards. **Map** p327 H12.
A cosmopolitan crowd, buzzing to the sound of fla-menco and rumba, throngs the Moorish arches, amid Andalucian tiles and a rogues' gallery of bull-fighters. Upstairs the rumba rumbles but doesn't dominate. Head up here for respite and a chat with the languid barman, but the frenzied guitar and pistol-shot hand-clapping will eventually lure you back.

FREE La Comedia

C/Principe 16 (91 521 51 64). Metro Sevilla or Sol. **Open** 10pm-3.30am daily. **Admission** free. **No credit cards**. **Map** p327 H12.
There's nothing funny about Bar de la Comedia. Instead expect a welcome change of pace on this frenzied strip. An international crowd do their thing to a steady soundtrack of hip hop, two step and R&B dancefloor grinders. The door staff are somewhat capricious in their admissions policy.

★ FREE Las Cuevas de Sésamo

C/Príncipe 7 (91 429 65 24). Metro Sevilla or Sol. **Open** 7pm-2am Mon-Thur, Sun; 7pm-3am Fri, Sat. **Admission** free. **No credit cards.** **Map** p327 H12.

It's easy to find this basement cavern at weekends – you just have to look for the queue that snakes out of the door. But it's well worth the wait for what's inside: las Cuevas is a sit-down affair, with live piano music from 9pm (except Monday), where punters take advantage of the cheapish drinks (the place is famous for its sangria) and friendly atmosphere. A good choice to start the night rather than a final destination, Las Cuevas is also a popular student venue.

FREE La Fontana de Oro

C/Victoria 1 (91 531 04 20, www.fontana deoro.com). Metro Sol. **Open** noon-6am daily. **Admission** free. **Credit** DC, MC, V. **Map** p327 H12.

As Madrid's oldest bar, this place used to be a real institution. These days, though, it's an Irish theme bar. It's run-of-the-mill by day, but everything changes when night falls. Then the crowd packs in, fuelling up for the night ahead and losing themselves to a mix of classic beer anthems and a variety of live music.

★ Mondo

C/Arlabán 7 (91 523 86 54/91 522 88 26, www.web-mondo.com). Metro Sevilla. **Open** 1am-6am Thur; 12.30am-7am Sat. **Admission** (incl 1 drink) €13 (€11 before 2.30am) Thur; €14 (€12 before 2.30am) Fri, Sat. **Credit** AmEx, DC, MC, V. **Map** p328 I11.

If you only go to one club in Madrid, make sure it's this one. Launched in 2000, Mondo has become one of the most lauded spots in the city for enjoying electronica and techno, but you can also expect to hear funk, house and disco on any given night. A regular stable of high-profile guest DJs play here, with previous guests including Carl Craig, Layo & Bushwacka and Alex Guerra.

Teatro Kapital

C/Atocha 125 (91 420 29 06, www.grupo-kapital.com). Metro Atocha. **Open** 11.30pm-6am Thur-Sun. **Admission** €12-€16. **Credit** AmEx, DC, MC, V. **Map** p328 J14.

The Godzilla of Madrid clubs, with splendid views of the main dancefloor from many of the upper balconies: dance voyeur heaven. Of seven storeys, each has something different to offer: the main dancefloor and bars are at ground level; the first floor has karaoke; the second R&B and hip hop; the third cosy cocktail bars; the fourth is Spanish disco; the fifth has a cinema and more cool sounds, and at the top is a terrace with a retractable roof. No trainers.

Torero

C/Cruz 26 (91 523 11 29). Metro Sol. **Open** 11pm-5am Tue, Wed; 11pm-6am Thur-Sat.

Admission free Tue, Wed; €12 (incl 1 drink) Thur-Sat. **No credit cards.** **Map** p327 H12.

Don't be put off by the forbidding exterior, the only thing not dancing inside Torero is a wall-mounted bull's head that stares down impassively at the mostly local crowd. The ground floor gyrates to a mixture of Spanish and Latin beats, while on the floor below house reverberates off the red-brick walls. No trainers.

RASTRO & LAVAPIES

If you're interested in some impromptu late-night flamenco, try **Candela** (*see p244*).

★ El Juglar

C/Lavapiés 37 (91 528 43 81, www.salajuglar. com). Metro Lavapiés. **Open** 9.30pm-3am Mon-Wed, Sun; 9.30pm-3.30am Thur-Sat. Concerts usually start at 10pm. **Admission** €5-€7. **No credit cards.** **Map** p327 H14.

Epitomising Lavapiés – a bohemian, cool and laid-back hangout for those who like the tempo of their evening to be energetic but not too frenetic. The bare red brick and chrome front bar provide a chilled background for the broad-based crowd and soundtrack of jazz and soul. After midnight the rhythm speeds up in the back as the resident DJ Señores de Funk spins a mix of souped-up soul, Latin and funk. Sunday nights see flamenco performed by students from the nearby Amor de Dios school. DJs start spinning at midnight.

FREE Kappa

C/Olmo 26 (no phone). Metro Antón Martín. **Open** 8.30pm-3am daily. Closed 10 days mid Aug. **Admission** free. **No credit cards.** **Map** p328 H13.

An unprepossessing and easily missed little hide-away, Kappa is amiable and intimate and, despite its complete lack of decor, somehow cosy. This chameleon of *locales* has built up quite a cult

---

INSIDE TRACK
PRICE TO PARTY

The ticket you are given on the door of a club is almost always valid for a drink, so don't just toss it away. Spain has recently seen a hike in prices across the board, and clubs have not escaped. Some of the swankier clubs will charge you as much as €12 for a long drink, and €10 for a beer. Remember though, the measures for long drinks are huge, so if you're looking to penny pinch, stick to the rum and coke. Before you head out, you might consider checking club websites for printable flyers that will get you in for a discounted fee.

ARTS & ENTERTAINMENT

following among those who feel life should have an unhurried pace, and is one of the better spots for indie music. This is an ideal pre-club launch pad or a haven where you can kick back and chill out when Madrid threatens to overwhelm.

FREE La Ventura
C/Olmo 31 (no phone). Metro Antón Martín. **Open** 10.30pm-2.30am Tue-Thur; 11pm-3am Fri, Sat; 8pm-2.30am Sun. **Admission** free. **No credit cards. Map** p328 H13.

You might not know the place's name, but if you've been in Madrid a while, you're sure to have been here at least once. Lounge on full-length floor cushions while soaking up the measured sounds of trip hop and dub. Later the pace hots up a little with breakbeat, electronica and house thrown in, and the dancefloor is filled by a cosmopolitan crowd of students, ex-students and the casually hip.

CHUECA

For gay clubs in Chueca (and elsewhere), *see pp226-229.*

FREE Areia
C/Hortaleza 92 (91 310 03 07, www.areiachillout. com). Metro Chueca. **Open** 1pm-3am daily. **Admission** free. **Credit** AmEx, DC, MC, V. **Map** p324 I9.

Once an Irish bar, Areia has been transformed beyond recognition into a chill-out space that has all the angles covered: by day it's somewhere to get lunch or a snack, in the afternoon it becomes a place to chill, and by the evening the vibe has hotted up enough for a cool crowd that passes through on their nightly tour of the city. The seductive

Eastern decor, along with sofas and cushions on which to lounge, can make it difficult to leave.

Pachá
C/Barceló 11 (91 447 01 28, www.pacha-madrid.com). Metro Tribunal. **Open** 11pm-6am Wed-Sat. **Admission** (incl 1 drink) €12-€17. **Credit** AmEx, DC, MC, V. **Map** p324 H8.

In a club scene that ditches the glitz, Pachá is the black sheep. The bouncers may claim it's for royal relatives and the jet set, but it mainly attracts rich kids and posers. Dress up to get in, and expect glamorous gogos, on-stage dance routines and themed parties, enacted to a soundtrack of soulful house. Wednesdays are hip hop nights, with appearances from the likes of local star Jotamayuscula. Not on a par with its Ibiza namesake, but fun for those who like a bit of glam.

Stromboli
C/Hortaleza 96 (91 319 46 28). Metro Alonso Martínez. **Open** 6.30pm-3.30am daily. **Credit** MC, V. **Map** p324 I9.

A very cool little lounge that's perfect for a mid-week drink or as a stop on your weekend tour of the town. Very much part of the hip scene around C/Hortaleza and C/Fuencarral, and a place where the club DJs of Madrid drop their big-room style and spin something a little more intimate.

MALASAÑA & CONDE DUQUE

★ FREE Démodé
C/Ballesta 7 (mobile 678 50 52 37). Metro Chueca. **Open** 11pm-3.30am Thur-Sat. **Admission** free. **No credit cards. Map** p323 H10.

The flyers let you know what you're in for – an elegant figure reclines against a backdrop of flock

Tupperware.

wallpaper in a juxtaposition of the übertrendy and the super-cheesy. This pre-club joint is housed in an old brothel. Faux oil paintings still adorn the walls, but red lighting, sofas and an ample sound system have transformed it into one of the coolest nightspots of the moment. DJs spin both underground house and electro for a mixed gay/straight crowd.

Morocco
C/Marqués de Leganés 7 (91 531 51 67, www.moroccoclub.es). Metro Santo Domingo. **Open** midnight-3am Thur; midnight-6am Fri, Sat. **Admission** (incl 2 drinks) €10. **No credit cards. Map** p323 F10.
Once owned by Movida legend Alaska, Morocco has two feet firmly planted in the past. From its '80s decor and crowd, everything here smacks of days gone by. The DJ mixes mainly classic Spanish pop with today's nu flamenco. Despite all this throwback action, it's still great fun, completely free of pretension and brimming with dancefloor energy.

Nasti
C/San Vicente Ferrer 33 (91 521 76 05, http://nasti.es). Metro Tribunal. **Open** midnight-6am Fri, Sat. **Admission** (incl 1 drink) €10. **No credit cards. Map** p323 G9.
The remit here is simple – pack out a small and smoky *sala* with a fiercely loyal crowd, and play anything from the Sex Pistols to Joy Division to make them dance. A riotous, grungy and alternative crowd find their home here, enjoying the live acts such as Fanny Pack or Humbert Humbert and the guest DJs such as 2 Many DJs.

FREE Oui
C/Marqués de Santa Ana 11 (no phone). Metro Noviciado. **Open** 11pm-3am Thur; 11pm-3.30am Fri, Sat. Closed mid Aug. **Admission** free. **No credit cards. Map** p323 G9.
A truly unique bar, Oui is damn difficult to find but worth the search. Its bizarre shape and eclectic music policy – expect anything from early techno to present-day electronica, together with a knowledgeable and loyal clientele, make this a gem among the sometimes mediocre bars of Malasaña.

★ El Perro de la Parte Atrás del Coche
C/Puebla 15 (no phone, www.myspace.com/elperroclub). Metro Gran Vía. **Open** 9.30pm-3.30am daily. **Admission** (min consumption) €6. **No credit cards. Map** p323 H10.
As the unusual name (it means the 'nodding dog') suggests, everything about El Perro is different. The music policy is a mix-up of everything, with hip hop, house, soul and funk played by the resident DJs. The live acts take in heavy metal, so you might hear Aretha Franklin songs one night and a Metallica tribute band the next. The crowd comes from all walks of life. A mix that shouldn't work, but really does.

FREE Radar
C/Amaniel 22 (no phone). Metro Noviciado or Plaza de España. **Open** 9.30pm-3.30am Wed-Sun. **Admission** free. **No credit cards. Map** p323 F9.
For those who get off on experimental electronic music, this is a must-visit venue. Small and dark, the decor – along the lines of minimalist 1980s computer-game chic – forms the perfect backdrop. When the DJs hit the decks at weekends the electronica, noise and techno enthusiasts flock, and like all good venues Radar manages to draw you completely into its world.

Siroco
C/San Dimas 3 (91 593 30 70, www.siroco.es). Metro Noviciado. **Open** 9.30pm-5am Thur; 9.30pm-6am Fri, Sat. Closed 3 wks Aug. **Admission** (incl 1 drink) €8-€10. **No credit cards. Map** p323 F8.
A wonderfully creative crew run Siroco, something that is abundantly clear from their flyers, their programme and the visuals of the club itself. Doubling as a live music venue, it starts to hot up after the concerts finish at around 2am, when a crowd composed mainly of wannabe b-boys, club kids and beardy young students get down to the soul, funk and rare groove seven-inchers deftly woven together by the resident DJs.

Tempo
C/Duque de Osuna 8 (91 547 75 18, www.tempoclub.net). Metro Plaza España. **Open** *Café* 5pm-3am daily. *Nightclub* 10pm-6am Thur-Sat. Closed Aug. **Admission** *Café* free. *Nightclub* €3 or free. **Credit** MC, V. **Map** p323 E9.
A very cool little venue that doubles as a café by day and a venue at night for live acts and DJs. In the pleasant upstairs café you can sit and have a bite, but as the night wears on, head downstairs, either to the dimly lit chill-out room or the dancefloor bathed with psychedelic projections. The in-house DJ is often accompanied by live percussion.

★ FREE Tupperware
C/Corredera Alta de San Pablo 26 (no phone). Metro Tribunal. **Open** 9pm-3.30am daily. **Admission** free. **No credit cards. Map** p323 H9.
Truly postmodern, this popular bar is outrageously kitsch but with a pop art sensibility that saves it from crossing over too far into tackiness. The fake fur, *Star Wars* pictures, 1970s toys and faux-cool psychedelia hang together surprisingly well, and there's a pleasant anything-goes music policy that brings all kinds of sounds from acid jazz to house to soul. The sociable crowd, slightly older and with less to prove, tend to chill out in the easygoing vibe. Something of a neighbourhood nightlife institution.

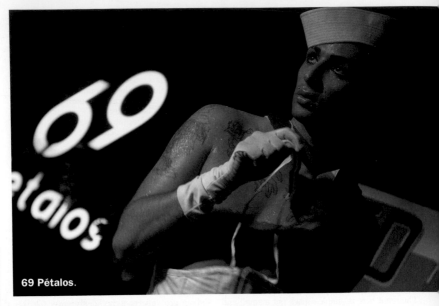

69 Pétalos.

ARTS & ENTERTAINMENT

SALAMANCA & THE RETIRO

Almonte
C/Juan Bravo 35, Salamanca (91 563 54 70, www.almontesalarociera.com). Metro Diego de León. **Open** 9pm-5am daily. **Admission** minimum consumption 1 drink. **Credit** AmEx, MC, V. **Map** p325 N6.
This 'flamenco disco' attracts a youthful crowd. The beautiful patrons flaunt it freestyle before *sevillanas* prompt a free-for-all. The evening is for dancing, the night is to be seen dancing. Try to work your way downstairs, where the most attention-grabbing dancing can be admired and – go on – attempted.

Ananda
Estación de Atocha, Avda Ciudad de Barcelona s/n (91 524 11 44, www.ananda.es). Metro Atocha. **Open** midnight-7am Fri, Sat. **Admission** (incl 1 drink) €12. **Credit** AmEx, DC, V. **Map** p328 K15.
This is the mother of all club terraces: the enormous 2,000-square-metre complex comes complete with two dancefloors (one indoors and one out), ten bars and plenty of cushion-strewn sofas and chairs, all of them done up in a bit of an Eastern theme. The regular clientele generally ranges from your usual fresh-faced clubby kids (especially on Sundays for the Sundance parties, where sounds are vocal and tech house) to older guys in suits out sharking for ladies. It isn't cheap, but from June to August you'd pay almost anything to stay cool in the city. As this guide went to press, the club was closed for a refurbishment, expected to open again in 2011.

NORTH & WEST

Argüelles

DU:OM
Sala Heineken, C/Princesa 1 (91 547 57 11, www. salarena.com). Metro Plaza de España. **Open** midnight-6am Fri, Sat. **Admission** varies. **Map** p323 E9.
A dual-personality club night, held at a well-known concert venue (*see p241*), with diametrically opposed sounds on each floor. Downstairs Iván Pica and Hugo Serra mix a bang-up-to-date selection of electro house tracks with whooshing high-level sweeps and pounding 4/4 beats that keep the crowd dancing all night long. Upstairs it's an anything-goes policy with Spanish pop (or *pachanga*) thrown together with commercial hip hop, cheesy dance tracks and eurotrance.

Chamberí

Changó
C/Covarrubias 42 (91 446 00 36). Metro Alonso Martínez or Bilbao. **Open** midnight-6am Thur-Sat. **Admission** (incl 1 drink) €10-€15. **Map** p324 I7.
One of Madrid's clubs converted from old theatres, Changó plays host to two top nights. First up is Nature, a long-running Thursday night dedicated to breaks, electro and techno. Second is Chill, attracting a supposedly more sophisticated crowd with its deep house. Third is L'Inferno, which moved to Changó in 2010, and has become one of the city's most popular club nights for dance music lovers.

Moma 56

C/José Abascal 56 (91 399 09 00, www.
moma56.com). Metro Alonso Cano or Gregorio
Marañón. **Open** midnight-6am Thur-Sat.
Admission (incl 1 drink) €12. **No credit**
cards. Map p321 J5.
If it's a bit of glamour you're looking for and you
actually feel up to the challenge of getting through
the door, then you should probably check out Moma
56. Multifunctional in a New York style, the venue
is a restaurant, bar and nightclub, with stylish decor
and a semi-celebrity crowd.

Shabay

C/Miguel Ángel 3 (91 319 76 92, www.
shabay.com). Metro Rubén Darío. **Open**
11.30pm-5am Tue-Thur; 11.30pm-6am Fri,
Sat; 9pm-3am Sun. Closed 2wks mid Aug.
Admission (incl 1 drink) €15. **Credit** AmEx,
DC, MC, V. **Map** p324 K6.
Full of Eastern promise, Shabay has lots of intricate
decoration and a carefully crafted atmosphere, with
oriental and Afrobeat sounds. From Tuesday to
Saturday the place functions as a nightclub, but on
Sundays the pace drops a few notches for a chill-out
session complete with incense, candles and a selec-
tion of treats from Indian and Thai cuisine.

Chamartín

69 Pétalos

C/Alberto Alcocer 32 (no phone). Metro
Colombia or Cuzco. **Open** 11pm-5am Thur;

11pm-6am Fri, Sat. **Admission** (incl
1 drink) €16. **No credit cards.**
Open in its current form since 2007, 69 Pétalos, not
far from the Bernabéu stadium, is a popular spot for
twentysomethings, who come for the mix of pop,
funk, latin jazz, house and indie nights (featuring
Depeche Mode et al). Pop-art style decor, stage performers and an interesting mix of people creates a
buzzing vibe from around 2am.

Macumba

Estación de Chamartín (91 733 35 05, 902
49 99 94, www.comunidadspaceofsound.com).
Metro Chamartín. **Open** midnight-6am Fri, Sat;
9am-8.30pm Sun. **Admission** (incl 1 drink) €12.
No credit cards.
Friday night here is Danzoo (*see p245*); Saturdays
see Sunflowers for an Ibizan vibe and lots of go-
go dancers; but Macumba's real crowd-puller is
Space of Sound on Sunday nights. It's the city's
biggest all-day party, and what a monster it is. The
crowd is weirdly territorial, with one area that's
mainly gay, another that's predominantly straight
and even a group of transsexuals claiming an area
by one of the bars. The sound system here is
unmatched and, along with the resident DJs – specialists in both tech and progressive house – the
promoters bring in the likes of Deep Dish and
Steve Lawler.

SOUTH OF CENTRE

Fabrik

Avda de la Industria 82, Ctra Fuenlabrada-
Moralejos de Enmedio (902 93 03 22,
www.grupo-kapital.com//fabrik). Metro
Fuenlabrada then bus 496, 497. **Open** 11pm-
6am Sat; 10am-midnight occasional Sun.
Admission (incl 1 drink) €18-€30. **Credit**
AmEx, DC, MC, V.
Fabrik is a converted warehouse kitted out with a
dazzling array of disco surprises: a 60kw sound system; a huge outdoor terrace complete with a fake
river and two covered dancefloors; and, in the main
arena, a vertical and horizontal megatron to shoot
freezing nitrogen into the crowd. The monthly
Sunday session Goa is the highlight (see www.trip-
family.com for info). It's a bit of a schlepp to get here,
but well worth the taxi fare.

INSIDE TRACK
SWEET ENDINGS

The *madrileño* chocolate and *churros*
tradition comes into its own in the
madrugada (pre-dawn hours). Old-school
fave **Chocolatería San Ginés** (*see p170*)
is open until 7am daily, and is a hive of
activity once the bars and clubs shut.

Sport & Fitness

A wave of new sports facilities has been matched with increasing enthusiasm to get active in the city.

It's been a good few years for Spanish football, with Spain winning its first UEFA World Cup in 2010, on top of the European Championship in 2008. The World Cup squad, although dominated by Barca players, included several Real Madrid stars, and the win was marked by night-long celebrations in this football-mad city. But the city's sporting scene is about more than just the beautiful game; Madrid is home to two of Spain's top basketball clubs, hosts one of Europe's most prestigious marathons, and is the setting for the finish of the Vuelta a España cycling race. What's more, the city is now on the Tennis Masters circuit, held in the purpose-built, avant-garde Caja Mágica.

Although Madrid was unsuccessful in both its 2012 and 2016 Olympic bids, these have led to the construction of new sports facilities in the city. Despite the summertime heat, *madrileños* are an active bunch. Head to the Parque del Canal de Isabel II to witness locals jogging, or playing football, golf or padel tennis – as with everything else in life, *madrileños* like to make keeping fit a sociable affair.

SPECTATOR SPORTS

Athletics/atletismo

Estadio de la Comunidad de Madrid
Avda de Arcentales s/n, Eastern suburbs.
Metro Las Musas.
This stadium, also known as Estadio La Peineta, was the centrepiece of Madrid's 2012 and 2016 Olympic bids, for which it would have been renovated had they been successful. The city council now hopes to persuade Atlético de Madrid to move here in some kind of part-exchange deal for the *rojiblancos*' current ground, the Vicente Calderón, which occupies a plot on the banks of the Manzanares river that the council wants to redevelop. In the interim, the council has talked of reopening the stadium for athletics and other events; but so far, little seems to be happening.

Maratón Popular de Madrid
Information MAPOMA C/Galileo 74, Chamberí (91 447 96 41, www.maratonmadrid.org). **Open** 10am-2pm, 4.30-7.30pm Mon-Fri. **Map** p323 F6.
Madrid's marathon, always held on a Sunday in late April, has grown year after year both in number of participants and prestige, and is now considered to be among the world's top ten. The halfway mark is

in the dead centre of the city; thousands of cheery folk collect in Puerta del Sol to egg on the tiring runners; an estimated million spectators annually take to the city streets to catch the race. A week or two earlier there is a half marathon, a 20km race, organised by Agrupación Deportiva Marathon (91 402 69 62, www.admarathon.es).

Palacio de Deportes de la Comunidad de Madrid
Avda Felipe II s/n, Salamanca (91 444 99 49, www.palaciodedeportes.com). Metro Goya. **Map** p325 O9.
This state-of-the-art 16,000-capacity sports palace was inaugurated in early 2005 and occupies the site where its predecessor stood until it was destroyed by fire four years previously. It is a multi-purpose venue which can host a wide range of indoor sports thanks to a modern system of retractable stands. As well as sports, you can catch spectacles such as *Disney on Ice* or any number of rock concerts: Springsteen, Depeche Mode and Coldplay have all performed here.

Basketball/baloncesto

Basketball is Spain's second most popular sport, and Madrid has two of the country's top teams:

Estudiantes is the city's best-supported club, while **Real Madrid**, affiliated to the football club of the same name, is traditionally the more successful. Both teams regularly qualify for the all-important league play-offs that run in May to eventually decide the annual champions.

CB Estudiantes

Madrid Arena, Avda de Portugal s/n, Casa de Campo (91 722 04 00, www.madridarena.org). Metro Alto de Extremadura or Lago. **Map** p326 A11/12.

Since the beginning of the 2005-06 season, 'El Estu' has made the city council-owned Madrid Arena its home. The less successful of Madrid's clubs, Estudiantes nevertheless has passionate supporters. Among them, the most vociferous are a group known as 'La Demencia' who make for a great atmosphere when the team plays at home and even away. You can order tickets (€20-€60) at www.clubestudiantes.com and choose where to pick them up, or simply go in person to one of the sales points listed on the website under 'Entradas' and 'Venta anticipada en tiendas'. Alternatively, you can buy tickets in person by visiting the club's student team venue, the Polideportivo Antonio Magariños at C/Serrano 127 (90 240 00 02, 10am-2pm, 4-7pm Mon-Fri).

Real Madrid Baloncesto

Caja Mágica, C/Camino de Perales s/n, Parque Lineal de Manzanares, San Fermín (91 722 04 00, www.realmadrid.com). Metro San Fermín-Orcasur.

Real Madrid's hoop stars have a trophy record to match that of the football team, and, after a few years in the doldrums look set to return to the top. The team lost its former home when former club president Florentino Pérez sold the land to pay off the football team's huge debts, but since summer 2010 the team has had an official new home in the Caja Mágica (*see p256*). Expect exuberant professional cheerleaders.

Cycling/ciclismo

La Vuelta a España (www.lavuelta.com) is an enormous deal in the cycling world, with the best international cyclists competing with a ferocity and determination only surpassed by their efforts in the Tour de France. La Vuelta finishes in Madrid, where a knowledgeable crowd awaits the arrival of the time-triallers.

Football/fútbol

Madrid has three top-flight clubs, the world-famous **Real Madrid** (known as 'El Madrid'), the sometimes-successful **Atlético de Madrid** ('El Atleti') and the modest **Getafe CF** from the southern suburbs. While Real Madrid has historically been Spain's and Europe's most successful club, boasting a dazzling collection of silverware, the club has not won the Champions League since 2002 and was defeated at the first knock-out stage of the competition for the sixth successive year in 2010. This despite lavish spending on a new generation of 'Galácticos', including Cristiano Ronaldo and the Brazilian Kaká. Perennial Champions League qualification is nevertheless practically certain for El Madrid, but while El Atleti may not be considered among Europe's elite teams, they overshadowed Real Madrid in 2010 by winning the Europa League. Getafe has also had some glory in recent years, reaching the final of the Copa del Rey for the first time in their history in 2007, then repeating the feat the following year.

Parque del Canal de Isabel II. *See p261.*

ARTS & ENTERTAINMENT

ARTS & ENTERTAINMENT

Since promotion in 2004, they have also become a mainstay in La Primera Liga.

League matches are played on a Saturday or a Sunday evening, from September to May or June; at least one of the teams plays in Madrid every weekend. Cup and European matches are held during the week. Tickets can be very hard to come by, especially for Real Madrid games; if you can't get one at the ticket office, you might have to resort to buying a *'reventa'* ('resale') from one of the touts outside the ground. For shirts and various bits of fan-junk, *see p203* **Área Real Madrid**, or try the club shops. Atlético's shop, 1903 Megastore, is housed in the stadium.

Good coverage of Spanish football is to be found weekly in Sid Lowe's column at http://football.guardian.co.uk.

Atlético de Madrid

Estadio Vicente Calderón, Paseo Virgen del Puerto 67, South of centre (91 366 47 07, www.clubatleticodemadrid.com/shop 91 366 82 37). Metro Pirámides. **Open** *Ticket office* 10am-2pm, 5-8pm day before match; from 11am till kick-off on match days.* **Tickets** €20-€42. **Credit** MC, V.

Now back in the first division, 'El Atleti' won the UEFA Europa League in 2010, defeating Fulham in the final and overshadowing arch rivals Real Madrid. The star player of the squad is currently the Uruguayan Diego Forlan. The loyal *'rojiblanco'* faithful create a vibrant atmosphere in the 57,000-capacity Calderón stadium and, although the football itself can often leave more than a little to be desired, it is not uncommon for tickets to sell out entirely. When available, tickets can now be bought via the website, or by telephone: 902 53 05 00. In 2006, a museum was added near Gate 23 (91 365 09 31, 11am-7pm Tue-Sun, admission €4-€8).

Real Madrid

Estadio Santiago Bernabéu, Paseo de la Castellana 144, Chamartín (91 398 43 00, www.realmadrid.com). Metro Santiago Bernabéu. **Open** *(guided tours)* 10am-7.30pm Mon-Sat; 10.30am-6.30pm Sun, on match days tours close 5 hours before kick off. **Tickets** *Stadium tours* €15-€15. *Match tickets* €30-€115. **Credit** AmEx, DC, MC, V.

The club has won no titles other than the Spanish equivalent of the Charity Shield in recent seasons. It has suffered all manner of behind-the-scenes shenanigans, including recent presidential elections the results of which are currently being disputed in the law courts. And the era of the 'Galácticos' is surely fading. Yes, Real Madrid's present and future look decidedly iffy. Fans are looking to a new generation of players to bring back glory, something they expect from a club that has won more domestic and European honours than any other. Tickets can only be bought over

the phone on 902 32 43 24, but getting hold of one can be extremely difficult as 90% of tickets are taken up by the club's members. For more information on stadium tours, call 90 230 17 09.

Getafe CF

Avda Teresa de Calcuta s/n, Getafe (91 695 97 71, www.getafecf.com). Metro Los Espartales. **Open** 10am-1.30pm, 5pm-8.30pm Mon-Fri in weeks before home games, 11am-half time match days. **Tickets** €40-€80. **No credit cards**.

With the current name dating only from 1983, after the merger of two locally based regional league clubs, Getafe CF reached the top flight for the first time ever in 2004. Against all expectations the *'azulón'* team has not only stayed there but, under the management of Bernd Schuster, is looking ever-more like solid upper mid-table material, able to mix it with the best. Getting tickets for the 14,000-capacity stadium is not usually a problem as the fan base is relatively small, but may be problematic when one of the bigger teams is visiting.

Motor sports

Circuito del Jarama

Ctra de Burgos (A-I), km 27, San Sebastián de los Reyes (91 657 08 75, www.jarama.org). Bus 171 from Plaza de Castilla to Ciudad Santo Domingo.

The last time the Jarama track hosted a Formula One race was way back in 1981, but it still has a full calendar of motorbike and truck racing.

Tennis

Caja Mágica

C/Camino de Perales s/n. Parque Lineal de Manzanares, San Fermín (91 722 04 00, www.madridcajamagica.com). Metro San Fermín-Orcasur.

INSIDE TRACK BREEDS APART

Most Atlético de Madrid football supporters pride themselves on their loyalty and have built the expectation of defeat into their collective personality. Meanwhile, Real Madrid fans, bloated until recently on a diet of almost constant success, are quicker to turn against their team when things are going wrong. At the Santiago Bernabéu stadium, there's more likelihood of a spectacular home win, and you even get warmed by vast gas fires in winter. At the Vicente Calderón, the warmth is more natural, and whatever the result, you're in for a better atmosphere and a more emotional experience.

The newest venue for top-level tennis, La Caja Mágica ('Magic Box') opened to much fanfare in 2008, replacing the Madrid Arena as the host venue for the Madrid Masters, the most prestigious event in the Spanish tennis calendar. It's retractable roofs are its most-celebrated feature.

PARTICIPATORY SPORTS

Bowling/boleras

Bowling Chamartín
Área recreativa, Estación de Chamartín, C/Agustín de Foxá (91 315 71 19, www. bowlingchamartin.com). Metro Chamartín. **Open** 10am-12.30am daily. **Admission** (incl shoe hire) €4.80. **No credit cards.**
A colourful 20-lane alley with a neon-lit bar, now the oldest and most central in the city. It gets crowded on Saturdays, when there's lots of whooping.

Football/fútbol

FC Britanico de Madrid
Originally made up of British expats, this men's football team, founded in 1972, is now multinational, and plays against Spanish teams at weekends. They're always open to new players; if you're in Madrid for a while and want to get involved, then go along to the training sessions that start at 8.45pm on Wednesdays at Polideportivo Barrio del Pilar (Avenida de Monforte de Lemos 13, Northern Suburbs). For more information, call 91 234 33 87, email fcbritanicodemadrid@gmail.com or visit www.fcbritanico.com.

Golf

Golf clubs around Madrid tend to be quite exclusive, and expensive, affairs. A full list of all courses in the Madrid region is available on the website of the Federación de Golf de Madrid, www.fedgolfmadrid.com, click on 'Campos' on the home page and choose from the many options that appear.

Club de Campo Villa de Madrid
Ctra de Castilla, km 2 (91 550 08 40, www.clubvillademadrid.com). Bus 160 or 161 from Moncloa. **Open** *Sept-July* 9am-6pm Mon-Fri; 8.15am-6pm Sat. *July, Aug* 8.15am-9pm Mon-Sat. **Rates** *Mon-Fri* €17 club entry, plus €60.30 course fee. *Sat* €35 club entry, plus €113.40 course fee. **No credit cards.**
Co-designed by Seve Ballesteros, this is considered the best and most difficult golf course near Madrid. As well as golf, for members there are squash and tennis courts, clay pigeon and range shooting, plus hockey pitches, polo facilities, horse riding and a swimming pool. It can be very crowded at weekends, with priority given to members.

Horse riding/hípica

Indiana Parque Recreativo Natural
Apdo Correos 32, San Martín de Valdeiglesias (91 861 27 99, 663 871 143, www.indiana-sl.com). By bus 551 from Estación Príncipe Pío/by car A-5 then M501 (58.5km). **No credit cards.**
Trekking here involves crossing rivers and reservoirs, and going up mountains. Beginners can take classes in the riding school, or there's climbing, archery and canoeing. It's worth the schlep out of town.

Las Palomas
Club Hípico, Ctra de Colmenar Viejo km 28.9 (91 127 21 28, 91 803 31 76, mobile 670 972 150, http://personaltelefonica.terra.es/web/chlaspalomas). By bus 721, 724, 725, 726 from Plaza de Castilla. **Open** 5-8pm Mon-Fri; 10am-2pm, 5-7pm Sat, Sun. **No credit cards.**
Riding courses for all levels (from €160 for 10hrs). A course must be booked a day in advance.

Skiing

Before heading off to the ski resorts out of town, *madrileños* like to practise their turns at the vast Xanadú indoor skiing centre just outside Madrid. *See also p216.*

Squash

Gimnasio Argüelles
C/Andres Mellado 21-23, Moncloa (91 549 00 40). Metro Argüelles. **Open** *Sept-July* 8am-11pm Mon-Fri; 9am-3pm Sat, Sun. *Aug* 10am-10pm Mon-Fri. **Rates** *Squash* €16/hr. *Gym* €8. **No credit cards. Map** p323 E6/7.
A fully equipped gym open to non-members, with a squash court for dedicated rubber-bashers.

Swimming pools/piscinas

There are many open-air swimming pools in Madrid: see the 'Deportes' section of the website www.munimadrid.es or pick up a leaflet at any municipally run sports centre. The most accessible are listed below. There's also a popular rooftop pool at the **Hotel Emperador** (*see p115; photo p120*), which non-guests can use for a fee (€30 Mon-Fri, €42 Sat, Sun). For Madrid's waterparks, *see p216.*

Open-air municipal pools
Piscinas Casa de Campo, Avda del Ángel s/n, Casa de Campo (91 463 00 50). Metro Lago. **Open** 11am-9pm daily. Closed Oct-May. **Admission** €4.35. **No credit cards.**
Landlocked Madrid is stiflingly hot in the summer months, so at weekends half the city seems to turn

ARTS & ENTERTAINMENT

up at this beautiful leafy complex with three open-air pools set in green meadows (expect queues on midsummer weekends). Topless bathing is tolerated, and there's an informal gay area. Of the other municipal pools, the Francos Rodríguez has a beach volleyball court, and the Barrio del Pilar and La Elipa have nude sunbathing areas; the latter has water chutes. All have the same hours and prices. **Other pools**: **Barrio del Pilar** C/Monforte de Lemos 13-15, Northern suburbs (91 314 79 43); **Concepción** C/José del Hierro, Eastern suburbs (91 403 90 20); **Francos Rodríguez** C/Numancia 1, Tetuán (91 459 98 71); **Moratalaz** C/Valdebernardo s/n, Eastern suburbs (91 772 71 21).

Centro Deportivo Municipal del Canal de Isabel II

Avda Filipinas 54, Chamberí (91 533 17 91, www.cyii.es). Metro Canal or Ríos Rosas. **Open** *Swimming pool* late May-early Sept 11am-8pm daily. **Admission** *Swimming pool* €4.20-€4.40. **No credit cards.**

This long-established sports club has olympic-sized and children's swimming pools, tennis and basketball courts, and a bar and restaurant, all with good wheelchair access. The place can get very crowded at weekends. It also hosts a variety of competitive sports teams. Just over the road is the popular Parque del Canal de Isabel II outdoor sports complex (*see far right*).

Bath Time

Madrid now has two superb hammams to help ease the stress of city life.

As traffic, work hours and the cost of living grows and the siesta diminishes, Madrid is turning to spas and alternative therapies with increasing frequency.

The shining star of Madrid's current health and relaxation infatuation is the **Medina Mayrit hammam**. An instant hit with *madrileños* from the minute they opened, the baths are still so popular you sometimes need to call weeks in advance for a weekend booking. They are an oasis of calm, located just minutes from the bustling Puerta del Sol. A series of pools span out beneath arched ceilings, half lit by flickering lamps. One shallow pool of warm water abuts another of hot water, with a deeper pool of cold water nearby for a chilly plunge.

The company behind the hammam, El Grupo Al Andalus, prioritises historic authenticity. Masons from Andalucía were hired to lay the stone floors, which replicate the streets of Granada's Albaicín (Moorish quarter). The mosaic walls at the entrance are designed in the red, blue and green tiles found in the Alhambra. Upstairs, a café/restaurant, La Colina de Almanzora, specialises in historic Arabic food.

Enthusiasts claim that the hammam provides relief for almost any ailment, from the common cold to arthritis and hangovers. The heat improves circulation, eliminates toxins and keeps the skin clean and supple. After a visit most people feel energised and refreshed, though if it's some deep relaxation you're after, book a 15-minute massage (for an extra fee).

In spring 2010, no doubt inspired by the success of the Medina Mayrit, Madrid's second authentic hammam opened, in the

upmarket Salamanca neighbourhood. The **Hammam Alaya** (*pictured*) claims to be the city's only really authentic hammam, with its steam baths pumping out eucalyptus and mint infusions, said to open the pores to release toxins, and with the use of traditional 'black soap' to exfoliate the skin.

Hammam Ayala

C/Ayala 126, Salamanca (91 187 52 20, www.hammamayala.com). Metro Goya, Lista or Manuel Becerra. **Open** 10am-8pm Tue, Thur; 1-10pm Wed, Fri, Sat; 1-8pm Sun. **Admission** *Basic ritual* €50. *Traditional ritual* €60. **Credit** AmEx, DC, MC, V.

Medina Mayrit

C/Atocha 14 (902 33 33 34, www.medina mayrit.com). Metro Sol or Tirso de Molina. **Open** 10am-2am (last entry midnight) daily. **Admission** *Baths* €24-€26. *Baths & massage* (from 4pm & all day Sat, Sun) €28-€38; before 4pm Mon-Fri €25; €23 concessions. **Credit** AmEx, DC, MC, V. **Map** p327 G12.

Tennis

Tennis in Spain is accessible and reasonably priced, with numerous council-run clay and tarmac courts for hire. At municipal *polideportivos*, €5.60 gets you a court for an hour. The best city-run complex is the **Tenis Casa de Campo** in the Casa de Campo, close to the boating lake (91 464 96 17), which boasts 15 floodlit courts. The **Barrio del Pilar**, **Concepción** and **La Elipa** swimming pools (for all, *see far left*) also have tennis courts, as does the **Canal de Isabel II** (*see left*; book in advance).

The growing raquet sport known as padel tennis is very popular in Spain; courts can be found around the city, including at the **Parque del Canal de Isabel II** (*see below*).

FITNESS

Madrid has over 50 city-owned and run sports centres. For details, see www.munimadrid.es; click on 'English' and then 'Sports'. Otherwise pick up a leaflet at any of them for information about others. Some are more basic than others, though the entrance fees are the same.

Runners should make a beeline for the **Parque del Canal de Isabel II** (*see below*).

Gyms & sports centres/
gimnasios & polideportivos

Bodhidharma

C/Moratines 18-20, South of centre (91 517 28 16, www.bodhidharma-gym.com). Metro Acacias or Embajadores. **Open** *Sept-July* 8am-11pm Mon-Fri; 9am-2pm, 6-10pm Sat; 10am-3pm Sun. *Aug* 8am-11pm Mon-Fri; 9am-2pm Sat. **Rates** €51 per mth. **Credit** MC, V.
A well-equipped health club for men and women, with a sauna, free weights, machines and aerobics classes.

Centro Deportivo
Municipal La Chopera

Calle Alfonso XII s/n, Parque del Retiro (91 420 11 54). Metro Atocha or Retiro. **Open** 8.30am-9.30pm Mon-Fri; 9am-9pm Sat, Sun. Closed Aug. **Admission** varies. **Map** p329 L12/13.
Shaded by the trees of the Retiro, La Chopera is a fine place to play tennis and 5-a-side football (*fútbol sala*).

Paidesport Center

Parque de Ocio Barrio Art Decó, C/Sepúlveda 3-5, Virgen del Puerto, South of centre (91 470 00 00, www.paidesport.com). Metro Puerta del Ángel. **Open** *Sept-July* 9am-11pm Mon-Fri; 10am-8pm Sat; 10am-3pm Sun. *Aug* 9am-11pm Mon-Fri; 10am-3pm Sat, Sun. **Admission** *Squash* €15/1hr. *Swimming pool* varies. **No credit cards**.
A slick, privately run complex down near the river, open to non-members and generally rammed with

earnest hardbodies pumping iron. It has racket courts, an open-air pool, a gym and weights room and an indoor sports hall. There are several other branches in and around the city; see the website for details.

★ Parque del Canal de Isabel II

Entrance on Avda de las Islas Filipinas, Chamberí (91 533 17 91, www.cyii.es). Metro Canal or Rios Rosas. **Open** *Oct-May* 10am-9pm daily. *June-Sept* 9am-11pm daily.
Open since 2007, this lovely outdoor sports complex/park – between Avenida de las Islas Filipinas, Calle de Santander and the Paseo de San Francisco de Sales – consists of a 1.5-kilometre running track and pedestrian pathway, a golf course, two football pitches, and eight *pádel* courts. It is beautifully landscaped with lavender, rose bushes, cypress trees, water fountains, benches and shaded areas, and there's a great vibe on summer evenings, when the park buzzes with runners, old folk on their evening strolls, families and more serious sporty types. Officially called the Centro de Ocio y Deportes Tercer Depósito del Canal de Isabel II, it's referred to by locals as simply Parque del Canal, or increasingly Parque Green Canal. *Photo p255*.

Yoga

Ashtanga Yoga

C/Juanelo 12, Lavapiés (91 369 00 33, www.ashtangayogamadrid.com). Metro Tirso de Molina. **Open** *Guided classes* 7pm Mon-Fri, Sun; 11am Sat. *Mysore self-practice* 8-10am Mon-Fri; 8-10pm Mon, Tue, Thur. **Admission** *1 class* €15. *4 classes* €50. *10 classes* €100. Monthly deals are also available; see the website for details. **Map** p327 G13.
An attractive and personal Ashtanga studio, popular with both locals and foreigners. The guided classes are suitable for all levels, through a combination of instruction and Mysore-style (self-practice).

City Yoga

C/Artistas 43, Tetuán (91 553 47 51, www.city-yoga.com). Metro Cuatro Caminos or Nuevos Ministerios. **Open** 10am-10pm Mon-Fri; 10am-2pm Sat; see website for times of individual classes. **Admission** *1 class* €15. *28 classes* €240.
This large centre offers a range of classes, covering different styles. Pilates classes are also held, and there's a selection of natural therapies and massage.

DISABLED SPORTS FACILITIES

The city sports authorities are slowly adapting their centres to allow full access for disabled users. The majority of indoor pools have been adapted, and many outdoor pools have ramps and full-access changing rooms. Those at Casa de Campo (*see p257*) and Concepción (*see p258*) have the best disabled facilities.

Theatre & Dance

No need for stage fright in Madrid's classic teatros and arty salas.

Madrid's theatre scene is a polarised affair: while Gran Vía is littered with Broadway and West End hand-me-downs – Spain's fervent passion for the blockbuster musical has not wavered – little theatres soldier on in the face of local government and city council limits on licences and funds.

Still, the fighting spirit of the fringe makes up for the mainstream's old-fashioned outlook – although to some outsiders, the alternative scene here can seem to be not that alternative, really; bear in mind that until the late 1980s there was virtually no non-mainstream theatre here at all.

As in the theatre world, the best thing going for Madrid's dance scene, meanwhile, is its festivals, such as the Festival de Otoño.

THE THEATRE SCENE

Look beyond the heavyweights, such as the **Teatro de Madrid** (*see far right*) and the **Teatro María Guerrero** (*see p264*), and you'll find that Madrid's has an active fringe scene, with the **Sala Triángulo** and **Cuarta Pared** (for both, *see p266*) the oldest of the *salas alternativas*, and the beleaguered **TIS** (*see p266*) a key player too. Other theatres to look out for include **Teatro Alcázar** (C/Alcalá 20, 91 701 02 30, www.gruposmedia.com/teatros.html), the **Teatro Calderón** (C/Atocha 18, 902 00 66 17, www/teatrohaagen-dazs.es) – recenlty renamed the **Teatro Häagen-Dazs**, following a sponsorship deal – the **Teatro Lara** (Corredera Baja de San Pablo 15, 91 523 90 27, www.teatro lara.com), for family entertainment, and **Teatro de Cámara Chéjov** (C/San Cosme y San Damián 3, 91 527 09 54, www.teatrochejov. com) for major classics.

THE DANCE SCENE

Three major companies are based in Madrid: the contemporary, but far far from radical, **Compañía Nacional de Danza**; the state **Ballet Nacional de España**, which specialises in Spanish styles of dance; and the **Ballet de la Comunidad de Madrid**, run by Victor Ullate.

As ever, contemporary dance teeters on an economic knife-edge, but spaces such as the **Pradillo** (*see p266*) continue to show good work. The two main contemporary dance companies are **10y10** (www.10y10danza.com), in residency at the Centro de Nuevos Creadores, and **Provisional Danza** (www.provisional danza.com), one of the pioneers of contemporary dance in Spain since 1987, led by the renowned choreographer Carmen Werner. The **Centro Danza Canal** (CDC) dance school and the **Víctor Ullate-Ballet-Comunidad de Madrid** company are based in new performing arts centre **Teatros del Canal** (*see p265*).

It's also worth noting that the **Teatro Real** (*see p236*) often stages dance productions, notably with the Ballet Nacional de España and the Compañía Nacional de Danza, as well as small pieces in the informal 'Café Danza'.

For Flamenco, *see pp46-49*.

INSIDE TRACK
TICKETS AND TIMES

Many of the mainstream theatres are closed on Mondays and most fringe venues only open Thursday to Sunday. Cheaper tickets are often available on Wednesdays and Sundays. Most theatres sell through telesales, and we list several in the shopping section, *see p204*. But you can also call the venue to check. The best places to find information are the *Guía del Ocio* and daily newspapers, especially in the Friday listings supplements that most of them publish.

VENUES

Mainstream theatres

Sala Mirador

C/Doctor Fourquet 31, Lavapiés (91 539 57 67, www.cnc-eca.es). Metro Atocha or Lavapiés. **Open** *Box office* 1hr before performance Thur-Sun. Closed Aug. **Tickets** €13-€16. **No credit cards. Map** p328 I15.

Doubling as theatre/dance school and performance space, this is also the site of the long-running *La Katarsis del Tomatazo*, performed every Friday and Saturday night at 10.30pm. The audience are given tomatoes as they enter, which they can use to express their feelings on this singing and dancing cabaret.

Teatro de la Abadía

C/Fernández de los Ríos 42, Chamberí (box office 91 448 16 27, information 91 448 11 81, www.teatroabadia.com). Metro Quevedo. **Open** *Box office* 5-9pm Tue-Sat; 5-8pm Sun. Closed Aug. **Tickets** €8-€20; concessions apply Wed. **Credit** V. **Map** p323 F6.

Housed inside an abandoned church, the award-winning Abadía dabbles in music and dance as well as theatre. It participates in the Festival de Otoño and Madrid en Danza festivals, and brings unusual one-offs to the regular programming.

Teatro Alfil

C/Pez 10, Malasaña (box office 91 521 58 27, information 91 521 45 41, www.teatroalfil.com). Metro Callao or Noviciado. **Open** *Box office* 1hr before performance daily. **Tickets** €9-€12. **No credit cards. Map** p325 G10.

Madrid's renegade theatre, the Alfil has been threatened with closure in previous years, but has battled on, and produces increasingly radical plays – both *The Vagina Monologues* and *Puppetry of the Penis* have been staged here. It's also one of the few venues to host stand-up comedy, including the Giggling Guiri English comedy nights (www.comedyinspain.com).

Teatro Fernán Gómez Centro de Arte

Jardines del Descubrimiento, Plaza de Colón, Salamanca (91 480 03 00, http://teatro fernangomez.esmadrid.com). Metro Serrano. **Open** *Box office* 11am-1.30pm, 5-7pm or until performance Tue-Sun. **Tickets** €5-€25. **Credit** AmEx, DC, MC, V. **Map** p324 K9.

The theatre in the city's purpose-built cultural centre shows an eclectic mix of concerts, opera, *zarzuela*, cinema, drama and dance. There are also jazz performances, workshops and children's puppet shows.

Teatro Español

C/Príncipe 25, Huertas & Santa Ana (box office 91 360 14 84, information 91 360 14 80). Metro Sevilla or Sol. **Open** *Box office* 11.30am-1.30pm, 5-7.30pm or until show begins Tue-Sun. **Tickets** €3-€20. **No credit cards. Map** p328 H12.

This grand theatre on Plaza Santa Ana dates back to 1745, but that doesn't mean it's old fashioned – in fact it has enjoyed some fairly radical programming in recent years. In 2010, the varied programme included a production of *Macbeth*, a modern tango show by the Mora Godoy Tango Company and a number of poetry performances.

Teatro Fernando de Rojas

C/Alcalá 42, Sol & Gran Vía (91 360 54 00, www.circulobellasartes.com). Metro Banco de

Teatro La Latina. *See p264.*

España or Sevilla. **Open** *Box office* 5.30-9pm
Tue-Sun. Closed Aug. **Tickets** varies.
No credit cards. Map p328 I11.
Housed in the Círculo de Bellas Artes, and not to be
confused with the unconnected Teatro de Bellas
Artes next door, the Fernando de Rojas stages three
or four works a season, mixing contemporary and
traditional, Spanish and international. The theatre is
one of the host venues for the Escena Contemporánea
festival (www.escenacontemporanea.com).

Teatro La Latina

*Plaza de la Cebada 2, La Latina (91 365 28 35,
www.teatrolalatina.net). Metro La Latina or
Tirso de Molina.* **Open** *Box office* 5-8pm Tue;
11am-1pm, 5pm until performance Wed-Sun.
Tickets €15-€30. **No credit cards.**
Map p327 F13.
Previously known for its home-spun comic theatre
(plenty of star names in farcical situations and lots
of banging of doors), this comfortable venue has
undergone a slight shift of image in recent years.
Although the programme now mainly consists of
quality drama (most of it 20th century), the theatre
also sometimes hosts less high-brow productions,
such as *Peter Pan*.

★ Teatro de Madrid

*Avda de la Ilustración s/n, Barrio del Pilar
(box office 91 730 17 50, information 91 740
52 74, www.teatromadrid.com). Metro Barrio
del Pilar.* **Open** *Box office* 5pm until performance
Tue-Thur; 11.30am-1.30pm, 5pm until show Fri-
Sun.* **Tickets** €12-€22. **Credit** MC, V.
The Teatro de Madrid specialises in bringing the
highest-calibre Spanish and international dance
companies to the city, staging a mixture of ballet,
contemporary dance and fusion performances such

INSIDE TRACK
A DIVIDED SCENE

The battle for the hearts and minds of
Madrid's increasingly polarised theatre-
going public is perhaps best illustrated
by the controversy that raged when the
Círculo de Bellas Artes put on Iñigo
Ramírez de Haro's *Me cago en Dios*
('I Shit on God' – a surprisingly common
Spanish exclamation). Cast members were
physically attacked, the Church weighed in,
and the playwright's sister-in-law, President
of the Madrid regional government
Esperanza Aguirre, asked the theatre
director to cancel the play. Undaunted,
Ramírez et al then took the production
to the maverick Teatro Alfil, where it later
opened and ran under a new title: *Me Cago
en la Censura* – 'I Shit on Censorship'.

---

as flamenco and tango. It is also home to the Nuevo
Ballet Español, the company of the fiery duo Ángel
Rojas and Carlo Rodríguez, and regularly stages
good children's shows around Christmas, as well as
a *zarzuela* in the summer. *Swan Lake* has been enjoying a long run over the past few years.

★ Teatro María Guerrero

*C/Tamayo y Baus 4, Chueca (box office 91 310
15 00, information 91 310 29 49, http://cdn.
mcu.es). Metro Colón.* **Open** *Box office* noon
until 6pm or until performance daily. Closed
Aug. **Tickets** €11-€18; half- price concessions
Wed. **Credit** AmEx, DC, V. **Map** p324 J10.
This beautiful late 19th-century theatre is the home
of the state-run Centro Dramático Nacional (CDN).
Having reopened after major renovations, it's retained
its red velvet plushness and is to host, among other
works, Buchner's *Woyceck* in 2011.

Teatro Nuevo Apolo

*Plaza de Tirso de Molina 1, Rastro & Lavapiés
(91 369 06 37). Metro Tirso de Molina.* **Open**
Box office 11.30am-1.30pm, 5-9pm Tue-Sat;
5-7pm Sun. Closed mid July-mid Aug. **Tickets**
€20-€30. **No credit cards** (except for purchases
exceeding €150). **Map** p327 G13.
In recent seasons, this venue has welcomed such
exciting acts as dancer Joaquín Cortes and the
Mayumana dance-percussion troupe. One of the big
shows in 2010 was a production of Bizet's *Carmen*
by the Ballet Flamenco de Madrid.

Teatro Pavón

*C/Embajadores 9, La Latina (91 528 28 19).
Metro La Latina.* **Open** *Box office* 11.30am-
1.30pm, 5-6pm daily. Closed mid July-early Sept.
Tickets €8-€16. **Credit** MC, V. **Map** p327 G14.
The Compañia Nacional de Teatro Clásico moved
here in 2002 while its real home, the Teatro de la
Comédia, is being restored. An impressive building
that sat semi-derelict for many years, it currently
stages classical productions by the Compañia
Nacional as well as by a number of invited compa-
nies. Here you'll usually get works by Spanish
Golden Age greats along with the occasional
Molière, Shakespeare or the like.

Teatro Valle-Inclán

*Plaza de Lavapiés s/n, Rastro & Lavapiés (91
505 88 01, http://cdn.mcu.es). Metro Lavapiés.*
Open *Box office* noon-6pm or until performance
daily. Closed Aug. **Tickets** €15-€18; €7.50-€9
concessions (half-price on Wed). **Credit** AmEx,
DC, V. **Map** p327 H14.
Occupying the space where the popular but tatty
Teatro Olimpia used to stand, the Valle-Inclán opened
its doors in early 2006 and is the Centro Dramático
Nacional's second venue after the María Guerrero. The
main theatre, with 510 seats, is equipped with the latest technology and offers a programme of contempo-

Speaking in Tongues

Spanish isn't up to scratch? Check out Madrid's English-language productions.

Even hardened theatre buffs quail before a show in a language they don't understand and, of course, almost all Madrid theatre is staged in Spanish. English-speaking visitors might get lucky, though, and happen on a touring production in the Festival de Otoño or Escena Contemporánea. In recent years the RSC has visited, Cheek By Jowl have brought *The Changeling* and the all-male Propeller Company staged a memorable *Winter's Tale*. But, best of all, English-language shows are available a few times a year, courtesy of local amateur groups, the Madrid Players and La Madrilera.

It would be easy to dismiss the former as expat ham-drams and frustrated thesps, but they firmly believe there is no such thing as an 'amateur performance' – especially for paying audiences. The **Madrid Players** (www.madridplayers. blogspot.com) with over 60 members of various nationalities, have been going for over 30 years and now regularly perform in some of Madrid's better-known fringe venues, such as the Teatro Triángulo and the Sala TIS. The staple earner, however, is the colourful, uproarious Christmas panto, which most years attracts total audiences of over 2,000, many of them Spaniards.

Serious drama also has its place: recent seasons have seen performances of Alan Ayckbourn, Samuel Beckett,

Thornton Wilder, Michael Christofer, Chekhov and Shakespeare. Some members have worked professionally, others have not, but enthusiasm and sheer hard work ensure high standards. This fact has not been lost on the media; the group has featured several times in major dailies and even made the national news on TV1 last year. It's worth pointing out that the idea of panto doesn't exist in Spain, and what local viewers made of a painted dame and several blokes in tights is anybody's guess.

Malasaña-based cultural association **La Madrilera** (www.lamadrilera.com; *pictured*) is a less formalised affair, but also puts on productions in English (as well as Spanish), and runs acting courses.

if you're in town for an extended period and fancy taking to the stage yourself, both groups welcome drama enthusiasts.

---

rary Spanish playwrights as well as works by authors such as Pirandello, Ibsen and Jean Genet. In the adjoining Sala Franciso Nieva, with room for 150 spectators, you are more likely to find works by newer writers.

★ Teatros del Canal

C/Cea Bermúdez 1, Chamberí (91 308 99 50, www.teatrosdelcanal.org). Metro Canal. **Open** *Box office* 11am-1pm; 5.30-9pm Mon-Sat; 5.30-8pm Sun. **Tickets** €12-€34; concessions 20% discount. **Credit** AmEx, DC, V.
Consisting of two theatres – the Sala Roja (Red Room) and the Sala Verde (Green Room) – the Teatros del Canal performing arts centre opened in the barrio of Chamberí a couple of years ago, to much excitement. The flashy avant-garde building, designed by Spanish architect Juan Navarro Baldeweg, utilises advanced audio-visual technology and has impressive interiors. A production of *Carmen* was being shown in 2010. The centre also houses the Centro

Danza Canal (CDC) dance school, and the Víctor Ullate-Ballet-Comunidad de Madrid dance company. Guided tours of the building are available for €4 (€3 concessions); call for information.

Fringe/alternative spaces

The **Teatro de las Aguas** (C/Aguas 8, 91 366 96 42) occasionally has productions in English. Small, more alternative spaces include: **DT Espacio Escénico** (C/Reina 9, 91 521 71 55, www.dtespacioescenico.com) for theatre, cabaret and dance productions on gay themes; **Nave de Los Locos** (C/Francisco Guzmán 28, 91 560 14 79, www.lanavedeloslocos.org), which hosts theatrical productions, workshops and forums in a bid to develop 'the creative imagination'; and **Lagrada** (C/Ercilla 20, 91 517 96 98, www.teatrolagrada.com), for kitchen sink dramas and contemporary plays.

Cuarta Pared

C/Ercilla 17, South of centre (91 517 23 17, www.cuartapared.es). Metro Embajadores. **Open** *Box office* 1hr before performance Thur-Sun. Closed Aug. **Tickets** €12; €8 concessions. *Children's shows* €5. **No credit cards.**
Cuarta Pared plays a crucial role in training and production. The resident company produces excellent work, it hosts visiting productions, is a major dance venue and stages acclaimed children's theatre.

El Montacargas

C/Antillón 19, Puerta del Ángel, South of centre (91 526 11 73, www.teatroelmontacargas.com). Metro Puerta del Ángel. **Open** *Box office* 30mins before show Thur-Sun. **Tickets** €12; €8 concessions. *Children's shows* €8. **No credit cards.**
Programming favours contemporary Spanish work, but it also hosts the Clown Festival in September.

Sala Triángulo

C/Zurita 20, Lavapiés (91 530 68 91, www.teatro triangulo.com). Metro Antón Martín or Lavapiés. **Open** *Box office* 30mins before show. **Tickets** €10-€13. **No credit cards. Map** p328 I14.
The original and probably the best of Madrid's alternative theatres, Triángulo is fiercely independent. There are always several productions going at once, usually including new writing and cross-art-form collaborations. It works closely with other theatres during festivals (it is the force behind La Alternativa in February, the Festival de Teatro Alternativo de Primavera in June and Al Fresco in July/August).

Teatro Pradillo

C/Pradillo 12, Chamartín (91 416 90 11, www. teatropradillo.com). Metro Concha Espina. **Open** *Box office* 1hr before performance. *Sept-June* Thur-Sun; *July, Aug* Wed-Sat. **Tickets** €9-€16; €6 concessions. *Children's shows* €4-8. **Credit** MC, V.
This fantastically intimate theatre, with just 120 seats, runs a varied programme throughout the year. A particular strength is dance – the Pradillo provided well-known dancers such as Manuel Liñan and Daniel Doña with their big breaks, and runs a dance programme for young audiences – while another strong point is children's theatre, and in particular puppet shows. It is one of the principal organisers of the Escena Contemporánea festival (www.escenacontemporanea.com), and runs a flamenco festival in August.

TIS (Teatro Independiente Sur)

C/Primavera 11, Lavapiés (91 528 13 59/664 345 789, http://galeria-tis.teatrotis.com). Metro Lavapiés. **Open** *Aug, Sept* 11am-2pm, 5-10pm daily. *Oct-July* 10am-10pm Mon-Thur, Sun; 10am-midnight Fri, Sat. **Tickets** €9-15. **No credit cards. Map** p328 H14.
The alternative (and often wacky) performances at TIS meet with mixed reviews, but it has put on plays by hundreds of international theatre companies in its comparatively short and sometimes precarious lifetime. Keep a look out for one of the theatre's most successful productions, *Jamming*, an entirely improvised affair where the audience is encouraged to participate.

SEASONS AND FESTIVALS

The **Festival de Otoño** (*see p210*) is the city's biggest event for theatre, dance and puppetry, attracting major international names and sometimes putting on shows in English. More alternative theatre and dance is showcased in January and February in the original **Escena Contemporánea**, the better-funded sibling to the slightly more avant-garde **La Alternativa** festival, while in June there's the **Festival de Teatro Alternativo de Primavera**. The summer **Veranos de la Villa** offers even more outdoor performances. The Centro Cultural de la Villa's **Apuesta por la Danza** attracts prestigious companies such as Ibérica de Danza and the Companhia Portuguesa de Bailado Contemporâneo. And, for a summer trip out of town, don't miss the **Festival Internacional de Teatro Clásico** in Almagro every July. The event pays tribute to Lope de Vega, Molière, Shakespeare et al with plays, workshops and street performances (call 91 521 07 20 or visit www.festivaldealmagro.com for details). The **Madrid Sur** festival is organised by the Fundación Instituto Internacional del Teatro del Mediterráneo (91 355 58 67, www.institutodel mediterraneo.es) and takes place in autumn.

DANCE CLASSES

If you take more than a passive interest in flamenco, you might want to try classes. Below are some of the more established dance centres.

Centro de Danza Karen Taft

C/Libertad 15, Chueca (91 522 84 40, 91 522 20 87, www.karentaft.com). Metro Chueca. **Open** *Oct-June* 9am-10pm Mon-Fri. *July-Sept* 9.30am-10pm Mon-Thur. **Map** p328 I11.
One of the foremost dance schools in Spain, offering classes in classical and modern dance, and flamenco.

Estudios Amor de Dios

C/Santa Isabel 5, 1º, Lavapiés (91 360 04 34, www.amordedios.com). Metro Antón Martín. **Open** varies (call for details). **Map** p328 I13.
The world's most famous flamenco school is now nearly 60 years old. It sits (or rather stamps) above the Antón Martín indoor market building.

El Horno

C/Esgrima 11, Lavapiés (91 527 57 01). Metro Tirso de Molina. **Open** 10am-11pm Mon-Fri; 10am-7pm Sat. **Map** p327 G13.
El Horno has a flamenco and *sevillana* leaning.

Escapes & Excursions

Segovia. *See p281.*

Escapes & Excursions

There's a whole other country out there.

It's a tough call. Spend the entire long weekend in Madrid in order to fit in all three of the mandatory museums? Or take advantage of one of the city's extraordinary day trips? Three words: change your ticket. Because you'll want to do both. In summer, the cool mountain air of the sierras beckons, along with excellent hiking and some of the best campsites anywhere. In winter, what better than to hole up in a traditional *mesón* in the stately cities of Toledo or Segovia, with red wine, a log fire and some suckling pig? Year round the palaces, monasteries and gardens at Aranjuez, La Granja, Riofrío and El Escorial make for a compelling visit.

The areas to the north and west of Madrid have the most spectacular landscapes, following the three main sierra ranges. The less dramatic country to the south and east – where dry tableland, tufty hillocks and fertile river basins gently intermingle – is full of fascinating towns.

GETTING THERE

By bus

Within the city, details of bus services are available by calling 012 (or on 91 580 42 60 from outside Madrid), and you can get also get information from tourist offices and on the regional transport website – visit www.ctm-madrid.es. A large number of buses depart from Estación Sur de Autobuses (C/Méndez Álvaro, 91 468 42 00, www.estacionautobusesmadrid.com, Metro Méndez Alvaro), but there are also five major interchange terminals (*intercambiadores*), where municipal bus services, regional bus services and Metro lines converge. The Plaza de Castilla terminal, straddling Tetuán and Chamartín, serves destinations to the north west; the subterranean bus terminal at Moncloa in Chamberí feeds destinations mostly to the south and west of Madrid; the Avenida de America terminus serves the airport and destinations to the north east; the Príncipe Pío interchange handles over 20 interurban bus routes; while from the Plaza Elíptica station in the south of the city, you can catch buses to Toledo, among other destinations.

By car

In 2004 many major roads changed name, and road map publishers and car-hire agencies were slow to catch up. 'National' roads, such as those formerly known as N-I and N-II, for example, became A-1 and A-2, except on toll-paying roads (*peajes*), where the prefix is now AP. The six notorious major roads, now numbered A-1 to A-6, can all be reached from the M-30 or the outlying M-40 ring road. The A-1 (Carretera de Burgos) leads to the eastern Guadarrama and Sierra Pobre, the A-2 Barcelona road goes to Alcalá de Henares, and the A-3 Valencia road to Chinchón. The A-42 (formerly the N-401) to Toledo can be reached from either the M-30 or the A-4. The A-6 La Coruña road leads to El Escorial, Segovia, Ávila and Salamanca.

Expect bottlenecks at weekends, especially for the return trip on Sunday evenings: streets can be gridlocked until midnight. Immense traffic jams and a substantial crop of accidents are also depressingly predictable during long holiday weekends (*puentes*). Don't even think about driving at the beginning or end of August, particularly on the A-3 Valencia road. For more on driving and car hire, *see p297*.

Toledo. *See p289.*

By train

The system of local trains (*cercanías*) runs to many interesting towns around Madrid; Alcalá de Henares, Aranjuez, El Escorial, Cercedilla and many more. The ageing but efficient single gauge extension line, the scenic C-9, wends its way up from Cercedilla through mountain pinewoods to Cotos, which adjoins ski slopes and a glacial lake. Services to other destinations leave from main-line stations Chamartín and Atocha, though many trains also stop between them at Nuevos Ministerios and Recoletos stations. It's also worth noting that the high-speed AVE and Talgo trains, from Atocha to Seville and Córdoba respectively, make a weekend or even a day trip to Andalucía a possibility. Depending on when you travel, there are often very good low-price fare deals as well. Several trains a day run to both cities.

RENFE information

902 320 320, 902 240 202, www.renfe.com. **Open** *Information* 24hrs. *Reservations* 5am-11.40pm daily. **Credit** AmEx, DC, MC, V. Tickets for long-distance services can be booked by phone with a credit card. Tickets can be delivered to a Madrid address for a small extra charge.

RENFE central sales office

C/Alcalá 44, Huertas & Santa Ana (no phone). *Metro Banco de España.* **Open** 9.30am-8pm Mon-Fri. **Credit** AmEx, DC, MC, V. **Map** p328 H11. Information and tickets for the AVE, Talgo and all other RENFE long-distance services are available from this office, which is a short walk from Plaza de Cibeles. It does not handle phone enquiries, which go through the central number above.

North & West

ÁVILA

It's an impressive sight; a forbidding stronghold encircled by thick 11th-century walls rising out of a boulder-strewn landscape. It is also the highest provincial capital in the country, with bitterly cold winters.

Despite its elegant buildings and well-to-do feel, there is something slightly sinister about Ávila's fortressed isolation; plaques around town celebrate Franco's victories and point out that this was the birthplace of Isabel 'la Católica' – the most powerful and merciless woman in the history of Spain. Proverbially a town of *cantos y santos* (stones and saints), it was also home to Spain's greatest mystic, Santa Teresa, the 16th-century religious reformer who founded 18 convents and revolutionised Catholicism, while living a life of spartan self-denial.

As well as a statue in the town centre, there are countless other reminders of her presence. The Baroque **Convento de Santa Teresa** (Plaza de la Santa 2, 920 21 10 30, closed Mon, admission free, museum €2) stands on the plot of the house she was born in, while the nearby Convento de San José contains the **Museo Teresiano de Carmelitas Descalzas** (C/Madres 4, 920 22 21 27, admission €1) where you can see her manuscripts and relics. General Franco is said to have kept the saint's mummified arm by his bedside in his final years.

The medieval city is a timewarp of cobbled lanes, sleepy squares, family mansions and stately religious buildings. The highlight is undoubtedly the stark fortified 12th-century **cathedral** (Plaza de la Catedral 8, 920 21 16 41, admission €4), embedded in the walls and rebuilt over the ages in Romanesque, Gothic and Renaissance styles. The **Basilica de San Vicente** (Plaza de San Vicente 1, 920 25 52 30, admission €1.40 Mon-Sat, free Sun), located outside the walls, is a similar hybrid of styles. Built on the spot where St Vincent and his two sisters were martyred in the fourth century, it has gruesome scenes of their torture depicted in relief around Vicente's tomb. Nearby stand the Romanesque church of **San Andrés** and the palatial but melancholy 15th-century Gothic **Santo Tomás monastery**, containing the alabaster tomb of Ferdinand and Isabella's only son and heir, Don Juan, who died aged 19.

The city's wonderfully preserved **walls** (920 25 50 88, closed Mon, admission €3.50), which were built after the knights had rid the city of the Moors, extend for one and a half miles and have nine gates and 88 watchtowers. For the best views go across the River Adaja to **Los Cuatro Postes**, a small Doric-columned monument perched on a knoll west of the city. The walls can be climbed at the Puerta del Alcázar just south of the cathedral and Puerta de San Vicente to the north.

Where to stay & eat

Among the major culinary delights to be found in Ávila are large steaks (*chuletones de Ávila*) from the fighting Iberian strain of black bulls, and delicious haricot beans (*judías* or *alubias*) from Barco de Ávila. Look out too for *cocido morañego*, a local variant on Madrid's famed winter stew; Ávila's own Castilian version of gazpacho, using fresh vegetables from the Tiétar Valley; roast lamb (*cordero asado*) and suckling pig (*lechona*). *Yemas de Santa Teresa* – rich sweets made from egg yolks and said to have been originally created by the saint herself in one of her rare moments of indulgence – are another of Ávila's specialities; you'll see them for sale all over town.

Ávila. *See p272.*

A good place to try them is the charming **Mesón del Rastro** (Plaza del Rastro 1, 920 21 12 19, mains €12-€20, set lunch €17), which has all the trimmings of a traditional Castilian tavern (boars' heads, log fires and so on) without the traditionally high prices. **El Rincón** (Plaza de Zurraquín 3-4, 920 35 10 44, restaurant closed Mon & all Feb, mains €10.50-€15, set lunch €9.65-€11.80) is another serving the same food as everywhere else, but at lower prices. **La Alcazaba** (Plaza Mosén Rubi 3, 920 25 62 90, closed 2wks in Jan, mains €18-€22) is more creative – try monkfish tournedor in Pernod sauce, or duck with caramelised apples. On the other side of the river, with a great view of the walls from its terrace, is **Mesón El Puente** (Bajada de la Losa 2, 920 22 50 51, closed Mon & all Jan, mains €12).

Many of the town's hotels are located in converted mansions and Renaissance palaces. The delightful **Parador Raimundo de Borgoña** (C/Marqués de Canales de Chozas 2, 920 21 13 40, www.parador.es, doubles €90-€140, mains €17) serves an exceptional breakfast, available to non-residents as well as guests. **Hospedería de Bracamonte** (C/Bracamonte 6, 920 25 12 80, www.hosp ederiadebracamonte.com, doubles €60-€80, restaurant closed last 2wks in Oct, mains €16, set lunch €15) has a seigneurial air and lots of game dishes. **Palacio de Valderrábanos** (Plaza de la Catedral 9, 920 21 10 23, www.palaciovalderrabanoshotel.com, doubles €75-€125) is a grander hotel located on the plaza with splendid views of the cathedral.

Getting there

By bus
Larrea (91 851 55 92, www.autobuseslarrea.com) from Estación Sur (91 468 42 00) has nine buses on weekdays, six buses on weekends. Journey time is 1hr 40mins.

By train
There are 20 trains daily from Chamartín or Atocha stations, 8am-10.30pm. The last return train is at 9.30pm. Journey time (Regional Exprés services) is anything between 1hr 15mins-2hrs.

Tourist information

Oficina de Turismo
Plaza Pedro Dávila 4 (920 21 13 87, www. turismocastillayleon.com). **Open** *Oct-June* 9.30am-2pm, 4-7pm Mon-Sat; 9.30am-5pm Sun. *July-Sept* 9am-8pm daily.

EL ESCORIAL

The grand, austere monastery of San Lorenzo de El Escorial never fails to divide opinion, but is indubitably one of the most significant buildings in the history of Spain. Many people see it as the outward manifestation of its founding monarch's mind – Philip II was at once fanatically religious and wildly ambitious, and so his legacy in stone is both spartan and vast. The gloomy building is also symbolic architecturally, and it was the grey slate and spiky turrets of El Escorial that inspired decades of the 'Herreran' style (also known as Castilian baroque).

Construction was completed in record time between 1563 and 1574, initially by Juan Bautista de Toledo – who died shortly after work started – and subsequently by Juan de Herrera. Everything here is on a grand scale: the main façade is 200 metres (700 feet) long, the overhead cupola measures 92 metres (302 feet), and there are 15 cloisters, 16km (10 miles) of corridors, 86 stairways, 88 fountains, 1,200 doors and 2,675 windows.

Philip conceived the palace as a mausoleum and contemplative retreat, built as a final resting place for his father, Charles I, and to celebrate the 1557 Spanish victory over the French at St Quentin on St Lawrence's day (San Lorenzo). It's laid out to resemble the grid-iron on which the saint himself was martyred. The jasper, gold and marble **Panteón de los Reyes**, designed by Gian Battista Crescenzi in the 1620s, contains all but two of the sovereigns who reigned over four centuries (absentees being Philip V, who was buried at La Granja, and Ferdinand VI, whose remains are in Madrid). The Basilica, with its notable *Christ Crucified* in Carrara marble by Benvenuto Cellini, has no fewer than 45 altars.

The main galleries are located on what was the lower floor of Philip's own austere rooms, above the **Basilica**. There is a small jalousie window overlooking the high altar so he could participate in Mass even if he was ill and confined to his surprisingly small bed. His cherished Hieronymous Bosch triptych was just a tiny part of a huge Habsburg art collection that includes celebrated works by Velázquez, Ribera, Alonso Cano and individual masterpieces like El Greco's *Adoration of the Name of Jesus* and Titian's *Last Supper*, concentrated mainly in the museum, church, chapterhouse and the ornate barrel-vaulted library – whose 50,000 volumes rival the Vatican's holdings.

The most refreshing section of El Escorial is the **Palacio de los Borbones**, remodelled by Charles IV in a light airy neo-classical style that contrasts with the general austerity and gloom. Highlights here are the tapestries designed by Goya and his contemporaries. Guided tours can be arranged on Fridays and Saturdays. It is worth noting that it can get very cold inside the building, even on warm days.

Two other small palaces lie in the spacious gardens and parklands surrounding the monastery and can be visited with prior reservation on the palace number: the **Casita de Arriba**, or Upper House (open Easter, July & Aug 10am-6pm Tue-Sun, admission €3.40, €1.70 reductions), and the **Casita del Príncipe** (Prince's House), with paintings by Lucas Jordan, a charming garden with 100-year-old sequoia trees, open at weekends only from April to September. The park is open year-round from 10am-6pm Tuesday to Sunday.

Outside the monastery El Escorial is really two separate towns. Down below, next to the train station, is **El Escorial de Abajo**, and at the top of the hill, alongside the monastery, is the grander **San Lorenzo**. Look out here for Charles III's 18th-century **Real Coliseo** theatre and the parish church of **San Bartolomé**. A couple of kilometres out on the road towards the Casita de Arriba is the **Silla de Felipe**, 'Philip's Seat', from where he used to watch progress on the building.

Real Monasterio de San Lorenzo de El Escorial

91 890 59 03/05, www.patrimonionacional.es. **Open** *Oct-Mar* 10am-5pm Tue-Sun. *Apr-Sept* 10am-6pm Tue-Sun. *Palacio de los Borbones* Guided tours *Apr-Sept* 4pm, 5pm, Tue-Thur; 4pm, 5pm, 6pm Fri; 10am, 11am, noon, 5pm, 6pm Sat. *Oct-Mar* 4pm, 5pm Tue-Fri; 10am, 11am, noon, 4pm, 5pm Sat. *Casita del Príncipe* Apr-June 10am-1pm, 4-6.30pm Sat-Sun. July-Sept 10am-1pm, 4-6.30pm Tue-Sun. **Admission** *Monastery* (incl guided tour) €10; (excl guided tour) €8; €4 reductions; Wed free for EU citizens. *Palacio de los Borbones* €3.60; €2 reductions. *Casita del Príncipe* €3.60; €2 reductions. **No credit cards**. Reservations are essential for the Palacio and Casita tours, at least 24 hours in advance.

Where to eat

Fonda Genara (Plaza San Lorenzo 2, 91 890 16 36, www.restaurantegenara.com, mains €16, set menu €13.50-€17) is a pretty if slightly pricey restaurant with old theatre posters around the walls. **Parrilla Principe** (C/Floridablanca 6, 91 890 16 11, www.parrillaprincipe.com, doubles €60-€80, restaurant closed Tue and Sun dinner, mains €20-€25, set menu €16-€18) is a small, peaceful 18th-century palace with a hotel on the upper floors and a blend of Castilian and seafood cuisine available in the restaurant

below. **Madrid Sevilla** (C/Benavente 1, 91 890 15 19, closed Mon & 2wks Oct, mains €11, set menu €14.50-€19.50) has simple but reasonably priced food, while **La Chistera** (Plaza Jacinto Benavente 5, 91 890 37 26, closed Mon night, set lunch €8.50, set dinner €16) is principally a tapas bar.

One of the nicest places for a drink or snack is the **Babel Café** (C/Juan de Austria 7, 91 896 05 22, www.babelcafe.com), with occasional live music, a small cinema club, exhibitions, internet access and a garden as well as good food. Up above the town in the Monte Abantos district, **Horizontal** (Camino Horizontal, 91 890 38 11, www.restaurantehorizontal.com, closed Tue-Wed dinner in Nov-Mar, main course €20) offers outdoor eating in summer and a seat by the fire in winter.

Where to stay

Designed by Herrera, the **Hotel Victoria Palace** (C/Juan de Toledo 4, 91 896 98 90, www.nh-hotels.com, doubles €80-€130) is an exquisite hotel with a charming garden just a couple of hundred yards from the monastery. **El Botánico** (C/Timoteo Padrós 16, 91 890 78 79, www.labuganvilla.es, doubles €65-€140) is a beautifully renovated summer house with a library, gardens and fine views of the monastery. A little cheaper, and right in the heart of San Lorenzo, the **Hotel Miranda & Suizo** (C/Floridablanca 18-20, 91 890 47 11, www.hotelmirandasuizo.com, doubles €60-€90) has reasonably appointed rooms looking out over the monastery and a bustling café.

Getting there

By bus
Herranz (91 890 41 00) buses 661 and 664 from the Moncloa interchange (journey time 55mins), every 15 mins 7am-11pm Mon-Fri, every 30mins-1hr 10am-10.15pm Sat, 10am-11pm Sun. Last return is at 9.30pm Mon-Fri, 9pm Sat, 10pm Sun.

By train
Cercanías C-8a, 27 trains from Atocha (journey time 1hr 15mins) 5.45am-11.30pm Mon-Fri; every hour 6.30am-11.30pm Sat, Sun. Last return 10.15pm daily. Trains run to El Escorial town, from where it's a 2km (1.25-mile) walk or bus-ride uphill to San Lorenzo and the monastery. The bus (L1) is much more direct.

Tourist information

Oficina de Turismo
C/Grimaldi 2 (91 890 53 13, www.sanlorenzo turismo.org). **Open** 10am-2pm, 3-6pm Tue-Sat; 10am-2pm Sun.

El Escorial. *See p273.*

ESCAPES & EXCURSIONS

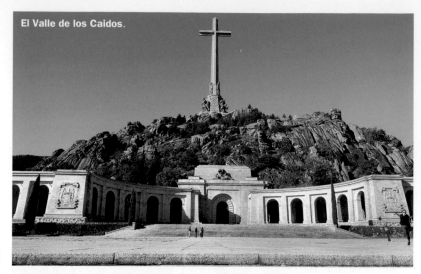

El Valle de los Caídos.

EL VALLE DE LOS CAIDOS

Built between 1940 and 1959 by Civil War prisoners of the defeated Republican army, Franco's giant mausoleum, the 'Valley of the Fallen' (the fallen on Franco's side, at least) stands in a forested valley a few miles from El Escorial. It was the *generalísimo*'s grand project, and its stark, grandiose, authoritarian style is worthy of the likes of Mussolini or Ceaucescu. It is easily spotted from up to 50km (31 miles) away by a huge 150-foot high cross (said to weigh over 180,000 tons) which itself is placed 150 metres above the main esplanade. The monument was completed at great financial and human cost and many Republicans perished while quarrying the dense granite rock needed to build it. Ironically, and to the grief of their families, many of the Republican prisoners' bodies probably now lie side by side with those of their oppressors.

Like it or loathe it, its cold, atmospherically lit underground chambers, lined with eerie cowled figures, do exert a certain mesmerising aura. The mausoleum is basically a huge tunnel, driven 260 metres (867 feet) into the granite rock. At its entrance are 16th-century monoliths, 12 metres (40 feet) high, while deep in the interior you can see bright-coloured tapestries of the *Apocalypse of St John*; a cupola decorated with mosaics showing heaven-bound saints and martyrs of Spain, and an altar-bound polychrome wooden sculpture of Christ crucified. It contains a subterranean church, an ossuary of six chapels bearing the remains of Civil

War dead and the tombs of two men – Franco himself and José Antonio Primo de Rivera, the rich young founder of the Falange who died in the early phases of the Civil War, thus conveniently leaving El Caudillo from El Ferrol unchallenged as leader. Both have fresh flowers placed on their graves daily, paid for by the state, to the disgust of most (though by no means all) of the Spanish population.

The views are quite staggering, especially from the base of the cross, reached via a funicular (€2.50 return).

El Valle de los Caídos

91 890 56 11, www.patrimonionacional.es. **Open** *Oct-Mar* 10am-5pm Tue-Sun. *Apr-Sept* 10am-6pm Tue-Sun. **Admission** €5; €2.50 reductions; Wed free for EU citizens. **Credit** MC, V.

Getting there

By bus
Herranz (91 890 41 00) bus 660 at 3.15pm Tue-Sun from San Lorenzo del Escorial (*see p273*). Return at 5.30pm. Journey time 10mins.

SIERRA DE GUADARRAMA

The Guadarrama range runs from El Escorial (*see p273*) in the south-west to Somosierra in the north-east, and separates the two Castilian *mesetas*, or plains: Castile to the north, and La Mancha to the south. For a selection of the many walks possible in the area, visit the information centre in the Plaza de Ayuntamiento in Guadarrama (*see p278*).

Until the 1970s, when a tunnel was built underneath it, the Puerto de Guadarrama pass was the only way out of Madrid to Segovia and Valladolid, and it would often be impassable for days on end in winter. Also known as the Alto de los Leones because of the lion that sits atop a plinth here (the lion is the symbol of the village of Guadarrama), the pass was the scene of bitter fighting during the battle for Madrid during the Civil War, and Hemingway set large parts of *For Whom the Bell Tolls* here. The remains of gun emplacements and bunkers from that era still litter the area.

A dirt road runs from the top of the pass, south-west for 30km (19 miles) to the charming and peaceful village of Peguerinos, from where there are buses and a fully paved road to El Escorial. Along the way there are several opportunities for camping. The track (signposted) veers off to the left from the Guadarrama direction, among a jumble of radio towers and satellite dishes. There is a restaurant called Alto de León on the side of the main road just at the turning. Coming the other way, the track is signposted 'Valle Enmedio'.

Another breathtaking walk, taking around three hours, runs from **Tablada** station. Walk up 2km (1.25 miles) – not all the way to the pass – to a post indicating km 56, and take a forestry track on the right, clearly marked with a stone sign, to the Peña del Arcipreste de Hita (1,527m/5,010ft). The track eventually descends again, to reach the station at Cercedilla.

Cercedilla is not an especially picturesque village, but it has managed to retain its own identity despite its popularity in summer, when the population swells from 5,000 to around 40,000. To find it at its most authentic, visit in winter, especially if you want to try any of the longer walks nearby. Additionally, rooms can be very difficult to find in summer. The village sits at the head of a valley that leads up to the **Puerto de la Fuenfría** (1,796 metres/5,895 feet), a pass that in turn forms a route across the Sierra dating back to at least Roman times. Along the way there is a Calzada Romana (Roman Road), which dates back to the first century AD, with two fine Roman bridges still standing at El Descalzo and Enmedio. The pass is also an important junction of carefully developed modern footpaths.

The most leisurely excursion from Cercedilla is on the old-world narrow-gauge *cercanías* line (C-9) that runs through fine scenery up to the Cotos ski station, a charming way to get up to and beyond the **Puerto de Navacerrada**, especially when it's snowing. Alternatively, from the *cercanías* station in Cercedilla, a 45-minute walk up the M-966 (the main road in front of you) will bring you to a stretch of open alpine woodland known as **Las Dehesas**, with

an information centre that's an essential port of call for visitors to the valley, with good free maps. Las Dehesas is a very popular picnic spot, with natural spring swimming pools, only open in summer, and freezing even then.

The nearby town of **Navacerrada** is a lively place with a mountain village feel, and several decent restaurants serving appropriately Alpine food (expect to be dipping your bread into lots of raclettes and fondues), making it a fun base.

Where to stay & eat

Camping Valle Enmedio (91 898 31 76, www.vallenmedio.com, closed Mon-Thur Oct-June, call for rates), 11km (seven miles) along the track to Peguerinos, is an isolated, idyllic and well-equipped campsite with wooden bungalows, set in a forest. In Peguerinos itself, **La Flor** (C/Espinar 7, 91 898 30 40) is a basic but friendly *pensión* with a small restaurant downstairs. For food, another good bet is the no-frills **Alto del León** (91 854 12 27, mains €13), on the crest of the pass.

Choices are much greater in Cercedilla. **Casa Gómez** (C/Emilio Serrano 40, 91 852 01 46, mains €10-€16, set lunch €12, 1-4.30pm Tue-Sun), opposite the railway station, specialises in wild mushrooms and game in season.

As you come out of the station, on the right is **Hostal Longinos – El Aribel** (C/Emilio Serrano 41, 91 852 15 11, www.hostalaribel.com, doubles €50). Book ahead in summer and at weekends.

In Navacerrada, one of the better hotels is the **Hotel Nava Real** (C/Huertas 1, 91 853 10 00,

Sierra de Guadarrama.

www.hotelnavareal.com, doubles €70, mains €12), which also has a more imaginative restaurant than most. **Restaurante Casa Paco** (Plaza Doctor Gereda 2, 91 856 05 62, mains €12, closed Wed) has tables outside overlooking the town square.

Getting there

By bus
The Larrea (902 22 00 52, www.autobuses larrea.com) bus 684 from Moncloa to Cercedilla

Take a Hike

As Madrid becomes more and more crowded, so its inhabitants have come to rely on escapes to the Guadarrama and Gredos mountain ranges to maintain their sanity. The mountains are within easy reach: whether by car, bus, or train, one can soon be up in alpine landscapes, 1,000 metres above sea level. Most villages in the sierras now have some kind of information centre, and simple illustrated guides to a varied range of walks (often signposted) are available. The town hall is also a good place to look for information. In summer it is advisable to take plenty of water and clothes offering protection from the sun, and in winter, waterproof, warm gear. Only experienced walkers should try the higher walks in winter. Also, weather in the mountains is notoriously changeable: check forecasts before you go. Buying food and water in Madrid before setting off is also a good idea.

Skiing around the Madrid region is a hit-or-miss affair. Of the resorts near Madrid, **Valdesquí** (902 88 64 46, www. valdesqui.es) usually has the best (and most) snow. La Pinilla (902 87 90 70, www.lapinilla.es) is directly north of Madrid near Riaza; the others are in the central Guadarrama. The only one with any accommodation is the **Puerto de Navacerrada** (902 88 23 28, www.puerto navacerrada.com). All-in package trips to these resorts can be booked at any travel agency in Madrid. These ski stations offer limited skiing only and are of little interest to intermediate or advanced skiers, but are great for day trips out of Madrid. Recorded information (in Spanish only) on snow conditions at ski resorts and out-of-season activities can be found on the Atudem phoneline (91 359 15 57, www.esquiespana.org).

leaves every 30mins (journey time 50mins-1hr) from 6.40am-11.30pm Mon-Fri, hourly 6.30am-11.45pm Sat, Sun. Last return is at 10.20pm. The Larrea bus 691 runs from Madrid to Navacerrada every 30 mins, from 7am-10.40pm Mon-Fri, and hourly from 8am-10.30pm Sat, Sun. Last return is at 10.30pm.

By train
For Cercedilla, take the train from Chamartín to Segovia. Trains run seven times a day from 8am-8pm Mon-Fri, and five times a day from 10am-6pm Sat, Sun; the last train back from Cercedilla is at about 9.35pm Mon-Fri and 7.30pm Sat, Sun.

Tourist information

Centro de Interpretación Turística
Plaza del Ayuntamiento, Guadarrama (91 849 47 03). **Open** 9am-8pm Mon-Fri; 10am-2pm, 4-8pm Sat; 10am-2pm Sun.

Oficina Municipal de Turismo Navacerrada
C/Prado Jerez 20 (91 856 03 08). **Open** *16 Sept-30 June* 10am-2pm, 5-8pm Fri, Sat; 10am-2pm Sun. 1 July-15 Sept 10am-2pm, 6-9pm Tue-Sat; 10am-2pm Sun.

VALLE DE LOZOYA

The wide, flat Valle de Lozoya runs northeast from below the pass of Puerto de los Cotos (1,830 metres/6,006 feet), to the main A-1 Burgos road. There is little to detain you in the village of **Rascafría** at the western end of the valley. For the most part, it has been drearily overdeveloped, with one exception – the stunning **Monasterio de Santa María del Paular** (91 869 14 25, tours noon, 1pm & 5pm Mon-Wed, Fri & Sat; noon, 1pm Thur; 1pm, 5pm & 6pm Sun, admission free) nearby. This Benedictine monastery, a short way south of the village, was founded in 1390 but was still being added to 500 years later. It is still partly occupied by monks, even though most of it is now an unobtrusive Sheraton hotel, and it remains a wonderful sight with its stunning backdrop of snow-capped peaks.

One of the many rewarding walks around here is along the GR-10 pathway from the monastery up to the Puerto de los Cotos, which winds its way through pine forests and a picturesque roe deer habitat. Heading in the other direction, the path runs two kilometres to some natural swimming pools at Las Presillas. In summer there is a small kiosk there, selling drinks. From the town itself, it's also possible to walk across the mountains to the palace of La Granja (*see below*).

La Granja.

Where to stay & eat

Casa Briscas (Plaza España 13, 91 869 12 26, www.casabriscas.com, mains €10.50, set lunch €10, closed Thur) is the best eating option in Rascafría's main square, and has a lively terrace arca. The 44-room **Santa María del Paular** (91 869 10 11, www.sheratonelpaular.com, doubles €109-€200, mains €20, closed Jan) occupies the former monastery cloister and is delightfully peaceful. **Los Calizos** (Carretera Miraflores-Rascafría km 30.5, 91 869 11 12, www.loscalizos.com, doubles €123 incl breakfast & dinner, mains €20) is a stone house by the Lozoya River, a short distance outside town.

Getting there

By bus

To or from Rascafría, take Continental Auto (902 33 04 00, www.continental-auto.es) bus 194, which leaves Madrid from Plaza Castilla interchange at 10am, 2pm, 6pm Mon-Fri; 8pm, 6pm Sat; 8pm, 3pm Sun. Last bus back is at 5pm Mon-Fri; 8.30pm Sat; 6.30pm Sun.

By train

For Puerto de los Cotos, take the hourly C-8b from Chamartín in Madrid to Cercedilla, then line C-9 to Cotos. There are five trains to Cotos daily (9.35am, 11.35am, 1.35pm, 3.35pm, 5.35pm). Last return is 6.43pm.

LA GRANJA

Another palace to start life as a hunting lodge, later to be converted by the Bourbons, is La Granja, about 11km (seven miles) from Segovia back towards Madrid on the N-101. It was built on the site of a former shrine, San Ildcfonso, by Philip V, homesick for his youth in Versailles. His wife Isabel Farnese also added some distinctive touches, not least of which are the famous fountains. The result is perhaps the loveliest of all the Bourbon palaces.

Work on the structure was carried out in record time between 1721 and 1723 by Teodoro Ardamaus, and on the extensive gardens over a longer period under thc main supervision of René Carlier. Amid the formal hedgerows, lawns and rows of trees you'll find voluptuous statues, limpid pools and the fountains, some of which spring to life three times a week in the summer and then all of which are turned on for one memorable evening each year, 25 August. Water comes from an artificial lake called El Mar, set in a woodland at the end of the estate and backed by the dramatic sheer wall of the Peñalara, the highest peak in the Guadarrama.

The palace itself, restored after a devastating fire in 1918, is an opulent maze of elegant salons and chambers that abound in classical frescoes, dazzling cut-glass chandeliers (made in the palace's own glass factory, which still functions today) and priceless *objets d'art*. The tapestry selection, though representing only a part of the Spanish and Flemish royal collection, is among the finest you'll see anywhere. Unfortunately visits are only via guided tours of up to 45 people at a time.

The charming village of **San Ildefonso** has long been a favourite resort for escaping the oppressive Madrid summer heat; if you have your own transport it offers a relaxing alternative to staying in Segovia. Among its imposing private houses is the **Casa de Infantes**, built by Carlos III for his sons Gabriel and Antonio.

Palacio Real de La Granja de San Ildefonso

921 47 00 19, www.patrimonionacional.es. **Open** *Oct-Mar* 10am-1.30pm, 3-5pm Tue-Sat; 10am-2pm Sun. *Apr-Sept* 10am-6pm Tue-Sun. Fountains operate Apr-Aug at 5.30pm Wed, Sat & Sun. **Admission** *Palace* €4.50; €5 guided tour; €2.50 reductions. Wed free EU citizens. *Gardens* free. *Fountains* €3.40; €1.70 reductions. **No credit cards**.

Where to stay & eat

It's essential to reserve ahead at the wildly popular **Casa Zaca** (C/Embajadores 6, 921 47 00 87, www.casazaca.com, closed dinner & Mon, mains €10); it offers home-style cuisine, so instead of the standard roast lamb or *cochinillo* there are gutsy casseroles and braised ox tongue. Alternatively try the tapas, in front of a roaring fire, at the colourful **La Fundición**

(Plaza de la Calandria 1, 921 47 00 46, closed lunch Tue-Fri, dinner Sun & all Mon in Jun-Sept; closed lunch Fri, dinner Sun & all Mon-Thur in Oct-May). **Hotel Roma** (C/Guardas 2, 921 47 07 52, www.hotelroma.org, doubles €65-€70, restaurant closed Tue, mains €13, closed Nov) is comfortable enough.

Getting there

By bus

There are around eight daily buses run by La Sepulvedana (91 530 48 00, 902 22 22 82, www.lasepulvedana.es) from the Príncipe Pío interchange in Madrid to Segovia (journey time 1hr15mins). From Segovia there are frequent connecting buses to La Granja (journey time 20mins).

RIOFRIO

After the death of Philip V, Isabel Farnese could not bear to stay on at La Granja with her stepson Fernando VI, and so had another palace built at Riofrío. She was to survive Fernando as well, however, and Riofrío was never completely finished. Later Alfonso XII came here to mourn the death of his new bride, Mercedes, and the whole palace still has a melancholy air, despite the warm pinks and greens of its exterior.

It was built in the middle of the best deer-hunting country near Madrid, and later sovereigns also came to this beautiful estate to blast away to their hearts' content. With this in mind, half the palace has been turned into

Monastery of El Parral.

a hunting museum – a mandatory and overlong part of the guided tour. Unless row after row of antlers and stuffed animals really rock your boat, it is probably best admired from outside, particularly with a picnic.

Palacio de Riofrío
921 47 00 19. **Open** *Oct-Mar* 10am-1.30pm, 3-5pm Tue-Sat; 10am-2pm Sun. *Apr-Sept* 10am-6pm Tue-Sun. **Admission** €4; €2.30 reductions. Wed free for EU citizens. **No credit cards**.

Getting there

By train
Segovia trains (*see belows*) stop at La Losa-Navas de Riofrío, about 2km (1.25 miles) from Riofrío.

SEGOVIA

Segovia combines beautiful architecture with visual warmth in a region more associated with austerity. In contrast with the traditional grey chill of Castile it glows, radiant and mellow. Make the approach by road across vast plains and it appears as if by witchcraft, rising on a burnished hillock like an acropolis or ship in full sail. The scene is dominated by the **Alcázar** fortress, with its sharply angled ramparts, spiky towers and high gables; a fantastical fairytale vision.

Impregnably poised on the edge of a hair-raising abyss into which a negligent nurse once accidentally dropped a 14th-century heir to the throne and then flung herself after him to avoid punishment, it was originally built as a modest stone fort 200 years earlier, and underwent radical changes over the centuries. Most of the world-famous fairy-castle architecture seen today is a brilliant work of restoration carried out after a disastrous fire in 1862. Though owned by the army, the bastion's purpose is now purely commercial and its chambers are open daily for the public to inspect the weapons, armour, tapestries and artworks on display.

Close by is the huge, airy and very light Gothic **Cathedral de Segovia** (Plaza Mayor, 921 46 22 05, admission €3). The current structure was built to replace a predecessor destroyed in a 1521 revolt. Inside there's a tiny museum that holds an interesting collection of tapestries, paintings and a wonderful 16th-century grandfather clock.

Very different, but just as extraordinary as the Alcázar, is the 728-metre-long (2,426-foot) Roman **aqueduct**, made of gleaming Guadarrama granite in rough-hewn blocks that mesh perfectly without mortar, though it no longer brings water from the Riofrío as it first did over 2,000 years ago. The **Plaza**

del Azoguejo below, where markets are now held, was a rendezvous for thieves and vagabonds in Cervantes' day. Steps rise up the wall at the place where the aqueduct merges into the hill, or you can spiral up the streets channelling traffic up and down. A warren of intricate lanes criss-crosses the old town like a demented spider's web, weaving you past squares, gardens, mansions, palaces and museums. The town is never short of tourists but is still resolutely traditional: in the Plaza Mayor the atmosphere of the past blends with real-life bustle and you can still find plenty of bars and cafés filled only with locals.

Of its dozen or so churches and convents, all built between the 12th and 16th centuries, **San Esteban**, noted for its striking bell tower, and **San Millán**, with its Moorish-influenced decor and elaborately carved wooden ceiling, stand out. Among its secular buildings the **Casa de los Picos**, with waffle-iron studs on its façade, can be found in the shopping streets downhill from the cathedral. Also not to be missed is the **Monastery of El Parral**, founded by Henry VI and now a national monument. One of the best views is from 13th-century **Iglesia de Vera Cruz** built by the Knights Templars with spoils from the Crusades.

Alcázar de Segovia
Plaza de la Reina Victoria Eugenia (921 46 07 59). **Open** *Oct-Mar* 10am-6pm daily. *Apr-Sept* 10am-7pm daily. **Admission** €4; €3 reductions. **No credit cards**.

Where to stay & eat

The **Casa Duque** (C/Cervantes 12, 921 46 24 87, www.restauranteduque.es, mains €17) is a long standing favourite with colourfully decorated dining rooms on several floors serving excellent Castilian fare. **Restaurante José María** (C/Cronista Lecea 11, 921 46 11 11, mains €14-€22) is a traditionally styled *mesón* serving first-rate *cochinillo* (suckling pig) and probably the best lamb in town. It also has a good tapas bar. **Cuevas de San Esteban** (C/Valdelaguila 15, 921 46 09 82, www.la cuevadesanesteban.com, mains €10-€15) is another place to avoid the tourist-trap market with reasonably priced Castilian food. For something different, **Narizotas** (Plaza Medina del Campo 1, 921 46 26 79, www.narizotas.net, closed dinner Sun, mains €15, set menu €13.90) has a selection of risottos and salads, as well as the usual parade of roast meats.

Los Linajes (C/Dr Velasco 9, 921 46 04 75, www.hotelloslinajes.com, doubles €98-€118) is an atmospheric 13th-century palace close to San Esteban church with beams, antiques and a lush patio, while the **Acueducto** (C/Padre

Claret 10, 921 42 48 00, www.hotelacueducto.
com, doubles €110) is a comfortable,
established hotel where some of the rooms
overlook the Roman aqueduct. Alternatively,
try **Las Sirenas** (C/Juan Bravo 30, 921 46 26
63, www.hotelsirenas.com, doubles €66-€99),
a homely hotel in the old town near San Martín
church. **Hostal Taray** (Plaza San Facundo 1,
921 46 30 41, www.hostaltaray.com, doubles
€37) is useful for those on a budget, as is the
very central **El Hidalgo** (C/José Canalejas
5, 921 46 35 29, www.el-hidalgo.com,
doubles €45-€50).

Getting there

By bus

There are around eight daily buses run by
La Sepulvedana (91 530 48 00, 902 22 22 82,
www.lasepulvedana.es) from the Príncipe Pío
interchange in Madrid to Segovia (journey
time 1hr 15mins).

By train

There are seven Cercanías trains Mon-Fri and
five trains Sat, Sun from Atocha or Chamartín
to Segovia, but it's a slow journey (2hrs 30mins).
Alternatively, you can catch the Ave fast train
connecting Madrid and Valladolid, which stops
at Segovia on the way. There are seven daily
trains and the journey is quicker (30mins)
but more expensive.

Tourist information

Oficina de Turismo

*Plaza Mayor 10 (921 46 03 34, www.turismo
castillayleon.com).* **Open** *July, Aug* 9am-8pm
Mon-Thur, Sun; 9am-9pm Fri, Sat. *Sept-June*
9am-2pm, 5-8pm daily.

MANZANARES EL REAL & LA PEDRIZA

La Pedriza is a rocky crag crisscrossed with
paths. Birthplace of the Manzanares river, it is
home to the Sierra's biggest colony of griffon
vultures, protected in the Parque Regional de
la Cuenca Alta del Manzanares. The area fills
up on Sundays, but don't be fooled – many
experienced climbers still get lost in La Pedriza,
and fatalities have been known. The starting
point for a hike is the town of **Manzanares
el Real**, dominated by the almost cartoonish
vision of a perfect 'Spanish' castle, the 15th-
century **Castillo de Manzanares el Real**,
once the stronghold of the Mendozas, one of
the most powerful aristocratic clans of medieval
Castile. Much of its interior is the product of
recent restoration work, but the castle retains
a fascinating mix of late Gothic and Mudéjar

features, especially in the courtyard and
the beautiful upper gallery, which has a
spectacular view over the valley.

Castillo de Manzanares el Real

91 852 86 85. **Open** 10am-4pm Tue-Fri; 10am-
6pm Sat, Sun. **Admission** €3; €1.50 reductions.
No credit cards.

Where to stay & eat

A kilometre or so out of town on the path
to El Yelmo is the small but well-appointed
Hostal El Tranco (C/Tranco 4, 91 853 04
23, doubles €50-€55, mains €12). Nearby are
a couple of lively bars with terraces. Another
option is **La Fresneda** campsite on the
Carretera M-608 in Soto el Real (www.
campinglafresnada.com, Sept-June open
weekends only, rates €4.50 per person,
including tent and car; €12 per pitch).

Getting there

By bus

Bus 724 from the Plaza de Castilla interchange,
operated by Herederos de J Colmenarejo (91 845
00 51, www.hjcolmenarejo.com) runs every 30
mins from 7am-11.30pm Mon-Fri, 8am-11.30pm
Sat, Sun. The last return is at 10.25pm.

SIERRA NORTE

In contrast to the majestic alpine landscapes
of the Guadarrama, this tract of rolling hills
some 60km (37 miles) north-east of Madrid
toward Guadalajara at first seems decidedly
the poorer relative. Isolated until the 1980s, the
Sierra Norte suffered from depopulation, with
many villages being abandoned, until it was
'discovered' by *madrileños* looking for a more
authentic, and cheaper, weekend retreat. The
Sierra Norte is also host to the region's finest
deciduous forests. Even at the height of
summer the area is never crowded.

The gateway to the area is **Buitrago de
Lozoya**, just off the A-1. What remains of its
walled medieval centre shows traces of Arab
times, and its cool and dignified Gothic 15th-
century **Iglesia de Santa María**, recently
restored after fire swept through it in 1936, is
also worth a visit. The real charm of Buitrago,
however, is the quirky little **Museo Picasso**
in the basement of its town hall (Plaza Picasso
1, 91 868 00 04, www.sierranorte.com/buitrago,
admission free), consisting of some 60 works,
especially centred on bullfighting themes, and
mostly from his later years. Picasso donated the
pictures to his hairdresser and friend Eugenio
Arias, a native of the town who met Picasso in
Toulouse, where they were both living in exile.

Segovia

Convento de las Carmelitas Descalzas
Iglesia de Vera Cruz
Monasterio de El Parral
Alameda del Parral
Casa de la Moneda
C/ARRAL
C/LOS MOLINOS
Monasterio de Santa Cruz la Real
C/SAN MARCOS
C/MARQUES DE VILLENA
COMENDA
Río Eresma
PASEO DE LA ALAMEDA DEL PARRAL
PASEO DE SANTO DOMINGO DE GUZMÁN
Hospital de la Misericordia
C/PUERTA DE SANTIAGO
C/DOCTOR VELASCO
C/CARDENAL ZÚÑIGA
Jardín de Mauricio Fromkes
PLAZA DE REINA VICTORIA EUGENIA
C/VELARDE
Casa Museo de Antonio Machado
Iglesia de San Esteban
Iglesia de San Quirce
Iglesia de San Nicolás
PASEO DEL OBISPO
Alcázar
RONDA DON JUAN II
C/DAOIZ
Museo del Palacio Episcopal
C/SAN NICOLÁS
CUESTA DE SAN BARTOLOMÉ
C/ZULOAGA
San Juan de los Caballeros
Iglesia de San Andrés
Ayuntamiento
Torre de Hércules
Iglesia de la Trinidad
C/REFITOLERÍA
PLAZUELA DE COLMENARES
Museo de Segovia
C/ARQUITECTO ARIO
PLAZA MAYOR
Iglesia de San Miguel
C/SAN AGUSTÍN
C/SAN FACUNDO
C/SOCORRO
Cathedral
C/ISABEL LA CATÓLICA
C/MARQUÉS DEL ARCO
Torreón de los Arias Dávila
Casa del Sol
C/BERMUDO
C/JUAN BRAVO
Museo de Esteban Vicente
Iglesia de San Sebastián
Casa de las Cadenas
CUESTA DE LOS HOYOS
C/POZO DE LA NIEVE
Convento del Corpus Christi
C/JOSE CANALEJAS
El Torreón de Lozoya
C/LOS BASOS
Río Clamores
C/HIPOLITO MORENO
C/SAN VALENTÍN
PASEO DE LOS TILOS
Iglesia de San Martín
C/COLÓN
C/OBISPO GANDÁSEGUI
Casa de los Picos
VÍA DE ROMA
Iglesia de San Justo
Palacio del Conde Alpuente
C/CERVANTES
PLAZA DEL AZOGUEJO
Aqueduct
PLAZA DE SAN JUSTO
C/OCHOA ONDÁTEGUI
C/SAN MILLÁN
C/CARMEN
PLAZA DE DÍAZ SANZ
C/MON ALMIRA
PASEO DE EZEQUIEL GONZÁLEZ
C/SANTO DOMINGO DE SILOS
Iglesia de San Millán
C/LAS CARRETAS
Iglesia de San Clemente
C/AVENIDA DE FERNÁNDEZ LADREDA
C/SAN FRANCISCO
C/INDEPENDENCIA
Academia de Artillería
To Train Station
C/SAN ROQUE
C/SOLEDAD
Bus Station
Jardincillos de San Roque
C/LOS COCHES
C/ROBLE
C/SAN ANTÓNTICO
Jardín Botánico
CARRETERA DE ÁVILA
CARRETERA DE MADRONA
C/SANTO TOMÁS

0   400 m
0   400 yds
© Copyright Time Out Group 2010

Castillo de Manzanares el Real.

Spires and Tyres

Religious recycling.

You may think you're doing your bit for the environment with that weekly trip to the recycling bins, but the average person's attempts at recycling pale into insignificance compared to the efforts of Justo Gallego, a pensioner in the small town of Mejorada del Campo, to the east of Madrid.

Back in the early 1960s, Justo took it upon himself to start building a cathedral, using stuff other people had thrown away. Neither builder, architect nor engineer, he was a farmer before entering the Convento de Santa María de Huerta, a Trappist monastery in Soria, northern Spain. He stayed there for seven years until he caught TB and the other monks politely if selfishly asked him to leave.

He was at something of a loose end after that, until 12 October 1961 – the feast day of Our Lady of the Pillar – when it suddenly came to him that he had been put on this earth to construct a cathedral in his home town. Justo flogged his belongings and started right away, on a patch of land he had inherited from his parents. Unsurprisingly, the money raised did not go very far, and soon he was using whatever he could scavenge. More than 40 years later, he is still at it. Local firms sometimes donate supplies they no longer need, but otherwise he has recycled the most unlikely of materials, helped along by occasional contributions.

It's a curious sight, but the structure does somehow resemble a cathedral, and mass has even been held there. It is, however, a long way from completion. Now in his 70s, Justo is desperate for more funds and materials to complete his mission while he is still able to do so. Local builders and architects are reluctant to take the project on because it never had planning permission – or, indeed, any kind of official authorisation. In fact, Justo himself readily admits he never drew up any sort of plans and there is no guarantee it won't fall down at any minute.

The structure could be described as neo-Romanesque, and is 40 metres (131 feet) high with 12 towers. It has a large nave, partly covered by a dome with a diameter of almost 12 metres (39 feet). There is also a crypt, cloisters, a library and various other as yet unspecified spaces. Columns are made from oil drums, arches constructed from piles of old tyres and towers built with bits of bricks and piping. Bicycle wheels have been transformed into pulleys to get materials up the structure. The main entrance is approached by mosaic steps and spiral staircases link different levels. The structure has become a symbol of the town and has attracted media attention from all over the world. If and when it will ever be completed, though, only God knows.

Catedral de Nuestra Senora del Pilar
C/Antoni Gaudí, Mejorada del Campo.
By bus *from Conde de Casal every 30mins weekdays, every 90mins Sat, Sun.*
By car *A-3, then M-203 (21km).*

For 26 years Arias cut Picasso's hair in return for his paintings and sketches, and on his return to Spain donated them to the town.

Among the first places of interest after Buitrago is **Montejo de la Sierra**, 16km (10 miles) to the north-east, and a good central point for excursions on foot. It has an interesting Renaissance church, but the jewel in its crown is a magnificent beech forest, 8km (5 miles) away at **El Chaparral**. It can be visited with guided tours, run from the **Centro de Recursos de Alta Montaña** information centre (C/Real 64, 91 869 70 58). It's a good idea to book places well ahead, especially from October to December. This is also popular mountain biking country, and the same centre has information on hiking routes.

An easy-to-follow bike route from Montejo, taking about three and a half hours, but which can also be walked in about twice the time, is along a dirt track that cuts off the road to La Hiruela uphill towards the signposted Puerto de Cardoso and Cardoso de la Sierra, in the province of Guadalajara, before turning back to descend again to Montejo. On the way there are inspiring views north to the Ayllón mountains, and the 2,129-metre (6,985-foot) Peña Cebollera. Further south, at the bottom of a magnificent valley in the very heart of the Sierra Norte, lies **Puebla de la Sierra**. With a population of less than 100, this mountain hamlet has been almost entirely restored, and probably looks better now than it ever has. There are many houses to rent at weekends, and it makes an ideal base for walks to the surrounding reservoirs. Information on walks is available at the Parador de la Puebla – not an official parador – in the centre of the village.

About 25km (16 miles) south-west of Puebla (as the crow flies, not as the road winds) is **El Berrueco**, with a 13th-century church and the huge El Atazar reservoir. **El Atazar** village is the starting point for more walks, and a range of water sports are yours for the asking at the reservoir. The picturesque villages of **Patones de Arriba** and **Patones de Abajo** sit on the southern edge of the Sierra, and are reached via the Torrelaguna road off the A-1 from Madrid. The former is a cluster of slate houses and narrow, cobbled streets, reached by a steep, twisting road, though most live in the latter. A restoration project in recent years has been a mixed blessing, saving many of the villages' ancient houses from decay, but attracting rich second-homers from the city. Patones (as they are collectively known) is thought to have once been a peculiar enclave within Spain, a diminutive Visigothic kingdom which held its independence until the 18th century. A road north-east from Patones leads 7km (4.5 miles) to the vast **Cueva del Reguerillo**, with prehistoric cave paintings around its underground lakes. The cave is unmarked, so be sure to ask directions before setting off, and a torch is helpful when you get there.

Where to stay & eat

Buitrago has the **Hostal Madrid-Paris** (Avda Madrid 23, 91 868 11 26, http://madridparis.com, doubles €45, restaurant closed Sat & dinner Sun, set meal €9-€19), an old stone house with 25 bargain rooms and a great-value restaurant. For old-fashioned food in surroundings to match, try **Asador Jubel** (C/Real 33, 91 868 03 09, mains €10.50). **Mesón del Hayedo** (C/Turco, 91 869 70 23, www.mesonelhayedo.es, rates €40, restaurant closed dinner Mon-Thur, Sun & all Mon, mains €15-€20) is small, with a crowded and lively restaurant, not always open to non-guests. **Taberna de Teo** (Plaza de la Constitución 10, 91 868 05 12, closed lunch Tue, dinner Sun, & all Wed) is a beautifully restored wine bar with excellent tapas.

In Puebla de la Sierra, the **Parador de la Puebla** (Plaza Carlos Ruiz 2, 91 869 72 56, rates €48-€54 incl breakfast, closed Tue) only has five rooms, so make sure that you book well in advance. However, staff will recommend other houses in the village that let rooms if you're out of luck. In upmarket Patones the restored five-room country house **Hotel del Tiempo Perdido** (Travesia del Ayuntamiento 7, 91 843 21 52, www.eltiempoperdido.com, weekends only, closed 2wks Aug & 2wks Dec,

doubles €100-€120) is as good as it gets. And for food, you can't beat the old-world charm of **El Rey de Patones** (C/Asas 13, 91 843 20 37, www.reydepatones.com, closed dinner Mon, Thur, Sun, all Tue, Wed & Aug, mains €13).

Getting there

By bus
Continental Atuo (902 33 04 00, www.continental-auto.es) bus 103 runs from Plaza de Castilla to Buitrago (9am or 5pm daily). Last bus from Buitrago back to Madrid is at 6.30pm Mon-Sat, 11pm Sun. Many local microbus services run from Buitrago.

Tourist information

Centro de Turismo de la Sierra Norte
Avda del Cabrera 36, La Cabrera (91 868 86 98, www.sierranorte.com). **Open** 9am-6pm daily. The impressive tourist office in La Cabrera, 18km (11 miles) south of Buitrago covers tourist information for the whole sierra and features its own botanical gardens.

South & East

ALCALA DE HENARES & AROUND

After the horrific terrorist attacks of March 2004, Alcalá de Henares was descended upon by the world's camera crews and catapulted to fame for all the wrong reasons. Centuries before, all eyes were on Alcalá as Spain's centre of learning and culture, with a superb university, founded in 1498, and later as the birthplace of Cervantes. As far back as Roman times, Complutum, as it was known then, was a large and important city.

The university moved to Madrid in the 19th century, but there is still a strong sense of the city's educational history here today. The streets in the old quarter are lined with **Colegios Mayores** – student halls of residence in the 16th and 17th centuries, now converted into hotels and restaurants. One of the most impressive is the **Colegio de San Ildefonso**, famous for its stunning Plateresque façade and its three-tiered patio, which is still the setting for the solemn opening of university terms and for the presentation of the Cervantes Prize for Literature.

The main square, named after the city's most famous literary son, is a great spot to relax over a coffee and admire the buildings that line it, such as the **Casa Consistorial** (town hall) and the **Capilla de Oidor**, a 15th-century chapel now used for exhibitions. If you want to know more about the creator of Don Quixote, head

ESCAPES & EXCURSIONS

to the author's birthplace, now the **Museo Casa Cervantes** (C/Mayor 48, 91 889 96 54, www.museo-casa-natal-cervantes.org, closed Mon, admission free). On the city's west side are the **Catedral Magistral** and the **Museo de Esculturas al Aire Libre**, an open-air museum with 50 or so sculptures.

One of the most entertaining ways to get to Alcalá is via the Tren de Cervantes (which runs weekends in autumn and spring, leaving Atocha station in Madrid at 11am, and returning at 7pm). Guides in Golden Age costume ply passengers with information about the city, and, on arrival, give them a tour of the town.

From Alcalá you can take a short excursion 17 kilometres (9.5 miles) down the M-204, to **Nuevo Baztán**. A peaceful little place, it was founded by a banker in the early 18th century and the entire village designed by renowned architect José de Churriguera, giving it a wonderfully harmonious feel.

Where to eat

Alcalá's best-known restaurant is the **Hostería del Estudiante** (C/Colegios 3, 91 888 03 30, www.parador.es, closed Aug, mains €20-€30, set menu €40), which occupies a stunning 16th-century *colegio* and specialises in hearty Castilian food – roast lamb and suckling pig, garlic soup and the Alcalá dessert speciality, *costrada*, which is something like a sweet millefeuille. At the back of the *hostería* and across a garden is the **Cafeteria El Restaurado** (Plaza San Diego s/n, 91 885 41 40, closed dinner, all Sat, Sun and Aug, set menu €7.20). It's handy and popular with students for a quick and cheap lunch. **Mesón Don José** (C/Santiago 4, 91 881 86 17, closed Mon dinner & 3wks Aug, mains €10, set lunch €10) is cheap and quite atmospheric. For good tapas washed down with draught *vermut*, check out the attractive, tiled bar **Cervecería El Hidalgo** (C/El Bedel 3, mobile 627 215 706, closed Wed).

In Nuevo Baztán, the **Mesón El Conde** (Plaza la Iglesia 5, 91 873 53 27, closed 2wks Sept, mains €10, set lunch €9) is a reasonably priced, traditional place with balconies over the square and tables outside in summer.

Getting there

By bus

Continental Auto (902 33 04 00, www. continental-auto.es/www.alsa.es) bus 223 leaves the Avda de América interchange every 5-10mins from 6.30am-11pm Mon-Fri, and every 15 mins from 7am-11pm Sat & Sun. Journey time approx 35 mins.

By car

On the A-2 it's approximately a 25min drive (31km/19miles).

By train

Cercanías C-1, C-2 and C-7 depart from Madrid's Chamartín station approx every 10mins (15-20mins weekends), from 5.20am-11.50pm daily. Journey time 35mins. From the station it's a 10min walk to the centre (go straight down Paseo de la Estación).

Tourist information

Oficinas de Turismo

Callejón Santa María 1, Plaza de Cervantes (91 889 26 94, www.turismo alcala.com). **Open** *Oct-May* 10am-2pm, 4-6.30pm daily. *June, Sept* 10am-2pm, 5-7.30pm daily. *July, Aug* 10am-2pm, 5-7.30pm Tue-Sun. *Plaza de los Santos Niños s/n (91 881 06 34).* **Open** *Oct-May* 10am-2pm, 4-6.30pm daily. *June, Sept* 10am-2pm, 5-7.30pm daily. *July, Aug* 10am- 2pm, 5-7.30pm Mon, Wed-Sun.

CHINCHON & AROUND

Out of season Chinchón is a sleepy little town, famous for its *anís* liqueur and pretty, arcaded Plaza Mayor, overlooked by wooden balconies all the way around, and occasionally used for bullfights. This is where you'll find the town hall, tourist office and, most importantly, plenty of balcony restaurants and bars, where the traditional lunch is lamb cooked in a wood-burning oven, washed down with red from the *cuevas* (cellars) and finished off with a glass of the famous local brew.

The neo-classical **Iglesia de la Asunción** overlooking the plaza houses Goya's depiction of the Assumption. Just next door is the **Teatro Lope de Vega**, where the playwright wrote *El Blasón de los Chavos de Villalba* and which now doubles as a cinema. Just outside the town is the 16th-century castle, built on the site of the original 12th-century fortress. Sadly, only the ground floor remains, and it's home to sheep and the local outdoor drinking scene.

Chinchón hosts an open-air folk festival in the plaza at the beginning of June, and during the fiestas in August the bulls run the Avda del Generalísimo (or C/Huertos as some residents prefer), and there are fireworks, a fairground and bands performing near the castle.

It's worth driving to **Colmenar de Oreja**, five kilometres (three miles) away on the M-311. A quiet, untouristy place, it has an unspoilt Plaza Mayor, again ringed with wooden galleries, though on a smaller scale than Chinchón's, and a handsome 13th-century church, the **Iglesia de Santa María**. The tower is by Juan de Herrera.

Garden Composition

The inspiration for Rodrigo's well-known concierto.

Inspired by Aranjuez's vast palace gardens, the *Concierto de Aranjuez*, composed in 1939 by Joaquín Rodrigo (1901-1999), is probably the best-known piece of Spanish music. Sneered at by classical snobs, it's nonetheless a 20th-century classic, covered by greats such as flamenco guitarist Paco de Lucia and, famously, Miles Davis, who used its 'Adagio' section as the cornerstone of his *Sketches of Spain* album. The *Concierto* has featured in commercials, World Championship-winning figure-skating routines, and even inspired Jack Black to start his 'School of Rock'.

Blinded after a diphtheria attack aged three, Rodrigo wanted the piece to depict the aural and olfactory pleasures he experienced in the Bourbon monarchs' summer retreat: 'the fragrance of magnolias, the singing of birds and the gushing of fountains'. Rodrigo drew on Spain's musical heritage – the formality of 17th- and 18th-century Baroque composers, as well as more passionate folk styles – to conjure up the magical flow of nature, as well as the splendour and darkness of the palace's history.

Unusual for pitting a solo guitar against a full orchestra, the *Concierto* comprises three movements. The first, 'Allegro con spirito', feels like an alfresco jaunt and is built on a series of switching elements – between solos and the orchestra, between the flamenco-tinged strumming of the guitar and the melody. The famous second movement, 'Adagio', is based on an Andalucían lament. Guitar and cor anglais swap the same mournful refrain back and forth, until it's taken up by the whole orchestra to deliver an aching climax. The third movement, 'Allegro gentile', reverts back to the opening jauntiness, a forthright mix of Baroque-like counterpoint and folk-dance melody.

'After listening to it for a couple of weeks I couldn't get it out of my mind,' said Miles Davis, in early 1959. He and collaborator Gil Evans set about reworking that haunting central 'Adagio' section for their third album together, *Sketches of Spain*. Rodrigo, reportedly, wasn't in the end all that impressed, but many other listeners were. In his autobiography, Davis recounts the story a woman had told him of a retired matador, now raising *toros* himself, who after hearing *Sketches of Spain* had got out of his chair, put on his old bullfighting gear, gone outside and fought and killed one of his bulls. 'He said that he had been so moved by the music that he just had to fight the bull,' Davis remembered. 'It was hard for me to believe the story, but she swore that it was true.'

The *Concierto* had its première in 1940 in Barcelona and brought Rodrigo worldwide fame. It is Aranjuez, though, that best commemorates the composer, with a statue off C/Infantas and, set into the pavement nearby, an inscription that includes musical notation from the *Concierto*. King Juan Carlos awarded Rodrigo the hereditary title of Marquis of the Gardens of Aranjuez in 1992. Rodrigo died in 1999 and was buried in Aranjuez's cemetery.

Where to stay & eat

The balcony restaurants lining the Plaza Mayor all offer similar Chinchón fare – garlic soup and roasted red peppers, roast lamb and suckling pig. **La Casa del Pregonero** (Plaza Mayor 4, 91 894 06 96, www.lacasadelpregonero.com, closed Tue, mains €15-€20), is slightly different – it uses local ingredients with some interesting twists, and has an attractive patio at the back. **Mesón Cuevas del Vino** (C/Benito Hortelano 13, 91 894 02 06, www.cuevasdelvino.com, closed Tue & 2wks Aug, mains €17-€26) is an atmospheric place, with an ancient oil press and some old carriages. For accommodation, try the delightful **Parador de Chinchón** (C/Los Huertos 1, 91 894 08 36, www.parador.es, rates €130-€160), in a 17th-century former Augustinian convent, or the slightly less luxurious, but still very comfortable **Hostal Chinchón** (C/Grande 16, 91 893 53 98, www.hostalchinchon.com, rate €48).

Getting there

By bus

Bus 337 operated by La Veloz (91 409 76 02) runs from Plaza Conde de Casal (Metro Conde de Casal, line 6). Buses leave every 30mins, 7am-11pm Mon-Fri; every hour, 8am-midnight Sat, and every 1hr 30mins, 9am-11pm Sun. The last return is at 10pm weekdays and Sun, at 11pm on Sat. Journey time approx 1hr.

ARANJUEZ

Aranjuez was the official spring residence of the Spanish monarchy and its hangers-on from the 17th to the 19th century. It was probably originally chosen for its setting and lush countryside – it is an oasis in the arid plains of central Spain, situated in a wide valley formed by the Jarama and Tajo (Tagus) rivers. The royals have long gone, but the Palacio Real is still the principal tourist attraction, along with the town's famous asparagus and strawberries.

Originally built as a hunting lodge for Charles I of Spain (Charles V of the Holy Roman Empire), the palace took its current shape under Philip II in the 1560s, and was extended in the 1770s by Charles III. It's a charming mix of Baroque and classical, and typical of the Bourbon palaces, with a sumptuous **throne room** and a cosy **ballroom**. It is the gardens, however, that provide the real attraction, particularly the 16th-century-designed **Jardín de la Isla** and **Jardín del Príncipe**. The gardens inspired Rodrigo's famous *Concierto de Aranjuez* (*see p287* **Garden Composition**) and the music continues today with a summer season of mostly open-air concerts and musical promenades, principally featuring Baroque music (*see p236* **Airs and Graces**). It is in the garden that you'll find the delightfully over-the-top **Casa del Labrador**, which was built for Charles IV. This early 19th-century folly – complete with painted ceilings, tapestry-lined walls, and porcelain and marble floors – is said to be one of the most important examples of neoclassicism in Europe.

In the town itself, **Museo del Toro** (Avenida Plaza de Toros s/n, 91 892 16 43) has recently been renovated. The museum aims to re-create the atmosphere of the bullfight and the traditions and entertainments of the court. If you're so inclined you can travel to Aranjuez on the Tren de la Fresa steam train, with hostesses in period costume plying you with cheery historical facts (*see p216*).

Palacio Real de Aranjuez

91 891 07 40, www.patrimonionacional.es. **Open** *Palaces* Oct-Mar 10am-5.15pm Tue-Sun. Apr-Sept 10am-6.15pm Tue-Sun. *Gardens* Jan-Feb, Nov-Dec 8am-6.30pm daily. First 2 wks Mar, Oct 8am-7pm daily. Last 2 wks Mar 8am-7.30pm daily. Apr-mid June, mid Aug-Sept 8am-8.30pm daily. Mid June-mid Aug 8am-9.30pm daily. **Admission** *Palace* €4.50; €2.50 reductions. *Guided tours* €5-€7; €2.50-€3 reductions. *Casa de Marinos* €3.40; €1.70 reductions. *Gardens* free. Free to EU citizens Wed. **Credit** MC, V.

Real Casa del Labrador

91 891 03 05, www.patrimonionacional.es. **Open** *Oct-Mar* 10am-5pm Tue-Sun. *Apr-Sept* 10am-6pm Tue-Sun. **Admission** (book in advance) €5; €2.50 reductions. **Credit** MC, V.

Where to stay & eat

Casa Pablo (C/Almíbar 42, 91 891 14 51, www. casapablo.net, closed Aug, mains €20) serves up superb seafood, while **La Posta** (C/Postas 23, 91 891 74 23, closed Sun & 2wks July, mains €11.50, set lunch €8.60-€14) is a good option.

To stay the night, the sleek **Príncipe de la Paz** (C/San Antonio 22, 91 809 92 22, www.nh-hotels.com, rates €77-€135) has stylish rooms overlooking the palace, though it is often closed to the public during the week, while the **Hostal Rusiñol** (C/San Antonio 76, 91 891 01 55, rates €34-€48) is a budget *pensión*.

Getting there

By bus

Bus 419 runs from Estación Sur every 25mins, 6.30am-11pm Mon-Fri; every 90mins, 7.30am-10pm Sat; every 3 hrs, 8am-10pm Sun. Last return 9.40pm Mon-Fri, 8.45pm Sat & Sun. Bus 423 from Estación Sur runs every 15-30mins, 6.30am-11.45pm Mon-Fri; every 30mins-1hr, 7am-midnight Sat, Sun. Last return 11.15pm Mon-Sat, 11pm Sun.

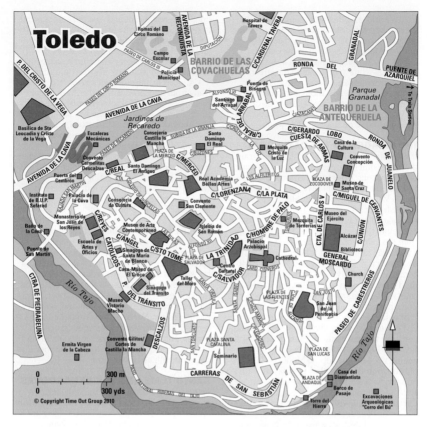

By train

Cercanías C-3 from Atocha, trains every 15-30mins 5.30am-11.30pm. Last return 11.30pm. The steam-powered 'Strawberry Train' (Tren de la Fresa) runs on summer weekends and holidays (*see p216*).

Tourist information

Oficina de Turismo

Plaza de San Antonio (91 891 04 27).
Open *Oct-Mar* 10am-6.30pm daily. *Apr-Sept* 10am-7.30pm daily.

TOLEDO

Once the imperial capital of Spain (1087-1561) and still the ecclesiastical heart of the country, 'Holy Toledo' represents two millennia of history and so holds incomparable cultural riches. Its impregnable hilltop position, tremendous fortified walls and the natural moat formed by the River Tagus have made this an important strategic stronghold for everyone from the Romans to the Visigoths, Muslims and Christians.

During the Middle Ages, Toledo was known as 'the city of three cultures' when the Jewish, Muslim and Christian population lived in a uniquely heterogenous society; many religious buildings still bear a strange palimpsest of crucifixes, stars of David and Arab script. Over time, these religions blurred into each other, creating the Mozárabes (Christians who lived under Muslim rule with a semi-Arabic liturgy), and later the Mudéjars, Muslims who did the reverse after the Christian conquest. This air of tolerance also attracted many world-class scholars, and Toledo became a famous centre of learning with prominent schools of science, mathematics, theology and mysticism.

Now enjoying a Golden Age of tourism, Toledo is by far the most popular daytrip from Madrid, and the steep, cobbled streets are mobbed with tour groups until the buses depart at sundown. The city is absolutely gridlocked for the duration of the Corpus Christi processions, during which the route is marked by white awnings over the streets and the cobblestones are strewn with rosemary, thyme and rose petals. Incense and chanting give the town an eerie medieval air, as do the period costumes and the priceless Flemish tapestries hung on the cathedral walls.

THE BISAGRA TO THE CATHEDRAL

If you come from Madrid by bus, car or train, the main point of entry to the old walled city is the imposing **Puerta de Bisagra**. This was built at the end of the reign of Emperor Carlos V to replace the original 11th-century Moorish gate and bears his imperial crest of the two-headed eagle, the symbol of Toledo. Before going into the old city proper, pick up a map from the tourist office opposite and walk back a little way down the main street to the **Museo de Tavera** (C/Cardenal Tavera 2, 925 22 46 77, admission €4.50). Housed in the 1541 **Hospital de Tavera**, with a fine chapel and Renaissance courtyards, it has works by Tintoretto, Zurbarán and the city's adopted son, El Greco. Part of it may only be visited by guided tour.

To avoid the steep climb from here to the city, take the free escalator (7am-10pm Mon-Fri, 8am-10pm weekends). Alternatively, behind the gate, the superb Mudéjar church of **Santiago del Arrabal** stands out, with an impressive brick tower and horseshoe arches. Part of it was once a mosque, but after the Christian reconquest it was rebuilt as a church. The maze of streets on either side as you head up C/Real del Arrabal was (as the name implies) the Arrabal – an area originally outside the Christian city. Off to the right on C/Cristo de la Luz are the gardens and stunning latticed brickwork of the **Mezquita del Cristo de la Luz** (925 25 41 91, admission €2.30). Built in 999, this mosque is the oldest surviving building in Toledo. According to legend, its name came from the fact that as Alfonso VI entered Toledo after the reconquest, his horse knelt at the door of the mosque, where, behind a stone in the archway, stood Christ, illuminated by the light of an oil lamp.

Dominating the skyline is the grim, black-turretted **Alcázar**, an enormous fortress built on the highest point of Toledo where Roman, Visigothic and Muslim forts stood before. Using the Alcázar as a landmark, head up C/Real de Arrabal and C/Cuesta de Armas to the social nerve centre of the city, **Plaza de Zocodover**. Originally known as the *suk-al-dawad,* or animal market, it became the site for *autos-da-fé* after the reconquest, but is now

lined with restaurant and café terraces serving everything from partridge to Big Macs. Nearby, the Renaissance **Hospital de Santa Cruz** (C/Miguel de Cervantes 3, 925 22 10 36, admission free) is now a museum housing tapestries, and works by El Greco and Ribera.

C/Comercio, the old town's main street, leads from the Zocodover to the Plaza Mayor, dominated by the **Palacio Arzobispal** (the Archbishop's Palace) and the jaw-dropping **Cathedral** (C/Cardenal Cisneros 1, Plaza del Ayuntamiento, 925 22 22 41, admission €7).

Spain's second-largest cathedral (after Seville) but for many the more beautiful of the two, Toledo's cathedral was completed in 1493 after 250 years of construction. A Christian church is said to have been founded here in the first century AD by Saint Eugene, the first Bishop of Toledo. Mainly Gothic in style with touches of Mudéjar, neo-classical and Baroque, the cathedral has 750 stained-glass windows, 70 cupolas and five naves, and is supported by 88 columns with 22 side chapels. You could easily spend a whole day exploring its dark interiors but some of its most extraordinary features include the sacristy's prestigious art collection (including El Greco's *The Disrobing of Christ*) the lavishly carved central choir and, behind the main altar, Narciso Tomé's unique 16th-century *Transparente,* a Baroque frenzy of bronze, stucco, coloured marble and painting lit by beams of light via a circular 'sunroof' dripping with alabaster putti.

SANTO TOME AND THE SYNAGOGUES

Just around the corner from the cathedral, the narrow alleys that lead to **Plaza del Salvador** are the most visited parts of Toledo. They are lined with shops selling Toledo's artisan products: Toledan steel has been famous for its strength since Roman times and C/Santo Tomé is packed with shops selling everything from flick-knives to sabres and plumed helmets. Equally ubiquitous is *damasquinado* – the Damascus style of decoration brought by the Moors, in which fine threads of gold and silver are hammered into blackened metal – which covers everything from chess sets to knife handles and jewellery. For the sweet-toothed, Toledan marzipan is sold in all shapes and flavours.

The first major building en route is the **Taller del Moro**, a Mudéjar workshop that used to house exhibitions of Toledo crafts; it remained closed for long-term renovations as we went to press. Behind the Taller, down C/San Juan de Diós, follow the crowds to the Mudéjar church of **Santo Tomé** (Plaza del Conde 4, 925 25 60 98, www.santotome.org, admission €2.30 reductions), which holds only one painting: El Greco's masterpiece, *El Entierro del Conde de Orgaz.*

Toledo. *See p289.*

Around the corner lies the **Casa-Museo de El Greco** (C/Samuel Leví s/n, 92 522 40 46, 925 22 44 05), although, despite the fanfare, it has never actually been confirmed that the artist lived here. The house – a reconstructed 16th-century Toledan home – is closed for restoration, but meanwhile its impressive collection of El Greco's later works is in the **Museo Victorio Macho** (Plaza Victorio Macho s/n, 925 28 42 25, www.realfundacion toledo.es, admission €3).

In medieval times this area was Toledo's *judería,* the Jewish quarter, once the world's most important centre of Jewish scholarship. Many of its finest works of Jewish-Mudéjar architecture were restored in 1992 as an act of atonement for the 500th anniversary of the expulsion of Jews from Spain. The most recent beneficiary of the makeover is the **Sinagoga del Tránsito**, a richly decorated multicultural blaze of Hebrew inscriptions, Gothic carvings and Moorish columns. It was built in 1357 and its immense size is a testimony to the huge Jewish population that once lived in Toledo. Today, there is not even the minimum number of adult males (ten) to hold a service. After 1492, the synagogue was used as a church, but it now pulls in large crowds with its fascinating museum of Sephardic Jewish culture, the **Museo Sefardí** (C/Samuel Leví s/n, 925 22 36 65, www.museo sefardi.net, admission

€3; €1.50 reductions) where displays include silver and crystal circumcision instruments and a 2,000-year-old ossuary.

The second of the surviving medieval synagogues, the **Sinagoga de Santa María la Blanca** (C/Reyes Católicos 4, 925 22 72 57, admission €2.30) lies at the opposite end of narrow C/Judería. Its small, plain interior, dominated by horseshoe arches, is extremely beautiful, in spite of the gaudy Baroque altar that was added later. Behind it, at C/Ángel 15, is a lovely bookshop dedicated to all matters Jewish, the Casa de Jacob.

The main street of the *judería* is now, ironically, called C/Reyes Católicos, and is topped by the very Catholic **Monasterio de San Juan de los Reyes** (C/Reyes Católicos 17, 925 22 38 02, www.sanjuandelosreyes.org, admission €2.30, €2 reductions). Built by Ferdinand and Isabella, it was originally intended to be the royal pantheon and has a dramatic Gothic cloister and an exterior garlanded with grim black chains; during the reconquest, these chains were supposedly taken from Christian prisoners and then used to hang Jewish dissidents.

Next to the monastery is a long stone balcony with impossibly romantic views over the River Tagus, the San Martín bridge and the typical *cigarrales* (Toledan country homes) on the hill opposite. For another great view, back over the whole city, head out of town over the River Tagus by the San Martín bridge, and turn right along the Carretera de Piedrabuena.

Where to eat

As Toledo province is the hunting centre of Spain, hearty game dishes dominate. Partridge (*perdiz*) is the most typical dish, and is usually served *a la toledana* – cooked slowly with onion, garlic and bayleaf – or else with *pochas* (succulent white beans) or pickled and eaten cold. Venison and wild boar stews are another speciality, along with roast suckling pig and *cuchifrito* (fricassee of lamb with egg and wine) and *tortilla a la magra* (cured ham omelette).

All these and more are on offer at traditional restaurants such as **La Abadía** (Plaza de San Nicolás 3, 925 25 07 46, www.abadiatoledo. com, mains €12.50-€16.50, set lunch €11) where a labyrinth of bars and dining rooms fill a 16th-century palace. If a whole pig seems a bit much, try their *pulgas* (bite-sized rolls). **Restaurante Aurelio** (C/Sinagoga 6, 925 22 41 05, www.casa-aurelio.com, closed Tue lunch, all Wed, mains €18) is in the heart of the Jewish quarter and filled with ancient farming tools. Part of a chain, it has three other branches in the city – check the website for details. After more than a century serving food, **Venta de Aires** (Paseo Circo Romano 35, 92 522 52 90, www.ventade aires.com, closed dinner Sun, mains €7-€17) must be doing something right. Particularly good at lunchtime when it's packed with locals feasting on excellent cod dishes and, naturally, partridge, is **La Perdiz** (C/Reyes Católicos 7, 92 525 29 19, closed dinner Sun, all Mon & 2wks Aug, mains €12-€24).

For a sophisticated twist on these local staples – quail fried with ginger and lemon or duck breasts with grapefruit sauce – **Los Cuatro Tiempos** (C/Sixto Ramón Parro 5, 925 22 37 82, www.restauranteloscuatrotiempos.com, closed Sun dinner, mains €18, set lunch €19.40) is located in a charming 16th-century National Heritage building. For a real treat, the famous **Adolfo Restaurante** (C/Granada 6, 925 25 24 72, www.adolforestaurante.com, closed dinner Sun, all Mon & 2wks July, mains €24.60) is worth a visit for its impeccable service, fantastic wine list and light cuisine such as tempura courgette flowers with saffron.

Shamelessly overpriced tourist feeding troughs prevail around the cathedral and Plaza de Zocodover but you can get a good, basic *menú del día* with the locals in the shady courtyard of **Alex** (C/Amador de los Rios 10, 92 522 39 63, closed Mon, mains €9, set lunch €13.50), or, if you're handy with a map, the places dotted around the **Corral de Don Diego**.

When planning your visit, bear in mind that most of Toledo's restaurants close for a fortnight in July or August.

Where to stay

Rooms in the old city can be hard to come by at weekends and in the high season, so it's best to book ahead, especially for Corpus Christi. With unbeatable views of the city, the luxury **Parador de Toledo** (Cerro del Emperador s/n, 925 22 18 50, www.parador.es, rates €130-€172) is about ten minutes' cab ride from the city. The splendid pool and top-notch restaurant make it worth allowing a day just to spend in the hotel. Right next to the Casa El Greco, the charming **Hotel Pintor El Greco** (C/Alamillos del Tránsito 13, 925 28 51 91, www.hotelpintorelgreco.com, doubles €54-€75) occupies a converted 17th-century bakery that combines an original façade and patio with mod cons such as satellite TV. More economical is the new and very central **Hostal Santo Tomé** (C/Santo Tomé 13, 925 22 17 12, www.hostalsantotome.com, doubles €52-€65) with ten comfortable rooms in an old Toledan townhouse. **Hostal Descalzos** (C/Descalzos 30, 925 22 28 88, www.hostal descalzos.com, doubles €49-€80) is also great value with en-suite, air-conditioned rooms around a sunny patio with swimming pool and jacuzzi.

Getting there

By bus

Around ten different Continental Auto buses (902 330 400, www.continental-auto.es, www.alsa.es) go to Toledo, from the Plaza Elíptica interchange terminal in Madrid. They leave every 30mins from 7am-10pm Mon-Sat, 8am-10pm Sun. Last return at 9pm. Journey time is around 50mins.

By train

There are ten daily trains to Toledo from Atocha station. The first train leaves at 6.50am Mon-Fri, 9.20am Sat, Sun. The last train out leaves at 9.50pm daily; returning, the last train is at 9.25pm daily. The average journey time is 30 minutes. From Toledo station, take bus 6 to the Puerta de Bisagra, or you'll face a long uphill walk.

Tourist information

Oficina Municipal de Turismo

Plaza del Consistorio (925 25 40 30).
Open 10am-6pm Tue-Sun.

Oficina de Turismo

Puerta de Bisagra (925 22 08 43, www.jccm.es).
Open *Oct-June* 9am-6pm Mon-Fri; 9am-7pm Sat; 9am-3pm Sun. *July-Sept* 9am-7pm Mon-Sat; 9am-3pm Sun.

Directory

Getting Around

ARRIVING & LEAVING

By air

Madrid's huge **Barajas Airport** is 13km (8 miles) north-east of the city on the A2 motorway. Thanks to the new Richard Rogers-designed terminal T4, the airport is used by around 50 million passengers per year. All airlines that are members of the OneWorld network (including BA, Iberia, Aer Lingus and American Airlines) will share T4 for national and international flights.

All other traffic is distributed between three existing terminals: non-Spanish airlines and flights on Spanish airlines from non-Schengen-area countries (such as the UK and USA, *see p308*) use T1; domestic flights and Spanish airline flights from Schengen countries use T2; some local flights and the Madrid-Barcelona air shuttle use T3. In T1 and T2 there are 24-hour exchange facilities, ATM machines and hotel booking desks. There is a tourist office (*see p308*) and rail reservations desk in T1, two tourist offices in T4.

For airport information, call 91 321 10 00, 91 393 60 00 or the premium rate number 90 240 47 04, or check www.aena.es, which has updated flight info. Phone lines are open 24 hours a day.

Airport Express

The city council's new express airport bus will run a daily 24-hr service (every 15 mins in the day and every 30 mins at night), once it kicks off in late 2010. The easily identifiable yellow buses – which will run between T1, T2, T4 and, in town, O'Donnell, Cibeles and Atocha – will take around 40 mins and the journey will cost just €2.
Aerocity *91 747 75 70, www.aerocity.com.*
Provides shuttle services between the airport and city-centre hotels. Handy for small groups and cheaper than taking several taxis. Prices vary between €17 and €38, depending on group size. The company has two airport reservation desks.
Bus from the airport *Avda de América terminal (information 91 406 88 10 or 91 406 88 00).*
Once the new Airport Express (*see above*) service is up and running in

late 2010, bus lines 200 and 204 will be combined into a single route running between the public transport hub on the Avenida de América and T1, T2 and T4. A single ticket costs €1.
Metro from the airport The metro is the cheapest way to get to central Madrid, costing only €2. Bear in mind that the Aeropuerto metro station is between T2 and T3, which means that if, as is very likely, you arrive at T1, you have a 10-15min walk to get there. From T4, take the shuttle to T2 (allow 20mins in total). From the airport it's four stops on metro line 8 (pink) and 12mins to Nuevos Ministerios. On outward journeys, if you are flying with Iberia, Alitalia and some other airlines you can also check in here. From Nuevos Ministerios it's around another 15mins to travel into the centre of Madrid. You can save money by buying a Metrobús ticket at the airport station.
Taxis from the airport Taxi fares to central Madrid should be around €19-€22 (depending on the traffic), including a €5 airport supplement (no luggage supplement). There are further supplements after 10pm and on Sundays (for both, 18¢ per km). There are lots of taxis at Barajas, but ignore any drivers who approach you inside the building, just use the ones at the ranks outside the terminal. Check the meter is at the current minimum fare (€1.85) when you begin your journey; it's a good idea to check a map first, and to have a landmark in mind in the area to which you are going. For more on taxis, *see p296*.
Train from the airport The new RENFE *cercanías* line from the airport was still being built when this guide went to print. Once completed, in 2011, it will take you from T4 to Sol in just 10 minutes.

By bus

Almost all international and long-distance coach services to Madrid terminate at the Estación Sur de Autobuses, C/Méndez Álvaro to the south of central Madrid (information 91 468 42 00, 91 468 45 11 from 6.30am to midnight or www.estacionautobuses madrid.com; bus companies also

have their own information lines). It's next to metro (line 6) and *cercanía* (local train lines C5, C7 and C10) stations, both also called Méndez Álvaro. Bus 148 also runs from there to the city centre (Plaza del Callao and Plaza de España). Taxi fares from the bus station carry a €2.50 supplement.

By train

Spanish national railways (RENFE) has two main stations in Madrid. Trains from France, Catalonia and northern Spain arrive at **Chamartín**, on the north side of the city, some distance from the centre. High-speed AVE trains from Andalucia, Barcelona (since 2008) and Valencia, express services from Lisbon and trains from southern and eastern Spain arrive at **Atocha**, at the southern end of the Paseo del Prado. There are exchange facilities at both stations, and a tourist office at Chamartín. Atocha is also the main hub of RENFE's local rail lines (*cercanías*) for the Madrid area (*see p268*), which have been expanding in recent years.

Metro line 10 is the fastest from Chamartín to the city centre, and Atocha RENFE (the train station; not the same metro as Atocha) is four metro stops from Sol on line 1. A taxi fare to the centre from Chamartín should be around €13, including a €2.50 station supplement. There are extra supplements at night and on Sundays (18¢ per km). The same need for caution with cabs at the airport (*see above*) applies to drivers touting for fares at main rail stations.

For more information on all Madrid-oriented rail services, *see p268*.

RENFE Information
90 232 03 20 or 90 224 02 02, www.renfe.es. **Open** *Information* 24hrs daily. *Reservations* 5am-10.30pm daily.
Estación de Atocha
Glorieta del Emperador Carlos V (Renfe information 914 68 83 32). Metro Atocha Renfe, Salamanca & the Retiro. **Map** p328 J14.
Estación de Chamartín
C/Agustín de Foxá, Chamartín. Metro Chamartín.

MAPS

Metro, local train and central area street maps are included at the back of this guide (*see pp335-336*). Metro maps are also available at all metro stations: simply ask for '*un plano del metro*'. The Consorcio de Transportes, the regional transport authority, publishes a range of good-quality free maps, especially the Plano de los Transportes del Centro de Madrid. This map should be available at tourist offices (ask for a transport map, rather than the inferior street map the tourist offices often give out to the unsuspecting). For good shops to buy maps, *see p189*.

In addition you can access bus and Metro maps online at the EMT (www.emtmadrid.es) and Metro (www.metromadrid.es) websites respectively.

PUBLIC TRANSPORT

To really get to know Madrid, it's best to explore on foot. Most of the main attractions are within walking distance of each other and for orientation purposes think of Puerta del Sol as the centre. Street numbers in Madrid all run outwards from Sol. Public transport is cheap and efficient – both bus and metro will get you where you want to go within half an hour, although it's best to avoid the buses during rush hour. Note: all transport and taxi fares are subject to revision in January.

For transport outside Madrid, *see p268*. For transport for disabled travellers, *see p299*.

Fares

Compared to fare structures in many other capital cities, Madrid's is simple – €1 for a single journey on the bus or metro (excluding Metro Sur, which is €1.75, and Barajas Airport, which is €2) within the capital, no matter how long the journey. On the metro you can change any number of times as long as you don't leave a station. The exceptions are trips to the stations Rivas Urbanizaciones, Rivas Vaciamadrid, La Poveda and Arganda del Rey (all Line 9), and all stations beyond Puerta del Sur on the new Metro Sur line, which circles the southern suburbs.

However, it's easier and more economical to buy a ticket for 10 journeys (*billete de diez/Metrobús*), which can be used on the bus and metro, available at all metro

stations and some *estancos* and *kioskos*, but not on the bus. You can share the ticket between two or more people and keep it for as long as you like (or until the prices go up). The current price of a Metrobús is €6.40.

On the metro, you simply insert the ticket into the machine at the gate that leads through to the platform, which cancels one unit for each trip – remember to collect it afterwards – and will reject expired tickets. There is no checking or collection of tickets at station exits. On buses, the Metrobús should be inserted arrow downwards into the blue and yellow machine just behind the driver.

Abonos – season tickets

If you're planning on staying much longer than a fortnight, a monthly season ticket is a good idea. Unlike the Metrobús, it is valid for *cercanías* trains as well as the metro and city buses, allowing you to use it on some trips out of town. Your first *abono* must be obtained with an identity card, available only from *estancos*, for which you will need two passport-size photos and must fill in a brief form. In succeeding months you can buy tickets to revalidate the card from metro stations and EMT kiosks as well as *estancos*. Note, though, that an *abono* is valid for an actual calendar month, not for 30 days from date of purchase, so that if your stay runs across two months, buying one may not be particularly economical unless you qualify for one of the different age discounts. Also, if you can, buy your *abono* before the start of the month to avoid the nightmare queues on the first of the month.

Unless you are intending to travel a lot outside the city, Zone A should cover everywhere you need to go. A standard one-month Zone A *abono* currently costs €40.45, and there are substantial reductions for young people and for over-65s. It can be used on the buses to the airport, for which *see p294*.

Metro

The metro is the quickest and simplest means of travelling to most parts of the city. Each of its 13 lines (including the Metrosur and Ramal lines) is identified by a number and a colour on maps and at stations. Metro stations also make essential reference points, and 'metro Sevilla', 'metro Goya'

and so on will often b. as tags with addresses.

The metro is open 6am-2a. daily. Tickets are available at all stations from coin-operated machines and staffed ticket booths. Trains run every three to five minutes during weekdays, and about every 10-15mins after 11pm and on Sundays. The metro can get packed in rush hours (7.30-9.30am, 1-2.30pm, 7.30-9pm).

Night buses (L1 to L11) run al ong the metro routes. *See p296* **Night buses**.

Metro information

C/Cavanilles 58, Salamanca & the Retiro (902 44 44 03, www.metro madrid.es). Metro Conde de Casal. **Open** 6am-1.30am daily.
There are customer service points at the airport, Atocha, Chamartín, Avenida de América, Nuevos Ministerios and Alto de Arenal stations.

Buses

Run by Empresa Municipal de Transportes (EMT; information 91 406 88 00 or 902 50 78 50, www.emtmadrid. es). **Open** 7am-9pm Mon-Fri; 7am-2pm Sat, Sun. See above for information about fares and tickets.

Most run from about 6am-11.30pm daily, with buses every 10-15mins (more often on more popular routes). Night buses then take over. You board buses at the front, and get off via the middle or rear doors. The fare is the same for each journey (€1), however far you go. Officially, there is a limit to how much luggage you can take on city buses, and trying to board with luggage during rush hours is almost impossible. Drivers are not obliged to give you the change if they don't have it (and if what you give them is more than five times the price of the ticket), nor will they allow you to travel for free. But they must write down your contact details for the bus company to send you the change later on.

For tourist buses, *see p53*.

Useful routes

No.2 From Avda Reina Victoria, above Moncloa, to Plaza de España, then along Gran Vía to Cibeles, the Retiro and Plaza Manuel Becerra. **No.3** From Puerta de Toledo up Gran Vía de San Francisco and C/Mayor to Sol, then up C/Hortaleza to Cuatro Caminos, C/Bravo Murillo; ends close to the Estadio Bernabéu.

a the
blón and
station.
al along
ocha,
,
na to

way up and ———— tellana from Embajadores via Atocha to Plaza Castilla.

C1 and C2 The 'Circular' route runs in a wide circuit around the city, via Atocha, Embajadores, Plaza de España, Moncloa, Cuatro Caminos, Plaza Manuel Becerra and the Retiro.

Night buses

Between midnight and around 5am in the morning there are 24 night routes in operation – N1 to N24 – called Búho (Owl) buses. All begin from Plaza de Cibeles and run out to the suburbs, and are numbered in a clockwise sequence. Although the Metro closes at nights, at the weekends special buses, called Metro Búho, cover the routes of the 11 central metro lines (L1-L11). The buses alight at the bus stop nearest to each metro station. The timetable for each line varies, but generally the buses run from 12.45am until 5.45am. L1-L11 buses run every 15 to 20 minutes. There are three buses that cover the L12 Metrosur route, which connects Alcorcón, Leganés, Getafe, Fuenlabrada and Móstoles. The L12 buses run every 30 minutes, from 1.15am to 5.30am.

EMT Information

C/Cerro de la Plata 4, Retiro (902 50 78 50/91 406 88 10, www.emtmadrid.es). Metro Pacífico. **Open** 8am-2pm Mon-Fri.

Cercanías/local trains

The highly efficient *cercanías* or local network of railways for the Madrid area has been expanding in recent years in order to link the suburbs with the centre more directly. It consists of 12 lines converging on Atocha, several of which connect with metro lines along their routes. The new Sol station opened in 2009 – and this will in the future link up with Gran Via metro station and T4 at Barajas airport, meaning that both the suburbs and airport can be reached directly from central Madrid.

As well as the suburbs, *cercanías* trains are useful for trips to Guadarrama and towns near

Madrid such as Aranjuez or El Escorial. Also, lines C-7a and C-7b combine (with one change at Príncipe Pío) to form a circle line within Madrid that is quicker than the metro for some journeys, and the RENFE line between Chamartín and Atocha is the fastest link between the two main stations. *Cercanías* lines run from 5-6am to 11pm-midnight daily, with trains on most lines about every 10-30mins. Fares vary with distance, but the lines are included in the monthly season ticket. For a map of the *cercanías* network, *see p335.*

TAXIS

Madrid taxis are white, with a diagonal red stripe on the front doors. The city has more than 15,000 taxis, so they are rarely hard to find, except late at night at the weekend or on days when it's raining heavily. When a taxi is free there is a *'Libre'* (free) sign behind the windscreen, and a green light on the roof. If there is also a sign with the name of a district in red, it means the driver is on his way home, and is not obliged to take you anywhere that isn't near that particular route. There are taxi ranks, marked by a blue sign with a white T, throughout the centre of Madrid. At the airport and rail and bus stations, it's always best to take a taxi from the official ranks; within the city, however, those in the know flag cabs down in the street, thereby avoiding the risk both of scams, and of station supplements. To avoid being swindled by a non-official taxi, make sure the driver has their licence number visible on the front and a meter, and always ask for the approximate fare before getting in.

Fares

Official fare rates and supplements are shown inside each cab (in English and Spanish), on the right-hand sun visor and/or the rear windows. The minimum fare is €1.85, which is what the meter should show when you first set off. The minimum fare is the same at all times, but the additional charge increases at a higher rate at night (11pm-6am) and on Sundays and public holidays, and there are extra supplements for trips starting from the bus and train stations (€2.50); to and from the trade fair complex (€2.50), and to and from the airport (€5). Also, the fare rate is higher for journeys to suburban towns in the outer tariff zone (zone B). Drivers

are not officially required to carry more than €12 in change, and some accept credit cards.

Receipts and complaints

To get a receipt, ask for *'un recibo, por favor'.* If you think you've been overcharged or have any other complaint, insist the receipt is made out in full, with details of the journey and the driver's signature, NIF number and licence plate, and the date. Make a note of the taxi number, displayed on a plaque on the dashboard. Take or send the receipt, keeping a copy, with a complaints form to the city taxi office at the address below. The form is included in the Taxi Information leaflet available from tourist offices. You can present the form at any Junta office and they will send it on (information 011, 91 588 10 00); one central office is Plaza Mayor 3, Los Austrias (91 588 23 43).

Oficina Municipal del Taxi

3rd floor, C/Albarracín 31, Eastern suburbs (91 480 46 23). Metro García Noblejas. **Open** 9am-1pm Mon-Fri.

Phone cabs

You can call for a cab from any of the companies listed below. Operators will rarely speak much English, so if you aren't at a specific address give the name of the street and a restaurant or bar that makes a suitable place to wait, or position yourself near a street corner and say, for example, 'San Agustín, *esquina* Prado' (San Agustín, corner of Prado). The operator will also ask you your name. Phone cabs start the meter from the point when a call is answered. Very few cabs will take credit cards.

Radio-Taxi Asociación Gremial *91 447 32 32/91 447 51 80.*
Radio-Taxi Independiente *91 405 12 13/91 405 55 00*
Radioteléfono Taxi *91 547 82 00.*
Teletaxi *91 371 21 31/902 50 11 30.*

CYCLING

Cycling in Madrid is only for the truly experienced (or the utterly insane) in view of the heavy traffic and lack of cycle lanes on any of the city's central streets (there are a few in parks and by the river). However, bike lanes are gradually improving, and bikes are a great idea for trips to the larger city parks (Retiro, Casa de Campo) and especially the

Madrid Sierras. Bikes can be taken free of charge on some *cercanías* lines and on the metro at weekends. Cycle hire shops often ask that you leave proof of identity (take a photocopy to avoid having to leave your passport) as well as a cash deposit. There are an increasing number of companies and associations in Madrid that are dedicated to cycling, including Pedalibre (www. pedalibre.org) and Ciclos Otero (www.oterociclos.es).

DRIVING

Driving in the city is rarely a quick way of getting anywhere thanks to traffic jams, and finding a parking space is another headache.

Signs & terms

cede el paso – give way
usted no tiene la prioridad – you don't have the right of way
único sentido – one way
cambio de sentido – indicates a junction that allows you to change direction
recuerde – remember
cinturón de seguridad – seat belt
ronda de circunnavegación – ring road

Car & motorbike hire

Car hire can be pricey, so shop around; there are often good weekend deals. Most companies have a minimum age limit (usually 21) and require you to have had a licence for over a year. You will also need a credit card (as opposed to a debit card), or leave a big cash deposit (sometimes up to €500). Check if IVA (VAT), at 16 per cent, and unlimited mileage are included. All the companies listed require you to take out a *seguro franquicia* – a fixed amount you have to pay in the event of an accident or any damage caused to the vehicle, and which is put on your credit card when you take the car (usually around half the hire cost – it is only charged if you return the vehicle damaged).

Avis *Estación de Chamartín, C/Agustín de Foxa s/n, Chamartín (91 314 19 81, www.avis.es). Metro Plaza de Castilla.* **Open** 8am-9pm Mon-Fri; 8am-2pm Sat, Sun. **Credit** AmEx, DC, MC, V.

Easycar *Barajas Airport (www.easycar.com).* **Credit** AmEx, MC, V.

Europcar *Paseo de la Castellana 193 (central booking number 902 10 50 55. www.europcar.com). Metro Plaza de Castilla.* **Open** 7am-9pm Mon-Fri; 8am-2pm Sat. **Credit** AmEx, DC, MC, V.

Other locations Barajas airport; Atocha station; Chamartín station; C/San Leonardo 8, Malasaña; Tetuán; Nuevos Ministerios metro.

BlaferMotos *C/Clara del Rey 17, Chamartín (91 413 00 47, www.blafermotos.com). Metro Alfonso XIII.* **Open** 8.30am-6pm Mon-Fri; 10am-1.30pm Sat. **Credit** AmEx, MC, V.
Motorcycle specialists.

National-Atesa *Plaza de España car park (1st floor) (91 542 96 10, www.atesa.es). Metro Santiago Bernabéu.* **Open** 8.30am-7.30pm Mon-Fri; 9am-1pm Sat. **Credit** AmEx, DC, MC, V.

Other locations: Barajas airport (91 393 72 32); Atocha station (91 506 18 46); Chamartín station (91 323 59 70).

PlanCar
C/Embajadores 216, South of centre (91 530 27 23, www.plancar.com). Metro Legazpi. **Open** 9am-2pm, 4.30-8.30pm Mon-Fri; 9am-1.30pm Sat. **Credit** AmEx, V.

Breakdown services

If you are planning to take a car to Spain it's advisable to join a motoring organisation such as the AA or RAC, which have reciprocal arrangements with their Spanish equivalent, RACE.

RACE (Real Automóvil Club de España)
Assistance 902 300 505, information 902 40 45 45, 91 592 74 00, www.race.es.
The RACE has English-speaking staff and will send immediate 24hr breakdown assistance. If you are outside Madrid, call the emergency freephone number, but you will be referred on to a local number. Repairs are carried out on the spot when possible; if not, your vehicle will be towed to the nearest suitable garage. Members of affiliated organisations abroad are not charged for call-outs, but non-members pay around €115 (on-the-spot membership) for the basic breakdown service.

Parking

For car-owning *madrileños* parking is a daily trauma. The city police (Policía Municipal) give out tickets readily (many locals never pay them). Be careful not to park in front of doorways with the sign *'vado permanente'*, indicating an entry with 24-hour right of access. The ORA (Operación Regulación

Aparcamiento) system now applies (*see below*) to the whole city centre (roughly between Moncloa, C/José Abascal, C/Doctor Esquerdo and Atocha). Residents park for free if they have an annual sticker.

ORA
Non-residents must pay to park in zones painted in blue or green from 9am to 8pm Mon-Fri and 9am to 3pm Sat (9am-3pm Mon-Sat in August). Pay-and-display machines are located on pavements. Maximum validity of tickets is two hours in blue zones and one hour in green, after which a new card must be used, and the car parked in a new spot. Cars parked in the ORA zone without a card can be towed away (*see below*). In the blue areas, tickets cost up to €2.55 for two hours and in the green areas, €1.80 for one hour. All streets in this zone that have no additional restrictions posted are ORA parking areas.

Car parks
Central car parks *Plaza de las Cortes, Plaza Santa Ana, C/Sevilla, Plaza Jacinto Benavente, Plaza Mayor, Plaza Descalzas, C/Tudescos, Plaza de España.* **Open** 24hrs daily. **Rates** €1.80 for 1hr, €3.60 for 2hrs, €10.76 for 5hrs, €27.60 for 12 to 24hrs (the maximum).
There are some 50 municipal car parks around Madrid, indicated by a white 'P'-on-blue sign. It's especially advisable to use a car park if your car has foreign plates. Car parks have disabled access. See also www.madrid movilidad.es for more details.

Towing away
Information 91 787 72 90/91 787 72 92, www.madridmovilidad.es.
Main pounds *Plaza Colón. Metro Colón.* **Map** p324 K9. *C/Velázquez, 87. Metro Nuñez de Balboa.* **Map** p325 M6. **Open** 24hrs daily.
If your car seems to have been towed away, call the central number and quote your number plate to be told which pound it has gone to. It will cost €144.70 to recover your car. You'll have to pay €1.85 per hour for the first ten hours, timed from the moment it was towed away. For each complete extra day in the pound it's €18.85. You can also locate your car by entering your registration plate number at www.madridmovilidad.es/ madrid_movilidad/bases.aspx. Bring your ID and all car papers when you pick it up.

DIRECTORY

Resources A-Z

TRAVEL ADVICE

For information on travelling to Madrid from within the European Union, including details of visa regulations and healthcare provision, see the EU's travel website: http://europe.eu/travel. Most government departments of foreign affairs also have websites with useful advice for would-be travellers.

AUSTRALIA
www.smartraveller.gov.au

CANADA
www.voyage.gc.ca

NEW ZEALAND
www.safetravel.govt.nz

REPUBLIC OF IRELAND
foreignaffairs.gov.ie

UK
www.fco.gov.uk/travel

USA
www.state.gov/travel

ADDRESSES

Individual flats in apartment blocks have traditionally been identified by the abbreviations *'izq'* (*izquierda*, left) or *'dcha'* (*derecha*, right) after the floor number (C/Prado 221, 5ª dcha) and occasionally *'int'* (interior, inward facing) or *'ext'* (exterior); in newer buildings they may be shown more simply (C/Prado 223, 4B). A building with no street number (usually huge places like stations or hospitals) has *s/n* (*sin número*) after the street.

AGE RESTRICTIONS

In Spain, you have to be 18 to drive a car, smoke or drink, and get married, but the age of consent is a startling 13.

BUSINESS

Administrative services

A *gestoría* is a very Spanish kind of institution, combining the functions of lawyer, accountant, business adviser and general aid with bureaucracy. They can be very helpful in seeing short cuts that foreigners are often unaware of. English is spoken at these *gestorías*.

Gestoría Calvo Canga
C/Serrano 27, Salamanca (91 577 07 09). Metro Serrano. **Open** 9am-2pm, 4.30-8pm Mon-Thur; 9am-3pm Fri. **Map** p325 L8.
A general *gestoría* that deals with the areas of labour law, tax and accounts, and residency.

Conventions & conferences

IFEMA/Feria de Madrid
Recinto Ferial Juan Carlos I,
Northern suburbs (902 22 15 15, www.ifema.es). Metro Campo de las Naciones. **Open** *Office* 9am-5pm Mon-Fri.
Madrid's lavish state-of-the-art trade fair centre has ten main pavilions, a 600-seater auditorium, a brand-new 10,000sq m convention centre and many smaller facilities, plus 20 catering outlets and no less than 14,000 parking spaces. By the entrance is the Palacio Municipal de Congresos, a 2,000-capacity conference hall.

Oficina de Congresos de Madrid
C/Mayor 69, Los Austrias (91 588 29 00, www.munimadrid.es). Metro Ópera or Sol. **Open** *Mid Sept-mid June* 9am-6pm Mon-Thur, 9am-3pm Fri. *Mid June-mid Sept* 9am-1pm Mon-Fri. **Map** p327 E12.
An office of the city council that assists those planning to hold a conference or similar event in Madrid. The Oficina de Congresos will facilitate contacts with venues and service companies.

Palacio de Congresos de Madrid
Paseo de la Castellana 99, Tetuán (91 337 81 00, www. palaciocongresosmadrid.es). Metro Santiago Bernabéu. **Open** 8am-9pm Mon-Fri.
This venue is longer established than the Feria de Madrid (*see above*) and used for several major international conferences. It has conference rooms and galleries of all sizes; the facilities are excellent.

Recintos Feriales de la Casa de Campo
Avda de Portugal s/n, Casa de Campo (91 722 04 00, www. madridespaciosycongresos.com/ recinto). Metro Lago. **Open** *Sept-July* 8am-3pm Mon-Fri. *Aug* 8am-2pm Mon-Fri.
An attractive site with three halls and open-air space.

Courier services

DHL
Ground services 902 12 30 30/air services 902 12 24 24, www.dhl.es. **Open** *Phoneline* 24hrs daily. *Pickups & deliveries* 9am-7pm Mon-Sat.

Motorecado
Avda del Manzanares 202, Southern suburbs (91 476 71 61, www.motorecado.com). Metro Laguna. **Open** 8am-7pm Mon-Fri.
No credit cards.

Trébol
C/Buenavista 32, Lavapiés (91 530 32 32, www.trebol.org). Metro Lavapiés. **Open** *Sept-July* 9am-8pm Mon-Fri. *Aug* 9am-3pm Mon-Fri.
No credit cards. **Map** p328 H14.

Office & computer services

Data Rent
C/Mesena 18, Northern suburbs (91 759 62 42, www.datarent.es). Metro Arturo Soria. **Open** *Sept-June* 9am-2pm, 4-7pm Mon-Fri. *July, Aug* 8am-3pm Mon-Fri.
Credit MC, V.
PCs, printers, OHPs etc for rent by the day, week or month.

Translators

Lionbridge Solutions
7th floor, Edificio Ofpinar, C/Caleruega 102-104, North of Centre (91 791 34 43, www.lionbridge.com). Metro Pinar de Chamartín. **Open** 9am-6.30pm Mon-Fri.
A professional translation service.

Polidioma
C/Cea Bermudez 6, 6° izq, Chamberí (91 554 46 20). Metro Canal.
In Spain, official and other bodies often demand that foreign documents be translated by legally

certified translators. Call for an appointment; rates are higher than for other translators. Some consulates (*see p300*) also provide these services or they can put you in contact with other translators.

Useful organisations

Bolsa de Comercio (Stock Exchange)
Plaza de la Lealtad 1, Retiro (91 709 50 00, www.bolsamadrid.es). Metro Banco de España. **Open** 9am-5pm Mon-Thur, 9am-2pm Fri. **Map** p328 J11.
See also p305.

Cámara de Comercio e Industria de Madrid
C/Ribera del Loira 56, Campo de las Naciones (91 538 35 00, www.camara madrid.es). Metro Campo de las Naciones or Mar de Cristal.
Has a useful information service for foreign investors in Madrid. You must make an appointment first.

Instituto Español de Comercio Exterior
Paseo de la Castellana 14-16, Salamanca (91 349 61 00/902 34 90 00, www.icex.es). Metro Colón. **Open** *Oct-May* 9am-2pm, 3-5pm Mon-Thur; 9am-2pm Fri. *June-Sept* 8.30am-2.30pm Mon-Fri. **Map** p324 K8.
The state-run ICEX (Spanish Institute for Foreign Trade) has an excellent information service to aid small- to medium-sized businesses.

COMPLAINTS

If you have a complaint, ask for an official complaint form (*hoja de reclamación*), which most businesses, shops, bars and so on are obliged to have available for customers. Fill out the form, leaving the colour copy with the business. Then take this, and any receipts or other relevant paperwork, to the official consumer office, listed below.

Oficina Municipal de Información al Consumidor
C/Gran Vía 24, Gran Vía (91 211 18 51). Metro Gran Vía. **Open** 9am-2pm, 4.30-6.30pm Mon-Thur; 9am-2pm Fri. **Map** p323 H11.
The official centre for consumer advice and complaint follow-up. You will need to make an appointment first.

CUSTOMS

If tax has been paid in the country of origin then EU residents do not have to declare goods imported into Spain from other EU countries for their personal use. However, customs officers can question whether large amounts of any item really are for your own use, and random checks are made for drugs. Quantities accepted as being for personal use include:
● up to 800 cigarettes, 400 small cigars, 200 cigars or 1kg of loose tobacco
● 10 litres of spirits (over 22% alcohol), 20 litres of fortified wine or alcoholic drinks with under 22% of alcohol, 90 litres of wine (under 22%) or 110 litres of beer.
Limits for non-EU residents and goods brought from outside the EU:
● 200 cigarettes or 100 small cigars or 50 cigars or 250g (8.82oz) of tobacco
● 1 litre of spirits (over 22% alcohol) or 2 litres of any other alcoholic drink with under 22% alcohol
● 50g (1.76oz) of perfume
● 500g coffee, 100g tea
There are no restrictions on cameras, watches or electrical goods, within reasonable limits, and visitors are also allowed to carry up to €6,000 in cash. Non-EU residents can also reclaim the Value Added Tax (IVA) they have paid on certain large purchases when they leave Spain. For details, *see p184*.

DISABLED TRAVELLERS

Madrid is still not a city that disabled people, especially wheelchair users, will find it easy to get around. However, the situation is steadily improving as new buildings are constructed with accessibility in mind and old ones are gradually adapted: technically all public buildings should have been made accessible by law, although in practice a great deal still remains to be done. Access to public transport is also patchy.
There is an excellent guide, *Guía de Accesibilidad de Madrid*, which is published by the Ayuntamiento (city council) in collaboration with the disabled association FAMMA. This booklet is available from the FAMMA office at C/Galileo 69 (91 593 35 50, www.famma.org), and can also be accessed via the city council website (www.madrid.es).

Access to sights

Some of the city's wheelchair-friendly venues are listed below.
Centro Conde Duque
Centro Cultural de la Villa
Museo de América

Museo de Cera
Museo de Historia
Museo del Libro
Museo Nacional Centro de Arte Reina Sofía
Museo del Prado
Museo Real Academia de Bellas Artes de San Fernando
Museo del Romanticismo
Museo Tiflológico
Museo Thyssen-Bornemisza
Palacio Real
Planetario de Madrid
Real Fábrica de Tapices
Santiago Bernabéu stadium

Buses

There are seats reserved for people with mobility problems behind the driver on most of the city's buses. Buses on many routes are now of the *piso bajo* (low floor) type, with low doors and spaces for wheelchairs. These are identified by the red on white stripes at the front and back of the bus and the slogan *'piso bajo pensado para todos'*.

Metro

All new metro stations have been built with access in mind, which means that those on newer lines (Line 8 to the airport, the Gregorio Marañón interchange, Line 7 to Pitis, the new Puerto del Sol stops) have good lifts. However, older stations in the city centre generally have a lot of steps, and although you may get on at a station with a lift, it may turn out to be impossible to get off at your destination. The metro map on p336 of this guide and the free maps available at metro stations indicate stations with lifts.

RENFE & cercanías

Of the mainline rail stations, Atocha, Chamartín, Nuevos Ministerios and Príncipe Pío all have good access. Cercanías trains have very limited access, but some newer stations such as Méndez Alvaro (by Estación Sur coach station) have lifts connecting metro, train and bus stations. There are also good interchanges at Moncloa and Plaza Castilla.

Taxis

Special taxis adapted for wheelchairs can be called through Eurotaxi on 630 02 64 78 or 687 92 40 27 and Teletaxi on 91 371 21 31 or 902 50 11 30. Make it clear you want an adapted model (ask for a

D I R E C T O R Y

DIRECTORY

Eurotaxi). The number of such taxis in Madrid is still very limited and the waiting time can be as long as half an hour. Fares are the same as for standard cabs, but the meter is started as soon as a request is received, so the cost can be quite high.

DRUGS

Many people openly smoke cannabis, but its possession or consumption in public are illegal. It's theoretically OK to smoke cannabis in private, but not to possess it; this law is rarely enforced. There's been a recent crackdown in bars, however.

ELECTRICITY

The standard current in Spain is now 220V, but a few old buildings in Madrid still have 125V circuits, so it's a good idea to check before using electrical equipment in older hotels. Plugs are all of the two-round-pin type. The 220V current works fine with British 240V products, with a plug adaptor. With US 110V appliances you will need a current transformer.

EMBASSIES

For a full list look in the local phone book under *embajadas*. Lots of embassies have moved to the Torre Espacio on Paseo de la Castella in the past few years.

American Embassy
C/Serrano 75, Salamanca (91 587 22 00, www.embusa.es). Metro Rubén Darío. **Open** *Phoneline* 24hrs daily. *Office* 9am-6pm (8am-1pm passports) Mon-Fri. **Map** p325 L6.
The general switchboard will put you through to the consulate.

Australian Embassy
24th floor, Torre Espacio, Paseo de la Castellana 259D, Northern Suburbs (91 353 66 00/visas 91 353 66 90/emergency phoneline 900 99 61 99, www.spain.embassy. gov.au). Metro Begoña. **Open** 8.30am-2pm, 2.30-4.30pm (visas 9am-noon) Mon-Fri.

British Embassy
Torre Espacio, Paseo de la Castellana 259D, Northern suburbs (91 714 63 00/visas 807 457 577/ passports 807 450 051, http://ukinspain.fco.gov.uk). Metro Begoña. **Open** 9am-5.30pm Mon-Fri. *Visa/passport lines* 9am-6pm Mon-Fri.
General commercial, economic and other information about the UK. For

information on British passports, call 807 429 026 (9.30am-5.30pm).

British Consulate
Torre Espacio, Paseo de la Castellana 259D, Northern Suburbs (91 714 64 00). Metro Begoña. **Open** 8.30am-1.30pm (until 6pm for emergencies) Mon-Fri.
For queries relating to passports, visas and legal problems.

Canadian Embassy
Torre Espacio, Paseo de la Castellana 259D, Northern Suburbs (91 382 84 00, www.canada international.gc.ca/spain-espagne). Metro Begoña. **Open** *Consular services* Sept-July 9am-12.30pm Mon-Fri. Aug 8.30am-2.15pm Mon-Fri. *Emergency services* Sept-July 8.30-1pm, 2-5.30pm Mon-Thur; 8.30am-2.30pm Fri. Aug 8.30am-2.15pm Mon-Fri.
Emergency number for citizens (reverse charge calls accepted) is 1 613 996 8885.

Irish Embassy
Paseo de la Castellana 46 4º, Salamanca (91 436 40 93/visas 91 431 97 84, www.irlanda.es). Metro Rubén Darío. **Open** 10am-2pm Mon-Fri. *Visas* 11.15am-1.15pm Mon-Fri. **Map** p325 L6.

New Zealand Embassy
3rd floor, C/Pinar 7, Chamberí (91 523 02 26, www.nzembassy. com/spain). Metro Gregorio Marañón. **Open** Sept-June 9am-2pm, 3-5.30pm Mon-Fri. July, Aug 8.30am-1.30pm, 2-4.30pm Mon-Fri. *Visas* 10am-1pm Mon-Fri. **Map** p321 L5.

EMERGENCIES

Madrid has a general number – 112 – to call for the emergency services (you also dial this number from GSM mobiles). Some staff speak English, French and/or German. However, you can be kept on hold for a long time; it's usually quicker to call direct. For more on the police, *see p304*.

Ambulancia (Ambulance) *061/092/ 91 335 45 45.*
Bomberos (Fire service) *Madrid capital 080. Whole comunidad 085.*
Policía Municipal (City Police) *092/91 588 50 00.*
Policía Nacional (National Police) *091.*
Guardia Civil *General 062/900 101 062.*

ETIQUETTE

Some of the stereotypes are true. It's all much more vivacious than at home, and certainly more vocal. It's normal to say 'Hola' to all

strangers; even when you're in a lift. Queues may look like free-form free-for-alls, but they're not. They first thing you must say, when taking your place in line, is '¿Quién es el ultimo?' Who is last in line? Make a mental note of which four-foot-tall old lady comes before you and be sure not to push in.

Packed rush-hour metro trains are common, so *madrileños* have a set way of alighting from them. Rather than just push past people, only to find they are also getting off, it's usual to ask those in front: '¿Va a salir?' ('Are you getting off?'). If they are not, watch in wonder as a path opens up before you.

GAY & LESBIAN

COGAM
C/Puebla 9, Malasaña & Conde Duque (91 522 45 17/91 523 00 70, www.cogam.org). Metro Gran Vía. **Open** 10am-2pm, 5-9pm Mon-Fri. **Map** p323 H10.
The largest gay and lesbian organisation in Madrid, COGAM is one of the main organisers of Gay Pride and campaigns on various issues. The on-site café is a great place to chill and find out what's new on the scene. At the time of writing, the organisation was in a temporary address on the Plaza Puerta del Sol (3rd floor, No.4).

Fundación Triángulo
1st floor, C/Melendez Valdés 52, Chamberí (91 593 05 40, www. fundaciontriangulo.es). Metro Argüelles. **Open** 10am-2pm, 4.30-8.30pm Mon-Fri. **Map** p323 E7.
A gay cultural organisation that campaigns on equality issues. It also runs a helpline (91 446 63 94, same schedules as above) and offers legal help and health and AIDS prevention programmes.

HEALTH

EU nationals are entitled to free basic medical attention if they have the European Health Insurance Card (EHIC), which replaced the old E111 form in January 2006. Travellers from the British Isles should apply for one online at www.dh.gov.uk (providing name, date of birth, and NHS or NI number) at least ten days before leaving home. Citizens of certain other countries that have a special agreement with Spain, among them several Latin American states, can also have access to free care. These arrangements won't cover all eventualities, so always take out private health insurance.

Accidents & emergencies

In a medical emergency go to the casualty department (*urgencias*) of any of the city's major hospitals (*see below*). All are open 24 hours daily; Clínico or Gregorio Marañón are most central. If you have no EHIC or insurance, you can be seen at any casualty department (pay on the spot and get reimbursed back home by presenting the invoices and medical reports). In a non-emergency, pharmacists are very well informed.

For an ambulance call **061**. You can also try the Red Cross (Cruz Roja 91 522 22 22, www.cruzroja.es) or the SAMUR service (reached via the Municipal Police on 092).

AIDS/HIV

Free advice is available on freephone 900 11 10 00 (10am-8pm Mon-Fri)
Centro Sanitario Sandoval
C/Sandoval 7, Chamberí (91 445 23 28). Metro Bilbao or San Bernardo. **Open** 8.45am-noon Mon-Fri. **Map** p323 G/H7.
An official clinic that carries out free, confidential HIV tests.

Hospitals

Hospital Clínico San Carlos
C/Profesor Martín Lagos, Moncloa (91 330 30 00, www.hcsc.es). Metro Moncloa.
To get to the Accident and Emergency Department, enter from C/Isaac Peral, which is off Plaza de Cristo Rey.
Hospital General Gregorio Marañón
C/Doctor Esquerdo 44-46, Salamanca (91 586 80 00, www.hggm.es). Metro O'Donnell.
Hospital Universitario La Paz
Paseo de la Castellana 261, Chamartín (91 727 70 00, www.hulpes). Metro Begoña.
The hospital is Plaza Castilla to the north of the city.

Complementary medicine

Instituto Albertos de Medicina Integral
Puerta de Alcalalá, Plaza Independencia 4, Salamanca (91 576 26 49, www.iami.biz). Metro Retiro. **Open** 9am-1.30pm, 5-7.30pm Mon-Fri. **No credit cards.** **Map** p324 J6.
There are several English-speaking practitioners at this clinic, which provides treatments ranging from homeopathy to acupuncture.

Contraception & women's health

Condoms (*profilácticos, condones* or *preservativos*) are available from most pharmacies, and vending machines and supermarkets.
Asociación de Mujeres para la Salud
Avda Alfonso XIII 118, Chamartín (91 519 56 78/91 519 59 26, www.mujeresparalasalud.org). Metro Colombia. **Open** 9am-2pm, 4-8pm Mon-Thur; 9am-3pm Fri. Closed Aug.
A feminist medical association offering free advice and counselling.
Clínica Duratón
C/Colegiata 4, Los Austrias (91 429 77 69, www.duraton.info). Metro Tirso de Molina. **Open** *Sept-July* 9.30am-1.30pm, 4.30-8.30pm Mon-Fri. *Aug* 4.30-8.30pm Mon-Fri. **Map** p327 G13.
Family-planning centre run by women doctors and staff.

Dentists

Dentistry is not covered by EU reciprocal agreements, so private rates apply.

Clínica Dental Cisne
C/Magallanes 18, Chamberí (91 446 32 21/24hr emergencies mobile 661 857 170, www.clinica dentalcisne.com). Metro Quevedo. **Open** *Oct-May* 10am-1.30pm, 3-8pm Mon, Tue, Thur; 2-8pm Wed; 9am-3pm Fri. *June-Sept* 10am-1.30pm, 3-8pm Mon, Tue, Thur; 9am-3pm Wed, Fri. **Credit** AmEx, DC, MC, V. **Map** p323 G6.
British dentist Dr Ian Daniel is based at this clinic. Hours may vary in summer, and the clinic sometimes closes in August.

Doctors

Centros de salud are local health centres with three or so doctors and various specialised clinics. Waiting times can be long and consultations brief, but if necessary you will be referred to a hospital. Usually open 8am-9pm Mon-Fri and 9am-5pm Sat. These are some of the most central:

Centro de Salud Alameda
C/Alameda 5, Huertas & Santa Ana (91 420 38 02). Metro Atocha. **Map** p328 J13.
Centro de Salud Argüelles
C/Quintana 11, Argüelles (91 559 02 23). Metro Argüelles. **Map** p322 D11.

Centro de Salud Las Cortes
C/San Jerónimo 32, Huertas & Santa Ana (91 369 04 91). Metro Sevilla. **Map** p328 I11.

Opticians

See p202.

Pharmacies

Pharmacies (*farmacias*) are signalled by large, green, usually flashing, crosses. Those within the official system of the College of Pharmacies are normally open 9.30am-2pm, 5-8pm Mon-Sat. At other times a duty rota operates. Every pharmacy has a list of the College's *farmacias de guardia* (duty pharmacies) for that day posted outside the door, with the nearest ones highlighted (many now show them using a computerised, push-button panel). Duty pharmacies are also listed in local newspapers, and information is available on 010 and 098 phonelines (*see p308*) and www. cofm.es. At night, duty pharmacies may look closed; knock on the shutters to be served.
There are two 24-hour pharmacies, open every day; *see p203.*

Private health care

Unidad Médica Anglo-Americana
C/Conde de Aranda 1-1° izq, Salamanca (91 435 18 23, www.unidadmedica.com). Metro Retiro. **Open** *Sept-July* 9am-8pm Mon-Fri; 10am-1pm Sat. *Aug* 10am-5pm Mon-Fri. **Credit** AmEx, MC, V. **Map** p325 L10.
Offers full range of services, including dentistry. Will make house/hotel calls.

HELPLINES

Alcoholics Anonymous
C/Juan Bravo 40 2°, Salamanca (91 309 19 47, www.alcoholicos-anonimos.org). Metro Diego de León. **Map** p325 N6/7.
English-speaking group meets 8pm Tue and Thur and 7.30pm on Sat.
Narcotics Anonymous
C/Doctor Piga 4 (902 11 41 47, www.narcoticosanonimos.es). Metro Lavapiés. **Map** p328 I14.
English-speaking meeting every Sunday at 5.30pm.

ID

Foreigners should carry national ID or a passport with them at all times, although a photocopy is usually OK.

You'll be asked to show the passport itself or a driving licence when paying by credit card in shops.

INSURANCE

EU nationals are entitled to use the Spanish state health service, provided they have a European Health Insurance Card (see p300), which must be applied for well in advance of travel. This will cover you for emergencies, but for short-term visitors it's often simpler to avoid dealing with the state bureaucracy and take out private travel insurance before departure, particularly as this will also cover you for stolen or lost cash or valuables.

Some non-EU countries have reciprocal healthcare agreements with Spain, but, again, for most travellers it will be best to take out private travel insurance before arriving. For more on health services, see p300.

INTERNET

Internet access options keep evolving, but the basic choice is between internet service providers (ISPs) that offer free basic access, such as Orange (www.orange.es) and those that charge a fee for better service, such as Ono (www.ono.com). Gonuts4free (807 51 70 45, www.gonuts4free.com) is an Anglo-Spanish free ISP. In both cases you pay for your internet time in your phone bill.

Madrid has plenty of cybercafés, particularly around Puerta del Sol. In summer 2010, it was also announced that Plaza Santo Domingo and Plaza Mayor are now free Wi-Fi zones.

WORKcenter
C/Alberto Aguilera 1, Malasaña (91 121 76 28, www.workcenter.es). Metro San Bernardo. **Open** 24hrs daily. **Credit** MC, V. **Map** p323 G7.
An office centre where you can send or receive faxes and emails, access the net, make copies or get ID photos. Internet access is pricey, charged at €1.95 for 30 mins once you've bought a connection card for €1.
Other locations Paseo de Castellana 149, Salamanca (91 121 76 30); C/Conde de Peñalver 51, Salamanca (91 121 56 60); C/María de Molina 40, Salamanca (91 121 56 80).

LEFT LUGGAGE

Barajas airport
Terminals T1, T2 & T4 (information 902 40 47 04).

Open 24hrs daily. **Rates** €3.90 first 24hrs; €3.90 (small locker) & €5 (big locker) per day thereafter.
Estación Sur (buses)
Open 6.30am-11.30pm daily. **Rates** €1.25 per case per day. A staffed office.
RENFE train stations
Open *Chamartín* 7am-11pm daily. *Atocha* 6.30am-10.30pm daily. **Rates** €2.40-€4.50 depending on locker size.

LIBRARIES

Madrid has a great number of municipal public libraries, but few are in the centre of the city and, not surprisingly, they generally have limited selections of books in English. For a full list of libraries, check 'bibliotecas' in the local *Páginas Amarillas* (*Yellow Pages*), call 010 or visit www.madrid.org/bpcm.
Biblioteca Nacional
Paseo de Recoletos 20, Salamanca (91 580 77 00 or 91 580 78 23, www.bne.es). Metro Colón. **Open** 9am-9pm Mon-Fri; 9am-2pm Sat. **Map** p324 K10.
Spain's national library has early books and manuscripts on display (in the Museo del Libro), and is also the home of the Hemeroteca Nacional, the national newspaper library (see below). To use the library regularly you need accreditation from a university or similar institution, but a one-day pass is quite easy to obtain (you will need to take a passport or residency card, however).
Biblioteca Pedro Salinas
Glorieta de la Puerta de Toledo 1, La Latina (91 366 54 07). Metro Puerta de Toledo. **Open** *Oct-June* 9am-9pm Mon-Fri; 9am-1.45pm Sat. *July-Sept* 9am-9pm Mon-Fri. **Map** p327 E15.
The most attractive and convenient of Madrid's public libraries. Books can be taken out on loan.
British Council
Paseo del General Martínez Campos 31, Chamberí (91 337 35 00, www.britishcouncil.es). Metro Iglesia. **Open** *Sept-June* 9.30am-6.45pm Mon-Wed; 9.30am-8.45pm Thur; 9.30am-5.45pm Fri. *July, Aug* 9.30am-2.45pm Mon-Fri. **Membership** Call for details. **Map** p324 J6.
The best place for English-language books in Madrid, the library in the British Council study centre has a massive selection of books and videos in English, as well as CD-Roms, internet access and daily newspapers.

Hemeroteca Municipal
C/Conde Duque 9-11, Conde Duque (91 588 57 72/75, www.munimadrid.es/hemeroteca). Metro Noviciado. **Open** *Sept-July* 9am-8.30pm Mon-Fri. *Aug* 9am-1.30pm Mon-Fri. **Map** p323 F8.
If you just have to track down that essential piece of information, the city newspaper library in the Centro Conde Duque is the place to do it. You need a researcher's card to get in, for which you must provide a copy of your passport and two ID photos.

LOST PROPERTY
Airport & rail stations

If you lose something before check-in at Barajas Airport, report the loss to the Aviación Civil office (AENA) in the relevant terminal, or call the lost property office in T1 (91 393 61 19, 8am-9pm) or T4 (91 746 64 39, 7am-11pm). If you think you've mislaid anything on the RENFE rail network, look for the Atención al Viajero desk or Jefe de Estación office at the main station nearest to where your property went astray. The Centros de Viajes in the Chamartín and Atocha train stations are the official lost property centres for the municipal train network. Call 902 24 02 02 for both and ask for the Centro de Viaje or information on *objetos perdidos*.
EMT (city buses)
C/Cerro de la Plata 4, Salamanca (91 406 88 43, www.emtmadrid.es). Metro Pacífico. **Open** 8am-2pm Mon-Fri. *Phone lines* 8am-9pm Mon-Fri.
The lost-property office for items that have been lost on Madrid's city or airport buses.
Oficina de Objetos Perdidos (Madrid City Council)
Paseo del Molino 7 & 9, South of centre (91 527 95 90). Metro Legazpi. **Open** *Oct-May* 9am-2pm Mon-Fri. *July-Sept* 9am-1.30pm Mon-Fri.
This office mainly receives articles found on the metro or in taxis, but if you're lucky, something lost in the street may turn up here.

MEDIA
Newspapers

Spanish newspapers may come in tabloid size, but they are far from light-hearted, preferring heavy political commentary. Sensationalist, celeb-dominated stories are reserved for the *prensa de corazón* (press of the heart), such as *¡Hola!*, *Diez Minutos* or *¡Qué me dices!*. Free daily papers *Metro*, *20 Minutos* and the gossipy *¡Qué!* are handed out outside most central metro stations. The plethora of other free newspapers now on offer includes *Latino*, aimed at the South American market, and *Gol!*, a round-up of the weekend's sport.

ABC
ABC's journalists have the highest professional reputation. Read by Madrid's most respectable citizens.

Marca & As
Sports-only (in fact, mostly football-only) papers. *Marca* is usually the country's bestselling daily paper.

El Mundo
This centrist, populist paper made its name by unearthing many corruption scandals under the Socialists during the 1990s. Friday's 'La Luna de Metrópoli' supplement is a good source of listings and information on the cultural agenda.

El País
The liberal *El País* is the established paper of record, and also carries good daily information on Madrid, with Friday's 'Tentaciones' supplement great for music and popular culture.

La Razón
Right-wing and sensationalist daily with much of its editorial coming from ABC.

English-language

Foreign newspapers are on sale in **FNAC** (*see p184*), all **Vip's** stores (*see p184*) and at most kiosks around Sol, Gran Via, Calle Alcalá and the Castellana.

InMadrid
A free monthly aimed at English-speaking residents – you can pick it up in pubs, bookshops, universities, language schools and tourist offices. Good articles on the Madrid scene, plus listings information, events, reviews and small ads.

Listings & classifieds

Local papers carry daily film and theatre listings, and the Friday supplements of *El Mundo* (Metrópoli) and *El País* (Tentaciones) give fuller information, reviews and so on. For monthly music listings look out for the Barcelona-based magazines *Mondo Sonoro* and *Go* (in bars and music shops).

Segundamano
www.segundamano.es
'Second-hand' comes out three times

a week and is the best place for small ads of all kinds.

Guía del Ocio
www.guiadelocio.com
A weekly listings magazine with cinema, arts, entertainment, concerts, nightlife and restaurant listings, and a good galleries section. It's handy, but can be inaccurate.

Music & style mags

Undersounds, *Rockdelux*, the Spanish version of *Rolling Stone* and the new *MTV* magazine are mainly sold in kiosks or music shops and at festivals. A few free mags to look out for are clubbers' zine *AB*, the smarter monthly *Cartel* and *Mundo Sonoro*.

Radio

The Spanish are avid radio fans; you'll hear radios blaring out in bars, cafés, buses and taxis.
  Radio Nacional de España stations to listen for include RNE-2 (96.5 FM, classical music) and RNE-3 (93.2 FM, an excellent and eclectic mix of rock and world music). There are dozens of other local stations.
  The main commercial broadcaster is **SER** (Sociedad Española de Radiofusión), which controls four networks: SER, a news network, and two music channels.
  One specific English-language programme to look out for is Radio Circulo's Madrid Live on Tuesdays from 8.30pm to 9pm (repeated on Friday at 10pm), which can be found on 100.4FM. Produced and presented by radio journalist Ann Bateson, it focuses on the city's arts, entertainment and social scene.
  The BBC World Service can be found in the evenings on 12095 kHz short wave.

TV

There are seven main channels, which pump out an endless diet of tacky game shows, talk shows, really bad imported *telenovelas* (soaps) from South America and badly dubbed American movies. Just about the only redeeming feature is the news, although **Canal 2** does show some good documentaries and films.
  Non-Spanish films and shows on some channels can be seen in undubbed versions on stereo TVs; look for VO (*versión original*) in

listings and a 'Dual' symbol at the top of the screen.

TVE 1 (La Primera)
The flagship channel of state broadcaster RTVE has a reputation for toeing the government line. However, the recent appointment of a committee assigned with restructuring the network comes with the promise from Prime Minister Zapatero that the era of political bias in the broadcaster has come to an end. Time will tell.

TVE 2 (La Dos)
The least commercial of all the TV channels, La 2 is good for documentaries and late-night movies (often in VO).

Antena 3
A private channel with an emphasis on family entertainment mixed with late-night salaciousness.

Tele 5
Another private channel. This celeb-obsessed station is the one to blame for the Spanish Big Brother, *El Gran Hermano*. It is also the Formula 1 channel, which has become a national obsession since the rise and rise of one Fernando Alonso.

Telemadrid
Madrid's own station. Good for live football on Saturday and the Megahit movie on Sunday nights, but bad for political bias. It functions as a mouthpiece for the local PP administration to such an extent that opposition PSOE politicians boycotted the station in early 2007.

digital +
A subscriber channel with a good selection of sport, movies and US hits. Many hotels and bars receive it.

Cuatro
This new channel, which filled the gap left by Canal+, is aiming squarely at people in their twenties with its mixture of American imports, flashy news programmes and chat shows.

La Sexta
La Sexta's launch was plagued by the need to retune everyone's receivers – particularly important given they showed some of the more significant matches in the 2006 World Cup. Now they're up and running, their programming focuses on a mixture of documentaries, films and the obligatory American imports.

MONEY

Spain is part of the euro zone. One euro is made up of 100 *céntimos*. One thing to remember is that the

British/ US practice on decimal points and commas is reversed (so 1.000 euros means one thousand euros, while 1,00 euro is one euro). There are banknotes for €5, €10, €20, €50, €100, €200 and €500, in different colours and designs. Then there are three copper coins (five, two and one *céntimo*), three gold-coloured coins (50, 20 and 10 *céntimos*) and large coins for one euro (silver centre, gold rim) and two euros (gold centre, silver rim).

Banks & exchange

Banks and savings banks (*cajas de ahorros*) readily accept cash and travellers' cheques (you must show your passport however). Commission rates vary, and it's worth shopping around before changing money (although banks usually give the best rates); also, given the rates charged by Spanish banks, it's often cheaper to get money from an ATM machine by credit or debit card rather than with travellers' cheques. It is almost always quicker to change money at larger bank offices than at local branches.

There are many small bureaux de change (*cambio*), particularly on Gran Via and Puerta del Sol. Exchange rates are usually worse than in banks.

Bank hours

Banks and savings banks normally open 8am-2pm Monday-Friday. From October to May many branches also open from 9am to 1pm on Saturday. Hours vary a little between different banks, and some have branches that stay open until around 5pm one day a week (usually Thursday). Savings banks often open late on Thursday afternoons, but are less likely to open on Saturdays. Banks are closed on public holidays.

Out-of-hours services

Outside normal hours you can change money at the airport (terminals T-1 and T-2, open 24hrs daily), at main train stations (Atocha, 9am-9pm daily; Chamartin, 8am-10pm daily), in El Corte Inglés (*see p184*), in hotels, at private *cambios* and at the places listed below. At the airport, Chamartin and outside some banks in Gran Via and Puerta del Sol there are automatic cash exchange machines that accept notes in major currencies, in good condition (be careful if you need to use these at night).

American Express

Plaza de las Cortes 2, Huertas (902 37 56 37). Metro Banco de España. **Open** 9am-7.30pm Mon-Fri; 9am-2pm Sat. **Map** p328 I12. The usual services, including money transfer worldwide in 24 hours.

Other locations throughout the city.

Western Union Money Transfer

Change Express, Gran Via 25, Sol & Gran Via (90 063 36 33). Metro Callao. **Open** 10am-11pm Mon-Sat. **Map** p324 G11. The local Western Union agent. It's the quickest if not the cheapest way to have money sent from abroad.

Other locations throughout the city.

Chequepoint

Plaza de Callao 4, Sol & Gran Via (www.chequepoint.com). **Open** 9am-11pm daily. **Map** p323 G11. An international exchange company.

Credit cards

Major credit and charge cards are accepted in most hotels, shops and restaurants. You can withdraw cash with major cards from most bank ATMs, which provide instructions in different languages. Exchange rates and handling fees often work out more economical than exchanging cash or travellers' cheques. Banks will advance cash against credit cards over the counter, but prefer you to use an ATM.

Lost or stolen cards

American Express *freephone 902 37 56 37.*

Diners Club *902 40 11 12.*

Mastercard *freephone 900 97 12 31.*

Visa *900 99 11 24.*

Tax

There are different rates of sales tax (IVA): for hotels and restaurants, the rate is eight per cent; in shops, it's generally 18 per cent, but on some items four to seven per cent. IVA is generally included in listed prices – if not, the expression '*mas IVA*' (plus tax) must be stated after the price. In shops displaying a 'Tax-Free Shopping' sticker, non-EU residents can reclaim tax on large purchases (*see p184*).

OPENING TIMES

Eating, drinking and shopping all happen late in Madrid. The siesta has faded to a myth, but *madrileños*

do operate to a distinctive schedule. Most shops open from 10am to 2pm, and 5-5.30pm to 8-8.30pm, Monday to Saturday, although many stay closed on Saturday afternoons. Food markets open earlier, around 8am. In July and especially in August most shops and services (such as the Post Office and administrations) close in the afternoon. August is also the time when most shops, bars and restaurants close for their annual holidays (from two weeks up to the whole month). Major stores and malls are open from 10am to 9pm without a break, Monday to Saturday (for the vexed question of Sunday shopping, *see pp183-184*). Big supermarkets (Al Campo, Carrefour) open from 10am to 10pm Mon-Sat and the first Sunday of each month.

Madrileños still eat, drink, go out and stay out later than their neighbours in virtually every other European country. Most restaurants are open 1.30-2pm to 4pm, and 9pm to midnight, and many close on Sunday nights and Mondays, and for at least part of August. Many businesses finish at 3pm in the summer. Most museums (state ones) close one day a week, usually Monday.

POLICE

Spain has several police forces. In Madrid the most important are the local Policia Municipal, in navy and pale blue, and the Policia Nacional, in darker blue and white uniforms (or all-blue combat gear). Each force has its own responsibilities, although they overlap. Municipales are principally concerned with traffic and parking problems and local regulations. The force with primary responsibility for dealing with crime are the Nacionales. The Guardia Civil, in green, are responsible, among other things, for policing inter-city highways, and customs.

Reporting a crime

If you are robbed or attacked, you should report the incident as soon as possible at the nearest Policia Nacional station (*comisaria*), where you will be asked to make an official statement (*denuncia*). It is extremely unlikely that anything you have lost will ever be recovered, but you will need the *denuncia* in order to make an insurance claim. Very few police officers speak any English.

Comisaría del Centro
C/Leganitos 19, Sol & Gran Vía
(information 060, station 91 548
79 85, operator 902 10 21 12).
Metro Santo Domingo or Plaza de
España. **Map** p323 F10.
The Policía Nacional headquarters
for central Madrid, near Plaza de
España. Some other police stations
in the city centre are listed below;
all are open 24hrs daily.
Chamberí
C/Rafael Calvo 33 (91 322 32 78).
Metro Iglesia. **Map** p324 K6.
Huertas/Retiro
C/Huertas 76-78 (91 322 10 17).
Metro Antón Martín. **Map** p328
J13.
Salamanca
C/Príncipe de Asturias 8 (91 444
81 20). Metro Manuel Becerra.

POSTAL SERVICES

If you just need normal-rate stamps
(*sellos*), it's easier to buy them in an
estanco (*see below*). Post offices now
have automatic stamp dispensing
machines (with a weighing system)
but they do not always work.
**Oficina Principal de Correos
en Madrid**
Paseo del Prado 1, Retiro (91 523
06 94, www.correos.es). Metro
Banco de España. **Open** 8.30am-
9.30pm Mon-Fri; 8.30am-2pm Sat .
Map p328 J11.
The central post office relocated
from the magnificent Palacio de
Cibeles, to this building nearby in
2008. All manner of postal services
are available at separate windows.
Faxes can be sent and received at
all post offices, but rates are
expensive, so use a private fax
bureau. Not all services are
available at all times. Mail sent
poste restante should be addressed
to Lista de Correos, 28000 Madrid,
Spain. To collect, bring your
passport. For express post, say
you want to send a '*carta urgente*'.
Other city centre post offices are
at El Corte Inglés, C/Preciados 1-4,
Sol & Gran Vía; Carrera de San
Francisco 13, La Latina; C/Mejía
Lequerica 7, Chueca; C/Jorge Juan
20, Salamanca, and at Terminal
1 in the airport.

Postal rates & postboxes

Letters and postcards up to 20g cost
30¢ within Spain, 58¢ to Europe and
North Africa, and 78¢ to the rest of
the world. Note that you will pay
more for 'irregular' shaped
envelopes (basically, not
rectangular). Cards and letters to
other European countries usually
arrive in 3-4 days, those to North
America in about a week. Normal
postboxes are yellow with two
horizontal red stripes. There are
also a few special red postboxes for
urgent mail, with hourly collections.
Postal Exprés
Available at all post offices, this
efficient express mail offers next-
day delivery within Spain of
packages up to 1kg (2.2lb), for
€10-€12, according to distance
and dimension.

Estancos

The main role of the tobacco shop
or *estanco* (look for a brown and
yellow sign with the word '*tabacos*')
is, of course, to supply tobacco-
related products. But they also sell
stamps, phonecards and Metrobús
and monthly *abono* tickets.
Estancos are the only places to
obtain official money vouchers
(*papel de estado*), needed for
dealings with Spanish bureaucracy.
Some have photocopiers/
fax facilities.

QUEUING

Despite appearances, Spaniards
have a highly developed queuing
culture. People don't always bother
standing in line, but they generally
know when it is their turn. Common
practice is to ask when you first
arrive, to no one in particular,
'*¿Quién da la vez?*' or '*Quién es
el último/la última?*' ('Who's last?');
see who nods, and follow on after
them. Say '*yo*' (me) to the next
person who asks.

RELIGION

Anglican

**St George's (British
Embassy Church)**
C/Núñez de Balboa 43,
Salamanca (91 576 51 09,
www.stgeorgesmadrid.com). Metro
Velázquez. **Services** 7.30pm Wed;
10.30am Fri; 8.30am, 10am, 11.30am
Sun. Consult the Grapevine section
of the website for latest service
times. **Map** p325 M8.

Catholic (in English)

Our Lady of Mercy
C/Drácena 23, Chamartín (91 350
34 49, www.ourladyofmercy.info).
Metro Pío XII. **English Mass**
11am Sun.
No shortage of Spanish Masses, but
this is the Catholic church for the
English-speaking parish of Madrid.

Jewish

Sinagoga de Madrid
C/Balmes 3, Eastern suburbs (91
591 31 31). Metro Iglesia. **Prayers**
8am Mon-Fri; 9.15am Sat; 9am Sun
& at dusk daily.

Muslim

**Centro Cultural
Islámico de Madrid**
C/Salvador de Madariaga 4,
Eastern suburbs (91 326 26 10,
www.ccislamico.com). Metro Barrio
de la Concepción. **Open** 10am-8pm
Mon-Thur, Sat, Sun; noon-4pm Fri.

RENTING A FLAT

The price of flats to rent in Madrid
varies wildly, so it pays to shop
around. A room in a shared flat
costs upwards of €300 a month,
while a one-bedroom flat is around
€600 or more. Places to look for flat
ads are the papers *Segundamano*
and *Anuntis* and the English
language magazine *InMadrid*
(for all, *see p303*). Another option
is to look around for '*Se alquila*'
(to rent) signs.
Contratos de alquiler (rental
agreements) generally cover a
five-year period, within which a
landlord can only raise the rent
each year in line with inflation, set
in the official price index (IPC).
Landlords usually ask for the
equivalent of one month's rent as
a *fianza* (deposit) and a month's
rent in advance. Details of contracts
(especially with regards to
responsibility for repairs) vary a lot;
don't sign a *contrato* unless you're
fully confident of your Spanish
and/or a lawyer or *gestor* has
looked at it.

SAFETY

As in most major cities, street crime
is a problem in Madrid and tourists
are often targeted. One plus point
is that pickpocketing and bag-
snatching are more likely than
any violent crime. Places to be
especially on your guard are the
Puerta del Sol, Gran Vía, the Plaza
Mayor, the Plaza Santa Ana and,
above all, the Rastro and Retiro
park; watch out, too, on the metro.
The area around the junction of
Gran Vía and Calle Montera is a
centre of street prostitution, and
can feel uncomfortable at night.
Recently, the Lavapiés district has
acquired a reputation for street
crime, which has developed
alongside growing racial tension

in the area, with robberies often attributed to young, homeless North African illegal immigrants, even though most thefts reported by *Time Out* readers and local media seem to involve teenage eastern European or gypsy girls.

Street criminals prey very deliberately on the unwary, and their chances of success can be limited greatly by the following simple precautions.

● When sitting in a café, especially at an outside table, never leave a bag or coat on the ground, on the back of a chair or anywhere you cannot see it clearly. If in doubt, keep it on your lap.
● Give the impression of knowing what's going on around you, and – without getting paranoid – be alert and watch out to see if you are being followed.
● Wear shoulder bags pulled to the front, not at your back, especially in the underground. Keep the bag closed and a hand on top of it.
● Avoid pulling out large notes to pay for things, especially in the street at night; try not to get large notes when changing money.
● Be aware that street thieves often work in pairs or groups; if someone hassles you for money or to buy something, or pulls out a map and asks for directions, keep walking, as this can be a ruse to distract you so that the thief's 'partner' can get at your bag. This is often done pretty crudely, and so is not hard to recognise.
● Be extremely careful when you withdraw money from ATMs. Don't let anyone distract your attention while putting in your PIN code.
● Beware of fake policemen: if someone asks to see your ID, ask to see their identification first.

SMOKING

Spaniards smoke – big time. It's not unusual for a bank cashier to serve you while puffing on the first of the day. Likewise, it's unusual to find non-smoking areas in restaurants or bars, although smoking bans in cinemas, theatres, the airport and on mainline trains are generally respected. Smoking is officially banned throughout the metro system, but many people take this to mean on trains only, and not station platforms.

STUDY

Foreign students from the EU staying more than three months require a residency permit (Tarjeta de Residencia Para la Realización de Estudios); non-EU students may also need a visa. For more details, *see p307* **Studying in Madrid**.

Accommodation

RoomMadrid
C/Conde Duque 7, Malasaña (91 548 03 35, www. roommadrid.es). Metro Plaza España. **Open** 10am-8pm Mon-Fri. **Map** p323 E9. This agency specialises in finding rooms in shared flats, with a minimum stay of one month in summer and three months from September to June. Commission starts at €70. At busy times you'll need to make an appointment a few hours in advance.

Madrid Sal y Ven
C/Cochabamba 17 (91 457 47 79, www.salyven.net). Metro Colombia. **Open** 9.30am-2pm, 3.30-6pm Mon-Fri. **Map** p324 K10. Finds rooms in shared flats with a minimum stay of one week. The agency charges an inscription charge of €60 and commission on top of that.

Language learning

Carpe Diem
C/Fuencarral 13, 2°, Malasaña (91 522 31 22, www.carpemadrid.com). Metro Gran Vía. **Open** 10am-7pm Mon-Fri. **Map** p323 H11. A young, funky Spanish-language academy, with small groups and enthusiastic teachers.

Academia Actual Plus
Gran Vía 71, 1° izq, Sol & Gran Vía (91 547 56 08, www.actualmadrid. com). Metro Plaza de España. **Open** 9.30am-2pm, 4-8pm Mon-Fri. **Map** p323 F10. A central and highly recommended school. There are no more than eight students per class.

Escuela Oficial de Idiomas
C/Jesús Maestro 5, Chamberí (91 533 58 02/03, www. eoidiomas.com). Metro Islas Filipinas. **Open** 10am-2pm, 4-9pm Mon-Fri. Closed July, Aug. This government-run school offers courses in Spanish through the academic year. The school has several other centres in the Madrid area; call for a full list. Registration is in August/ September and April/May; competition for places is extremely stiff.

International House
C/Zurbano 8, Chamberí (902 14 15 17, www.ihmadrid.com). Metro Alonso Martínez. **Open** 9am-8.30pm Mon-Fri. **Map** p324 J8.

Offers Spanish courses at all levels. **Other locations** throughout the city.

Universidad Complutense de Madrid
Secretaría del Centro Complutense para la Enseñanza del Español, Facultad de Filología, Ciudad Universitaria (91 394 53 25, www. ucm.es). **Open** *Office* Sept-June 10am-1pm, 3-6pm Mon-Fri. July 10am-1pm Mon-Fri. Closed Aug. Three-month Spanish courses for foreigners are held during the academic year. Higher-level students can study linguistics, literature and culture; there are also intensive language courses.

Universities

Erasmus, Socrates & Lingua programmes
Information in the UK: British Council, 1 Kingsway, Cardiff (029 2092 4311, www.britishcouncil.org/ erasmus.htm).
The Erasmus student-exchange scheme and Lingua project (for language learning) are the main parts of the EU's Socrates programme to help students move freely between member states. To be eligible you must be studying at an exchange institution. Prospective students should contact their college's Erasmus co-ordinator.

Universidad de Alcalá de Henares
C/Escritorios, 4, Alcalá de Henares (91 881 23 78, www.lingua.edu.es). **Open** *Office* 9am-2pm, 4-7pm Mon-Fri. Offers Spanish courses for foreigners all year. Intensive month-long courses are offered between June and September and cost €680 for language-only courses or €850 for language and culture courses.

Universidad Autónoma de Madrid
Ciudad Universitaria de Cantoblanco, Ctra de Colmenar km15 (91 497 46 33, www.uam.es). **Open** *Office* 9am-2pm, 4-6pm Mon-Thur; 9am-2pm Fri. The UAM now competes in prestige with the Complutense.

Universidad Carlos III
C/Madrid 126, Getafe (91 624 60 00, 91 624 95 00, www.uc3m.es). **Open** *Office* 9am-2pm, 4-6pm Mon-Fri. One of Madrid's newest universities, with campuses in Getafe and Leganés.

Universidad Complutense de Madrid
Avda de Séneca 2, Moncloa (91 452 04 00, www.ucm.es). **Open** *Office*

9am-2pm, 4-6pm Mon-Thur; 9am-2pm Fri. The prestigious Complutense is Madrid's main university. The largest and oldest in Spain, it is home to 98,000 students, 3,000 of them from abroad.

TELEPHONES

Since the Spanish national phone company (Telefónica) was privatised, other companies – such as Jazztel and Ono – now compete with it in certain areas. Nevertheless, Telefónica remains the main player in the field as far as infrastructure is concerned, though its prices remain relatively high.

Dialling & codes

It is necessary to dial provincial area codes with all phone numbers in Spain, even when you are calling from within the same area. Hence, all normal phone numbers in the Madrid area are preceded by 91, and you must dial this whether you're calling within Madrid, from

elsewhere in Spain or from abroad. Calls from numbers beginning 90 can only be connected if dialled from within Spain. Numbers beginning 900 are freephone lines; 901, 902 or 906 numbers are special-rate services and can be very pricey, especially if dialled from a mobile phone. Spanish mobile phone numbers have six digits and begin with a 6.

International & long-distance calls

To call abroad, dial 00 followed by the country code, then the area code (omitting the first zero in UK numbers) and number. To call Madrid from abroad, dial the international code (00 in the UK, 001 from the USA), then 34 for Spain.

Australia *61.*
Canada *1.*
Irish Republic *353.*
New Zealand *64.*
United Kingdom *44.*
USA *1.*

Mobile phones

The Spanish are mobile (*móvil*) mad and just about everybody has one (or two). You can pay each month or use rechargeable pre-paid cards. Call costs depend on the type of contract you have. Mobile phones from other countries can be used in Spain with a 'roaming' system, which you need to activate before leaving home.
Spain Cell Phone
687 558 529,
www.puertademadrid.
com/rentacellphone.
Offers short- and long-term mobile phone rental. Call rates are low and incoming calls are free.

Phone centres

For international calls it's often worth using a call centre (*locutorio*). You don't need change (you are charged when you've finished your call), the booths keep out noise, and many offer international call rates cheaper than Telefónica's. There are many phone centres around Lavapiés, Huertas and Malasaña.

STUDYING IN MADRID

There are plenty of learning opportunities for foreign adults at Madrid's universities and private institutions. Unsurprisingly, many of these are Spanish-language courses.

Language schools offer intensive summer courses in general Spanish (from beginner level to advanced) lasting from one week to four months or more. **EleMadrid** (www.elemadrid.com), **Alba Language Consulting** (www.albalanguage.com) or **International House** (www.ihmadrid.com) also run specialised courses for job-related Spanish (in fields including medicine, law, commerce and hotel management) and for those who plan to become Spanish teachers. Many of the schools, such as **Acento Español** (www.acentoespanol.com), **Academia Contacto** (www.academiacontacto.com), **Academia InHispania** (www.inhispania.com) or **Idiomas Plus** (www.madridplus.es) balance the tuition programme with

leisure activities aimed at allowing students to learn about the city and Spanish culture. Schools can also help with accommodation.

For those who already have a reasonable level of Spanish, there are plenty of other interesting programmes around. **Universidad Complutense de Madrid**'s (*see p306*) prestigious summer lecture series have been taking place for the last 17 years in the mountain town of El Escorial. Lecturers have included luminaries such as poet Rafael Albertí, film-makers Pedro Almodóvar and Carlos Saura, and sculptor Eduardo Chillida, along with international artists, politicians, economists and scientists. Subjects are usually related in some way to current events, and have drawn on disciplines as varied as economics, art, politics, literature, psychology, sociology and environmentalism. Places on the lecture series are limited and fees are quite high (for details and fees, see www.ucm.es/info/cv). Students can apply for a

scholarship that covers costs of accommodation and meals.

The **Madrid Chamber of Commerce** offers a good selection of vocational courses. There are classes throughout the year in subjects ranging from business Spanish for foreign executives to Spanish wine-tasting and oenology (you'll need a good level of Spanish for the latter). These courses have a very good reputation, both in Spain and abroad. Tuition fees are reasonable and class sizes are limited, which means there can be some competition for places. Check out www.camaramadrid.es for more information (click on 'formación'). Or phone the Chamber of Commerce (91 538 38 38, 8.30am-8.30pm Mon-Fri).

Cooking courses are popular too. **Club Cooking** (www.club-cooking.com) is a fun and friendly school with classes in cookery for all standards (there are even courses for children). Courses cover topics such as cooking with cod, rice cooking, Moroccan food, and cakes and pastry.

Often other services – fax, internet, currency exchange, money transfer – are available. There is a directory of *locutorios* at www.ocio latino.com in the 'Guia Latina'.

Money Exchange
C/Infantas 1, Chueca (91 532 75 35). Metro Gran Vía. **Open** 10am-10pm daily. **Map** p324 H10.

Public phones

Payphones are plentiful in the city, although due to the traffic noise, it's often worth using a phone in a bar or café, even though they often cost 50 per cent more than regular booths. Most models of payphone take coins (from five *céntimos* up), phonecards and credit cards, and have a digital display with instructions in English and other languages.

The first minute of a daytime local call costs around 11 *céntimos*; to a mobile phone around 35¢; to a 902 number, around 18¢. You are usually given credit to make more calls without having to insert more money.

Kioskos and estancos sell €5 (up to 70 minutes of communication) and €10 (up to 140 minutes) phonecards by various companies. Many of the cards give you a free number to call; an operator or automatic system then connects you with the number you want and can tell you how much is left on your card.

Operator services

Usually, operators will only speak Spanish, though most international operators speak basic English.

National directory enquiries
11818, 11850, 11828, 11824, 11819

International directory enquiries & operator 11825
National operator 1009.
National operator for calls to Europe 1008.
National operator for calls outside Europe 1005.

Telefónica telephone faults service 1002

Time 1212

TIME

Spain is an hour ahead of UK time, six hours ahead of US EST and nine hours ahead of PST. Daylight saving time runs concurrently with the UK.

TIPPING

There are no rules or percentages for tipping and in general Spaniards tip very little. It is usual to leave five or ten per cent for a restaurant waiter, rarely more than €4, and people often leave a few *céntimos* of small change in a bar. It's also usual to tip hotel porters, toilet and cinema attendants. In taxis the norm is around five per cent, although you can give more for longer journeys, or if a driver has been especially helpful.

TOILETS

Public toilets are rare, although there are some with an attendant in the Retiro, by the lake; at Chamartín and Atocha stations; and in the Paseo del Prado. However, proprietors usually don't mind if you pop into a bar or café (better, though, if you ask first), and big stores such as El Corte Inglés or fast-food restaurants are a good bet.

TOURIST INFORMATION

The Centros de Turismo run by the city council, and the tourist office run by the regional authority (Comunidad de Madrid) provide similar basic information on Madrid and the surrounding region, plus free maps. The city also runs a phone information line for locals, 010 (*see below*), that can be useful to visitors. Tourist offices do not make hotel bookings but can advise on vacancies; for booking agencies, *see p129* **A Home from Home**.

Full information on what's on is in local papers, listings magazines and local English-language magazines (*see p303*). For useful websites, *see p311*.

Centro de Turismo de Madrid
Plaza Mayor 27, Los Austrias (91 588 16 36). Metro Sol. **Open** 9.30am-8.30pm daily. **Map** p327 G12.

Centro de Turismo Colón
Plaza de Colón, Salamanca (91 588 16 36). Metro Colón. **Open** 9.30am-8.30pm daily. **Map** p324 K9.
Located in the old pedestrian subway running under the Paseo de la Castellana, this is the largest tourist information office in the city. Smaller *puntos de información turística*, all connected to the same telephone number as the Centros de Turismo, are located at: the Plaza de Cibeles; the Plaza de Callao; just off the Plaza del Emperador Carlos V on C/Santa Isabel; and at Barajas Airport Terminals 2 & 4.

Oficinas de Turismo de la Comunidad de Madrid
C/Duque de Medinaceli 2, Huertas (91 429 49 51, 902 10 00 07). Metro Banco de España. **Open** 8am-8pm Mon-Sat; 9am-2pm Sun. **Map** p328 I12.

Summer information officers
During July and August pairs of young information guides, in bright yellow and blue uniforms, are sent to roam the central area ready to answer enquiries in a courageous variety of languages (8am-8pm daily). They also staff information stands at Puerta del Sol, Plaza del Callao, Plaza Mayor, by the Palacio Real and by the Prado.

010 phoneline
Open 8am-9pm Mon-Fri; 9am-2pm Sat.
A city-run information line that will answer enquiries of any kind on Madrid, and particularly on events promoted by the city council. Calls are accepted in French and English, but you may have to wait for an English-speaking operator. From outside Madrid, call 91 529 82 10.

VISAS & IMMIGRATION

Spain is one of the EU countries that is party to the Schengen Agreement (which includes all of the EU except the UK, Ireland or the countries that joined in May 2004). These countries share immigration procedures and have reduced border controls between each other. To enter Spain nationals from countries that are party to the agreement need only show their national ID card, but British, Irish, those from the new EU countries and all non-EU citizens must have full passports.

Additional visas are not needed by US, Canadian, Australian, New Zealand or Israeli citizens for stays of up to three months. Citizens of South Africa and some other countries do need a visa to enter Spain. They can be obtained from Spanish consulates in other European countries as well as in your home country.

WATER

Madrid's tap water is good and safe to drink, with less of the chlorine taste that you get in some Spanish cities. There are occasional water shortages in summer, and signs posted in hotels urge guests to avoid wasting water.

If you want tap rather than bottled water in a restaurant specify that you want *agua del grifo*.

WHEN TO GO

The climate of Madrid has justly been described as 'nine months of winter (*invierno*) and three months of hell (*infierno*)'. Many people can't cope with the summer heat, others love it – and the city is great fun during the fiestas. *See also pp206-211.*

Climate

Winter in Madrid can be very cold, although there's often bright, crisp sunshine and most rain falls in autumn and spring. Spring is unpredictable – February can often be freakishly warm, while in April, rain is likely. Summer temperatures range from hot to unbearably hot, although it's a dry heat with little humidity. In July and August it doesn't really cool down at night, making partying in the street great fun, but sleeping less so. Traditionally there's a mass exodus in August. Autumn weather is usually bright and warm and it's often possible to eat and drink outside well into October.

Holidays

On public holidays (*fiestas*), virtually all shops, banks and offices, and some bars and restaurants, are closed. There is a near-normal public transport service, though, except on Christmas Day and New Year's Day, and many museums do remain open, albeit with Sunday hours operating. When a holiday falls on a Tuesday or Thursday it's a common practice for people to take the day before or after the weekend off as well, in a long weekend called a *puente* (bridge). Many places are also closed for the whole of Easter Week. For the city's festivals, *see pp206-211*. The usual official holidays are:

New Year's Day/Año Nuevo 1 Jan; Three Kings/Reyes Magos 6 Jan; Good Friday/Viernes Santo; May (Labour) Day/Fiesta del Trabajo 1 May; Madrid Day/Día de la Comunidad de Madrid 2 May; San Isidro 15 May; Virgen de la Paloma 15 Aug; Discovery of America/Día de la Hispanidad 12 Oct; All Saints' Day/Todos los Santos 1 Nov; Virgen de la Almudena 9 Nov; Constitution Day/Día de la Constitución 6 Dec; Immaculate Conception/La Inmaculada 8 Dec; Christmas Day/Navidad 25 Dec.

WOMEN

Instituto de la Mujer
C/Condesa de Venadito 34, Concepción (91 363 80 00, www.inmujeres.es). Metro Barrio de la Concepción. **Open** 9am-2pm Mon-Fri.
A government organisation with a useful information servic (90 019 10 10, 9am-11pm Mon-Fri). The Institute has a legal office that deals with cases of discrimination (91 700 19 10).

WORKING

There is a huge number of foreigners living and working in Madrid. Ninety-five per cent of those from the EU are teaching English. To get a job in one of the academies with better pay and conditions, it's advisable to have a relevant qualification such as TEFL. Private classes are also available, but bear in mind that work often dries up over the summer and holiday periods.
There is a lot of red tape involved in working in Madrid; you can ignore the bureaucracy for a while, but in the long run it's best to sort things out. If you come here contracted from your country of origin, papers should be dealt with by your employer. The quickest way to deal with the state's love of form-filling is to resort to *gestorías*.
A ruling made in March 2003 effectively exempts many EU citizens living in Spain from the obligation to apply for and carry a resident's card (tarjeta de residencia). Students, along with contracted workers, freelancers, business owners or retired people who have already made Spanish Social Security contributions, are entitled to live in Spain and use their own country's ID card, or passport, for all dealings or transactions. Not all branches of the administration are aware of the ruling but it is clearly stated both on the British Embassy's website (www.ukinspain.com) and the Ministry of the Interior's (www.mir.es/SGACAVT/extranje).
Everybody in Spain, both nationals and foreigners, however, is obliged to carry a valid form of ID. In the case of those foreigners who do not have a national ID card, this means carrying your passport, which is risky. Technically not legal, but usually acceptable, is to carry a photocopy of the relevant pages. Alternatively, you can apply for a resident's card voluntarily, at the

foreigners' police station, the Comisaría de Extranjería. First you must obtain the NIE (*número de identificación de extranjeros* – foreigners' identity number). The process is simple – go to the Comisaría de Extranjería or a police station that deals with foreigners' affairs with your passport and a photocopy of the important pages, fill out an application form and you will be sent your number by post. The number is used for all financial dealings and is necessary for opening bank accounts, tax declarations and so on. For the residency card, you will then need three passport photos, along with your passport and a photocopy. Proof of income and medical insurance are no longer necessary.
Non-EU citizens have a tougher time. While in Spain on a tourist visa you are technically not allowed to work, though many do. If you are made a job offer while in Spain you must return to your home country and apply for a *visado de residencia* (residence visa). Without this you may not enter Spain to work. The process can take some time and applications aren't always successful. Once the visa has been issued, you can travel to Spain, take up the job and begin the lengthy application process for a resident's card and work permit (*permiso de trabajo*). On making the application, the following documents must be submitted along with the official application form: photocopy of a valid passport; a police certificate from your home city stating that you have no prison record (officially translated into Spanish by a sworn translator); an official medical certificate (obtained upon arrival in Spain); three identical passport photographs; where applicable, documents proving why you are more capable of performing the job than a Spaniard or EU citizen; where necessary, proof that you have the qualifications or training required for the job. Work permits and resident's cards, once issued, are initially valid for one year, the second for two, the third for three. After five years you will be granted a permanent work permit, which, though valid indefinitely, must be renewed every five years. Good legal advice is recommended throughout the process.
Comisaría de Extranjería
C/General Pardiñas 90, Salamanca (general 91 322 68 40/student 91 322 68 13/14/residency 91 322 68 01). Metro Núñez de Balboa. **Open** 9am-2pm Mon-Fri. **Map** p325 M6.

Vocabulary

DIRECTORY

Like other Latin languages, Spanish has different familiar and polite forms of the second person (you). Many young people now use the familiar *tú* form most of the time; for foreigners, though, it's always advisable to use the more polite *usted* with people you do not know, and certainly with anyone over the age of 50. In the phrases listed here all verbs are given in the *usted* form. For help in making your way through menus, *see p134 and p159*.

PRONUNCIATION

c, before an i or an e, and z are like the th in thin. c in all other cases is as in cat. g, before an i or an e, and j are pronounced with a guttural h-sound that does not exist in English – like ch in Scottish lo**ch**, but much harder. g in all other cases is pronounced as in get. h at the beginning of a word is normally silent. ll is pronounced almost like a y. ñ is like ny in canyon. A single r at the beginning of a word and rr elsewhere are heavily rolled.

BASICS

hello *hola*; hello (when answering the phone) *hola, diga;* good morning, good day *buenos días;* good afternoon, good evening *buenas tardes;* good evening (after dark), good night *buenas noches;* goodbye/see you later *adiós/hasta luego;* please *por favor;* thank you (very much) *(muchas) gracias;* you're welcome *de nada;* do you speak English? *¿habla inglés?* I don't speak Spanish *no hablo español;* I don't understand *no entiendo;* what's your name? *¿cómo se llama?;* speak more slowly, please *hable más despacio, por favor;* wait a moment *espere un momento;* Sir/Mr *señor* (*sr*); Madam/Mrs *señora* (*sra*); Miss *señorita* (*srta*); excuse me/sorry *perdón;* excuse me, please *oiga* (the standard way to attract someone's attention, politely; literally 'hear me'); OK/fine/(or to a waiter) that's enough *vale;* where is... *¿dónde está...?;* why? *¿porqué?;* when? *¿cuándo?;* who? *¿quién?;* what? *¿qué?;* where? *¿dónde?;* how? *¿cómo?;* who is it? *¿quién*

es?, is/are there any... *¿hay...?* very *muy;* and *y;* or *o* with *con;* without *sin;* open *abierto;* closed *cerrado;* what time does it open/close? *¿a qué hora abre/cierra?;* pull (on signs) *tirar;* push *empujar;* I would like... *quiero...* (literally, 'I want...'); how many would you like? *¿cuántos quiere?;* I like *me gusta* I don't like *no me gusta;* good *bueno/a;* bad *malo/a;* well/badly *bien/mal;* small *pequeño/a;* big *gran, grande;* expensive *caro/a;* cheap *barato/a;* hot (food, drink) *caliente;* cold *frío/a;* something *algo;* nothing *nada;* more/less *más/menos;* more or less *más o menos;* the bill/check, please *la cuenta, por favor;* how much is it? *¿cuánto es?;* do you have any change? *¿tiene cambio?;* price *precio;* free *gratis* discount *descuento;* bank *banco;* to rent *alquilar;* (for) rent, rental *(en) alquiler;* post office *correos;* stamp *sello;* postcard *postal;* toilet *los servicios*

GETTING AROUND

airport *aeropuerto;* railway station *estación de ferrocarril/ estación de RENFE* (Spanish Railways); Metro station *estación de Metro;* entrance *entrada;* exit *salida;* car *coche;* bus *autobús;* train *tren;* a ticket *un billete;* return *de ida y vuelta;* bus stop *parada de autobús;* the next stop *la próxima parada;* excuse me, do you know the way to...? *¿oiga, señor/señora/ etc, sabe como llegar a...?;* left *izquierda;* right *derecha;* here *aquí;* there *allí;* straight on *recto;* to the end of the street *al final de la calle* as far as *hasta;* towards *hacia;* near *cerca;* far *lejos*

ACCOMMODATION

do you have a double/single room for tonight/one week? *¿tiene una habitación doble/para una persona para esta noche/ una semana?;* where is the car park? *¿dónde está el parking?;* we have a reservation *tenemos reserva;* an inside/ outside room *una habitación interior/exterior;* with/ without bathroom *con/sin baño;* shower *ducha* double

bed *cama de matrimonio;* with twin beds *con dos camas;* breakfast included *desayuno incluido;* air-conditioning *aire acondicionado;* lift *ascensor;* swimming pool *piscina*

TIME

morning *la mañana;* midday *mediodía;* afternoon/evening *la tarde;* night *la noche;* late night/early morning (roughly 1-6am) *la madrugada* now *ahora;* later *más tarde* yesterday *ayer;* today *hoy;* tomorrow *mañana;* tomorrow morning *mañana por la mañana* early *temprano;* late *tarde* delay *retraso;* delayed *retrasado* at what time...? *¿a qué hora...?* in an hour *en una hora* the bus will take 2 hours (to get there) *el autobús tardará dos horas (en llegar)* at 2 *a las dos* at 8pm *a las ocho de la tarde* at 1.30 *a la una y media* at 5.15 *a las cinco y cuarto* at 22.30 *a veintidós treinta*

NUMBERS

0 *cero;* 1 *un, uno, una;* 2 *dos;* 3 *tres;* 4 *cuatro;* 5 *cinco;* 6 *seis;* 7 *siete;* 8 *ocho;* 9 *nueve;* 10 *diez;* 11 *once;* 12 *doce;* 13 *trece;* 14 *catorce;* 15 *quince;* 16 *dieciséis;* 17 *diecisiete;* 18 *dieciocho;* 19 *diecinueve;* 20 *veinte;* 21 *veintiuno;* 22 *veintidós;* 30 *treinta;* 40 *cuarenta;* 50 *cincuenta;* 60 *sesenta;* 70 *setenta;* 80 *ochenta;* 90 *noventa;* 100 *cien;* 1,000 *mil;* 1,000,000 *un millón*

DAYS, MONTHS & SEASONS

Monday *lunes;* Tuesday *martes;* Wednesday *miércoles;* Thursday *jueves;* Friday *viernes;* Saturday *sábado;* Sunday *domingo* January *enero;* February *febrero;* March *marzo;* April *abril;* May *mayo;* June *junio;* July *julio;* August *agosto;* September *septiembre;* October *octubre;* November *noviembre;* December *diciembre* spring *primavera;* summer *verano;* autumn/fall *otoño;* winter *invierno*

Further Reference

READING

Art & architecture

Hugh Broughton *Madrid*
The capital's architecture analysed for a lay audience.
Jonathan Brown *Velázquez: Painter and Courtier* The most comprehensive study in English.
JH Elliott & Jonathan Brown *A Palace for a King: The Buen Retiro and the Court of Philip IV* A vivid reconstruction of the life, culture and spectacle of the Habsburg Court, and the grandest of Madrid's palaces.
Robert Hughes *Goya* A dynamic biography of Madrid's favourite son.
Michael Jacobs *Madrid Observed* A lively survey by one of the best current foreign writers on Spain. A good walking companion.

Food & drink

Alan Davidson *Tio Pepe Guide to the Seafood of Spain and Portugal* An excellent pocket-sized guide, with illustrations, to Spain's fishy delights.
Sam and Sam Clark *Moro* The best modern cookbook available in English for reproducing the tastes of Spain.

History, politics & culture

Phil Ball *Morbo* A fascinating history of Spanish football, with a good section on Real Madrid.
JH Elliott *Imperial Spain, 1469-1716* The standard history.
RA Fletcher *Moorish Spain* Varied account of a little-known period in European history.
Ronald Fraser *Blood of Spain* An oral history of the Spanish Civil War, the most vivid and human account of Spain's great crisis.
Juan Lalaguna *A Traveller's History of Spain* A handy introduction to the country.
John Hooper *The New Spaniards* The best survey of post-1975 Spain, updated to cover changes in the 1990s.
Paul Preston *Franco*; *Comrades!*; *Doves of War* Exhaustive portraits of the key players on both sides of the Spanish Civil War. The same author's *The Spanish Civil War* is a good concise account of the war.

Hugh Thomas, ed *Madrid, A Traveller's Companion* A great anthology of writing on Madrid from the Middle Ages to the 1930s, by authors as varied as Casanova, Pérez Galdós and the Duke of Wellington.
Giles Tremlett *Ghosts of Spain: Travels through a Country's Hidden Past* Now an essential read if you're interested in Spain's history and culture over the past century.

Literature

Pedro Almodóvar *Patty Diphusa Stories and Other Writings* Frothy, disposable, but full of the sparky, sexy atmosphere of the Madrid of La Movida.
Camilo José Cela *The Hive* Nobel-prizewinner Cela's sardonic masterpiece on Madrid in the aftermath of the Civil War.
Miguel de Cervantes *Don Quixote* The Golden Age classic, and still an entertaining read. Now available in an excellent and lively new translation by Edith Grossman.
Benito Pérez Galdós *Fortunata and Jacinta* The masterwork of Spain's great 19th-century realist novelist, a story of love and class of great depth set amid the political conflicts of 1860s Madrid. If you like *War and Peace*, you'll like this.
Antonio Múñoz Molina *Prince of Shadows* A psychological thriller based on the legacy of the recent past in modern Madrid.
Tim Parfitt *A Load of Bull: An Englishman's Adventures in Madrid* An entertaining memoir on *madrileños* and their customs.
Arturo Pérez Reverte *The Fencing Master*; *The Flanders Road*; *The Club Dumas* (also published as *The Dumas Club*) Elegant, unconventional mystery novels by one of the most lauded of current Spanish writers.
Benjamin Prado *Not Only Fire* Examination of post-Civil War intergenerational relationships by one of Spain's bright young hopes.
C J Sansom *Winter in Madrid* An insightful portrait of life in Madrid following the Spanish Civil War.

MUSIC

Plácido Domingo *Romanzas de Zarzuelas* One of his several recordings of lush tunes from the *zarzuelas* that have played a big part in the recent revival of Madrid's own comic operas.
El Gran Lapofsky *Spain is Different* A fantastic selection of Latin, bossa, nu-jazz and funk-infused tracks – some otherwise unavailable rarities – interspersed with skits from Spaniards telling us just why Spain is different.
Ray Heredia *Quien no corre, vuela* One of the most original new-flamenco performers.
Los Jóvenes Flamencos Several CDs in this series, bringing together all the best *nuevo flamenco* artists of the last 15 years, have been issued by the Nuevos Medios label. One at least is available outside Spain with the title *The Young Flamencos*.
El Lebrijano, con la Orquesta Arábigo Andaluza *Casablanca* Fascinating crossover recording by flamenco *cantaor* El Lebrijano, accompanied by Moroccan musicians and using traditional themes from Muslim Andalusia.
Carmen Linares *Antología* Classic flamenco themes sung by one of the best younger *cantaoras*. Another CD, *Carmen Linares, Cantaora*, may be more widely available outside Spain.
Corazón Loco *40 Joyas del Pop Español* Excellent intro to the perky, occasionally daft and sometimes pretty cool soundtrack of modern Madrid.
Paco de Lucía *Luzía*, or any of the many recordings by the greatest of modern flamenco guitarists.

MADRID ONLINE

www.madrid.es The Madrid Ayuntamiento's functional website, with some information in English.
www.madrid.org Equivalent site of the Comunidad: practical information on local services, in Spanish only.
www.esmadrid.com Useful website with information on all visitor attractions.
www.ctm-madrid.es Madrid transport information.
www.lanetro.com Concerts, clubs films and reviews.
www.lecool.com Weekly round-up of the city's quirkiest, coolest events.
www.renfe.es Spanish Railways' site, with online booking.
http://madrid.lanetro.com The hippest and best of local Spanish-language events and listings sites.

Content Index

INDEX

INDEX

Venue Index

INDEX

INDEX

Advertisers' Index

Please refer to the relevant pages for contact details.

Sopa de Ganso

INDEX

Maps

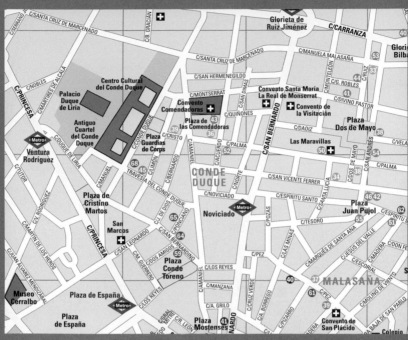

Area name....................................... **CHAMBERÍ**	
Place of interest and/or entertainment...........	
Park	
River	
Square	
Highway...	
Main road	
Pedestrian road.....................................	
Teleférico...	
Hospital or college.................................	✚
Church	✚
Tourist information................................	ℹ
Metro station	◆Metro◆

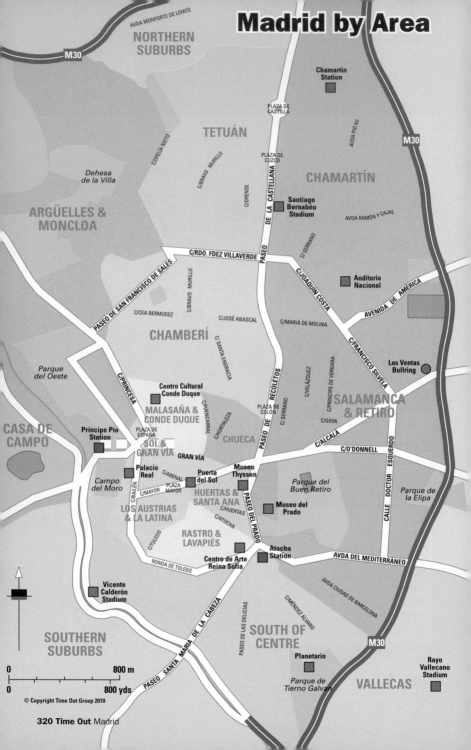

Madrid by Area

AVDA MONFORTE DE LEMOS

NORTHERN SUBURBS

M30

Chamartín Station

PLAZA DE CASTILLA

AVDA PIO XII

M30

TETUÁN

PLAZA DE CUZCO

CHAMARTÍN

Dehesa de la Villa

C/OFELIA NIETO

C/BRAVO MURILLO

C/ORENSE

PASEO DE LA CASTELLANA

Santiago Bernabéu Stadium

AVDA RAMÓN Y CAJAL

ARGÜELLES & MONCLOA

C/RDO. FDEZ VILLAVERDE

C/SERRANO

C/JOAQUIN COSTA

Auditorio Nacional

AVENIDA DE AMÉRICA

PASEO DE SAN FRANCISCO DE SALES

C/BRAVO MURILLO

C/CEA BERMUDEZ

C/JOSÉ ABASCAL

C/MARIÁ DE MOLINA

C/FRANCISCO SILVELA

CHAMBERÍ

C/SANTA ENGRACIA

Las Ventas Bullring

Parque del Oeste

C/PRINCESA

Centro Cultural Conde Duque

PASEO DE RECOLETOS

C/VELAZQUEZ

C/PRINCIPE DE VERGARA

SALAMANCA & RETIRO

CASA DE CAMPO

Príncipe Pío Station

PLAZA DE ESPAÑA

MALASAÑA & CONDE DUQUE

C/FUENCARRAL

C/HORTALEZA

PLAZA DE COLÓN

C/ SERRANO

C/GOYA

SOL & GRAN VÍA

GRAN VÍA

CHUECA

C/ALCALÁ

C/O'DONNELL

Palacio Real

C/ARENAL

Puerta del Sol

Museo Thyssen

PASEO DE RECOLETOS

Parque del Buen Retiro

CALLE DOCTOR ESQUERDO

Parque de la Elipa

Campo del Moro

C/BAILEN

C/MAYOR

PLAZA MAYOR

HUERTAS & SANTA ANA

Museo del Prado

LOS AUSTRIAS & LA LATINA

C/HUERTAS

C/ATOCHA

PASEO DEL PRADO

RASTRO & LAVAPIÉS

C/TOLEDO

Atocha Station

AVDA DEL MEDITERRÁNEO

Centro de Arte Reina Sofía

RONDA DE TOLEDO

Vicente Calderón Stadium

PASEO SANTA MARIA DE LA CABEZA

PASEO DE LAS DELICIAS

C/MÉNDEZ ALVARO

AVDA CIUDAD DE BARCELONA

SOUTHERN SUBURBS

SOUTH OF CENTRE

M30

Planetario

Rayo Vallecano Stadium

Parque de Tierno Galvan

VALLECAS

0   800 m

0   800 yds

© Copyright Time Out Group 2010

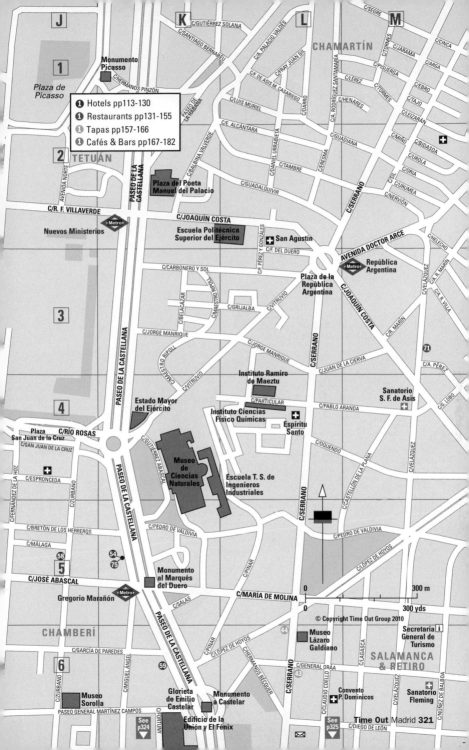

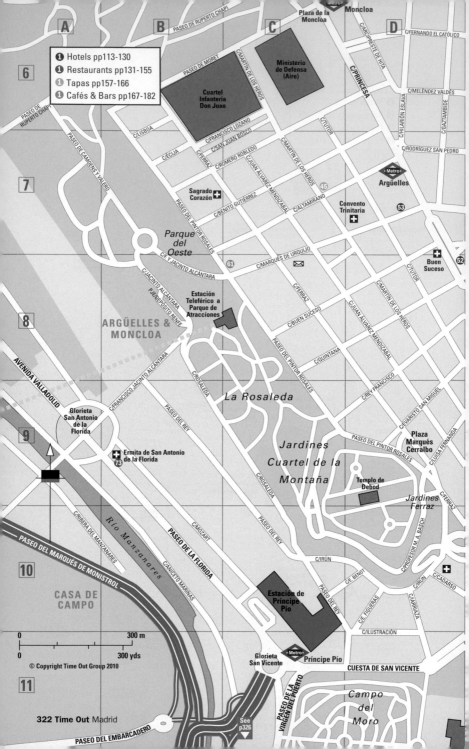

Legend

1 Hotels pp113-130
1 Restaurants pp131-155
1 Tapas pp157-166
1 Cafés & Bars pp167-182

A **B** **C** **D**

6 **7** **8** **9** **10** **11**

PASEO DE RUPERTO CHAPI
Plaza de la Moncloa
Moncloa
C/FERNANDO EL CATÓLICO
PASEO DE MORET
Ministerio de Defensa (Aire)
C/ARCIPRESTE DE HITA
C/PRINCESA
C/MELÉNDEZ VALDÉS
PASEO DE RUPERTO CHAPI
Cuartel Infantería Don Juan
C/MARTÍN DE LOS HEROS
C/CHILARIÓN ESLAVA
C/GAZTAMBIDE
C/LISBOA
C/FRANCISCO LOZANO
C/TUTOR
PASEO DE CAMOENS Y VALERO
C/ÉCIJA
C/ERAZ
C/SAN JUAN BOSCO
C/ROMERO ROBLEDO
C/JUAN ÁLVAREZ MENDIZÁBAL
C/MARTÍN DE LOS HEROS
C/RODRÍGUEZ SAN PEDRO
Sagrado Corazón
C/BENITO GUTIÉRREZ
45
C/ALTAMIRANO
Metro
Argüelles
53
PASEO DEL PINTOR ROSALES
Convento Trinitaria
Parque del Oeste
C/F. Y JACINTO ALCÁNTARA
61
C/MARQUÉS DE URQUIJO
C/FRAZ
52
Buen Suceso
C/JACINTO ALCÁNTARA
C/TUTOR
PJE. DEPÓSITO RENFE
Estación Teleférico a Parque de Atracciones
C/BUEN SUCESO
C/JUAN ÁLVAREZ MENDIZÁBAL
C/MARTÍN DE LOS HEROS
ARGÜELLES & MONCLOA
C/FRANCISCO JACINTO ALCÁNTARA
C/ROSALEJA
PASEO DEL PINTOR ROSALES
C/QUINTANA
C/REY FRANCISCO
AVENIDA VALLADOLID
PASEO DEL REY
La Rosaleda
C/EVARISTO SAN MIGUEL
Glorieta San Antonio de la Florida
Ermita de San Antonio de la Florida
73
Jardines
PASEO DEL PINTOR ROSALES
Plaza Marqués Cerralbo
C/LUISA FERNANDA
Cuartel de la Montaña
Templo de Debod
Jardines Ferraz
C/FRAZ
C/ROSALEJA
C/MOZART
PASEO DEL REY
C/RIBERA DE MANZANARES
C/ANICETO MARINAS
Río Manzanares
C/IRÚN
C/PROFESOR M. A. BASCH
C/CADARSO
PASEO DEL MARQUÉS DE MONISTROL
C/F. BENOT
C/IRÚN
C/AMARIZ
C/LUZÓN
CASA DE CAMPO
PASEO DE LA FLORIDA
Estación de Príncipe Pío
C/E. FIGUERAS
C/ILUSTRACIÓN

0   300 m
0   300 yds
© Copyright Time Out Group 2010

Glorieta San Vicente
Metro
Príncipe Pío
CUESTA DE SAN VICENTE
PASEO DE LA VIRGEN DEL PUERTO
Campo del Moro

See p326

PASEO DEL EMBARCADERO

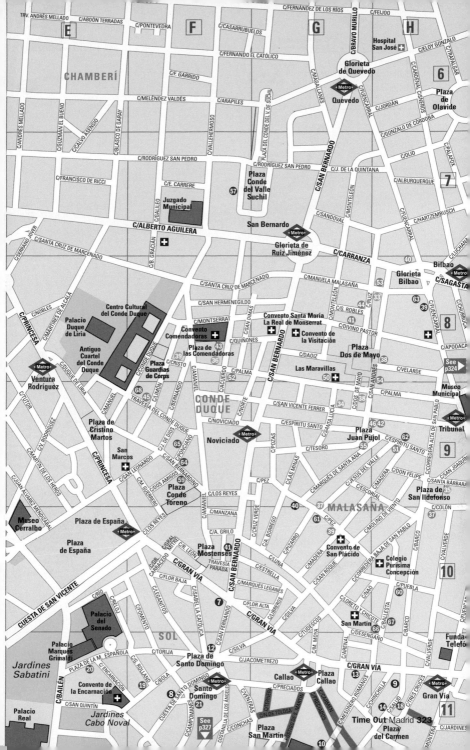

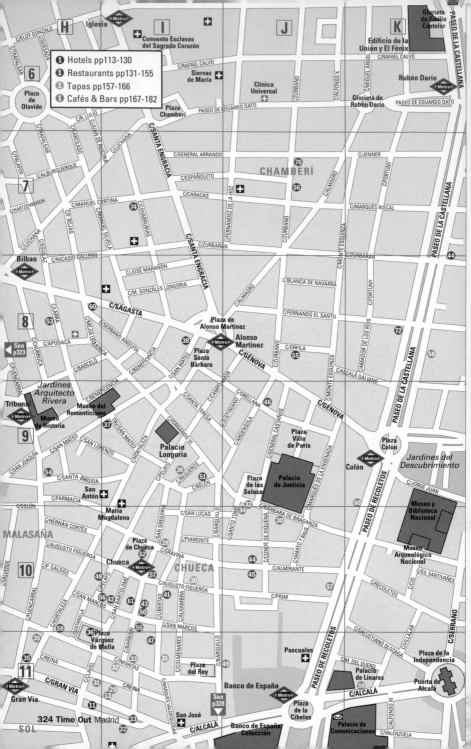

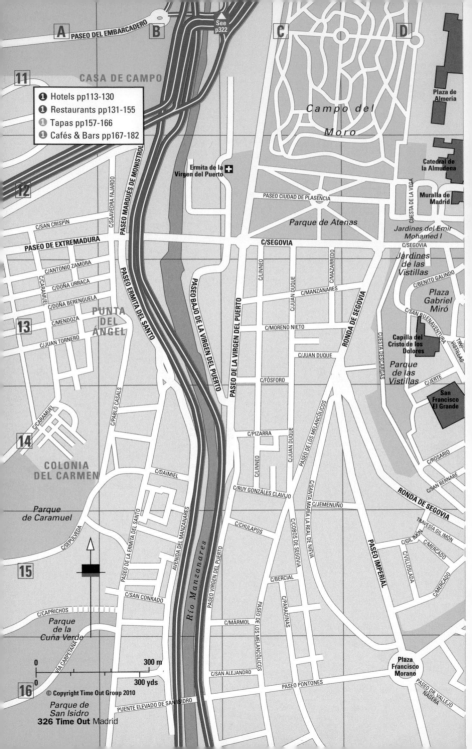

A PASEO DEL EMBARCADERO **B**

See p322

C

D

11 CASA DE CAMPO

❶ Hotels pp113-130
❶ Restaurants pp131-155
❶ Tapas pp157-166
❶ Cafés & Bars pp167-182

Plaza de Almería

Campo del Moro

Ermita de la Virgen del Puerto

Catedral de la Almudena

12 PASEO CIUDAD DE PLASENCIA

C/SAN CRISPÍN

PASEO DE EXTREMADURA

C/ANTONIO ZAMORA

C/DOÑA URRACA

C/DOÑA BERENGUELA

C/MENDOZA

C/JUAN TORNERO

13

PUNTA DEL ÁNGEL

Parque de Atenas

C/SEGOVIA

Muralla de Madrid

Jardines del Emir Mohamed I

C/SEGOVIA

Jardines de las Vistillas

C/BENITO GALINDO

Plaza Gabriel Miró

C/SAN BUENAVENTURA

Capilla del Cristo de los Dolores

Parque de las Vistillas

San Francisco El Grande

C/LINNEO

C/JUAN DUQUE

C/MANZANARES

C/MAZARREDO

C/MORENO NIETO

C/JUAN DUQUE

C/FÓSFORO

RONDA DE SEGOVIA

CUESTA DESCARGAS

C/JERTE

C/ROSARIO

14

COLONIA DEL CARMEN

C/PABLO CASALS

C/CARAMUEL

C/DAIMIEL

C/PIZARRA

C/LINNEO

C/JUAN DUQUE

C/RUY GONZÁLES CLAVIJO

PASEO DE LOS MELANCÓLICOS

C/SANTA MARÍA LA REAL DE NIEVA

C/JEMENUÑO

RONDA DE SEGOVIA

TRAVESÍA GIL IMÓN

C/GIL IMÓN

C/MERCADO

C/VILLOSLADA

C/SAN BERNABÉ

15

Parque de Caramuel

C/SEPÚLVEDA

PASEO DE LA ERMITA DEL SANTO

AVENIDA DEL MANZANARES

C/CHULAPOS

C/COBOS DE SEGOVIA

C/BERCIAL

C/PARADINAS

PASEO IMPERIAL

C/MERCADO

C/CAPRICHOS

C/SAN CONRADO

Parque de la Cuña Verde

VÍA CARPETANA

Río Manzanares

C/MÁRMOL

PASEO VIRGEN DEL PUERTO

PASEO DE LOS MELANCÓLICOS

Plaza Francisco Morano

PASEO DR VALLEJO NÁGERA

0   300 m

0   300 yds

16 © Copyright Time Out Group 2010

Parque de San Isidro

326 Time Out Madrid

C/SAN ALEJANDRO

PASEO PONTONES

PUENTE ELEVADO DE SAN ISIDRO

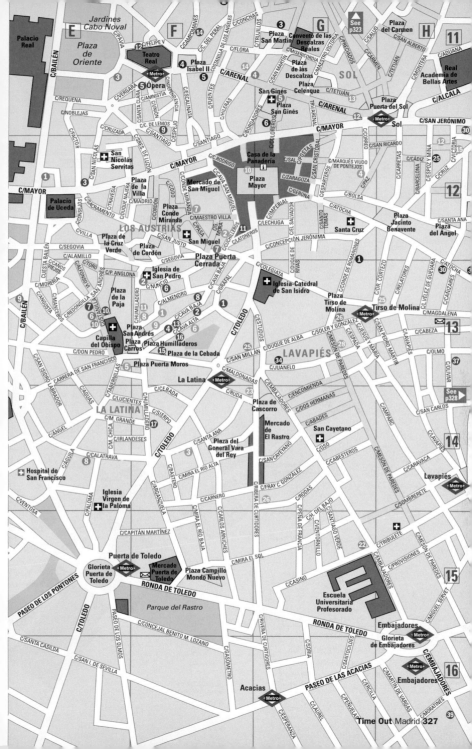

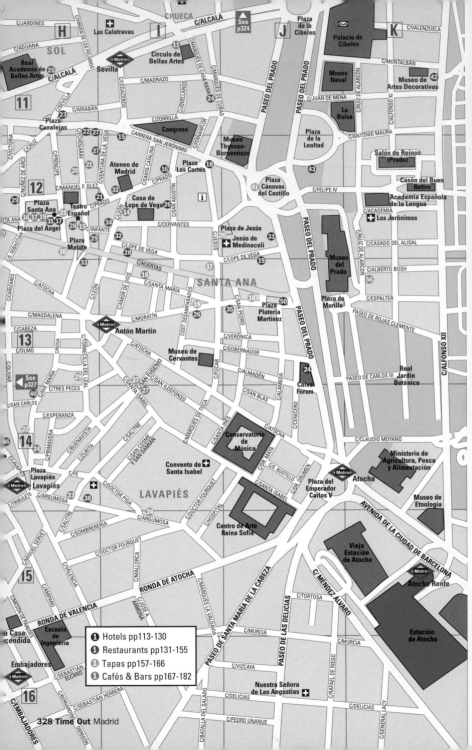

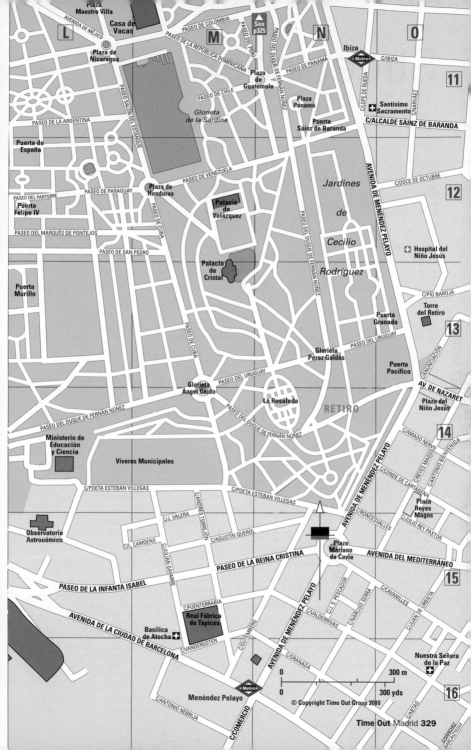

Street Index

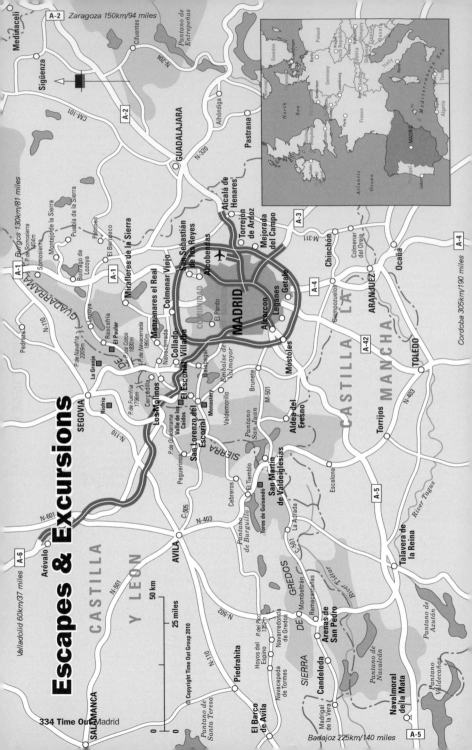

Escapes & Excursions

© Copyright Time Out Group 2010

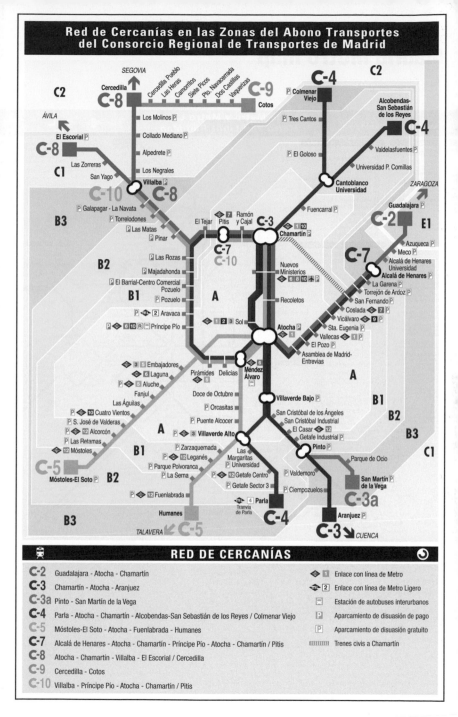

Red de Cercanías en las Zonas del Abono Transportes del Consorcio Regional de Transportes de Madrid

RED DE CERCANÍAS

C-2 Guadalajara - Atocha - Chamartín

C-3 Chamartín - Atocha - Aranjuez

C-3a Pinto - San Martín de la Vega

C-4 Parla - Atocha - Chamartín - Alcobendas-San Sebastián de los Reyes / Colmenar Viejo

C-5 Móstoles-El Soto - Atocha - Fuenlabrada - Humanes

C-7 Alcalá de Henares - Atocha - Chamartín - Príncipe Pío - Atocha - Chamartín / Pitis

C-8 Atocha - Chamartín - Villalba - El Escorial / Cercedilla

C-9 Cercedilla - Cotos

C-10 Villalba - Príncipe Pío - Atocha - Chamartín / Pitis

◈ 1 Enlace con línea de Metro

🚋 2 Enlace con línea de Metro Ligero

▭ Estación de autobuses interurbanos

Ⓟ Aparcamiento de disuasión de pago

Ⓟ Aparcamiento de disuasión gratuito

||||||| Trenes civis a Chamartín

Madrid Metro map

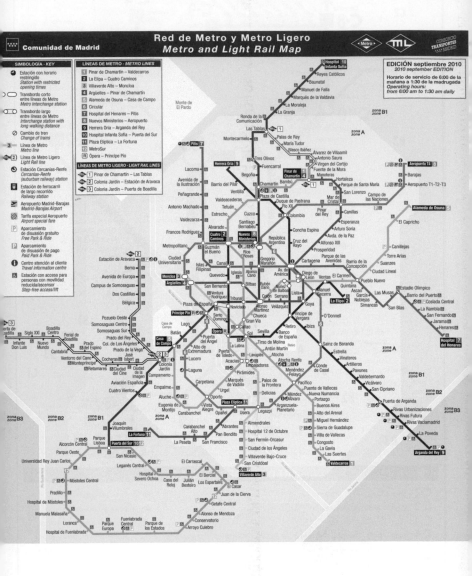